NEWMAN
THE PILLAR OF THE CLOUD

1. JOHN HENRY NEWMAN, 1844
From the drawing by George Richmond

NEWMAN
THE PILLAR OF THE CLOUD

BY

MERIOL TREVOR

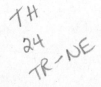

DOUBLEDAY & COMPANY, INC.
GARDEN CITY, NEW YORK
1962

NIHIL OBSTAT

Joannes M. T. Barton, S.T.D., L.S.S., Censor deputatus

IMPRIMATUR

E. Morrogh Bernard, Vic. Gen.

Westmonasterii, die 25 Novembris, 1961

LIBRARY OF CONGRESS CATALOG CARD NUMBER 62-13341
COPYRIGHT © 1962 BY MERIOL TREVOR

TO

THE FATHERS

OF THE

BIRMINGHAM ORATORY

PAST, PRESENT, AND TO COME

ACKNOWLEDGEMENTS

FIRST of all I should like to thank the Fathers of the Birmingham Oratory who have allowed me to read anything and everything from their Archives, and given permission to print from many unpublished letters and memoranda. My view of Newman is my own and I alone am responsible for what I have said of him; my gratitude for this privilege is all the greater. I am especially grateful to Father Stephen Dessain for all his help and for his kindness in allowing me to use his notes, compiled for the volumes of Collected Letters which he is editing for publication. I would like to thank Father Denis Sheil, who went to the Oratory School in 1875 and was received as a novice by Newman in 1890, for his reminiscences, unique in interest; Father Humphrey Crookenden for his photographs and other Fathers for their interest, information and assistance.

My thanks are also due to the Provost and Fellows of Oriel College, Oxford, for permission to use their files of College Correspondence, and to Mr. H. T. Lambrick who so kindly arranged for me to see Newman's rooms and the famous Common Room. I should also like to thank the President, Fellows and Librarian of Magdalen College for the use of Bloxam's Scrapbooks.

I am very grateful to Father Juvenal Matthews and the Fathers of the London Oratory for their kindness in letting me use and quote from their files of letters; and to the Oblates of St. Charles, of St. Mary of the Angels, Bayswater, for allowing me to consult the Manning Papers, and to the Abbé Chapeau of the Institut Catholique of Angers, who is rearranging them after the disasters of the war, and made it possible for me to see them.

I would like to thank Mr. Basil Johnson for the use of letters written to his grandfather, 'Observer' Manuel Johnson, for the Observer's portrait and for much interesting information and research notes; my thanks too to Mgr. Gilbey of Cambridge for his picture of the Oxford and Cambridge coach in 1830.

I am very grateful to Miss Dorothea Mozley and her brother Mr. John Mozley, grandchildren of Jemima Newman, for interesting information and photographs and permission to quote some family letters. Grateful thanks, too, to Lady Pigott, for permission to reproduce the portrait of J. W. Bowden, and to Mr. Harold Giberne for the miniature of Miss Giberne.

Finally I should like to thank for their kind assistance the Rev. Mother Provincial and Community of the Cenacle Convent, Grayshott, and Mrs. Bell the librarian there; the Rector of Oscott, Mgr. Foster; the Rev. Mother and Community at Maryvale; Mr. and Mrs. Morby of Ravenhurst Farm; Mr. and Mrs. Hill of St. George's, Littlemore; Mr. and Mrs. Evans, Miss Joan Ash and Miss Evelyn Self.

CONTENTS

HOME AND OXFORD
(1801–1828)

CRISIS
(1828–1833)

THE MOVEMENT
(1833–1839)

THE TRANSITION
(1839–1846)

ROME AND BIRMINGHAM
(1846–1850)

Contents

TRIAL BY FURY
(1850–1853)

ILLUSTRATIONS

HOME AND OXFORD
(1801–1828)

1801–1816

Beginnings

In the autumn of 1805 a child of four lay in his cot and stared at the candles stuck in the windows of his home, flames against the dark, in celebration of the victory of Trafalgar. It was one of the first events that John Henry Newman remembered by its date in history, at once definite and mysterious. Light within and darkness outside, victory far off at sea : the image remained in his mind.

The house and the world in which he lay belonged to the eighteenth century ; in England the old order reigned, though the nation was profoundly disturbed by the repercussions of the French Revolution and the birth pangs of industrialism. John Henry Newman was born with the nineteenth century and died at the beginning of its last decade ; he was to see the whole face of his country and of Europe change and he was one of the few who foresaw something of the century to come. Not that he was a prophet of events, but his profound insight into the conflict of ideas behind the transformation enabled him to forecast the trend things were likely to take.

We are beginning to realize that the spectacular events of our own time are but the developments of the ideas and discoveries of the first half of the nineteenth century, a period of revolutionary energy comparable only to the sixteenth. Perhaps the continuity of scientific and political theory has been more readily recognized than that of religious and cosmological ideas relating to the nature of man, his place in the universe and the meaning of his existence. We are still trying to understand the implications of the great theory of evolution, the most fundamental of nineteenth-century discoveries, which alters the whole context of our thought. As the astronomical theories of sixteenth-century scientists destroyed the concept of the earth as static and central in space, shaking in men's minds their image of the external poles of good and evil, so the nineteenth-century evolutionary theories have shattered the idea of the world as static in time, and man's image of himself as master of his fate. Newman frequently

3

compared these two revolutions of thought which are indeed complementary and so radically alter our perspective as to seem at first destructive of all traditional beliefs and values.

The scientific theory of biological evolution, which first became widely known with the publication of Darwin's book, *The Origin of Species*, in 1859, and which so shocked and alarmed the majority of Christians, who thought it contradicted the truth of the Bible, did not disturb Newman. For more than sixteen years he had been pondering his own evolutionary theory — of the development of ideas, and especially those ideas which activate the Christian society within the larger society of mankind. His mind had already made the transition from the static to the dynamic view of the world which his contemporaries for the most part found it so hard to make. He had transferred the idea of growth from the individual to the group on the highest, the personal level, before it was discovered on the lowest and basic level of biology.

But while the nineteenth century was the first act of the age of evolution, it was also the last act of the age of individualism, set loose by the renaissance in men and in nations. Thus, in his rediscovery of the collective entity of mankind, its common development and destiny, Newman was misunderstood by the liberals of the time, who regarded themselves as the leaders of intellectual and moral progress. Extreme individualists, they put him down as a reactionary and an authoritarian, looking towards the past rather than the future. Throughout the whole of Newman's long life the tide seemed to be running against him, and he expected it to run further still ; yet he could write in a verse of 1833 : 'But now, I see that men are mad awhile, And joy the Age to come will think with me'.

To an extraordinary degree Newman's thought and his life were one ; his own story is one of development, in ideas, in action and in personality. It is possible to trace the course of this growth because of his exceptional self-awareness, which some have considered self-preoccupation. But a self-centred man is not himself the centre of a wide circle of friends, as Newman was from his boyhood to his death, friends of both sexes and all ages, and from different social and national backgrounds. The self was the centre of action, as it must be for everyone — and he knew more about its motives than most — but the centre of love was in another : in Christ.

Newman has been called a complex and subtle character, and in the sense that he was endowed with a nature capable of manifold and various emotions and activities, this was so. But in a deeper sense

he was simple, and it is his very simplicity which has deceived clever
people into making a mystery of him.   A lifelong victim of misrepresentation he was exceedingly suspicious of biographers who, he
said, insisted on interpreting Lord Burleigh's nods. 'Let the facts
speak' was a favourite maxim, and for this reason he thought lives
were best told in letters, each reader making his own judgment. Yet
no man ever suffered more from people who read into his letters
feelings and intentions he never entertained.

This has to be said before telling of Newman's early years, because
almost everyone approaches them through the medium of the *Apologia*,
and that famous book, written to lay the phantom which, as Newman
said, 'gibbers instead of me', itself raised another troop of ghosts
which glide from one study of him to another.   In the *Apologia*
Newman was not telling the story of his life but of his religious opinions. It is not *Confessions*, whether on the model of Rousseau or of St.
Augustine.   Hasty critics at the time called it egotistic, but in fact
Newman effectively effaced himself behind his ideas. He told nothing
of what he had done, and very little of what he had felt, except in
relation to his public decisions ; consequently he inadvertently gave
the impression that he did nothing but think — or that he was under
the delusion that only thought matters.   For those who had never
met him the picture was created of an intellectual recluse, a dreamer
of dreams from earliest childhood. And because he carefully recorded
the influence of others upon him, and never mentioned his upon them,
he appeared passive, reacting rather than acting.   Some reviewers
were mystified, wondering how he could ever have been the leader
of a movement which had caused a religious revolution in the
educated classes of England.

'I used to wish the Arabian Tales were true,' Newman wrote in
the *Apologia*, of his childhood : 'my imagination ran on unknown
influences, on magical powers and talismans. I thought life might
be a dream, or I an Angel, and all this world a deception, my fellow
angels by a playful device concealing themselves from me and deceiving me with the semblance of a material world.'

Since he did not balance this picture of the inward world of his
childhood with memories of the external world — these are scattered
haphazard in letters to friends — readers might be forgiven for
thinking him so isolated in his own imagination as to be, as one
modern writer has said, 'alienated' from reality. Yet he was so observant of the external world that he could remember the plan of houses
he had left before he was five, and the border of the dining-room

wallpaper which he admired before the birth of his sister, when he was not quite three. He remembered coming downstairs saying, 'This is June', and seeing the breakfast things shining on the table ; he remembered the loft at his grandmother's, with apples on the floor and a mangle. It was the same child who recited 'The Cat and the Cream Bowl' to the assembled company on his fourth birthday, and Cowper on his sixth, and who sent his mother a broom flower when his second sister was born in May 1807. And who made a servant laugh by the heavy sigh with which he forecast his future of school, business and marriage.

The house where the candles were stuck in the windows to celebrate Trafalgar may have been 17 Southampton Street (now Place) near Bloomsbury Square, or Grey Court House at Ham, not far from Richmond, which was the family's country retreat. Both were Georgian, the Ham house big and square, three storeys high and standing in its own garden, next to the Royal Oak Inn, where the carriage horses were probably stabled. There were several other houses near, bigger still, and a little way off Ham House itself and the river. Newman loved this house so much that he said he could have passed an examination in it. 'It has ever been in my dreams.' It was given up before he was seven, and soon afterwards he was sent to school ; the double break isolated for him the Golden Age, the time before time, that lies at the beginning of all lives. Years later he wrote that when he dreamed of heaven, as a boy, it was always Ham. Happy the man to whom heaven is home.

His home, his childhood, were indeed exceptionally happy. John Henry was the eldest of six children, born in London on February 21st, 1801, and baptized in the church of St. Benet Fink. Church and house have long disappeared ; the site of the latter is now under the London Stock Exchange. Next to John came Charles, then Harriett, Francis, Jemima, and lastly Mary, who was nearly nine years younger than John.

Their father, John Newman, was a banker, the son of a Cambridgeshire man from Swaffham, who had come to London and done well enough in the grocery trade to give his son a better education than his own. The Newman forebears, traced out with difficulty quite recently, were small farmers and village tailors in the seventeenth century ; there were Newmans in East Anglia back to the late Middle Ages, none in the least distinguished. Grandfather John Newman died just before his son married, but Grandmother Elizabeth (born Good) and her daughter, Aunt Betsy, were well known to the children, who often stayed with them. The mother of the six was Jemima Fourdrinier, the only girl in a family of brothers, the daughter of a paper manufacturer of French Protestant stock. She brought her husband a dowry of five thousand pounds, which she kept intact through many vicissitudes, leaving one thousand to each of her surviving children. The Fourdriniers were perhaps of slightly higher social standing than the Newmans, but both families were good bourgeois, rising with every generation to more importance in the English scene.

In England, manners and education have always raised people in the social scale more certainly than money, and the young Newman couple were both musical, fond of plays, of dancing, of reading and of conversation. They went to 'routs', to concerts and theatres, and John Newman belonged to the Beefsteak Club. He was thirty-three when he married, and prosperous enough to take the big house at Ham as well as his town house ; his bride was twenty-eight. They were a well-matched pair and devoted to each other ; when adversity came it only drew them closer together. They both delighted in their children. Mr. Newman was an easy-going, straightforward man, impatient of anything he could not understand, but tolerant and generous. He was inclined to be irascible, but his temper quickly subsided. He was conventional, conservative in habit, liberal but not radical in opinion, belonged to the established Church and disliked intensity in religion. The Newmans have often been described as Evangelicals ; they certainly were not. Evangelicals of the day frowned on theatres and dancing and would have considered the banker's household worldly and frivolous.

In a family picture of the Fourdriniers, Mrs. Newman, as a young girl, stands by her father, gay and graceful, with dark ringlets and a French air, recalling her ancestry. She would have been considered handsome, observed a family friend, had she not been marked by the smallpox. Her letters show her as affectionate and lively, engrossed in her little domestic world. John Henry remembered her agitation when she missed her husband on a journey to Brighton ; she was lost without him. She was a sensible woman, but not a managing dominant type. She and her husband were intelligent and cultivated, but in no sense intellectuals ; nor were they ambitious for themselves or their children — they were content with their position in the world. This created the best possible background for their clever, imaginative and lively children ; there was no forcing, moral or intellectual, no strain of living up to high adult standards. The memories of childhood were happy for all of them.

John Henry seems to have inherited his nose and chin from the Newmans, his wide mouth with its full lips from the Fourdriniers. His eyes were grey, or grey-blue, his hair brown, straight and thick, of that soft and fine quality which will not stay in place. It grew forward over his forehead and it is evident from photographs that it would not stay combed back for long. Of the others Jemima was most like him in looks, unfortunately for her, since those strong features did not look well in a woman. In character she was the most gentle and retiring of the family. There was a mathematical ability in the family which she shared and passed on to a brilliant son. Like John, she was musical. In contrast to her younger sister, Harriett was small and neatly built ; she was considered delicate, was highly strung and given to headaches ; but she was clever and practical, with a large share of the family obstinacy. Charles carried this trait to an extreme ; he was wilful and unpredictable, and seems to have had some defect of character, not of mental equipment, for he was clever and argumentative, but of feeling. He seemed incapable of feeling for other people. Later his personality became alarmingly unstable, but doctors declared he was not insane, and after middle age he became more settled. He had a beak of a nose. Francis was considered the most handsome of the family, with features less rugged than John's, piercing blue eyes and straight black hair which he wore rather long. Intensely serious, intellectually brilliant, humourless, as he himself admitted, with a strong will and capable of passionate idealism, he and his brothers could never get on easily. Charles, while criticizing everybody, never failed to take John's side against Frank in any difference. Their mother was to say to John of Frank, 'He is a piece of adamant, but you are such a sensitive being'. The youngest of the family, Mary, was cheerful and gay ; nothing could damp her high spirits and breathless fun. She was everyone's favourite, but not spoilt.

John, the eldest, was often also the leader ; but neither of his brothers yielded an inch of independence ; they argued and tussled and went their own way, each determined he was right. Even Harriett would answer anyone back. Thus John was never in any danger of becoming the despot of the family ; there was give and take from the first. And they were all too close together in age for him to live an isolated life. What a contrast is this natural family life to that of so many famous people of the century — to the motherless Brontës with their eccentric father and ingrowing existence, to John Stuart Mill, forced by his terrible father into premature intellectual development, made to teach his own brothers and sisters and to despise feeling as feminine weakness. These came from the same middle-class background as the Newmans; among the upper classes neglect was more frequent than forcing — the future Lord Shaftesbury was a lonely child, his affections centred entirely on his old nurse, a simple puritan.

John Henry certainly had a strong will. Jemima once told Anne Mozley, her sister-in-law and John's first biographer, of an early tussle with authority in which he lost the day. 'You see John,' said his mother, 'you did not get your own way.' — 'No,' said John, 'but I tried very hard!' This story made Anne smile; she thought it so typical.

If the nose and chin, later such a mark for *Punch* cartoonists, were signs of will-power, the full and expressive lips, so rarely tightly closed, seem indicative of the feelings equally strong with which he was endowed. It is revealed by the struggles with his temper recorded in the early journals that he had inherited his father's irascibility, a quick-come and quick-gone impatience at what crossed his will, which he himself called 'impetuousness'. In his youth this anger could be so passionate that the effort to control it made him tremble and feel faint. Most people who met him later in life had no idea of this naturally quick temper, but he was under no illusion himself that he had eradicated it; he knew the small things in which the tendency continued to show itself. But it was progressively overcome, not by mere suppression, but by the gradual expansion of other and more loving feelings.

From the beginning he loved people and places with extraordinary tenacity; not just one or two, but many. Much of his energy was spent in loving and in delighting in being loved; gratitude for the love of others, and a continual surprise that they should expend it on him, was a constant reaction all his life. But love comes to those who give it; those who complain that they are not loved, do not realize that it is because they are unloving. Newman's letters from early days, and other people's to him, show how affectionate he was by nature, and how eager to do things to please those he loved, how miserable if he was forced to cause them pain. It was unusual that anyone with such high intellectual gifts should also possess such an affectionate heart; more unusual still that both developed so fully, not crossing or stunting each other.

Newman had very keen and perceptive senses which, since he did not dull them with excess or narcotics, remained acute almost into old age. He was especially alive to scents and flavours, the most delicate and easily lost of sense experiences. He had a discriminating eye for colour, a sensitive ear for music, and a great love for wild landscape and wide views. He had, in fact, all the physical and mental equipment of a poet, keenly observant of the external world and with the creative imagination which can express the mysterious union between what is outside and what is inside man. At the same time he had a mind capable of the clearest abstract reasoning, logical and mathematical. This combination is rare indeed, and when it occurs one faculty almost always takes the life out of the other. Reason tends to dry up imagination, as William Blake, the most spiritually perceptive of English poets, saw with indignation. Newman had the power to be a poet or a philosopher ; because he became so wholeheartedly a priest he never threw the whole force of his personality into either ability. But though this prevented him from becoming a professional in either sphere, it allowed both faculties to develop together, fertilizing each other in such a way that his mind came very close to the mind of the great Greek Fathers, and yet exercised itself in a wholly modern way upon the questions of the present age.

Feeling and imagination, of course, were strongest in the child at Ham ; other faculties developed quickly at school, where he was sent when he was seven. He was lucky in that school did not break the trusting and loving disposition that had thrived in the psychological security of his home. It was not one of the public schools, haunts of savagery in those days, but a private (boarding) school at Ealing run by a Dr. Nicholas. It was quite a fashionable place in its day ; Marryat and Thackeray at different periods were there, and a contemporary and friend of Newman's was Westmacott, the designer of the Hyde Park Arcades. Discipline was mild and Dr. Nicholas a kind and cultured man.

All the same, John Henry, like most little boys, started his school career by being teased and bullied by other little boys. He arrived on May-day 1808 and his first term cannot have been happy, for when he came back in the autumn he was afraid to go into the room where the other boys were. When he was an old man over eighty, sending materials to Anne Mozley for her biography, he told William Neville how, when his father and mother had gone, he hung about in the hall. Dr. Nicholas 'passed by and said, kindly enough, "Hadn't you better go into the big room ?" — "No, no, I won't, they'll bully me so, they'll do all sorts of things to me though I can't help crying." "Oh no, nonsense, they won't." At last,' Neville

wrote down, 'he said, "But they will! Only come into the room and
see for yourself." Then he caught hold of Dr. Nicholas' hand and
dragged him into the room saying, "Come with me, sir, and then you
can judge for yourself". In they went together, hand in hand, and
no one said or did anything.' In Anne Mozley's version, only bullying words, not deeds, were mentioned. John Henry's innocent trust
says much, not only for the kindness of Dr. Nicholas, but for his own
father, and the simple confidence he must have inspired.

This action, naïve as it was, did not make little Newman unpopular ; he settled down well and made many friends, with whom
he kept in touch after they had all grown up. In the brief memoir
Newman wrote in 1874, expecting Ambrose St. John to be his
biographer, he said that he became greatly attached to Dr. Nicholas.
It is clear from the anecdotes that Neville recorded that Dr. Nicholas
became equally fond of his clever scholar ; he used to call him John.
'Once Dr. Nicholas said, "Why, John, it's your birthday — won't
they be drinking your health at home to-day ? I must go to London
to-day — suppose you get up behind the carriage and then you can
say I shall be glad of a dinner too." John quite appreciated the
proposal.'

Dr. Nicholas became quite a friend of the family, and when Mr.
Newman was in difficulties over the failure of the bank, he was most
kind about the payment of the fees and would say 'when it suits'.
He was paid in full. He shared with Mr. Newman a love of music
and used to have musical evenings. John and a friend used to creep
up outside the door to listen. Once they made some little noise and
Dr. Nicholas threw open the door and discovered them. 'What, do
you like it ?' he said, looking at them. 'Come in and sit down.' And
he gave them leave to come to the music whenever they liked. When
John was ten his father gave him a violin and he took lessons. Thus
his music was encouraged both at home and at school, something very
unusual in those days.

Ealing was undoubtedly a civilized school, and when there was
talk later of sending John to Winchester he begged off, supported by
his mother. This is yet another indication of Mr. Newman's happy
relationship with his children ; how many boys of the time would
have been allowed any say in the matter at all ? John Henry, as
Dr. Nicholas used proudly to say, passed more quickly up the school
than any other boy, and reached the top of it by the time he was
fifteen. Charles and Francis followed John, and soon on prize days
they were all reciting, John in Greek. But though he was so clever at

work, John was not a slave to it; he spent much of his playtime reading, but he read poetry and novels. Sir Walter Scott's novels excited him so much that when he woke early on summer mornings he used to read them in bed.

Nor was he always perfectly amenable to authority. He could be cheeky. 'He never was birched,' Neville recorded, 'though once he had his name ordered for six, which was ordinarily the utmost — it was for a bit of impudence to a master — the head master took no notice of the order — the under master never forgave him and always had a spite against him in consequence.' Six strokes as a maximum was a very mild punishment. Even some twenty years later Dr. Arnold of Rugby was to give eighteen to a boy he thought had told a lie.

In December 1811 the ten-year-old John wrote exuberantly to his aunt, 'Already in imagination I pay my respects to the mince Pies, Turkies and other good things of Christmas. In the mean time the Notches on my wooden calendar diminish apace.' Home and food, as with most boys, were major preoccupations at school. But Newman always had a taste for good things, and was later to think himself greedy for it. He once recalled a visit to Ham in 1813 with his father and brother, when his father told him to choose first from the three apricots the gardener offered, and he chose the biggest; he said it still made him ashamed to think of it. It was typical of Newman to tell someone else this piece of greed. And in the fifties, writing in his Irish university magazine, an imaginary conversation with an Epicurean, he recalled gooseberries in the garden and 'how difficult it was to stop'.

John did not care for games — which were then casual, not organized activities — marbles, skipping and ball games. Francis, who was nearly five years his junior, remarked with scorn in the recollections he wrote in his old age, that he was never seen to *swim*. But Newman's schoolboy diary was full of entries of Bathing; to him it meant plunging into the water, not swimming. He went on doing this, in one form or another, almost all his life, and remarked once, when he was about sixty, that he never liked the moment of the plunge, but the sensation of exhilaration after it. Although he did not care for games, he was not an inactive boy. He learned to ride; it was then almost a necessity. He went on riding, to get about or for exercise, till he was nearly forty. By the time he went to Oxford he was already a tough walker, ready to go seventeen miles before breakfast to visit friends. Boating on the Thames was another activity of his boyhood, and there is a casual reference to an attempt, when he was about fifteen, to row round the Isle of Wight in a fog. He did not say whether this adventure was undertaken alone. When he was only about nine he and Charles climbed up the cliff at St. Leonard's and nearly got stuck there.

Nor was he a solitary at school, avoiding or avoided by others. He was the ringleader of a club, secret of course, and the indefatigable editor of a series of newspapers, modelled on the *Spectator* — his were called *Spy* and *Beholder*. Another, the *Portfolio*, was political and contained a contribution from the American Minister, John Quincy Adams, whose son was at the school. A cartoon of the Spy Club, done by 'our enemy' survives, in which Newman, nose already prominent, appears very much in command of the meeting. Charles was a member (critical, of course), but Francis was too young. In 1845 when John went over to Rome, they ludicrously agreed that it was the logical consequence for one who so young had coveted secret power. The Spy Club, after some exciting wars, had to be broken up, but the papers were continued by the eager and prolific young journalist.

Newman did not retail these early adventures in leadership in the *Apologia*, any more than he enlarged on his physical recreations or his music ; but they are very significant. As a child, imagination and feeling had ruled him, but as a boy he quickly developed his latent powers of intellect and action. Boys do not accept as leader one whom they do not respect, and they are not apt to be very respectful of the merely clever, or the bookish dreamer. Newman's youthful letters are high-spirited, often written in a consciously high-flown style whose periods conclude with laughter at his own cleverness. He had a great sense of fun, and when he began writing plays for his brothers and sisters to act, they were usually comedies. He even wrote an opera — and it was a burlesque. Some years later, at Oxford, he wrote a song, to oblige a friend, for a comedian called Fat Jack. At school, too, the boys acted Latin plays by Plautus and Terence ; Newman later edited them for his own school at Edgbaston. He was then over sixty, but the boys never forgot what vigour he put into teaching them to act. One of their plays was the *Eunuchus*, which Newman had expurgated and entitled *Pincerna* ; in 1874 he reminded Jemima that it was the one in which he 'acted at Ealing in 1814, a woman's part, which amused Anne Withy so much'. It struck Anne as irresistibly funny that the wonderful John, nose and all, should pretend to be a girl. John was evidently a good actor, for on the great occasion when the Duke of Kent, the father of the future Queen Victoria, gave away the prizes, he was put on to recite. The master apologized for the fact that the boy's voice was breaking. 'But his action was so good,' said the Duke. This must have been in John's last year at school, when he was fifteen.

When the *Apologia* appeared and readers heard only of Newman's sense of separation from the world, many of them imagined he had lived in a world of fantasy, remote from the normal savagery of boyish existence. The reviewer in the *Reader* conjectured that he was 'wanting in a certain elemental vitality', and asserted 'his roots do not go deep into common human soil'. It was not Newman's intention to dig up his common roots for the inspection of the multitude. But there was plenty of elemental vitality in the boy who tried to row round the Isle of Wight, the ringleader of a secret club, the spirited comedian.

And now this happy security was suddenly shattered. The Bank failed.

1816

The First Crisis

THE failure of the Bank was no fault of Mr. Newman's. The end of the Napoleonic wars brought economic crisis and many other private ventures failed. The doors were closed on March 8th, 1816, and the partners managed, though with difficulty, to pay all the depositors. But Mr. Newman was left in reduced circumstances and with no very good prospects. He was nearly fifty and had no experience outside banking. The house in Southampton Street was let and by the autumn Mr. Newman had settled his family in Alton and was trying to manage a Hampshire brewery. The shock of his failure profoundly affected him ; he lost confidence in life and was never again to succeed in any undertaking.

The three little girls went first to Grandmother at Vine Cottage, but soon that beloved place had to be given up too, and they joined their parents at Alton. Only John was left at school all the summer holidays. He had been fetched home earlier to hear the news, but sent back to Ealing. Perhaps he was left there because he had an illness about this time, probably infectious. It cannot have been serious, for no one showed any anxiety, but he must have run a high temperature and suffered after effects of depressive lassitude, for he remembered it all his life, and the experiences 'before and after, awful and known only to God'. The sick room at school became the symbol of horror and desolation ; it at once returned to his mind when he was in Sicily in 1833, alone and desperately ill with fever. Now the family disaster, the uncertainty of the future, loneliness and feverish sickness, suddenly opened an abyss in his happy and active life. As he expressed it much later : 'I was terrified under the heavy hand of God'.

This cruel revelation of the insecurity of human existence came with all the more force to the boy because he had lost the simple faith of his childhood. As a child he had been very responsive to the numinous world of the spirit, and to the religious teaching he was given, mostly, it seems, by his grandmother and aunt, the most pious of the family. It may have been at their house that he experienced, perhaps before he was five, a moment of intense awareness, when self-consciousness and conscience awoke all at once in his mind. 'What am I ? What am I doing here ?' he asked himself.

He thought this experience common to everyone, and did not realize that to less alert minds it can come so gradually that no moment of apocalypse is remembered. But about the age of five all children make a great leap forward in mental activity, often asking abstract and metaphysical questions ; then the spring of energy begins to flow through thought into action and the child is absorbed in his first social activities. To Thomas Traherne, the seventeenth-century contemplative, this transit appeared primarily as the passage from eternity into time, and the loss of the innocent eye in the deceits of the world. The same psychological change came to the child Newman in a more active form ; as soon as he was aware of himself, he knew he was capable of deliberate action, right or wrong. This was the realization of conscience, the light that lights every man coming into the world — as much part of his nature as will or appetite or reason. Newman ever found the most cogent argument for the existence of God in this universal interior light.

In the awakening of his mental energies at school Newman had lost the sense of spiritual presences and powers that had haunted his childhood. His intellectual curiosity led him early beyond the bounds of the traditional piety he had picked up at home ; by the time he was fifteen he had reached a general scepticism which required only a step to become conscious atheism. In 1811, five years before Newman's crisis, Shelley, aged eighteen, was sent down from Oxford for writing *The Necessity of Atheism*. Newman was about eight years his junior, but intellectually even more precocious, and in his omnivorous reading was exposed to the same kind of influences. When he was fourteen he read Tom Paine's tracts against the Old Testament, and some of Hume's Essays : 'so at least I gave my father to understand, but perhaps it was a brag', he wrote modestly in the *Apologia*. He copied some French verses denying the immortality of the soul and thought, 'How dreadful, but how plausible !' And he decided that he would like to be virtuous, but not religious.

It was the classical ideal, exalted by the philosophic moralists of the time, who identified the Christian religion with social and mental oppression. There was every excuse to do so, since the Church, whether Protestant or Catholic, had been so long in subordination to the State as to become enfeebled and worldly. Establishment was a more effective instrument of destruction than persecution. To an idealist like Shelley comfortable clergymen could never be types of Christ and it was more noble to serve mankind than a deity whose sole function seemed to be to reinforce earthly tyrannies. Newman felt the same disgust at worldliness and tyranny, not only as a boy, but all his life. The genesis of the Oxford Movement lay in his desire to free the Church from this inward corruption and external servitude.

In 1859, when Newman was in the throes of another spiritual crisis, his mind returned to the crucial event of 1816, and he wrote in his private journal, addressing the Creator : 'Thy wonderful grace turned me right round when I was more like a devil than a wicked boy . . .'. To many people 'a devil' is just a dramatic way of saying 'a bad person', but Newman meant it literally. He thought that his state at the age of fifteen was more like that of an evil spirit than of a bad human being. 'Was any boyhood so impious as some years of mine ?' he wrote in a meditation. 'Did I not in fact dare Thee to do Thy worst ?' His likeness to the devil lay in the intellectual pride that can so easily become an arrogant self-sufficiency. Some have thought he attributed excessive importance to the evil element in his youthful scepticism, but it later appeared to him a form of self-will, leading to the substitution of human reason for the divine creative spirit, to a self-centred universe and a final alienation from all love. Like St. Teresa of Avila he 'saw his place in hell'.

He was turned right round, converted to God. This mysterious event, to him for ever more certain than that he had hands or feet, he never attempted to describe. God 'mercifully touched his heart' — it was his whole being that was changed. Yet because he did not go through the particular experiences associated with conversion by the evangelicals of the time, many of them afterwards assured him that he had never been converted at all. To them it was an apocalyptic event and it would have surprised them to learn that even then he gave it in his mind a duration of five months, from August to December 1816.

Newman himself called it 'a great change of thought' and as such he dealt with it in the *Apologia*. The catastrophe at home and the illness that terrified him, opened his mind to the ideas of a young clergyman teaching in the school, whom he already liked and respected because, although he was religious, there was no cant about him. Walter Mayers had come to Ealing some eighteen months before.

He had cherished worldly ambitions of a clerical career till a dramatic moment when his horse shied at a steam-boat and nearly threw him into the Severn. Henceforth he devoted himself seriously to the service of God, but he did not repudiate intellectual cultivation. He lent Newman books not tracts. What Newman learned from them gave his thought a direction which it never lost.

Chief among these books were *The Force of Truth*, by Thomas Scott, Milner's *Church History*, Beveridge's *Private Thoughts*, Newton's *On the Prophecies* and Doddridge's *Rise and Progress*. Mr. Mayers gave him Beveridge on the last day of 1816, and it became a close companion; it contained apologetics based on a rational approach to religion. Newton deeply impressed on Newman's mind the idea of Prophecy in religion — intuitive insight into the divine scheme — but the book also injected the current Protestant interpretations of certain eschatological predictions of Scripture : that the Pope was Antichrist, the lawless king who set himself in the place of God. Newman recorded that even after he had reasoned himself out of this belief it left a stain on his imagination : such an identification touches some of the most primitive forces in human nature. Later, Newman was to focus on himself much of the irrational hatred roused by this projection of evil on the representative person of a particular system.

The authors who most profoundly influenced Newman were Scott and Milner. Scott was the grandfather of Sir George Gilbert Scott the architect ; he was the tenth of thirteen children of a Lincolnshire grazier, a poor man who made his way entirely by the force of his own character. Through great difficulties he attained the comparative ease afforded by ordination in the Church of England, only to throw away his worldly advantages by scrupling to swear to the Thirty-Nine Articles. *The Force of Truth* was the record of his progress from the Unitarian belief that Jesus was a man only, to the full Christian doctrine that he was the divine Word, or Son, of the Triune God, become a man. Scott not only implanted in Newman's mind the doctrine itself, but presented religious truth as a quest, and the understanding of it as a personal development. Newman used some of Scott's sayings almost as proverbs : 'Holiness before peace', and 'Growth the only evidence of life'. From the start Christianity was for Newman not simply a system to be accepted, but a way to live.

Milner's history had an equally profound effect, for in it Newman first discovered the Fathers of the Church, the great thinkers of the fourth and fifth centuries. He was instantly attracted to this 'paradise

2. 17 SOUTHAMPTON PLACE

3. GREY COURT HOUSE, HAM

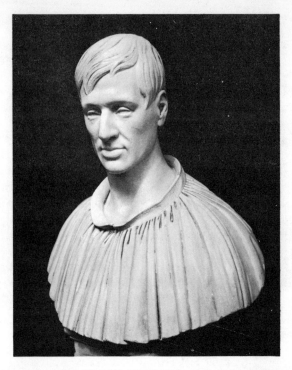

4. BUST OF JOHN HENRY NEWMAN, 1841, BY WESTMACOTT

5. THE OXFORD AND CAMBRIDGE COACH, 1830

of delight' as he significantly called it. He compared the action of
their thought upon him to music, his favourite art. In them Greek
clarity of reasoning met the concrete symbolism of the Hebrews in a
marriage of unparalleled fecundity, and this fusion of intellect and
imagination answered the unusual balance of Newman's mind in
which these forces were equal. It was an unique meeting, for at that
time the study of the Fathers had fallen into desuetude, even in the
Catholic Church, as a result of the excessive concentration on the
rational, in religious as in secular studies. The ordinary reaction to
this rationalism was a flight into the irrational extreme — in literature
from classic to romantic, in religion from formalism to emotional
revivalism. The Fathers showed Newman the way into a world
where the supreme mysteries were neither devitalized into an abstract
system nor subject to the degenerative process of uncontrolled feeling.
Many problems of religious thought in our own day are being solved
by a return to the methods of the Fathers, used with all the increased
resources of knowledge ; in the secular sphere Jung uses a similar
approach to symbols in his psychological theories. Newman was to
be a pioneer of this new outlook, the opener of the gate.

At fifteen he did not know what he had found, except that it was
music and paradise to his mind. But the discovery of the Fathers at
this critical moment of his development released into conscious
activity the deep imaginative power dormant since his childhood.
It soon slept again, as the Fathers also slept, while he pursued the
prescribed course of classics and mathematics, but the way was open
for its return. It had a personal effect too. Newman, as an exceptionally clever boy in an age of reason, was always in danger of becoming over-intellectual, and putting so high a value on knowledge and
thought as to lose touch with other aspects of reality. His love of
music, poetry and drama kept him in the world of image and symbol,
but the Fathers had the unique power of actually translating these
into the world of reason, revivifying it, and relating it to action. It
is a fact that at every crisis of his youth 'the Fathers rose before him'
as he was to put it later ; after each period of constriction, they were
the medium through which his renewed creative energy began to
express itself.

Closely connected with the mysterious union of reason and intuition is another element in Newman's first conversion which mystified
his Protestant contemporaries when they read of it in the *Apologia* : his
conviction that God willed him to live a single life. He called it 'a
deep imagination' — an exact phrase, indicating neither a mere fancy

nor a rational decision, but something rising from the depths of the
self beyond conscious awareness. Newman referred to it with reluctance and with bald simplicity, because it touched the centre of
himself, but he told it, because it was an essential part of his conversion and of his subsequent development.

Newman's Victorian critics treated the admission with amusement
or pity, sometimes with scorn. One review ran the heading 'The
Boy Celibate'. The idea that God might will such a life for a man
was not dismissed as nonsense — it was simply not considered.
Newman's will, not God's, was assumed to be the only factor in the
situation. To the English society of the time the idea of a man
devoting his life to the work of the spirit was simply unnatural;
there was no place for monk and mystic — Eastern sages had not yet
become fashionable. To Newman's contemporaries a single life was
a negative conception, and most of them concluded that the Boy
Celibate was 'lacking in elementary vitality'. By the time he wrote
the *Apologia* Newman knew what their reaction would be.

In the years of his adolescence he thought of the single life as a
practical necessity, and it was linked in his mind with the hope that
he might serve God as a missionary. Protestant missions were new
adventures then, and to the ardent boy seemed a more heroic ministry
than preaching to the respectable in his own country. To face danger
and death to bring Christ to the heathen in China or Africa was indeed
a noble ambition in 1816; nor did Newman give up all idea of it till
his father died in 1824, and he realized that to go would be to evade
his responsibilities at home. By then his career was fixed in Oxford,
and as Fellows of Colleges were not allowed to marry, celibacy, if
only temporary, was their inevitable lot. Newman's obscure intuition
that God willed him to remain single was not transformed into a
conscious resolution till he was twenty-eight; even then it was still
primarily a symbol of separation from worldly ties and ambitions.

It is remarkable how Newman's spiritual crises coincided with
the phases of physical, emotional and mental growth. In the successive metamorphoses of youth his personality developed evenly,
though not without stress. The form of these metamorphoses,
common to everyone, is dramatic: in the first act there is a concentration of forces, a narrowing that sometimes seems a failure of
vitality; then comes the outburst of new energy and finally the full
exploration of it in action. All the elements of personality are involved and at every crisis of growth one or other may become stunted
or twisted, so that the person develops unevenly, sometimes psycho-

logically crippled for life, but more often only lopsided, perhaps not permanently. The ancients, who observed men from the static rather than the dynamic angle, recognized the same phenomenon when they classified types according to the preponderance of one or other element. Where a modern psychologist would speak of a mental age of fourteen in an adult man, a pagan sage would have classified him as a man of instinct and impulse. Then there are the people, often of high mental development, whose emotions remain those of adolescents. We are used to this lack of balance in ourselves and in others, but we admire most the most complete person.

To Christians, however, even the most fully developed man is as much in danger of losing his soul as the most stunted or neurotic — perhaps in worse danger, since he is the more likely to feel himself self-sufficient. Natural growth in this fallen world needs the continual power of God to keep it true to the Spirit. God gives the power, but man is free to take it or leave it. At each crisis of his natural growth Newman, like everyone else, was faced with a spiritual choice, when he might have made himself the centre of his own life. What is remarkable in him is his awareness, so sensitively alive to the mysterious demand, and so whole-hearted in his response. Each time he turned to God, and with the entire force of his being. Of course there was always a certain falling back. To Newman himself it always seemed that in his boyhood he had fallen so far from the vision of his childhood as to be in danger of absolute spiritual loss. The conversion at fifteen was so much a new birth that he seemed to himself, even as an old man, a different person before and after it. It was this experience of regeneration that made it easy for him at first to accept the peculiar doctrines of the evangelicals along with those essential to any form of Christianity ; yet his conversion was not the personal assurance of salvation, subjective and irreversible, which went by that name among them, but conversion as it is known among Catholics, a special turning to God which determines the course of life to come.

Though his danger was spiritual and intellectual, Newman wrote that God had touched his *heart* — the traditional centre of being and the seat of love. There was not only a new knowledge of truth, but a new energy of love. Newman had a great dislike of facile talk about love, whether for human persons or for God ; he said little about his own. But as a boy he poured out his feelings in pages of close, rapid, unformed writing, prayers and confessions, aspirations and praises, often in the words of Scripture which he already began to know by heart. He tore out and threw these away later, all but a few pages belonging to the year 1817, his first at Oxford. Few as they are, they give a vivid impression of this youthful outburst of emotion.

But the emotion of love was not the only form of his response to the divine touch ; from the first moment his will moved to obey the will of God. As his mind was directed to the system of Christian truth, and his love to the supreme lover, so his will was set on spiritual action. What is light to the mind, is love to the heart, and in action is life. Newman's journals show how passionate and persevering were his attempts to do and to be what he saw and knew of truth. This threefold response meant that every force of his being was centred on God — in the Trinity, through Christ.

In November 1817, in the pages already mentioned, he addressed God in thanksgiving — 'for Thy goodness in enlightening my soul with the knowledge of the truth ; that whereas I was proud, self-righteous, impure, abominable and altogether corrupt in my sinful imagination, thou wast pleased to turn me to thee from such a state of darkness and irreligion by a mercy which is too wonderful for me, and to make me fall down humbled and abased before thy footstool. Oh ! merciful Saviour continue thy grace and let me so run the race that is set before me that I may lay hold of everlasting life ; let me be a faithful soldier. . . .' The passage continues with a realization of the communion of saints ; even at this necessarily individual point of personal development, Newman had grasped the social nature of Christianity, the idea of adherence in a mystical body.

This was the point then, when he became aware of the deep imagination that it was his destiny to live a single life for God ; the force behind it was positive, not negative. It was an intention of love, not a rejection of love. And not of love to God only, but of love to others, since he thought of it as a mission. But of the meaning of all this he was aware only obscurely.

At the end of this momentous year Newman was still not yet sixteen, but boyhood was over. In December 1816 he was matriculated as a commoner of Trinity College, Oxford.

1817–1820

Three Years at Trinity

'TRINITY? a most gentlemanlike college.' With these words Dr. Nicholas reassured John when he returned to school and timidly mentioned the name of his college — he himself had never heard of it before. His going to Oxford was altogether a haphazard occasion. With the post-chaise at the door Mr. Newman had not decided which university to make for. The casting vote was given by a Mr. Mullens, Curate of St. James', Piccadilly. He went with them to Oxford but was unable to secure a vacancy for John at his own college of Exeter. They entered him at Trinity. But though he was matriculated, he had to wait till the following June before he was able to go into residence.

Full of enthusiasm he arrived just when everyone was going down, and he had some difficulty in cornering his tutor, Mr. Short, to get advice on his reading. The first thing he did was to buy his gown — a commoner's. He wrote home exuberantly, fascinated by the variety of dishes at dinner, and the fat cook, astonished at the amount everyone drank and self-conscious at being 'silently stared at'. Excitement and too much reading made his eyes hurt. Perhaps it was now that he acquired the spectacles which he wore all the time until middle age. He was short-sighted.

During this brief prologue to his Oxford life Newman met John William Bowden, who was to be his greatest friend in these early years, and who remained a faithful ally until his death in 1844. Bowden was told off to instruct Newman in the ways of the college. They discovered that their birthdays were on the same day, though Bowden was three years older. He was nineteen, Newman sixteen, but Bowden, easy-going, slow and steady, did not seem so much the elder. In fact Newman took the lead from the beginning. Bowden was the eldest son in a wealthy family, his father was a director of the Bank of England. He was a handsome youth, with a Byronic mop of hair and an amiable smile. They became, as Newman said, 'inseparables, reading, walking and boating together'.

It was lucky for Newman that he made this friend at once, for his first year was in many ways a difficult one. He was two or three years younger than the men of his own year and came from a very different background from most of them. It was not till many years later that he realized the implications of the epithet 'gentle-manlike', as applied to Trinity. At that time what scholarship there was in the university was concentrated in a few colleges, chiefly in Christ Church and Oriel, where the tutors were also the Examiners. Trinity was not one of them, and the undergraduates there were mostly the sons of good families sent to get through their adolescence with the minimum of trouble to all. Newman retained an affection for his old college, and for kind Mr. Short, and so he never put on public record the consequences of his having started his academic course so unpropitiously. But he wrote a note on it, during his time at the Irish university. Mr. Short was continually surprised at his knowledge and had little idea how to guide his reading ; Newman and Bowden made their own plans of work, and as Newman realized later, it was not always what would have been of most service to them in the schools. Bowden was ahead, even in mathe-matics, which Newman regarded as his best subject ; he was am-bitious and 'fagged' as he called it, to keep up with and surpass his friend.

Fagging meant early rising and long hours of study, which put a severe strain on him just at the time when he must have been growing and developing in physique. He suffered from sudden bouts of faintness ; once he had to be taken home from St. Mary's by the man sitting next to him. Sometimes his overworked mind refused to go on and he fell suddenly asleep over his books. Sudden faintness and sudden sleep were to be characteristics into middle age. He used to go to the cold plunging bath in Holywell, recording his visits in his journal, which he kept for a while in Latin, for practice and to foil the curiosity of servants. As an old man he noted, amused, 'I seem to have bathed very frequently through this winter'. It was considered good for the health. He also went for long walks with Bowden, and in the summer boating on the river. His other recreation was music ; he kept up his violin and went to concerts in the Holywell Music Room. Later he joined a small private orchestra.

But the gentlemanlikeness of Trinity affected his social as well as his educational life. It must be remembered that the Oxford of Newman's youth was by no means what it was even during the

years of the Movement, let alone after the reforms of the mid-
century. The level of scholarship was low, except for a few outstanding individuals. Fellows of colleges were not allowed to retain
their posts if they married, consequently lecturers and tutors were
mostly young men filling in a few years before taking a living — for
they were all clerics, actual or potential. They did not take very
seriously their responsibilities towards the undergraduates, but were
willing to undertake private tuition if paid for it. On the whole
only the brilliant or the poor men who wished to advance themselves, worked ; the great majority of young men idled. Eighteenth-
century social habits lingered and the most noticeable of these was
drunkenness. Even Heads of Houses habitually got drunk at
dinner ; the undergraduates threw wine parties of a riotous nature.

Getting drunk, of course, has always been a favourite initiation
ceremony for young men wishing to assert their independence, and
when Newman wrote his memoir in 1874 he treated the subject
lightly, out of his own mature tolerance. But he remembered also
how strongly he had felt about it in his youth, and why. In the
early years of the century drunkenness was not a mere outburst of
high spirits but had become a social ritual ; anyone who did not join
in became an outsider, ridiculed and despised. Not only so, but the
parties were devoted simply to getting drunk, so that they were, in
a trivial way, mere orgies. Perhaps there was a psychological necessity for them ; the irrational getting its own back on the over-
reasonable and common-sensical attitude of the day. But Newman,
whose imagination never lost touch with the mysterious side of the
world, was under no such necessity. His control was not simply
the result of external habit, but of his own deepest will. The whole
process of systematic drunkenness was pointless and disgusting to
him, and became hateful when he found that the worst traditional
ritual orgy of the year took place at the Gaudy, the college feast on
Trinity Sunday and the next day. On Sunday there was communal
Holy Communion ; on Monday the community saturnalia. Nobody thought twice about the juxtaposition ; so completely had the
participation in Christ's sacrifice become a mechanical observance.
But to Newman, fresh from his first deep contact with divinity, it
was a horrible desecration. He surprised a contemporary by saying
passionately that drunkenness was like murder. He did not mean
a like crime, but a similar violation of life in the soul.

Horrible as it was to him, however, it was hard to stand altogether aside at first. The social pressure was intense and he was

just at the age when ridicule hurts most, and to be despised seems
the ultimate catastrophe. Newman paid the penalty for his exceptional awareness by acute self-consciousness. Nor was he cold and
aloof by nature, able to retire into a proud solitude, convinced of
his superiority to those who scorned him. He was sociable, and
liked to be liked. His greatest difficulty as a leader of others was
that he was so anxious to please everybody that he sometimes
annoyed all of them. Consequently the wine parties became an
ordeal in his first term ; the attitude he took would determine his
position among his immediate associates as well as affecting his own
character. The test was the more searching as he did not yet know
about the Gaudy ; parties were just parties.

Thus he accepted an invitation to one in November, perhaps
the more hopefully as he was asked to bring his violin. Perhaps he
expected something like Dr. Nicholas' musical evenings. He wrote
down in his journal afterwards what had happened. 'The first
thing that surprised me on entering the room was to see a long
table ; the next to hear a smothered laugh at my conductor's announcing "Mr. Newman and his fiddle". I was offered a chair, a
glass and a decanter.' He realized at once that they had invited him
merely to make a fool of him for their own amusement. Playing
the fiddle, as he probably had not discovered then, was not considered an accomplishment for a gentleman. Determined not to be
a butt, he steadily refused their requests for a tune. But he soon
found that their other purpose was to make him drunk. No doubt
they expected such a very young and innocent freshman would not
have any idea how much he could take and it would be all the more
comic to see him succumb. They kept passing the bottle and
pressing wine on him. But Newman was very cautious. He drank
only three glasses and then rose to say he must take his leave. They
all shouted that he must not go ; but he went all the same.

It was not the end of the incident. The jokers were annoyed to
lose their sport and about ten days later a band of them, in a fit of
mob violence to which youths are notoriously prone, paid a sudden
uninvited call on the virtuous Mr. Newman. Newman wrote indignantly in his journal : 'Is it gentlemanly conduct to rush into my
room, and to strut up and down at the farther end of it, and ask
me in a laughing tone how I do ; and then after my remaining
some time in silent wonder, to run and bolt the door and say they
are hiding from someone'.

Laughing or not, they were plainly in what a later generation

would recognize as a 'debagging' mood. Locking themselves in
with him, they obviously meant to scare him if they could. The
ringleader was a formidable fellow '6 feet 3 or 4 inches high and
stout in proportion', as Newman noted. Probably they expected
the youthful fiddle player to take fright, or get in a fuss, but Newman
kept his head and his silent stare put them off.

'Then, to tell me they have come to invite me to wine, and when
I answered in the negative, pressing and pressing me to come, and
asking me in a gay manner if I do not mean to take a first class, telling
me I read too much and overdo it, and then to turn from me suddenly
and hollow out "Let him alone, come along" and to throw open the
door ? I said such conduct was not the conduct of gentlemen and
ordered them to leave the room. One then said he would knock me
down if I were not too contemptible a fellow.' This was humiliating,
even for a sixteen-year-old facing a lout six-foot-four. But Newman's
coolness had won the day ; the rioters went off and next day the giant
came to apologize, saying 'a sudden gust of passion had overset him'.
He told Newman he had 'seldom or never seen anyone act more
firmly'. This must have been gratifying. 'I told him to think no
more about it. He shook hands and went.'

After this Newman was left alone ; he had won the respect of
those who could have made life a torment for a more timid youth.
Some seventy-odd years later Newman's friend and ex-curate
Bloxam wrote to ask if he remembered one Alfred Roberts, rather
uncouth and eccentric. 'He was somewhat ill-treated by the Roughs
of the College at that time, and you were kind to him ; and gave him
a religious book.' Perhaps this was the 'poor despised awkward
man' who was one of the few who stood with Newman in refusing to
take part in the Gaudy. So that Newman not only succeeded in
braving the social ridicule he brought on himself by his virtue and
his fiddle, but even dared to compromise himself still further by
befriending the unpopular odd man out. He did not find this sort
of thing easy, bitterly accusing himself of feeling embarrassed to
be seen about with an oddity, perhaps this very man. But still, he
did it.

To finish the story of Newman's resistance to the ritual orgies :
at his first Gaudy, attending in all the glory of his newly won scholar's
gown, when he saw that the sole object was to get drunk, he walked
out and never went to another. Already people began to take a lead
from him, and during the next year quite a party grew up which
affected to despise the custom. But when Trinity came round again

the opposition crumpled up. 'There has been weakness and fear of ridicule,' Newman wrote to Mr. Mayers. 'Those who resisted last year, are going this. I fear even for myself, so great a delusion seems suddenly to have come over all.' But still he did not go. He did not attack those who did ; sometimes he felt this was cowardice. But his refusal to take part was in itself a protest, and earned him a certain amount of enmity. It had its effect all the same, in the following years.

In telling this incident in his memoir of 1874 Newman treated it lightly, but he remarked in passing that ' in spite of his gentleness of manner, there were in him at all times *"ignes suppositi cineri doloso"* which as the sequel of his life shows, had not always so much to justify them . . .' Fires under the deceptive ash — many people were to discover that, with surprise.

Newman's first year ended gloriously with his winning a college scholarship which had then for the first time been opened to all comers. Although he was only seventeen Mr. Short pushed him into it, almost at the last minute. Since he had little time in which to be anxious, he did well, though others told him he turned pale when called for his interview. He kept the news secret from home till he could tell of his success, and when he went back to Alton for the summer his proud father greeted him, beaming, 'What a happy meeting this !' The scholarship was worth £60 a year for nine years — no mean sum in those days : it was more than Newman was to receive as Vicar of St. Mary's.

Typically he rushed out from his interview to buy his scholar's gown, sign of his triumph, and the other candidates asked him if it was decided. 'What was I to say ? "It was." "And who got it ?" "Oh, an in-college man," I said, and hurried away as fast as I could. On returning with my newly earned gown I met the whole set going to their respective homes. I did not know what to do. I held my eyes down.' He was too shy to say 'I won it'.

With his scholarship to his credit Newman launched into his second year with confidence and enjoyment. His intellectual curiosity was such that he could not resist studies quite unrelated to his examinations. Sciences then in their infancy attracted him. Mr. Kinsey, the Dean, took him to Professor Buckland's lectures on geology ; he attended others on mineralogy ; like Shelley he became interested in chemistry, read manuals and tried experiments. He read Gibbon, whose style he admired ; he read Locke and other philosophers. He analysed the plays of Aeschylus according to the principles of Aristotle's Poetics. The Bible was not neglected ; he studied, meditated, and learnt by heart long passages which he could recite even in old age. He speculated, rather crudely, on creation in the light of the new geological discoveries.

In 1819 he and Bowden collaborated to produce a periodical they called *The Undergraduate*. It started somewhat pompously, but got more comic with every issue ; funny verses were contributed by a friend. But after several numbers were out (and selling quite well) the secret got out that 'Newman of Trinity was editor'. The bashful journalist was so alarmed at this publicity that he handed over the concern to the printers and it soon died. Newman grumbled that it was his name and not Bowden's which got out, but he was already noticeable, while Bowden was born to be a Horatio.

Another collaboration the same year was a poem, issued in two parts, and entitled *St. Bartholomew's Eve*. In his old age Newman described it with amusement as 'a romance founded on the Massacre of St. Bartholomew. The subject was the issue of the unfortunate union of a Protestant gentleman with a Catholic lady, ending in the tragical death of both, through the machinations of a cruel fanatic priest, whose inappropriate name was Clement. . . . There were no love scenes, nor could there be, for, as it turned out to the monk's surprise, the parties had been, some time before the action, husband and wife by a clandestine marriage, known, however, to the father of the lady.' Newman said that Bowden was responsible for the historical and picturesque parts, and he for the theological. But he marked the passages, and the truth emerges : Bowden wrote the dull descriptions and Newman most of the romantic and dramatic episodes. For though there were no declarations of love, it was Newman who wrote of the last tragic meeting of the ill-fated pair. The lady hears his step :

> And Florence knows — see! see! the quick-drawn breath,
> The cold cheek sickening with the hues of death —
> The starting eye — the feeble tott'ring frame —
> The faint wild shriek with which she sounds his name —
> 'Julian!' — 'My wife, my dearest, then again
> I see thee, love! I have not pray'd in vain!'

It was Newman, too, who had most to say about the wicked priest Clement. But there was a passage on silence, music and the angels, which could only be his.

> There is a spirit singing aye in air . . .

It is not surprising that during this year, when Newman was eighteen and beginning to feel his powers, he became less eager to take Orders and more ambitious for a career in the world. His father had always intended him for the Law, and it was the entrance, for those not born to power, into the administrative and political life of the nation. The Union was not founded in Newman's day — he was one of those who suggested a university debating society ; but if it had existed he would undoubtedly have been a member. He went to some History lectures because he heard that the names of those present were sent to the Minister ; this piece of worldliness, forgotten by everyone else, he set down in his memoir. Bowden, too, who took his schools this year, was to read Law in London. Most of Newman's best friends all his life were lawyers. In 1829 when he was campaigning about Peel's election, someone remarked that he would have made a good Lord Chancellor. This kind of career appealed to the active side of his nature ; the faculty of leadership which kept drawing people to collect round him in whatever sphere he entered.

But in the summer of 1820 he gave up these secular ambitions. It was another, though minor crisis. Schools were in sight, and he was fagging away, sometimes twelve or fifteen hours a day. Bowden was gone, whose presence introduced an atmosphere of relaxation. Newman was alone ; the entries in his journal all became very serious. Before the scholarship examination he had prayed not for success, but for 'good'. Now he read over his journals and saw how, after his success, he had gradually dropped his standards ; he thought he had become vain, self-seeking and ambitious. He began to be afraid that if he won honours in the Schools the same thing would happen all over again. He tried to pray not to succeed if it would mean spiritual failure ; but on the other hand he desperately needed to do well, not only for himself, but for the sake of his harassed family, for the brewery scheme was not a success and things went ill for them. They had returned to London, and Mr. Newman was trying to manage a Clerkenwell brewhouse, but his position was deteriorating all the time towards the bankruptcy of the next year.

The strain was too much for Newman and he broke down in the examination. He was called up a day sooner than he expected, lost his head and retired before the end, unable to continue. Even so he could hardly believe in his own humiliation when he saw the list : 'his name did not appear at all on the Mathematical side of the paper, and in Classics it was found in the lower division of the second class

of honours, which at that time went by the contemptuous title of
"Under-the-line", there being as yet no third and fourth classes'.
He was only nineteen, and most of the other candidates were twenty-
two, but everyone had expected him to win honours. Trinity men
had said that if he did not, it was no use anybody from their college
attempting it.   It was a dreadful shock.

'It is all over and I have not succeeded,' he wrote to his father,
overwhelmed at the thought of the disappointment he was causing
them.   Father and mother wrote anxiously, hearing the note of
anguish and despair, and he pulled himself together to reassure them.
'Very much I *have* suffered, but the clouds have passed away.'
Indeed, the situation was not irreparable.   He still had his scholarship, which would enable him to stay at the university till he was old
enough to take Holy Orders ; he could earn money coaching pupils,
and perhaps try later for a Fellowship.   His failure was due to nerves,
not to laziness or stupidity.   But it meant that nothing was to come
to him easily.   So many less gifted than he, born into the upper and
ruling class, who never had to worry about money, passed comfortably into whatever career they chose to enter ; Newman had to slave
for all he gained, and to suffer humiliating defeats for every prize.

Morally his present defeat did more for him than success. Meeting the blow with courage, he suddenly matured from youth to
manhood.   A certain boyish precocity and an alternation of moods of
hilarity and solemnity, stabilized as responsibility settled, so early,
on him.   The change, which was begun by his failure in November
1820, showed itself more clearly the next year, not long after his
twentieth birthday.   For, having got through the restless and excitable
period of adolescence without any interior disasters, he soon found
himself engaged in a fierce struggle with a host of invisible enemies
within his own soul.   This battle for spiritual integrity was all the
more exhausting because it synchronized with his equally intense
battle with his adverse circumstances in the external world.

1821–1822

The Devil and the Flesh

NEWMAN always had great resilience ; in the Christmas holidays, far from moping over his failure he amused himself going to the theatre. By the next year he had read Wilberforce on Christian living and was shocked at his own laxity. The puritan attitude to the arts and entertainment is apt to become negative and self-righteous, but the true basis of it is the necessity for the Christian to be on his guard against slipping into a life of God-eclipsing self-indulgence. It was as an ascesis that Newman accepted this outlook, which proved a passing phase. Even so he never gave up his music, and concerts, or adopted a censorious attitude to those who did frequent light entertainment. 'Signor Giovanni Enrico Neandrini has finished his first composition,' he announced, on returning to Oxford. He was pleased with his harmonies.

That term, in reaction to his concentrated fagging of the year before, he returned to mineralogy and scientific experiments, and thought of learning Persian. But after Easter he spent a very serious summer term reading (Evangelical) theology, studying the Bible and making collections of texts on various themes. He was puzzled to find his conversion did not fit the descriptions he read. He did not doubt its reality, but nor did he yet doubt the theories he had learned to associate with it. All the same the Calvinist doctrine of predestination, which he had never put in a high place, began to fade from his mind. In any case he had not dwelt on the idea of others being irrevocably destined to damnation ; he had thought only of God's mercy to him.

But his mind was occupied more deeply with the essentials of Christian doctrine, especially the mystery of the Trinity. It is significant that he had a dream in which a spirit came and spoke to him so wonderfully of the Trinity that he fell on his knees in gratitude. The threefold being of God was present to him not merely as a theological idea, but as an image of transforming psychological power, and a spiritual reality evoking an act of adoration.

At the same time he was struggling with the psychological difficulties of regular prayer. 'I can read religious books, the most
spiritual, with great pleasure, and, when so engaged, feel myself
warmed to prayer and thanksgiving ; but let the appointed hour of
devotion arrive, and I am cold and dead. My head is full of God
during the day, and particularly of the salvation of others, and I can
offer up heartfelt prayers in my solitary walk, but this dreadful listless-
ness comes on me morning after morning and evening after evening.'
But he persevered in these exercises in spite of the refusal of his
emotions to take part in them.

When he went home in August he and Francis determined to
take the Sacrament once a fortnight during the vacation. Frank
was now about sixteen, and in the first fervour of his conversion ;
he too had come under the influence of Mr. Mayers, and he had
picked up a great deal more than John of the teaching peculiar to
the Evangelicals of the day. He was a brilliantly clever boy, but
unlike John he had very little imagination, or it was early swamped
by feeling and abstract reasoning. He had that passionate idealism
which is apt to disregard facts, and especially those most stubborn
of facts, actual persons. Adolescents, knowing little of the world,
tend to be doctrinaires anyway. In September Francis created a
scene in the family by refusing to copy a letter for his father on
Sunday. Mr. Newman appealed to John, and when he backed up
his brother, transferred his anger to him. 'A scene ensued more
painful than any I have experienced,' John wrote in his journal. 'I
have been sadly deficient in meekness, long suffering, patience and
filial obedience.' In fact, his temper was as quick as his father's,
and he argued the case with warmth.

It was typical of both that everything was made up the next day.
'My father was reconciled to us to-day,' John recorded. 'When I
think of the utter persuasion he must entertain of the justice of his
views of our apparent disobedience, the seeming folly of our opinions,
and the way in which he is harassed by worldly cares, I think his
forgiveness of us an example of very striking candour, forbearance
and generosity.'

Not only John's father, but his mother was displeased with him.
'She seemed to think I was righteous overmuch,' Newman had
written in August, 'and was verging upon enthusiasm. I was also
leading Francis with me.' His parents thought it unnecessary to
approach the Sacrament so often. Mr. Newman also criticized his
eldest son for leaving out Charles. It was difficult to get Charles

in, for he was in process of rejecting religion, and tended to argue
and scoff. But John tried, and after a fortnight felt he was succeeding better. Also, he noted that 'so cold a veil does not seem to
separate me from my Father'.

Undoubtedly his present religious fervour irritated his father,
but John was unlike some youthful enthusiasts in realizing his own
deficiencies. How easily he might have adopted a self-righteous
attitude to a father who was not 'converted'! He might annoy him,
but he did not condemn him. On the other hand he was merciless
in analysing himself. In August he wrote, 'I am very deficient in
spirituality in prayer, in brotherly love, meekness, humility, forgiveness of injuries, charity, benevolence, purity, truth and patience. I
am very bad-tempered, vain, proud, arrogant, prone to anger and
vehement'. Mr. Mayers, whom he visited at Ealing in September,
probably gave him advice and encouragement, but in some ways
John must have already outgrown Mayers' guidance.

He was very much alone in struggling with his moral problems.
He adopted from books methods of examining his conscience, and
confessed his sins regularly and in some detail to his journal. 'The
time has come round for the celebration of the death of my dear
Saviour', he wrote before the Sacrament service. '. . . How deficient I am in any good thing . . . I am enclosed in a net . . . I
look down on others whom I do not know, and those I meet in the
streets, who appear of an inferior rank to myself, with ineffable
contempt, and look up with meanness, I may say, and awe to those
who seem above me. I am horribly vain of my attainments, abilities
and performances. And as to pride, it is leading me every minute
into ill nature, anger, lying and uncharitableness. . . .' It is not
unusual for a clever young man to be snobbish and vain, but it is
uncommon for him to admit it. Conceit and snobbery are not
among the sins that people like to boast of.

This side of Newman's life, which so much preoccupied him just
now, was not apparent to others except in occasional impatience and
obstinacy in his opinions. Jemima was at Strand-on-the-Green,
where Aunt Betsy had started a little school for young ladies, and
just after the row over the Sunday letter John was writing to her,
'Talking of Harriett leads me to observe that she is a girl possessed of
rashness (the pun I cannot claim) but she is looking quite herself,
smiling, sitting on the sofa, with pretty pink cheeks and blue eyes —
(the wording is not mine) — I am obliged to keep Francis off by
main force, the boy is now snorting in my ears. . . .'

Francis was to go back to Oxford with John, to live with him in lodgings and be coached by him for the university. John was determined that he should have this chance, and reckoned to pay for his keep by taking private pupils. Peace was restored with Mr. Newman, and, aware of his imminent bankruptcy, he warned John to take away all his personal belongings. But John did not understand the hint, and in November everything had to be sold, including John's music, which they bid for and lost. When Newman was an old man a lady bought his music and inquired why he should have parted with it. He told Jemima that for his father's sake he was 'obliged to shuffle', saying that he could not answer for a boy's negligences fifty years ago. It *was* negligence, he told his sister, for he ought to have been more alert. He always tried to keep his father's failures secret 'for his sake who laboured and spent himself for us', as he wrote in a note on Alton. The Bank crash was not Mr. Newman's fault, and to start a new life at fifty proved too much for him. Nor were his easy-going nature and irascible generosity the qualities to advance him in the competitive world of London trade.

John wrote affectionate, if somewhat solemn, letters home when the bankruptcy was declared, saying how lucky they were that their troubles came from without and not from within; they were so united a family. Whatever happened must turn out well in the end, for 'God will give good'. But he was anxious to do as much as he could to help. He already had a plan: to stand for a Fellowship at Oriel. His Trinity friends thought it madness after his failure in the Schools. Oriel had the highest reputation for learning; it was said that 'the common room stank of logic'. But the Dean's cousin, an Oriel man whom Newman met at dinner, told him that 'the principal thing at the examination for Fellows was writing Latin'. Newman felt confident he could do that, and when, in December, he saw an essay by a rival, he thought he could do better.

But the idea roused desires so strong as to alarm him. 'How active still are the evil passions of vain glory, ambition etc. in my soul!' he wrote in his journal. 'After my failure last November I thought they never would be unruly again. . . . Alas! no sooner is any mention made of my standing for a Fellowship, than every mound and barrier seems swept away, and tides of passion spread and overflow and deluge me in every direction, and without Thy help, O Lord, what will be the end of this?'

Nevertheless he could not put the audacious idea out of his mind.

He could not help feeling he belonged in that logical common room, where learning was prized, and drunkenness considered boorish. 'Porter, does the kettle boil?' the Oxford men shouted, passing what they believed to be a tea-drinking community. Newman made up his mind to try for a Fellowship next Easter, and began to practise himself in composition. If he could win it, he would have a settled income, relieve his father's burdens and secure Frank's future.

Yet for all his good intentions, when he went home, all the tensions of the summer were apparent again. The Southampton Street house had had to be given up, and the family were living in lodgings. Much of their personal belongings had been sold. Mr. Newman was broken in spirit. Charles was no use at all; his father had pronounced gloomily that he would never make his way in the world. The two younger girls lived with Aunt Betsy, whose finances were also somewhat precarious. The brothers were all growing up and their very diverse temperaments were bound to grate on each other and on their parents.

Early in January 1822 John went to Kentish Town Chapel and was much impressed with a sermon in which the preacher said that 'to come out of an affliction is an awful thing, for calamity either leaves us better or worse'. He came home and poured it all out. Mr. Newman was irritated and delivered a lecture, which his son afterwards wrote down in his journal. 'Take care,' said Mr. Newman. 'It is very proper to quote Scripture but you poured out texts in such quantities. Have a guard. You are encouraging a nervousness and morbid sensibility, and irritability, which may be very serious. I know what it is myself, perfectly well. I know it is a disease of the mind. Religion, when carried too far, induces softness of mind. You must *exert* yourself and do everything you can. Depend upon it, no one's principles can be established at twenty. Your opinions in two or three years will certainly, *certainly* change. . . . Take care, I repeat. . . . The temper you are encouraging may lead to something alarming. Weak minds are carried into superstition, and strong ones into infidelity. Do not commit yourself. Do nothing ultra. . . . I know you write for the Christian Observer. My opinion of the Christian Observer is this, that it is humbug. You must use exertions. That letter was more like the composition of an old man, than of a youth just entering life with energy and aspirations.'

John wrote it all down. He did not think he would change his opinions. What young man does? But his reaction was not to justify himself but to turn to anxious prayer. 'O God, grant me to pray earnestly against any delusive heat, or fanatic fancy, or proud imagination of fancied superiority, or uncharitable zeal. Make me and keep me humble and teachable, modest and cautious. I have sadly neglected till lately to pray against fanaticism, spiritual pride etc.' A few days later, looking back on that Christmas vacation, he felt he had been 'generally hot and violent', and that he had been once 'particularly undutiful to my Father — once to my Mother'. He had apologized on both occasions, 'but what little good does that do', he commented shrewdly.

An incident of the year before shows the way in which Mr. Newman could be irritated by John, and misunderstand him. At the trial of Queen Caroline John had taken the side of the King. His father was exasperated. 'Well, John! I suppose I ought to praise you for knowing how to rise in the world. Go on! Go on! Persevere! Always stand up for the men in power! And in time you will get your promotion!' This comment was recalled by Francis Newman, in the rambling and bitter reminiscences he wrote after his brother's death, when he was nearly ninety himself. He then shared with his father the misconception that John worshipped authority *in se* and in any form.

After this uncomfortable vacation Newman returned to Oxford; when his mother wrote to say Francis was not coming again he was dreadfully disappointed, and set it down as a 'punishment to me for the wicked ill nature and moroseness with which I treated him last term'. He was glad when his parents relented and Francis joined him after all. But for the next few years his journal was punctuated with confessions of ill temper towards Frank, ill humour, and later 'cruelty'. These records are extremely revealing of Newman's natural temperament and the way he dealt with it, for he struggled with it ceaselessly, and when things seemed to go better he acutely observed that it was probably because he then saw less of his brother. He never felt he had succeeded in overcoming what he considered a serious sin.

A superficial reading of the journals suggests that John was unkind, sarcastic, cross and altogether a mental bully to his younger brother. No criticism of Frank's behaviour was recorded, so that he seems the innocent victim of jealous bad temper. But from what is known of Frank when a few years older, it is plain he could be very annoying indeed. He was so earnest, so certain he was right, so rigid in putting principles into practice, and so censorious, especially, it may be noticed, of his eldest brother. Frank was always abnormally sensitive to the fact that John was his senior ; perhaps it was a disguise for the fear that he might in some way be his superior. Even when Frank had won himself a respected position among London liberal intellectuals and was a Professor in London University, he would occasionally burst out aggressively in peevishly resentful letters. Only when John appeared to be a failure was he able to be friendly, and then in a somewhat condescending way. Yet any pressure from John in early years was unconscious. At this very period John even encouraged Francis to criticise him by suggesting that he should give him the hint with a look if he noticed him slipping into 'hastiness or heat in conversation'.

It is a surprise to read, after the wicked ill-nature of the first term, the entry for December 1821 : 'I have gone on day after day so grievously sinning in ill temper, that I have come to the resolution through God's grace to make an open confession to Francis, the first time I do so again'. Francis, therefore, was so unaware of all this ill temper that to confess it to him would be a salutary humiliation. And indeed, when John in 1845, before making his general confession to the priest who received him as a Catholic, wrote to ask Frank's forgiveness for his cruelty, Frank, who was not given to making allowances for him, replied that he could not remember any. And even in his Recollections, when he was trying to smash the public image of the Cardinal, he spoke of him as a generous and kind brother. What annoyed him in John had nothing to do with cruelty.

If most of this ill temper never got out in words, still less in actions, was Newman morbidly exaggerating ? Whether it affected Frank or not, it certainly affected him. In December 1822 he copied into his journal what he had said or written to his mother : 'I have felt while with Francis at Oxford, a spirit of desperate ill temper and sullen anger rush on me, so that I was ready to reply and act in the most cruel manner to intentions of the greatest kindness and affection. So violent has this sometimes proved, that I have quite trembled from head to foot, and thought I should fall down under excess of agitation.' It was not so much the violence of the passion that made him feel faint, as the equal violence with which he met and suppressed it. To yield to an aggressive impulse is less exhausting at the moment than to resist it ; the difference made in the character can only be judged by effects, and over a long period.

Two things are particularly noticeable in Newman's youthful battle
with his own temper : the clarity with which he saw his own defects,
and the entire lack of censoriousness towards those of others.

The battle took place at a time when he was in a state of chronic
fatigue and nervous tension. He worked so intensively to earn money
that he only allowed himself four hours sleep at night ; shockingly
inadequate for a young man of twenty, especially as his mind, during
his waking hours, was nearly always at full stretch. To increase the
strain he had another tiresome pupil. In 1856 he wrote in pencil in
his journal, 'My pupil was a little wretch, aged 17', and then crossed
it out, perhaps thinking it savoured of self-justification. 'Let me
praise that excessive Mercy which has blessed me with so strong a
frame', he wrote in 1823, in his birthday check-up of the preceding
year. 'I have sometimes quite trembled, on retiring to rest, at my
own exertions.' Everyone knows how fatigue increases irritability ;
but Newman did not make it an excuse — the observations appeared
in different connexions in his journal.

It was natural that at this period Newman should be troubled by
other passions besides anger ; in youth instincts are awakened which
have yet to be orientated and humanized before they can be dignified
by the name of love. Everyone has to go through the transformation
of instinct into personal love, if he is not to remain immature indefinitely, but there is more than one way of making the transition. In
Newman's day all respectable young men were expected to marry
when they reached a suitable age, and settle down to rear a family ;
but until then, so long as they were reasonably discreet, a temporary
licence was extended to the lusts of the flesh. Ordinary worldly
people expected this pattern of behaviour, and in the upper classes
even marriage was far from being considered the end of amorous
adventure ; indeed, for women it was only the beginning. But for
young men growing up a certain amount of promiscuous indulgence
was taken for granted, though not mentioned in polite society, and
the two universities each had their well-known houses, and succession
of famous whores. Like drunkenness, such behaviour was expected
and overlooked by the authorities.

This background of casual sexual morals and not the stricter code
of later decades of the nineteenth century, was that in which Newman
grew up and set himself to follow the Christian ideal of chastity. He
always took a simple view of the temptations likely to beset a youthful
Christian in this respect ; he associated youth with lustfulness in its
basic and primitive form — maturity had other and subtler trials.

It was not a question of love, but of subpersonal physical desires, blind demands for satisfaction, innocent in animals but at the human level selfish and regressive. Everyone knows how strong they can be, deriving their force from the hunger for life that, properly organized, generates the energy for all forms of human love.

In 1849, after long experience in guiding young men during this phase of their development, Newman wrote a sermon on *Saintliness the Standard of Christian Principle*, in which he traced the growth of a saint — any man consistently aiming at holiness and afterwards recognized as having attained it to a high degree. For the period of youth, he took three instances of young men tempted not by any complicated subtleties, but simply by lustful suggestions which they did not want to entertain, but from the violence of their reactions evidently felt to be a danger. One was a Roman martyr — the Romans were particularly resentful of the chastity, and especially the virginity of Christians. Another was St. Thomas Aquinas, whose brothers, hoping to distract him from his vocation, shut him up for days and then sent a harlot to seduce him. St. Thomas chased her off with a burning branch from the fire. The other exemplar Newman chose was St. Benedict, whose trial, in his solitary life, was psychological rather than actual, but none the less dangerous for that.

In this sermon Newman wrote of the saint : 'He grows up, and he has just the same temptations as others, perhaps more violent ones. Men of this world, carnal men, unbelieving men, do not believe that the temptations which they themselves experience, and to which they yield, can be overcome.' By the time he wrote this he knew only too well the opinions of worldly men on the subject. They think a resolute Christian, he said, 'a hypocrite, who practises in private the sins which he denounces in public ; or . . . they consider that he never felt the temptation, and they regard him as a cold and simple person, who has never outgrown his childhood, who has a contracted mind, who does not know the world and life, who is despicable while he is without influence and dangerous and detestable from his very ignorance when he is in power'.

Newman knew that this was what was said of him, during the days of his influence at Oxford. Since no one could discover anything scandalous in his life, his chastity was put down to defective nature — either he was in this respect an overgrown child, or otherwise abnormal. There is no defence against such an imputation. That Newman resented its injustice is indicated in a sermon of 1840, when, in reference to the ideal of celibacy, he spoke of the 'slurs' cast on those who attempted it.   By that time, for all the reserve he maintained, he was known (and much hated) as a champion, not only of chastity, but of virginity vowed to God ; no one was in a better position, in the masculine society of the university, to know the commonplace reactions.   Newman always thought that much of the hostility he had to face in Oxford was due less to his theological opinions than his uncompromising preaching of such an unpopular virtue.   The fact that he lived up to his ideal himself only infuriated the more those who felt it a threat to their own laxity.   'Slurs' on the natural virility of the standard-bearer were the inevitable, if dishonourable, self-defence of the average man.

However, by the time he had to face this Newman was a mature man, though his comments reflect back on his own youth.   His own battle, in 1820 and the next few years, was necessarily personal and private.   As far as can be told from his journal his temptations, like St. Benedict's, were on the psychological level, and came in the form of what he called 'bad thoughts'.   Since his standard was high, the thoughts were probably not very evil, not vicious or particularly sensual.   Nor, since he noted the attacks among his sins, did he voluntarily indulge in them ; but he had a vivid imagination, and he was not 'a cold and simple person' ignorant of life.   These attacks of 'bad thoughts' tended to come when he went home in the vacation, perhaps because of the emotional tensions there.   Although they never were as persistent as the attacks of bad temper, or the continual struggle with intellectual pride and vanity, they recurred during several years.   In 1825, when he was just ordained and twenty-four years old, Newman wrote, almost with surprise : 'I seem more pure in heart than I was.   I say it with trembling, but this year past God has been most gracious.   I do not recollect one grievous attack — one or two momentary temptations I have had, but I have been able to turn my back on them.   Doubtless my incessant engagements is one advantage ; besides, I am getting older.   What an age I seem to be !   It is quite dreadful.'

This entry in the journal tells indirectly much more of Newman than he realized when he wrote it.   First, he prayed against this form of temptation :   he believed that the power of deliverance from it was God's, not his.   Secondly, he turned his back — shifted his attention instead of engaging in a direct battle of will against desire.   This is the classic method adopted by experienced Christians through the ages.   To rely on the conscious personal will is considered a dangerous mistake, though a common one.   Desires simply suppressed by force of will often take an humiliating revenge, not always in the sexual sphere. Ancient saints and modern psychologists seem to agree in this diagnosis. Newman, with neither to guide him, somehow found the right path, so that his instinctive energy, restrained from expending itself in blind obedience to casual desires, was yet not repressed with disgust or dismissed from consciousness, but was slowly transformed into human love and sympathy.

Newman was never at any time in his youth unaware that he was liable, like everyone else, to suggestions of a sexual nature which could not be entertained willingly, far less indulged, without sin. Considering the intensity of his conversion to God and his passionate desire for holiness, without which no one can hope to see the supreme object and source of love, Newman's attitude to these bad thoughts of his was remarkably balanced. He did not magnify them out of all proportion — he always knew the spiritual sins were more dangerous; but neither did he repudiate them, as distasteful dreams for which he could not be held responsible. Twenty years later he showed the same common sense dealing with the same subject, in some Latin prayers he wrote to help an adolescent boy he was teaching at Littlemore. The prayers are directed against specific youthful difficulties, but with great brevity and simplicity, and God is invoked as *caritatis amator* — the lover of true love.

The spiritual danger to the chaste, as medieval writers frequently insisted, is pride. It is easy for the chaste to think themselves above the common herd and to be disgusted with the sensual behaviour of others. Never at any time in his life did Newman show any sign of this form of pride. He spoke severely in sermons of intemperate living, but he was far more concerned to show the dangers of compromising with the attractions of the world, the corruptions of seeking power and the false idolatry of reason. He was always understanding of those whose weakness led them into sins of the flesh which had not been his. Perhaps his realization of the importance of sins of the mind and imagination helped him there. He sometimes talked as if he had committed all the sins of youth, because he knew himself capable of committing them. It was this self-knowledge, this admission that in his irritations with Frank, in his bad thoughts, were the seeds of evil which could issue in murders and sexual sins, that Newman learned both humility and sympathy with the sinful — and a clear sight of the nature and working of moral evil.

For strength in attacking the roots of evil in himself he relied on God. In future years, if he mentioned the trials of adolescence, it was in gratitude to God for bringing him through them, never in self-congratulation at having conquered. Yet passions and appetites are not brought into conscious control by remaining passive ; the struggle was constant and continued. Many of Newman's contemporaries, who translated their bad thoughts into action and then forgot them till the next time, would have considered it better for him had he done the same ; and no one can deny that it is more tiring to restrain the passions than to yield to them. Nor was it less exhausting, possibly it was more so, to wrestle with them in the soul before they expressed themselves in action. But chastity, which is integrity of body and mind, is an expression of obedience, and to purify the heart is to purify the whole person.

Newman's voluntary purgatory, so searching and so persevering, went on all through these years of intense labour, to get learning and to get money to help his family — years when most young men he knew were simply enjoying themselves, whether innocently or not. He thanked God for his strong frame, and it must have been strong to stand the life he led it ; such a strain might have injured permanently a nature in which there was some marked weakness, of body or mind. Newman was reckoned as tall among his contemporaries ; he must have reached his full height about now. He was always thin, but with that wiry toughness which often has more staying power than brawn and muscle. He had a tremendous nervous energy, which on occasions of stress and anxiety could prevent his sleeping — though normally he slept well for the few hours he allowed himself. But it carried him through formidable undertakings, and after any shock, mental or physical, he would recover extraordinarily quickly from near-prostration. If his body was tried too hard he lost consciousness, either in a faint or in sudden sleep. He walked fast, he worked fast ; his letters were rapid talk. But he thought things out slowly, not content till he had got right to the bottom of every difficulty. At this time his affections were almost wholly absorbed in his family, especially in his sisters. At Oxford he was lonely, going for solitary walks ; his Trinity friends had gone down, and he had not yet found others.

In February 1822 he was twenty-one and in April he stood for the Oriel Fellowship.

1822–1824

Oriel and Ordination

NEWMAN nearly repeated the collapse of his Schools at Oriel. It only made him the more anxious that he had a feeling he would succeed. On his twenty-first birthday he wrote in his examination of conscience : 'Thou knowest my heart — I am in Thy presence. Thou seest how fondly, and I fear idolatrously, my affections are set on succeeding at Oriel. Take all hope away, stop not an instant, O my God, if so doing will gain me Thy Spirit.' He remained hopeful till he had written to the Provost for permission to stand, and then reaction set in. 'Yesterday and to-day I find I cannot write Latin at all. See, God can take away the fruit of my labour at a stroke. Surely I have set my heart on success.' A week later : 'I think most certainly I shall fail, and therefore have cause to look forward for some great trials this next year ; for how am I to live ? The Lord is my Shepherd ; I shall not want. I am obliged to spend every day ; but whether from being unused to want, or from my natural temper, I feel no anxiety.'

The first day of the examination was Saturday April 6th and at the end of it Newman felt worn out and harassed. He took the Sacrament next day, Easter Sunday. His anxiety was so great he thought he was going to be ill ; his back seemed inflamed at night, but at last he went to sleep and felt better when he woke. The day went badly. 'In the middle of the day (and I was kept in 9 hours or more) I was so ill I could do nothing, and was obliged to walk about' — up and down Oriel Hall. This 'illness' as Newman himself noted later, was a 'nervous affection', the effect of over-excitement. In despair he went to see his tutor. Kind Mr. Short was having an early dinner in his room ; he made Newman sit down and eat lamb cutlets and fried parsley, and told him he was doing very well. Thus encouraged he went off to construe in the *viva voce* 'with very great readiness and even accuracy'. The examination finished on Thursday and he went home, comforted by a motto in one of the windows of Oriel Hall : *Pie repone te.* 'Thank God I am going to bed and have been very calm the whole evening. How can I sufficiently praise Him !'

The next day, Friday April 12th — 'of all days most memorable' — he was in his lodgings in Broad Street, playing his fiddle, when the Provost's butler arrived. 'He had, he feared, disagreeable news to announce, that Mr. Newman was elected Fellow of Oriel and that his immediate presence was required there.' Apparently this was the usual formula, but Newman did not know it and thought he was trying to be impertinent. He said briefly, 'Very well', and went on fiddling. The butler, afraid from such a cool reception that he had told the wrong man, asked if he had mistaken the rooms ; Newman reassured him. But as soon as the bewildered messenger had gone, he jumped up, 'flung down his instrument and dashed downstairs with all speed to Oriel College'. And he long remembered the eager bows of the tradesmen as he hurried by : Oxford was a small place and they knew all about it.

When he arrived at the Common Room he was overcome with shyness at meeting his new colleagues. He wrote to Bowden, 'when Keble advanced to take my hand, I quite shrank, and could nearly have sunk into the floor, ashamed at so great an honour'. This was his vanity in practice ! Keble was barely thirty, but already as well known for his goodness as for his brilliance — at eighteen he had taken a double first and soon afterwards won two Essay prizes and an Oriel Fellowship. Yet he was the humblest and gentlest of all that brilliant circle.

Back to Trinity went Newman, to find the college in an uproar, bells set ringing in three towers ('I had to pay for them', he wrote) and congratulations on every side. The eventful day ended with his taking his seat in Oriel Chapel and dining in Hall, where he sat next to Keble, and tried to get used to being called 'Newman' by his distinguished colleagues, abashed to learn that he must treat them with equal familiarity. He wrote in his journal, 'I have this morning been elected Fellow of Oriel. Thank God, thank God.' He remembered the date with gratitude all his life.

But although he now had a home, an income and a career before him, there was no let-up in work. Till next year he was only a probationer ; he still lived in lodgings and worked all through the summer with his 'little wretch' of a pupil, even through the Long Vacation : 'How I longed for it to be over !' he wrote in pencil in 1856. This was the time when he only had four hours' sleep at

night. He spent an hour a day reading the Bible and prayed on his
solitary walks 'for all friends and for all mankind'. It was a hard
time. 'I find it very irksome to be so tied down as I am. I am too
very solitary. . . . Pound me, Lord, into small bits grind me down,
anything for a meek and quiet spirit.'

In 1823 he was admitted actual Fellow of Oriel, but still lived in
lodgings with Francis, who went to Worcester College in May, his
expenses paid by his brother, who had never failed to find pupils
enough for their support. This year Newman met the first of
his new friends, Edward Bouverie Pusey, who although six months
his senior, was elected the year after to an Oriel Fellowship —
Newman was thankful he had stood the year before, feeling he could
not compete with Pusey. He was a Christ Church man and so had
been from the first in the intellectual circles from which Newman,
by his being entered at Trinity, had been cut off. Newman first
saw him dining at Oriel with his friend Jelf, also a Fellow. In his
memoir he described him : 'His light curly head of hair was damp
with the cold water which his headaches made necessary for comfort ; he walked fast, with a young manner of carrying himself, and
stood rather bowed, looking up from under his eyebrows, his
shoulders rounded, and his bachelor's gown not buttoned at the
elbow but hanging loose over his wrists. His countenance was very
sweet and he spoke little.' He spoke a lot, however, on their walks
together. Newman, while admiring his goodness and humility, had
some Evangelical doubts as to whether he was 'regenerate'.

Pusey's background was very different from Newman's. His
family were wealthy landowners ; the Bouveries had come from the
Low Countries, the Puseys were so indigenous that the place where
they lived was called Pusey. Edward's father was a despotic eccentric, who had refused to marry while his mother lived. When she
died he was in his fifties ; his late chosen bride, Lady Lucy, was
devoted to her children, but even as an old lady she sat on straight-
backed chairs and never showed her feelings. Luckily for Edward,
with his studious tastes, he was not the heir, but the second of three
sons. Lady Lucy brought him up in the old High Church tradition
and he had always intended to devote himself to the ministry and
to learning. He had the true scholar's mind for collecting and
arranging a mass of information, but nothing of Newman's creative
imagination and intuitive power. His headaches and delicate health
were partly the result of his autocratic father's disapproval of the
young lady with whom he had fallen in love when scarcely more

than a boy. Mr. Pusey disliked the politics of Maria Barker's father.
Edward remained dutiful to him, but also faithful to his love ; the
tension affected his health, but not his large-scale plans for study.

Newman could talk away to Pusey, but in Oriel Common Room
he was struck dumb with shyness, so that the Fellows began to
wonder if they had not made a mistake in electing him — especially
when they heard he played in an orchestra. The great Whately
undertook to see what he was made of ; he liked to lick cubs into
shape if, like the dogs of King Charles' breed, they could be held
up by one leg without yelling. Richard Whately was not, strictly
speaking, any longer a Fellow of Oriel, for he had recently married,
and had a living at Halesworth. But Suffolk did not agree with his
delicate wife, and Oxford was much more congenial to a man of
intellectual interests, so Whately put in a curate at Halesworth. He
was thirty-five and his reputation was rising. He was already a
great Oxford character, known as the White Bear, Bear because of
his manners and White because of a rough coat he wore. He was
a huge man with a huge appetite and his dogs, Bishop and Sailor,
were the subject of many anecdotes.

This was Whately as he appeared, the picture of the hearty
extravert. But he was a more interesting character because he had
made himself almost the opposite of what he was by nature. He
was very much the youngest of a family of nine, coming six years
after the rest, and unexpectedly. As a child he was so puny and
sickly that he did not know what it was like to feel healthily hungry
till he was twelve. He was shy, timid, unhappy at school. He had
brilliant intellectual gifts and retired into his own mind with his
mental calculations and 'castle-building'. It was Copleston, now
the Provost, who, when he came up to Oxford, brought him out,
and Whately remained always devoted to him — 'my beloved
tutor', as he called him. He cured himself of his shyness by an act
of will, saying to himself, 'If I am a bear, let me be an unconscious
bear'.

These early difficulties gave Whately a certain penetration into
the character of young men, and a somewhat astringent sympathy
with the shy ones. He was an exceedingly good teacher and tutor
because, although he liked to mould the opinions of his pupils, he
took a real interest in them. His success in teaching himself not to
care about the impression he made gave him, however, a certain
moral arrogance ; there is an aggressive, self-satisfied tone behind
his aphorisms, shrewd and witty as they are. He cured himself of

over-sensitiveness by becoming almost insensitive to the feelings of others. A great intellectual, small-talk bored him ; he could not be bothered to remember or notice practical details. He was a botanically minded observer of nature and used to get up at five in the morning and go out for energetic walks before chapel.

Newman survived the ordeal of being metaphorically held up-side down in mid-air ; he remarked slyly in his memoir that Whately 'was a great talker, who endured very readily the silence of his company'. Whately pronounced Newman to have the clearest mind he knew — his highest praise. He got Newman to assist him in hammering out his articles on Logic for the *Encyclopaedia Metro-politana*, which he afterwards made into a highly successful book. Finding out how hard-up Newman was, he got him the entrée to the *Encyclopaedia*, for which in the next few years he wrote several articles, on Cicero, on Miracles, and later on Apollonius of Tyana. Whately was the first person Newman had met who questioned the right of the State to control the Church, and this principle, of the Church's sacred independence, sank deep into his mind and became one of the chief tenets of the founders of the Oxford Movement. In fact it was almost wholly Newman's contribution, for till he advanced it Froude had adhered to Keble's traditional Anglican Church-and-King line. How annoyed Whately would have been, had he realized that he had contributed to the formation of the party he so intensely disliked !

For Whately was a strong liberal, and bid fair to be the leader of the new party of progressive men in the Church ; he was am-bitious too, and did not think it wrong, as he was later to tell Hampden, 'to wish to rise in his profession'. He regarded it as a moral duty for reformers to take the highest positions they could get, and a bishopric to him was an opportunity for public service. He did not look on the Church as a sacred society preserving a divine doctrine, but as a kind of moral order within civil society. It was not establishment he objected to, but Parliamentary inter-ference ; he advocated a standing commission to deal with Church matters, composed entirely of Anglicans, for once Catholics and Dissenters were admitted to Parliament it was ridiculous to allow it to control the Church. Newman's mind, essentially more radical, did not stop at this practical compromise, but penetrated to the root of the difficulty — the nature of the Church and the source of its authority.

It is significant that Newman felt Whately, for all his liberalism, had a more permanent influence on him than Lloyd of Christ Church, afterwards for a few years Bishop of Oxford, whose theological lectures for graduates Newman and Pusey attended this year. Lloyd was Regius Professor of Divinity, and belonged to the old High-and-Dry school. He took to Newman (so that Newman was soon confessing in his journal the pride he felt at being noticed by him) but he found his Evangelical opinions irritating, and tried to bully him out of them. Newman wrote in his memoir : 'As he moved up and down his room, large in person beyond his years, asking them questions, gathering their answers and taking snuff, as he went along he would sometimes stop before Newman, fix his eyes on him as if to look him through, and then make a feint to box his ears or kick his shins, before he went on his march to and fro'. No wonder the shy young man felt 'constrained and awkward' in his presence! But he had his share in the sifting of Newman's youthful opinions, which was the result of his introduction into the Oriel circle.

Newman went home in August of this year, 1823, but it was not a very happy visit. Once he walked with Charles from Turnham Green to Knightsbridge, and discovered how far he had already repudiated religion. Charles was reading the works of the Socialist Owen, and thought reason a sufficient guide in everything. John fell into an argument with his father, too, and confessed in his journal to 'unbecoming violence'. He analysed his own behaviour acutely. 'I was not, I believe, at all warm, but I have got into a way of asserting things very strongly — "so and so is most *unjust*", another thing "most illogical etc.". Not that I give hazardous opinions or hasty judgments, but my manner is hasty and authoritative. This manner proceeds from pride. But he thinks it is worse than it is. I have accustomed myself to laughing sometimes when I argue to prevent my engaging too seriously in dispute, becoming angry etc., but this may certainly degenerate into a contemptuous manner and as such he takes it.'

That autumn was very wild, there were storms and snow at the end of October. Newman's lodgings were in the High Street 'some way from Oriel', he told his mother, 'so you may fancy it is very inconvenient to paddle to dinner in thin shoes and silk stockings'. Later that winter he was writing to his sister : 'Tell my Mother I have been speaking to my laundress about my shirts but she is too much for me — and argues most plausibly that a frill which tumbles immediately it is put on is nevertheless very well got up. If Mary were with me I would get *her* to put the matter to rights.' (Mary was then about fourteen.) The costume for the evening was still that of the period of Jane Austen's novels ; long trousers were not yet in vogue. Gentlemen wore stocks, not collars, and the clergy's were always white. Tom Mozley told a story of the eccentric Dornford (of Oriel) who told a disapproving bishop that his light trousers had faded from the prescribed clerical hue — 'and I suppose your tie has faded black', observed his lordship dryly.

In one of his letters Newman said something about Frank's getting on with his tasks, upon which Frank added his own comments : 'So you see ! who would have thought it ! only think ! Jemima ! ! impudence ! he knows nothing *about* my tasks !' So John was by no means always in a state of irritation with his young brother, and Frank was not at all in awe of him.

Newman was very much in need of money at the beginning of 1824 ; his wretched pupils delayed settling with him and his debts began to weigh on him. 'O Lord Thou doest all things well,' he wrote on February 9th, 'I owe much ; many bills should have been paid long ago ; the very forbearance of the persons concerned in asking for their money distresses me. Francis too is coming up. Yet I am fully confident Thou wilt relieve me — how mercifully I have been delivered hitherto !' The same day he was able to add, 'O gracious Father, how could I for one instant mistrust Thee ? On entering my room I see a letter, containing £35 !' In spite of his efforts to earn extra money by writing he was harassed by debts right up to the time of his ordination as a deacon, which was fixed for June. At last he resolved, reluctantly, to ask the Oriel Treasurer for a loan ; he missed him in the morning and before dinner received £40. 'The joy shed over my mind by this great deliverance is such that I could willingly undergo the same anxiety for the same delightful surprise.' Many times yet he was to go through that anxiety!

Newman had taken advice as to whether to take Orders as soon as he was old enough. Mr. Mayers, who was now curate of Over Worton, a tiny place seventeen miles north of Oxford, advised it, on the ground that the clergy needed all the help they could get. Hawkins, on the other hand, the Vicar of St. Mary's and future Provost of Oriel, was against it, as tying the young man down. Newman decided in favour of the step. In preparation for it he began fasting. Since there is no earlier reference to the practice, perhaps this was the first time. On his birthday check-up he had written : 'It may be well to watch myself whether I am not very selfish . . . what is most absurd, I am so in eating, not that I eat much (tho' this is sometimes the case) but that I am dainty, greedy, indulge my palate etc.'. His first attempts at fasting ended ignominiously : 'I could not get myself through the most childish greediness. . . . At last I have to-day. God grant it may be a means of grace.' In June, just before the ordination, he was fasting again.

When Anne Mozley was putting her volumes together in 1885, Newman sent a note on his feelings about his ordination — he was not thinking then about the Apostolical Succession, he said. 'I was dedicating myself for ever, consecrating myself, to the service of Almighty God.' This appears from the journal too. 'Make me Thy instrument . . . make use of me, when Thou wilt, and dash me to pieces when Thou wilt. Let me, living or dying, in fortune and misfortune, in health and sickness, in honour and dishonour, be Thine.' This he wrote on Friday ; on Saturday 'how hard my heart is, how dead my faith. I seem to have an unwillingness to take the vows, a dread of so irreparable a step, a doubting whether the office is so blessed, the Christian religion so true.' But the next sentence was, 'I am fasting to-day'. Doubts and anxieties did not deter him from his preparation. The heaviness of his misgiving is the measure of the intensity of his dedication.

The ceremony took place on Trinity Sunday, June 13th, 1824. 'It is over. I am Thine, O Lord ; I seem quite dizzy and cannot altogether believe and understand it. At first, after the hands were laid on me, my heart shuddered within me ; the words 'for ever' are so terrible. It was hardly a godly feeling which made me feel melancholy at the idea of giving up all for God. At times indeed my heart burnt within me, particularly during the singing of the Veni Creator. Yet, Lord, I ask not for comfort in comparison of sanctification. I feel as a man thrown suddenly in deep water.'

How deeply he was affected can be realized from a little scene on the following day, when the brothers were beginning their prayers together. John asked Francis if he had been at the ceremony ; he had, and his answer made John realize he had been praying for him, 'for me, *me* who at the time was so hard and miserable'. He began to cry and could not go on reading, but went on sobbing, unable to stop, while Frank finished it. 'O the evil of my heart, so vile, so proud. How I behave to *him*! "For ever" words never to be recalled. I have the responsibility of souls on me to the day of my death. . . . What a blessed day was yesterday. I was not sensible of it at the time — it will never come again.'

At once he began his new work, for in May, after some hesitation, he had accepted the offer of the curacy of St. Clement's ; it carried a stipend of £45 a year and surplice fees. It was no easy position. He was only a deacon. The Rector, Mr. Gutch, was eighty and often bedridden ; the population, entirely of poor people, had doubled in the last year owing to the increased trade brought by canal traffic. The church was small and old and a subscription was to be raised to build a new one ; a curate would be 'a kind of guarantee to the subscribers that every exertion will be made when the church is built, to recover the parish from meeting houses and on the other hand from alehouses'. Newman thought it 'likely to give much trouble'. He wrote in his journal : 'When I think of the arduousness I quite shudder. O that I could draw back, but I am Christ's soldier.'

Newman's first sermon was preached in the tiny church at Over Worton. Either this one or the first in his first parish, was on the text 'Man goeth forth to his work and to his labour until the evening'. He chose to preach his last sermon as an Anglican on the same text. That was the evening of a day nearly twenty years long, and he began as he went on, preaching, teaching and visiting the people in their homes. Mr. Newman doubted the propriety of this visiting, which to him savoured of 'ultraism' — 'Do nothing ultra', he kept telling his son. John assured him that most of the people liked to be visited, and told his mother that he always spoke as kindly as possible of the dissenting minister and praised the good he had done. It was not his object to get the people to church by polemics.

But he was young and inexperienced. He started out with some little books with clasps, given by Mr. Gutch, with printed columns for tabulating information about the parishioners, but very soon he was scribbling in the back of his diary, and copying notes into a larger exercise book that was not so cramping. Most of them concerned the sick, whom he visited regularly. Pusey recorded that the first shut the door in his face. 'Newman persevered. The man died penitent.' Sometimes he was taken in. One pious invalid turned out to be drinking heavily. And there was a Mrs. Bradby, whom a sick girl, to Newman's surprise, did not like. In 1840 at Littlemore he noted that he had seen her again : 'She has a nasty smooth unnatural manner, and I cannot conceive how I could have been taken in by her. But I took things on faith — i.e. I had faith that God's presence ever was, where people spoke in a certain way. I viewed things through the imagination in a remarkable degree.'

Of the girl who did not like Mrs. B. Newman wrote : 'The case
is very painful — it is like a sword going through my heart. Her
mother has since told me she said that when I entered her room she
thought of Jesus Christ in the picture. I should not have put this
down did not St. Paul say to the Galatians, "Ye received me as
Jesus".' Few received him like this ; mostly they were either unctuous or suspicious. Newman's object was to bring them to penitence
and to the Sacrament ; he often had to teach them the elementary
doctrines of Christianity. Since he was only a deacon, he had to
bring in another clergyman to administer the Sacrament ; sometimes
old Mr. Gutch managed it. He had failures here too. After having
given the Sacrament to a painter called Appleby he heard that he had
run away from his wife and children and had used shocking language
immediately after Newman's visits. But he also had some unexpected
successes. Swell, 'a very bad character', who had been a rich farmer,
but had cancer of the throat, wanted the assurance of religion without
penitence, and after a time told Newman he was doing him no good
and had better not come. Some time later Newman met him and in
tears he begged him to call. 'His poor frame was horribly emaciated.
He begged me to pray for his release.' He asked forgiveness of his
wife and all he had injured ; he received the Sacrament in peace and
the physician was surprised at the fortitude with which he bore his
sufferings.

Some of the illnesses these poor people suffered were terrible and
disgusting. A 'female perhaps forty', called Rippington, had such
dreadful ulcers on her legs that they were almost decayed and people
in the street could hear her screams. She found great peace in
receiving the Sacrament, and putting her hand on her breast said,
'He is here, He is here'.

The most striking case of Newman's arriving just when he was
needed — a thing that happened with him, sometimes uncannily, all
his life — was that of a young married woman who had consumption.
When he first called she was not interested, not liking to be interrupted in her work. When he came again she was very ill. 'Her eyes
looked at me with such a meaning I felt a thrill I cannot describe —
it was like the gate of heaven.' She died half an hour after he left
her, and he heard that she had told her friends 'she had had so
pleasant a conversation with me, and was so glad she was alone with
me'. She knew little, and was much comforted by his readings from
St. John, and the prayers he used. Another young woman, a widow
of about thirty, also very ignorant, asked again and again when he

was coming, enlightened by his readings from Scripture. Newman
was with her the day she died. 'No case has afflicted me like this.'

The sick and dying were not his only care at St. Clement's. He
was supposed to collect for the new church, and succeeded in getting,
from people with money, no less a sum than between five and six
thousand pounds. He left before it was built and was not responsible
for the designs. Meanwhile he did what he could in the old church.
Pusey, who was well-off, paid for a gallery to seat the children,
ninety-five of them, whom Newman had collected. It was always
his first care in any parish. He taught them for confirmation, and
many of these children never forgot him — two even turned up in
Birmingham and became Catholics. Miss Gutch, the Rector's
daughter, helped Newman with the children and the parishioners
immediately fixed up a match between the two, and were surprised
it did not come off. Miss Gutch continued to live in Oxford and
when Newman came back as a Cardinal, she was one of the persons
he visited.

Needless to say, the active young curate came in for some criticism. A row developed with the singers, who walked out. Newman
received a letter from 'an old inhabitant of St. Clement's parish' who
assured him, on behalf of others that 'there is not one but thinks it
very strange that a *young curate* should so show his authority over
an old Rector'. They had had a meeting and threatened action at the
next visitation. Newman started his whole congregation singing
together, probably the psalms in metrical version. Pusey helped
with the services when he was in Oxford, but at that time he was
much in Germany, studying the liberal theology there.

Newman made out schemes of prayer for his private use for each
day of the week ; the people prayed for included relations, friends,
his old headmaster, his colleges, his parishioners, dissenters, romanists, and those without religion. The things he prayed against and
the things he prayed for, in his own life, are interesting. The keynote
for Saturday was *Usefulness*. 'Pray for — in the parish, vigilance,
alertness, unweariedness, presence of mind, *meekness* of *wisdom* —
simplicity — quickness, power of reply — love, humility, discerning
of spirits. In visiting sick ; lowliness, mercy, dependence on Christ,
judgment, knowledge, firmness, candour. In catechizing etc. —
patience, gentleness, kindness, cheerfulness, clearness in teaching,
wisdom. Towards dissenters — humility, charity, mercy, forbearance, wisdom, a word in season.'

He also prayed for the necessary gifts for preaching. He found

two sermons a week very exhausting. In his journal he wrote :
'Those who make comfort the great subject of their preaching seem
to mistake the end of their ministry. *Holiness* is the great end. There
must be a struggle and trial here. Comfort is a cordial, but no one
drinks cordials from morning till night.' Already, while he was
still only a deacon, 'gownsmen' began to come to hear these astringent
sermons, and introduced a new danger. 'All this puffs me up', he
wrote anxiously in his yearly confession in the journal. 'I have not so
much opportunity of displaying pride, yet I am very proud.' He
could not have been so *very* proud, since he noticed thus every
stirring of vanity.

In September 1824 Mr. Newman died, after a short illness. John
got to London in time to see him. 'He knew me, tried to put out his
hand and said "God bless you".' He died peacefully, two days after
speaking his last words, to his wife. '"God bless you, thank my God,
thank my God — and lastly "my dear".' His family were praying
round him. Newman wrote : 'On Thursday he looked beautiful,
such calmness, sweetness, composure and majesty were in his countenance. Can a man be a materialist who sees a dead body ? I had
never seen one before.'

They buried him the next week and John wrote in his journal :
'When I die shall I be followed to the grave by my children ? My
Mother said the other day she hoped to live to see me married, but *I*
think I shall either die within a College walls, or a Missionary in a
foreign land — no matter where, so that I die in Christ.' Immediately after his ordination in June he had gone to make inquiries at
the Church Missionary Society in London, where they told him that
short sight and a weak voice would not prevent his acceptance. But
he knew he could not go yet, with Francis only beginning his Oxford
education. The inquiry was more a sign of renewed dedication than
an immediate intention. And when Mr. Newman died, not yet
sixty, leaving John the only earning member of the family, the prospect
of dying a Missionary in a foreign land became extremely unlikely.

1825–1826

'High and Mighty Youths'

WHEN her husband died Mrs. Newman had her dowry of five thousand pounds and probably very little else. Temporarily she and Harriett joined the other girls at Strand-on-the-Green, with Aunt Betsy and Grandmamma. The grandmother was now very old; she died in the spring of 1825, just before John's ordination as priest — the wish of her heart, to see him in the ministry, was satisfied. Aunt was no business woman, and her little school was not prospering. Charles, who ought to have been able to help, was a liability. As soon as his father died he left the family, saying they were too religious to live with, but he was incapable of finding a job even to keep himself. Bowden's father was a director of the Bank of England, and through his influence John was able to secure a clerkship for Charles. He kept it about five years, longer than he was to keep any job afterwards. Francis, though responsible enough, was only nineteen, and was costing money at Oxford rather than being in a position to earn it.

Then there were the girls: Harriett was twenty-one, Jemima seventeen and Mary fifteen. Their education, formally sketchy, was supplemented by John, who advised on their reading and sent them problems by post — mathematical for Jemima, grammatical for Mary. 'Jemima is an ingenious girl', he said, 'and has invented a very correct illustration of the generation of the asymptotic curve.' Harriett was reading Gibbon and Tasso. Once John had gained the Oriel Fellowship he was confident he could support them all. In the winter of 1822 he said to his father, 'Everything will — I see it will — be very right, if only you will let me manage'. To which his mother replied that she always began and ended their discussions by saying, 'I have no fear, John will manage'.

John managed. He continued to coach private pupils, he wrote more articles for the Encyclopaedia; later, he accepted Whately's offer to make him Vice-Principal of St. Alban's Hall; Whately had just been appointed Principal. Although the Hall consisted of only

about a dozen students, these were among the most idle and dissipated in the University, who had been refused everywhere else —
the place was known as 'Botany Bay'. Newman dined there three
times a week and read the prayers ; he also tried to get to know the
undergraduates. His chief task was to get the accounts in order and
to assist Whately in cleaning the place up. In this they were so
successful that Newman's successor the next year considered the
reform already established.

It was worth Whately's while to accept this appointment, for
he became Head of a House (however small) with a seat on the
Hebdomadal Board and a voice in the affairs of the university. At
the same time he was made a Doctor of Divinity. He continued
to hold Halesworth, run by his curate. He was now well on the
road to high position in the Church and in choosing Newman as
his assistant he was placing his foot on the same ladder of preferment. Newman's successor, Hinds, went to Dublin as Whately's
chaplain and became Bishop of Norwich. Hinds was Whately's
most amenable cub ; he was known sometimes as the Black, sometimes as the Little Bear, in contrast to his master. This was the
career Newman might have had, if he had kept his eye on the main
chance.

In those days an academic career was also ecclesiastical, and
both were closely integrated with the political life of the nation.
Clever and ambitious young men stood for Fellowships, and after a
few years became Tutors, at a higher salary. Having established his
worth in the university, the promising cleric would then take a
college living and marry ; with any luck he would soon return
(appointed by the Government) as a Professor, a Canon of Christ
Church, or as Head of a House : only these posts could be held by
married men. Bishops were nearly always chosen from among
these, and in those days a Bishop not only had a very large income,
but his seat in the House of Lords carried with it a political power
and responsibility it has since lost. State and Church being so
closely integrated, Bishops were more than merely ecclesiastical
figures. Even at a later date *Punch* caricatured them as often as
politicians. Consequently Oxford was in the full stream of the
social and political life of the country ; what men thought and did
there had an immediate effect in London.

Newman worked to support Whately and was grateful for the
extra money, but he never looked forward to this sort of career.
His only ambition was to stay in the University. Although he

laboured so hard in his parish he regarded teaching as his real vocation. Yet it was his parishioners who first shook his confidence in
the specifically evangelical doctrines ; the coachmen, pub-keepers,
young females and the rest just would not fit into the categories of
Saved and Unsaved. The change of mind was completed through
the agency of Edward Hawkins, a Fellow of Oriel twelve years
Newman's senior, and then Vicar of St. Mary's. The two of them
were left together in Oxford during the Long Vacations of 1824
and 1825, looking after their parishes, and talked much. Common
sense was Hawkins' chief characteristic. He criticized, in Newman's
sermons, his division of humanity between darkness and light.
'Men are not saints *or* sinners', he said. 'They are not as good as
they should be, and better than they might be.' By the next year
Newman realized he was right ; most of his St. Clement's people
'were in that condition as if they had some spiritual feelings, but
weak and uncertain'.

Newman himself had always behaved in a manner more con-
sonant with belief in progressive sanctification than in a sudden and
irreversible assurance of salvation. Evangelicals insisted that this
subjective experience was the necessary entry into the kingdom of
Christ ; yet Christ himself had commanded the rite of baptism, so
objective that it was traditionally applied to a baby. Newman argued
it out with Pusey on their long walks. Hawkins had made him realize
the importance of Tradition : that the Christian faith was an objective body of teaching handed on from one generation to another.
No doubt to Hawkins this was a habit of thought, and religious
tradition not very different from the other traditions in which he
was brought up, but to Newman it was an Idea, and one which
brought a new orientation to his other ideas. In acknowledging so
gracefully the origins of his principal ideas Newman omitted to
mention the transformation they underwent in his own mind.
Whately did not recognize his idea of a self-governing established
Church in Newman's repudiation of all civil authority over a divine
institution ; Hawkins was unaware that in emphasizing the importance of habitual loyalty he had started Newman off on the path
which led to the Apostolic Deposit of Faith and the Church as its
infallible interpreter. It is interesting to notice how far these
ideas had developed in Newman's mind before he became intimate
with Froude and Keble ; how far in fact he influenced these two
friends — though he never said so — by the turn he gave to the
High Church Tradition : a conversion of habits into ideas most

characteristic of a mind that could not rest till it found the first
principles of every train of thought.

Newman had made this important change, from a subjective to
an objective view of the scheme of salvation, before his ordination
as priest, which took place on Whitsunday, May 29th, 1825.   It
was a calmer occasion for him than the diaconate. That had expressed his personal break with the world ; this came as a consecration. 'What a divine service is that of Ordination !' he wrote in his
journal. 'The whole has a fragrance in it ; and to think of it is
soothing and delightful.' This time, too, he was able to believe of
his fellow candidates that 'all might be in some degree spiritual'.
Thus his change of opinion altered his outlook.

At the beginning of August he celebrated the Holy Communion
service for the first time, and for the first time Jemima and Mary
took the Sacrament, and from him.   They had come with his mother
and Harriett from London and stayed in Oxford till the end of
September — there was another Communion on their last Sunday.
'O how I love them', Newman wrote in his journal. 'So much I
love them, that I cannot help thinking Thou wilt either take them
hence, or take me from them, because I am too set on them. It is a
shocking thought.'

Scarcely more than two years were to pass before Mary's sudden
death.

After the family left, Newman took a brief holiday with Bowden
at Southampton. 'Bowden meets with many infidels in the Law',
he recorded. Bowden read Butler and then Sumner, on Newman's
recommendation — Hawkins had made Newman read Sumner.
Bowden comfortably followed his friend's opinions, but brother
Francis was shocked at his backsliding in the matter of baptism and
discussed it with Mr. Mayers. Evangelicals thought an emphasis
on the objective value of sacraments dangerous formalism. The
High-and-Dry tradition seemed to them to have turned religion into
a mere morality and worship into meaningless repetition. They
regarded themselves as the exponents of 'vital' religion — with some
justification, since they counted among their leaders such fine Christians as William Wilberforce, the Liberator of the slaves, and young
Lord Ashley (Shaftesbury) the social reformer. They were at this
time the most influential party in the Church of England, but they
were suffering the fate of all successful movements in becoming
shallower as they spread wider. They lived too much on the emotions
generated by Wesley's great revival, and phrases which had once

expressed personal experience tended to become mere catchwords. Francis Newman was unable to distinguish between basic Christian doctrines and those peculiar to the Evangelical party. He thought John was heading straight for the idolatries of Rome and refused to accept a print of a Madonna by Correggio, which John gave him for his rooms. So John kept it — for the rest of his life.

In January 1826, just before Newman was twenty-five, Jelf left Oriel to become private tutor to the Prince of Cumberland, and Newman succeeded to the College tutorship, with an income of over £600. Since he had always felt his vocation lay in teaching, he gave up St. Clement's at Easter, and St. Alban's Hall too, though Whately offered to make up his salary to the equivalent of a tutor's, so keen was he to keep him. Without a thought of his career Newman gave this up. He now had exactly the position he wanted and a much better income; prospects were brightening and his letters home became more and more lively, written off full speed at odd moments.

'I am out of breath with business — all through that old fellow who will never have done : — he talks, talks on incessantly and is an old chatterbox and tiresome old chap. . . . When your parcel with the cake arrived I could have blushed as I received it from the servant its smell was so tell-tale, but it 'eat' so well I would not you should have sent it for anything. . . . Frank has failed at Worcester [for a scholarship] — he is quite well and impudent.' And he mentioned a project which might take 't ! e !! n !!! . . . years ? ? ? — to trace the sources from which the corruptions of the church, principally the Romish, have been derived'.

Mary wrote to him, 'Dear John, how extremely kind you are. Oh, I wish I could write as fast as I think. I cannot tell why, but whatever I write to you I am ashamed of. I think it must be vanity ; and yet I do not feel so to most others. And *now* all I have written I should like to burn. Thank you for your long letter which I do not deserve. I wish I *could* see your rooms. Are they called generally by the titles you give them ? I hope the "brown room" is not quite so grave as the name would lead one to suppose . . . I did not imagine, John, that with all your tutoric gravity and your brown room you could be so absurd as your letter (I beg your pardon) seems to betray. . . . Well, I think I have found out the secret of my difficulty in writing to you. It is because I never told you that difficulty. At least I find I write much easier since that confession.'

In June Frank went in for his finals and scored a double first —

in classics and mathematics. His future was assured. But although he was off his brother's hands 'the rest are now heavier', as Newman noted. Since there was no St. Clement's this year to keep him in Oxford, during the Long Vacation, he took the duty for an ex-Oriel Fellow, Samuel Rickards, in his parish of Ulcombe near Maidstone, in Kent. Ulcombe is a tiny place on a ridge of hill, overlooking mile upon mile of the Weald ; in the old church there is a squint from the side aisle upon the altar, so that the elevation at mass could be seen. The Vicarage was large and rambling ; many of its eighteen rooms have now been pulled down. Samuel Rickards was a character, original and amusing, and his wife was charming. Harriett, who was housekeeping for her brother, stayed on when the Rickards came back, and the sisters soon became friends and favourite visitors. In November Rickards told Newman that the village people were quite determined never to forget him.

He was answering a letter from Newman in which he had mentioned some difficulties at Oriel owing to the indisposition of the Provost, Copleston. But, Newman said, 'my spirits, most happily, rise at the prospect of danger, trial, or any call upon me for unusual exertion ; and as I came outside the Southampton coach to Oxford, I felt as if I could have rooted up St. Mary's spire and kicked down the Radcliffe'.

The trials to which he was returning were more personal than those he mentioned, though Copleston's imminent departure — as it seemed then — to a Bishopric, and the fact that his chief assistant, Tyler, left the college, meant that Newman began his tutorship in a kind of interregnum. He took his duties as Tutor seriously, a thing rare among Tutors then. College tutors took little interest in their pupils and asked extra fees if they coached them ; otherwise they gave general lectures and let them get on as they could. Newman was determined that his pupils should be properly tutored without having to pay for it. But, having studied the Statutes, he also regarded himself as responsible for their moral welfare, and it seemed to him that much needed to be done in this direction. This attitude was an advantage to serious young men who intended to study — unfortunately for the new tutor these were in the minority.

'The College is filled principally with men of family, in many cases, of fortune', Newman wrote in his journal, on becoming a tutor. 'I fear there exists very considerable profligacy among them.' Tom Mozley, the son of a Derby printer and publisher, and by no means a prig, came up as a freshman in 1826, and observed in a letter written in December that the undergraduates of Oriel were 'getting so dreadfully dissipated ; perhaps as bad as any in the University'. The 'gentlemen commoners' had many privileges. They wore silk gowns, and gold tassels, if they were noblemen, on their caps. They dined at High Table with the dons. They broke the rules with impunity, keeping packs of hounds in the town and throwing wine parties which lasted to all hours. As at Trinity, what Newman felt most strongly about were the drunken parties before and after the compulsory general communion. When he told Tyler, the Dean, of this he said, 'I don't believe it, and, if it is true, I don't want to know it'. When he asked the Provost if there was really an obligation for all the men to communicate, Copleston said briskly, 'That question, I believe, has never entered their heads, and I beg you will not put it into them'.

Newman found himself alone in his disgust at this sacrilege ; he was only a junior tutor and was discouraged and snubbed by authority. Provost and Dean favoured the lawless young aristocrats. He must therefore either yield to circumstances, or make his stand alone, and with little prospect of success. It was courting unpopularity to reprove those whom the Provost did not think it necessary to check. Nevertheless Newman took this course. When he was writing his memoir for St. John, in his seventies, he laid the blame for the troubles that followed on himself, saying that 'he behaved towards them with a haughtiness that incurred their bitter resentment'. It was his habit to accuse himself of failing in manner on occasions when he was convinced he was right in matter. But in 1885, when he was eighty-four and a Cardinal, one of his ex-pupils, and a ringleader of this wild set, Lord Malmesbury, wrote his Reminiscences, and the newspapers extracted a passage in which he made out that Newman had been a helpless dummy as a tutor, quite incapable of dealing with the pranks of his juvenile tormentors. Newman, old as he was, was roused to answer what he considered an unfair attack on his courage. Another ex-pupil, Frederic Rogers Lord Blachford, got in first to defend him ; letters passed between them which tell more than Newman had told in his memoir.

'He used to allow his class to torment him with the most helpless resignation,' said Lord Malmesbury. 'Every kind of mischievous trick was to our shame played upon him — such as cutting his bell rope and at lectures making the table advance gradually till he was jammed into a corner. He remained quite impassive and painfully tolerant.' The table turning, as Blachford pointed out, was a story told against Dr. James, a don who was certainly ragged. Blachford told another tale of him saying to his teasing pupils, 'Paulus Aemilius, Mr. Wobinson, was a noble Wôman'. Of Newman in those days Blachford wrote, 'He was very kind and retiring, but perfectly deter-mined . . . a tutor with whom men did not venture to take liberties, and who was master of a formidable and speaking silence calculated to quell any ordinary impertinence'. He told Newman privately that he used the last phrase because he knew very well that 'the FitzHarris set (with the Provost at their backs) might have insulted you in some way which made it difficult for you to meet them with self-respect'. (Lord Malmesbury, in his pupillage, was Lord FitzHarris.)

In one of the drafts of a letter to the Press Newman wrote that his activities as a new broom 'roused the indignation of some high and mighty youths who, relying on the claim of family and fortune, did their best to oppose me and spread tales about me. I don't consider that on the whole I got the worst of it and what Lord Malmesbury calls "helpless resignation" and "painful tolerance" I may interpret to have been the conduct of a gentleman under great provocation.' In another draft he wrote, 'That indignities and even insults in and out of lectures were contemplated and even attempted against me (being the first year that I was Tutor) which became in the course of time fables about what had been done I have granted freely . . .'. He told Blachford the real bell rope incident ; it was the wire outside his door they cut, and it was done at night when he was asleep. Blachford thought he showed too much feeling. 'I am sorry you dislike "high and mighty",' replied Newman. 'I could find nothing else to intimate that from the first they thought me "only a tutor" and that "of course" their conduct cowed me.'

What annoyed Newman was that Malmesbury's account sug-gested that nothing important was at stake, and that the young men were acting out of mere high spirits and not out of indignation that he, a don and a nobody, should oppose their amusements and dare to reprove them for immoral behaviour. A passage Newman left out of his final letter, no doubt as being too personal, shows what the atmosphere must have been. He wrote it in several forms before abandoning it. 'Can your Lordship recollect no times that you showed indignation in your very countenance on one occasion when I sent for you and is that compatible with my impassiveness ? . . . I used words of severity to you and I still remember the expression with which you received it.' It is easy to see how an eminent old nobleman might remember all this as boyish pranks — when he did finally apologize he still talked about 'the too indulgent and patient tutor who has since become one of the most vigorous literary athletes of the age' — to the annoyance of Blachford, who felt he was simply repeating his original assertion in another form, and thought Newman let him off too easily. To Malmesbury the whole episode was unimportant, but to Newman it represented one of his first battles with the world.

He acutely observed to Blachford that another story of Malmesbury's — that he had been nearly turned from High Table by an irate Copleston, shouting at him for 'mutilating' a haunch of venison — was probably 'a mythical representation of what was the fact — viz., that I was not supported in my reforms by the high authorities of the College'. Snubbed by the Provost, evaded by Tyler, despised as only a tutor and faced with resentment and insult by the outraged youths, Newman continued to uphold his standard, and gradually won at least respect from his juniors. At a later date Lockhart recorded the tale of a gentleman commoner summoned for some misdemeanour and coming out of Newman's room considerably subdued. 'What did he say to you?' — 'I don't know, but he looked at me.' This was the 'formidable silence' which Blachford remembered — from personal experience, though he was a favourite pupil.

It was the prospect of going back to all this that Newman had in mind when he so gaily told Rickards that his spirits rose to battle, and that he could have rooted up St. Mary's spire and kicked down the Radcliffe.

1827–1828

Mary

THERE was some discussion as to whether Mrs. Newman and the sisters should settle in Brighton or nearer London. John, who had a special liking for the south coast all his life, went to prospect in Brighton. 'I prefer it to Bath,' he wrote home '— it is magnifiquo — and the waves are breaking so soft, bluey green and white.' But in March 1827 he was writing that he was 'much distressed by Charles' indisposition. Do make Harriett say seriously and on deliberation, whether she does not think our being near town and his having a home would not (in spite of that inward inquietude which wears him) be a very great comfort to him ? Harriett thinks and judges much more dispassionately and rationally than I do.' But they finally decided on Brighton, and it was John who found the house and made the arrangements, ordering wallpaper, upholstery and so on. It was not ready when promised, and Mrs. Newman and the girls stayed on in the lodgings they had taken in Eastern Terrace till August, moving into No. 11 Marine Square in the autumn.

Harriett and Jemima went to stay at Ulcombe in the middle of July, and in August Mrs. Newman and Mary joined John in Hampstead, where he was taking duty for a clergyman named Marsh, and coaching a new pupil, Charles P. Golightly, for his entrance into the university. Golightly, very young and solemn, stayed with the Newmans ; his family had a large property at Godalming and he had been at Eton. The house turned out to be crawling with bugs, and Mary and John were in fits of laughter over the awfulness of it, the smell, and poor Golightly's valiant attempts to ignore it all. 'I wish you could see the faces John and I make at each other at dinner', Mary wrote to her sister. Her letters rattled off gaily, full of jokes, mimicry, teasing and nonsense. 'It is all John's doing,' she grumbled in one, '— he came looking over me and repeating "Rev. Wolf Rickards ! Wolf ! Wolf !" till at last he made me write Rickw — If Mr. Ric were to know this how he would be amused. Goodbye sweet Mum my mum.' This was her nickname for Jemima. On the same sheet John wrote : 'My dear Jemima Mary says I must not write to Harriett so I am forced to write to you. I have generously let her write on three sides and on the turndown of my letter so am pent up in this corner.'

They had some musical evenings in Hampstead, and a little boy, son of a Mr. Cazenove, remembered one occasion all his life, and nearly half a century later, when Newman was a Cardinal, wrote to remind him of it.

Newman's letters this year were overflowing with high spirits and he teased his sisters affectionately. 'Love to all, *s*aucy H, *s*ly J, and *s*illy M,' he scribbled in one letter, and in the next, 'by way of making amends — Love to sensible H, sober J, and sprightly M.' At the end of April he had written to Jemima : 'The clock has struck nine breaking in . . . I am hungry — I have already had two interviews with men this morning, one about Hebrew, one about Sophocles during my writing — I am going to eat — I have a Latin composition lecture with a pupil at ten, from eleven to two I hear the candidates in the Tower construe. I am going to eat. I have a third pupil coming at two with Sophocles — and doubt whether I shall get a walk to-day. I wish I was out of Oxford — goodbye — I am going — to *eat*! With love to all I fly on the wings of hunger.' In May : 'Tell my mother I *cannot conceive* what she *is* to do with the contents of my portmanteau. Certain it is that I want the portmanteau and *empty* too — I am laughing so much I cannot write.' To his mother he wrote : 'Does the sea blossom ? Are green leaves budding on its waters, and is the scent of spring in its waves ? Do birds begin to sing under its shadow and to build their nests on its branches ? Ah! mighty sea! Thou art a tree whose spring never yet came, for thou art an evergreen. There is a pastoral!'

This kind of thing was all mixed up with the agonies of dentistry, plans for reading the Fathers, his pupils, the new Fellows and Bishop Lloyd's wig — for Lloyd had been made Bishop of Oxford and looked quite unrecognizable when he appeared in St. Mary's in his wig — 'People say he had it on hind part before'. One of the new Fellows was a Spaniard, an ex-priest called Blanco White, with whom Newman began to play Beethoven quartets. As usual he was doing too much, but at least he did not have two conflicting tasks, of teaching and parochial duties.

Not all his pupils were like the Malmesbury set. There was Tom Mozley, clever but indolent and careless, later to marry Harriett.

6. MARY NEWMAN 　　　 7. EMILY BOWLES IN YOUTH

8. MARIA ROSINA GIBERNE IN 1820
From a miniature by De La Cour

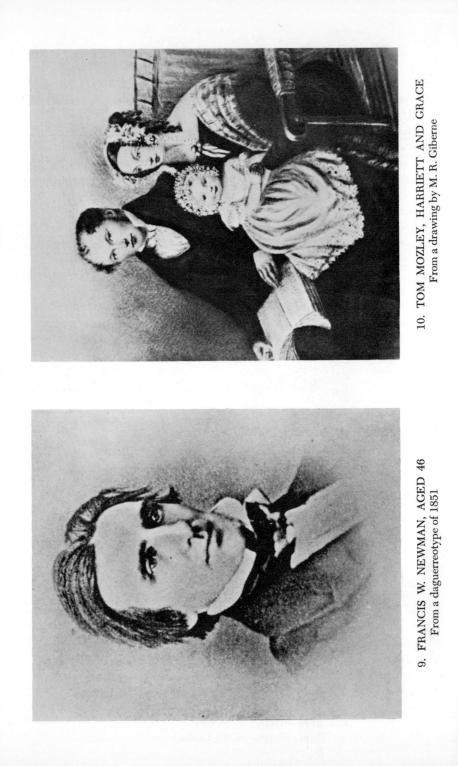

10. TOM MOZLEY, HARRIETT AND GRACE
From a drawing by M. R. Giberne

9. FRANCIS W. NEWMAN, AGED 46
From a daguerreotype of 1851

There was Henry Wilberforce, youngest son of the Emancipator, who came up in the Michaelmas Term of 1826. His brother Robert had been elected a Fellow that year. Henry was 'small and timid, shrinking from notice, with a bright face and intelligent eyes', Newman wrote after his death in 1873, in a short memoir undertaken at the request of his widow. He and Henry took to each other at once, and Newman gave him private coaching, at Hampstead, and in the following long Vacations. Henry was only temporarily timid, partly because he had never been to school. By nature he was cheerful and sociable, and particularly fond of the company of young ladies — he found Oxford dreadfully devoid of them. He soon became a favourite of the Newman sisters. 'I am just wishing to be able to write as fast as H. Wilberforce speaks; in two minutes I should cover this sheet I am sure,' remarked Mary. In another letter she said, 'Mrs. W. made a face several times just like H.W. biting her underlip, you know how'. And she shrewdly compared the two Wilberforce brothers. 'R.W. with all his quietness and gentleness is as bad as H.W. and worse because he is not so honest — H.W. says I am impudent, I am a torment, and he is so. R.W. says "I am gentlemanly and timid" and he *is*—impudent and tormenting!'

One of Henry's private tutors had been John Sargent, the Rector of Lavington, who possessed a quartet of beautiful daughters; Henry never recovered from the impact and was later to marry the youngest. He was twenty in 1827, with a round, snub Wilberforce face. He was clever, though he turned out less of a scholar than his brother Robert, and less a public man than his brother Samuel, who had just gone down, a brilliant speaker in the newly established Union. Sons of the great William, to whom they were all devoted, their careers were assured. Newman met the famous old man before he died and was touched by his sons' affection and veneration for him. He combined the deepest evangelical piety with the happy disposition he had bequeathed to Henry. In his last illness Henry looked so like his father that it gave Newman quite a shock to see him.

Robert Wilberforce joined Newman at Ulcombe for a fortnight in September. Mrs. Rickards wrote to Harriett that John looked very tired, but would not rest, spending his time studying or talking with her husband. But she added : 'And now here is John, come to keep me company, or rather to be plagued with the children. I wish you only could see him with both on his lap in the great arm-chair, pulling off and then putting on his glasses.' This was Newman's favourite game with small children, though he was also a good story-teller. He was a popular visitor with the children of his friends all his life.

It was earlier that summer, in Brighton, that Maria Giberne met Newman for the first time ; she was to be another lifelong friend, not without some ups and downs, for she was an enthusiastic and romantic person. She was a year younger than Newman. She came of a large Evangelical family of French extraction, and one of her sisters had married Mr. Mayers and gone to live at Over Worton. While she was staying there in 1826 Francis Newman walked over from Oxford — he was then twenty-one — and immediately fell passionately in love with Maria Rosina, who was about three years his senior. She was a tall handsome girl with dark ringlets and features which in middle age were to remind a sea-captain of Napoleon. She played the harp and sketched ; she was lively and had a great sense of humour : when she felt 'conversion' coming on she hastily finished Sir Walter Scott's novels, knowing they would be considered too frivolous afterwards. Her sisters morally forced her to be 'converted' but she was sincere, in spite of her airs and graces. Maria Giberne was much impressed with Francis Newman's good looks, his black hair and piercing blue eyes, and with his virtue and religious fervour ; but she had already given her heart to a young officer, Robert Murcott, who had gone to India, hoping to make enough money to return and ask for her hand. So Frank was destined to an unrequited love. He could not yet contemplate marriage, and he was soon to jeopardize his career for conscience sake, scrupling to swear to the Thirty-Nine Articles. He was thinking of becoming a missionary ; John assured him that he would willingly shoulder all responsibility for the family to allow him to do so. But he did not go yet ; he went over to Ireland instead, to give private tuition.

Meanwhile Miss Giberne met the Newman sisters. She was a little put off by Harriett, who seemed to know more than she did about everything, but took a great fancy to the lively Mary, who wanted to learn drawing from her. John was the last she met, and she had taken a dislike to him before the meeting because she had heard he was 'a stiff churchman'. She may have heard his back-slidings discussed sadly at Over Worton. So she thought him stiff and cold when she did meet him and was surprised, though rather impressed, that he paid more attention to his mother and sisters than to her, a young lady used to being the centre of attraction. When she found he was to escort them home she tried to avoid being the one whose arm he took, and secretly put out her tongue when she lost the manœuvre. The walk was as silent as she had feared, and when they came in sight of her aunt's house she thankfully assured Newman he need come no farther — expecting, of course, a gallant compliment. But he said, 'Now that I have come so far I may as well go on to the end!'

In spite, or perhaps because, of this unpromising beginning Maria Giberne was fascinated, and watched him closely 'to see what sort of man he was'. She was sure he could not be really religious, because he never prayed extempore. She wrote these recollections in French and English, when she was an old nun in France, and Newman a Cardinal. They were interspersed with such comments as : 'Has he not heaped coals of fire on my head by laying me under an eternal obligation to him ? (Bless the Monk ! ! !) in spite of my ill will to him (oh! oh! oh!).' Maria Giberne was an uninhibitedly emotional creature, but she had a determined will and a good deal of common sense ; she could be an embarrassment to her friends, but never a liability. People laughed at her devotion to Newman all through her life, and at one period he was to find it somewhat tiresome himself ; but, as with all his friends, he did not drop her when things became difficult, but persevered till they settled down again.

In the autumn of 1827 Newman was appointed a University Examiner. He felt this appointment redeemed his failure in the Schools, and worked hard to prepare for it. Now, suddenly, came shattering news from Strand : poor Aunt had come to the end of her resources, she was nearly £700 in debt — in danger of bankruptcy. Although in the event Frank was able to help to pay this debt, at the time it seemed likely to fall entirely on John, who had already found he had had to pay out more than he expected for the house in Brighton. It was a crushing blow, and on top of it came the disturbing news that Copleston had at last got the Bishopric he had been so long angling for — it was only Llandaff but he was to be Dean of St. Paul's as well — and Oriel would have to elect a new Provost. To get the right man was vitally important to Newman, who had the intellectual and moral improvement of the College so much at heart. The news came to him on Friday, November 23rd, while he was in the Schools, and it precipitated a kind of breakdown, partly physical and partly nervous. On Monday he found his mind a blank and had to leave in the middle of the day.

Afterwards he tried to describe his sensations in his journal. 'I was not in pain exactly ; nothing acute, nothing like a rheumatic

headache ; but a confusion, an inability to think or recollect. Once
or twice indeed, when my head was on my pillow, I felt a throbbing
so distressing, though it was not violent, as to make me sensible I had
never experienced a real headache. It was not pain, but a twisting
of the brain, or the eyes. I felt my head inside was made up of parts.
I could write verses pretty well, but I could not *count*. I once or twice
tried to count my pulse, but found it quite impossible ; before I
had got to 30, my eyes turned round and inside out, all of a sudden.'

He said nothing of this alarming experience to his mother ; only
that he was overtired. The doctor bled him with leeches on his
temples, and Robert Wilberforce took him off on the Wednesday
for two days at his home, Highwood. He introduced Newman to
their family medical adviser, Mr. Babington, whom Newman consulted from now until his death in 1856. Babington diagnosed 'a
determination of blood to the head arising from over exertion of
the brain, with a disordered stomach', and said he must not return
to Oxford. He stayed only a week at Highwood and then went
down to Brighton. Writing to say he was coming, he said little of
himself, but asked his mother to be kind to Pusey, who was in
Brighton recovering from an illness. This illness was chiefly the
result of his prolonged separation from Maria Barker ; luckily it
scared old Mr. Pusey into allowing the engagement at last.

As soon as he was at home Newman began writing eagerly to
friends about the election of the Provost. In his view, Hawkins
was the man to undertake the necessary improvement of discipline.
The only other candidate was Keble. At this time Newman did
not know Keble well, for he was not living in College but helping
his old father in his parish of Fairford. Newman thought Keble
too gentle to control the wild set. He made one of the Fellows
laugh by saying that if they were electing an Angel it ought to be
Keble, but they were only electing a Provost. He also assumed that
Keble would not want the post. But Keble would have liked it ;
he was hurt at Newman's assumption, though he laughed it off in
his usual way. To Hawkins himself, at the end of December, Keble
wrote, 'Having brought all into a sum, as George Herbert says, I
have pretty well satisfied myself that greatly as the college would be
benefited were the choice of the majority in this important matter
to fall on me, it may yet do very well, provided you are a good boy,
and do your *very very* best'.

It was Newman's influence that determined the younger Fellows,
though Hurrell Froude, elected Fellow with Robert Wilberforce in

1826, was for Keble, whose pupil he had been. Thus Hawkins largely owed to Newman his election to the Provostship which he was to hold through half a century, dying in 1882 at the age of ninety-three. For Oxford it was to be one of the stormiest of all periods, not only because of the strife aroused by the Movement, but because of the changing nature of English society and education. In helping to put Hawkins rather than Keble at the head of his college, Newman was unknowingly cutting his own throat, for the Provost was to prove one of the stiffest of his opponents. For Keble, it meant a lifetime of obscurity in country parishes. The actual election took place on January 31st, 1828, and was celebrated on the annual Gaudy-day, February 2nd, feast of the Purification of the Blessed Virgin Mary, under whose patronage Oriel had been founded. With Hawkins' promotion Newman became Vicar of St. Mary's, the University Church.

But by then he was writing in his journal : 'O my dearest sister Mary, O my sister, my sister, I do feel from the bottom of my heart that it is all right — I see, I know it to be, in God's good Providence the best thing for all of us ; I do not, I have not, in the least repined — I would not have it otherwise — but I feel sick, I must cease writing. . . .'

Mary died, quite suddenly, at Brighton, on the eve of the Epiphany 1828. She was only just nineteen.

Maria Giberne was with them on the fatal evening ; fifty years later she wrote to Newman : 'Dear Mary sat next to you, and I was on the other side ; and while eating a bit of turkey she turned her face towards me, her hand on her heart, so pale, and a dark ring round her eyes, and she said she felt ill and should she go away ? I asked you, and she went : I longed to accompany her, but dared not, for fear of making a stir. . . .'

There were other guests dining ; no one realized how serious it was ; Newman even made a joke about the doctor's fees. Even next morning Harriett went for a walk with Miss Giberne and only said Mary had had a bad night. It seems she may have had appendicitis. She was a strong, healthy girl. Miss Giberne had a painful session with the dentist, dined elsewhere, and returned about nine to a silent house, and no one about but Newman 'who offered us chairs and leant himself against the table facing the fire', as she wrote in her memoirs. 'I see him now, his serious eyes fixed on the fire, his cheek deathly pale, his lips firmly closed except when in speaking to prepare us for the sad truth they quivered, his hands crossed and closed.' She did not at first realize what he was trying to tell them, and asked him to pray with them for Mary, secretly thinking, 'Now I shall see by his prayer whether he is like other religious people.— Stupid fool that I was, unfeeling hardhearted wretch !!!' she cried in retrospect. 'And then he said, "I must tell you the truth : she is dead already."'

'Then you went to fetch vinegar,' she reminded him fifty years later, 'which I did not need, for I felt turned to stone.'

She never forgot the selfless kindness of all the family, Mrs. Newman's care that she should be given soft food while her agonies of toothache lasted. She made arrangements to leave as soon as possible, but before she went she made a drawing of Mary lying dead upstairs, in her little frilled cap. The sisters came in often and Harriett, leaning over the bed, whispered, 'Dear cold creature'. Once John stood by her, to look at the drawing, and at last he said in a low voice, 'It is *very* like'.

John read prayers for them, the prayers of the burial service ; but now Miss Giberne did not judge the depth of his feeling by his inventive eloquence, or lack of it. She went away, and the family were left to their grief.

Mary had been strong and well, full of life and intelligence ; she made another girl laugh by asking her if she liked thinking. She was eagerly learning by heart the poems of Keble's *Christian Year*, which came out in 1827. It was John's copy, and when it came back to him, he saw in it the marks of her black kid gloves. Her death was sudden and unexpected. Yet Newman wrote : 'For some time I had a presentiment more or less strong that we should lose dear Mary. I was led to this by her extreme loveliness of character and by the circumstance of my great affection for her. I thought I loved her too well, and hardly ever dared to take my full swing of enjoyment in her dear society.' At that time Mary was probably the person he most loved, and his affections were always both strong and deep ; it is likely too that, loving as she was to all her family and closest to Jemima, he was then first with her. When Newman was over eighty he could not think of Mary without tears coming into his eyes. Now, when he went back to Oxford, he wrote : 'Here everything reminds me of her. She was with us at Oxford, and I took a delight in showing her the place — and every building, every tree, seems to speak of her. I cannot realize that I shall never see her again.'

Newman was just twenty-seven when Mary died and he became the Vicar of St. Mary's.

CRISIS
(1828–1833)

1828–1829

New Friends and New Beginnings

THE double shock of Mary's death and his own nervous collapse profoundly affected Newman, coming just at that point in his development when, as he put it himself, he came out of his shell. The shell was that period of youth when the world is seen as it is reflected in the desires and feelings — an intense, adventurous, but subjective time. The person emerging into his first maturity is as different from what he was before as schoolboy is from child, or young man from boy. For the last year or two Newman's entries in the journals were less frequent ; even the yearly confessions were becoming records of events, though still accompanied with brief but severe self-criticisms. Now, unless he totally destroyed further records, which he scarcely ever did, they stopped. Ideas began to crystallize in notes and sermons. He had reached the point, inwardly and outwardly, where the world becomes objective and a man active rather than passive towards it.

Once more this metamorphosis of nature coincided with a spiritual crisis. The double shock, he briefly noted in the *Apologia*, awakened him from a dream. 'I was beginning to prefer intellectual excellence to moral ; I was drifting in the direction of liberalism.' This was just what Frank suspected, and good Mr. Mayers, who died suddenly, quite young, in this spring of 1828. But how could Mary's death or a nervous collapse affect this intellectual drift ?

The loss of Mary revived all Newman's sense of the overpowering reality of the unseen world. In May, riding by doctor's orders about the green country round Oxford, she was ever in his mind. 'I wish it were possible', he wrote to Jemima, 'for words to put down those indefinite vague and withal subtle feelings which quite pierce the soul and make it sick. Dear Mary seems embodied in every tree and hid behind every hill. What a veil and curtain this world of sense is ! beautiful, but still a veil.' A feeling so intense as to make him feel sick, and a sense of the reality of the supernatural world so vivid as to make the world of nature — which nevertheless he observed with an artist's keen and loving eye — seem a veil : such a spirit and imagination could never fit itself into the world of common-sense morality and intellectual abstraction inhabited by Whately and his friends of the liberal school.

Mary's going out of this world strengthened Newman's sense of exile in it, which success had been undermining ; that it was Mary who went, deeply affected his attitude towards people. He loved her — too much, he feared ; their sympathy was very close. The day of Newman's collapse Mary was writing from Ulcombe : 'How I long to see you ! . . . I can fancy your face — there, it is looking at me.' It is impossible to say how this relationship would have developed, had she lived. Complex and various are the changes through which such affections pass. In one way Mary's early death meant that Newman never lost her ; and yet he lost someone who might have understood him when others turned away. But because she died when they were in perfect accord the loss made him realize to the full how much he loved her, and how lovable she was. This in itself was a check to over-intellectualism. He was forced to feel intensely just when he was putting most of his energy into thinking. The death of Mary did for him what falling in love does for some people — opened his heart to a more sensitive sympathy with others. Sometimes, to lose a loved person, makes for a deeper understanding of love than can be realized in a relationship where there is no frustration. The pain can be fruitful.

Other experiences were to continue this process, but this was crucial, as Newman recognized when he coupled it with his breakdown and listed them among the three illnesses which had so much changed him : the first at fifteen, which 'made him a Christian' and the third still to come, in Sicily. Although all three had immediate physical causes Newman felt them to be intimately connected with his psychological and spiritual state, at once precipitating and expressing what was within. Each was a death and resurrection. Now he discovered that the intellect he had begun to rely on too much was only an instrument, and could in a moment go horribly wrong, leaving him helpless. His mind was vulnerable, his heart was vulnerable ; he had been relying on himself and his own powers — now sickness and death made him realize his weakness. It was a question of turning again from the world and the self to God. Because Newman answered so quickly to the divine touch it seems almost inevitable that he should ; but these two blows, humbling

and painful, might have been met in a very different mood. Rebellion or resentment are often the reaction to what seems unfair
and arbitrary suffering. They have a narrowing and depressive
effect. But Newman was enlarged, and in time revivified by the
suffering he felt to the full but accepted.

Two of his best friends got married this year. Pusey was offered
the Regius Professorship of Hebrew, which carried a Canonry of
Christ Church. He was only twenty-eight, but already his erudition
was becoming known and he had begun to publish books. This post
made it possible for him to marry, and although Mr. Pusey incon-
veniently died just then, his son evidently felt filial duty had gone
far enough, and did not put off his wedding. He was rapidly ordained
and married and left Oriel to live at Christ Church. He was to
remain there for the rest of his life. His bride was much loved by all
their friends ; many found her easier to get on with than her husband,
who, humble and gentle though he was, seemed to live in a world of
his own. Newman did not get to know her at once, but next year he
was writing home that she had called on him to apologize for not
dining and that he 'had had a long gossip with her. She is a *very*
pleasing person ; and if I knew her well, I daresay I might use
towards her the same terms which I once applied to another Lady.'
What those terms were, and who the Lady, was evidently known to
his family, though not to us ; but he was soon very friendly with
Mrs. Pusey. They called each other Maria and John, though with
an effort — Newman put 'Maria' in inverted commas in his letters.
In 1830 she was helping him to find a home near Oxford for his
mother.

Bowden also got married ; his bride was Elizabeth Swinburne,
aunt-to-be of the poet Algernon Charles Swinburne. She is perhaps
the Mrs. B. of whom Newman wrote home that she was 'a very
elegant refined select person, most persons would think her very
pretty — she is much less cold and stiff than when I saw her before —
and then her coldness and stiffness was not *at all* like the coldness of
awkwardness but of self-possession. I have reason to think it really
arose or arises from a sort of retiring diffidence or something like it.'
If this was Mrs. Bowden, she probably felt shy of meeting Newman,
of whom she had heard so much. But whenever he went to London
he stayed with the Bowdens, and she soon lost her shyness. Newman
was an adaptable friend, easily accepting and accepted by the wives
his friends had chosen. Bowden and his wife called him 'the great
man' and 'Joannes Immortalis'.

It was in 1828 that Newman began to know Hurrell Froude well. In the general shuffle when Copleston left, Froude and Robert Wilberforce were appointed junior tutors, and Newman became one of the two seniors — the other was the eccentric Dornford. Thus their work threw them together, and so did the fact that Newman had been ordered by the doctor to ride for exercise. He learned to jump about this time, and enjoyed the exhilaration of it. Froude was a bold rider, and Tom Mozley, just elected a Fellow and enjoying the privilege of being able to keep a horse, said, 'He would take a good leap if he had the chance and would urge his friends to follow him, mostly in vain'. Mozley added, 'Newman rode well enough to come to no mishaps'. At one time Newman owned a mare called Klepper, 'a pretty creature with Arab blood', who had some dangerous tricks and needed careful handling. Tom knew what he was talking about, for she was later passed on to him.

Richard Hurrell Froude was two years younger than Newman, the eldest son of a Devonshire Archdeacon, who lived the life of a conscientious and cultured country gentleman of ample means, at Dartington. Hurrell had a brother close to him in age, with whom he shared school-days, who died when they were undergraduates at Oriel. He also had several younger brothers and sisters, the youngest being James Anthony, the future historian. His mother died when Hurrell was just growing up. When he was a boy she wrote a querulous epistle, directed at him, but written in the third person, complaining of his whistling and his teasing his little brother and what he called 'funny tormenting'. Illness perhaps made her oversensitive to boyish noise and nonsense. The Archdeacon was proud of his eldest son, followed his career with the closest interest, and nursed him in his last illness. Hurrell was on very good terms with him, writing home from Oriel to 'Dear Maister', as he called him affectionately in Devonshire style, teasing and careless letters, as often as not asking for cash or cheering on the arrival of wine from the Dartington cellar. He was so excited when he got an Oriel Fellowship that he accused himself of getting 'quite drunk and upset by it, and am so ashamed of the fact that I shall think and say as little about it as possible'.

Frederick Oakeley, one of Froude's contemporaries at Oriel, described his 'sunny cheerfulness' and could find no epithet more suitable to him than the French 'riant'. Tom Mozley remembered him as 'tall, erect, thin'. His eyes were very bright, grey, ironic and keen. He was daring, high-spirited, strong-willed and gay. He delighted to poke fun at solemnity and shock people with outrageous remarks ; slang and nonsense enlivened his conversation. He had a keen sense of honour and an aristocratic disdain for any kind of shuffling or mealy-mouthed talk. He grew up in the country, riding, shooting, fishing and sailing. He was brought up in the old High Church and High Tory tradition, and Keble, when he went to him as a pupil, continued him in his Cavalier principles, while spiritualizing his aims. His religion became a kind of discipline of chivalry, and he was strongly affected by the artistic revival of interest in medieval-ism ; at one time he was continually sketching Gothic architecture. His attempts to curb his appetites, recorded with the utmost sim-plicity in his journals, and his self-criticism, shrewdly directed against the worldly code of his class, were undertaken in a spirit of passionate determination, and his failures provoked corresponding outbursts of remorse. But this discipline was hidden from the world by his light-hearted manner.

Froude was utterly remote from the Protestant middle-class London in which Newman had grown up ; he was never anywhere near Evangelicalism, which he laughed at, or Liberalism, which he hated. This background gave his ideas a coherence, accidental but solid, which Newman's never had ; it also made it difficult for him to sympathize with people who held opinions he disliked. When he liked anyone, he would not believe in any difference of opinion, as Newman soon discovered. Both Newman's nature, and his back-ground, helped him to understand people unlike himself and ideas the opposite of his own ; it also forced him to think out his views with a thoroughness Froude never attempted.

They were in some ways so very different that it was not surprising they had not yet made friends. 'Newman is a very nice fellow indeed, but very shy', Froude told his father, when enumerating his new colleagues after his election in 1826. Like Newman himself, Froude was lonely when he was first a Fellow ; for a while his letters home were more frequent and full. In Common Room, he said, 'I sat in a corner as I generally do and said as little as I generally do'. He met Henry Wilberforce and thought him 'a silly fellow ; certainly he is very forward and obtrusive'. All the same he was soon friendly with the Wilberforces, especially Robert. Presently he was writing, 'Newman has foiled my analytical skill ; I cannot make him out at all, but have got far enough to see that he is not my sort'.

No letters home remain to tell how he discovered that after all Newman was his sort ; in the next, of 1830, the friendship was already established, and Newman mentioned as out riding with him, or coming in from St. Mary's with an anthem by Boyce, which Froude copied for his sister Peg. The correspondence between Froude and Newman shows that once the initial step was taken they soon got to like each other. By January 1829 Newman was writing home that on his way to Oxford he had changed places with an undergraduate who wanted to smoke — Newman travelled outside because it was cheaper — and 'on tumbling into the coach', he said, 'I found Froude opposite me. He formed an agreeable companion "*in* course" — but rather spoiled the correctness of my Thursday evening anticipations as to the loneliness of my supper on arrival — so much so that although candles, furniture, magazines, letters, papers and provisions answered faithfully to the account I gave, I did not think of that account nor (pro pudor) of my listeners till F's departure when the Brighton party and our love-lighted converse came into my mind.'

Much later Newman spoke of wanting to get a spark by collision with Froude; the metaphor expresses the effect of the meeting of two such different and yet congenial minds. Froude was an empiricist by nature; he was not interested in theology and philosophy, as Newman was; he liked history, politics, actual events and things. Music was Newman's art; Froude's was drawing. He was not attracted to the early Church and the Fathers, but was always a medievalist. The Church as a great Fact appealed to him, its hierarchical structure enshrining Christ in Sacraments and Saints. St. Thomas à Becket was his favourite study: the pull of forces between ecclesiastical and civil power. Newman called him 'an Englishman to the backbone' in this preference for the concrete. Was it partly from his French ancestry that Newman derived the logical clarity and order of his thinking? Yet there was an empirical English side to him too, and Froude, at a critical moment, helped to consolidate this. Newman met him just when his own mind was beginning to centre on the concrete; Froude accelerated the process — he did not initiate it.

Newman was always so anxious, after Froude's death, to win at least posthumous recognition for his high qualities, that his emphasis on Froude's influence has given to some the impression that he was passive to a dominant personality and took over Froude's views — Keble's views — wholesale. This was not so. Newman had already left behind the religious individualism of the Evangelicals; he had accepted the idea of a visible society, bound together by sacraments of objective value, and holding a tradition of teaching. What Froude did was to give particularity, historical reality and a certain romance of adventure to these ideas ; even so, Newman did not accept his views all at once. He had to go his own pace. The impact of Newman's personality on Froude is less obvious only because Froude left no *Apologia* in which to trace his influence. But Newman must have communicated to him, as well as theological and philosophical ideas, something of his own amazing gifts of understanding and tolerance of people. In the excitements to come Froude encouraged Newman's fighting qualities and laughed him out of his diffidence ; Newman gave Froude, in the purgatory of patience his illness imposed on his active spirit, sympathy of the most invigorating kind by making use of his powers to the utmost. It was a friendship of equals and a steady and equable one ; they sometimes argued the point, but never quarrelled. As to Newman's being passive in any way, it is clear enough from the letters of his contemporaries, whether friendly or hostile, that he was the centre of action, and his friends, even Froude, regarded as allies and subsidiaries.

That Newman was becoming a centre of influence distinct from Whately and even in opposition to him was first generally realized after the great Peel row, which split Oriel and the university in 1829. Hawkins was an ardent Peelite, and when the Prime Minister resigned on the Catholic Emancipation issue, he went up to London and without consulting his colleagues, pledged the college, not to say the university, to support his re-election in order to pass the measure. Newman suddenly became leader of the opposition ; his letters home were scribbled off in a great state of political excitement. He regarded it as an insult to the university that Peel should expect it to keep pace with his changes of policy. It was state interference with the Church's university which offended Newman ; not the question of Catholic Emancipation, about which he had no strong feelings. And so successful was the campaign that Sir Robert Inglis was returned as the Oxford member — Peel, of course, getting a seat, for the close borough of Westbury.

Perhaps it was the young Fellows' success that made Hawkins so angry — for angry he was. He even called the Tory party itself 'their cabal'. Whately, too, was disgusted with Newman, his protégé, for taking up the cause of intolerance and stupidity. He showed his disapproval in a typical gesture ; he invited Newman to a party of all the stupidest old Tories he could collect — the two-bottle orthodox — sat him between 'Provost This and Principal That' and asked him

how he liked his company. Newman treated this episode humour-
ously in the *Apologia* ; nevertheless he said that the Peel row made a
formal break between Whately and himself, and that Whately was
'considerably annoyed at' him. Whately, both then and later, attributed Newman's defection, as he considered it, to ambition — the
desire to make himself leader of a party of his own. Newman characteristically defended himself against this charge by remarking that
he had not collected a party, the party — his friends — had come to
him. This was true, but has been misunderstood. It has been taken
out of context as evidence for Newman's supposed self-centred
passivity, whereas it tells the other way. A party does not collect
round anyone who is not a centre of activity, nor friends come to the
sensitive egotist. Whately thought desire for power was Newman's
motive, and not dedication to a new idea, but he was under no
illusion as to who was the leader of this ginger-group.

It was difficult for Whately to see that Newman had not lapsed
into what Froude called 'mere conservatism' but was building up a
new ideal, because Whately regarded himself, and was regarded by
his friends, as the leader of the new liberal movement in the Church.
The Archbishopric in Dublin so removed him from the English
scene that his later life passed into comparative obscurity, but his
was undoubtedly the most shrewd and keen mind the liberal Churchmen were to possess for a long time to come. Men of liberal opinions
were rare in the Church of England at the time, but they were the
intellectual *élite*, and knew it ; they had a strong conviction of their
own rectitude, and were sure that since their views were enlightened
they would in time prevail. They were reformers, and in moral and
charitable affairs were full of energy — but so were the Evangelicals,
so were to be the members of the Movement, so even the atheists and
agnostics : it was the temper of the age. Liberal Churchmen had
no monopoly of the social conscience, though they were more concerned with politics than other parties in the Church. What really
distinguished them was their approach to the doctrines and history
of Christianity. In effect, if not always in theory, they gave the
highest authority to Reason.

But Newman had just come to believe that Reason, improperly
exercised to judge the data of a divine revelation, was the chief
instrument of the World in the modern age — the World of which
Satan was the ruler : nature, human and non-human, so far as it is
in rebellion against God and in opposition to the kingdom of Christ.
During 1829 and 1830 his sermons in St. Mary's expressed these

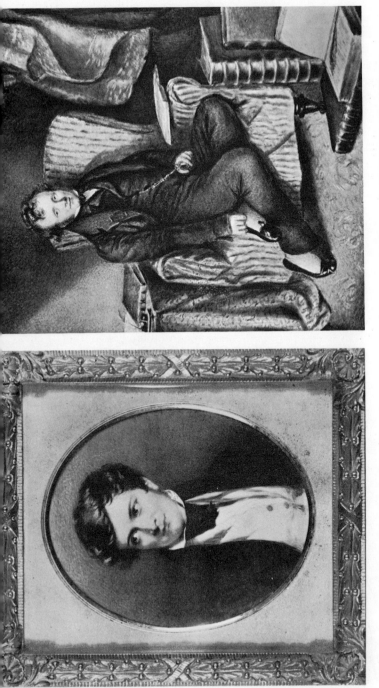

11. JOHN WILLIAM BOWDEN

12. HENRY WILBERFORCE AT OXFORD

13. MANUEL JOHNSON,
THE RADCLIFFE OBSERVER
From a drawing by George Richmond

14. FREDERIC ROGERS
From an engraving after Richmond

15. TOM MOZLEY IN 1832
From a drawing by M. R. Giberne

ideas of the World and the Church, which were basic to his thought
for the whole of his life. He published his last words on the subject
when he was eighty-four and quoted some of these early sermons.
With his clear mind — Whately himself had said it was the clearest
he knew — Newman foresaw the general development of the liberal
idea in religion, as in fact it has come to pass. Wherever reason is
made sole judge of religious truth, faith weakens and in logical
minds is destroyed ; not because the Christian faith is irrational or
false, but because it is something given to the human mind, not
discovered by it. Reason is within the scheme, not superior to it.
Perhaps Newman saw this so clearly because of his own early
scepticism ; Christianity could never be to him merely an habitual
frame of reference, within which the individual critical reason could
be let loose without danger. But to most of the liberal Churchmen,
this was just what it was ; they were critics by conviction and
Christians by habit. Later generations shocked them by losing the
habit. Newman was not shocked, though he was grieved, because
he expected it. In fact, he began by expecting general scepticism
to arrive sooner than it did.

Whately never understood the nature of Newman's opposition
to Liberalism. He thought Newman abandoned the liberal cause
for orthodoxy because orthodoxy was in power, that his motive was
worldly ambition ; yet the truth was that Newman parted company
with the liberals because he saw that their principles, though they
did not realize it, would betray the Church to the World.

Although Newman probably felt the break with Whately more,
because he liked him, it was the break with Hawkins that immediately affected him. Hawkins' hostility to Newman's tutorial scheme
was far more obstinate than the occasion warranted, and was born
of his resentment at the success of the younger man's political campaign. In writing of these early battles, whether in the *Apologia* or
in his memoir, Newman's tone is so detached, his criticism of his
opponents so light and of himself so severe, that it is sometimes
quite difficult to recapture the atmosphere of the actual occasion.
Hawkins was not an easy man to deal with when he was in a mood
of determined hostility. Many left on record that they found him
stiff, formal, ever on his dignity ; he was an inveterate manager, a
meddler, some said, in affairs political and of the university. He
was not improved by acquiring authority. In his memoir Newman
said that before his election Hawkins had been something of a
Tribune of the People, advocating the participation of the tutors

and Fellows in the affairs of the university ; but as Provost he saw
the advantages of the *status quo* and declared that the interests of
the Fellows were sufficiently represented by their Head. In fact,
he was the type who cannot resist concentrating power in his own
hands, cannot believe anyone else is efficient, and is suspicious of
other able men as possible rivals. He was not above some rather
doubtful manœuvres to secure his ends, as his part in Pusey's condemnation in 1843 shows. His self-importance showed in little
things ; he used the authoritative 'we' so often that the younger
Fellows nicknamed him 'the College'. It showed in his manner
too. 'He could not endure free and easy ways', Newman wrote in
a passage of his memoir which he did not send to Anne Mozley,
'and was disgusted with slang ; what others only thought to be
humour would instantly bring a strange rigid expression to his
face.' Needless to say, Froude was frequently guilty of rigidifying
the Provost.

Even in autumn of 1828, when he was working out his new plan
for the tutors, Newman feared Hawkins would not approve it and
did not discuss it with him. He thought if the scheme was put
into operation and the results turned out well, the Provost might
accept it — he had the opportunity of judging the results as it was
he who conducted the terminal examinations. The table of lectures
and classes was complicated, but the principles of the reform were
simple. Each tutor was to be responsible for a certain group of
pupils, and they were to have first claim on his attention, for classes
and for private (unpaid) coaching. This superintendence would
make possible a certain moral supervision also, which was provided
for in the Statutes, but had fallen into disuse. The old, or rather
the decayed, system which Newman inherited, was that in which
the tutors had become mere general lecturers and scarcely knew
their pupils. The first classes which had won Oriel its reputation
had been gained under Tyler, who had asked fees from the most
promising scholars for private tuition. The new scheme was entirely
Newman's ; he carried Dornford along by moral force. Neither
Froude nor Wilberforce was keen to teach, though they certainly
agreed that if they must, Newman's was the best method to use.

The new system was put into operation in the Lent term of 1829 ;
the Peel battle intervened, and when the matter was mentioned to
the Provost the next term the tutors were 'much surprised and
disconcerted at the rude way in which he received the intelligence',
Newman wrote in his memorandum drawn up in 1830, 'without

any kind of deference to us, or any enquiry into the reasons which had swayed us in making our new arrangement'. He abruptly told them they must alter things next term. After the long vacation he repeated his command 'in the same authoritative absolute tone. A long discussion ensued, in which I plainly told him I considered my office a University office and under University sanction, and that it was a matter of conscience with me not to give my time and exertions to the system he upheld.' Newman considered himself responsible to the university as preparing candidates for the Schools.

Hawkins was adamant. He refused to see anything in Newman's system but 'favouritism' — he was making favourites of his clever pupils at the expense of the others. Hawkins himself was inclined to favour the gentlemen commoners, who were not usually candidates for academic honours. He exchanged stiff letters with the tutors; neither side would budge. Finally Hawkins decided to crush the opposition by force. He refused to send the tutors any more pupils. He was within his rights, but it was a high-handed action, and he had no very suitable substitutes. Dornford gave in, and returned to the old system, or lack of system. The others did not. Hawkins sent the pupils who should have gone to Newman to a liberal friend of his, Renn Dickson Hampden, who was married, but living in Oxford. This was also a somewhat dubious expedient, justified in Hawkins' eyes by his disapproval of Newman's influence. Newman went on coaching his remaining pupils till the time came for their Schools; they all came through with flying colours. Indeed, educationally, Hawkins was cutting his own throat — the number of first classes fell during the following years and Oriel never regained its lead in the university. And in the end the old system had to give way to a reform very similar to Newman's. By 1830 all was over; Hampden was tutor in Newman's place and he had lost the position that had meant so much to him and several hundred pounds a year as well. He was excluded from exercising what he felt was his vocation, the teaching and pastoral care of young men.

The atmosphere during the prolonged campaign was extremely trying. In his memoir, written in his old age, Newman accused himself of feeling fiercely on the subject 'that secular education could be so conducted as to become a pastoral cure'. Contrasting his behaviour with Froude's, he said, 'Newman, on the contrary, when he had a clear view of a matter, was accustomed to formulate it, and was apt to be what Isaac Williams considered irreverent and

rude in the nakedness of his analysis, and unmeasured and even
impatient in enforcing it'.   Isaac Williams, however, was not only
a fervent disciple of Keble, but by nature inclined to take up
an attitude of passive resignation to adversity.   Newman's natural
reaction to opposition was to fight, and his immediate feeling when
faced with arbitrary commands which he did not think justified
was indignation.   This he tried hard to keep in check.

Newman may have felt fierce, but Hawkins, as can be seen even
from Newman's pacific summing up in his memoir, was exceedingly
rude to him, not to say unkind.   Knowing his poverty, he 'let it
appear' that a tutor's salary was of more importance to him than it
could be to Wilberforce and Froude.   Newman charitably put this
down to the kindest motive he could discover — that Hawkins
wished to detach him from Froude, whom he thought a bad influence.   Hawkins disliked Froude's slang and his views almost equally.
Whately also thought him a bad influence and jeered at him as
'Boy Tutor', comparing him to the eldest girl in a poor family who
lost her shape by carrying her little brothers about.   Froude took
this in good part, but he enjoyed baiting the great Whately all the
same.   The more Froude was attacked, the more closely Newman
stuck to him.   This loyalty to friends in the teeth of his own interests
was always to be a characteristic of his.   Sticking to his principles
and sticking to Froude he lost his last chance of keeping the favour
of those who had the power to advance him in the university and in
the Church.   He never mentioned this aspect of the affair ; probably
it never even occurred to him.   At no time in his life did he understand the gentle art of getting on in the world.

Even more irritating to Newman than hints about his poverty,
as he admitted in a private note to his memoir, was Hawkins' refusal
to take seriously his assertion that it was a matter of principle with
him to make the tutorship 'a fulfilment of his ordination vow' — a
pastoral as well as a teaching office.   Hawkins put down Newman's
views to an unhealthy attitude caused by overwork.   He was always
asking him 'how he felt to-day ?'   Newman said it became a joke
among the tutors, but surely a very tiresome joke for the victim,
whose deepest convictions were thus ridiculed in public.   Hawkins'
downright, dry temperament and his seniority gave him an overwhelming advantage ; he could administer humiliating snubs and
Newman had to take them as best he could.

'All my plans fail', Newman wrote gloomily to Froude in September 1830.   'When did I ever succeed in any exertion for others ?'

Yet out of the ruin of his hopes he made a sermon on 'Jeremiah, a Lesson for the Disappointed', meditating on a recurring theme — that Christians must expect disappointment in this world : to the world Christ himself was a failure.

With his usual resilience he planned to use his new leisure studying modern French Mathematics, and he said to his mother : 'The Fathers arise again full before me'.

1829

The Idea of Virginity

NEWMAN gave the year 1829 as the date after which he had no more doubts that he was called by God to live a single life. Before that he had sometimes wavered, 'with a break of a month now and a month then', as he said in the *Apologia*, provoking some mild ribaldry from the reviewers. 'When, it may be,' remarked one, 'a pretty face, a gleaming eye, an ensnaring ankle, came between him and his resolution.' The ensnaring ankle is a nice period piece, perhaps more suitable to 1864 than the pre-Victorian age of Newman's youth. Where the critic went wrong was in imagining that Newman had made a resolution. He had not, and was very definite on this point. Until 1829 the 'deep imagination' he had felt at fifteen remained in the background of his mind as an 'anticipation'. In 1829 it was transformed into a resolution by an act of conscious choice. Froude was the agent of the change, for it was from him that Newman learned the Catholic ideal of Christian Virginity.

In his description of Froude in the *Apologia* Newman said, 'He had a high severe idea of the intrinsic excellence of Virginity ; and he considered the Blessed Virgin its great Pattern'. In a cancelled passage he wrote that he 'was taught the Catholic belief of the moral superiority of the single life' by Froude. He added, 'I determined to be "a pilgrim pale in Paul's stern girdle bound"'. That he determined to be such a pilgrim, emphasizes the element of choice. The verse quoted is from the poem *Our Future* written at Tre Fontane, near Rome, in April 1833. The place is associated with the martyrdom of St. Paul, always Newman's hero, the greatest of all missionaries and teachers, and an Apostle who was not married, but spent his whole life and energy for Christ. In the first verse of the poem Newman supposes that the sight of our own future 'would break The youthful spirit, though bold for Jesu's sake'. The second runs :

> But Thou, dear Lord!
> Whilst I traced out bright scenes which were to come,
> Isaac's pure blessings and a verdant home,

Didst spare me, and withhold Thy fearful word ;
Wiling me year by year, till I am found
A pilgrim pale with Paul's sad girdle bound.

Whether the girdle was stern or sad, the sacrificial aspect is stressed,
and so is the almost accidental course towards the decision which
Newman felt had been his. But the decision itself was not accidental.

Froude ought to be revered among their Founders by Anglican
monks and nuns, for the rediscovery of this special Christian vocation was his own contribution to the Catholic Revival in the Church
of England. Even Keble did not share his view, and was soon to
get married himself, rather to his pupil's disappointment. Through
Newman, principally, Froude's ideal spread, less among his immediate contemporaries, than among those fifteen or twenty years younger.
He must have got it from his medieval reading, probably about the
year 1826, when he was first a Fellow of Oriel. At any rate, by 1827
he was arguing with his friends on the subject, for a letter of Sam
Wilberforce's survives of that date, teasing him for being 'almost a
Roman Catholic'. Sam had just got engaged to the beautiful Emily
Sargent, one of the daughters of the Rector of Lavington, and
remarked on 'my practical difference from those doctrines of yours
with respect to matrimony which I have often combated in argument
with you'. He confidently expected that Froude would be cured
of his notions and denied that it was 'dread of you that keeps me
from Oxford', as his brother Robert jokingly maintained. Robert
too teased Froude after not hearing from him for some time, at the
beginning of 1827, 'Are you married ?' The idea, then, was fixed
in Froude's mind before he knew Newman well — indeed, at the
time when he had decided Newman was not his sort.

In his brief allusions to the question in the *Apologia* Newman
only referred to 'the intrinsic excellence of Virginity', and not
understanding the reference to the Blessed Virgin, his Protestant
and agnostic readers perhaps naturally assumed that he meant to
exalt mere singleness at the expense of marriage — and the corollary
was of course understood that the sexual union of man and woman
was, if not sinful, at least in some way a degradation of the spirit.
It was this supposed attitude to marriage that roused the wrath of
Kingsley and many others who did not know Newman personally,
and imagined that he must be someone who feared and hated natural
processes, or himself a woman-hater and perhaps effeminate, the
term commonly used then to cover a variety of deviations, whether
pathological or moral, from the norm of masculinity. Nobody who

actually knew Newman, however hostile to his views, ever classed him as effeminate. It was a charge only made by those, personally unacquainted with him, who misunderstood his views on celibacy and felt their own belief in the supreme value of sexual love challenged.

There is nowhere in Newman's writings, public or private, any depreciation of marriage as such, or of love between the sexes ; contrary to rumour, he welcomed the marriages of his lay friends and gained the friendship of their wives rather than losing theirs. When Bowden married he was still Newman's closest friend, since his friendship with Froude was then only beginning. After Bowden's death Newman told his widow that the Christian goodness and happiness of their married life had for some time 'hindered' his accepting the view that any state could be higher. Ten years after her father's death Marianne Bowden was clothed as a Visitation (contemplative) nun and Newman, who had baptized her, was asked to speak at the ceremony where, dressed as a bride, she received the habit signifying her total dedication to Christ. This sermon, of 1854, remains as an unpublished draft : it is a meditation on creation and love. 'The very idea of matrimony is possession,' he said, '— whole possession — the husband is the wife's and no other's, and the wife is the husband's and none but his.'

Of virginity he wrote then : 'To make a single life its own end, to adopt it simply and solely for its own sake, I do not know whether such a state is more melancholy or more unamiable, melancholy from its unrequited desolateness (like a Mohammedan's God who from eternity has had no exercise of love) and unamiable from the pride and self-esteem on which it is based. This is not the Virginity of the Gospel — it is not a state of independence or isolation, of dreary pride or barren indolence or crushed affections ; man is made for sympathy and for the interchange of love, for self-denial for the sake of another dearer to him than himself. The Virginity of the Christian soul is marriage with Christ.'

The relation of the Church to Christ and of the soul to God has been expressed, from the time of St. Paul, in the imagery of marriage. Christians believe that Christ introduced the world of natural experience into a new dimension. Sexual union was transformed into one of the seven mysteries of the new life, and the partners became mediators to each other of eternal as well as of natural love. But virginity also could be raised from a natural and passive state to one of action and fruition in the spirit, by an act of self-dedication to the Lord of life and love. Christ himself announced this new form of life when he distinguished from eunuchs who were so born, and eunuchs made by men, those who would be eunuchs for the sake of the Kingdom of Heaven. They would forgo the privilege of marriage and the generation of children in order to give themselves entirely to God and through him to bring many to birth in the spirit. Christ, who lived on earth as a virgin, is called Father of the World to Come.

This positive idea of Christian virginity which Newman first learned from Hurrell Froude, offered an opportunity of self-dedication to love as concrete as marriage, though in a different sphere. As marriage humanizes the instincts, so a virginity freely chosen for love can expand the personality in a way that too often does not happen in those who are virgins by accident, whether of circumstances or through some natural defect. The higher form of love orientates and organizes the lower, though not necessarily without difficulties. People have to adjust themselves to whatever form of life they choose to live. The difference between natural and Christian virginity is manifest in the act of choice. It is easily expressed for a woman by the symbolic rite in which she becomes the Bride of Christ. There cannot be so simple an outward expression for a man, though the choice is the same ; but vows, as in marriage, express the voluntary loyalty to a person. Of a man who is to be a priest it might be said that he is identified with Christ, and therefore his bride is the Church ; this symbolism is often used of bishops. Faithfulness and sacrifice are the elements of a promise of chastity freely made.

Newman made no promise in 1829, not even a private vow, for at that time he regarded vows as showing lack of trust in God, on whom he relied for help to continue him in the chosen way. Nevertheless the way was chosen ; his acceptance of this Catholic ideal was a definite act ; this is indicated by his assigning a date to the point at which his 'anticipation' became a resolution, and associating it with the doctrine he received from Froude. But although he 'determined to be a pilgrim pale', Newman did not throw himself into the ideal with the emotional enthusiasm of one who feels he has discovered the answer to all his problems. On the contrary, there is a marked hesitation on some aspects of the subject, which shows perhaps especially in his verses, during the next few years. Newman never accepted any idea completely till he had lived with it for several years ; ideas were not adopted, they were assimilated. Even during the early years of the Movement, when all he wrote was alive with the ferment of newly discovered Catholic doctrine and practice, his view of clerical celibacy still emphasized separation from the world more than spiritual perfection.

In the early thirties Newman was writing popular articles in the *British Magazine*, later collected as *The Church of the Fathers*. On St. Basil, founder of eastern monasticism, and his friend St. Gregory Nazianzen, he found much to say ; with St. Gregory he had a fellow-feeling all his life. Gregory was no firebrand — he stayed in Athens, shirking the mud and bleakness of Basil's mountain retreat ; he liked gardening, writing poetry ; he was domestic and literary in his habits and later came to grief in the world of imperial and ecclesiastical politics where Basil, tormented with illness, cut his forceful way so fearlessly. 'One might say', Newman wrote of these two Christian Greeks, 'that Gregory's abandonment of the world arose from an early passion, as it may be called, for a purity higher than his own nature ; and Basil's from a profound sense of the world's nothingness and the world's defilements. Both seem to have viewed it as a sort of penitential exercise as well as a means towards perfection. . . . When they had once resolved to devote themselves to the service of religion, the question arose, how they might best improve and employ the talents committed to them. Somehow the idea of marrying and taking orders, or taking orders and marrying, building or improving their parsonages, and showing forth the charities, the humanities and the gentilities of a family man did not suggest itself to their minds.'

Humour was never far off when Newman was thinking of the state of clerical life in England, though he did not give it full rein in print till he wrote *Loss and Gain* in 1847, when he was a Catholic priest and an Oratorian novice in Rome. It was mild satire even then, for he loved the kindly parsonage life even while he teased it. What made him impatient was its being held up as the only possible ideal for a Christian priest — its domestic comfort and comparative ease contrasted so sharply with the life of God on earth. Monasticism arose as a protest against worldliness and a corrective of its corruptions ; the difference between the Roman Empire of the fourth century and England in the nineteenth determined the different form of the ascetic ideal followed by Newman and Froude, but the protest was essentially the same. English worldliness was not so spectacular as that of ancient Rome, and Froude did not retire to a mountain like St. Basil. There were no startling indecencies of social or ecclesiastical behaviour to castigate, nor were Oxford clergymen tempted to commit sensational sins in pursuit of material power and pleasure. The world presented its attractions in a more subtle form. There was nothing wrong, there was much that was good, in the clerical career followed by the majority.   But in those days it was a gentleman's life, and on the whole an easy one.   Marriage anchored the clergyman in the ruling class ; his service of God and his fellows was conditioned by the necessities of bringing up his family in the culture suitable to their social station.   It was in itself a virtuous life — but it was noticeably unlike St. Paul's.

But just because it was a good life and socially acceptable it had attractions which could not be dismissed as temptations, because they were not sinful.   To judge from many verses and remarks in his letters Newman found the idea of a domestic life attractive ; he was very much a man of his period in his love for home, the intimate circle where highest and smallest things are naturally enjoyed together. He had been brought up in a happy home and was affectionate by nature, fond of children and liking to have women about — when he was old he was quite envious of his friend Woodgate, who had six daughters as well as his wife to care for him in illness ; Newman did not think much of men as nurses and his highest praise was that one was almost as good at it as a woman would be.   These characteristics do not appear romantic in modern eyes, but Newman shared them with most of his contemporaries ; indeed, in any age, a man without them is not likely to be happy in married life.   Newman, at all times in his life, fitted most comfortably into his friends' family circles, and one of his favourite themes on the nature of the Oratory was its homeliness.

Nor did he despise the pleasures of human love.   A charming and unexpected excursion occurs in some philosophical notes he was making in 1861 on the power of sudden feelings of doubt.   He paralleled the experience with the force of illicit loves in youth, thinking of Thackeray's novels.   He said : 'It has been my own happiness not to have known them experimentally, but I can easily understand there must be an ecstatic sweetness in the first unlawful kiss given, which to the very end of life will carry with it its own (seeming) evidence of its innocence and allowableness ; and to bear down all idea that God could mean to punish such pleasant vices ; the truth is, religion is something supernatural ; and, from nature being closer to us than it, may easily be brought home to our imagination as unnatural.   Sight is closer than faith ; reason is closer than authority ; human affection is closer to us than devotion, and passion than mortification.   And since sight, reason, affection and passion are all natural, they are all from God, and have that impress of divinity on them that they *do* carry an evidence with them of their own innocence *in se*. It is the when and the where and the with whom and the under what circumstances constitute the question of sin or not sin. . . . Of course to the end of life, except in the case of saints and very perfect Christians, nature is easier than the way of grace. Hence the great difficulty of persevering.'

There are many other evidences that Newman could 'easily understand' the sweetness of love between the sexes. As far as his personal life was concerned, besides the women he got to know well because they married his friends, or because they wrote to him for advice, there were others whom he met and liked at once for themselves: Anne Mozley was one. These became friends, because he so willed it. But he did not regard himself as immune to the chances of love.

In 1832 Froude wrote to Newman from Devonshire, 'I am getting to be a sawney [sentimentalist] and not to relish the dreary prospects which you and I have proposed to ourselves — but this is only a feeling — depend on it I will not shrink — if I buy my constancy at the expense of a permanent separation from home'.

Newman answered: 'What can you mean by your "feeling" against our dreary prospects? Were you myself, I should say you were falling in love — but I hardly suspect you of that. Your words are quite unintelligible, for what do you propose to stand to that you have not commenced already? and how can you ever be required to give up your friends of kin, where you do not now? Unriddle.'

Froude unriddled in his usual straightforward way. 'As to my sawney feelings — I own that home does make me a sawney — and that first eclogue runs in my head absurdly — but there [is] more fun in the prospect of becoming an ecclesiastical agitator than in "at nos hinc alii etc" — and the rest may be regarded as irrelevant.'

This exchange — not printed in the *Remains* of course — shows that Newman felt himself liable to fall in love, and rather more liable than Froude who had made a chivalrous ideal out of what Newman had long regarded as a hard necessity. Now Froude turned out to have qualms, and it was home that brought them on — one of his sisters got engaged about that time. Neither of them drifted into the celibate life because it happened to suit them; though they chose it, and chose it as a high ideal, yet it was still in many ways 'a penitential exercise' and a 'dreary prospect'. Newman's qualms were to come later, in 1840, when Froude was dead and his other friends married, so that he not only felt lonely, but was forced into a position of unpopular singularity most unwelcome to him. By then he had no real intention of giving up his chosen path, to which he had already adapted his life, for a woman's sympathy, such as only a wife could give, but he wrote in his journal 'yet not the less do I feel the need of it'. It was typical of Newman to admit that he felt the need of a particular human sympathy which he nevertheless willingly gave up for the sake of the kingdom of heaven ; he never would disown his natural feelings, even if they appeared to run counter to the supernatural ideal. Many of his contemporaries, even his friends, were puzzled by this emotional honesty ; they did not admit to feelings contrary to the ideals they professed, did not recognize them except possibly as temptations.

In discussing Newman's vocation to celibacy some, in our biological age, have confused the attraction of marriage with the need to satisfy physical desires ; because he did not confess to the latter, his confession of the need for the intimate personal sympathy of marriage has been dismissed as meaningless. But it had meaning for him. We have no right to assume we know what he felt or did not feel on the physical plane ; but at the level of personal love we should not ignore the fact that there were times when he found the sacrifice hard, and that just because his idea of marriage was high — it was whole possession, each of the other, exclusive and perpetual.

Newman's capacity for love can be measured by the love he inspired in others, for no one is loved who is not lovable, and no one is lovable who is not loving. In youth the power to love is ready and strong, though often selfish in scope, but if nature is left to itself it diminishes with age, the person becoming circumscribed, sometimes totally imprisoned in his own habits and wishes. In spite of his shyness and the difficult gift of self-awareness, Newman's sympathy with others did not narrow as he grew older, but increased and deepened and included ever more various types of person. This enlargement of heart, which cannot happen to anyone if he remains merely passive to experience, Newman won by the way he passed through the successive crises of his personal development. Often the power to love was threatened with constriction and even extinction : in his youth from within, by the dangers of intellectualism and self-will ; after he had passed his physical prime by reiterated blows from without, ordeals by rejection. He not only survived these crises, some very severe, but each time came out more alive and with greater power of sympathy. The signs of the struggle marked his features, but so, increasingly, did the resulting gentleness.

To understand Newman's youth it is sometimes necessary to look back at it from his old age. The aged Cardinal, loved by so many, grew out of the young man who chose, among other difficult choices, to be what he called 'a pilgrim pale'. He could not have been what he became had this choice been based, consciously or unconsciously, on any defect, or weakness, or selfishness, or revolt against the demands of nature. It was a choice slowly made, deeply felt, completely conscious — made not without hesitations, but for love.

The very idea of matrimony was whole possession, Newman said to Marianne Bowden, in his maturity. 'And this it is to be married to Jesus. It is to have Him ours wholly, henceforth and for ever — it is to be united to Him by an indissoluble tie — it is to be His, while He is ours. . . . Such has the Highest deigned to be to His elect ; to all of them in the world to come, and to those of them in their degree by earnest or anticipation who are called to follow the Lamb whithersoever He goes. . . .' He might not have so expressed it in 1829, but the desire to follow Christ wherever he went was, then and always, the motive power of his resolution to live a single life. Nothing less positive and vital could have carried him through the storms to come, when he became the representative figure of the religious celibate in a society which hated and feared and despised nothing so bitterly.

1830–1832

Ancient Fathers and Ladies' Albums

AFTER his final defeat in the tutorship row, in July 1830, Newman told Froude he thought of setting up for a great man. 'It is the only way to be thought so. I have ever been too candid and have in my time got into all sorts of scrapes. I shall learn wisdom rapidly now.' He never did learn this particular wisdom. The letter was cheerful ; he laughed at himself for having told in detail a mishap when his horse stumbled, riding to Brighton, without saying in so many words that he had fallen off. He cut his nose with his glasses, and the horse its knees, 'So I finished by walking above 21 miles in a broiling sun on the dusty road'.

Later that summer, just when his income dropped, he was busy establishing his mother and sisters in a house at Iffley. He would have preferred them to stay at Brighton, where he liked to spend a holiday, but they could not bear to be so far from their 'guardian angel' as his mother called him. For the last three years he had taken summer cottages in the villages round Oxford, giving extra coaching to Henry Wilberforce, who flirted mildly with the Newman girls. In the end, though Newman suspected (what turned out to be the case) that they would not really see more of him by living where he worked, he gave in to his mother's wishes and found them Rose Hill, in Iffley. Later, they moved to a house called Rose Bank. As usual it was he who superintended the alterations, the painters, the paperers and the removal, which took place in the late autumn. In October, after coping with all this on top of his other work, he admitted to Jemima that he was 'supremely tired'.

At this critical moment in the family fortunes Frank announced that he was going on a missionary expedition to Persia with a party of 'saints'. For in the last few years he had become involved in the fortunes of a nascent sect, now known as Plymouth Brethren, who gathered about the magnetic figure of J. N. Darby, an evangelical clergyman of the Church of Ireland, who gradually gave up his connexion with the establishment and became the apostle of an absolute return, as he conceived it, to primitive Christianity. When Frank was in Ireland in 1827 he met this strange man, lame, earnest and learned in his way, devoted to preaching his gospel. Later, Frank brought him over to Oxford and introduced him to the evangelical set. He became a sort of father confessor, said Frank in later years. 'There was no end of secret closetings with him.' He may have introduced him to John, for of John he remarked, 'He never showed any strong attraction towards those I regarded as spiritual persons : on the contrary I thought him stiff and cold towards them'.

Francis Newman was about twenty-two when he met Darby, and as Mr. Mayers died soon after, he transferred to the Irish clergyman all his admiration and devotion, took up his ideas and began to meet his disciples. The Persian expedition was to be made up of some of these : Mr. Parnell, afterwards Lord Congleton, and in later years the owner of a fine bird's nest beard of the Edward Lear variety ; Mr. Groves, 'a well-known dentist from Devonshire', and Mr. Cronin, a doctor, whose sister was engaged to Parnell. She was to accompany them, with Cronin's mother and his wife — but his wife died on the eve of departure. He took his baby with him. None of the ladies survived the expedition. They started from Dublin with an enormous pile of luggage, including a library of books, a large medicine chest and a lithographic press for printing tracts.

Frank's decision to be a missionary was influenced by the fact that Maria Giberne, faithful to her absent Indian officer, had refused his offer of marriage. He consulted none of his family about his decision to go abroad. '*After* making up his mind, he nakedly tells me the *fact*', John said to Jemima. Though he would have answered as he had done in 1827, that it would be a privilege to bear the whole responsibility of the family to allow his brother to go, he was hurt at not being consulted. Frank's peculiar views worried him, but he hoped that would not matter too much in converting the heathen. He did not doubt it would involve self-denial for Frank, 'though from F's great dissatisfaction with everything as it is I doubt not it will be a relief to his mind to be free from the irritation that everything around him occasions. . . . All I can say is, he never has thrown himself on my confidence and (I trust) never will, and be disappointed in me.' He added a postscript : 'Frank has offered Froude some of his books as not needing them any more. *He has made no such offer to me.* One would have thought I had a prior claim.' This was all the criticism he made of his brother, who was leaving him with a depleted income and in sole charge of mother, sisters, poor bankrupt Aunt and the unpredictable Charles.

Charles was writing John argumentative letters, trying to convert him to atheism. He said he knew John was busy, but as his engagements sprang principally from his religious views, he wished to put an end to them by undeceiving him as to those views. John was annoyed with Charles for having played a practical joke on a blind clergyman, but when he answered in September it amused him to turn the tables and demand that instead of attacking Christianity Charles should try to prove the truth of atheism. For, he told Jemima, he thought 'unbelievers took an unfair advantage in always *assailing* things, as if *they* had not also an hypothesis to maintain, and greater difficulties (as I think) to surmount'. He described their exchange high-spiritedly in terms of a schoolboy tussle.

Charles was a problem. He had visited his mother in August. 'Charles comes frequently of an evening', she wrote to John. 'He looks very ill. I wish he would consult Mr. Babington. I have hinted at it, but who can administer to the mind ? He, poor fellow, is more perplexed than he will allow. He is as earnest in Mr. Owen's plans as Frank can be in his "good cause" yet it is very striking how similarly self-willed they each are. They each consider that they *alone* see things rightly.'

In spite of disappointment and harassing business Newman was very cheerful. On the turn-up of his letter about his paper-battle with Charles he told Jemima about Pusey's brother's election to Parliament. Both the Puseys were inevitably lampooned as Pussy. 'The opposite party got together a number of cats and put *his* ribbons on them ∿ ∿ that's a laugh.' Laughter made his pen slip.

When Newman realized that his career as a tutor was over he turned all his teaching energy into his sermons at St. Mary's. When he came to publish his sermons he took more from 1831 than from any other year — twenty-seven in all. The theme of obedience runs through all these parochial sermons, obedience to conscience as the path to the understanding of truth, and obedience to God to putting his commandments into action. Many deal with the use and misuse of emotion in religion, with warnings against relying on feelings much needed then in the heyday of the Evangelicals. Typically, Newman did not merely denounce emotion ; he recognized its use in providing an initial impetus to action but showed the danger of identifying holiness with feeling good.

Newman preached to his parishioners — High Street shopkeepers with leanings towards dissent — on the dangers of emotion ; he preached to the university of the dangers of reason. The university sermons, delivered in the afternoon by a rota of selected preachers, were expected to be of high intellectual standard and were attended by a large number of important persons as well as the younger dons and undergraduates. To preach to such an audience was a great test, and Newman, the first time he was called to do it, could not sleep the night before. He was twenty-five ; it was Act Sunday, July 2nd, 1826. His subject was 'The Philosophical Temper, first enjoined by the Gospel', and his text the words of Jesus : 'I am the light of the world'. Gracefully, he introduced the motto of the university : *Dominus Illuminatio Mea* — the Lord my light. Afterwards, as he recorded, 'I lay on my sofa writhing, at the thought of what a fool I had made of myself'.

There were two other sermons in the next few years, and then from Advent 1831 to Advent 1832, Newman was appointed one of the Select Preachers. He was never appointed again. The most famous preacher in Oxford, perhaps in England, was carefully excluded from the university pulpit by the authorities. The six further sermons to the university (printed with the others in 1843) were preached at the appointment of friends, mostly on saints' days — two on Whit-Tuesdays. The only two on Sundays were preached in the mornings, and before the beginning of term. Even in the year when he was Select Preacher efforts were made to arrange his turns so that they did not fall in full term, and he noted as an old man that several of the set on Faith and Reason were preached to half-empty benches. Yet they contain some of Newman's deepest thought ; he reissued them almost without alteration in 1871, the year after he had published his mature reflexions on the same problems in the *Grammar of Assent.*

Nothing could make clearer the disapproval of the university authorities than this treatment of Newman from the very beginning of his career. It is plain enough why liberals like Whately disliked his teaching — less plain why the Heads, who were far from any taint of liberalism, were so afraid of it. Perhaps the reason lurked in the disconcerting fact that the World, against which Newman preached with such penetration, was all too like the prosperous society in which they were contentedly settled. He brushed aside decent moral behaviour as perfectly possible to pagans and even to atheists ; Christians who were only virtuous were not worthy of the

Christ who had come to sow fire on the earth, a life of supernatural love as far beyond ordinary human virtue as that was beyond the instinctive life of animals. A moving exhortation on these lines was one thing, but practical directions on the road to perfection were another. It was all much too *ultra* for elderly men in authority.

'The usurpations of Reason may be dated from the Reformation', Newman announced to his afternoon university audience on Sunday, December 11th, 1831. It was Froude who had brought to his notice the disintegration effected by the sixteenth-century Reformers in their attempts to purify the Church, but it was Newman who traced out the development of ideas from that rebellion against authority. To him the rebellious human reason was the instrument of the World in the present age of the perennial battle with the kingdom of God. But it was not the use, it was the usurpation of reason which he attacked. Faith could make usurpations too. 'It would be an absurdity to attempt to find out mathematical truths by the purity and acuteness of the moral sense. It is a form of this mistake which has led men to apply such Scripture communications as are intended for religious purposes to the determination of physical questions.' (Here he proposed the solution, now commonly accepted, of that debate on the truth of the Bible which began to be fashionable thirty years later.) But in the same way that faith could not dictate to reason in the pursuit of scientific truth, so reason could not dictate to faith in matters of religious truth. Why not ? Because Christianity is not what men have found out about God, but what God has made known to men. It is a revelation of objective truths, which can be accepted or rejected, but cannot be criticized piecemeal as if it were some system of human philosophy.

In the *Apologia* Newman tried to give Keble the credit for his theories on Reason and Faith, but he had to admit that it was partly dissatisfaction with Keble's approach that led him to elaborate his theory of assent. Keble was not a philosopher ; faced with young men who had doubts he told them to do their duties and turn aside from doubts as from temptations. Newman had always emphasized the importance of conscience in the pursuit of truth, but he thought some intellectual difficulties honestly demanded an answer and deserved to get one. What he did was to formulate the conditions under which inquiry could usefully be made. Reason must be put in its place, but it had a place, and an important one, in religious inquiry. Reason could judge the probabilities that a revelation had taken place ; reason could also explore the meaning and connexion of the revealed truths. What it could not do was to set itself up as judge of the relative value of this or that part of the revelation. The whole question was closely connected with that of the authority of the Church, and Newman's two great Essays, on the *Development of Doctrine* and on the *Grammar of Assent*, deal with two different but related aspects of this complex double problem.

Froude used to say that he was like the murderer who had done one good deed in his life : he had brought Newman and Keble to understand each other. Newman owed less intellectually to Keble than he tried to make out, but he was indebted to Froude for gaining him a friend whom he loved and admired as much as anyone he knew in all his life. Keble was a living exponent of the seventeenth-century Anglican tradition, a spiritual descendant of George Herbert and many other country parsons, poets, scholars, gentle, quiet men — and great individualists. As a Catholic Newman was to follow Philip Neri, one of the most individual and homely of saints, and he thought that in his own English setting Keble was just such another. Small, bright-eyed, with a youthful look that lasted almost into old age, humorous to the point of oddity on occasion, hating pomposity and pretence so much he could sometimes be abrupt in manner, Keble's kindness and goodness made it impossible for anyone to remain hostile for long. Once Froude had made him realize that Newman was neither an enthusiastic evangelical nor an incipient liberal, Keble soon took to him, it was not long before he was writing in his casual, charming style — asking him to send some shoes left behind at Oriel, or demanding criticism 'for I can't get it out of my head that you are a real honest man'.

It was probably of Keble Newman was thinking when he wrote, in his sermon on *Personal Influence, the Means of Propagating the Truth*, of the hidden saints, who, unknown to the world, were the instruments God used to bring about his purposes for mankind. It was by this humble propagation of faith among the weak and oppressed that Christianity had conquered the great Roman Empire, when all the imperial power and the learning of the philosophers had been concentrated on its extermination. Newman was already meditating on the mysterious growth of the kingdom of Christ in the world of time.

In the summer of 1831 Newman went to stay with Froude at Dartington. They travelled by boat to Torbay, and as Newman disliked the crowded cabins they slept on deck, rolled up in their

cloaks under a starry sky.   Froude caught a cold which Newman
afterwards believed to have been the beginning of his illness.   Newman
had never been in Devonshire before and its luxuriant beauty stupe-
fied him.   He wrote to his mother : 'Limestone and sandstone rocks
of Torbay are very brilliant in their colours, and sharp in their forms ;
strange to say, I believe I never saw real rocks in my life.   This
consciousness keeps me very silent, for I feel I am admiring what
everyone else knows. . . . Really I think I should dissolve into essence
of roses, or be attenuated into an echo, if I lived here.   What strikes
me most is the strange richness of everything.   The rocks blush
every variety of colour, the trees and fields are emeralds, and the
cottages are rubies.   A beetle I picked up in Torquay was as green
and gold as the stone it lay upon. . . . Nay, my very hands and fingers
look rosy, like Homer's Aurora, and I have been gazing on them with
astonishment. . . . The exuberance of the grass and the foliage is
oppressive, as if one had not room to breathe, though this is a fancy
— the depth of the valleys and the steepness of the slopes increases
the illusion, and the Duke of Wellington would be in a fidget to get
some commanding point to see the country from. . . . The scents are
extremely fine, so very delicate and yet so powerful, and the colours
as if they were all shot with white.'

In this earthly paradise Newman wandered about alone, for the
Froudes had all been having influenza and Hurrell was nursing his
cold.   Newman found the close, cornered richness fascinating, but a
little suffocating ; Devonshire was to remain for him always an
enchanted garden, dangerously alluring.   He wrote verses in the
album of one of Froude's lively and charming sisters.

> There stray'd awhile, amid the woods of Dart,
>   One who could love them, but who durst not love.
> A vow had bound him, ne'er to give his heart
>   To streamlet bright, or soft secluded grove.
> 'Twas a hard humbling task onwards to move
>   His easy-captured eyes from each fair spot,
>   With unattach'd and lonely step to rove
> O'er happy meads which soon its print forgot : —
> Yet kept he safe his pledge, prizing his pilgrim-lot.

In another album there he wrote *Seeds in the Air*, in lighter style.

> Could I hit on a theme
>   To fashion my verse on,
> Not long would I seem
>   A lack-courtesy person . . .

> Bright thoughts are roaming
>   Unseen in the air ;
> Like comets their coming
>   Is sudden and rare.

After describing how these could be nursed by the Muse he ended :

> All this is a fiction ;
>   I never could find
> A suitable friction
>   To frenzy my mind.
> What use are empirics ?
>   No gas on their shelf
> Can make one spout lyrics
>   In spite of oneself !

One of these girls was soon to die of the illness which also threatened her brother, though it was known to neither at the moment. Newman felt one of his obscure intuitions of doom among this happy family party, which he could not explain and which depressed him. He had to write a sermon while he was there, which he did not want to do ; when Froude read it in print, some time later, he was surprised to find how appropriate it was to their real but then unsuspected fate.

Making gentlemen write verses in their albums was the favourite pursuit of young ladies then, and Newman was good at it. He had a light touch. Two girl cousins presented him with tiny albums, in 1829. In one he wrote :

> Fair Cousin, thy page
> is small to encage
> the thoughts which engage
> the mind of a sage
>   such as I am ;

> 'Twere in tea-spoon to take
> The whole Genevese lake
> or a lap-dog to make
> the white Elephant sac-
>   red in Siam.

> Yet inadequate though
> To the terms strange and so·
> lemn that figure in po-
> lysyllabical row
>   in a treatise ;

> Still true words and plain
> of the heart not the brain,

in affectionate strain
this book to contain
        very meet is.

So I promise to be
a good Cousin to thee,
and to keep safe the se-
cret I heard, although e-
        v'ry one know it ;

With a lyrical air
my kind thoughts I would dare,
and offer whate'er
beseems the news, were
        I a poet.

That same year, 1829, he wrote for his sisters 'My Lady Nature and her Daughters', comparing ladies' delight in dress and dancing and their round of homely tasks to the beauties and activities of nature. But in answer to the question 'Where shall work-day souls repair ?' he concluded :

High-born Nature answers not.
Leave her in her starry dome,
Seek we lady-lighted home.
Nature 'mid the spheres bears sway,
Ladies rule where hearts obey.

In the sixties, when Newman, in answer to many requests, repub-lished his verses in a volume, one of his converts, Father Coleridge, the Jesuit editor of *The Month*, demanded in great disappointment why he had left this one out. Newman said he had feared people would think it rather frivolous for a grey-headed priest. He put it into the later editions.

Music meant more than verse-making to him. One of his star pupils, Frederic Rogers, lodged in Iffley in 1831, and used to visit Rose Hill to play with Newman and his sisters. Later his own sisters got to know them, and one remembered into old age Newman's playing of a sonata of Beethoven. No professional violinist heard afterwards ever quite brought it home to her in the same way. Beethoven, only recently dead, was Newman's favourite composer, then and always — 'like a great bird singing', he said once. Mozart, Haydn, Corelli were all his familiar friends.

Frederic Rogers was the eldest son of another Devonshire family living at Blachford, near Ivybridge ; he was sent to Eton and came up to Oriel in 1827 just after the practical joker FitzHarris (Lord

Malmesbury) went down. Rogers was clever and shrewd, with a
keen wit, and his mind matured early. He was ten years younger
than Newman and at present found the gap too great for intimacy,
but later he was to be his closest friend after Froude's death. He
seems never to have intended to take Orders, and aimed at a political
career, which he afterwards successfully followed. At this time
Newman was giving him extra tuition — free. 'He informed me in
an embarrassed kind of way that he hoped I understood that I was
reading with him as a college pupil and friend', Rogers wrote home.
Rogers had trouble with his eyes, sometimes serious, and in 1832
Newman spent hours reading not only with him but to him ; this
became a Herculean labour when he caught cold and lost his voice.
But Rogers justified his tutor's devotion with a brilliant first class.
He was the last of the ill-fated experiment.

Another friend with whom Newman played Beethoven was the
Spaniard Blanco White. A priest of liberal sympathies who had
lost his faith, in England he tried to accept the Anglican tradition,
but was later to turn to Unitarianism, becoming increasingly
sceptical. He was of a sensitive and nervous temperament and had
an exile's touchiness about being given presents, especially of food.
'What, send me jam ? am I come to that, Newman ?' he said once,
and it became a family saying, repeated by Newman when his
mother sent him a 'sweet present'. Newman liked Blanco White
and Blanco White liked him, but was suspicious of his views. He
told him that if he went on like that he would end up a Roman
Catholic ; Frank Newman thought this was evidence straight from
the horse's mouth, confirming his own worst forebodings. Blanco
White also liked Froude, and was later to maintain that Newman
had led him astray ; he said Froude tried to laugh off his most
extravagant opinions. White was probably misled by Froude's
dislike of solemnity, for in many ways he was more intransigent
than Newman. Whately was Blanco White's friend and patron,
so far as he would allow himself to be patronized, and when
Whately, in the autumn of 1831, left Oxford for Dublin, White
presently followed to be tutor to his children. 'Adieu, my Oxford
Plato', he wrote affectionately in one of his letters to Newman.

Whately was now an Archbishop, but he was wasted in Dublin —
so thought Thomas Arnold, ex-Fellow of Oriel, and the liveliest of
the liberal Churchmen, now relegated (as he felt it) to Rugby School,
where he had no intention of staying for ever. 'It was an evil hour
which took Whately from Oxford where he was doing great and

certain good,' he wrote to Hampden in 1836, 'to exhaust his powers
in what is but an attempt to raise corn out of the sea-sand.' Whately,
however, continued to take a keen interest in what went on in Oxford,
and the year after he left he sent Hawkins some typical advice. He
did not like Dornford, the one Tutor who had compromised, because
of his offensive manner. 'You will find Hampden a firm man as
well as an able tutor,' he said, 'and though not engaging in manner,
yet not offensive. To gain his intimate confidence would cost you
much trouble, he is very reserved ; but I think he is worth it.'
Hampden was to be used continually by Hawkins to thwart Newman,
and became the occasion of the first great row of the Movement.
'If you catch the *young* Fellows as they are elected,' Whately went on,
'and coax them into tameness (which is what I do to my clergy) you
will in time find a tractable set around you. Who need despair when
I tell you that *I* am more popular than, considering the existing state
of parties, could have been expected of *any*, the most accomplished
courtier ?'

But Hawkins was not as good at taming young Fellows as Whately,
and had nothing like the attraction Newman so tiresomely had, even
though Newman was not aiming at producing a tractable set but a
band of Christian apostles. Nearly all the younger Fellows were
drawn into Newman's orbit, for many years to come. Perhaps this
was why Hawkins became more and more determined in his manage-
ment of affairs outside the college, in order to crush the influence of
Newman in the university. The hostilities, of course, were conducted with the utmost politeness, which has permanently veiled the
ferocity of the campaign. It was a one-sided battle as far as the acts
of the chief combatants were concerned, for it never occurred to
Newman to undertake manœuvres in his turn, in counter-intrigue.
To Hawkins, however, everything Newman said or did appeared in
the nature of an offensive because he thought his ideas and his
influence deplorable — and this influence, the unseen power which
Newman wielded, and which frightened his opponents into extraordinary acts of injustice, was growing all the time.

As well as pouring all his teaching energy into his sermons Newman during these two years was writing his first book. Rose and
Lyall, editors of the new Theological Library, asked him to write a
volume on the Councils of the Church. Hugh James Rose was a
Cambridge man, the Editor of the *British Magazine*, and it shows
how promising was Newman's reputation already that he was asked
to contribute to this series. He had certainly read much in the

period, so little explored at that time, though he was afterwards to say that he had learned less than he should because he went about it the wrong way.   In 1828 he had begun reading the Fathers again, this time chronologically.   His ex-pupils gave him further folios to add to those Pusey had bought him in Germany for a shilling each — the price indicates how little they were then prized.   Newman soon realized that the field covered by all the early Councils was too vast to be tackled in one book ; he gradually contracted his view till the work became *The Arians of the Fourth Century*.

It was out of the intellectual dissensions of that time that the orthodox doctrine of the Trinity was formulated and received authoritative definition at the Nicene Council.   But Newman got so interested in the development of the Arian party and the activities of St. Athanasius, the lonely champion of orthodoxy, that the council itself was relegated to a summary at the end.   Froude, when he heard of the length of the introductory portion, became alarmed that Newman would never arrive at his subject.   'Recollect, my good sir,' Newman retorted, 'that every thought I think *is* thought, and every word I write *is* writing, and that thought tells, and that words take room, and that though I make the introduction the *whole* book, yet a book it is.' The only snag was that it was not the book he had been asked to write.   It was too long for inclusion in the series, too.   In the end, he published it himself in 1834.

The Arians were to turn up again in the history of Newman's mind and help to change the course of his life ; even now they had a strong effect on him.   The image of the Church emerged powerfully from his study of these early conflicts — and it was quite as much an historical as a theological study.   It was ideas in action that fascinated Newman, the genealogical tree of any heresy, the twists given by this or that national character, the reaction of the civil power, and the slow mysterious life of the main body of Christians, gradually assimilating into itself certain ideas, and throwing off, sometimes violently, others which turned out to be alien to its composite, collective, yet living and united mind.   At present he studied them without realizing fully the implications of his own views.

Newman worked so unrelentingly at his book that he had spells of faintness.   Sometimes he felt dizzy and had to lie down ; occasionally he lost consciousness completely for a few moments.   This was to happen to him in nearly every concentrated application to his work, but the writing of *The Arians* remained in his mind ever after as *the* example of such occasions ; every similar crisis was compared to it.

This summer, of 1832, there was a threat of cholera, and there were cases about Oxford, but the visitation proved a light one and none in Newman's parish caught it. Newman went off on a brief visit to Mr. Rickards, who had left Ulcombe for Stowlangtoft. On the way he stopped at Cambridge, surprised and delighted at its beauty. He felt there was nothing like King's College Chapel in Oxford. 'Surely there is a *genius loci* here, as in my own dear home,' he wrote to his mother.

Years later he was accused of deserting his parish in a cholera epidemic. The winter before, when it threatened, he and his mother had laid plans ; she was going to take a cottage and run it herself as a hospital. Had there been any danger, Newman would not have left his mother to face it alone. But so little was apprehended that it was not considered dangerous for the invalid Jane Mozley to stay in Oxford on her way home from Teignmouth, where she had been staying, with her brother Tom for company— for the ebullient Tom had collapsed under the strain of his first curacy and had to recuperate by the sea.

Tom Mozley was a Fellow now, elected in 1829, and his younger brother James was an undergraduate at Oriel. A whole bunch of Mozleys descended on Oxford, were 'lionized' over it, and visited the Newmans. The girls made friends at once. This was the first time the Mozley sisters, among them Anne, Newman's future biographer, had met Tom's ex-tutor, about whom they had heard so much, and Froude, equally famous to them. They came prepared to admire these learned young clergymen, but were all the same surprised when the two of them walked into breakfast one Saturday morning. 'Striking entrance, the whole not to be described,' Miss Jane recorded in her diary, while Anne, in a later note, remembered their 'marked individuality' and 'unconscious dignity of aspect'.

Poor Jane did not recover her health. She died the next winter, another victim to that scourge of the age, tuberculosis. It was now that Froude told Newman that the doctors feared he had the same disease, then nearly always fatal. His brother Bob had already died of it. This terrible news, and the threat of cholera still in the air, made them feel when they parted that they might never meet again. Such partings, like those that separate friends in war-time, make people realize their feelings for each other more fully than ordinarily. Newman wrote long after, in a note on this occasion, 'I shook hands with him and gazed into his face with great affection': and he referred to one of his verses as composed with this occasion in mind.

> And when thine eye surveys
> With fond adoring gaze
> And yearning heart, thy friend,
> Love to its grave doth tend.

Newman's friends were afraid he was in danger from the cholera. In answer to Rogers he said he was more or less a fatalist in such matters, but that he had a strong impression that he was destined for some work, as yet undone. 'Surely my time is not yet come. So much for the cholera.' It was one of his curious premonitions ; apparently unjustified by the present situation, for there was no sign of any particular future for him except possibly as an author, and his first book was as yet unpublished. His interests were still very much within the university. 'That wretch H. W.', he continued cheerfully to Rogers, referring to Henry Wilberforce, who had also gained a first class in his Schools, 'instead of settling to some serious work has been falling in and out of love in Yorkshire'.

At this point Charles Newman suddenly threw up his job in the Bank of England. His employers had been very patient with his eccentricities, but he was extremely aggressive about his socialistic opinions, and would never allow any criticism of his work. He was haughty with his family about it, but consented to see his mother. Very unwisely she handed over to him his thousand pound share of her dowry. While Newman was out of England Charles was to squander the lot. Newman cannot have approved his mother's action. He said in a note of 1873 that there had been family disagreements about the way to treat his brothers, and this must have been one of them. 'I always consider poor Charles' case so hopeless,' said his mother. It was hopeless, but throwing away a fifth of her income did not help anybody.

Fed up with Charles, exhausted by his book, and with the last of his pupils off his hands, Newman now suddenly received an invitation from Froude to accompany him and his father on a winter trip to the Mediterranean. 'It would set you up', said Froude, who felt his friend was overworking to the danger of his health. And for himself, he still hoped to stave off his disease. Newman was at first rendered sleepless by the proposal ; he had never dreamed of such a holiday and wondered if it was right to take it. But if he was ever to travel, this was a good moment, when he had no urgent commitments, and some money in hand — provided he did not spend more than £100. He was shy of Archdeacon Froude, but on the other hand it was a relief to think that he would not

have to arrange anything himself. At last he made up his mind
to go, and preached his last sermon to the university at the beginning of December. It was on 'Wilfulness, the Sin of Saul', a subject later to be charged with special meaning for him.

He set off for Falmouth immediately afterwards, pursued by a
series of minor accidents which he cheerfully related in the first of
many long letters home : a rent in his cloak, the buckle of his
carpet bag breaking, the key sticking in the lock, his portmanteau
ripped and finally 'Harriett's purse has torn itself'. But — 'a night
journey through Devonshire and Cornwall is very striking for its
mysteriousness ; and it was a beautiful night, clear, frosty, and
bright with a full moon. . . .' He travelled on top of the coach,
as usual, and embroiled himself with someone 'called by courtesy
a gentleman' who was making advances to 'a silly goose of a maid-
servant'. Newman intervened and was called a damned fool by the
'gentleman' — who was under the impression that he was being
ousted by a rival! The scene ended peaceably with a handshake.

And so, hurrying and tearing and breaking things, scribbling
verses in waiting-rooms, Newman met the Froudes and embarked
on the *Hermes*, and sailed away from familiar home, out on the wild
sea, image of the unknown.

1833

Verses and Visions in the South

AT sea Newman wrote poetry, sets of verses as he called them, one almost every day right through from December to February, and afterwards too, though there was less opportunity. Ostensibly they were written for Rose's *British Magazine*, and in fact many did appear in it, and were published in the *Lyra Apostolica* under the Greek sign δ. But the inspiration of them was this voyage into the unknown, image of the last voyage of death, for they began to come in Oxford, in November, when the journey was first suggested. Newman had no very high opinion of his verses which he wrote to please album addicts or to amuse himself. He could only compose when the pressure of other work was relieved. Writing, to order, a hymn on Purgatory while crossing to Ireland, he told Ambrose St. John that composition always came easier when he was feeling slightly seasick!

This particular series has a special interest since Newman expressed in these verses many of the ideas and feelings of the Movement to come. Some have a power of their own, though his mind worked more creatively in prose. The sermons, as literary creations, are like an avenue of wonderful trees ; the poems stark as bits of stone in a field. Yet they have a directness and simplicity which has its own attraction. Here is the parallel to the sermon on Personal Influence, written at Malta on Christmas Eve and entitled 'The Course of Truth'.

> When royal Truth, released from mortal throes,
> Burst His brief slumber and triumphant rose,
>> Ill had the Holiest sued
>> A patron multitude,
> Or courted Tetrarch's eye, or claim'd to rule
> By the world's winning grace, or proofs from learned school.
>
> But, robing Him in viewless air, He told
> His secret to a few of meanest mould ;

They in their turn imparted
The gift to men pure-hearted,
While the brute many heard his mysteries high,
As some strange fearful tongue, and crouch'd, they knew not why.

Still is the might of Truth, as it has been :
Lodged in the few, obey'd and yet unseen.
Reared on lone heights, and rare,
His saints their watch-flame bear,
And the mad world sees the wide-circling blaze
Vain searching whence it streams, and how to quench its rays.

There was more in many young ladies than a liking for pretti-
ness, and one, Emily Bowles, recorded that when she read Newman's
verses in the *Lyra* they seemed like 'startling oracles or newly discovered inscriptions in a strange character', quite different from the
'running water' of Keble's gentle hymns. There was certainly a
fierce ring to some of the lines, and a prophetic strain in their attack
on the contemporary scene. The chief heroes were the patriarchs
of Israel and St. Paul. But some were intensely personal, and concerned with guilt, penitence, and absolution. 'The priest' appears
in Gothic guise, like a character out of a romance, to pronounce
(in capital letters) ABSOLVO TE. The priest was not as real to
Newman as Moses and Jeremiah and the rest, whose trials made
him understand his own ; he was an anonymous medieval character
in an 'austere garb'. Holy Church kindly told the penitent that
she well understood how he might shrink 'from urgent rule and
severing vow . . . Gay hopes flit round and light thy brow, Time
hath a taming hand!'

So they sailed, in mid-winter, down to Gibraltar. Newman was
fascinated with the colours of the sea, with the mountains of Spain,
interested in the officers of the ship, the way the crew washed the
decks : his letters home brimmed with details of everything. 'Do
I not write well, considering the sea is rocking up and down, up and
down ?' He turned out a reasonably good sailor, better than Froude,
and much better than the poor Archdeacon, who was in bed for
some days. Newman had no more than qualms, but it was a new
feeling to him, and so he was interested in it, describing it exactly,
and how funny it seemed to him, so that he could do nothing but
laugh at it. It did not even stop him taking his meals — 'On I ate
. . . on I drank, but in so absurdly solemn a way . . .' His cabin
was very small, and he kept knocking his head and arms ; his berth,
five feet from the floor, was like a coffin and dark. The scenery of

Portugal, seen from afar, seemed like a dream, clear and distant.

It was on this voyage that Newman gained a deep impression of the difference between the North and South of the earth, which appears in many of his writings. It was not peculiar to him but a common preoccupation of English writers in the middle of the nineteenth century. We have now a similar contrast in our minds between East and West. Such divisions are based partly on external, partly on psychological fact; certain human characteristics are associated with geographical orientation. To nineteenth-century travellers from Northern Europe the South meant the Mediterranean, and its civilization. It seemed to them the region of the sun, of passion and all things primitive and mysterious. It was also a mother-land, for from those shores had come the culture accepted in the north, and the ruins of the ancient classical world remained there; from there too the Christian religion had come, and there it still retained the form that to Englishmen was associated with the Middle Ages, an era so alien and forgotten as to turn monks into characters of romance and saints' lives into fairy tales. Thus to go South meant to return to the childhood of the race, to the region of myth and vision, and as some might say nowadays, to the primeval images, the realms that lie so often below the threshold of consciousness.

Newman was by nature a poet, a seer, and his awareness of the self embraced a wider and deeper field than that of the average man; it was not surprising that the South manifested to him inward visions, as well as an appearance to the senses and associations to the cultured mind. His long letters were full of detailed observation of people and places, politics, history, past and present, and the daily incidents and moods. The visions were more rare and are only distinguishable from the rest by the sense of mystery they created in his mind, and the way they remained in it, long after, symbols.

At Gibraltar they had introductions to the officers of the garrison; they went about, the Archdeacon in a gig, Froude and Newman riding, saw the monkeys and gazed across at the mountains of Africa. Newman had books with him, the *Odyssey* sailed with him over the Mediterranean, Thucydides landed in the Peloponnese and in Sicily, Virgil wandered about Naples and Rome. The Mediterranean, true to its ancient character, changed rapidly from stillness to violent storms, like that which not long since had drowned Shelley, sailing with Keats' poems in his pocket — but it might just as well

have been the *Odyssey*. The sea was so clear at Gibraltar that they
watched the fishes playing under the water; next day, porpoises
dived round them and they had an awning on deck. The *Hermes*
was a steamer, but a small one — they were the only passengers
and there were no ladies in the ladies' cabin, which they used in
consequence. One of the advantages of modern science enjoyed by
the steamer was that it was able to sail much nearer the coast, and
the travellers had fascinating views of the African landscape, of
Algiers, and the site of ancient Carthage. Yet before they reached
Malta a gale blew up so severe as to make not only the three tourists
but half the sailors sick. The engines were damaged, which might
have had serious consequences; in the middle of one night they
stopped, but the *Hermes* survived and made harbour at Malta on
Christmas Eve. There were stringent quarantine regulations and
they were not allowed to land; they were distressed that the boat
had to spend all Christmas morning coaling, and that the only celebration was Christmas dinner in the evening. All the bells pealing
in the churches only made Newman feel more sad.

On they went to Zante and Corfu, again entertained by English
officers; at Corfu Newman described them as 'dandy officers, aides-
de-camp etc, brimful of the indifference which is now the fashion'.
He talked to one, a German scholar 'passionately fond of Weber's
music' who felt somewhat out of place among the others (whose
pursuits were 'baser'), but he seemed to Newman to substitute
refinement for religion. Wherever he went Newman always got even
more interested in the people than the scenery, watching and describing the men he and Froude saw in the taverns, the peasants at work,
the exiled officers, and fellow travellers. They discussed the political
situation of Greece and the Islands, they visited Greek churches and
tried to find out the state of the clergy and what kind of habits and
prayers the people used. Newman wondered no longer at the wars
of ancient Greek cities, but at how they had ever become one nation
in such wild mountainous country, how, even, they had managed to
fight in so rough a terrain. The steep mass of mountains on the
mainland where they briefly landed, astonished him. But there were
some fine highroads in Corfu — 'on Macadam's plan'. He and
Froude went for long rides. There was a ball in Corfu while they
were there which amused Newman by its incongruity; it was
intended to be Greek, but English costume was thought the most
fashionable, and the ball was a copy of London's smart ways in this
wild romantic place.

After this they went back to Malta and the *Hermes* sailed away, back to England, and Newman felt quite sad at seeing her go — 'a sort of home'. He thought he would almost like to find himself 'suddenly transported to my rooms at Oriel, with my oak sported, and I lying at full length on my sofa'. He was feeling tired, for the weather had been abnormally rainy and rough, and he had slept little at nights and done a great deal by day ; so much seeing of new places, too, was tiring : 'I had much rather *have* seen them than *see* them', he told his mother, 'though the while I am extremely astonished and almost enchanted at them'.

The greatest enchantment was to see Ithaca, the home of Odysseus, the home to which all his voyaging, delayed twenty years by the avenging gods, was directed. Already as a very small boy at Ham, Newman had learned by heart some poems on Odysseus and his dog Argus, and the sight of Ithaca took him back not only to Homer, but to Ham. He stared at the 'barren huge rock' and could hardly believe it was the reality of what had been the earliest vision of his childhood. 'I thought of Ham, and of all the various glimpses which memory barely retains and which fly from me when I pursue them, of that earliest time of life when one seems to realize the remnants of a pre-existing state.' That was when the angels hid behind the trees and perhaps walked in the garden when he was not looking. Heaven was Ham in childish dreams, and now Ithaca appeared, like a vision, a symbol of that timeless awareness our minds first inhabit, the shadow of the last, the home of eternity. In Corfu Newman collected the seeds of flowers for his mother's garden in Iffley. The furthest reach of their voyage touched the earliest shore of memory.

Now they had to stay a fortnight in the Lazaret at Malta, in a suite of large bare stone rooms, with meals sent in from an hotel, and a hired servant. They were locked in at night, but by day were allowed to row about the quarantine harbour. The Archdeacon and Hurrell painted and touched up their sketches ; Newman sent out for a violin, which although it was not a good one, sounded very grand in the vast stony spaces. They kept hearing footsteps at night, sometimes close round their beds. Once Newman heard a crash and thought it might be thieves, he sat bolt upright and shouted 'Who's there ?' Profound silence, while he sat still a long time, wondering. From this episode, he thought, came the cold which now descended on him and gave him the worst cough he had ever had in his life — caught 'speaking to a ghost', he said afterwards. It was annoying that it came just as they left quarantine, and when they moved to Valletta he had to keep his room — the Archdeacon would not hear of his going out, even on Sunday. Froude offered to stay and read to him, but Newman insisted on their both going out; when they did, sight-seeing in the morning and dining with acquaintances at night, he felt depressed, and had a fearful struggle with 'a blister' which he put on his chest, feeling he needed four hands for the operation. Mrs. Newman, on receiving what he had said in his gloom, was quite annoyed with Froude, and Newman had to assure her it was only his own inconsistency, and no unkindness in his friends. A doctor gave him some powerful medicine which banished the cough; as usual he recovered rapidly and was in good spirits by the time they set sail for Naples via Palermo, in a very smart steamer with a crowd of foreign nobility on board.

All these grand people streamed off at Palermo and secured the best apartments; the English trio thought theirs unbearably filthy, but after a trip inland, so quickly did their standards fall, pronounced them very fair. This expedition was to Egesta (Segesta) to see the ruins, and it was this vision that haunted Newman and brought him back alone in April, to fever, nearly to death. 'It has been a day in my life to have seen Egesta.' They went forty-three miles by carriage, and then eight or nine to and fro on mules, all this on nothing but a few eggs taken *en route*, and some coffee and bread on starting. Tourists were tough in those days.

At the climax of the long journey they came up through a rich valley to a bare hillside where lay the ruins of the once great city, and standing on the crown of a circular hill, a roofless temple, alone: 'six gigantic pillars before and behind, twelve in length . . . the whole place is one ruin except this in a waste of solitude. . . . On the hill on which the theatre stood was a savage-looking bull, prowling amid the ruins. Mountains around and Eryx in the distance. The past and the present! Once these hills were full of life! I began to understand what Scripture means when speaking of lofty cities vaunt-ing in the security of their strongholds.' All Sicily was to him, almost more than Greece, the vision of the pagan world, the world without Christ, the natural world so full of beauty, so haunted with death.

> So let the cliffs and seas of this fair place
> Be named man's tomb and splendid record stone . . .

Another thing he saw in Sicily was human misery in its most squalid hopeless form. 'Oh, the miserable creatures we saw in Sicily! I never knew what human suffering was before. . . .' At Calatafimi, where they slept after the vision of the temple, 'I dare not mention facts. Suffice it to say the poor children of the house slept in holes dug into the wall, which smelt not like a dog-kennel, but like a wild beast's cage, almost overpowering us in the room upstairs.' He was glad to see some people looking well and clean 'and outside the towns much washing was going on'. They were eaten up with bugs wherever they went.

So they went on to Naples, where they arrived on February 14th, and in storms of rain, which continued for days. They were disappointed with the scenery even when they could see it ; it was nothing to Corfu or the bay of Palermo — 'lumpish hills like bolsters' said Newman. Froude had his handkerchief stolen ; Newman's was half pulled out, but he was evidently too quick for the pickpocket. Newman's conclusion was that Naples was 'a *watering-place* with watering-place scenery, and will be admired chiefly by watering-place people'. He was the more surprised when they had made a trip to Salerno and Amalfi, where he thought the scenery really beautiful. They saw the excavations at Pompeii and Herculaneum, and were pleased to see the country people looked strong, handsome and well-dressed. They also heard of two English travellers, a husband and wife, shot and robbed by these peasants, whom they partially excused from intentional murder after hearing the circumstances. In those days, however, there was a good deal of sporadic banditry in Italy.

They arrived in Rome on March 2nd, driving along the way of the Via Appia, through the Campagna — 'a desolate flat, the home of malaria. . . . The flat waste goes on ; you think it will never have done ; miles on miles the ruins continue. At length the walls of Rome appear ; you pass through them ; you find the city shrunk up into a third of the space enclosed. In the twilight you pass buildings about which you cannot guess wrongly. This must be the Coliseum ; there is the Arch of Constantine. You are landed at your inn ; night falls, and you know nothing more till next morning.' Newman loved Rome at first sight ; it was the only city he had praised abroad, he said. 'And now what can I say of Rome, but that it is the first of cities, and that all I ever saw are but as dust (even dear Oxford inclusive) compared with its majesty and glory ? Is it possible that so serene and lofty a place is the cage of unclean creatures ? I will not believe it till I have evidence of it.' The first evidence, the next day, Sunday, at St. Peter's was pleasant. 'Everything is so bright and clean and the Sunday kept so decorously.'

Ithaca was childhood, Sicily was nature and pagan man, Rome was

religion — it was at once the scene of the great triumph of the
martyrs, and the place, so Newman felt, of the deepest human corruption : it contained the extremes of Christianity.   A few days later
he was writing of the early time : 'We need no Tower of Babel ; the
immense extent of the ruins ; the purposes to which, when in their
glory, they were dedicated ; the arena where Ignatius suffered ; the
Jewish candlestick on the Arch of Titus ; the columns, with the
proud heathen inscriptions still visible, brand the place as the vile
tool of God's wrath and Satan's malice'.   Thus he saw the Babylon
of St. John's Apocalypse.

Present Rome was a different matter.   The English visitors knew
very little of the ecclesiastical life of Rome, and what they saw they
were half inclined to approve, especially after Sicily and Naples,
where standards were appallingly low.   Priests, schools, orphans,
seminarists, all seemed quite respectable.   Mrs. Newman evidently
felt he was too lenient to the Church of Rome, for in April he wrote
to her : 'As to the *Roman* Catholic system, I have ever detested it so
much that I cannot detest it more by seeing it ; but to the Catholic
system I am more attached than ever, and quite love the little monks
of Rome ; they look so innocent and bright, poor boys !'   These
were the young seminarists, whom they met out walking.   He thought
that in spite of corruptions of Christian teaching, mass and purgatory
being the chief of these, there was 'a deep substratum of true Christianity ; and I think they may be as near truth at the least as that
Mr. B., whom I like less and less every day'.   Mr. B. was the English
chaplain, 'a perfect watering-place preacher, semi-evangelical', and a
sad contrast to Mr. Bennett at Naples, who was 'an accomplished
man ; has travelled much, speaks various languages and is liberal' —
liberal in culture, not in his religious opinions.

At Easter they went to some services, but not knowing much
about them Newman's description was similar to that of other
English travellers ; except that he was very interested in the music,
and retailed it to Jemima.

In Rome they met English friends, William Wilberforce, junior,
and his family (the eldest brother of Robert and Henry, a semi-invalid)
and others ; also the Prussian Count Bunsen, a great figure in religious circles in those days.   They caught up with English news, and
were shocked to discover how far the Government was going in its
proposals to reorganize the Church of Ireland, drastically abolishing
Bishoprics and adjusting revenues, as if the Bishops were civil servants to be axed as redundant.   Froude and Newman were very

indignant. Newman wrote to Tom Mozley, 'I hate the Whigs (of course, as Rowena says, in a Christian way) more bitterly than ever', and longed to know what people in Oxford thought of 'the atrocious Irish sacrilege Bill'.

Among other English and Irish Roman Catholics they met Nicholas Wiseman, the brilliant and charming Rector of the English College, who was just their own age, born the year after Newman and the year before Froude. They talked vaguely about reunion, and left feeling it quite impossible while Rome remained what she was. Froude, who was better disposed towards that Church than Newman, was also more shocked by the conduct of the priests he had seen in Naples; going home, he called the Catholics 'wretched Tridentines everywhere'. Trent, the Council of the sixteenth-century Catholic reform, was regarded then as an impassable barrier; later, when they had actually read the decrees and the official Catechism, some people changed their minds. People in England were to think Froude and Newman had almost been made papists in Rome, but in fact they were blissfully ignorant of both doctrine and practice in the modern Church, for their knowledge of it, except as seen by Anglican writers, stopped short at the point where England had thrown off the yoke of papal supremacy. They held strongly that there was one true Faith, an objective body of doctrine handed down from the time of the Apostles, by means of a visible church with a ministry of bishops and priests, but they thought that corruption had set in everywhere, and that unity had been lost through human weakness. In this view of things any Church which retained the ancient forms and creeds had a right to call itself Catholic. Newman and Froude had no desire to introduce Roman teaching and practice, but ardently wished to restore the damaged Catholicism of their own Church.

The Froudes had decided to give up the tour they had planned in Sicily and return overland. Froude had not lost his cough, and Newman wrote home that he feared he had counted too much on merely missing the English winter, and that the discomforts of travel, and the exceptional rain and storms they had encountered, could not have done him any good. He himself had set his heart on Sicily; his earlier glimpse of its wild beauties had only whetted his appetite for more. An acquaintance, Edward Neate, at first thought of going with him, but when he gave up the idea, Newman decided to go alone. The Froudes did not actively advise against it, but it was plain they would have liked him to return with them, and thought his expedition

'over-ventursome'. In spite of this, and of his knowledge, from
their trip to Egesta, of the discomforts of travel there, he was determined to go back. Bugs, bandits, foreign food, foreign talk, loneliness, nothing put him off. In fact, as he admitted to Jemima, one of
his secret reasons for going was to see what it was like 'to be solitary
and a wanderer'. He *wanted* to rough it alone. At least, part of him
wanted it ; at moments he dreaded it. When he left England he had
felt glad the Archdeacon was arranging everything ; now he stuck
obstinately to his own plan. It was a careful plan too, discussed with
helpful advisers whose advice was to prove often misleading. What
was more, it was to be no easy tourist's visit. He would take a servant
and mules and his own provisions and walk and ride round the island,
visiting all the most famous ancient sites. This was really an extraordinary plan for an Oxford don who had never been out of England
before, and was worthy of the toughest professional travellers of the
time.

Newman knew this was a strange episode in his life from start
to finish, but this aspect never seems to have struck him. Either
he took his own courage for granted, or it did not occur to him
that he needed courage to undertake an expedition so unlike anything he was accustomed to do. He was used to riding and walking
long distances — on a muddy fifteen-mile walk in Oxford recently
he had worked out a new method of writing his sermons. But he
knew that Sicily was a wild place and that people quite frequently
got murdered there. Yet the only thing that worried him before
going seems to have been the inevitable discomforts.

Much stranger was the complete break with the whole habit of
his mind. For years all his acts had been ruled by duty and determined by circumstance, which he had accepted as God's will. But
no duty called him to Sicily. Circumstances rather suggested a
return with the Froudes to the duties at home, especially with the
Whigs threatening the Church with sacrilege. It was perhaps the
only time in his life he acted upon an urgent wish of his own, and
yet he hardly knew himself why he was so determined on it. In
the event the whole adventure perfectly realized in action the
psychological and spiritual crisis within, resolved the uncertainties
and renewed the life in him, so that he went back to England charged
with a new power. Perhaps that obscure intuition of his drove
him back to the beautiful terrible island he called man's tomb.

1833

Journey into the Underworld

HIS friends left Rome before he did. 'I wandered about the place after the Froudes had gone with a blank face', he told Jemima. For about half an hour he repented his decision. 'I was going among strangers into a wild country to live a wild life, to travel in solitudes, and to sleep in dens in the earth — and all for what ? for the gratification of an imagination, for the idea of a warm fancy which might be a deceit, drawn by a strange love of Sicily to gaze upon its cities and mountains.' His farewell gesture to Rome was to visit once more the scene of St. Peter's martyrdom, 'and for the last time went through the vast spaces of his wonderful basilica, and looked at his place of burial and then prepared for my departure'. But next day, travelling through beautiful country to Naples, his spirits at once rose, and remained high. Naples seemed to him as dull as ever, to look at, but this time he felt more friendly to it, although he was held up for some days waiting for a boat, and in spite of the fact that it began to rain again, 'with a boisterous wind and a vehemence of pour which I have not seen since leaving Corfu'. This time he found the people amusing. 'They are very clever, and humorous. They are quite Punches. Just now a ragged boy persecuted me with a miserable whining for coppers, following me for a minute or so. When he found that would not do, he suddenly began to play a tune on his chin, with great dash and effect.'

Before the rain set in Newman climbed Vesuvius with Mr. Bennett, the chaplain, and Anderson, with whom he had travelled from Rome. They had a tiresome slippery climb to the first crater, where they cooked beef and drank the local wine, which Newman liked. Then they went over some sulphur beds and up the second cone to view the awesome sight of the recesses of the earth steaming and curling with sulphurous smoke. 'The utter silence increased the imposing effect which became fearful when, on putting the ear to a small crevice, one heard a rushing sound, deep and hollow,

partly of wind, partly of the internal trouble of the mountain.' They
made a descent of three hundred feet, half suffocated with sulphur,
and Newman suffered painfully from his loose foreign shoes, which
filled with hot ashes, so that he had to hang on with his hands.
His hands and feet got badly blistered. 'I assure you I quite cried
out with the pain', he told Jemima. But he went down to the bottom,
where it was cool, and up again, and walked with the rest of the party
about three miles round the outer crater looking at the views. 'It
was grand to look down a sheer descent of 800 feet, which began
at one's foot, the walking place being a narrow ledge almost per-
pendicular on each side.' Newman's shoes, filling up with (cold)
ash, delayed his descent, but he was jubilant, not least that the
whole thing had cost only four shillings. 'This is the most wonderful
sight that I have seen abroad.' A few days later there was a slight
earthquake shock and he looked expectantly towards the mountain,
but it did not oblige with an eruption.

It was a suitable beginning to his classical expedition to make a
descent into the underworld, especially as he was about to make a
similar descent into the soul. The depths of the earth have always
been associated with the depths of the human soul and with the
loss of light and vital power. To the pagans, whose only real world
was the world of nature, the underworld was the place of lost people,
shadows who longed for blood, the essence of life. To the Christians,
who lived with Christ's immortal blood in them, and who knew that
only by their own fault could they lose that supernatural life, a
deeper underworld was revealed, where loss was the consequence
of deliberate choice, involving guilt and torment. Pagan hell was
cold, divided by dark rivers ; Christian hell was fire, for the uprush
of life hurts what hardens against it and love becomes fearful to
those who refuse to surrender themselves.

The symbolism is a true one, because it is a fact that underneath
the fertile fields the earth is dark and on fire, and it is a fact too
that everyone has a volcano in his own heart. Hatred, anger, resentment, envy, selfish indulgence, no one approves but everyone feels,
and can see how they exclude love, harden and diminish the person
and destroy its integrity. The ultimate expression of life destroying
itself is the fire of hell. We are familiar with this process on the
mental level, where the mind becomes disrupted and decayed, and
to those to whom reason is the highest principle in human life
lunacy is the only hell, more terrible than the Christian hell because
no one can say that it is deserved. To warn people against falling

into lunacy would be superfluous ; nobody wants to be mad, any more than to be cancerous, and the misery and subhumanity of the condition is plain to all. But the moral disease and spiritual madness of hell are not so immediately discernible ; and since it can be avoided, to understand the predispositions is even more necessary than in the case of bodily and mental diseases.

When Newman at last got home in July, he preached, not on the immediate situation which was so exciting everybody, including himself, but on the difficulty people have in realizing, even when they believe in it, their immortal destiny. One sight of hell, he said, would force upon a man's attention the real nature of evil tendencies he had thought excusable. There were those then, as later, who were shocked to find someone like Newman trying (they thought) to terrify people into good behaviour with the threat of eternal fires ; it was particularly inappropriate and superfluous in addressing a virtuous and intelligent Oxford audience. But it was just to the respectable that Newman always spoke on hell, with the intention of waking them out of the spiritual sleep of self-satisfaction. Hell being the denial of love, the complacently good are in as much danger as the morally weak, sometimes more. The volcano is dormant, but not extinct, and to ignore the fires below is to court destruction. Newman did not exclude himself. He went down that crater too.

From the beginning things went wrong with his plans. He failed to get a berth on the smart steamer, and had to take one instead on an English merchantman, the *Serapis* of Yarmouth, and as it was a sailing vessel, they had to wait for a suitable wind. Newman remained cheerful ; it would be cheaper, he would not have the same experience of rich passengers securing all the best accommodation on landing, and it was better to spend the bad weather in Naples than Messina. So he told his mother, in the letter about the Naples people being like Punches. Getting to like the food better he ate some tempting cheese at night, which he thought gave him nightmare.

'First a weight and horror fell on me, after which I found myself in the tower at Oriel. It was an audit and the Fellows sat round.' Newman shook hands with them all, ending with those who had been made tutors in place of himself and his friends, and one of these introduced the new Fellows. At this time Newman was thinking much about the election, which had then already taken place ; he was exceedingly anxious that Rogers should have been elected. It

was horrifying then in his dream to see 'two of the most clumsy
awkward-looking chaps I ever set eyes on, and they had awkward
unintelligible names. With great grief of heart, but a most unem-
barrassed smiling manner, I shook hands with them and wished
them joy, and then talked and chatted with the rest as if nothing
had happened, yet longing to get away, and with a sickness of heart.'
But when he did get away he could not find Froude, or Christie,
another Fellow and friend. He wanted to run away into the shrub-
beries at Ham to recover, 'but it was not allowed me'. Instead he
was in his rooms 'or some rooms, and had continual interruptions',
a father whose son was intending to stand for a Sicilian scholarship
and 'a brace of gentlemen commoners with hideous faces, though I
was not a tutor', and lastly Anderson, with whom he had travelled
from Rome, 'with a lady under his arm', whom Newman thought
he knew but could not remember. This was not all the dream, he
said, hoping it was poetical, not historical, and determined that after
all Rogers must have succeeded. This miserable succession of
thwartings, such as any dreamer is familiar with, Newman remembered because it was a caricature of the very real thwartings he had
actually experienced in the college.

He ended this letter on April 19th — 'Half-past 7 a.m., the wind
is fair. I am off suddenly.' This was the last anyone at home was
to hear of him till June.

The first thing that happened was that the wind dropped and
the ship was becalmed off Stromboli ; but not before the brisk breeze
of the day before had made Newman very sick. The three other
passengers, Frenchmen, amused him with their conversation with
the Captain, 'a thorough Englishman'. It was all at cross purposes
in a mixture of tongues. The colour of the sea and the coast of
Calabria were so beautiful he was quite happy. But when at last
they made Messina at 5 o'clock on Sunday morning, he failed to
find the English chaplain, and so had no service, and discovered
that he would have to wait till next day for his passport and papers.
On Monday, however, he got them and was off by noon on the first
stage of his expedition, down the eastern coast of the island towards
Taormina and Catania.

'On setting off from Messina I felt amused and almost ashamed
of the figure I was cutting', he wrote to Harriett a few days later.
'I was chief of a cavalcade consisting of a servant, two mules and
several muleteers (though the latter were soon reduced to one, who
was to go with us through), and when I happened to catch sight of

my shadow, the thought of my personal equipments, at least as regards my hat and my coat, was still more perplexing. My neckcloth was the only black thing about me, yet black without being clerical.' If only he had described the coat and hat! He had with him an old blue cloak, dating from 1823, a dear familiar object which went through everything with him and survived to lie on his bed at Littlemore. The servant, Gennaro, was an ex-Peninsular War veteran who had been sixteen years with one English family, but unfortunately had no knowledge of Sicily. He proved a faithful and honest man, his only failing being, according to Newman, an occasional over-addiction to the bottle.

The first night was spent among the usual fleas, but the lodging was better than Newman had expected. The next day was a great success. They went twelve miles before breakfast and then climbed up to ancient Tauromenium. It was a bright day. 'I never knew Nature could be so beautiful; and to see that view was the nearest approach to seeing Eden. O happy I! It was worth coming all the way, to endure sadness, loneliness, weariness, to see it. I felt, for the first time in my life, that I should be a better and more religious man if I lived there.' More beautiful landscapes opened before him as he went on : 'Etna was magnificent. The scene was sombre with clouds, when suddenly, as the sun descended upon the cone, its rays shot out between the clouds and the snow, turning the clouds into royal curtains, while on the one side there was a sort of Jacob's ladder. I understood why the poets made the abode of the gods on Mount Olympus.' In that marvellous land even the frogs were musical, trilling like nightingales.

The night, however, was very uncomfortable and Newman got little sleep. 'In England we have no idea what a Sicilian flea is.' The next day he climbed up to look at some famous chestnuts, but found they had been cut down, and the rest of the day's march was longer than they expected, across baking lava fields, to Nicolosi, where he decided against going up Etna. The visitors' book at the inn was full of dissuasions from disillusioned adventurers, Newman had strained his leg walking, Gennaro was tired, and there was a lot of snow up there. The inn here, he told Harriett, was 'the most forlorn place I ever was in'. Newman had brought his own provisions, but they were not in very good condition and his 'spirits of wine' ran out, with which he dressed it. Gennaro had gone out to fend for himself. 'I lay down on my so-called bed, and thought of the sick room at Ealing, and my mind felt very dry, and I thought,

"What if I should lose my reason?" and I was in dreadful irritation
from the renewed attacks of the fleas.' He thought the wretched
bed, with dirty coverings, was going to come to pieces. But the
faithful Gennaro, on his return, poached him some eggs and 'threw
down water under my bed against my enemies' so that after all he
slept heavily for eight or nine hours and woke feeling much better.
They walked downhill to Catania for breakfast, and in Catania he
had an introduction to Signor Gemellaro from the Froudes.

At the Corona d' Oro he had a good wash and in spite of blisters
and weariness went to see Gemellaro, who promised to show him
Sicilian medals on his return from the trip he intended to make to
Syracuse. Everyone advised him to do this by boat, which would
only take him a few hours, whereas it was forty-odd miles round the
bay, and bad going, especially now after the phenomenal rain this
season had brought. The boat was a *speronaro*, a thirty-five-foot
sailing craft with an awning over the stern; there were fourteen
people on board. Bad luck again pursued Newman, for instead of
the voyage taking a few hours, a *scirocco* sprang up and they were at
sea all day, and unable to land that night. They lay to, and spent the
night in the boat, fleas just as plentiful as in the inns. Newman had
no food with him, but the sailors had a little bread and some wine,
which they shared. They came into Syracuse in the small hours,
but of course had to wait for 'pratique'.

Newman had an introduction to the Consul; he and Thucydides
equally directed his sightseeing, which was quite arduous and
included rowing up the Anapus in a boat to gather papyrus. He had
meant to stay over Sunday, but the wind for Catania called. He
finished his letter to Jemima with some verses he had made up in the
speronaro, which he felt wanted ease and spirit. In them he asked
himself if all the visions he had seen had been no more than the
'marvel to have found This blighted world so fair'?

> Store them in heart! thou shalt not faint
>   Mid coming pains and fears;
> As the third heaven once nerved a Saint
>   For fourteen trial-years.

St. Paul's third heaven he did not expect, but even the vision of Eden
at Taormina was not to be what really nerved him for the trial-years
to come.

He felt very tired, and in fact must have been already sickening
for the fever. At the hotel in Syracuse he met three Englishmen who

had come from Malta on their way overland from India. They asked Newman to dinner and took him to a wedding party, the son of a judge being married to the Russian consul's daughter. 'I went in traveller's dress, thinking, goose as I was, to be incognito and merely a sightseer. You may fancy we were all lions. Though by no means a brilliant party, it was such a contrast to ancient Syracuse that I thought of Corfu.'

Again he was unlucky with the *speronaro* ; the wind changed, and for the second time he had to sleep, as well as he could, in the boat. Unable to make Catania they got off at Agosta, the ancient Hybla, at breakfast time, but were so delayed over passports that it was three in the afternoon before they set off, on mules, for Catania, in the belief that it was some twenty-two miles away. By the time they had gone fourteen it was dusk, and they then discovered that their goal was still eighteen miles away, that there were three rivers ahead to ford or ferry, a deep sand to traverse, 'and the danger of being plundered', as Newman told Rogers in the first letter written after his illness. 'When we got to the most suspicious part of our journey our guide lost his way.' The sun had been broiling by day, but the night was damp ; Newman had had nothing to eat all day since breakfast, and when they finally reached Catania, somewhere near midnight, he felt 'more dead than alive'.

He slept all right, but not feeling very well in the morning, rested, visited the theatre and Signor Gemellaro, deciding to cut across country to Girgenti (Agrigentum) on the south-west coast, and from there return to Palermo on the north. He was assured that none of the roads would be as bad as those he had already sampled. He finished his letter to Jemima, praising Gennaro as 'a treasure — very sharp-witted and ready. . . . He cannot read or write.' Describing how, when they were lost in the night they 'got among shepherd's tents under Mount Etna, the dogs barking at us', he said, 'I like what I see of the people ; dirt, with simplicity and contentment'. There was a slight earthquake that day ; it was close and hazy, as on the day of the quake at Naples. The next day Newman and his illiterate old campaigner set off inland. It was the first of May.

After a wet twenty miles they stopped at Adernò. For the first time the insects left Newman alone ; he realized afterwards it was because he had the fever, but at the time he did not know it. He put down his discomfort and low feelings to lack of sleep and food and his rough journeying. The day before in Catania, unable to eat for a choking in his throat, he thought it was due to ginger. He was so

unused to this kind of life that it did not occur to him that he was ill,
and no doubt Gennaro thought it was all due to English gentlemanliness, always an unpredictable quality.

When they started from Adernò it was fine and, as Newman
wrote in his private account afterwards, 'the scene was most beautiful
— hills thrown about on all sides, and covered with green corn in all
variety of shades, relieved by the light (raw sienna) stone of the hills.
The whole day the scene was like the Garden of Eden most exquisitely
beautiful, though varying, sometimes with deep valleys on the side,
and many trees, high hills with towns on top. . . . I set out walking,
the mules coming after — and fell to tears thinking of dear Mary as
I looked at the beautiful prospect.' Beautiful country always brought
Mary to his mind, the girl lost just in the flower of her youth ; Eden,
the paradise of a world still innocent, the earth fresh from angelic
hands, and Mary were all related in one recurring pattern of experience. But by now he was already ill, without knowing it. He had to
lie down and rest at midday. Most of the time he was riding ; they
went some forty miles and he was chafed and in pain. Walking again
by evening, he came to Leonforte and found the good inn occupied
by a Sicilian Duke 'and I was forced to wander about for a lodging for
the night'. He got one in a miserable place, his room opening on
another where lay a sick man, but sick from an accident. Newman
could not sleep, and next morning when he tried to get up he 'fell
back and could not'.

However, when the Sicilian Duke had gone he managed to dress
and go down to the better inn, where he went to bed in a 'gaily
ornamented room'. Now he dimly realized that he was not well and
wondered what medicine to take. There were no shops in Leonforte.
He asked for camomile 'as being tonic and stomachic', for he had a
pain in his bowels, and luckily Gennaro succeeded in getting this.
He made tea out of the leaves, which to Newman in his now feverish
hypersensitive state seemed rough. 'Next he made me some with
the flowers which I thought beautiful.' He told Gennaro that he was
better, but the old campaigner felt his pulse and said he had fever.
'Oh no,' said Newman firmly, he knew himself better.

'As I lay in bed the first day many thoughts came over me', he
wrote in his private notes, *My Illness in Sicily*. 'I felt God was
fighting against me — and felt at last I knew *why* — it was for self
will. I felt I had been very self willed — that the Froudes had been
against my coming, so also (at Naples) the Wilberforces — perhaps
the Neates and Andersons — I said to myself Why did no one speak

out ? say half a word ? Why was I left now to interpret their mean-
ing ? Then I tried to fancy where the Froudes were, and how happy
I should have been with them — in France, or perhaps in England.
Yet I felt and kept saying to myself "I have not sinned against light".
And at one time I had a most consoling overpowering thought of
God's electing love, and seemed to feel I was His.'

The next day, May 4th, a Saturday, was terrible. Gennaro went
out and left him locked in, with the key turned, alone. Whether the
man took fright and went to get a drink, drank too much, or what,
never transpired. He came back, and did not desert his temporary
master for so long again. Newman was in high fever but did not
realize it. He thought the same thing was happening to his mind as
happened in 1827, and to a much slighter degree during the Oriel
examination when he had had to walk up and down the hall. He
wrote : 'I forced myself up to keep my mind from thinking of itself . . . . I kept counting the number of stars, flowers etc. in the pattern
of the paper on the walls to occupy me.' In this state of acute nervous
tension he was further tormented by a Sicilian beggar's whine outside
the door. 'Who can describe the wretchedness of that low feeble
monotonous cry, which went on I cannot say how long (I unable to
do anything) till my servant released me after a time.'

Some time during this day, perhaps bringing on this nervous
distress, Newman's 'self reproaching feelings increased. I seemed to
see more and more my utter hollowness. I began to think of all my
professed principles and felt they were mere intellectual deductions
from one or two admitted truths. I compared myself with Keble, and
felt that I was merely developing his, not my convictions. I know I
had *very* clear thoughts about this then ; and I believe in the main
true ones. . . . Still more serious thoughts came over me. I thought
I had been very self willed about the Tutorship affair — and now I
viewed my whole course as one of presumption. It struck me that
the 5th of May was just at hand, which was a memorable day, as
being that on which (what we called) my Ultimatum was sent in to
the Provost. On the 3rd anniversary I should be lying on a sick bed
in a strange country. Then I bitterly blamed myself, as disrespectful
and insulting to the Provost, my superior. So keenly did I feel this,
that I dictated to myself (as it were) a letter . . . stating in strong terms
my self reproach ; and I was not to preach at St. Mary's or anywhere
for a length of time as a penitent unworthy to show himself. I
recollected too that my last act on leaving Oxford was to preach a
university sermon on the character of Saul against self will.' He even

felt that he had blasphemed the Sacrament, going to it with resentment in his heart against the Provost, and that his sickness was a
punishment, but afterwards he could not remember whether he
thought this at Leonforte at the beginning, or in Palermo at the end.
'Yet still I said to myself "I have not sinned against light".'

He saw himself as hollow at heart, full of theoretical knowledge
unrealized in action, as self willed to the point of presumption,
carrying his resentment to the sacred communion with Christ; but
he clung to the knowledge that he had not seen what he had been
doing, his intention had been to serve God, he had acted blindly, not
preferring darkness to light, but falling into it unawares.

In his 'lowest distress' he was relieved first by the music of some
travelling performers outside, and then by the return of Gennaro, who
took him out for a walk. Newman was in a dazed state. He sat on a
bank by a fig tree 'and wondered how it should be I was there'.
Gennaro was sure he had fever and wanted to get him along to some
more suitable place. He talked about a litter to remove him, and,
convinced he was going to die, began to indulge in reminiscences
about a sick officer in Spain who left him all his baggage and then
went and got well. He had his eye on Newman's effects, but wanted
them legally bequeathed. Newman wrote out Froude's address for
him, in case of his death, so that Froude should break the news to his
mother. But he did not think he was dying. He said to Gennaro he
was not going to die — 'God has still a work for me to do'. Gennaro
was not impressed. There was serious fever about and he knew the
Englishman was stricken.

The next day, however, Newman had an hallucination that he
was perfectly well, and only weak from want of food — he had not
eaten for two days. 'I quite laughed to myself through the night at
the news I should have to tell in England, how ridiculous and shameful, that I had missed seeing Girgenti from such neglect.' He kept
on eating all through the day under this delusion and Gennaro took
him out in the evening on his mule, presumably to see how he would
stand a move. Newman was quite determined to start next day
for Palermo. 'I had a strange feeling on my mind that God meets
those who go on in *His way*, who remember Him in His way, in the
paths of the Lord, that I must put myself in His path, His way....'
In fact he actually started the next morning, almost before sunrise,
having drunk some toast and water. But they had barely gone half a
mile before he insisted that he was so weak Gennaro must unpack the
food and give him some; he was so obstinate that the man most

unwillingly had to obey. Presently 'a great thirst came on'. He
sucked oranges that grew by the wayside and they were so good he
kept thinking what he would say about them to his mother 'not
sweet or tart, but a fine aromatic bitter'. The fever was burning him
and he felt he was suffocating — 'at last I took to eating the leaves
of the trees as I went on'. He blamed the toast and water, said it
was rough bread, and he must have water. He was obviously so ill
that Gennaro took him off the road to a hut built like a tent of poles,
spread his blue cloak on the mud floor and there he lay.

'How long I lay, hours probably, I do not know . . . when I
opened my eyes I saw the men and women, young and old, hanging
over me with great interest — and apparently much rejoiced to see
me a little better. At length, as I lay, I felt fingers at my pulse.'
God had met him in the way and sent a doctor who was treating fever
cases in the neighbourhood.

1833

Sicilian Purgatory

THE doctor told them to give Newman camomile, lemon and sugar and to take him on to Castro Giovanni, the ancient Enna, which was only a few miles off. Newman recovered sufficiently to hear that a diligence was passing with English passengers, on its way to Palermo — some days' journey. He said he must speak to them. Gennaro objected, but Newman was so obstinate and commanding that at length he fetched one, who turned out to be German, but spoke English. Quite delirious Newman pressed on him the letter of introduction he had to an Englishman at Palermo and thanked him fervently for his kindness without either of them quite knowing what he was doing. By this time it was evening and they put Newman sideways on a mule and, holding him there, set off up the steep hill to the town. His parting with the poor people was so affectionate that Gennaro burst into tears, 'though I should not have thought him especially tender', Newman noted retrospectively. Actually from this moment Gennaro accepted his lot, fatalistically saying to the nurse who was engaged, 'If we get the fever we get it', and quite soon he developed a protective feeling for his helpless patient, whom he was certain was going to die. Newman still had outbreaks of obstinacy, but grew meeker as he grew weaker, till Gennaro in the end got quite the upper hand.

Up they went, and in the town could get no room, except a damp, dark place which Gennaro spurned. He did well in the end, securing a large room in the house of a man called Luigi Vestivo, and there Newman was put to bed, still sufficiently alive to notice some camomile flowers and beg that they might not be taken away. The doctor who had found him in the tent, who was the best in the district, 'was out of the way' and another was brought 'who was said to be inferior, but I made much of him. He had moustaches and a harsh voice.' He ordered lemonade, where Gennaro advocated tea. Newman became suspicious of the old campaigner and thought he was altering the prescriptions. His memory became confused about this time, and he lost all his little Italian, but retained his Latin, and wrote questions on a piece of paper which the doctor contrived to answer in the same tongue. His Latin was atrocious, but Newman's, even at such a crisis, was quite respectable, though the doctor laughed at it. Apart from ordering lemonade the doctor was able to help with a purge and to relieve a retention of urine which was giving Newman acute pain. Otherwise there was not much done. The first thing the doctor attempted was to draw off some blood, Newman suspiciously and perhaps wisely insisted on his taking it from his instep ; at the somewhat nervous jabbings that ensued Gennaro suddenly fainted away. Not much blood was removed in the end ; Dr. Babington afterwards said scornfully so little as to be no use at all. Perhaps it was lucky Newman was not further weakened.

Now the fever was increasing and he lost count of time and everything else, but he remembered a jumble of impressions with extraordinary vividness. Restless and flushed he tossed about and had miserable dreams 'sitting on a staircase wanting something', and about home. He dreaded the sleepless nights and wanted someone to sit up with him, but Gennaro, who had a bed in the room, firmly slept on it, and the nurse would not stay. The muleteer was pressed into service once, and Newman long remembered 'his great bullet tips of fingers' as he put vinegar to his nose to revive him in the fainting spells that came over him. He longed for cold water and tried to outwit Gennaro who would only allow vinegar.

At the beginning of his illness the doctor when he felt his pulse used to shake his head and say, 'A — ah, A — ah debil, debil'. A priest visited him, and Newman, delirious, told Gennaro 'he wished to dispute with him'. Hypersensitive to sound he could not bear the daily mass bell ; 'I used quite to writhe about and put my head under the bed clothes'. He wanted it stopped ; Gennaro answered with a laugh of surprise that it ought not to annoy him. Newman's reactions to priests and mass bells and anything religious probably, he thought afterwards, made them think he, a heretic, was tormented by holy things.

The noise of the bell was supplemented by the noise of a fair, under his window, and guests talking in the room next door. The landlord, hearing he liked music, actually employed some performers to play to him from the next room. 'It was very beautiful, but too much for me.' This may have been when he was getting better.

He was aware of the day of the month again by the 19th, knowing it was Jemima's birthday, but the crisis had taken place a day or two before. It was about May 17th. At one point he began to itch so much he thought the fleas had returned to feed on him, but it may have been the skin peeling, as it did on his hands and face. His lips peeled, his hands were yellow and the nails discoloured. But he was not going to die.

Slowly coming back to life after ten days' delirium his memory kept failing; he could not remember the order of events. He had fantastic dreams of armies marching about in which he was on one side or the other, and of talking to the Russian Empress and suddenly thinking with embarrassment that he ought not to have initiated conversation with a great person — how ill mannered! He was visited by the magistrates of the town who were curious to see the Englishman who had caused quite a lot of litigation, involuntarily, for Gennaro had taken disputes before them, first with the muleteer about his wages (he had won, and gone off) and then about the presents Newman gave to the doctor and the landlord. He gave away things in gratitude with too much abandon, Gennaro thought, though it was he who suggested a thank-offering to the poor. Probably everyone assumed that the Englishman was rich, Englishmen always were. The Lady Bountiful of the town was sick of the same fever, and died of it; Newman was informed daily of her decline and then of her death, and finally heard her funeral bell. Nothing was stolen from him as he lay helpless, and a note was sent to Palermo requesting £20 English, all of which came safely to hand.

When the crisis was past Newman was left so weak he could not raise his hand to feed himself. Gennaro had to do everything for him. Newman remembered he could not bear him to go out of the room, and when he did, used to call him 'Gen-na-rooooo!' But 'Gennaro ruled me most entirely — I was very submissive, and he authoritative'. This evidently amused Newman afterwards, and possibly caused the old campaigner a smile, recollecting Newman's obstinacy and peremptoriness at the beginning. He fed Newman at first on chicken broth and when he was getting better an egg baked in wood ashes and some tea for breakfast, and cakes. Of the tea Newman said, 'How I longed for it! I could not help crying out from delight. I used to say, "It is life from the dead!" I never had such feelings.'

Gennaro was evidently determined to get him to Palermo as soon as possible, for on the 20th he got him out of bed and made him walk in the room, and then in the next room. He was very weak, and at the time, from a cough which had come on, imagined that he had got inflammation of the lungs. He also got a fancy that the blood was mounting to his head, and he must not sleep. But on the whole he recovered, as ever, remarkably quickly. Next Gennaro helped him down the stairs and put him in a chair outside 'looking out across somewhat of a space, so I seem to think, to a pillar which he said was Roman. As I sat in the chair I could not command myself, but cried profusely, the sight of the sky was so piercing.' Some poor people gathered round to look at him.

Newman himself was now anxious to move. He managed to walk as far as the Cathedral, leaning on Gennaro and with a stick. Then they went a little way in a carriage. At the time when he had the fancy about his blood going to his head a letter had come up for him from Palermo. It was a sheet of thin paper written in tiny writing by five people from home. Newman eagerly seized it and peered at it without his glasses looking for news of Rogers' election — 'you unworthy fellow' he told him in the letter he wrote soon after — but it was not there, and the effort 'brought on the determination of blood to the head'. He was really not well enough to move, but now he was driven by the desire to get home. A carriage was hired and at last on Whitsunday, May 25th, they left Castro Giovanni, three weeks after Newman had been brought up the hill delirious with fever, and dying, as everyone thought. Presents and largesse distributed, the name and address of the landlord taken (Newman wrote him a Latin letter from England) they started for Palermo.

The first day they went twenty miles. 'My joy, however, was too great for me at first. I never saw such a country. The Spring in its greatest luxuriance. All sorts of strange trees — very steep and high hills over which the road went ; mountains in the distance, — a profusion of aloes along the road — Such bright colouring — all in tune too with my reviving life. I had a great appetite and was always coaxing (as I may call it) Gennaro for cakes.' But he was very weak. The next day they went sixty miles. At one of these inns the landlord came and sat opposite Newman and stared at him so long he frightened him. The next morning he sat by his bed crying bitterly 'and all I could say was that I was sure God had some work for me to do in England. . . . My feeling was intense and overpowering — and my servant of course could not understand me at all.' It was the last lap.

Next day, before noon, they arrived in Palermo, and put up at
Page's hotel, where Ann Page, a motherly person, was horrified at
the sight of her visitor and made him sago and tapioca puddings to
restore him to true English life. He was so weak he could hardly
speak without drawling, so that the wine merchants he consulted
thought him a dying man. Judging from their reactions and that
of the landlord on the road, he must have looked like one. When
he arrived he could not get out of the carriage by himself, but soon
he was moving about with a stick, and one of the hotel servants said,
'Come sir, cheer up ; you will get quite young again'.

His memory of how he had got to Castro Giovanni was at first
confused ; he only with time established continuity. For the first
days in Palermo he could not think or write easily. On June 1st he
wrote some verses, and after that composed a set a day. Three
days later someone lent him an old paper and at long last he saw
the news of Rogers' election, and wrote to him, the first account of
his wanderings, which, however, he did not send till he got to
Marseilles. He did not write home for days, expecting to go off at
any moment ; but no ship came. His first letter to his mother was
brief and cheerful and made no mention of his illness. Since it was
not able to go on its way at once, she only received it on July 1st,
the first news of him since his letter of April 19th on setting sail
from Naples for Sicily. When Newman saw the news that Rogers
was a Fellow of Oriel he was so delighted he kissed the paper. The
other to be elected was Charles Marriott, afterwards a stalwart of
the Movement.

Newman now longed to get home, and in the weakness of con-
valescence the desire to return became so insistent that every delay
chafed him ; yet, as he afterwards realized, he was not really strong
enough to take the long journey alone. Gennaro was going home
to his wife and family in Naples. He got drunk in Palermo, but
insisted he was not drunk. He wanted Newman's old blue cloak
'a little thing for him to set his services at — at the same time a
great thing for me to give for I had an affection for it'. Gennaro
did not get the cloak, but he got £10, a large sum then, over and
above his wages, and a written character. He afterwards got a post
in England with Lord Carrington's family. 'He was humanly
speaking the preserver of my life', Newman wrote in 1840, finishing
his account at Littlemore, with the old blue cloak on his bed. 'He
nursed me as a child. An English servant never could do what
he did.'

To recruit his strength Newman used to go out in a boat every
morning, and often he would walk with his stick to the public
gardens, or to the beach outside, and sit on a bench in the shade.
Sometimes the trying scirocco blew, 'the wind like a furnace. And
the clouds were blue, the tawny mountains looking wondrous.' He
dined out with an Englishman, and visited the German with whom
he had spoken outside Leonforte, supposedly dying in the hut in
the midst of a sympathetic circle of peasants. Sometimes he went
into churches, and sitting there his burning impatience died down.
He knew nothing then of the presence of the Blessed Sacrament,
but was calmed and felt at peace. He wrote :

> Oh that thy creed were sound !
> For thou dost soothe the heart, thou Church of Rome,
>   By thy unwearied watch and varied round
> Of service, in thy Saviour's holy home.
>   I cannot walk the city's sultry streets,
>   But the wide porch invites to still retreats
> Where passion's thirst is calmed, and care's unthankful gloom.
>
>   There, on a foreign shore,
> The home-sick solitary finds a friend :
>   Thoughts, prisoned long for lack of speech outpour
> Their tears ; and doubts in resignation end.
>   I almost fainted from the long delay
>   That tangles me within this languid bay,
> When comes a foe, my wounds with oil and wine to tend.

This was written on June 13th, the day he at last embarked, on
an orange boat bound for Marseilles. A few days later this sailing
vessel was becalmed off Sardinia, in the Straits of Bonifacio. There
was nothing to do but write verses, several sets a day. And here it
was, stationary in the still sea when he longed to be on his way,
that Newman wrote the famous poem which he called 'The Pillar
of the Cloud' but which is always known as 'Lead Kindly Light'.
It is a prayer, and under its general forms, intensely personal to
Newman, and he could never quite get used to its extraordinary
popularity with his English contemporaries. In the first verse he
prayed to be led on step by step in the darkness, not asking to see
'the distant scene'. In the second he confessed that he had loved
to choose and see his path : 'Pride ruled my will : remember not
past years'. The third verse expressed the hope that he would be
led on through the wilderness till he saw again the angels of his
childhood, the inhabitants of heaven — and Ham. Perhaps it was

the image of finding one's way in the dark that appealed to the Victorians, lost in a spiritual wilderness in the midst of a powerful development of material resources. But as far as Newman was concerned it expressed a new, or renewed, humility and a resignation to experience which had come to him in Sicily, through his illness.

Newman always associated three feverish illnesses with three spiritual crises in his life. The first, when he was fifteen 'made him a Christian' and turned him away from scepticism; the second, when he was twenty-six, checked an incipient liberalism, when he felt he had been coming to prefer intellectual to moral excellence. These are Newman's own brief analyses, but he left none similar of the third and worst sickness, which nearly killed him, and which he regarded always as of the deepest importance to him. That was why, at intervals over the next seven years, he put down what he could remember of what had actually happened. Anne Mozley, his biographer, and Dean Church, whom she consulted, were puzzled by the details, physical and psychological, he had recorded; but Newman had an instinctive feeling for reality and a suspicion of deciding what was irrelevant in experience; often in later life he had to rewrite letters to leave out personal detail which it was his natural impulse to include. Having the fever and going through a crisis were all part of the same experience; it deeply affected the whole of his being and his life — perhaps that was why he did not epitomize it in a sentence, as he did the others. They had shifted his direction but this altered the attitude in which he accepted the direction, and so it was not something he passed through once, but which went on changing him.

When, about 1826, Newman had come out of his shell, it was no wonder he was in danger of over-valuing the intellect, his own being so exceptional. His mental collapse as Examiner, and Mary's death, resetting his course, predisposed him to receive from the Fathers, from Froude and Keble, the idea and image of the Catholic Church as founded and maintained on divine authority to mediate to men a new supernatural life. This was the Truth, which he held all his life. The new danger lay not in missing, or in distorting the Truth, but in so holding and teaching it as to stultify real spiritual growth. When he lay alone that miserable day in Leonforte, locked in, hearing the beggar whine outside, he traced the course of his wilfulness back from the actual return to Sicily, to his conduct over the Tutorship, not wrong in principle, but in the way he felt about it. He thought afterwards that delirium might have heightened his offences in his own eyes, and certainly took none of the exaggerated measures for publicly humiliating himself which then suggested themselves to his feverish imagination ; but he remained convinced there was truth in his self-accusation, and acted on it.

Preaching on Saul's self-will, and all the time full of it himself, an expert on humility in theory but not in practice : this made him see himself as a hollow sham, and not on this one point alone, but on all. He had seized on Keble's religious principles and worked them out, professing them 'as I might sing a tune which I liked — loving the Truth but not possessing it — for I believe myself at heart to be nearly hollow — i.e. with little love, little self denial'. This was what he thought the next summer, 1834, when he first began to write a private account of his illness in Sicily, for it took time for that experience to sink into his heart and bear its fruit. Of course this ability to work out in theory what is not yet worked out in practice is a danger to anyone with an active mind and vivid imagination. In this respect Newman judged himself harshly, for other people did not think him a hollow sham. Among his pupils he roused admiration and love, for they felt, as Rogers said, that he drew the very best out of them, by his own interest in them, and affection for them. Keble himself, 'the hidden saint' whom Newman feared he was exploiting, felt affection and respect for him. Whately and his friends, of course, did think him hollow, but for a different reason : they thought he was singing the tune not because he liked it, but because he could gain power by it.

Newman's temptation was more subtle than that, an insidious form of spiritual corruption, with which we are more familiar in a political context. Devotion to a cause can easily become devotion to a theory at the expense of reality, and the devoted person is perhaps the more easily deluded the better his cause is ; we know from past, if not from present history, how idealists can abuse authority and attempt the coercion, physical or moral of others, in the name of Humanity, or of Truth, or of God. And this, not from a simple love of power, but of the state of affairs they wish to bring about, and believe, perhaps justifiably, would be the best for all. Newman was on the point of emergence from university circles into the wider sphere of national life, and he was obscurely aware of this, though without in any way making plans for it. The revival of Catholic life and thought which he was going home to promote could easily become, and did in a sense become, a party of men devoted to certain principles of which he was the most famous exponent. He would be in imminent danger of identifying his cause with himself so that it was no longer a work of God's but a work of his, and to someone so devoted to God's service as he was, the way this was likely to happen was in his so ardently throwing himself into teaching and promoting ideals as to lose touch with reality in his own personal life.

Newman never fell under this delusion ; he was so resolutely un-party-minded as to suffer for it both as an Anglican, when many accused him of desertion, and as a Catholic, when some believed him a traitor. But it was not that he was in no danger : at Leonforte he saw himself not only as in danger, but as already fallen, a hollow man teaching others to do what he was not doing himself. The fever acted as a purge of the heart and spirit. Through it he recognized the evil at work in himself and instead of refusing to admit his guilt and dismissing the whole thing as a sick fancy, he confessed the worst and set about living in a new way : one step at a time, God leading, he submissive to experience. Of course it took long to learn, but really he had already begun to live like that, putting deeds above words ; now it only became a deeper and more sensitive and more conscious obedience.

The immediate reaction to this lesson in patience was impatience. The fever had burned up the last of the complex of feelings roused by the college quarrel, and released a tremendous spring of energy, welling up from the spirit before his body was equal to sustaining it. Mere verses could not express it. But they expressed something, a kind of ante-echo of the action to come, and a passionate love of the Christian community, warred on by the world, scorned by the clever and powerful. In some Newman put his anxieties as to whether it was right to take an active part in the struggle ; although he reminded himself continually that zeal must be coupled with gentleness he always came to the conclusion that to stand aside for fear of contamination was not humility but cowardice. St. Paul, always his hero, pointed the way. If he had stayed at home, where should we be to-day ?

> And so on us at whiles it falls, to claim
>   Powers that we dread, or dare some forward part :
> Nor must we shrink as cravens from the blame
>   Of pride, in common eyes, or purpose deep ;
> But with pure thoughts look up to God, and keep
>   Our secret in our heart.

In this respect, as in so many, he certainly got what he expected.

And there he was, unable to begin to spend all his new energy, becalmed. Who kept him back ? 'Really it seems as if some unseen power, good or bad, was resisting my return', he wrote to his mother from Lyons, again delayed. '. . . God is giving me a severe lesson of patience, and I trust I am not altogether wasting the opportunity of discipline. It is His will. I strive to think that wherever I am, God is God and I am I.' He felt there was a bad resistance to his return, as well as God's restraint. The more he thought over his experience during the year that followed the more convinced he became that Satan had made a special assault on him in Sicily. When he began his account he wrote, 'Well, in an unlooked for way I come to Sicily and the devil thinks his time is come. I was given over into his hands. From that time everything went wrong. . . . I could almost think the devil saw I am to be a means of usefulness and tried to destroy me. . . . Now it certainly is remarkable that a new and large sphere of action has opened upon me from the very moment I returned. . . . O my God, keep me still from being the sport and victim of Satan.'

Christ called Satan the prince, or ruler of this world ; the Passion was his hour when he beset Christ with all possible evils. Christ warned Peter that Satan would try to sift him as wheat ; when Peter expressed the human wish that Christ should avoid suffering, He addressed Peter as the representative of Satan. The Adversary uses the weaknesses of men to destroy unity, personal and communal ; the Apostle warned Christians not to give room to Satan in their hearts. Newman thought that his self-will had put him in Satan's power. God had allowed him to be sifted like St. Peter, preserving him because he had not 'sinned against light' — deliberately cut himself off from the divine love. The devil was cheated of his prey by the very assault he made : Newman saw the danger of becoming a hollow man and he was not even removed by death from the scene of action at that critical moment. So the enemy was reduced to annoying him in lesser ways — a familiar trick of evil spirits when they are thwarted. The result of the attack, physical and spiritual, was a man renewed, on his guard against the most subtle form of inward corruption and psychological sterilization, and more determined than ever to give the whole of himself to God as an instrument in His work.

At last the wind blew and the boat went on, and Newman disembarked at Marseilles, not without remembering to take with him some oranges for his ex-tutor Ogle's little girls in Oxford — some thirty years later their younger brother, on reading the *Apologia*, wrote to say they had not forgotten the oranges. Newman dashed on to Lyons, too quickly, for his feet swelled up so badly that he had to be helped from the carriage, and he suffered from cold sweats at night. But nothing could stop him now, and in a day or two he was off again, travelling night and day, never stopping till he reached Oxford and his mother's house. It was July 9th ; Frank had arrived from Persia a few hours before.

On Sunday Keble preached the Assize Sermon in St. Mary's, on National Apostasy.

THE MOVEMENT
(1833–1839)

1833

'Choose your side!'

It was Newman who started the fashion for dating the beginning of
the Oxford Movement from the delivery of Keble's sermon on
National Apostasy. Keble's principles were the foundation of the
Movement, and the influence of his personality affected the shape it
took in the eyes of the world, but the sermon itself was no call to
action and would not have started anything. Although he lamented
'fashionable liberality' and feared that duty to the Church might
become irreconcilable with duty to the State, his advice to 'the
Church's children' was resignation. But Froude and Newman had
come home burning for action, and soon found like-minded men,
Hugh James Rose among them. There were some hurried meetings
and plans made for associations, petitions and so on. Newman had a
profound suspicion of such methods; he thought energy frittered
away in talk and argument. Froude went to the initial conference,
Newman did not. Instead he sat down and addressed to the clergy
A Tract for the Times. In fact, he wrote several straight off, in simple
straightforward language, arranged with headings and capitals: incen-
diary pamphlets would be a better description than tracts. In capitals
appeared the caption: CHOOSE YOUR SIDE!

'I am but one of yourselves, a Presbyter; and therefore I conceal
my name, lest I should take too much on myself by speaking in my
own person. Yet speak I must; for the times are very evil, yet no
one speaks against them. . . . Should the Government and the country
so far forget their God as to cast off the Church, to deprive it of its
temporal honours and substance, *on what* will you rest the claim of
respect and attention which you make upon your flocks? Hitherto
you have been upheld by your birth and education, your wealth, your
connexions; should these secular advantages cease, on what must
CHRIST's ministers depend?' Having posed the question Newman
answered it. 'CHRIST has not left His Church without claim of its
own upon the attention of men. Surely not. Hard Master He

cannot be, to bid us oppose the world, yet give us no credentials for so doing. There are some who rest their divine mission on their own unsupported assertion ; others who rest it on their popularity ; others on their success ; and others who rest it on their temporal distinctions. This last case has perhaps been too much our own ; I fear we have neglected the real ground on which our authority is built — OUR APOSTOLICAL DESCENT.'

The first tract ended with the warning : 'Fear to be of those whose line is decided for them by chance circumstances, and who may perchance find themselves with the enemies of CHRIST, while they think but to remove themselves from worldly politics. Such abstinence is impossible in troublous times. HE THAT IS NOT WITH ME IS AGAINST ME AND HE THAT GATHERETH NOT WITH ME SCATTERETH ABROAD.'

'Are we to speak when individuals sin and not when a nation, which is but a collection of individuals ?' demanded the second tract. 'Must we speak to the poor, and not to the rich and powerful ? . . . Are we content to be the mere creation of the State ? . . . Did the State make us ? Can it unmake us ?' Although the occasion of their protest was the attack on the temporal possessions of the Church, actual and threatened, by the Reformers, the founders of the Movement were not concerned with retaining secular power and privilege, but with spiritual authority. Newman kindly wished the Bishops 'the spoiling of their goods and martyrdom' at the same time as he proclaimed 'Exalt our holy Fathers the Bishops, as the Representatives of the Apostles and the Angels of the Churches'.

As soon as the tracts were written Newman had them printed and by the beginning of September started their distribution by the simple method of sending bundles to friends and ex-pupils, then mostly at home for the vacation, telling them to circulate them in their neighbourhood. He himself, shyness forgotten, rode round Oxfordshire and Northampton delivering his anonymous pamphlets by hand to unsuspecting clergymen of every variety of opinion. Even Miss Giberne in London was pressed into service, and while her mother paid calls, nervously shoved into the hands of surprised maids packets to be delivered later to the mistress of the house. As her mother's friends were all evangelicals she had an uphill task, but some, like the Laprimaudayes, became keen supporters, and afterwards Catholics.

'Newman is becoming perfectly ferocious in the cause', wrote James Mozley in September to his sister Anne. 'We'll do them,' he says, at least twenty times a day — meaning the present race of

aristocrats and the Liberal oppressors of the Church in general.'
Both the Mozleys, Tom and James, enjoyed the excitement of being
'ecclesiastical agitators', as Froude called it.   Froude himself, his
health not improved by his tour, wrote from Devonshire 'I think I
have my paw on another fellow'. It would be a great loss if, as
seemed likely, he would have to go abroad again.   Newman, finding
he had already offended some, wrote to him, 'Yet what can one do ?
Men are made of glass — the sooner we break them and get it over
the better.'   He, the leading spirit in all this activity was thirty-two,
and his abettors were either contemporaries or younger.   He drew
up some notes to assist them in campaigning.   'Our object is to get
together immediately as large a body as we can in defence of the
substance of our spiritual rights and privileges, our creeds etc — but
we wish to avoid technicalities and minutenesses as much as possible.
The posture of affairs will not admit of delay.   We wish to unite the
clergy and create channels of correspondence among them.'   He
advised caution about 'the Apostolical ground' and general tem-
perance.   'Recollect we are *supporting* the Bishops — enlarge on the
unfairness of leaving them to bear the brunt of the battle.'

It was perhaps not surprising that the Bishops did not quite know
what to make of their new reinforcements ;   one spent hours trying
to decide whether or not he believed himself to be a successor of the
Apostles.   Martyrdom was no aspiration of theirs ;   it was revolution
they feared.   In the riots before the passing of the Reform Bill the
mob in Bristol burned down the Bishop's house, and the Bishop
might have suffered a similar fate if he had not made a hasty retreat
from the back.   The mob identified the Bishops, not with the
Apostles, but with Tory Government — so did most of the Bishops,
except for a few liberal Whigs like Whately.   To disassociate the
temporal from the spiritual power of the Bishops, despising their
alliance with the State while exalting their authority in the Church,
was so unfamiliar a line as to puzzle many, and finally alienated both
liberals and tories, the private-conscience men and the establishment
men.   But at first a good many of the latter rallied to the standard of
the Church's rights, in the hope of preventing further depredations.

The Tracts caused an immediate stir ;   there were comments in
the newspapers.   Everyone began reading them.   Anne Mozley was
annoyed at criticisms of Newman's style as too simple and plain.
'He enters upon his subject with the same humble quiet manner
with which he enters a room before one is aware', she wrote indignantly to James.   The liberals did not think so ;   Newman's quiet

manner was slyness to them. His tracts were anonymous, but he was known to be the editor of what soon became a series — Keble, Bowden and others were pressed into service as writers, but for some time the majority were his own. What Whately had seen threatening had now come to pass, a reactionary party was forming at Oxford, of which Newman was the activating centre, and it was drawing into itself the very men, young and brilliant, who should be coming to the support of the liberals.

The first to cross swords was Thomas Arnold, himself a notable leader and inspirer of young men. Not only his sixth-form boys, but his younger masters at Rugby were under the spell of his idealistic energy. He lamented Whately's withdrawal from Oxford as a loss of influence on the rising generation. He was convinced, as Whately was, that Newman had thrown himself into the cause of conservative reaction, the cause of the powerful, against those who were fighting for freedom and reform ; such a step looked to him like moral perversion — and Whately called Newman a Judas. When Arnold heard that in Rome Newman had said, 'But is Arnold a Christian ?' his wrath boiled over. He launched into a verbal duel, conducted through a second, Grant, who had been present on the occasion of Newman's delivering this insult.

'The natural tendency of such an insinuation is to disturb the minds of parents', Arnold said indignantly. He regarded it as a calumny, an imputation on his character rather than a censure of his opinions, likely to lead plain men to think he was professing Christianity but laughing at it in secret, like the sceptical Spanish clergy Blanco White had told them of. 'I do not suppose Newman to be so utterly wicked as to have intended such a calumny as this — but he chooses to use the word Christian in a sense of his own and excludes from any claim to it those who differ from him in their notions of Church government. . . . Let Newman say or write or print, any where and every where, that in his view I do not understand what Christianity is. . . . But let him not use language which from its necessary ambiguity had all the ill effects of falsehood, not without some portion of its guilt.' The letter was intended to be shown to the delinquent.

'It ought to be you', Newman wrote to Froude, who enjoyed saying outrageous things. He could not remember saying the words himself, but accepted Grant's word for it. The conversation had been private, no more than four people being present, and they had been discussing the principles of Old Testament criticism. Some-

one had said of a German expositor of whose soundness they were
dubious, 'Arnold says he is a Christian', meaning that he held
orthodox opinions. Newman had laughed and said something like
'Arnold must first show he is a Christian himself'. Grant afterwards confirmed this, and said unhesitatingly that he had never
thought it implied any imputation on Arnold's belief in Christ.
Arnold made no secret of his views. To him Christianity was a
moral discipline rather than a teaching. 'Scripture is to be used
for lessons more than for Truths', he said in a letter. Recently he
had publicly advocated the use of parish churches by all the Christian sects (except the papists) in turn ; Newman made fun of this
to a friend in a letter from Rome, suggesting the inclusion of Jews
and Mohammedans, who could be fitted in the more easily as their
holy days were on Saturday and Friday. Even Whately said of
Arnold that 'with his enormous energies (he) is as indolent as any
one in accurate reasoning ; but he has not the advantage of being
sensible of this'. He was something of an *enfant terrible* to the liberal
Churchmen.

Newman thought of writing to him direct, but decided to continue the correspondence through Grant as it enabled him to express
himself less disrespectfully. He said that he did not apologize for
his words since they were said in private, and that neither he nor his
hearers meant to impugn Arnold's personal faith, but only to criticize
the unorthodoxy of his opinions on the interpretation of Scripture.
But he ended, 'I believe my words had no direct reference to Dr.
Arnold's ecclesiastical principles, though I should not duly respond
to the frankness of his letter if I did not plainly declare that as far
as I understand them, I think they are unscriptural, unchristian
and open to ecclesiastical censure.'

This merely confirmed Arnold in his opinion that Newman was
an arrogant bigot, and a cowardly one, who played with the meaning of words and made his slanders ambiguously. He was to make
these charges again in public. To Arnold a Christian was any
decent man with a devotion to Christ ; he argued on the assumption
that the Church was a religious society formed by men in a similar
way to civil societies, but, as Whately would say 'he had not the
advantage of being sensible' of its being an assumption. He never
realized that it was this very assumption, of which he was unconscious, that Newman contested ; therefore he concluded that
Newman was preaching a form of human tyranny crushing to the
conscience, and was setting up his own opinion as the one standard

of truth. But even arguing from his own principles he was not justified in accusing Newman, as he did, of using words in an equivocating sense, or of advocating persecution. These became commonplace charges against Newman ; as he never answered personal attacks, or retaliated on his opponents, his reputation suffered. The Verses show he had expected to be accused of seeking power, but the charge of dissimulation took him by surprise, and he found it hard to bear. Dishonesty in any form was so foreign to him that he could not easily understand how his words and actions could be so misinterpreted. He was good at grasping the ideas of those with whom he did not agree, but not at guessing their emotional reactions to his own ideas, or indeed to himself.

Arnold's opposition he expected, though hardly his making such a fuss over a joke in a private conversation, but disagreement among friends was much more trying. The learned Palmer of Worcester, author of a famous work on liturgical origins, expressed himself against the Tracts, and there was much dissension over the form of the proposed Petition, and the organization of the association. 'The Tracts give offence I know', Newman wrote to Froude on November 13th, '— but they also do good. . . . I want advice sadly. I have no confidence in any one. If I could be sure of 5 or 6 vigorous co-operators in various parts I would laugh at opposition, but I fear being beaten from the field.' Soon after he wrote anxiously, 'My dear F, I so fear I may be self-willed in the matter of the Tracts — pray do advise me according to your light'. He did in fact stop publication at Palmer's disapproval. Froude was horrified. 'As to giving up the Tracts, the notion is odious . . . we must throw the Zs overboard.' The Zs were the establishment men, the Ys were the Evangelicals or Peculiars, and the Xs the Apostolicals. Froude was full of cheerful pugnacity. The Petition, as even the Archdeacon said, had turned out mere milk and water — 'Do make a Row about it'.

Froude encouraged Newman to fight when he looked like faltering from fear of forcing his own will on others ; always this was his anxiety, and much more now since his experience in Sicily. Yet there was nothing demoralizing in Froude's friendly pushes. It was a great loss to Newman when he left England at the beginning of that winter for Barbados, so far away, just as it was for him the greatest trial he could undergo, for in exile he could not effectively pursue his ambition to be an ecclesiastical agitator. He went away cheerful, however, teasing Newman for signing himself classically

Usque ad cineres (yours till he is ashes, till death). 'Why do you say *usque ad cineres* — if I am wrecked on Ash Wednesday you will be the cause of it.' Off he went to a year and a half of solitude, months away as far as consulting him was concerned, with no one but Zs to talk to. 'Love to all the Apostolicals', he said.

Newman was left to face all the crises, public and private, that came thick and fast in the next year, alone.

1834–1835

Cutting Brothers and Friends

WHEN Newman came back from Sicily people meeting him in the
street hardly recognized him.   He was very brown and thin, James
Mozley wrote home.   His hair all fell out and he had to wear a wig
till it grew again ; when it came it was darker.   But the real change
was the great rebound of energy which drove him through the first
critical months of his new work.   It was his supreme confidence in
the truth of his principles which carried him on ; yet even in the
first excitement he would have stopped the Tracts, his own distinctive contribution, and the one which was making their ideas
known in the world, rather than force his own way against the
opinion of others.   If Froude and Keble had not urged him on, he
would have given up this weapon of incalculable power.

But whatever was yielded, the sermons at St. Mary's went on.
Many of those written in these first years were published in the
second and third volumes ; the third contained several on subjects
distinctive of the Movement, such as the use of daily services and
how Christians should adapt to their day the zeal of the Jews of old
in maintaining the purity and unity of the Lord's people.   It was
sermons such as these that shocked the liberals of Oxford, and spread
the legend of intolerance and bigotry which was the chief weapon
used against the Tractarians during the first years.   Newman certainly was not tactful in his way of announcing this method of
maintaining unity ; he drew out the most bloodthirsty episodes of
Hebrew history, exterminations of women and children in the name
of the Lord.   It was then of little use to say that for Christians force
must be banned, and the way to deal with offenders, those who
broke up the unity of the Church by forming sects founded on
human opinions, was to refuse to meet them socially and exclude
them from such services of the Church as they wished still to make
use of.

All the Apostolicals felt strongly on this subject.   They thought people had lost the idea of a visible Church which maintained an objective Truth with divine authority ; everyone thought he had a right to his own opinion as to what Christianity was. To make a stand, not only in theory, but in practice, was a duty. Keble himself was most strict in applying the rules to dissenters. But Keble lived in the country, and his dissenters were too low in the social scale to make a noise about it. As so often it was Newman who drew the fire. It could scarcely be otherwise, since he had a parish church in the middle of Oxford ; but he was unlucky in having a dissident brother in his own family.

Frank Newman came back from Persia after three years' absence, three hours before his brother's return from Sicily. He heard that Miss Giberne's Indian officer had died the year before, and went straight off to make her a second proposal. She was moved by his devotion, his intense silent gaze, his cold hand ; but she refused him again. She had not yet recovered from the shock of Robert Murcott's death. Their marriage was more or less arranged, and she was making her wedding clothes, when her mother had to tell her that Robert had died of fever on the eve of his return. Stunned by the news, Maria went upstairs and earnestly prayed that she might see him again. She fell asleep after midnight and, as she wrote long after in her French memoir, 'Voilà que j'ai vu mon Robert'. In her dream they talked long of their sad separation and when she woke she made a picture of him which she kept until, as an old woman over sixty, about to be professed as a contemplative nun, she was advised to destroy it ; she burnt it.

Refused yet once more by Maria Giberne, Frank went down to Devonshire to visit Sir John Kennaway, one of those impressed by Darby and his search for primitive Christianity. Kennaway also had a beautiful daughter called Maria, more gentle and submissive than Maria Giberne. In September 1833 Froude reported Devonshire gossip that Sir John insisted on Frank's giving up any idea of a missionary life. 'For his own sake I hope he may be going to do a commonplace thing ; yet from what I know of him I cannot doubt but he has some scheme such as he hinted to you. As to any conflict between his views and ours, I apprehend no evil from him, however painful it may be ; anything that sets people agog is on our side ; I deprecate a calm.' Newman replied that Frank had given up his missionary scheme of his own accord, but he said no more.

Frank had certainly been disillusioned with missions ; instead of converting anyone to Christianity the first seed of disbelief in the Trinity had been implanted in his mind by a Mohammedan. His mind was already unsettled, but his crusading ardour had not abated, and he was still emotionally involved in religion. He had taken from Darby the ideal of primitive Christianity, but for a time he found this compatible with doubt about certain doctrines, which he was able to consider a later accretion. He soon found that he had gone too far for Darby, who told the Brethren to excommunicate him. By this time Frank had secured a post as Classics Tutor in Bristol College, and for some time wandered among the many Protestant sects established there. He occasionally let his family into his opinions ; hearing that he had openly denied that the Holy Spirit was God, and the duty of praying to Christ as God, Newman wrote to him : 'Indeed my dear Frank, you are in a net which I do not like to think of. I do feel it to be a snare of the devil. . . . As to your still holding regeneration, I value it not a rush — such doctrines have no substantive existence. They may remain on your mind a while after you have given up the High Mysteries of the Faith but will not last longer than the warmth of a corpse. I write in great grief, not knowing what best to say.' He saw, long before Frank, where 'the wretched principle of private judgment' would take him.

At the end of his letter Newman added a postscript : 'I hope you understand that decidedly as I object to meet you in a familiar way or to sit at table with you, yet should you be coming here and wish to have any talk with me (not disputation) or in like manner of course write to me, I shall be most happy. If I can be your servant in any way, so that I do not countenance your errors, you really may command me — at least I trust so.'

This postscript illustrates Newman's dilemma. Frank was making a division by his active promotion of a sect ; therefore, according to the Apostolicals' principles, he must be avoided. But it was not natural to Newman to behave so stiffly, so he tried to soften it by offering any private assistance he thought might be acceptable. Some years later he had to apply the rule again in the case of George Spencer, a clergyman converted to Rome before the Tractarian Movement began, who came to Oxford, as a Catholic priest, to collect prayers for Reunion. Newman refused to dine with him, because he was, in his view, a schismatic in the opposite direction from Frank ; but he gladly met him in private and was so friendly that poor Mr. Spencer did not know what to make of it all. Newman

and his friends were in an impossible position, since the majority of
the members of their own communion regarded the Church as a
merely human society, subject to such modifications and revolutions
as civil societies.   This, however, did not become plain at once.   But
it was plain enough that everyone was shocked at Newman's bigotry
in refusing to meet his brother.

Frank, in his bitter recollections, did not complain of the principle, but did complain that Newman's action cut him off from his
mother and sisters.   His memory must have strayed, for they did not
approve of John's method with the erring sheep, and Frank stayed
at Rose Bank at least once when John was not there.   He hurt his
mother by refusing to go with her to communion in the Church of
England ; this he regretted after her death.   Jemima wrote to John,
'We get on as well with Frank as the consciousness of having some
forbidden subjects will allow. . . . Poor fellow, it is very difficult for
him to know what to say to please us, when he thinks so differently.
He is now making hay in the orchard.   Get well John, and fat as fast
as you can.'

Frank had no scruples in lecturing John, in 1834, on his worldliness in keeping their mother and sisters in more comfort than was
strictly necessary ; he did not see why they should have a man-
servant.   John replied that what he gave them was a free gift, but
that in fact much of it went in charity.   'If they had lived in lodgings
where would be the kitchen for Littlemore, with broth and messes ?
where the rice and tapioca from the housekeeper's closet ?'   He
added, 'I suppose my money goes further than yours in journeying
to Persia'.   Criticism as to how John spent his money came somewhat
ill from Frank.   'As to myself personally I shall say nothing,' Newman
ended.   'You know little either of my principles or practice if you
think I go by the mere fashion of society.'

Frank's job in Bristol enabled him to marry Maria Kennaway.
Mrs. Newman was delighted.   'They are marrying in such a true
Christian spirit that I doubt not a blessing will be on their union, and
perhaps we may greet them both again in the bosom of our own true
spiritual soothing Church.   I intend to propose their coming here
after their marriage at Christmas.'   But Frank's bride fell ill, the
visit was postponed, and never took place.   Maria's health was the
reason Frank gave for not attending his mother's funeral, some
months later.   In the break with his family he was at least as active
as John.

In his recollections Frank said that his mother and sisters made

an idol of John, but in fact at this time Newman was just discovering
that they did not like the distinctive principles of the Apostolicals.
In these two years the domestic scene was not so happy as it had been.
Mrs. Newman never had liked what she regarded as the more extreme
ideas, especially John's determination not to marry, which she always
quietly deplored. In a short note written in 1873, called *Apology
for Myself*, Newman briefly touched on the causes of disagreement.
They did not like some of his friends — he did not say who was
unpopular ; and his mother thought his treatment of Frank wrong.
He may have thought her policy towards Charles mistaken. While
Newman was abroad Charles had squandered all the £1000 she had
given him. For one awful moment they thought Charles was married
to some undesirable character, but he was only living with her, and
when old Aunt descended on his squalid lodgings, consented to be
separated from her and started on a new career as a teacher in boys'
schools. He went from job to job, still lecturing his family from
time to time, in extraordinary letters.

In his note Newman mentioned that there were disagreements
about his brothers, but he was inclined to think a deeper cause for
difficulties was in their having come to Oxford expecting to share
more of his life. Of course, since he was very busy, they saw less of
him sometimes than when he had taken special holidays, devoting
his attention solely to them. When he came out to Rose Bank he was
often tired and preoccupied, and their loving interest became impor-
tunate. 'I got worried — I got worried by their affectionateness,'
he admitted. Yet he also said : 'These differences, though they tried
to make the best of them, made me very sore. They had a full right
to their own views ; but I did not imitate them in bearing patiently
what could not be helped.' Possibly he was as patient as they were.
Harriett actually wrote him letters to tell him he had not behaved as
affectionately as they thought he ought to have done. She was a
very determined young woman, and the one who opposed his ideas
most forcibly. She had also involved herself in the episode of Henry
Wilberforce's marriage, in a manner which hurt and annoyed her
brother considerably.

Henry, without any malice, contrived to injure Newman's reputation in Oxford almost as much as his enemies. He had been elusive
ever since Newman's return from Sicily, 'afraid to be brought into a
party', Newman surmised to Froude. He had written a 'kind but
curious' letter on the dangers of schism. Soon after 'H. W. has
slipped through my fingers, left me in the lurch, and gone without

answering my letter to Scotland. Report says the Lord Chancellor
is to give him a living in Yorkshire. If he takes one from him, I
pronounce it will be against his conscience.' The Wilberforces, from
their father's prestige, were certain of preferment, especially from a
Whig government. Then there was such a long silence on Henry's
affairs that Froude, from Barbados, wrote, 'Tell me when you have
any news of that wretch Henry', and even began to wonder if he had
deserted to the Zs. Newman replied in June 1834: 'H. W. engaged
to marry Miss S. last December, was afraid to tell me and left Oxford
without — spread abroad I had cut Ryder for marrying. He now
wishes to go into orders but *cannot get a title*, *because* he wants one
with a house and £100 a year. Precious nonsense and foolery — it
makes one half beside oneself. Yet he has not ratted and will not
(so be it). Marriage is a sin which it is sinful to repent of.' In July
he added, 'G. Ryder and bride passed through Oxford yesterday —
he seems proud of showing her off; which I suppose is proper'.

George Ryder, son of the Bishop of Lichfield, was one of Froude's
pupils, and had made open professions on the ideal of clerical celibacy.
He then fell in love with Sophia Sargent, one of the siren band of
Lavington, the beautiful daughters of the Rector who had tutored the
Wilberforces. Sam Wilberforce had already carried off one, and
Henry fell in love with Mary. That left Caroline, who was snapped
up by Manning in 1834, when, after being the Rector's curate, he
succeeded, on his death, to the living. So far from cutting Ryder,
Newman had written to him in 1832: 'It is quite absurd to suppose
that you are not at liberty both to marry and to go into the church —
indeed I think that country parsons ought, as a general rule to be
married — and I am sure the generality of men ought, whether
parsons or not. The celibate is a high state of life to which the
multitude of men cannot aspire — I do not say that those who adopt
it are necessarily better than others, though the noblest ethos is
situated in that state.' Expecting a time of revolutionary turmoil, he
added practically, 'Is it not worthwhile to ascertain whether your
hoped-for partner is prepared to be a pilgrim?' Forcing penitential
ideals on young mothers of families was no part of his programme.

Newman was not unreasonable on the subject of clerical celibacy,
but it was certainly a deeply cherished desire that others would follow
Froude and himself in aiming at this total dedication, and his friends
knew it. Henry therefore felt guilty over his engagement, and was
afraid Newman would be angry with him for deserting the difficult
path. It was simply moral cowardice not to tell him; to go away and

leave him to make a fool of himself, as he did, by denying the reports of it on the score that Henry would certainly have told him such important news. But Henry had made everything much worse, first by letting Harriett into his secret, and then by telling everyone he met in Oxford that Newman had cut Ryder for marrying, and was sure to cut him ; he even said in a letter to Rogers, 'I suppose he will cut me'. Harriett, as Newman wrote in a little note of 1860, when he was going through old letters, 'triumphed over me in her heart, and I knew she did'. He said no more, but imagination supplies the atmosphere. As for the general talk, Oxford was a small enclosed society, and it was not only Harriett who triumphed. Newman became an object of ridicule to the unfriendly, and was saddled with the unpleasant reputation of cutting his friends for marrying. Having carelessly scattered his unfounded gossip abroad, Henry then bemoaned Newman's unkindness in putting principles above friendship.

This was too much for Newman and he wrote off a letter, wrote it again differently and yet again — and then did not send it, probably because he felt it was too full of self-justification. But he kept it, so it must have expressed what he felt. He started off in a bantering tone, 'My poor dear foolish Henry — dear, for auld lang syne, — foolish for being suspicious of me, — poor, because I suppose you have been pained at your own suspicions'. But he was unable to keep that up. 'When have I ever questioned the propriety of your marriage or dared to interfere with your Christian liberty ? . . . the single thing I said was I thought you would do better to wait awhile — not that here I did more than state my opinion when asked.'

Then he went on to Henry's reproach that he was breaking up friendships for the sake of a principle. 'But you surely are inconsiderate — you ask me to give you my heart, when you give yours to another — and because I will not promise to do so, then you augur all sorts of ill treatment towards you from me. Now I do not like to speak of myself, but in self-defence I must say, it is a little hard for a friend to separate himself from familiarity with me (which he has a perfect right and perhaps lies under a duty to do) and then to say, "Love me as closely, give me your familiar heart as you did, though I have parted with mine". Be quite sure that I shall be free to love you, far more than you will me — but I cannot, as a prudent man, forget what is due to my own comfort and independence as not to look to my own resources, make my own mind my wife, and anticipate and provide against that loss of friends which the fashion of the age

makes inevitable.   This is all I have done and said with respect to
you — I have done it to all my friends, as expecting they will part
from me, except to one, who is at Barbadoes.   I dare not even towards
my sisters indulge affection without restraint.   Now is it not hard,
when I a poor individual see what the chance is of my being left
alone, and prepare for it, that I then should be said to be the breaker
of friendships ? it is the story of the lamb and the wolf ; unless you
think I have that confidence in myself that I could calmly contemplate putting the whole world into Coventry.   You know very little
of me if you think I do not feel at times much the despondence of solitariness — (if I had had no experience of it this last year) and why
may I not arm myself against what is inevitable ?   Why must I give
my heart to those who will not (naturally it would be a bad bargain
for them) take charge of it ?   God grant all this discipline will make
me give my heart more to Him — but it is hard to be accused of
inflicting it on others.

'You are ever in my prayers and will not cease to be — and I trust
you will never forget your present principles, nor the sentiment of
Keble's in which you seemed fully to acquiesce, that "celibacy and
marriage were accidents, and did not alter by one jot or tittle a true
Christian's mode of acting".

'My dear H, — you really have hurt me — you have *made* a
difficulty in the very beginning of our separation.   You should have
reflected that to remove it, you would not only have to justify it to
yourself but explain it to me. . . . P.S. At first I intended not to write
lest I should say what would seem unkind.   But that itself seemed
unkind — so I changed my mind.   This is not the first letter I have
written.   I plucked it. . . .'   This was plucked too.

Perhaps it was a pity it did not go, for Henry complained afterwards that he had not realized what Newman thought, and consequently had made matters worse.   Newman was always inclined to
credit other people with his own imaginative intelligence ; Henry
surely would know how his behaviour had hurt him.   Besides this,
he always had a great dislike for easy talk about love, whether of man
or of God ; it was deeds not words that love was really made of.
Thus, though he did not send his feelings to Henry, he showed them,
as he thought, a week or so later that same January 1834.   Isaac
Williams, Keble's disciple, who was acting as his curate, had a bad
cough and thought his health would not stand the work.   Newman
at once wrote to Henry, offering the job to him ; it would carry no
money, of course, but it would give him opportunities of using St.

Mary's pulpit, and Newman suggested finding a house on Rose Hill,
which would advance the possibility of marriage and make him twice-
over his neighbour.   Then Williams decided his cough was not fatal,
but mainly nervous, and Newman had to apologize to Henry for
being too precipitate.   'All I can say is that my very writing, even if
inconsiderate (which I hope it was not) at least shows the desire I had
still to be near you as heretofore.'   They met in the summer and
Henry was evidently already feeling a certain sadness at being cut
off from the centre of activity in Oxford ; however, he went off and
married his Mary and got a curacy in the New Forest.   He tried to
keep in with what went on in Oxford as well, and wrote a pamphlet
for Newman on the question of admitting Dissenters to the University.

But the episode was not even than at an end.   Henry had done
nothing to counteract the rumours he had set in motion, but Newman
was willing to forget that.   But Henry felt uneasy, and kept stirring
up the embers.   He felt cut off from things and accused Newman of
not writing to him any more.   Newman's reply was that he was so
pressed for time that even correspondence with Froude got left, who
as an exile had first claim on him.   Then, at the beginning of 1835,
Henry told Rogers that Newman was refusing to write to him till he
had made explanations, but that Henry did not know what explanations to make.   This was too much for Newman, who began to try
again to tell him what he felt.   Three drafts remain of his attempts, but
none went in the end — only a few lines and a letter about the pamphlet.   Henry had suggested that Newman was indulging in unchristian
resentment towards him.   Newman could think of nothing that
warranted this except possibly a message he had sent through Rogers
to ask him if he could do anything 'to remove certain misapprehen-
sions you had created concerning me in people's minds, and which
you scarcely deny creating.   Your letter to Rogers just seen by me
says plainly "that you cannot do so".   With this answer I am quite
contented and drop the subject for ever.   Still I do not see what there
has happened to be unchristian in me, except the fact of my asking
you to undo what I at least, to say nothing of you, thought you had
done.'   This was in the letter he did not send.

But in June he did write a letter which he sent.   The occasion
of it was some approach Henry made through Harriett.   'I am
surprised and hurt at the inconsiderateness which has led you, in
spite of the unkindness I experienced last year from you and my
sister, to make me the channel of messages to her and her to me,
as if to force upon me the recollection of what I fain would forget.'

He briefly said that he wanted to have nothing to do with their intimacy and was going to bind himself to a definite line of conduct towards Henry for three years, dating from the offence, 'which I less mind doing because, for what I know, it may inconvenience myself'. He said he wrote to 'show to you my feeling about the matter and to relieve for myself feelings, which, if pent up within me, may do me harm'.

Henry, not having read the other letters, or guessed his feelings, and not knowing them now (for there were still no explanations) was shocked and horrified, especially at Newman's mysterious 'line of conduct', which he assumed must be severe. He did not answer for nearly six weeks, when the birth of his son made a suitable opening. He said he had no idea Newman had been annoyed with him for telling Harriett, and that it was all his own fault for refusing to hear explanations. But what really upset him was the decision to take up a special attitude, and he delivered a long and anxious lecture, warning Newman against transferring his principles about shunning schismatics 'to those who have behaved with *personal unkindness* to yourself. . . . I must deliberately say that it does not seem to me compatible with our Blessed Lord's teaching for a man to resolve to retain the memory of a *personal wrong* and to mark that memory in his conduct for three years, nor for three days.' He thought that Newman might come to blame his own conduct in this respect, and that other people saw him in danger of becoming 'stern and rigid' against persons as well as principles. But he ended by saying that the loss of Newman's friendship would be insupportable, and by telling him of the birth of his son.

Replying to this, Newman plucked three letters, and the draft that remains was not as sent, for the final effort was 'more gently and kindly worded'. 'I never can feel otherwise than obliged at any advice or hint which you or anyone else can give me about myself — though not useful in the way intended, it must always be of some use or other — if it were only to humble one.' He felt Henry's advice, however, was as wide of the mark as his would be 'on the subject of making steam vessels or railroads'. Still, he did not tell Henry in what way he had missed the mark, because he felt : 'If there is anything which feeds a misunderstanding it is an explanation ; and for this reason I always whether hear or give them with a very heavy heart. The true Christian way is to forgive and forget, not to prove yourself right — though there is no harm in showing you have an opinion. This you abundantly showed when you acted towards me as you did in Christmas 1833 — and so that you understand I have an opinion the other way, I am ready that you should keep your own view without molestation — so that you will not oblige me to argue on the subject. As you must know, whenever we have been together since that time, especially in June 1834, my manner towards you has been what it was before, and my feelings have been the same. You have not allowed me to rest, but have in one way or other (if I may say it) forced upon me your slightness of feeling on the subject — and then gone on to accuse me with bearing it in mind, in neglecting to write to you etc., which was a fancy. . . . We have made mutual accusations — do let us forget them.' He had already given up his protest at Harriett's request.

Henry was melted by the more gentle version of this which he received, 'It brought tears into my eyes at seeing I had given you pain'. He was not quite sure they understood each other's point of view even yet 'but notwithstanding all this your letter was so kind and affectionate that it almost overpowered me'. He asked Newman to be godfather to his baby, whom he wished to name John Henry William Wilberforce. Newman accepted this office with pleasure and in September was remarking, 'I hope my godchild is a good boy'. Thus the only serious misunderstanding of their long friendship was closed.

Henry had certainly missed the mark in thinking that Newman was in danger of dehumanizing himself by too stern an adherence to principle; his real difficulty was not to let his feelings run away with him and land him in a morass of emotional self-indulgence. The language of the day must not be misunderstood; it is only in our own time that the term 'love' has become almost exclusively the property of passionate love; up to, and including, the nineteenth century it was in general use for the affection between friends, brothers and sisters. Newman had determined not to canalize the energies of love in marriage, in order to direct all towards Christ, and through Christ to the people to whom he was sent. But there was a danger, to someone whose feelings were so strong, in partially relapsing into a dependence on the affection of a circle of personal friends; not in loving some people more than others, which Newman always maintained was natural to a human being and sanctioned by Christ Himself, but in depending on their love for him and inadvertently putting the highest value on their approval. He had to learn how to adjust his emotional relationships so as to assist and not retard the development of spiritual love, which is choked by selfish and demanding feelings. His plea to Henry (not sent!) to understand his psychological position, how he must make his own mind his wife and be prepared to lose close familiarity with friends who married, shows that it cost him a struggle. Whether anyone marries or not he must feel an emotional response to everyone he meets, either of liking or disliking : indifference is the sign of psychotic self-absorption. By nature we follow our likes and avoid our dislikes, in the matter of persons as of everything else; a Christian has to learn to control and transcend both in a love which is more detached from the self — of course the process of a lifetime, and only successfully achieved through the love of Christ.

It was hard for Newman that he had to wean himself from grasping at the affection of friends just at the time when he most needed encouragement, when Froude, the only one who fully shared his ideal of self-dedication, was far away, and when all the hostile reactions roused by the Apostolical movement tended to be focused on him. But he came through this critical time without having lost a single friend, and he kept them all (recovering even those who broke away from him in 1845) to the end of his life. He managed to love them still, and love them positively and individually, without demanding an intense or exclusive love in return. But it was not easy.

1834–1835

Persecuting Dissenters

'I HAVE got a most audacious scheme about myself which will not bear to be put on paper — the ink would turn red', said Newman to Froude in the first flush of the enthusiasm of September 1833. The scheme to make the ink blush was that he should stand for the Professorship in Moral Philosophy. 'Don't you think I should make a good Professor? At all events let us look out for one. I do not see anyone we could so well put forward (!) But if you think you would do as well yourself, n'importe. You shall be the man.' He then suggested others. But he was so eminently suited for the post that he did in the end stand for election. It would give him a definite position in the university, an opportunity of lecturing and teaching again, and more money, which he badly needed. No one else was standing, so the thing seemed decided.

But at the last moment a group of those who disliked his opinions, headed by Provost Hawkins, put up a rival candidate, none other than Renn Dickson Hampden, who had already been used to evict Newman from the Oriel tutorship. The selection board was not large. Old Martin Routh, the fabulous President of Magdalen, who was then about eighty and was to live to be a hundred, was extremely annoyed at this manœuvre. He wrote to Hawkins to say that he hoped Mr. Newman would be returned unopposed, but that if a division was made, he intended to come down and vote for him. Routh carried on at Magdalen the tradition of the seventeenth century; he was one of the few Heads of Houses who approved of the Movement, and of Newman, whom he supported throughout his Oxford career. His vote, however, was not sufficient to turn the scales. Hampden, James Mozley wrote home disgustedly, 'being a Bampton lecturer, and an Aristotelian, and a Head of a House, and a Liberal, and, moreover, a stupid man in his way, was of course the successful candidate'. Hampden was Principal of St. Mary's Hall, a small institution attached to Oriel; this gave him a place

on the all-powerful Hebdomadal Board. Newman took his failure
lightly enough. 'I have so much to do I cannot be sorry', he told
Froude.

This was in March 1834, the month the first volume of Parochial
Sermons came out. Soon after, Newman made himself a lecture
room, since the university would not provide one. The ancient
chapel of the Oriel Founder, Adam de Brome, was at that time
partitioned off from the nave of St. Mary's and used as a mere dump.
Newman had it cleared out and cleaned, benches put in and a reading-
desk, and proceeded to give theological lectures to anyone who
chose to come. There were a hundred at his first lecture, but some
fell off. William George Ward was there, at first hostile, but soon
brought round to Newman's views. A large and self-confident youth,
his fixed stare, his nudgings and audible comments so put off the
lecturer that he had the benches turned round the other way. Ward
was a brilliant abstract thinker; he gained a Fellowship at Balliol
and remained a figure in Oxford life till the famous scene in 1845
when he was deprived of his degrees for writing *The Ideal of a
Christian Church*.

Newman's lectures were on the subject of Justification; later
he rewrote them for publication. This doctrine, the chief issue
between Protestants with Lutheran views and those holding the
Catholic tradition, Newman took with the intention of making the
parties to the argument realize that they misrepresented each other,
and especially that Evangelicals misunderstood the Catholic teaching,
which was not so inimical to their own as they thought. 'The
saving Cross crucifies us in saving', he said. Evangelicals condemned Catholics as relying on their own efforts to acquire holiness,
Catholics replied that God did not give an external holiness but
required the free co-operation of men in the gradual process of
making them holy. 'O easy and indulgent doctrine', Newman said
to the Evangelicals, 'to have the bloody cross reared within us, and
our hearts transfixed, and our arms stretched out upon it, and the
sin of our nature slaughtered and cast out!' Yet this was done
only by Christ: 'Our crosses are the lengthened shadow of the
Cross on Calvary'. Thus in the lectures as in his sermons he tried
to raise again the standard of self-discipline and self-denial, as the
response of love to the overwhelming love of God. To him self-
denial was the test of religious feeling, as of all real love.

Later that year he started reading Matins daily in the Church.
John Keble and his brother Tom, Rector of Bisley, had begun the

revival of this practice. Newman began bravely, and continued
year after year, but he never had much more than half a dozen in
his daily congregation (he noted the numbers), and years afterwards
he admitted that it became increasingly 'dreary' to him. It did not
have the moving intensity of the early communion service on
Sundays, which he later started, a great innovation, attended by
many young dons and some undergraduates. He also found it
trying to his voice, especially on days when the litany had to be said.
He had a clear, but not a very resonant voice ; under strain he was
inclined to go hoarse or lose it altogether. The sermons did not
owe their fame to any natural eloquence, but to what he said, as
was proved by their wide sale to people who had never heard him.
His personality deeply impressed many who actually listened, but
that was a different matter. The sermons are alive now in the way
that only creative thought expressed in its right imaginative form
can live.

The first volume of sermons was dedicated to Pusey. Newman
wanted to gain Pusey, who was reluctant at first to throw himself
wholly into the Movement. Isaac Williams remembered him
'smiling and wrapping his gown round him as he used to do. "Oh
no," he said in a playful manner, "I will not be one of you !"' He
wrote one of the early Tracts on fasting, and a later one on Baptism
which became a treatise, and signed them with his initials in order
to dissociate himself from the anonymous Apostolicals. But the
identity of E. B. P. was easily guessed, and it was naturally assumed
that as Professor of Hebrew and Canon of Christ Church Pusey
must be the leading spirit behind the Tracts. Popularly the Tractarians were christened Puseyites. In this typically roundabout way
did Pusey become a Puseyite.

Although Pusey was a most unassuming man, he had some of
the qualities of a party leader. He was extremely tenacious ; his
life became a series of rearguard actions against liberal encroach-
ments, political and ecclesiastical, on the Church and the university.
At Christ Church he had an independent position, with no cure of
souls, no Bishop to consult, no authority over him but the Crown
— a fact of which he was proud. He was not averse to advising
and directing others, humbly, yet with the utmost reliance on the
authority he felt was his as a priest of the Church of England, which
he regarded as part of the Catholic Church. He had not Newman's
drive, his simplicity in presenting ideas and ideals, the personal
attractive power which so fascinated his friends and made his

enemies so suspicious ; but he had an immovable will ; the nineteenth century roared and flowed round him but he remained
stationary, and somehow permanently optimistic — sanguine, Newman called it. The immediate difference made by his advent to the
Movement was that the Tracts, from airy little missiles, became a
heavy bombardment, tomes of learning and argument. Newman
wrote fewer and fewer, though he remained Editor, and sometimes
suggested the subjects to the earnest authors. He paid tribute in
the *Apologia* to the solidity given by so much scholarship to the
Movement, but his own gifts lay in stirring people to action ; when
he turned to deeper things it was to think out the basis of Faith, or
meditate on the process by which Christianity had unfolded in the
world.

Just after the summer term ended Newman was plunged into his
first public row. Coming into college one evening, he found a note
requesting him to perform the marriage ceremony next day for the
daughter of a pastry-cook named Jubber. He was a Dissenter and
had refused to have his children baptized. Newman went round at
once and explained that he could not perform the marriage ceremony
for someone who was not baptized ; it would be meaningless. He
apologized for seeming harsh towards the girl. The obvious remedy
would be to have her baptized first, but Jubber felt strongly on the
subject and got her married in some other church. A paragraph
appeared in an Oxford paper in which the intolerant Vicar of St.
Mary's was said to have declaimed, 'I will not marry her for she is
an outcast !'

'No, I did not say this', Newman protested, writing to the editor.
But he stuck to his point, that baptism made a person a member of
the Christian Church and that no unbaptized person could make a
Christian marriage. To the public this was all nonsense ; baptism
was the usual way of naming a baby, but it was ridiculous to make it
a test of Christianity, which as everyone knew meant good moral
behaviour. Miss Jubber was a respectable girl and had every right
to be married in Church. Newman was attacked by anonymous
writers.

> 'Who could affront a Lovely Woman ?
> Who, why the Reverend Mr. No Man
> A pretty Jesuit of a Vicar
> The Reverend Ruffian was in liquor.

'An outcast ! ! !   The unworthy priest should be cast out.'
Another rhymester wrote :

'There's not a rubber
Where *outcast* Jubber
Is not thought an injur'd Woman
There's not a party
Where young Men Hearty
Would not horsewhip Mr. Newman.'

This was addressed 'To the Revd. Parson Purblind, alias Paul Pry'.

The affair did not stop at Oxford but was taken up by the national press, even by *The Times*, and caused a minor summer scandal. Questions were asked in the House. More letters of abuse came in ; one lurid effusion painted the flames of hell and demanded what use it would be to Newman then to call on the Pope. His persecuting behaviour was instantly put down to incipient popishness. Abuse from the gutter, censure from *The Times*, was not pleasant, but worst of all was the discovery that his Bishop disapproved. 'In these reforming days such conduct was only calculated to disgust', he said to a third party. Newman at once wrote to explain that had there been time he would have consulted him before acting ; the Bishop, ignoring the question of principle, replied, perfectly truly, that the Vicar of St. Mary's had no legal right to refuse to marry Miss Jubber. Such was the result of the bondage to the State which Newman detested.

He wrote to his mother, 'Till the last hour I have felt like one man against a multitude. No one, apparently, to encourage me, and so many black averted faces that unless from my youth I had been schooled to fall back upon myself I should have been quite out of heart. I went and sat twenty minutes with Mrs. Small (the old Dame schoolmistress at Littlemore) by way of consolation.' However, he was now able to report that Keble and Pusey had written to him in support of his position. 'I seem as if I could bear anything now. I felt that I could not have done otherwise than I did. Yet it is very distressing to be alone. . . . I am more pleased at these letters than I can say. I had taken my vexation as a sort of punishment for my many sins, and did not expect thus to be comforted.'

A few friends might approve, but the great British public thought a parson who believed Sacraments more binding than human laws deserved to be horsewhipped. The persecuting Newman was showered with abuse and had to endure the contempt of his acquaintance, the persecuted Miss Jubber was married in Church just the same. And the Bishop backed public opinion and the State.

To Froude Newman wrote cheerfully, 'K. and P. and Williams

take my part, else I am solus, abused beyond measure by high and low — threatened with a pelting and prosecution — having anonymous letters — discountenanced by high church and low church. It should be you.' Later that year, in answer to Froude's request for further information, he told him 'nothing more came of it except some letters in the papers and plenty of most abusive articles in the vulgar town prints of Sunday'. Every now and then he wrote letters full of news and gossip for Froude which he called 'disgraceful trash' but hoped would amuse him. He also made a scrapbook of cuttings to send him. Some, he said, 'made me laugh most heartily as I stuck them in'.

Miss Jubber's was a case of conscience for Newman, and therefore he bore the imputation of bigotry as best he could, but in the same year it was noised all over Oxford that he had absented himself from Oriel Chapel so as not to receive communion with Whately. This rumour showed how completely the Apostolical rule about the treatment of separatists was misunderstood. People thought Newman cut his friends for holding divergent opinions. Whately himself wrote in October to know the truth of the matter. Newman was able to say that the sole reason for his absence from Oriel on that occasion was his having to administer the Sacrament in St. Mary's. But although he did not dream of separating from anyone who had not actively separated himself from the Church, Newman felt it would not be honest to pretend that he did not think Whately's principles extremely dangerous. At the same time Whately was his senior, an Archbishop, and had been kind to him. The correspondence is printed at the end of later editions of the *Apologia*.

Newman was careful to exonerate Whately himself from errors to which he believed the liberal principles led, but Whately chose to think Newman implicated him, and quoted a letter of his from eight years back, asking why he had not had it out with him, frankly, and asserting that it was Newman who had changed, not he. Newman, in reply, tried to explain, without being rude, that he had been very young when Whately took him up, that he had only gradually come to realize how fundamental their difference was, and that he did not like to remonstrate with someone who had been kind to him, or argue with an Archbishop about his views and acts. For the fact was that Whately had supported the Whig government in its suppression, the year before, of the Irish Sees. Newman, remembering Whately's opinion of the State's unwarrantable interference with the Church, would not believe at first that he had countenanced this act. But to

Whately it made a good deal of difference which party was in control of the actions of the State ; nor did he believe in real divine authority vested in the Church. His letters to Newman contain criticism of his personal conduct, Newman's the assertion of his right to hold views which implicitly criticized the opinions, not the conduct, of his old friend and teacher.

Whately never changed his opinion that Newman was aiming at power. He told Hawkins that he thought the extracts he had seen from Newman's sermons 'very little different from Romanism except in not placing the Pope at *Rome*'. In 1843–45 he became extremely rabid against the Tractarians and Newman in particular, saying that he could have had nothing to learn from 'the *Slanderer* Himself'. This was in a private letter to Hawkins, but he said plenty in public too. All the same, when Newman went to Dublin to found the Catholic University he approached a mutual friend to ask whether he might not call on Whately. He was warned off, twice. He told Henry Wilberforce of the 'anguish' it cost him to have to pass Whately in the street without a greeting ; but it was Whately who cut Newman, not *vice versa*. Yet when in 1874 Newman wrote the memoir of his Oxford days for St. John to read — afterwards used by Anne Mozley — there was no bitterness in his account of Whately, no hint that he had ascribed such base motives for Newman's difference from him.

At the turn of the year between 1834 and 1835 Newman wrote about eleven sermons for his second volume, published soon after. They were all on the theme of witnessing in word and deed to the objective Revelation lodged in the visible Church. At the same time he picked up his private account of what had happened to him in Sicily, begun in August, and wrote the passage on his own hollowness, as it seemed to him, in failing to *be* what he *knew*. He thought of himself 'as a pane of glass which transmits heat being cold itself' and wrote of the terrible day when he felt he must count the stars on the wallpaper to prevent himself losing his reason. Thus he used the humiliations of the self-knowledge forced on him by the fever, to keep himself straight while writing to rouse the conscience of others.

That January he had a painful return of one of the symptoms of his illness and had to go to London to consult a specialist. He wrote to Froude saying that 'it turns out to be something which might be serious, — but not if taken in time — so I am under discipline here, and have a field of pain opened upon me, which has thrown a new

light on the whole subject of martyrdom. . . . However I am very well
and in spirits, the worst is over and I trust to be set right altogether.'
Froude was alarmed by his vagueness. 'I wish you had been more
distinct in your last — you have set my imagination fancying all sorts
of horrible things . . . when I opened your letter I hardly recognized
the handwriting but I will hope for the best.' He was back in England
before Newman could explain what caused him such pain, so no other
record of it remains except a reference ten years later in a letter to
Jemima when he suddenly said, 'This day is memorable to me —
since ten years ago it was the day on which I had one of the most
formidable attacks of illness I ever had, though you at Rose Hill
knew so little about it'. He must have made his usual quick recovery.
It was soon after this that Henry began complaining to Rogers that
Newman was cherishing unchristian resentment against him for his
behaviour over his marriage. Apart from the letters which he did
not send to Henry, Newman did write to him about his pamphlet
The Foundations of the Faith assailed at Oxford. For they were in
the thick of another battle, this time about the admission of Dissenters
to the university.

This conflict of opinion, like nearly all Newman took part in at
Oxford, was unfortunately mixed up with the affairs of Dr. Hampden.
The Whigs, full of tolerance and kindness, wished to introduce a
measure suspending subscription to the Articles (the indispensable
condition of entering the university of Oxford) with the intention of
opening its amenities to intelligent Dissenters. The orthodox,
whether Zs or Apostolicals, opposed the measure on the ground that
it would introduce religious errors into what Henry Wilberforce truly
called 'the nursery of the Church of England'. To them it was a
question of truth and error in religious teaching ; to the liberals, of
liberty for the individual. It raised the question whether education
in the university was to continue to be conducted on Christian lines,
or to be secularized.

Hampden began the controversy in November 1834 with a
pamphlet advocating the admission of Dissenters on the ground that
differences of theological opinion were not important. 'No communion as such can be the one Church of Christ, since the separation
into distinct communions is an effect of discordant opinions ; and
the greatest disagreement of opinions may take place consequently,
without any real violation of the Unity of the Church. . . . Our
dissensions belong properly to our theological opinions, not to our
religion.' In effect he considered it made no difference what a man

believed about the nature of God, or of the Church, so long as he expressed confidence in Christ and behaved decently. He sent a copy of his pamphlet to Newman, who read it and replied, 'While I respect the tone of piety which the pamphlet displays I dare not trust myself to put on paper my feelings about the principles contained in it, tending (as they do in my opinion) altogether to make shipwreck of the Christian Faith'. Hampden answered, 'I thank you for your candour', and thought more free discussion desirable. He said he was 'quite ready to hear any arguments that may be alleged against my notions, to examine any such with freedom — and admit my error if I can be proved to be wrong'.

It was Henry Wilberforce who undertook to marshal the arguments against such a view. Newman gave him some advice, and Henry was careful to attack Hampden's 'notions', not his sincerity. But Hampden was a man who never saw the implications of his opinions, and was exceedingly annoyed to have them pointed out. The lively H. W. equated his view with Lord Brougham's dictum : 'That man shall no more render account to man for his belief, over which he himself has no control'. This Apostolical Tract came out anonymously, like all the others, and did not appear till May, when the situation had reached its highest pitch of excitement, for the measure was to be voted on in Convocation on May 19th. On the question of admitting Dissenters to the university the Apostolicals had all the establishment men on their side, throwing the liberals into a small minority. Orthodox Church-and-King men came up from the country to vote, cheered on, to the liberals' great disgust, by a mass of undergraduates gathered outside the Sheldonian Theatre. Arnold was revolted but not surprised by Oxford conservatism. 'I often think of the instructive Fact', he wrote to Hampden, 'that the Reformation was carried out by a Reforming Government supported by a small minority of the clergy, against the Majority of the Clergy, the Country Gentlemen and the Populace.' This was just what infuriated Froude about the Reformation, and it was most suitable that he should have arrived in England just in time to rush to Oxford and record his vote against the motion.

Anne Mozley, who was staying at Rose Bank, was in the town with Mrs. Newman and saw Froude 'as he alighted from the coach and was being greeted by his friends. He was terribly thin — his countenance dark and wasted, but with a brilliancy of expression and grace of outline which justified all his friends had said of him. He was in the Theatre the next day, entering into all the enthusiasm

of the scenes, and shouting his *Non Placet* with all his friends about
him. While he lived at all, he must *live* his life.' A day or two later
he left Oxford, never to return. From Devon he wrote cheerfully to
Newman, 'People don't look so horribly blank at me as they did,
though perhaps that is only from being accustomed to my grim
visage'. But the sight of him had been a shock to Newman. He
wrote to Rogers, 'Dear fellow, long as I have anticipated what I
suppose must come, I feel quite raw and unprepared'.

Froude came and went, the Dissenters were kept at bay, but
Hampden could not get over his rage at being attacked in *The Foundations of the Faith assailed at Oxford*. He was sure Newman was behind
it, but was temporarily baulked when Henry Wilberforce gave his
name. He succeeded in making Henry admit he had had assistance,
but Henry refused to divulge the name of his assistant. This was
just at the time when he was feeling that Newman was indulging in
unchristian resentment ; he was not in Oxford and his wife was
approaching her first confinement. But whatever he felt about Newman in private he stuck by him in public. Hampden was very cross.
'It is but right that society should have its eye on persons who can so
unfeelingly scatter their venom under a mask' ; he wrote to Henry,
'that at least one may not mistake them for *friends*'. Newman
authorized the publishers to give his name on inquiry, not of course
as author, but as editor.

In June Hampden boiled over. Newman copied his violent and
insulting letter, together with his own reply, for Froude's benefit.
'Sir, I have heard with disgust of the dissimulation, falsehood and
dark malignity of which you have been guilty', wrote Hampden.
He accused Newman of publishing lies and calumnies, of concealing
his name till it was extorted by the publishers. 'You have been
among the "crafty firsts" who have sent their "silly seconds" to
fight their mean and cowardly battles by their trumpery publications.
You have worked the machine but hid yourself behind it. . . . I
charge you with malignity because you have no other ground of
your assault on me but a fanatical persecuting spirit. I have done
no wrong or unkindness to you, but on the contrary have always
treated you with civility and respect. Have you (to take the lowest
ground) acted towards me in the manner of one gentleman to another ?
Would you have dared to act in such a way had you not taken
advantage of the sacred profession ?' Froude regarded this as the
nearest thing to a challenge one clergyman could make to another.
At that time duelling had not quite died out in England ; the code

of honour which upheld it was still very much alive : a gentleman
was considered directly responsible, at the risk of his life, for all his
words or actions.   Hampden was accusing Newman of using his
priesthood to shield himself from the consequences of dishonourable action.   Perhaps he had temporarily forgotten that he also was
a member of the sacred profession as well as a gentleman.   Insult,
in any case, could hardly go further.

The letter continued : 'I would readily submit to the heaviest
charge of erroneous doctrine which your proud orthodoxy could
bring against me, rather than exchange for your state of mind my
conscious satisfaction at having neither willed nor thought nor done
anything to hurt the feelings of a single person by what I have
written.'   He demanded that Newman should put his name to the
pamphlets, or he would take steps 'to expose' him.   He ended,
'Why did you employ coadjutors if you are ashamed of them, and
why should they be ashamed of such a master ?'

Such an angry letter was difficult to answer without getting
involved in recriminations or excuses.   Newman wrote his reply in
the third person, no doubt to insulate the quarrel as far as possible
from passions and keep it in the realm of facts.   He answered the
charges briefly ; he was Editor not author of the Tract — both
he and Wilberforce had given their names when required.   They
were not attacking Hampden but the opinions he had publicly put
forward, inviting discussion.   Newman reminded him that he had
expressed his own view directly and openly to Hampden himself,
as soon as he had read his pamphlet.   Still using the third person, he assured Hampden that he did not want to make their difference personal : 'At the same time, he certainly does recognize as
conceivable the existence of motives for approving or disapproving
the conduct of another, distinct from those of a personal nature'.
This distinction was lost on Hampden, who, in spite of holding
that differing opinions did not matter, invariably assumed that
people who attacked his own did so from mere malice.   He never
could see that his liberal principles might 'distress' others, as
Newman put it at the end of his letter, implying that Hampden
ought not to be too sure he had never hurt anyone's feelings.
Hampden was not even logical about anonymity, for when Woodgate, a solid Tractarian who remained an Anglican all his life,
published a signed pamphlet and wrote to him first to assure him
that no personal ill-feeling was intended, he angrily called him a
hypocrite.   Anyone who attacked his ideas was attacking him ; as

if anyone could really care about an idea! What had he done that people should be so unkind as to criticize him in public?

Newman was in trouble all round. Provost Hawkins had been told he had been preaching against him in St. Mary's and wrote a dignified remonstrance. Newman replied, 'I trust it is very unlike me to make charges against my superiors and seniors in the University publicly, in their absence, in the course of my parish teaching'. The sermon in question had been written before the dissension on Subscription, and had a general not a particular reference. But while Newman was accused of every kind of mean and cowardly and arrogant behaviour, he never, even in his private letters, ascribed to his opponents any unworthy motives or criticized their conduct or character. Rare was any humorous comment, even, like this to Froude on a stranger, the chaplain to the Bishop of Winchester: 'A specimen of donnishness grafted on to spiritualmindedness, i.e. a constrained way of behaving which is redolent of both conceits. At confirmation he sprawled about like the statues in St. John Lateran. Consider all this unsaid, carissime, and bury it in the folds of your mind: and really I reproach myself for my severity.'

1835–1836

'*Vale, dilectissime . . .*'

FROUDE was home, but not for long. In nine months he was dead.
Newman saw him only once, going down to Devonshire in September 1835. His long exile had not saved his health and had been to
him a hard trial, relieved only by long rides in strange country and
some mild teasing of a Z Bishop. His letters were nearly always
cheerful, but he suffered sometimes from feeling forgotten, especially
when a box of books and letters from Oxford went astray.

'My dear F, be comforted,' Newman said in November 1834,
'be sure that I, and I doubt not others think of you twice a day.
How I long to see you again, if so be ; I wish you knew how very
angry I am ; but, I suppose all this is for your good — you want a
taming in various ways — I suppose this discipline is to wean you
from overinterest in politics — I miss you continually in advice but
of course one is fond of what one does well, so you see you are
being taught to unlearn the world, the ecclesiastical as well as the
worldly world.' Having said that, he then proposed his latest plan
for Froude, that he should be a Bishop in India : 'there you might
be a Catholic and no one would know the difference'. The idea
amused him, but also made him think how many 'posts' there were
in the Kingdom of Christ. 'It is quite impossible that in some
way or other you are not destined to be an instrument of God's
purposes. Though I saw the earth cleave and you fall in, or heaven
open and a chariot appear, I should say just the same. God has ten
thousand posts of service. You might be of use in the central elemental fire, you might be of use in the depths of the sea. I wish I
knew in what state of mind you are. I so fear you are out of sorts.'

As a matter of fact Froude was out of sorts then. At Christmas
he wrote : 'There was a passage in a letter I have just received
from my Father that made me feel so infinitely dismal that I must
write to you about it. He says you have written to him to learn
something about me, and to ask what to do with my money. It

17. JOHN KEBLE
From an engraving after Richmond

16. EDWARD BOUVERIE PUSEY
From the drawing by Richmond

18. RICHARD WHATELY
From an engraving

19. THOMAS ARNOLD OF RUGBY
From the portrait by Thomas Phillips

20. ORIEL COLLEGE, SHOWING NEWMAN'S ROOMS
(middle row on right)

really made me feel as if I were dead, and you were sweeping up
my remains; and by the by, if I was dead, why should I be cut
off from the privilege of helping on the good cause?' Not so long
after, Newman was 'sweeping up the remains' and the book he
made of them precipitated the crisis of the Movement, both internally
and externally. Froude dead had a wider influence than Froude alive.

Froude felt starved of news. 'Do you know I am hungry and
thirsty for news of you?' he complained. Newman replied in
January 1835, after that year of difficulties and misunderstandings
(and now he was ill as well), 'I could say much, were it of use, of
my own solitariness now you are away . . .'. But he did not say
much. At this very moment Froude was writing, of an earlier
letter; 'I am ashamed of myself at having grumbled at you; your
letter almost made me cry. My blue devils are my only excuse,
and you may guess I have had a good dose of them.' Then at last
the lost box turned up with Newman's letter of gossip and news
from the summer before. 'What can have put it into your head
that your style is dry?' he said. 'The letter you wrote me in the
box was among the most amusing I ever received.'

Of course, as soon as he was back, letters went to and fro rapidly.
Newman was anxious to get his opinion on everything that turned
up, but alas, Froude was sometimes too ill to answer. 'I am sick
of expecting a letter,' Newman wrote in acute anxiety, 'for the last
week I have every day made sure of one and been disappointed. I
cannot help fearing you are not well. . . . I must (so be it) come
down to you before vacation ends, to get some light struck out by
collision.' It must have been heart-rending to read Froude's cheerful excuses: 'My dearest Newman, I am afraid you will be grumbling
in your heart at me for putting off writing so long. But really I am
not to blame, as I have not put pen to paper for a fortnight, except
yesterday, when I began a letter to you upside down.'

Newman's delay in coming down to Devonshire was due partly
to his being busy, not only with his private work, but with his parish,
the confirmation and other duties; partly too it was due to lack
of cash. 'Ricarde Frater . . .' he scribbled, explaining this. Latin
forms of address, classical or from the Pauline epistles, came into
their letters about this time. 'Dulcissime . . .' Froude wrote;
'Carissime . . .' Newman replied. It expressed the affection they
felt, already knowing there was little time left to say anything, but
the habit was not exclusive to them. 'Mi amicissime, N has left
me these lappets,' Keble wrote on the flap of one of Newman's

letters, '. . . we are very snug but want you, yours lovingly JK.'
Newman scattered his 'Carissime' lavishly among his friends ; even
James Mozley became 'Carissime' on occasion. But the younger
ones did not quite feel able to reply so familiarly. 'Antiquissime',
said Rogers whimsically.

Froude's letters, when he could write, were as forceful and full
of fun as ever. 'I have heard from my sisters the efficacy of your
opuscula in leading captive silly women', he teased Newman, telling
how an invalid girl was converting Peculiars with Newman's sermons,
and how 'a learned lady (a very good and sensible person, by the
bye) was poking away industriously at your "Arians".' Newman
was anxious not to go too far in an article on Monasticism he was
writing for Rose's *British Magazine*. Froude said : 'I cannot see
the harm in losing influence with people when you can only retain
it by sinking the points on which you differ from them. What is
the good of influence except to influence people ?' And on another
question : 'You lug in the Apostles' Creed and talk about expansions.
What is the end of expansions ? Will not the Romanists say that
their whole system is an expansion of the Holy Catholic Church
and the Communion of Saints ?' He protested too at what he considered Newman's 'cursing and swearing' against Rome. 'What
good can it do ? I call it uncharitable to an excess. How mistaken
we may ourselves be on many points that are only gradually opening
to us.'

At last, on September 15th, Newman went down to Dartington
and stayed till October 11th, as long as he could before term began.
Indeed, as the coach at Exeter was full and he had to wait till the
next day, he was actually late, for the first time in his history, causing
surprise and alarm to Provost Hawkins, who was used to his always
being there, the only senior member who never missed. For just
over three weeks, in the warm green Devon which still seemed to
Newman a place of dangerous enchantment, the two friends were
able to talk and argue and plan to their hearts' content, no longer
dependent on tiresome mails, boats and coaches — but for the last
time. At the end of their correspondence Newman afterwards
noted : 'I took my last farewell of R.H.F. on Sunday in the evening,
sleeping at Exeter. When I took leave of him his face lighted up
and almost shone in the darkness, as if to say that in this world
we were parting for ever.'

After he had gone Froude wrote : 'Don't be conceited if I tell
you how much you are missed here. . . . Now you are gone I

clearly see that a step has been gained. Even I come in for my
share of the benefit in finding myself partially extricated from the
unenviable position hitherto occupied by me — that of a prophet
in his own country.' In spite of his anxiety Newman responded
with letters full of humour. Bunsen, the famous Lutheran they
had met in Rome, was in Oxford, talking ceaselessly and pro-
nouncing on the Movement. 'He says that, if we succeed, we shall
be introducing Popery without authority, Protestantism without
liberty, Catholicism without universality and Evangelism without
spirituality. In the greater part of which censure doubtless you
agree.'

Unable to get down at Christmas he sent Rogers as a substitute.
'We had many arguments and proses', said Froude when he had
gone. 'I do believe he hates the meagreness of Protestantism as
much as either of us.' Rogers told him a tale of woe from Oxford ;
'Golius (Golightly) has rebelled, Rogers says, and the Theological
meetings go flat, and old Mozley won't work'. Newman would not
have it so, writing on Christmas Eve : 'As to our being out of joint
here — no ! Golius would not *goliare* or γολίζειν i.e. be *golius*
unless he acted as he did. At present he goes about declaiming
against my patronage of Clement of Alexandria, my incaution, my
strange sayings ; so very unsatisfactory, such a pity, as hurting my
influence etc. He is such as to take a keystone for an excrescence
and insist on its removal.' Wishing them a happy new year a week
later he remarked of a town meeting at which he had had to preside,
as Rural Dean, that it had 'opened a new view'. 'I suspect the
Dissenters here are hating me with a perfect hatred. I hear there
is a large party of people who abominate me, others speaking more
favourably. I have been told I am "a marked man ; there is
no question of it." I am getting callous. I believe all this would
have made me quite sick at one time, but somehow I wag on
sluggishly. . . .'

Froude and Rogers laughed over these letters, and Rogers went
back to Oxford fairly hopeful of him. But Froude's spirit, so
strongly alive, deceived him ; for he was fast wasting away. His
last letter, no different from usual, came at the end of January 1836.
'I don't gain flesh in spite of all the milk.' On his own birthday
Newman wrote to Jemima : 'God is teaching me, it would seem,
to depend on Him only ; for as perhaps Rogers has told you I am
soon to lose dear Froude — which, looking forward to the next
twenty-five years of my life, and its probable occupations, is the

greatest loss I could have. I shall be truly widowed, yet I hope to bear it lightly.'

'All hope of his recovery is gone,' wrote Archdeacon Froude at last. 'But we have the comfort at seeing him quite free from pain. His thoughts turn continually to Oxford, to yourself and Mr. Keble.' A few days later : 'Your friend is still alive. . . . On no account, my dear Mr. Newman, would I have you come down.' The fatal news was written at last, on February 28th, 'My dear son died this day'.

'Newman opened the letter in my room,' Tom Mozley wrote to his sister, 'and could only put it into my hand, with no remark. He afterwards, Henry Wilberforce told me, lamented with tears (not a common thing for him) that he could not see Froude just to tell him how much he felt he had owed him.' Newman wrote to Bowden : 'He was so very dear to me that it is an effort to me to reflect on my own thoughts about him. I can never have a greater loss, looking on for the whole of my life ; for he was to me, and was likely to be ever, in the same degree of familiarity which I enjoyed with yourself in our Undergraduate days. . . . Everything was so bright and beautiful about him, that to think of him must always be a comfort.' To Miss Giberne he wrote, 'As to dear Froude I cannot speak of him consistently with my own deep feelings about him, though they are all bright and pleasant. It is a loss such as I can never have again. I love to think and muse upon one who had the most angelic mind of any person I ever fell in with — the most unearthly, the most gifted. I have no painful thoughts in speaking of him (though I cannot trust myself to speak of him to many) but I feel the longer I live, the more I shall miss him.'

At the back of his diary in 1837, when he was preparing Froude's *Remains* for publication, are the scribbled lines : '*Vale dilectissime, desideratissime, usque ad illum Diem qui te, paucissimis notum, omnibus patifaciet qui fueris*'. (Farewell, most loved, so much missed, until that Day which shall make you, known to so few, manifest to all as you were.)

1836

The Persecution of Hampden

IN the quiet little church of Ewelme there is a memorial tablet to Burton, Regius Professor of Divinity in the University of Oxford; next on the list of incumbents is the name of Renn Dickson Hampden. Nothing to show now the tremendous storm that succession evoked, revealing, as by a flash of lightning, the landscape of religion in England. The post, which carried the living of Ewelme with it and a fine house there, was a Crown appointment, and one of great responsibility in the days when the university was the only training ground of the clergy. In 1836, when Burton died, the Whigs were in power. Lord Melbourne received a list of names from Howley, Archbishop of Canterbury, which was said to include the names of Keble, Pusey and Newman. The Archbishop had read, and liked, *The Arians*, which perhaps accounts for Newman's name.

Newman was anxious that Keble should have the position, and wrote to press him not to refuse it even if offered by a liberalizing government. About his own chances he wrote to Froude, then still alive: 'For myself, Carissime, I think I may say with a clear conscience I have no desire for it. . . . I am too indolent and like my own way too well to wish it. . . . I should be entangled in routine business, which I abhor. I should be obliged to economize and play the humbug in a way I should detest, and I have no love for the nuisance of house and furniture — adding up bills, settling accounts, hiring servants and getting up the price of butcher's meat. I covet £200 or £300 a year more and that is all — all this does not apply to Keble who is already entangled in these delights' — (Keble had just got married) — 'who, moreover, would not have the unpopularity, the fame of being a party man which I have, nor the care of the Tracts and the engagements of agitation. I am more useful as I am; but Keble is a light too spiritual and subtle to be seen unless put on a candlestick. Yet at the same time, were the office actually offered me, I should be in a puzzle — and would trust you to decide for me.'

Lord Melbourne did not dream of offering it to him ; he wanted a Liberal, and wrote to Whately and Copleston for advice. They told him Hampden was a safe man. Melbourne, ignoring the Archbishop's recommendations, appointed him.

'We were electrified by the intelligence!' wrote Palmer in 1843, recapitulating the history of the Movement. It was not Hampden who was electrifying, but the appointment to such an important post of a man of novel religious views who advocated the admission of Dissenters to the university. Conservatives were angry at having a Liberal thrust on them ; even the Evangelicals were suspicious because he belonged to the school which applied critical principles to Scripture. This made a large majority against the appointment, and a committee met in Corpus Christi College, under the chairmanship of Vaughan Thomas, to discuss ways and means of opposing it. It was by no means composed of Apostolicals, but Newman and Pusey were on it. They dissuaded the committee from making any personal attack on Hampden through the newspapers, insisting that it was not the man but his theology which constituted the danger.

Newman was asked to get up a pamphlet explaining these dangers to the public. He sat up all night to write it, and it was printed within a few days. Newman put in one column statements from Hampden's Bampton Lectures of 1832 and in the other his own elucidations of their implications : it became known, by the first word of its title, as *Elucidations*. Thus he demonstrated in the simplest way that liberal principles logically issued in viewing Christianity as no more than a system of human philosophy. For instance, Hampden's statements carried to their conclusion would support the Socinian heresy that Jesus was no more than a man. This was the teaching of the Unitarians, at that time rapidly increasing in numbers and influence, since they attracted many intellectual people who baulked at the supernatural but admired the character of Christ. But Newman was careful to exonerate Hampden from personal heresy. 'It is not hereby insinuated that he himself agrees with them in their peculiar errors', he said.

He was in some difficulty in publishing this pamphlet, from the unfortunate personal relations between Hampden and himself. He did not want the personal issue confusing the theological, yet he had no wish to shirk responsibility for what he said. The pamphlet was issued anonymously, but in the preface he said that the author's name would be given on inquiry at the publishers. Thus he hoped that the general public would read it for the views it contained, while in

Oxford it would be known who was responsible. As the row quickly
spread to London and national newspapers secured correspondents
in Oxford, his authorship became immediately and generally known,
and the anonymity was called cowardice and dissimulation. Since
he had ensured that all the opponents he was likely to meet would
know the truth, this was hardly fair, but popular journalism has never
been noted for just discrimination. After *Elucidations*, all the pamphlets on the Tractarian side were signed ; it was Hampden's supporters who were, almost to a man, anonymous.

This did not prevent Hampden from taking all attacks on his
opinions as slanders against his character ; righteously indignant he
wrote to beg interference from the Duke of Wellington, Oxford's
Chancellor, and to the Archbishop of Canterbury, demanding redress.
The Duke remarked dryly that he had no seat on the Hebdomadal
Board, whereas Hampden had ; he advised him to prosecute his
own case. The Archbishop, with dignity, let him understand that
there were other places besides Oxford where liberal religious views
were unpopular. Hampden could not understand it ; he pursued the
Archbishop for months with protestations of belief in God and the
Church of England, and of his own moral rectitude, and at last
published the whole correspondence in the conviction that it showed
what an injured man he was. He had the satisfaction that his own
view, that he was a blameless man suffering persecution, was widely
shared by his fellow-liberals, and by the popular press.

Pamphlets were hurled to and fro. Whately was amused at a
supposed encyclical from the Pope addressed to his Oxford col-
laborators. 'Softly, John!' was the title of another, 'Or a word of
caution to Calvin not to set up for pope in a Protestant university'.
Whately remarked cheerfully to Hampden, 'Your works appear to
some Socinian — so does the Bible'. He called Newman and his
friends 'the Protestant papists'. But the biggest outburst came after
the meeting of Convocation in March at which a Statute was proposed to suspend the new Professor of Divinity from some of his
faculties. This was not the work of the Tractarians, who thought it
directed too much against the person and too little against the
opinions of the Professor. But none of them were Heads of Houses
or had seats on the Hebdomadal Board, which decided the question.
The Statute was a Z measure, but the Apostolicals were prepared to
vote for it, in default of another. There was a great uproar in Convocation and it was plain the Statute would have been carried, had
not the Proctors interposed their veto. Not beaten, the Corpus

Committee was determined to bring the matter up the following term, when new Proctors would be in office.

Five days before the March Convocation, at the end of the Lent term, Hampden gave his Inaugural Sermon in St. Mary's ; it was printed and widely distributed. St. Mary's was crowded ; Tom Mozley said all the university was invited. Hampden now had the opportunity to defend his liberal principles, as the bold Thomas Arnold would undoubtedly have done. Instead, while stating that he repudiated nothing, he astonished his audience by making a personal declaration of faith in almost Evangelical terms, and an emotional appeal for fair play. 'I come to you under a cloud of suspicion and clamour', he said. 'I am at all times ready to meet fair and free discussion, but to misrepresentation and violence with God's help I will never yield.' He never, during the whole episode, discussed anything or attempted the slightest defence of his opinions ; he was too busy defending himself. He found an able defendant in Arnold, who wrote up the scene, at which he was not present, for the *Edinburgh Review*. 'As the Professor looked round upon his audience he saw the well known faces of his persecutors', said Arnold dramatically ; including, of course, that of the Grand Inquisitor and fanatic for 'Church Government', the Vicar of St. Mary's.

Arnold seized the occasion for a full-scale attack on the Apostolicals ; his article entitled 'Oxford Malignants' appeared in the April number of the famous Whig periodical, unsigned, as was the custom, but everyone soon knew the author. Arnold started from the assumption, which he believed self-evident truth, that all progress must be good : 'the heresy of one period becomes the orthodox faith of another'. The Reformation, the Revolution of 1688 which was the beginning of Whig ascendancy, were steps in enlightenment of which the Liberals were now the heirs ; they had been consistently opposed by the lumpish inertia of the multitude and by the intrigues of a pernicious Church party representing religious atavism and human tyranny which 'always defeated in the end has yet always impeded the progress of the good'. On this view the Apostolicals appeared as 'a few obscure fanatics' inheriting the mantle of the non-jurors, who had refused to break their oaths to James II, papist though he was, and retarded the Whig cause by remaining an anomalous obstinate minority, like a cancer in the political body. Through one of the non-jurors, Arnold was able to get in a hit at Newman. 'Hickes, a man like one or two of the Oxford conspirators, much vaunted by his party for the pretended holiness of his life, because he used a sentimental religious style of excessive religious feeling in his prayers and other compositions, found his religion perfectly compatible with falsehood and malignity.'

Arnold made no attempt to answer, or even to grasp, the intellectual principles of the party he was attacking; indeed, he could not believe they had any. 'If it was merely *intellectual error* it would have to be confuted firmly and plainly but with tenderness to the persons of those who held it, but the attack on Dr. Hampden bears upon it the character not of error but of *moral wickedness*. When they run down a good and pious individual . . . we see nothing of Christian zeal but much of the mingled fraud and baseness and cruelty of fanatical persecution. And for such persecution the plea of conscience is not admissible; it can only be a conscience so blinded by wilful neglect of highest truth, or so corrupted by the habitual indulgence of evil passions that it rather aggravates than excuses the guilt of those whom it misleads.'

Lesser papers than the *Edinburgh Review* took up the cry of persecution, nor did they, like Arnold, disdain to mention the name of the cowardly author of *Elucidations*. It was a gift to the journalists to discover from Oxford informants that Newman was Hampden's 'disappointed rival'; that settled it that he had got up the whole agitation out of jealousy and the desire for revenge. But there was Popery behind it too. 'Mr. Newman is said to be aiming at establishing a quasi-Catholic scheme', said the *Globe*, on April 28th, and went on next day to be shocked at 'the moral terrorism with which this intellectual tyranny is enforced'. They had allowed Newman to be honest and sincere, but published a letter from an indignant correspondent who maintained 'Honesty and sincerity afford no valid plea on behalf of persecution'. The persecutor, he said, 'harasses and destroys those who differ from him in opinion . . . visiting others as sincere and honest as himself with deprivation of office, forfeiture of goods, fines, imprisonment, torture and death'. He hastened to add that he 'disclaimed imputing to Mr Newman the least sinister motive'. He need not have feared, if he did, a retort from Newman that he had never suggested that Hampden should be tortured; for Newman made it a point of honour never to reply to personal attacks unless they also involved an attack on the Faith. After his pamphlet he never published another word on Hampden's case, though it looked as if he did because a tract he had written earlier, on the Apostolical Tradition, in opposition to the views expressed in the Bampton Lectures, came out while the row was on.

Newman's *Arians* suddenly came in for a great deal of publicity, as it was found a convenient mine of 'papistical doctrines'. The *Edinburgh* had already given it a long review, in the course of which the liberal view of Christianity and the Reformation was declared more fully than was usual with its defenders. 'The Reformation was achieved in the name and by the authority of *Reason*. . . . It asserted and for ever established the right of every man to judge and decide for himself what Scripture reveals and requires.' Why Scripture should reveal anything was a question which had not yet occurred to them, though the anti-rational Mr. Newman was already considering it. 'A particular theory of metaphysics can never be the sign of those that love Jesus', said the Edinburgh Reviewer. 'And therefore we strenuously war against Creeds because they chain down men's minds to one single form of speculative truth.' Yet he became excited at the idea of anyone loving Jesus without subscribing to the particular metaphysical theory that he was God. He firmly believed in the right of Parliament to decide religion ; the Reformation and the Revolution of 1688 had 'alike proclaimed that every society is supreme over all human affairs, and possesses both the right and the power to create, modify, or abolish all offices and institutions whatsoever'. He was thinking of the past but Newman was looking to the future. In just these two principles, that the individual human reason is the supreme authority in the world of ideas, and that the civil society is the supreme authority in the realm of action, Newman saw intellectual and moral chaos coming upon mankind. Yet Arnold thought he was obsessed with Church Government and Hampden that he was jealous because he was not a Moral or a Divinity Professor at Oxford.

In April the Corpus Committee issued a manifesto in answer to all these bitter attacks in the press. 'No imputation has been thrown on Dr. Hampden's personal religion.' They had come forward 'with deep reluctance, without one feeling of bitterness, or arrogant desire to condemn others, but under a keen sense of duty which they owe to the character and office of the university ; to the students placed under their care ; to the rising generation of the clergy ; to the Nation and to the Church'. The second Convocation was held on May 5th ; a great many non-resident members of the university, especially country clergy, came up to record their votes against the innovator. Arnold thought them, as he told Hampden, 'about as capable of listening to Truth and Reason as the irrational and inanimate instruments by which they are con-

veyed to Oxford'. The Statute was passed by a huge majority. It
was a triumph for the Zs rather than the Apostolicals, but they were
regarded by the general public as the engineers of it. On the spot,
however, Evangelicals were heard to say that they hoped next time
they would be voting against the 'handful of semi-papal divines'
as the papers called them.

The Statute in fact made little difference to Hampden. He was
appointed by the government and not removable by the university ;
he was soon exercising his functions as Divinity Professor without
hindrance. In the following December Newman himself had to
come before him to sign the Articles on taking his B.D. He did not
have to dispute, because he had done so earlier, obliging Arnold
when he could not find an opponent. The disputations were displays of talent, not tests of orthodoxy, but Hampden later indulged
in a little persecution of his own by refusing to approve candidates
who professed Apostolical opinions.

Hampden's martyrdom did not prevent him from doing very
well for himself out of his plurality of offices. He did relinquish the
chair of Moral Philosophy, but for eleven years he remained Regius
Professor, Rector of Ewelme, Canon of Christ Church and Head
of St. Mary Hall. To retain a Canonry at the Cathedral while
Head of a Hall was unprecedented, even in those days. At the end
of this period, in 1847, he became Bishop of Hereford, in the teeth
of an almost united episcopal opposition, still proclaiming his ill-
treatment with injured innocence. In 1836 he evidently confided
his ambitions to Whately, who told him it was 'natural to wish to
rise in his profession'. Whately confessed his own desire for literary
fame and originality, but said he tried to act 'as if he were actuated
only by a pure single desire of serving the public'. A Bishopric
to him was a particular kind of political post, as it was to Copleston,
the ex-Provost of Oriel. But Copleston, a more cautious man than
Whately, advised Hampden to proceed with equal caution, and
warned him against telling an ignorant public the full extent of his
views : thus practising the policy of economy and equivocation so
much censured in the Tractarians.

But if Hampden gained by being persecuted, Newman certainly
lost by his part in the persecution. His general reputation as an
arrogant bigot and crypto-papist was now firmly established. He
made no public defence of himself but he answered private accusations, such as that brought against him by Grenfell, an Oxford man
and once a pupil of Froude, now teaching at Rugby, who wrote

and reproached him for cutting him on a mere matter of Church
Government. Newman said it was a matter not of government but
of principle, but he would not enter into argument by letter. 'Next
I do not at all know what you mean by "separation". That I am
very much grieved by your mode of viewing things is certain, and
that it is impossible (as is plain) that a man holding views so practically different from yours as I believe mine to be, can be very
familiar with you, but as to separating from you, it seems to me that
separation is not justifiable except from those who openly and distinctly act the part of heretics and schismatics. . . . Believe me, I
had no intention of withdrawing from you when you were in Oxford.
If I did not call on you in return it was because I did not know
where you were. . . . Nor had I any intention of behaving uncivilly
to you in the Theatre, which you seem to think — and which, if
so, I am very sorry for. I heartily wish we could talk together,
not that any direct end would be answered by it, but that you might
see I am not what rumours may have led you to think me.'

1836

'God intends me to be lonely'

THIS was a year of change for Newman. In the middle of the Hampden row, in April, Jemima was married to John Mozley. Although not the eldest of the many Mozley brothers, John was the one chosen to succeed his father in the family printing business. He was not sent to Oxford, but he had visited it the year before, when the Mozleys came down in force to see young James receive the coveted Essay prize, and were 'lionized' over Oxford by the Newmans. John Mozley was square-faced and solid, with none of Tom's irresponsible charm. Tom was nearly late for the ceremony; he had lent his best trousers the night before to Henry Wilberforce for an evening party. Being a husband and a father had not changed Henry much, said James Mozley; 'he is just the same perfectly irresistibly ludicrous person as he always was'.

The wedding party, as described by Maria Mozley, was very gay. She it was who made Mr. Newman wear white gloves and put his black ones in his pocket, in spite of Tom, who said he never would. Much to Harriett's annoyance Newman was not there to ride with his sister; he had gone off walking across the fields. Everything went well and the breakfast was a great success: 'Mr. Newman cut the bride cake as if he was used to it', and Golightly was there talking all about his aunts and his aunts' wills, to Anne's amusement. Maria was sorry she had not brought her music 'but I had no notion Mr. Newman had any time to play. He wished I had brought Beethoven's long trio from my description.'

Jemima and John Mozley went off to begin their married life in Derby and Anne stayed to keep Harriett company. Less than three weeks afterwards, Mrs. Newman, who had not been well for some time, suddenly collapsed. Anne Mozley mentioned the strain of the recent entertaining, but not what she must have found harder to bear, the shocking publicity of the newspaper attacks on John. At first it was not realized how seriously she was ill, and a note to

John went astray, so that he only knew her danger a couple of days before the end. He at once called in a second medical opinion, but her case was pronounced hopeless. Short as her illness was, her mental wandering so distressed the family that they felt death came as a release. She died on May 17th ; John and Harriett were both with her.

She was not an old woman, and her sudden death was unexpected and a great shock to her eldest son. He was haunted by their recent misunderstandings ; even in their last conversation she had been hurt by something he said, mistaking his meaning. He thought of the time, two years ago, 'after I had fainted away', as he told Jemima, 'my Mother most kindly stooping down to take up my feet and put them on the sofa. I started up — I could not endure it. I saw she was hurt, yet I did not know how to put things right. I felt it something quite shocking that any one, above all she, should so minister to me. Nay, when I seemed rude it often arose from feelings very different from what appeared.' Now it was too late to put these little things right.

Up to the time of the funeral, James Mozley wrote home, 'Newman was dreadfully dejected, his whole countenance perfectly clouded with grief'. Anne remembered how at the service 'he remained still kneeling at the altar when all was over, lost in prayer and memory, till at length Mr. Williams, who had officiated, touched his shoulder to recall him to the necessity of joining the mourning train'. But when they came back from the funeral 'the sun was in the house again', and he made a resolute effort to resume his usual manner. For the next few days he stayed at Rose Bank and took them for long walks to Shotover and Bagley Wood. The sight of the summer country recalled to him the wonders of the Sicilian landscape, and he told Anne something of his illness there. Always at moments of crisis the vision of Sicily and what had happened there would return to his mind.

It was right that Sicily should be remembered, because the effect of this visitation, three years later, was to separate him further from the affairs of this world and centre his life yet more intensely on the work God had then given him to do. Everything was mysterious. Last year, he confided to Jemima, when he was so hard up for money, he had earnestly prayed that 'God would either give me the means of doing what I wished to do towards you all or remove the necessity'. He was thinking hopefully of something like a legacy, but now he felt as if, unawares, he had been praying

for his mother's death. 'To pray seems to be using an edged tool.'
Yet had she lived another ten years, how much they both would
have suffered! Jemima's marriage was a happier answer to his
prayers. Now Harriett went to stay in Derby, and the sisters were
anxious lest John should be lonely. 'I am not more lonely than I
have been for a long while', he replied. 'God intends me to be
lonely.'

A week later the break with the past was completed when Tom
Mozley proposed to Harriett and was accepted. Tom wrote to
Newman for his consent and the reply must have been warm for
he was soon scribbling in joyful surprise : 'I have scarcely time to
say anything, but if I had a day I could not express the delight your
lines afforded me. I confess I marvel to see the confidence with
which you commit your sister to one so weak and dependent as I
am. I knew of course I should only see a fresh example of your
tenderness and affectionateness, but I hardly could calculate on
such an expression of your opinion of me.' Harriett wrote, 'Everyone is delighted and surprised at your exalted notions of Tom and
your affection'.

In spite of his consent, Newman was anxious about Harriett ;
she was talking a great deal about duty, having talked before so
much of taste and feeling. He had no idea she cared for Tom,
though Jemima had been teasing her about it for months. Letters
passed between him and Jemima : 'I thought it came suddenly
upon her, the very idea — and she could not all of a sudden begin
to look at a person in a different light from what she had done', he
said. But it was he who had to adjust himself to the idea, not
Harriett. Tom seemed so young, and Harriett was his senior. But
then 'everyone took Harriett for a child', because she was so small
and lively ; most people thought Jemima the elder sister. He
could not help a sigh of disappointment that some plan of his own
for Harriett had come to nothing ; apparently he had introduced
someone hoping that he and Harriett might 'form an attachment'.
Was this Rogers, who never intended to follow a clerical career ?
Whoever it was, brotherly artifice failed ; Tom was the chosen man.
Newman comforted himself with the thought that his mother's
feelings towards Tom (whom she had not liked) had changed
during the last few months. After all, he concluded, 'one cannot
have everything one's own way ; one cannot pick and choose in
this life and where was a match without something in it which
might have been altered for the better ?'

Once convinced that Harriett's decision was not only guided by duty, he was generous with assistance. He sent her £30 for her trousseau, wishing it was more, and wishing he had been able to give the same to Jemima. He hoped Tom would accept the furniture and plate from Rose Bank; it would be 'the greatest comfort to be free from the charge of both without any breach of duty'. Next there was the question of finding a living for Tom; there happened to be a college living vacant at Cholderton, near Salisbury. 'Tell Tom I went on receipt of his letter to the Provost feigning some indifferent business and when I nabbed him letting out Tom's purpose as to Cholderton. . . . I assure you it affected him greatly and he replied as if in sudden pain that he must take time to think of it. So I was dismissed and am quite disconsolate.' But Tom got Cholderton. Newman related how he had teased Eden, a contemporary of Tom and an odd character. 'Eden has some lionesses here for a week and talked in such a strain about them, I thought they were three old women — they turn out to be two young ones, and not bad looking — so I taxed him with it to-day when he was in the midst of one of his pshaws about them, and told him I feared he would think better and take Cholderton at which he fell so complimented, abashed etc that I was obliged to tell him Cholderton was gone. . . . Tell H,' he ended, 'if she manages to make T. M. read she will do what *I* have never been able to do.'

This was all in July, but when he heard they planned their marriage for September he did not like its being so soon after their mother's death. 'Perhaps I am superstitious about these things, but I do not like it.' However, he merely expressed his opinion, and when they preferred their own, said no more. He was in good spirits. Sending his love to all the Derby Mozleys he said, 'Which please to give always for I always mean it, and understand that the twirl of the J of John in my signature means it in cipher' — and gave the J a much bigger twirl than usual.

The marriage took place in Derby on September 27th, and proved a happy one. Jemima was soon receiving letters from Harriett telling how Tom had chased her all round the house and put her in the pigsty, and only consented to let her out because guests were coming to dinner. Both were full of energy and high spirits. Tom, who fancied himself as an expert on architecture, was soon happily employed in altering the parsonage and rebuilding the church. The house was comfortably large, but the church was tiny; on crowded Sundays men sat on the altar and the font was used as an umbrella

stand.   High time for a Tractarian Vicar, even such an unclerical one
as boisterous Tom.   He was very popular in the village, and at the
Coronation feast for the young Queen the next year, someone chalked
up on a wall, 'Long live Mr. Mozley, Beef and Strong Beer!'

So now the Iffley house was given up, and Newman for the first
time since he was twenty-three was free of the responsibility for his
family.   He was thirty-five, and now had no other home but Oriel.
He lived in his two rooms, inferior to many of the sets then given to
undergraduates, next to the chapel in the corner of the quadrangle
opposite to the Provost's lodgings.   Opening out of the bedroom
there was a narrow way through behind the oriel window into the
gallery of the chapel, making a sort of passage or cupboard to the set.
Whately used to hang dried herrings on a string in there, when he
had the rooms.   Newman in 1830 had a shower bath in it and later
used to say his prayers there.   Tom Mozley asserted that he once
heard him doing so from outside in the quad, and told him, but it
might be one of his tall stories.   In here Newman kept a picture Miss
Giberne sent him of the saints praying round the throne of God.   He
told her that whenever he went in there he was 'tempted to say
"What? are you all at it still?" if that were a reverent and proper
speech.   It seems an impressive emblem of the perpetual intercession
of the saints perfected, waiting for Christ's coming.'

Newman's sitting-room was not big, with a window on each side
and a moulded ceiling.   It was full of books, and the only sign of
luxury was a clean towel to wipe them with.   He had a crucifix, with
the figure removed, over his fireplace, his favourite picture of Charles
I, the Anglican martyr, and some others.   He entertained friends in
the Common Room, giving breakfasts and dinners to streams of
visitors who wanted to talk to him.   In one sense it may have been
a lonely life, but in others it certainly was not, and he sometimes
began to feel it was too comfortable and wish for a more monastic
discipline.   Probably this desire was increased when he began to read
regularly the offices of the Breviary.   It was Froude's Breviary.   The
Archdeacon had asked him to choose a book as a keepsake; he had
asked for Butler, but it was bespoken.   Rogers, who was with him,
said, 'Take that', indicating the Breviary.   The little volumes became
familiar companions.   There was not much in them that seemed
corrupt; he only hesitated to use the antiphons of the Blessed
Virgin, ancient and simple as they were, and devoted as he was to her.
It was not the Anglican usage to address her directly, and he felt it
would be disloyal to do so without authority.   He kept this rule till

he left the Church of England.   The daily office was all psalms, which
he knew and loved so well already, and lessons, either from the Bible
or from the Fathers or from legends of the saints and martyrs.   To
use this form of prayer every day could not but mould him ever more
deeply in Catholic faith and practice.

Meanwhile, as well as writing Tracts and books and sermons to
help on the Movement, he had his parish.   Attached to St. Mary's
was a village called Littlemore, some four miles out of Oxford on the
road to Henley.   The places had been connected since the Middle
Ages, when there was a Mynchery or nunnery, of Our Lady of Littlemore, which Newman believed had been instrumental in the foundation of St. Mary's.   At the Reformation the nunnery had been dis-
solved and fell into ruins, and the village which had grown up round
it was left isolated and without church or chapel.   So it remained till
Newman became Vicar of St. Mary's.   He used to walk out and visit
the people, and when his mother and sisters moved to Iffley they
became very active in the village, started a school and gave food and
clothing where it was needed.   Littlemore had about 200 inhabitants,
all poor labourers.   There was no gentleman's house anywhere near.
It was considered a rough, wild place, and the children like little
bears.   It was Newman's ambition to build a church for them, and
the foundation stone was laid by his mother in 1835, with much local
ceremony and interest.   Miss Giberne sketched the scene, with
people crowding round the edge of the quarry-like foundations, and
Newman in a tall hat.   Now, after his mother's sudden death, it was
completed and ready for the dedication ceremony, which took place
a few days before Harriett's wedding, on September 22nd, a festival
kept every year afterwards.

It was a plain little building in Gothic style, like a barn with a
pointed roof and narrow lancet windows, later filled with painted
glass.   There was a stone altar and in the centre panel of the arcading
on the wall behind it, a stone cross.   This was considered exceedingly
popish.   When Newman was adjusting this cross a shy young Fellow
of Magdalen, John Rouse Bloxam, came timidly in at the door.
Newman turned round and saw him, and asked him if he thought it
looked right.   Bloxam, who had a passion for liturgical furniture, and
had gazed enviously after Newman and Rogers as they walked round
Addison's Walk talking eagerly, was overjoyed to be noticed.   He
became one of Newman's curates and friends.   When they were both
very old men he used to write every year on the Littlemore feast, as
often as not happily recalling this incident.

The little church was quite crowded, with Oxford people on one side and villagers on the other, for the consecration, and Bishop Bagot came. 'Williams read and I preached,' Newman wrote to Bowden. 'The east end was quite beautiful. We had a profusion of bright flowers, in bunches, all about the chapel. The Bishop was much pleased.' He asked to read the sermon afterwards. Flowers were considered a frivolity only suitable to popish chapels in those days. Twenty years later Hawkins wrote disgustedly to Charles Marriott about St. Mary's : 'What can make you dress it up with *flowers*!' But then even a surplice, if worn in the pulpit, carried fearful implications of Romish priestliness.

Newman was no ritualist ; as a Catholic he often made mistakes of detail. As an Anglican he celebrated the communion service from the north end of the altar, and preached in his gown, as Protestant as anyone could please. But since people were convinced of his popery, imagination supplied the missing setting. Of course he was continually genuflecting to his stone cross, of course he had been seen in St. Mary's 'with a cross down the back of his surplice — a rich illuminated one', said an excited person in Ilfracombe. In Truro it was whispered that lights burned day and night in Littlemore chapel. Newman prayed to St. Mary from St. Mary's pulpit — it was too appropriate not to happen. Newman collected these stories, which amused him. A few years later they had grown to fantastic legends. The Catholic belief in the Eucharist as the continuing mystery of Christ's sacrifice filtered into suspicious Protestant minds as a conviction that the Tractarians 'made sacrifices'. Pusey was once travelling in a coach and was astonished to hear a woman assert that she knew for a fact that Dr. Pusey sacrificed a lamb on Fridays. In vain he earnestly said, 'Madam, I am Dr. Pusey, and I assure you I do not know how to kill a lamb'.

In 1839 Newman told Henry Wilberforce of a Cheltenham lady who was sure they offered sacrifices every morning at Littlemore. Her acquaintance suggested Morning Prayers. 'No, she said, it was not that. She knew for certain we killed something, she did not know what. (qu. little children ? or each other ? or frogs and spiders ? or what ?).' All this nonsense made Newman laugh, but it showed, what he did not quite realize then, how deep-seated in English people was the horror of Catholicism. His preaching was stirring up not only the reasoned opposition of liberal-minded people but a mass of irrational fears which gave birth to these strange fantasies, and a fierce hatred directed not so much on ideas as at the men who embodied them. And Newman, going on his own way, not knowing where he was going, was becoming more and more the representative figure on which these feelings were focused.

But now, unaware of this, his spirits rose as he found himself free to devote his energies entirely to his special work; the next few years were to see the peak of his achievement, and the period of his greatest influence. Yet, with his uncanny prevision he wrote to Jemima: 'For what I know I may in a year or two be cast aside as a broken tool having done my part. Not that I expect this, but God's ways are so wonderful.'

1837–1839

Apostle in Action

'LET every one who hears me ask himself the question, what stake has *he* in the truth of Christ's promise ? . . . We know what it is to have a stake in any venture of this world. We venture our property in plans which promise a return ; in plans which we trust, which we have faith in. What have we ventured for Christ ? . . . I really fear, when we come to examine, it will be found that there is nothing we resolve, nothing we do, nothing we do not do, nothing we avoid, nothing we choose, nothing we give up, nothing we pursue, which we should not resolve, and do, and not do, and avoid, and choose, and give up, and pursue, if Christ had not died and heaven were not promised us. I really fear that most men called Christians, whatever they may profess, whatever they may think they feel, whatever warmth and illumination and love they may claim as their own, yet would go on almost as they do, neither much better nor much worse, if they believed Christianity to be a fable. When young, they indulge their lusts, or at least pursue the world's vanities ; as time goes on they get into a fair way of business, or other mode of making money ; then they marry and settle ; and their interest coinciding with their duty, they seem to be, and think themselves, respectable and religious men ; they grow attached to things as they are ; they begin to have a zeal against vice and error ; and they follow after peace with all men. Such conduct indeed, as far as it goes, is right and praiseworthy. Only I say, it has not necessarily any thing to do with religion at all. . . .'

A young man of twenty, Richard Church, heard this sermon, *The Ventures of Faith*, preached by Newman on his birthday just before Froude died in 1836, and was fired to make his venture for Christ. Two years later he was elected Fellow of Oriel and gradually became one of the most devoted of Newman's younger friends. An exact contemporary of his, Ambrose St. John, was a Student of Christ Church, but did not meet Newman personally till after he had left Oxford to be Henry Wilberforce's curate. Frederick Faber and William George Ward were also up, and stayed at Oxford with Fellowships in this period. A few years later came a group born about 1818–20, the two sons of Keble's friend Judge Coleridge, John Hungerford Pollen, and among others John Dobrée Dalgairns, a youth from the Channel Islands later to be closely connected with Newman's ventures. It was the generation most directly influenced by Newman, fifteen or twenty years younger than himself, the generation of Queen Victoria's contemporaries, the rulers of the new age.

Sixty years of extraordinary expansion were ahead for Britain, hardly dreamed of when it began ; a vast transformation, far greater than the changes of the first sixty years of our own century, which we hear so much about. All that we now think new is merely the acceleration of a process which began then. The young men came up to Oxford in the age of the horse ; in ten years' time England was covered in railroads. Industrial towns grew like mushrooms, London spread in a few decades from a city you could walk through to a vast agglomeration of suburbs and slums. A society stratified fairly simply on an agricultural basis and essentially unchanged for centuries, was forced, half consciously, into a quite different and far more complex formation. The whole economy, culture, aims and thought of the nation was shaken by a series of crises and shocks, first by threats of revolution, by famines, plagues of cholera and the horrors, experienced or vicarious, of the Crimean War, and afterwards, in a time of greater prosperity and more control of the huge new powers of industry, by what may perhaps be called earthquakes of the mind, the most famous and most far-reaching in its results being that occasioned by the publication of Darwin's *Origin of Species* in 1859, which made known to educated people the first form of the scientific theory of the evolution of animals, including man, by natural process, from similar ancestors of indeterminate antiquity.

The rich young men from the rulers' houses who, unknown to themselves, were to face the moral issues of this unparalleled upheaval, met at the outset of their course someone who seemed very like a John the Baptist, preaching repentance of sins to respectable people who had no notion they were sinners, and felt quite comfortable, whatever they were ; but instead of romantically wearing goatskins he wore a swallow tail coat and spectacles. And that was typical of the effect he had, fascinating them at once by his uncompromising obedience to Christ in all the forgotten rigours of penance, fasting and prayer, and the natural way he fitted into the world with which they were familiar, both intellectual and social. There was nothing of the fanatic about him and nothing, either, of the dignity of a man conscious of a position to keep up.

The Tracts, the polemical books, the public excitements of the Movement, were as nothing to Newman's personal influence, extended through the printing of his sermons to thousands who never met him. And this influence, though it certainly affected people's ecclesiastical views, was essentially spiritual ; he communicated a tremendous energy of will directed towards the true following of Christ, a sense of the urgency of immediate personal combat with the forces of evil, in the world, but still more in the individual soul. His sermons are directions for the campaign, warnings of common failures of understanding and practice, advice for their correction, pictures from Scripture of those who had taken wrong turnings set against others of divine or apostolic example, and expositions of the great mysteries that are the life of the wayfarer. Sam Wilberforce, and his brother-in-law, Henry Edward Manning, thought Newman's sermons too stern ; Sam told him so at length in several letters. But to Newman it seemed worse than useless to attempt to fight the father of lies with comforting generalizations, and a betrayal of Christ to live at ease with the world which condemned Him. He said with Ignatius the martyr, 'My Love is crucified'.

But Newman's impatience with mere respectability did not lead him to denounce selfish ease so much as to suggest a self-denial at once practical and relentless. Making gestures in moments of emotion was useless without an everyday discipline of prayer and self-control carried out faithfully even in the absence of feeling and in the midst of distractions. This insistence on persevering action in the details of ordinary life and on the eternal issues which depend upon the moral choices which mould the character, was the 'strictness' so often complained of ; he would let none forget their freedom and responsibility — 'the destiny of accountableness, the fate of being free, the inalienable prerogative of choosing between life and death, the inevitable prospect of heaven and hell'. People did not like to be reminded that sacrifice for love is possible in little and inward things, and that Christ's words about taking up the cross *daily* meant something definite. 'They are sure to say we carry things too far, when we carry them home to themselves', said Newman, in *Ventures of Faith*.

To this period belong the many published recollections of Newman in St. Mary's, some by those who knew him, others by strangers. Visitors often came out of curiosity, expecting to see some strange and imposing figure, elaborately ceremonial, dramatically declaiming medieval doctrines. But before they were aware he was coming, he was suddenly there. He moved so quietly and quickly that several used the word 'gliding' to describe his progress, which sounds perhaps affected. But he always walked fast, not lifting up his feet much, nor making the most of his height, as Tom Mozley said, by 'holding his head aloft'. In later years, when he was even more famous, his light tread and unassuming entrance still took visitors by surprise; he was beside them before they saw him. 'Gliding' would have seemed an odd description to the fairly hostile memorialist Tuckwell who said he well remembered meeting Newman in the street, 'striding along with an emaciated but ruddy face'. Lockhart, a young man of twenty in 1838, who afterwards joined Newman at Littlemore and then became a priest of the Institute of Charity, thus described his entrance in the Church: 'When he reached the lectern in the middle aisle he would drop down on his knees and remain fixed in prayer for a few moments'. Perhaps this was the origin of the tales about his supposed genuflexions before the altar.

Newman not only moved fast in Church, he read the service at a speed that was considered shocking by pious Evangelicals. A friend of Frank thought he must have another service to get through elsewhere. But it was then considered reverent to mouth addresses to God with great solemnity. Newman could not bear unnatural diction, either in or out of Church, or a special manner when speaking of religious matters. When reading the lessons he did not declaim them, but read as if meditating their meaning, as indeed he was. Many who listened could never afterwards hear certain prophetic passages from Isaiah, or the story of the Passion without inward echoes of his voice. Those who became Catholics thought of it when they first heard the Passion sung at High Mass on Palm Sunday; Newman's reading combined in the same way liturgical simplicity with the intense drama of the narrative.

His voice was clear, and of tenor pitch, so distinctive that everybody noticed it, all through his life. It was subtly expressive of change of feeling, missed by the more insensitive of his listeners, but to some more moving than a wider dramatic range. He would deliver a rapid sentence and then pause; after this brief silence the next he let fly reached the target with the force of an arrow. It was not a trick of delivery, but a habit of giving himself time to think what he was saying, but sometimes it had a thrilling effect. He used no gestures, which was unusual in those days, and read his sermons, which was then the common practice in Oxford. But although his aim was to rouse not the emotions but the will of his listeners, that did not mean he felt nothing himself, and perceptive observers noticed that as he got more deeply into his subject there was a kind of intensification of tone, an almost trembling tension of feeling under the severe control. Some people never observed this, and were disappointed ; expecting emotional excitement they thought the sermon very 'ordinary'. The suspicious, finding nothing of the popish doctrine they expected, were convinced that the preacher was concealing his real views and that these moral sermons were a mere blind, while he carried on his subversive activities privately But Lockhart spoke for the great majority of the young men who heard him, whether or not they afterwards became Catholics : 'He effaced himself. It was like God speaking to you.'

It was not surprising, perhaps, that having wakened the consciences of his young listeners, Newman should presently be approached by those who wished to make a general confession and a new start. He heard the first, with the greatest reluctance, in the Lent of 1838. He firmly believed in the right of members of the Church of England to confess to a priest, but he had not what he called 'a clear view' of what was implied by Absolution. However, when pressed by the young man whose conscience was troubled, he told him that whatever he, Newman, thought, 'anyhow the act was *God's*, and He could as really use me as His instrument, though ignorant, as He could the inanimate element in Baptism'. When first approached he said he 'should feel it painful, both from the responsibility and the distressing trial of hearing it', and it is clear that neither of these feelings wore off with time ; even as a Catholic priest with the training and the authority of the Church behind him, he continued to feel both, sometimes more, sometimes less. Perhaps because he knew so much of what went on in people's minds, he was overwhelmingly conscious of the difficulties and dangers of dealing with them, even under the more or less formal conditions of the confessional. This distress and anxiety was a trial to him, but did not affect those penitents who came to him. In Oxford Pusey became something of an expert, in his own peculiar way, as a confessor and director ; Newman was always hesitant. Nevertheless, he must have heard many confessions during his time there, at the north end of the altar rails in St. Mary's, and afterwards at Littlemore. But he would not hear any confessions from ladies. The ladies went to Pusey.

Newman did not preach what he did not practise ; indeed he practised a far more severe self-discipline than he thought it wise to preach to his mixed congregation. Since he either did not write, or did not preserve, journals of self-examination at this period, no evidence remains of the continual warfare with the failings noted in earlier years, but that it was carried on is witnessed by the retreat notes from Littlemore a few years later. The only witness to this interior discipline is the outward one of fasting, which he noted in his diary under the cryptic letters 'fb, fd, ft', — fasted breakfast, fasted dinner, fasted tea. He made some notes on his method of fasting, for it was all an experiment and he did not know what would be the effect of these privations before he began. He guided himself by what he read of the habits of the ancient church, but had to adapt their very different regimen to modern life, and what was more difficult, to conditions of living in a nineteenth-century Oxford college.

The last thing he wanted was to attract attention, and thus he had to break his rules to dine with the Provost, the Iffley Trustees and his friend Williams, in 1839, the Lent he first kept notes on. Dining in hall he made it a rule not to take a second helping of meat, and avoided eating pastry, sugar and other delicacies, but he did not give up wine. On Wednesdays and Fridays he simply missed out breakfast and dinner, ate nothing till 5 p.m. but had an egg for tea. In Passiontide he tried to leave off butter and milk ; in Holy Week he ate practically nothing at all but bread and biscuit and water at tea time. 'The only great inconvenience I have found has been face ache — for which I have used sulphate of quinine pills successfully.' This Marathon was nothing to what he attempted the next year, alone at Littlemore. 'Gratias tibi Domini — whither art Thou leading me ?' he wrote on St. Matthew's Day 1839, having discovered he could eat nothing till 8 p.m. without feeling weak. 'I do not intend to keep this so strict', he noted at the same time.

Fasting was the simplest way to share the hardships of Christ in a too comfortable Christian world, to do penance for sin, his own and others', but it was never an obsession with Newman, as it became to one of the most eccentric of the Tractarians, John Brande Morris, Faber's friend, who lived in Exeter tower and was known as St. Simeon Stylites. In the Long Vacation of 1839 Newman left him in charge of St. Mary's while he was away, and he chose to exercise his monomania on St. Michael's day by advocating that animals ought to be made to fast too. 'May he (*salvis ossibus suis*) have a fasting horse next time he goes steeple chasing', said Newman, exasperated, in a letter to Bowden. In consequence of this aberration the Vice-Chancellor, as a protest and to preserve his family from contamination, removed them from St. Mary's congregation. Morris was incorrigible. At Littlemore Newman remembered with amusement how 'Morris once at a breakfast table after a long silence turned round to a nice and pretty young lady who was next to him and said with his peculiar smile that he thought it not worse to burn a man for heresy than to hang him for sheep-stealing!' It was the antics of those who professed to be Newman's admirers which were the origin of many silly tales about him.

Of course Newman's unpopularity with the Heads of Houses only increased his appeal to the younger generation. The authorities' fear of him was so acute that some actually changed the times of dinner in hall to prevent the undergraduates attending St. Mary's evening service. In after years someone, explaining why he had not gone to hear Newman, hastened to add that it was *not* because he did not want to miss his hot dinner. The choice between hot dinner and hearing Newman must have presented some of his disciples with their first chance of undertaking fasting and penance. The pettiness of the opposition, and the underhand methods chosen made it no less determined ; the authorities were simply afraid of Newman, but their unfairness reacted against them. He was just the right age to exert influence on young people growing up — not to be classed with the elderly and dull, but strong in that maturity so much desired by the young, positive in idea and in action. He himself was not anxious to collect followers among the undergraduates, conscious that they were often under age and not officially in his charge. It was the young Fellows, the newly fledged graduates that he liked to draw into Apostolical circles. It was they who came to the early communion services every Sunday, a sort of catacomb worship almost in the dark, before the ordinary English Sunday had got on its easy-going way. He got them to help in any schemes afoot, from the translations of the Library of the Fathers, which he and Pusey had begun, to helping with the visiting at Littlemore. Many of them walked out there with him, more for his conversation than anything else. They had a job to keep up, he walked so fast.

In February 1837 James Mozley wrote home : 'Newman gives a tea party now every Monday evening in term. Last night went off very well . . . conversation flowing continuously and everyone at his ease. Newman can manage this kind of thing better than Pusey.' He was a good host, because he liked to make other people talk ; shyness only attacked him on public occasions. He hated any sort of pretence or self-importance, any donnishness as he called it, and so those who were younger found themselves soon getting on familiar terms with him. Sometimes they took advantage of this. James Mozley, without any excuse, was late for his deacon's examination in 1838 ; naturally this carelessness reflected on Newman, whose protégé he was known to be. 'N. took it into his head to feel hurt about it', James wrote home airily. 'I have made up the affair with him . . . but he looked amazingly black at first.' No wonder ; such a casual attitude was very different from his own, years ago, and was sure to be censured by those who were hostile to the Movement. But the blackness soon lifted, for he scribbled a note to James : 'Carissime, I send you my surplice not knowing whether or not you want it. It is that in which I was ordained deacon and priest.'

James was kept out of Fellowships by hostility to Newman and the Tractarians ; it worried Newman, and he was relieved to be instrumental in getting him at last, in 1840, a place at Magdalen. Meanwhile Pusey took him in, rather to his embarrassment ; later Pusey and Newman took a house in High Street for several young men similarly circumstanced. Newman called them 'the young monks', but it was he, not they, who had yearnings after a monastic life. In 1837 he read Manzoni's famous novel, *I promessi sposi*, and found it inspiring ; he said afterwards, 'the friar stuck in my heart like a dart'.

Religion was not the topic at the Monday evening tea-parties ; Newman later, in *Loss and Gain*, drew a satirical picture of Evangelical tea-parties, where unctuous religious conversation was accompanied by the tinkling of teaspoons. The talk was general, and very varied types were fascinated by the wide range of Newman's interests. The tea-parties had a social object, in introducing people to each other, but of course this facilitated the growth and consolidation of the Tractarian group in Oxford. Newman did not directly angle for adherents to the cause, but people thought he did, and parents outside Oxford imagined him as a religious Pied Piper, charming their children away. Tom Mozley was amused to be asked if Newman was a *good* man. Miss Mitford, the author, recorded that she had once been alarmed to hear that a young relative had been introduced to the arch-conspirator. He was a poor plodding scholar, ready to starve to get learning ; Newman asked him to breakfast every week, 'and he gives me the best advice possible', said artless Frank. 'What about ?' anxiously enquired Miss Mitford. 'Everything,' replied Frank ; 'the classics, history, mathematics, general literature. He thinks me in danger of overworking at Greek — he, such a scholar ! — and tells me to diversify my reading, to take exercise and to get as much practical knowledge and cheerful society as I can . . . he talks to me of every sort of subject except what is called Tractarianism, and that he has never mentioned.' Much relieved, Miss Mitford gave Newman a good mark for honourable behaviour.

Newman could not resist teasing the solemn. Rogers showed Anne Mozley a letter telling of a tease, but he suppressed the victim's name ; it may have been Berkeley of Pembroke, whose primness and pomposity always amused Newman. 'I saw [him] for a day last week,' said Newman, 'and was as grave (yet natural) as a judge the whole time, except for one instant, when, to try him, I suddenly on a pause broke out with a sentence like this, turning round sharp : "So, you wish, it seems, to change the monarchy into a republic ?" [He] shrunk up as if twenty thousand pins had been thrust into him ; his flesh goosified, his mouth puckered up and he looked the picture of astonishment, awe, suspicion and horror. After this trial I went back to my grave manner and all was well. Now don't you see that, for his own good and comfort, one must put on one's company coat for him ? he cannot bear one's shirt sleeves.'

Berkeley, as Faber remembered eleven years later, had invited Newman to dine after his university sermon on *Faith and Reason contrasted as Habits of Mind*, which had annoyed the Heads of Houses. Faber, who had preached for Newman at the ordinary service, was invited too. 'You scandalized him by making rabbits on the wall ;' he reminded Newman, 'and when he scolded you, you went fast asleep in your chair.'

Two earnest Cambridge Tractarians were once surprised when Newman refused to put on his conversational company coat for their benefit. They came to spend the evening with Pusey in Christ Church, and Newman was there. Expecting serious talk and spiritual edification they sat down at a table with Pusey. But Newman retired to an armchair with the two little Pusey children, Lucy and Philip, on his knees, putting his spectacles first on one and then on the other, to their great delight. The astonished visitors from Cambridge heard him telling them the story of a magic broomstick, most useful to the owner, which broke in half and subsequently became two broomsticks.

Mrs. Pusey brought up her children on the teaching of Newman's sermons. In 1835, writing to her husband about his complex and learned Tract on Baptism, she said : 'There are some things that come to one at once as truth as soon as they are proposed, and those are the things one really believes unhesitatingly. Other things (and your Tract is one of them) in greater or lesser degree stir up against themselves in one's mind doubts and difficulties and perplexities. Mr. Newman's (I beg pardon, *John's*, I might almost say St. John's) sermons are full of truths of the first sort, and perhaps that is one reason why I so like them.' Pusey humbly replied, 'I see many reasons which you do not why John's statement of truth should be attractive, mine repulsive : he has held a steady course, I have not.' He then listed his defective actions, exalting his friend. It was very like Pusey to put faults of exposition down to moral, rather than literary, failings. Newman told Miss Giberne in 1836 that Pusey was the nearest thing to a Saint in modern times. Saints, to him, meant the Patriarchs of Israel, the Apostles and the Fathers ; he later compared Pusey to 'a Father'. Pusey was a sort of good-tempered St. Jerome, so learned, so austere. He and his wife gave up all entertaining and going out to parties, and Mrs. Pusey sold her jewels. Out of the money they saved they gave very large sums to charity and the building of churches.

Miss Giberne was a constant correspondent of Newman's. She was now in her thirties, a striking, handsome woman, tall and self-possessed. She was still receiving proposals of marriage ; it amused her, as an old nun, to remember these conquests, and the speed with which her suitors had consoled their broken hearts with someone else. Living in Evangelical circles as she did, she involuntarily became a siren to earnest young ministers who disapproved of the Movement, almost a Scarlet Woman. One, leaning over her at an evening party, announced the end of his infatuation in tragic Scriptural terms : 'the snare is broken !' Her family teased her about her correspondence with Newman and insisted she must want to marry him. With hauteur she replied that if she did, she would not write to him ! Their letters were free and lively, but not emotional. They both enjoyed a straight fight and a good joke. He encouraged her, isolated as she was among Peculiars. 'It amuses me beyond measure how angry these people are made by their very incapacity', he wrote in 1837. 'They put me in mind of a naughty child put atop of a bookcase, very frightened, but very furious. You see, when one knows one has all the Fathers round one, let be that little mishaps and mistakes may befall, yet on the whole one feels secure and comfortable.' He was supremely confident then, and in high spirits : 'Everyone of us has his own prey. I might disgust some people with my sermons and take with others. . . . If your letter was untidy, what is mine ?' The letters of that period were all written off in a legible, even, but sprawling hand. 'As to fasting this week I confess to be emaciated,' he remarked, 'but the Influenza is the cause.'

Miss Giberne was anxious to have her prey too ; at the end of 1836 she had suggested writing a story for children. 'Your plan is the very thing I have been wishing', said Newman. 'I am sure we shall do nothing till we get some ladies to set to work to poison the rising generation — so I hope you will begin at once.' Full of enthusiasm Miss Giberne (on her knees) wrote the tale of Little Mary. Newman took endless trouble to see it through the press. It was anonymously published ; some people thought it was his, or his sister Harriett's, for she too began to write tales for children. She wrote several and had a mild success with them, but Miss Giberne went back to her painting. It was left to Charlotte Yonge to be the great poisoner of the rising generation — but it was a later generation, for she was only fifteen herself now, a clever girl preparing for confirmation under her adored teacher, Keble, in whose parish her father, General Yonge, resided. *The Heir of Redclyffe*, best-selling Tractarian novel, did not come out till 1853, and her stories for children later still.

'The mind of the composer', said Sam Wilberforce, reviewing Newman's contributions to the *Lyra Apostolica*, 'has probably lived too much apart from the tenderness and sympathies of domestic life.' Newman, said James Mozley, was highly amused. He often gave the *Lyra* to ladies and involved himself in one of the *anti*pathies of domestic life when he gave one to Frank's wife ; Frank was incensed. His angry letter arrived just when Charles had suddenly turned up in Oxford, walking to London in midwinter 'without clothes' as his brother put it ; 'he declared he did it for health and exercise'. At first Newman put Frank's letter in his pocket in disgust, saying nothing, but afterwards he showed it to Charles. Frank had been 'all this while fidgetting about my giving a book to his wife. Why not say so then ? I am sure it gave me trouble enough', he wrote to

Jemima. 'He speaks as if I were treating *her* as I would not *him* —
i.e. more kindly. Why I have done everything *through* him, and
through delicacy would not even write to her. When the book was
received *she* wrote to me and I then answered it — which has excited
F's displeasure.' Charles gladly joined the fraternal fray and told
John that Frank was telling people in Bristol that he was setting up a
new sect for himself in Oxford. 'What a very uncharitable thing it is,
saying I want to make a sect', said Newman to Jemima. 'I say
nothing of *him*. I judge him in no way. I only say that God tells me
to avoid persons who make divisions — and he makes a division.'
The *Bristol Morning Chronicle* quoted Frank as saying his brother
was the author of an article on Dr. Wiseman. 'I do not care who
knows it — people are very much out if they think I do, but how did
F know ? it is like him to go chattering about, not very decent to have
one brother speaking against another in mixed society. If he does it
on religious grounds I have nothing to say of course ; only I should
find fault with his taste.'

'Frank is fundamentally wrong in setting himself up as a judge
of the English Church', announced Charles, who nearly always sided
against Frank in any family dissension. 'To be consistent, he ought
to be an unbeliever.' This was true, but surprising from Charles.
But since his mother's death he was having a slight return of religious
feeling. John watched anxiously ; what worried him most was that
Charles went to receive the Sacrament, not only without penitence,
but apparently without belief. 'He seems to take religion as a
medicine, which may be beneficial though he were an atheist', said
John to Jemima. 'I say all this, dear J, because we ought all to think
of him much in prayer. Of course Satan wishes to keep him.' It was
not long before Charles returned to his now habitual atheism. Even
in 1825 Newman had written to his Aunt of Charles, 'He is madly
rushing along a dark and dangerous cavern thinking he must find
light *at the end* of it — but he will never arrive at that end'.

Charles' brothers and sisters did not at this time think him mentally unbalanced, but a few years later they were very much afraid
of it. He reached the point of his greatest psychological disturbance
while his eldest brother was at Littlemore in the early forties ; after
that his mind seemed to stabilize in its own eccentricity. When
Newman, in 1855, drew the portrait of Juba in his novel *Callista* he
may have been dramatizing Charles' spiritual state. Juba, the son of
a Roman veteran and an African witch, deliberately chooses to make
his own will his supreme guide ; despising the sensual cruelty of the

old woman his rash pride yet puts him in her power ; under her
curse he flees, possessed by an evil spirit, through forest and wilderness, unable to control his actions.   Exorcized at last by the power
of the martyred Callista, he is left at peace, but feeble-minded.
Newman may or may not have come to feel that his brother Charles
was in some sense under the domination of an evil spirit, but he
treated him differently from the way he treated Frank, who was, and
wished to be, responsible for his opinions and actions.   Sin, madness
and disease — death in spirit, mind and body — were all referred
ultimately to the prince of this world by Christ, who alone had power
to raise all these dead to life.   Whether or not Satan had this particular
grip on Charles Newman, John certainly believed that his scoffing at
religion put him in great danger ; just as Frank's making his own
critical intellect his only guide put him in a different kind of danger —
in a 'net' which prevented free spiritual action while leaving him in
the light of reason ;   Charles was in the dark, running in an endless
tunnel.   Of course Newman did not regard himself as safe ; but he
knew his own danger, of becoming a mere 'pane of glass', knowing
without doing, or being.   He prayed to be kept from becoming the
'sport and victim of Satan'.

1837–1839

Controversial Leader

ALL this time there were 'the engagements of agitation', as Newman had called them to Froude. In 1838, trying to find an editor for the *British Critic*, a monthly magazine which he did not wish to see come to an end, Newman was landed with the job himself. Rose, though no Z, was more cautious and conservative than the Oxford members of the Movement wished to be ; his health was delicate and he had to give up the *British Magazine*, where so many of the Lyra poems had appeared, and Newman's sketches of the lives of the Fathers. He died in 1839, just after Newman had dedicated to him the fourth volume of Sermons. Newman was a good editor, he allowed his contributors plenty of latitude, often publishing things he did not quite approve himself, rather than suppress anyone else's opinions. The *British Critic* became the organ of the Movement, spread its influence about, and made it possible for Apostolicals to make public comments on events, books and ecclesiastical policy. But it meant a great deal more work for Newman.

The year before, 1837, he had brought out a book which expressed the Tractarian theory of the nature of the Church. *The Prophetical Office of the Church* set out the Via Media, the ideal middle way of the Anglican Church, avoiding the errors of Protestantism on one side and the corruptions of Rome on the other. Newman was not under the illusion that the Church of England was the perfect mean, but he thought it could be, and hoped it would be so. The book was based on lectures given in Adam de Brome's chapel, and was occasioned by the necessity of explaining why the Tractarians, who were so anti-Protestant, were not thereby pro-Roman, as everyone thought they were. It was the more necessary to define their position in relation to Rome, as in 1836, during the great Hampden row, the long silence of Romanists in England was suddenly broken by Nicholas Wiseman, the brilliant young Rector of the English College whom Newman and Froude had met in Rome. Wiseman gave a

series of public lectures in London on Catholicism, which were
attended by a large crowd of surprised and interested Protestants ;
it was an unheard-of thing for a Catholic to dare to expound his faith
in public. Wiseman, who was an attractive lecturer, and a genial as
well as a cultured man, had a great success, but Protestants commented : 'Mr. Newman is doing Dr. Wiseman's work for him in
Oxford'.

'I say nothing, I believe, without the highest authority among
our writers,' Newman wrote to Jemima, 'yet it is so strong that
everything I have yet said is milk and water to it and this makes me
anxious. It is all the difference between drifting snow and a hard
snowball.' The snowball was intended to be hurled at the reigning
'popular Protestantism' of the day, but what made it Newman's
biggest success so far was his criticism of Rome. Although he
attacked Rome chiefly in order to be able to strike the harder at
Protestantism, as he afterwards admitted, yet his language in de-
nouncing Rome's corruptions was sufficiently strong to put his
Anglican readers at ease ; this was the true seventeenth-century
tradition and no mistake. Newman had indeed taken his views on
Roman corruptions from the old Anglican divines and when he later
found some of these controversial doctrines and practices flourishing in the works and times of the Fathers, he felt cheated, and as
if he could 'bite off their ears' for misleading him. Instead, he
bit off his own, in the famous retractation of 1843. In 1877, at the
age of seventy-six, he reissued the book as the first volume of the
Via Media, with footnotes, sometimes amusing, and a preface on
the nature of the Christian Church, as calm and clear as the view
from the top of a mountain.

In 1837, however, he was full of confidence in his position.
The Church had been undivided for the first five centuries or so ;
later through the weakness of its members parts had broken off
and pursued a life of their own, developing differently from each
other. The Eastern and Orthodox Churches were the first great
branches ; England in medieval times had been part of the Roman
branch, but was separated at the time of the Reformation and continued on its own. The Roman branch had gone its own way,
intensifying its particular corruptions, the Anglican had suffered
some severe curtailments and a certain infusion of error, but had
maintained its continuity with Apostolic organization, and the Creeds
which enshrined the Catholic doctrines. There was no single
Church with the monopoly of truth, but it was possible to use

Antiquity as the standard by which to purge present errors and revive a purer Catholicism. The two principal corruptions of Rome were the worship of the Virgin Mary and the Saints, and the doctrine that the living (Roman) Church was the infallible authority, and not the Church of Antiquity. These two objections, of course, are still felt to-day by Christians not in communion with Rome. For Newman himself, Antiquity, his chosen standard, was to answer both questions, as he read and meditated the history of the early Church; his theory of Development grew out of these studies. As a Catholic, he wrote again on these two subjects in his *Letter to Pusey* (on Mary) and his *Letter to the Duke of Norfolk* (on Infallibility). But even now he could write 'Rome retains the principle of true Catholicism perverted; popular Protestantism is wanting in the principle'. He dedicated the book, by permission, to old Martin Routh, the President of Magdalen.

In 1838 was published Froude's *Remains*, which Keble and Newman edited together. Neither of them expected the explosion of feeling which followed. Dead, Froude perfectly fulfilled his ambition to be an ecclesiastical agitator, which, alive, divine providence had not allowed him to pursue. He was the catalyst, starting many reactions, both inside and outside the Movement, crystallizing the opinions of the hostile and the friendly, and dividing those who repudiated the Reformation from those who found that they adhered to it. He had this effect because Newman and Keble presented him as he was, without toning down his vigorous expressions. The previous summer Archdeacon Froude had sent Newman his son's early journals, and Newman read for the first time his friend's youthful attempts at self-discipline, so like his own though pursued in such a different background. The Archdeacon gave the editors a free hand. After some hesitation Newman published extracts from these journals in the first volume, along with a selection of letters. He expected criticism of his editing, and some of Froude's views, but he was taken by surprise at the horror and alarm expressed by John Bull, faced with this popish cuckoo in the nest. A young man of good family, fasting! Hesitating to buy himself an overcoat! Criticizing his own gentlemanliness! Worse still, a clergyman jeering at the Reformers, calling Jewel a Dissenter, praising monks — it was indecent, unnatural, dangerous, perverted: in a word, Romish.

The Reformers were national heroes, and the Reformation considered the dawn of English liberty; Newman expected general anger at Froude's uninhibited criticisms of them and their mission. But he had not expected to shock adherents of the Movement itself. Yet it turned out that many thought the Reformers had purified the Church of England from the corruptions of medieval Romanism. Some shocked Tractarians could not contain their feelings. One of them, Churton, came to Newman's room and let fly at him. Newman wrote to him : 'You are very kind to be so frank in the expression of your opinion about me. I hope never to be distressed at it except what must arise from differing in any matter from any one like yourself. While we hold the same faith I should be a fool if I did not allow you to have your own opinion about matters which are not of faith, about historical events and characters. . . . Still less have I any right to complain of your censuring me in matters of conduct and judgment, when I claim the right to censure our predecessors in the Church.'

He told Churton he did not repent publishing the *Remains* and was glad that people now knew what he thought about the Reformers. 'You know your bargain now ; at least I am no hypocrite. I cannot help fancying that you were easier after speaking out in my room : give me credit for the same state of mind.' As for the Reformers and their spiritual descendants : 'I do detest the talk that is made, to me the odious hypocritical talk (*not to others* for they believe) about certain things and persons — and if I did not try to rule myself I could say very violent things, and astonish you as much perhaps as you astonished me when last I saw you. And this con- sideration, while it quite removes (I trust) all pain from my mind at anything you said, may perhaps tend to soften you towards me. Is all the strong feeling, all the expression of it, to be on one side only ? Why should we not bear with each other, agreeing so clearly in main matters as we do ?' Churton must have been softened, for the next letters proceeded in peace.

A friend might be softened by Newman's reasonableness, but people in general remained horrified by Froude's views and person- ality. Faussett, the Margaret Professor of Divinity, was actually roused from his habitual indolence to write an attack on Froude's view of the Eucharist, strategically bringing it out at the end of term. 'He has been firing away at us in gallant style', said Newman cheerfully. He sat up all night to write a reply, defending both Froude and Catholic doctrine ; it went into a second edition and sold 750 copies to Faussett's 500. 'Who would have thought persons would buy an *answer* without a *question* ?' said Newman innocently, to James Mozley. 'He is very angry in the Preface to his second edition — talks of my flippant suggestions etc. . . . Rogers reports an amusing saying of a lady he knows about my Letter. "Now Dr. Faussett will be quite pleased and convinced by this, and obliged to Mr. Newman, if he is a nice kind of man."'

The Professor was far from being obliged, and he had powerful support outside the university. Lord Morpeth, a great champion against Popery at Oxford, launched an attack in the House, duly reported in the papers, and went out of his way to mention Newman's name. Telling this to James Mozley, Newman added that the *Dublin Record* had called the Movement '"a sect of damnable and detestable heretics of late sprung up at Oxford ; a sect which evidently affects Popery and merits the heartiest condemnation of all true Christians . . . we do not hesitate to say that they are essentially heterodox". — That we are *what ?*' commented Newman, amused. But battle always raised his spirits. 'We must expect a volley from the whole conservative press. I can fancy the Old Duke sending down to ask the Heads of Houses whether we cannot be silenced.'

Another result of Froude's delayed action on his contemporaries was the familiar Martyrs' Memorial at Oxford, raised in honour of Cranmer, Latimer and Ridley, burnt in the reign of Queen Mary. We owe this monument to the zeal of the Rev. C. Portales Golightly, who, while others merely held up their hands in horror, went into action, collecting money for what was, originally, intended to be a Church built in honour of the Reformers. In Oxford it was regarded as 'a good cut at Newman' and nobody was more surprised than Golightly when Pusey put his name down for a subscription. Later, friends persuaded him that his support might be misconstrued as a change of front, and he withdrew, but he never understood what Newman and Keble felt about the Reformers, and some years later was shocked all over again when he discovered it. He had a singularly comprehensive mind, in which ancient Fathers, Romanist devotional writers and Reformers, whether Lutheran or Calvinist, lay down together, the lion eating straw like the ox. Of the Reformers he said to Newman that he thought 'we owe our peculiar position as adherents of primitive antiquity to them'. It was the great moment of division within the Movement, though it was not quite realized at the time. In the event all those who followed Froude in repudiating the doctrines and separatism of the Reformers, 'went over to Rome'. The only exception was Keble.

Golightly was something of a deserter from the cause. He had got into Oxford through Newman's coaching, at that hilariously verminous house in Hampstead ; Newman stayed with him at Godalming on his return from Sicily and wrote him letters as eager and friendly as those to Henry Wilberforce or Frederic Rogers. When the church was being built at Littlemore Golightly suggested himself as curate. Newman was always glad to have his ex-pupils helping in the parish and to give them a chance of preaching in St. Mary's ; once he had as many as four. Money was no object to most of these young clergymen, who all had private incomes and were much better off than he was. Tom Mozley said he was careless about formalities, saying, 'You be my curate', when anyone was wondering what to do with himself.

Golightly was rich, an ex-Etonian ; in after years he did not take a living but settled in Oxford. He offered to send Newman two of his sermons to read, so that he could know his views. He imagined Mrs. Newman saying, 'O John ! What a Peculiar you have got at Littlemore !' His tone was such that no one would have thought he *was* a Peculiar, and Newman never gave it another thought ; nor did he bother to read Golightly's sermons. He liked his curates to have 'full swing' — a favourite phrase — and did not demand rigid agreement with himself. Even when Golightly began to speak in public against *The Arians* he only joked with Froude and Rogers that Golius wouldn't be Golius if he didn't *goliare*. But when Golightly preached in Oxford against Pusey's views on Baptism, Pusey told Newman that 'he would never do'. Then Newman wrote to Golightly and told him it would be better if he did not come to Littlemore. Golius was very annoyed indeed, and never forgave him, though it is difficult to see why he wanted to be curate to someone so wrong in his ideas as he thought Newman to be. Perhaps he took it as a personal slight. At any rate after this he became an implacable enemy of the Tractarians and particularly hostile to Newman, though Newman did not realize it for a long time, and could not take his enmity very seriously, even when it was doing him irreparable harm.

Golightly's antics did not worry Newman, and external opposition was simply a challenge, even opposition within the Movement was better brought into the open, but what really did shake him was a censure, as he felt it, from his own Bishop. Some hard things were said about Bagot by members of his own Church, and he was considered weak and inefficient, and called 'King Log' ; but Newman always spoke of him, in private and in public, with respect and even

affection. Bagot's kind intentions outweighed for him everything
else. On this occasion Bagot had been so badgered about the supposed Romanism rampant in his diocese that he made some sort of
investigation ; all he found was a cross embroidered on the stole of
Seager, Pusey's eccentric assistant in the School of Hebrew. Seager
promised never to allow such a thing to happen again. But in the
Charge reporting this satisfactory state of affairs, the Bishop went on
to grumble mildly at the Tracts, as a possible source of error to those
less learned than their authors. It was the first open sign of episcopal
displeasure and Newman was immediately anxious, writing off twice
in one day to Keble, for advice. To Bowden he wrote, 'What he has
said is very slight indeed, but a Bishop's lightest word, *ex cathedra*,
is heavy. The whole effect was cold towards us . . . it was negation :
there was no praise.'

He wrote off at once to the Archdeacon, offering to withdraw the
Tracts from circulation if the Bishop desired it. The Archdeacon
hastily referred him to the Bishop himself, who, totally unused to
being treated with Apostolic submission, assured Newman, quite
alarmed, that he wished nothing so definite done. Newman, thinking
it over on his own lines, wrote to Keble that probably the Bishop
really agreed with the teaching of the Tracts, but had been alarmed
by the current attacks, 'and (not thinking of our feelings at all, any
more than if we were the very paper Tracts themselves) he propitiates
the popular cry against us with a vague disapprobation, just as men
revile Popery in order to say strong Catholic things. . . . Also I am
not sure if he was not rather annoyed with me when he delivered his
Charge, whether on account of the *Remains* or for other reason. I
think he has not considered that a Bishop's word is an act, that I am
under his jurisdiction, that he cannot criticize, but commands only.'
Poor Bishop Bagot ! Such obedience had never entered his head,
such readiness to sacrifice influence, not to speak of income, at the
first hint of disapprobation.

When Pusey was old he used to say that Newman had depended
on the Bishops, while he himself had looked to God's providence
acting through the Church. But what would the Fathers have said
to a Church where God's providence omitted to act through the
Bishops ? Newman depended on the Bishops only in the sense that
he depended on them to maintain true doctrine. It was of no avail
for a priest to assert something if his Bishop contradicted it ; such
was not the teaching of Catholic Antiquity, not to speak of St. Paul.
He was thinking of the divine institution of the office, as descending

from the Apostles, when he wrote, 'Sometimes when I have stood by as he put on his robes, I felt it would have been such a relief if I could have fallen at his feet and kissed them'. Bishop Bagot was spared the embarrassment of such a passionate declaration of loyalty; Newman had too much common sense and humour thus to act out what he felt, but the feelings were there. When he came to kiss the Pope's foot, a symbolic gesture if ever there was one, he afterwards related with amusement that he hit his head on the papal knee. Incongruity of feeling and action always did amuse him.

When he had made the offer to suppress the Tracts Newman wrote to his old friend in London, 'Well, my dear Bowden, has not this come suddenly and taken away your breath? It nearly has mine. But I do not think I can be wrong and I think good will come of it. . . . It will make people see we are sincere and not ambitious.' So he thought, but most of his friends felt he had acted with unnecessary quixotry. To them the doctrine of the Apostolic Succession was more important than a mere Bagot. They did not relate the idea to the person. But to Newman it was impossible to preach submission to Bishops and not to practise it. 'My good fellows,' he said, '*you* make me the head of a party — that is your external view — but I *know* what I am — a clergyman under the Bishop of Oxford, and anything more is accidental.' It was perhaps easier for Pusey to take less account of actual Bishops while upholding the Apostolic Succession, since he held his Chair and his Canonry from the Crown and was not directly under any Bishop; he could not be deprived even by the university. He had no obvious person to be obedient to and was thus able to elaborate his individual position indefinitely.

Troubles did not come singly, and in the autumn of 1838 there was a secondary row, within the Movement; symbolically, the cause was the Roman Breviary. Since Newman had begun to use Froude's Breviary he had been impressed with its liturgical riches. A Tract came out on the Breviary which was such a success that it was decided to make an English translation. Samuel Wood (brother of the future Lord Halifax), Frederick Oakeley, now the Vicar of Margaret Chapel in London, and Robert Williams — no relation of Isaac's — were the chosen translators. But very soon a powerful opposition developed, led by Keble's brother Thomas, Rector of Bisley, the ideal parish of the early Tractarians, whose praises were ever sung by Isaac Williams, once curate there. Another leader was Isaac's brother-in-law, the Rev. Sir George Prevost, an influential 'squarson' who had thrown in his lot with the Movement. They were not keen on the Breviary at all, but if it had to be translated they wanted it radically cut and altered.

Newman, as Editor of the Tracts, found himself the centre of the storm, attacked on both sides and offending both. But he offended the country party more, because he could not see what principle to use in adapting the Breviary ; were they to rely after all on private judgment, and if so, whose private judgment ? Anxious above all not to be made the judge himself he wrote to Keble : 'I will do whatever you suggest. . . . If you tell me to make any submission to any one, I will do it. . . . If you will tell me what not to do, I will not do it. I wish parties would seriously ask themselves what they desire of me. Is it to stop writing ? I will do anything you advise. Is it to show what I write to others before publishing ? It is my rule already. . . . Is it to stop my weekly parties, or anything else ? I will gladly do so.' He was willing to surrender anything for peace, but he told Keble his feelings as well. 'People really should put themselves into my place, and consider how the appearance of suspicion, jealousy and discontent is likely to affect one who is most conscious that everything he does is imperfect, and therefore soon begins so to suspect everything he does as to have no heart and little power to do anything at all. Any one can fancy the effect which the presence of ill-disposed spectators would have on some artist or operator engaged in a delicate experiment. Is such conduct kind towards me ? is it feeling ? If I ought to stop I am ready to stop, but do not in the same breath chide me (for instance) for thinking of stopping the Tracts, and then be severe on the Tracts which are actually published.'

Keble, however, though always ready to sympathize, was not the man to dictate to his friends, and he was in a particularly difficult position since his brother, to whom he was devoted, was one of those most annoyed with Newman for 'going too far'. Newman might be willing to obey, but in a situation like this there was no authority to command his obedience. The question of the Breviary was not a mere matter of policy, but carried with it doctrinal differences, just as the *Remains* had done, and again the Reformation was a dividing line : did it constitute a purification of the Catholic Church in England, or a corruption ? Newman and the Breviary translators believed the influence introduced by the Reformers was destructive, and wanted to restore Catholicism, though without the Pope, since they believed his power to be a human corruption within the divine institution. To Prevost and his friends, as to Pusey, the Reformation was a true reform, reverting to a more primitive and pure

Catholicism than that represented even by the ancient offices of the Breviary.

It was particularly painful to Newman that Rogers, who was now his closest friend, took the Prevost side. At such times of disagreement, Rogers told Anne Mozley when they were all old, Newman had 'a certain flinty way', and added, 'but then you occasionally saw what this flintiness cost him. And when you came to frank explanation there came from the rock a gush of overpowering tenderness.' The phrase comes oddly from the dry, reserved man of the world that Rogers became, and it came from the other side of a much deeper breach than this. Rogers, like Henry Wilberforce, imagined that Newman hardened himself towards a friend for disagreeing with him; in reality the hardness was exercised against himself for fear his feelings might make him betray his principles and give up a position which ought to be held. He hated quarrelling, and flintiness was a defence against it. While he seemed flinty to Rogers he was writing to Bowden, who had consulted his opinion on the Breviary : 'I am so bothered and attacked on all sides by friends and foes, that I had much rather say nothing. . . . I mean, I distrust my judgment and am getting afraid to speak. It is just like walking on treacherous ice : one cannot say a thing but one offends someone or other — I don't mean foe, for that one could bear, but friend. You cannot conceive what unpleasant tendencies to split are developing themselves on all sides, and how one suffers because one wishes to keep well with all, or at least because one cannot go wholly with this man or that.'

The translation of the Breviary hung fire ; part was indeed printed, but privately, and not till some years later.

These differences and uncertainties had slipped, not wholly resolved, into the background by the next year, 1839, but they may have had something to do with Newman's attempts to keep a severer fast that Lent, and with his increasing desire to live according to some kind of religious rule. He and Pusey often discussed the possible revival of the idea of monastic community. Pusey had great plans to found a 'college' for priests living together, to work in some industrial town : the needs of these places were much in the minds of the Tractarians. Pusey would sketch his plan to the last detail, long before he knew if there were men who would carry it out ; Newman, on the other hand, felt that if the thing was to be alive and real, it must grow up naturally. The most he thought of was buying land at Littlemore in case of need.

Meanwhile he tried to regulate his own life, but it was extremely

difficult while living at Oriel, called on by all and sundry, and busy
from morning till night. The diaries are like graphs of the endless
business of his everyday life, with the spare pages at the end a shore
on which the flotsam and jetsam were cast. Baptisms, burials,
marriages ('married the waiter at the Star'); duties as Rural Dean
('went over St Peter-le-Bailey'); visiting the sick, week after week
('sat with so-and-so'); confirmation classes; walking out to Littlemore and back; daily Matins in St. Mary's; the weekly communion;
this went on while he wrote books and sermons and tracts, edited
the *British Critic*, and corresponded with Tractarians in ever widen-
ing circles: the names overran the compartments of the diary,
written along the side. At the end there were lists of 'people I must
be civil to' — more invitations, all ticked but two. Notes on Anti-
christ and Pantheism followed hard on jotted accounts: umbrella,
washing, charity, medicine, letters, parcels, the early communion
collections which went to clergy charities, and a memo of powder for
toothache.

People later got the idea that Newman lived at Oxford a secluded
scholar's life, sheltered from the rough realities of the world. Nothing
could be farther from the truth. The books that influenced so many
were written at high pressure in the midst of a life of overflowing
activity. No leader of a political party could have suffered more
trials from public attacks, private dissensions, personal disappoint-
ments, discoveries of intrigue without and misgivings within: in
personal relations alone Newman was dealing every day with men of
all kinds, ages and opinions, from London lawyers to the High Street
shopkeepers of his vestry, who glared in hostile silence when he
showed them the gift of a chalice. People who read the sermons, or
saw him once in St. Mary's imagined sometimes that anyone who set
such a high value on spiritual things must live in a rarefied atmosphere,
insulated from the trivial wear and tear of ordinary existence and
from its sudden emergencies and rude shocks. The hostile suggested
that his gentleness was in fact weakness, a hypersensitive shrinking
from unpleasant situations and people who opposed him — a form of
cowardice and selfishness, however disguised with phrases about the
sensitivity of genius. But in Oxford, in his own college, Newman
had to face permanent and increasing personal hostility; he did not
evade it. Sometimes he was confronted with sudden situations
requiring a simpler courage. Lockhart remembered one incident, in
that time of Town and Gown rows where heads were often broken on
both sides — it was, after all, a revolutionary era. Newman was

walking alone up the High Street when from Carfax a mob of men
bore down on him, led by a brawny and drunken butcher, shouting
blasphemies. Some friends hurried after Newman to effect a rescue.
But he walked straight up to the ringleader and said calmly, 'My
friend, if you thought of the meaning of your words, you would not
say them'. Lockhart commented with admiration : 'The savage was
tamed on the spot, touched his hat, turned round and went back'.

Anthony Froude, Hurrell's youngest brother, is a good witness to
Newman's character and behaviour at Oxford, since after 1845 he
repudiated the ideas of the Movement, and for some time was sceptical
of all religion. In 1849 he wrote *The Nemesis of Faith* which enjoyed
a brief *succès de scandale*. It was his second attempt at an autobiographical novel — the first had been bought up by the horrified
Archdeacon. The doubting young man in *Nemesis* falls in love with
a married lady ; when her child dies she suggests elopement, which
so overcomes the hero with guilt and horror that he rushes off to the
Lake — Italy is the appropriate setting for passion — to commit
suicide by drinking a poisoned cup. From this fate he is saved by
the sudden appearance of Mr. Frederick Mornington — Newman, in
thin disguise, who dashes the poison from his hand. 'What a figure
you cut in poor Froude's book !' Faber remarked to Newman in 1849.
Ludicrous as the situation is, the picture of Newman shows the
immense power his image exercised over Anthony Froude's mind —
which it retained, in more mature form, to the end of his life.

'Markham Sutherland' looks round : 'And the figure he saw, and
the glance he met, was hardly calculated to give him back his courage.
How well he knew it ! How often in old college years he had hung
upon those lips ; that voice so keen, so preternaturally sweet, whose
very whisper used to thrill through crowded churches, when every
breath was held to hear ; that calm grey eye ; those features, so
stern, and yet so gentle !' Markham meekly follows Mr. Mornington
away from his chosen place of suicide and pours out his woes. 'His
listener's sympathies were so entire, so heartfelt, he seemed himself
to have passed through each one of Markham's difficulties, so surely
he understood them.'

When he had regained a certain national Protestantism, and had
won fame with his histories, Anthony Froude put these same qualities
on record in an essay on *The Oxford Counter-Reformation*. He
emphasized Newman's qualities of leadership, his candour, his
'world-wide' mind, his carelessness of his personal prospects, his
tender-heartedness with the erring and anxious — to Froude it was

a blessed thing not to have doubts treated as a form of moral wickedness. 'He was never condescending with us, never didactive or authoritative. . . . Ironical he could be but not ill-natured. Not a malicious anecdote was ever heard from him. Prosy he could not be. He was lightness itself — the lightness of elastic strength. . . .'

Newman's sympathy was not only extended to anxious young men ; his friends knew they could count on him in a crisis for positive support. The friend who needed it most at this time was Pusey. When he was first married Pusey weighed only eight stone and was in very delicate health ; but as he grew stronger his wife grew weaker. She began to be ill in 1837. At the beginning of 1838 their only son Philip was desperately ill. He survived, but crippled and deformed for life, and deaf. Mrs. Pusey grew worse and worse ; her illness was long drawn out and Pusey suffered agonies. In the spring of 1839 he knew all hope was gone. He wrote to his mother, 'God's will be done ! ever ! ever ! My poor children ! Yet He will provide.' He was so worn out with the long strain that Newman, who was devoted to them both, could write when she died, without pain, on Trinity Sunday, 'It is a great relief'. Pusey was so shattered with grief he felt he could not bear to see anyone, but his mother sent for Newman. He came at once and after he had gone Pusey said, 'It was like the visit of an Angel'. He came every day to walk or sit with Pusey ; he was the only person Pusey could bear to see ; even to Keble he could not speak of his loss. The funeral was on the first of June, and for long after Pusey used to walk across the Quad with his head down, trying to escape the memory. 'I used for some time (I know not how long) to see on my way to Cathedral prayers, the white of the pall wave, as it had waved with the wind on that Saturday, at that particular spot.'

After his wife's death Pusey gave up all social visiting and lived in seclusion, leaving the great drawing-room unused, and wearing crape on his hat from now on and a black scarf (stole) in church. When one of their babies had died he had regarded it as a 'chastisement', and now he worried both Keble and Newman by taking his loss as a punishment. Newman wrote : 'You must not think any punishment is meant. Why should it ?' And he added, perhaps thinking of Mary : 'How many whom we love are taken out of our sight by sudden death, however healthy. . . . I do not think you must look on it as some strange thing. Pray do not.' But Pusey developed a fixed idea that he was being punished, and must live as a penitent. For this reason he persistently refused to have his portrait taken, even at the request of friends, to the end of his life. Under the anonymous title of penitent he built and endowed the famous church of St. Saviour's, Leeds, where the pugnacious Hook was the high Tractarian but very anti-Roman Vicar.

The church was to be a memorial to his wife, and alas, by the time it was opened, it also commemorated his daughter Lucy. She was ten when her mother died, and had five more years to live, the last in illness and suffering. There was one healthy child, Mary, the youngest, who grew up and married. The children were cared for by governesses and did not live much in Oxford; Pusey took holidays with them, often at Ilfracombe, a devoted, if rather sad father. It was his curious temperament to be very hopeful about the Movement and very gloomy about himself. In 1846 he showed Keble a code of penitential behaviour he had drawn up for himself, which included not smiling; in vain Keble pointed out that this would be imposing a penance on other people. Pusey lived in a world of his own and rarely realized the effect of what he said and did.

Far otherwise was it with Newman, intensely aware of other people's reactions.

THE TRANSITION
(1839–1846)

1839

The First Hit from Rome

'I LOVE our Church as a portion and a realizing of the Church Catholic among us,' Newman had written to Hugh James Rose in 1836 after the Hampden affair. He did not, as some were to complain, love it for its own sake, in the spirit of 'my country right or wrong'. His conversion at the age of fifteen is crucial to the understanding of his development. He did not grow up, as so many do, in a half-conscious habit of religious practice. He turned directly from a boyish but real scepticism to the worship of a transcendent Creator, and determined to serve Him, the Way, the Truth and the Life, with all his heart, mind and soul, according to the divine will. He came to accept, because he was convinced it was part of the revelation of that will, the idea of a society, at once divine and human, in which Christ worked to restore and re-create mankind. For years he had been fighting the errors which, coming in at the Reformation, had, as he believed, corrupted the faith of the English people, both in understanding and action. It was natural to assume that churches in other countries were equally corrupted, though from an excess rather than a deficiency of faith. The True Faith was to be found in the Creeds hammered out by the great Councils of the first five centuries ; if the Church of England followed Antiquity it could not go essentially wrong.

In the summer of 1839 Newman settled down to study the doctrine of the Incarnation and the theological conflicts which resulted in its definition. Particularly important to its understanding were the Monophysite heretics, who believed that if Christ was God he could not be man too : his humanity was only an appearance. It was theology that Newman was considering, but it was history that rose up and hit him. In common with all later Christians who accepted the creeds he believed these men were wrong, and had mistaken the truth handed down by the Apostles — a mistake which reacted on Christian living. What surprised him was that it was the orthodox

party, sanctioned by Rome, which introduced new terms to clarify
the old doctrine, and that besides the active Monophysite (One-
nature) faction there was a large body of conservatives who regarded
the new terms with suspicion as innovations, thought peace more
important than an accurate definition of truth, and consequently
were strongly supported by the civil powers. Here was the Via
Media in the fifth century and it was on the wrong side! The
Church now, including the Anglican Church, believed what Rome
believed then : why ? Suddenly Newman's angle of vision shifted
and he saw the Church, not as it looked from England since the
Reformation, but as it looked, always, from Rome. 'Rome was where
she now is.' Years later he wrote in the *Apologia* : 'My stronghold
was Antiquity. Now here, in the middle of the fifth century, I found
as it seemed to me, the Christendom of the sixteenth and nineteenth
centuries reflected. I saw my face in that mirror and I was a Monophysite.'

It was a disturbing sensation. He mentioned it to Henry Wilberforce when they met at the dedication of the new church at Otter-
bourne, in Keble's parish, built by Charlotte Yonge's father. But
soon he was writing his usual carefree letter, retailing the rumour that
an elderly don was to marry : 'You see it is never too late. Yet I
want people to believe me, which they sometimes won't, when I say
I do not mean to marry at 60.' A novel had given him dreams of
being 'a sort of brother of charity in London'. He was just going off
on a round of vacation visits when a worried friend pressed on him a
copy of the *Dublin Review*, the Catholic quarterly recently founded
by Wiseman, and containing an article by him on another controversy
of Antiquity, that of the Donatists' schism. 'It is all the old story,'
said Newman, not interested, because he saw no Via Media parallel.
But the friend kept repeating the phrase Wiseman quoted from St.
Augustine : *Securus iudicat orbis terrarum* (the whole world is a
safe judge). The words went on sounding in Newman's ears like the
Tolle, lege (take it, read it), St. Augustine himself had heard the
child crying over the garden wall, in his torment of indecision. The
phrase was not the expression of a new idea, for Newman already
believed the decisions of the whole *ancient* world to be a safe guide,
but it now came to someone who saw his own position as similar to
that of a party which had been condemned by the judgment of that
very world. Why was Rome always on the right side ? Again,
suddenly and irrevocably, Newman saw the question as Rome saw
it : the side was right because Rome was on it. Rome claimed that

God had given her Bishop, as St. Peter's successor, the privilege and duty of acting as supreme authority on earth, as Vicar of Christ. 'Rome is the divinely appointed centre of unity and judge of controversies,' as he put it, four years later, to Harriett, when he was certain.

Now he was not certain, but he was so startled by this new vision that he could not keep it to himself. He told it to Rogers, and to Henry Wilberforce, walking with him through the New Forest. 'A vista has opened before me,' he said, 'to the end of which I do not see.' It was 'a thunderstroke' to Henry, who cried out he would rather Newman died than deserted to Rome. Newman said he would indeed ask his friends to pray that he might die rather than do it, if it were not the will of God. He so prayed himself, later. At present he had no intention of trusting this sudden illumination ; it must be examined carefully and without emotion. 'After a while I got calm,' he said in the *Apologia*.

Back in Oxford he found Wiseman's article was causing alarm and despondency ; it was a new thing to have a Catholic of his learning taking part in their controversies. Newman set to work on an essay for the *British Critic*, which he prefaced with a brief and pithy dialogue. The Anglo-Catholic says, 'Our teaching is the true, because it is the primitive ; yours is not true, because it is novel'. The Roman Catholic replies, 'Our teaching is true, for it is everywhere the same ; yours has no warrant, for it is but local and private.' 'We go by Antiquity', says the Anglo-Catholic. 'We go by Catholicity', says the Roman. Newman was trying to prove that whether or not the Anglican Church was wrong, Rome was wrong too. He convinced himself for the moment, but the Monophysite ghosts were not to be laid so easily. They too had said their teaching was true because it was primitive. The novelties of Rome, the technical terms of its definitions, were a barrier to accepting its claims just as long as they were seen as arbitrary additions to primitive truth ; but if in the fifth century they had been elucidations of that truth, was it not possible that they might be so in the sixteenth, at that wretched Tridentine Council ?

1840

'*I am going up to Littlemore*'

AT the beginning of 1840 Newman published *The Church of the Fathers*, a collection of his sketches from the *British Magazine*. It became very popular with young Apostolicals of both sexes, who found in it for the first time the inspiration of the lives of saints, as real and human as if they were still alive, as indeed they were to Newman. 'Strong meat, but sweet meat too', he called it to H. W. and thought it his 'prettiest book'. To the world, whether hostile or friendly, he was still a rising star ; his power and prestige had never been higher. It was now that he decided to go up to Littlemore and spend Lent there alone.

It happened by accident. Bloxam, then acting as his curate, had to give up because his father was ill. 'What a loss I have in you!' Newman wrote, warmly thanking him for all he had done. But it gave him an opportunity of an experiment in retirement from the world, such as he had wished for so long. He lodged in the village with a Mrs. Barnes, away from the distractions of Oxford. Here he could undertake unobserved a more rigorous fast ; it was in fact far too severe, though it took him several years to find out where he must relax it or seriously impair his health. He did not dine out, did not read the newspapers and, a nineteenth-century touch, did not wear gloves. He breakfasted on bread and hot milk with an egg ; dined on cold bacon, bread, cheese and water, supped on barley water, bread and an egg. Bacon was his only meat. This sugarless, butterless diet, without fruit or pastry, or even fish, and without tea or coffee or wine, he kept up throughout Lent. On Wednesdays and Fridays he ate nothing at all till 6 p.m. and then had an extra egg for supper. On Sundays he had some tea and a glass of wine. All through Holy Week he fasted till six, and on Maundy Thursday and Good Friday ate nothing at all but bread and water in the evening. 'I have felt rather weak in the limbs,' he remarked calmly at the end. 'I have been able to think, write and read as usual.' He took a few quinine pills and had no 'face or teeth ache'. He made, however, no attempt at this time to curtail sleep, or sleep on the ground, or to endure cold. But he did not sleep long, writing letters at night and rising very early. He used the full Breviary office, privately, all through Lent.

This was the voluntary cross he set himself to carry in secret while he plunged into the work of the parish. 'For myself,' he wrote with enthusiasm to Bloxam, 'I am so drawn to this place, though I have been here but a week, that it will be an effort to go back to St. Mary's. How one is pulled in twain! Why cannot one be in two spheres at once? however, I have various plans to effect this object, of multiplying myself.... Everything is so cold at St. Mary's. I have felt it for years. I know no one. I have no sympathy. If it were not for those poor undergraduates, who are after all *not* my charge, and the Sunday communions, I should be sorely tempted to pitch my tent here. . . . The children are vastly improved in singing and now that the organ is mute, their voices are so thrilling as to make one sick with love. You will think I am in a rapture. I fear I am writing hyperbolically. . . .' He had taken the children in hand immediately, teaching them 'Gregorians'. 'I have rummaged out an old violin and strung it,' he told Jemima, 'and on Mondays and Thursdays have begun to *lead* them with it, a party of between twenty and thirty great and little in the schoolroom.' The children seemed to take to the chant, 'though they have not learned it yet — for I see it makes them smile — though that may be at me'. On Sundays in the church, he taught them their faith. 'Newman's catechizing has been a great attraction this Lent,' James Mozley wrote home, 'and men have gone out of Oxford every Sunday to hear it. I thought it very striking, done with such spirit, and the children so up to it . . . all unanimous on the point of the nine orders of angels.'

But even with the children everything was not easy. There was a fine printed 'System' but it was not followed ; many children whose names were down did not come ; some were mere babies of two or three and even the older ones could not answer Newman's simple questions when he first went to the school. In some notes he wrote that Mrs. Whitman, the schoolmistress, was 'a dawdle and a do-nothing — and what was worse, she attempted to be obsequious to me . . .'. To Tom Mozley he said, 'I'm afraid my schoolmistress drinks', and later admitted, 'She *does* drink, badly'. The children were badly behaved and dirty. In a postscript to Henry he wrote : 'For several days I have been saying to myself, O that Henry would bring his wife to put my school to rights! I see the girls' hair wants combing, but cannot go further in my analysis of the general air of slatternliness which prevails.' To Jemima he remarked, 'I find I am not deep in the philosophy of school-girl tidiness.'

At this point he was struck down by 'a most unpleasant cold, which has clean taken away my voice. . . . This evening my reading the service was not audible to the little children close to me — my throat is choked up ; and I have been sucking liquorice all day to my great disgust and without any perceptible benefit. . . . Mrs. Barnes comforts me by telling me that if I take some precious mess (which now stands on my fender till I go to bed) for *three* nights, I cannot tell the good it will do me.' But next day he had to report that Mrs. Barnes' prescription had proved a failure. He tried steaming his mouth with camomile, but ended, 'I believe patience is the only recipe'.

It was cold ; there was a fall of snow on March 25th, feast of the Annunciation. Newman told Jemima news of the Littlemore people, all poor, whom he visited. They were too simple to have views about religion like the High Street shopkeepers ; they accepted what he said and what he did, and the only thing special they remembered about him was his goodness and faith. One woman was sure he had said something at the burial of her baby which convinced her it was in heaven ; others recalled the Good Friday services. Perhaps it was to them that Newman preached in 1842 a sermon on the Crucifixion designed to bring home the sufferings of Christ to people too familiar with the story to feel its horror. With great simplicity three pictures are presented, an animal cruelly killed, a child tortured, and a venerable man subjected to shame and violence : 'Why are you so shocked at the one, why are you not shocked at the other?'

No wonder they did not forget him. Anne Mozley, going back in 1849, was surprised to find how much they had loved him — like so many she imagined 'his power lay in a different class'. They resented all the changes after he left. Even in 1875 an old couple sent messages : 'Tell him we be old too — husband in his seventy-nine. Lawkadaisy! you be older than Mr. Newman.' He was always finding jobs for them, making use of his richer friends in this way, ready to help in this world as well as to prepare them for the next. This first Lent he had a bright idea for encouraging cleanliness in the girls, he got pinafore patterns from Mrs. H. W. for them to make up themselves 'with directions it would do your heart good to see', he told Jemima 'about lappels and frock sleeves'. When Easter came the white pinafores were set off very prettily with pink bonnets and white tippets, which he gave them. 'I have effected a great reform (for the time) in the girls' hands and faces', he told Jemima triumphantly. 'Lectured with unblushing effrontery on the necessity of their keeping their work clean, and set them to knit stockings with all their might.'

'I came up here as a sort of penance during Lent', he wrote to his aunt. 'But though without friends or books, I have as yet had nothing but pleasure. So that it seems a shame to spend Lent so happily.' Part of the penance of going to Littlemore, then, was to do without books and friends for a while. Perhaps an incident which occured at Christmas made him feel he was too dependent on the sympathy of friends. He wrote a dedication for the *Church of the Fathers* to Rogers and sent it to him. Since it was destroyed it is not possible to recover the wording, but Rogers was embarrassed by it and replied in a flippant, jeering tone. Ordinary society, he said, would 'think it a conclusion on the mooted sanity of Oxford divines. ... If I knew the "dearest, sweetest, etc" was to be contained in those two little volumes I should never be able to see their very backs without colouring up to the eyes.' He even said he did not see how 'to convince an ordinary sensible well-disposed person you were compos'. Whatever Newman said in reply provoked a defensive retort, and it was only a week of silence which drove Rogers to apologize for his manner, not his opinion, for he still thought that Newman 'living exclusively among Oxford friends and reading very much was not aware of the degree of strangeness' in his expressions. He was relieved when Newman answered. But the book was dedicated to Isaac Williams : 'the sight of whom carries back his friends to ancient, holy and happy times'. Isaac was taken by surprise, but was delighted.

But Rogers was now leaving Oxford for good. He was nearly thirty, he had found his feet in the London world, and was ambitious for a political career. When Newman saw him off in March, on the London coach, he reflected that he had had just seven years of his company — *contubernium*, as he called it, when people live in the same house and share daily life together — the same span as that allotted to his friendship with Froude. Rogers' failure of sympathy, perhaps partly due to irritation at Newman's Roman misgivings (for Rogers had nothing but antipathy for Rome), and his going away to London and politics, left Newman feeling lonely. On that snowy Annunciation day he took out the old exercise book in which he had

written the account of his illness in Sicily and suddenly finished it.
That was the end of Sicily; and the beginning of a new process of
dying and renewal. Now he remembered the simple faithfulness of
Gennaro, who had only asked for an old cloak as his reward. But
Newman had given him far more than its worth, and kept it. 'I have
it still. I have brought it up here to Littlemore, and on some nights
I have had it on my bed. I have so few things to sympathize with me
that I take to clokes.'

Out of his loneliness he wrote : 'The thought keeps pressing on
me, while I write this, what am I writing it for ? For myself, I may
look at it once or twice in my whole life, and what sympathy is there
in *my* looking at it ? Whom have I, whom can I have, who would
take an interest in it ? I was going to say, I only have found one
who even took that sort of affectionate interest in me as to be pleased
with such details — and that is H. Wilberforce, and what shall I ever
see of him ? This is the sort of interest a wife takes, and none but
she — it is a woman's interest — and that interest, so be it, shall never
be taken in me. Never, so be it, will I be other than God has found
me. All my habits for years, my tendencies, are towards celibacy. I
could not take that interest in this world which marriage requires. I
am too disgusted with this world — And, above all, call it what one
will, I have a repugnance to a clergyman's marrying. I do not say it
is not lawful — I cannot deny the right — but, whether prejudice or
not, it shocks me. And therefore I willingly give up the possession
of that sympathy, which I feel is not, and cannot be, granted to me.
Yet, not the less do I feel the need of it. Who will care to be told
such details as I have put down above ? Shall I ever have in my old
age spiritual children who will take an interest such as a wife does ?
How time is getting on ! I seem to be reconciling myself to the idea
of being old. It seems but yesterday the Whigs came into power —
another such to-morrow will make me almost fifty, an elderly man.
What a dream is life. I used to regret festival days going so quick.
They come and they are gone ; but, so it is, time is nothing except
as the seed of eternity.'

Three weeks earlier, just before Lent, he had preached on *The
Power of the Will*; whether he spoke, or only wrote in for publication,
as he often did on controversial subjects, some remarks on celibacy,
they certainly belong to the mood of this time. 'I will not be inconsiderate enough to make light of the power of temptation of any kind,
nor will I presume to say Almighty God will certainly shield a man
from temptation for his wishing it ; but whenever men complain, as

they often do, of the arduousness of a high virtue, at least it were well
that they should first ask themselves the question, whether they desire
to have it. We hear much in this day of the impossibility of heavenly
purity ; — far be it from me to say that every one has not his proper
gift from God, one after this manner, another after that ; — but O ye
men of the world, when ye talk as ye do, so much of the impossibility
of this or that supernatural grace, when you disbelieve in the existence
of severe self-rule, when you scoff at holy resolutions, and affix a slur
on those who make them, are you sure that the impossibility which
you insist on does not lie, not in nature, but in the will ? . . . Say not
. . . that you cannot be other than Adam made you ; you have never
brought yourselves to will it — you cannot bear to will it. You cannot
bear to be other than you are. Life would seem a blank to you, were
you other ; yet what you are from not desiring a gift, this you make
an excuse for not possessing it.'

He had chosen his way, and would not turn back for the hardness
of it. And yet it was hard. Now he was completely alone in it ;
Froude had died ; Henry had married, Keble had married ; Rogers
had gone away into the world. There was no sign of anyone else
choosing the same path. It looked as if he would be left a solitary
eccentric, no different in appearance from any odd old don who had
simply remained a bachelor for no particular reason. Already he was
much older than the other Fellows at Oriel, and he felt the awkwardness of it — his sister Jemima could not understand why. He was
just at the age, nearly forty, when the psychological horizon closes in
and the contours of experience and personality are more or less
defined, when the natural energy of life is no longer expanding and
if a human being is to grow, it must be in mind and spirit. Newman
had always felt the speed and shortness of time passing, but it is
different to realize, physically and emotionally, what was known only
to thought and imagination.

Some people might have given up, out of loneliness, the ideal
which brought only ridicule and 'slurs' and appeared to serve no
particularly high purpose in a society which had no use nor place for
priests and monks ; this was not really a temptation to Newman now
that he had held his course so long. But there was perhaps a less
obvious danger that he might sink into the position assigned to him
by others, and be the mere academic bachelor they thought him.
What could have been easier than to slip into a comfortable donnish
life, a famous author and preacher, visiting friends, going abroad for
holidays, slowly becoming respectable as he got older, perhaps even

ending up as a Professor of Divinity ? It could have happened. Instead, when he felt lonely, Newman gave up friends and books for Lent, and went out to live with rigorous austerity in a dull village, where the schoolmistress drank, the children were dirty and the people quarrelled in their homes. And it snowed, and he got a cold. But it was a time of happiness.

On Easter Eve Bloxam came to tea, and Newman broke his fast with him, after three days of nothing but bread and water. Then they got out the altar cloth that Jemima and the Mozleys had been working in Derby. Mrs. Barnes was in ecstasies over it — she dreamed of it of a night, she told Newman. He and Bloxam went up to the little church and arranged it with care, and how beautiful it looked, he told its makers. 'We have got some roses, wallflowers and sweetbriar and the chapel smells as if to remind one of the Holy Sepulchre.' And next day there were the children in their new pink bonnets and white pinafores, singing the Psalms in Gregorians, and Easter communion, and new life for Littlemore, and for Newman too. 'Indeed,' he wrote to Jemima, 'we are all so happy we are afraid of being too happy.'

1840–41

Taken up by 'The Times'

'It is a great joy to me and fitted to this season,' Newman wrote to Jemima after Easter, 'that I have made it up with Frank.' He felt he was able to do this because Frank had given up the Brethren, and was in a state of simple dissatisfaction with religious bodies. But it was difficult to effect a thorough reconciliation, not because Frank did not wish it, but because the two brothers were so different that they never could get on easily. Newman took a great deal of trouble not to offend Frank, as the struggling drafts of his letters show, but he could not help the chief offence which was being himself, and older than his brother. 'I know it is harder for an elder brother to bear opposition but it seemed to me as if you could not endure it,' said Frank, 'and while I feel this I cannot be easy. It is not that I want to contradict you when I am with you ; but I want to feel that I am *at liberty* to do so if I like ; else it is slavery, not society on equal terms.' As a matter of fact, to judge from his letters he never could resist contradicting John ; and though John never preached his own opinions at Frank, Frank certainly let fly his at John. He liked argument as much as John hated it. 'I do not value Chrysostom any more than I value Dr. Wiseman, but rather less', he announced belligerently. John answered by switching his attention to Charles, responsibility for whom was the one bond they shared to the end of their lives. They were still trying to find a place in society for Charles. The Mozleys would make no allowances for him and refused a testimonial to help him to secure a commercial situation.

This year Frank got the post of Classical Professor at Manchester College. In the autumn John, on his way up to Derby, met him in Cheltenham and they travelled as far as Birmingham together ; all went off well. At Manchester all the most prominent and clever people were Unitarians ; Frank soon became a friend of Dr. Martineau. The moral earnestness and rationalistic attitude of the Unitarians appealed to Frank, who soon shed the remnants of his

Evangelicalism. But now, as well as doubting the truth of theological doctrines, he began to question the historical foundation
of Christianity — he was soon to go too far for the Unitarians, discarding not only worship of Christ as God, but even admiration for
him as a man. However, at present he only doubted the resurrection.
'It is most painful indeed . . .' Newman said to Jemima. 'Indeed I
do not see *where* he is to stop. . . . Whether Anglicanism leads to
Rome, so far it is *clear as day* that Protestantism leads to Infidelity.
With a clear-headed impartial man, or with a body of men in the long
run, there is no resting place short of it.' To Frank himself he said,
'I think your reasoning irresistible, granting certain latent principles
which you all along affirm. And since I anticipate that these will be
generally affirmed by the coming age, as they are in great measure
ahead, I am prepared for almost a downfall of Christianity for a time.'
And he added, in almost the very words he was to use nearly forty
years later, when he was made a Cardinal at Rome : 'I have no fears
for the ultimate fortunes of Catholicism ; I do but grieve and sigh
over those destined to fall by the way in the wilderness'.

A great many would fall in the wilderness for want of being
warned of the way they were going, and whenever he got the chance
Newman issued warnings. An opportunity to address a much wider
audience than ever before came suddenly at the beginning of the
next year, 1841, while he was working on his tract on the interpretation of the Thirty-Nine Articles, No. 90 of the series. John Walter,
editor of *The Times*, thought it time the Tory leader Peel was taken
to task for his growing radicalism, and his son, another John Walter,
who had just gone down from Oxford a great enthusiast for Newman,
suggested that he would be the very man. Newman wrote seven
letters, signing them *Catholicus*, which appeared in February and
were, much later, published under the title of *The Tamworth Reading
Room*, for they were an attack on Peel's speech at the opening of that
admirable institution. Sir Robert had let off a few high-flown phrases
in praise of education ; how knowledge refined people, improved
their characters, raised their standards and so on. Newman picked up
these dull remarks and by indicating their origin in Lord Brougham's
philosophy was able to attack the principles to which he was most
opposed. Peel, who had no idea of the implications of his own
platitudes, was so annoyed that at the third letter young Walter had
to write to Newman to suggest stopping. He acquiesced, 'though of
course I should not have begun unless I expected to finish. Do what
you will with No 4, perhaps you had better burn it.' But everyone

was discussing the brilliant letters and speculating on the author's identity, and in the end the series was continued, with a leading article 'to satisfy people they are not intended to serve political purposes'. Newman certainly had no political purpose, nor did he attack Peel personally ; his speech was a mere excuse to hold up to ridicule the fashionable idea that education was going to make people morally better. And it was done in high spirits ; Newman was at the top of his form.

'It seems that all "virtuous women" may be members of the Library,' he teased the humanitarians. 'A very emphatic silence is maintained about women not virtuous. What does this mean ? Does it mean to exclude them, while bad *men* are admitted ? Is this accident or design, sinister and insidious, against a portion of the community ? What has virtue to do with a Reading Room ? It is to *make* its members virtuous ; it is to "exalt the moral dignity of their nature" ; it is to provide "charms and temptations" to allure them from sensuality and riot. To whom but to the vicious ought Sir Robert to discourse about "opportunities" and "access" and "moral improvement" ; and who else would prove a fitter experiment, and a more glorious triumph of scientific influence ?'

But the letters were not all teasing. Man could not improve himself morally by increasing knowledge ; his sins would but become more subtle. 'You do but play "hunt the slipper" with the fault of our nature till you go to Christianity. . . . If we attempt to effect a moral improvement by means of poetry, we shall but mature into a mawkish, frivolous and fastidious sentimentalism ; — if by means of argument, into a dry, unamiable long-headedness ; — if by good society, into a polished outside, with hollowness within, in which vice has lost its grossness, and perhaps increased its malignity ; — if by experimental science, into an uppish, supercilious temper, much inclined to scepticism.' An education has been achieved since Newman's day which seems to produce all these results.

At that time people were only beginning to think that scientific methods alone could arrive at truth in all spheres ; to-day this is almost an axiom. Religion is a subject for investigation, God a proposition to be proved, Christ an object of historical argument and saints cases for psycho-analysis. Some people then thought that increased knowledge of nature would also increase knowledge of God, and that God could be scientifically discovered from nature. Newman said, 'The truth is that the system of Nature is just as much connected with Religion, where minds are not religious, as a watch or a steam-carriage. The material world, indeed, is infinitely more wonderful than any human contrivance ; but wonder is not religion, or we should be worshipping our railroads. What the physical creation presents to us in itself is a piece of machinery, and when men speak of a divine Intelligence as its Author, this God of theirs is not the Living and True, unless the spring is the god of the watch, or steam the creator of the engine.' He warned of a danger which many were to fall into, of ceasing to believe in God when science found no direct evidence for His action in nature. 'Religion', he said, before the great confusion had really begun, 'never has been a deduction from what we know ; it has ever been an assertion of what we are to believe. . . . Christianity is a history supernatural, and almost scenic : it tells us what its Author is, by telling us what He has done.'

'Catholicus' made a great impression — his identity was kept secret — especially as it seemed as if *The Times* had taken up the Movement. This was influence, this was respectability ! And to the Liberals this was danger. The *Morning Chronicle* said : 'Puseyism claims to be a god upon earth and commands intelligence like a slave'. They saw danger in an alliance between the hard intellect of Oxford and the vague traditionalism of the Tories. 'Puseyism is an iron mace, Toryism a rope of sand.' Puseyites were in earnest, as obstinate as Thomas à Becket. How delighted Froude would have been at the comparison ! Newman wrote to H. W. : 'You should have seen the late article in the *Globe* silently alluding to Catholicus. It seems as if hitherto they had thought Puseyism a thing of copes and lighted tapers. Geese, they never read a word till the fist is shaken in their face.'

He was delighted with the result. Lord Morpeth shook a fist in retaliation, making in the House what Church called to Rogers 'a savage attack on Oxford as being a place where people who were paid for teaching Protestantism were doing all they could to bring things nearer to Rome.' Right in the middle of this excitement Tract 90 was published.

1841

'I am in a regular scrape about that Tract 90'

IT was a hard cold winter, Lent had just begun and Newman's birthday had fallen on Quinquagesima Sunday. 'I never had such dreary thoughts as on finding myself forty,' he wrote to Jemima. 'Twenty-one was bad enough.' The Tract came out on Saturday February 27th, the day before the anniversary of Froude's death. Newman had written it for the benefit of those who, like himself, believed the Church of England to be essentially Catholic, and found difficulty in accepting some of the Thirty-Nine Articles. 'But what do you make of the Articles?' people often said to him. Like Froude he thought the authority of the Articles on a different plane from that of the Creeds; he believed that they were a Protest not against Catholic doctrine, but against medieval abuses. The Tract was not a polemic, but a short treatise in which the author openly stated that he was not concerned with the intentions of the framers, but with interpreting the Articles according to the faith of the Church Universal, so far as this could be done without violating the literal and grammatical sense. He felt himself the more justified in doing so as the predominant evangelical party had adopted doctrines of regeneration and justification difficult to reconcile with some of the articles; indeed, this was the reason why Frank Newman had been unable to sign them and was now in Manchester instead of in Oxford.

Newman never expected the storm that now burst over his head. One of the reasons for it was that for a long time nobody had given a thought to the Articles, but they had been generally assumed to be a bulwark against Catholicism. Newman, who had sworn to them both as a member of the University and as Vicar of St. Mary's, was too honest to shelve the problem, but as soon as he put forward the only interpretation possible to those who thought Protestantism a corruption alien to the true Church of England, he was widely and furiously accused of dishonesty. Hampden and his friends now had the satisfaction of hearing Newman's dissimulation and guile proclaimed all

over England ; for over twenty years this was the common charge
against him and to the great majority of his countrymen he became
the very embodiment of craft and subtlety.

Newman called Golightly the 'Tony-fire-the-faggot' of the agitation. As soon as the Tract appeared he read it, horrified, and bought
up so many copies, Church reported, that Parker the bookseller could
hardly keep up with him. These he sent round to everyone he could
think of, including a number of Bishops, underlining the popery of
the Tract and the evasive hypocrisy of the author. In Oxford it was
through his efforts that four senior tutors met and issued a public
letter, on Monday, March 8th, a week after the publication of the
Tract, demanding the name of the author. Two of the tutors were
Evangelicals, two Liberals ; one of the latter was Tait, who was to
be Arnold's successor at Rugby and afterwards Archbishop of Canterbury. On the Friday before this appeared Newman was already
writing to Bowden, 'People are so angry they will attempt anything.
The Heads of Houses are on the move.' Yet he did not 'repent it
unless indeed it should get Pusey involved'. After the four tutors'
demand, on 11th, he wrote to Henry Wilberforce, 'Do you know I
am in a regular scrape about that Tract 90 ? *All* through Golius, who
has solely *proprio motu* stirred up the world which else would have
slept. What is to come I know not. Heads of Houses are sitting
upon it. . . . People know me now. That's a comfort.' To Harriett
he wrote next day, 'I fear I am clean dished. The Heads of Houses
are at this moment concocting a manifesto against me. Do not think
I fear for my cause. We have had too great a run of luck.'

He had started an explanatory letter, addressed to Dr. Jelf, Pusey's
friend, but before he could get it printed the Heads were meeting
again. Pusey asked Hawkins to get the Hebdomadal Board to delay
proceedings twelve hours to allow Newman's defence to appear, but
they were much too angry to wait, and wanted no explanation. (Years
later Pusey reissued the Tract with an appended history ; Hawkins
swore it was not a question of twelve hours ; they appealed to
Newman who said he could not remember.) The Heads, on March
15th, promulgated a resolution which was printed under the University Arms and signed by the Vice-Chancellor, in which it was stated
that the Tract 'evading rather than explaining the sense of the
Thirty-Nine Articles and reconciling subscription to them with the
adoption of errors, which they were designed to counteract' was
inconsistent with the due observance of the University Statutes.
This was to say that no one who held the Articles in that sense had

the right to be a member of the university.   Church thought that the
Board took this authoritative line because the Heads were afraid of
an open fight in Convocation.   On the same day Newman sent his
reply.

'Mr. Vice-Chancellor — I write this to inform you respectfully
that I am the author, and have sole responsibility of the Tract, on
which the Hebdomadal Board has just expressed an opinion ; and
that I have not given my name hitherto, under the belief that it was
desired I should not do so.

'I hope it will not surprise you if I say, that my opinion remains
unchanged of the truth and honesty of the principle maintained in
the Tract, and of the necessity of putting it forth.

'At the same time I am prompted by my feelings to express my
deep consciousness, that everything I attempt might be done in a
better spirit, and in a better way ; and while I am sincerely sorry for
the trouble and anxiety I have given to the members of the Board, I
beg to return my thanks to them for an act, which, even though
founded on a misapprehension, may be made as profitable to myself,
as it is religiously and charitably intended.

I say all this with great sincerity and am, Mr Vice-Chancellor,
your obedient servant, John Henry Newman.'

Church, who was keeping up a running commentary for the
benefit of Rogers, thought this 'must have let new light into these
excellent old gentlemen. . . . It softened many people : even the
Provost, who is very strong, thought it necessary to butter a little
about "excellent spirit under trying circumstances etc."' (Hawkins
called it, to a friend, 'a manly letter'.)   James Mozley, however,
thought it too meek, and that the Heads would think it humbug.
'A general confession of humility was irrelevant to the present
occasion.'   His sister Anne disagreed, as usual.   'There is a Catholic
spirit of humility in it that one finds in some books and longs to see
practised,' she said.

Newman wrote to Bowden : 'Do not think all this will pain me.
You see no *doctrine* is censured, and my shoulders shall manage to
bear the charge.   If you knew all, or when you know, you will see
that I have asserted a great principle, and I ought to suffer for it.'
On the flap of Church's long letter to Rogers he wrote : 'I am now
in my right place, which I have long wished to be in, which I did not
know how to attain, and which has been brought about without my
intention, I hope I may say providentially, though I am perfectly
aware at the same time that it is a rebuke and punishment for my

secret pride and sloth. . . . I cannot anticipate what will be the result
of it in this place or elsewhere as regards *myself*. Somehow I do not
fear for the *cause*.'

Meanwhile his explanatory *Letter to Dr. Jelf* had come out, and
many people in Oxford felt he had been treated unfairly and too
precipitately. The newspapers, however, took up the case in a frenzy
of indignation. '*The Standard*', reported Church, 'has attacked
Newman personally with all the spite which its dulness enabled it to
put forth.' *The Times*, with the Catholicus letters just behind it, was
in a nasty quandary, and tried to keep the balance by praising the
good conduct of all concerned. But the general opinion was that
Popery had been unmasked at Oxford. 'What do you mean by
"the sensation I am causing in the world?"' Newman asked Jemima.
'Have they caricatured me yet?' They had; Harriett was disgusted.
'J. H. N. is shockingly thin,' she wrote, when he came to stay after
Easter, 'and set down on paper would look as old every bit as that
awful representation of him.'

His thinness was not entirely due to strain, as she imagined, for
he was keeping the same strict fast as last year, except for Sundays,
and was now even watering the milk he had allowed himself at breakfast; the only difference was that as he had to dine rather often in
hall he took fish for dinner; at Littlemore he had suet pudding —
for he was spending Lent there again. 'MUCH tried at times,' he
noted at the end. In Oxford he had to do so much talking, which
relaxed his throat. Once he had a stranger to breakfast, and so he
drank tea with him. Nobody knew he was doing all this, and all the
time letters were pouring in from friends and supporters all over the
country — very encouraging to find so many, but they all had to be
answered. However, Newman was in good spirits, as he always was
in a fight; he minded nothing till the Bishop came into it.

The Bishop could not help it; he was inundated with furious
letters from Evangelicals, demanding that he should take action about
the popish plotter he was harbouring in his diocese. And when he
wrote for advice from the Archbishop of Canterbury he got a vague
reply which ended suddenly, 'It would be desirable that the publication of the Tracts should be discontinued for ever'. There was
nothing for it but to intervene; he used Pusey as his intermediary
with Newman. His first request was that Tract 90 should be with-
drawn and the series discontinued. Notes passed to and fro. The
more Newman thought about it the more he felt he was being pushed
into a position where he must either defy his Bishop or deny his

principles — for to suppress the Tract publicly, at the Bishop's bidding, would imply its official censure. He told Pusey he would have to give up his living. 'If it was condemned as to doctrine I should feel I had no business in his diocese. I should not be signing the articles in the sense he meant them to be signed.' Two days later he said sadly, 'It is vain to deny that I shall be hurt and discouraged beyond measure if the Tract is suppressed at all'. Bagot melted, as usual, and a compromise was effected. Tract 90 was to remain in print, but the series was to end with it, and Newman agreed not to make any further comments on the Articles, after he had written a public Letter to the Bishop, in which he was to make it clear that he repudiated the claims of Rome. On his side the Bishop gave Newman to understand that if this was done, the Tract would not be censured.

Newman dated his *Letter* to the Bishop from Oriel, March 29th, and wrote it in such a hurry that the first sheets were in the press before he had finished the last. It was distasteful to him to bring up the old arguments of Roman corruptions, but he still believed in them, and to show that he thought Rome wrong was the only way to prove he was a *bona fide* member of the Church of England. His positive view he thus expressed: 'I think that to belong to the Catholic Church is the first of all privileges here below, as involving in it heavenly privileges, and . . . I consider the Church over which you preside to be the Catholic Church in this country.' The Bishop was pleased, and said he would never regret it. Newman wrote to Keble, whom he had of course consulted about his answer, 'We are all in very good spirits here'. Catholic doctrine was not censured, the Bishop was obeyed, and the Tract was selling like hot cakes. Newman added, 'Pusey is writing ; I wish he were not'.

Not only Pusey but everyone seemed to be writing, on all sides. Golightly was making Popish extracts from Newman's works in imitation of the *Elucidations* ; Ward on the other side was startling the Balliol Senior Common Room ; Hook, the peppery Vicar of Leeds, High but anti-Roman, whom Newman had also consulted, was addressing his Bishop. Pusey, however, took the prize for length and complexity, as usual : *his* Letter to Jelf (everybody's favourite public correspondent, perhaps because he did not reply) was 186 pages plus 41 of appendix. Pusey had once more been surprised by Newman's views. Newman wrote to George Ryder, 'Pusey has just discovered that I dislike the Reformers'. He had never even read Keble's preface to the second volume of Froude's *Remains*. In spite of the shock he was loyally determined to defend Tract 90 and its author.   The battle was enjoyed by most of the Tractarians, who felt they were giving as good as they got.   'What a glorious clamour it has made!' wrote Miss Giberne.   'As the Blessed Froude says some-where, "I deprecate a calm".   I hope it is not wrong, but I cannot for the life of me help enjoying the fun of the row.'   Newman himself wrote cheerfully to Jemima, 'We are like ducks in a pond, knocked over, but not knocked out'.

Some criticisms came from within the Movement, however, from those who did not like to repudiate the Reformation as entirely as Newman, and they took what was to become the hackneyed line of blaming him, not for his ideas, but for what they imagined were his motives in putting them forward.   To Keble's friend, Judge Cole-ridge, Newman replied : 'Of course everyone has a right to form his own view. . . . I am much obliged by your frankness — and quite feel that a far more unfavorable and severe view of my conduct might be taken.   At the same time I do believe you have not hit the matter at all when you attribute what you disapprove to a "tendency to self love and self approval".   Not that I deny those tendencies in me — but their operation in the particular case which you bring them to account for.'

On April 9th, which was Good Friday, after an even more severe Holy Week fast than last year, Newman preached on *Christ's Cross the Measure of the World*.   'It is the death of the Eternal Word of God made flesh, which is our great lesson how to think and how to speak of this world.   His Cross has put its due value upon everything which we see, upon all fortune, all advantages, all ranks, all dignities, all pleasures ; upon the lust of the flesh and the lust of the eyes and the pride of life.   It has set a price upon the excitements, the rivalries, the hopes, the fears, the desires, the efforts, the triumphs of mortal man.   It has given a meaning to the various, shifting course, the trials, the temptations, the sufferings of his earthly state.   It has brought together and made consistent all that seemed discordant and aimless.   It has taught us how to live, how to use this world, what to expect, what to desire, what to hope.   It is the tone into which all the strains of this world's music are ultimately to be resolved. . . . Thus in the Cross, and Him who hung upon it, all things meet ; all things subserve it, all things need it.   It is their centre and their interpreta-tion.   For He was lifted upon it, that He might draw all men and all things unto Him.'

And the Cross was like the heart, the source of life, but hidden :

hidden in the world, which seemed to promise so fair and turned to sorrow and bitterness, and hidden in the soul of the Christian, circulating in him the new supernatural life. As for the deceiving world, 'They alone inherit it, who take it as a shadow of the world to come, and who for that world to come relinquish it'.

What could the world do to one whose standard, in fact as in word, was the Cross ? It could make him carry it.

1841–1842

Bishops Charging

NEWMAN was content with his bargain, and was so scrupulous in carrying it out that he resigned the editorship of the *British Critic*. Tom Mozley took it over. This was not a successful move, for Tom was so closely related that everyone thought Newman was still responsible for the magazine. Tom certainly did consult him often, but he did not always take his advice, and things were printed which Newman did not approve but which were generally taken to be his. A case in point was Faussett's, the Margaret Professor of Divinity. In June Newman wrote privately to Tom joking about him : 'Heads of Houses do *work* but F. is a fat dog who comes out to bark once to two years and *whose work* we are doing'. Tom, tickled at the idea, elaborated it into an Apologue between Growler and Fido, which he still thought funny when he read it again as an old man. But when Faussett's pamphlet appeared Newman wrote anxiously, 'Faussett is come out and is a mere tirade against *me* personally — so much so that I think he ought not to be noticed'. But Tom could not resist putting in his dialogue. His brother James thought it funny too, but neither of them had much imagination about other people's feelings. Keble was shocked. Many readers thought it was by Newman himself, puzzled, as one of them remarked that 'a person could appear so amiable at one time and so much the reverse at others'. Newman felt so strongly about it that he wrote out a prayer begging God's pardon 'if we have erred in our dealings towards G M P of Divinity in this University' — Godfrey Faussett, Margaret Professor. 'Thou savest, O Lord, those who sit still, and avengest those who suffer silently ; grant that no mischief befall us for that we have done, and keep us ever from taking into our own hands the things which belong to Thee.'

In the summer Newman retired to Littlemore again. He now definitely began to make plans to live there, hoping that by removing himself from Oxford he would make it plain that he wanted peace and not party strife, and that the angry feelings roused by Tract 90 would then calm down. He had stopped talking about a monastery, but this seemed a providential opportunity to begin to live according to some kind of rule. He could not do this in Mrs. Barnes' cottage. Down the road from the Church, just hidden by a bend, was a row of old stables, L-shaped on the corner of the lane, on the edge of the property he had bought. They had belonged to Costar, or Costard, who ran the Oxford to Cambridge coach. At first Newman had thought of converting them into cottages and letting them at a nominal rent. But now it occurred to him that he might very well live there himself. The boxes for the horses could be turned into rooms, and the barn along the short arm would do for a Library. The whole place was rough and plain, the roof so low he could almost touch it with his hand, the floors of uneven brick and the windows few and small. Except for animals only the poorest would consent to live in such a place. Newman decided it would do for him. But he could not move in at once ; a good deal had to be done to make the stables habitable by human beings, even by one determined on living as hard as possible. In the end the place was not ready till early spring the next year, and then Newman moved in before it was done, to 'fight the workmen out' as he called it. One of them was known as 'drunken Jim Blazy', so the man-hours he put in were probably an uncertain quantity. For this summer, then, Newman was still in lodgings in Littlemore.

He stayed this time in the ancient house called St. George's, belonging to a well-to-do farming family of the name of Giles. Upstairs, the back room, with its small seventeenth-century windows overlooking the garden, was his study, and a small front room is traditionally known as his oratory — it faces the road which ran past the stable-monastery. In the midst of the housing estates this old place remains among its green trees ; long before Newman stayed there recusant Catholics lived in it. Forty years ago there was a small diamond window pane on which his name was cut, but it vanished before the present owner completed his purchase, so that it cannot now be known whether the writing was Newman's or another's.

Newman was cheerful, teasing Henry Wilberforce, who had just got a living in Kent : 'I only hope your new preferment will not make you a shovel-hatted humbug. Beware of the Lambeth Livery.' Henry had a curate, Ambrose St. John : 'I like my Mr. St. John more and more', he said. In fact, he liked him so much that he proposed to call the new baby 'Ambrose Newman' after his old and new friends. 'I wish Newman had been a prettier name', wrote the owner of it. '"Melville" e.g.' About the same time he scribbled a note to Bloxam : 'My dear Bloxam — they tell me you are at present performing the character of mope — and that the due maintenance of that character forbids your coming so far as Littlemore. If you have nothing better to do I would come and mope with you at your rooms at dinner on St. Peter's day (Thurs.) at any time you please. I am, my dear Bloxam, your sympathetic mope, John H. Newman.'

Bloxam, a gentle timid creature, hated rows, and was shrinking under the impact of the popular fury roused by Tract 90. He had been reported to the Bishop for bowing down at High Mass at Oscott. Newman wrote to Bagot on his behalf. He insisted he had only been saying his own prayers in the gallery of the chapel. Poor Bloxam loved visiting Pugin's Gothic college and looking through their vestments ; no wonder he moped when accused of idolatry.

Bloxam's best friend among the papists was Ambrose Phillipps, who later took the name of de Lisle. The heir of a wealthy family, he became a Catholic at the age of fifteen. Nine years younger than Newman, he had been refused a place in Oriel in 1825, and went to Cambridge ; his father, fearing he might wish to become a priest, encouraged him to marry young. His bride, Laura Clifford, came from an old Catholic family, and shared all his interests. Phillipps called his house Grace-Dieu, and Pugin built him a Gothic chapel where the 'right' vestments were worn and the 'right' chants were sung — in order to have them sung properly Phillipps imported some Trappist monks from France, and was a little disappointed, when he had built them a monastery, to find that they had to stay in it. He got a chaplain instead, who tutored his boys, and took visitors to the monks' chapel as a treat. He built a school for his tenants and converted a lot of them. He was gentle, enthusiastic, with any number of bees buzzing in his bonnet, very well known in aristocratic society ; his portrait was drawn by Disraeli in *Coningsby*, as Sir Eustace Lyle, and his Gothic estate appeared as 'St. Genevieve'.

Phillipps was delighted with 'the Oxford men' and had visions of reunion, a Catholic England and High Mass in Westminster Abbey. He soon had Dr. Wiseman as enthusiastic as himself. For Wiseman had left the English College in Rome for England itself ; he was now a Bishop, coadjutor to old Bishop Walsh of the Midland District and Rector of Oscott. The old college had been hidden away in a valley outside Birmingham, the windows barred against possible attacks of anti-popish rioters ; in penal times its chapel was upstairs, tiny and

secret. Here Catholic boys had got some learning, and some prepared for the priesthood; here Bishop Milner had lived, with a
collapsible crozier in a little bag, and gone riding round his district
in knee breeches to administer confirmation and visit the groups of
Catholics gathered round their few and scattered priests. But in
1838, a sign of the new times of Emancipation, a great new college
was built up on the hill, proudly overlooking the distant but growing
sprawl of Birmingham, splendid with quadrangles and halls of red
brick and stone, and flaunting a towered gateway. Pugin, for once,
was able to let himself go with the chapel, which was rich with all
the detail he loved. This creation of enthusiastic faith made a suitable
setting for the genial Wiseman. A steady stream of interested Oxford
men came over to view this stronghold of the Romans.

Newman never went. Nor was he encouraging about Reunion,
when the eager Phillipps conducted a three-cornered correspondence
through Bloxam. 'While Rome is what she is, union is impossible',
he wrote. 'That we too must change I do not deny.' The chief
charge he levelled against Rome in England was lack of holiness.
'Alas! I see no marks of sanctity.' Instead, he saw O'Connell's
political alliance with the Liberals. 'Never can I think such ways
the footsteps of Christ. If they want to convert England, let them
go barefooted into our manufacturing towns — let them preach to
the people like St. Francis Xavier — let them be pelted and trampled
on — and I will admit that they can do what we cannot. . . . Let them
use the proper arms of the Church, and they will prove that they are
the Church by using them.'

Phillipps replied, through Bloxam: 'It is true we want a great
reformation in the English R. Catholick body, but I still think he
does not quite do us justice. The fact is he does not know us. I
could show him Men and Women who, I think, would surprise him
not a little. In the Cistercian monastery here, in the Benedictine
Nunneries generally throughout England, at Stonyhurst among the
Jesuits, I could show him individuals of solid piety, of heroick virtue,
who live only for God, and whose hearts are truly on fire with the
charity of Christ. . . . He knows us only through the medium of noisy
violent unholy Men who call themselves Catholicks but know nothing
of the Spirit of the Church.'

He was quite right; Newman did not know them. He did not
know that last Guy Fawkes Day a little Italian, Father Dominic
Barberi of the Passionist Order, had landed in England, and ignorant
of English ways began his work by doing just what Newman had

required, going barefoot into the manufacturing towns in his monk's habit and preaching in broken English to any one who would listen, with surprising success. But he was pelted too, with mud and stones. Later he adopted the ways of English Catholic priests in wearing ordinary clothes ; nor was Newman a stickler for bare feet — it was the spirit not the habit of the missionary friar he looked for. When he came to meet Father Dominic, he instantly recognized it ; but that event was still to come.

Phillipps and Wiseman were disappointed that Newman was so discouraging. Wiseman wrote a pamphlet on Tract 90 ; Newman complained, in a private letter, of unfairness ; Wiseman apologized, but complained in his turn. Newman said, 'It gives me very great sorrow to pain members of your communion in what I write ; but is not this the state of Christendom, that we are all paining each other ?' It was most painful to him to be told 'that we worship Christ in His Sacraments but that He is not there'. Only one Catholic really got through to him and that was Dr. Russell of Maynooth. Ironic, after what Newman had said of O'Connell, that he was an Irishman ! But Newman was to understand the Irish case better later. Russell was ten years Newman's junior, about the age of Rogers ; he was a clever man, but humble. He wrote because he could not bear to think that Newman should be imagining the gross horrors Protestants thought were implied by the doctrine of Transubstantiation, and he wrote on Holy Thursday, his whole letter breathing a deep love of Christ in the Eucharist and assuming that Newman felt the same. In this way he at once reached Newman's heart. He was doubtful of the doctrine, but assured Russell he did not believe the horrors, though he thought the framers of the Articles did, and were protesting against them, not against the Mass itself. But even to Russell he said, 'That your communion was unassailable would not prove mine was indefensible.' He felt too great a horror of the principle of private judgment to separate from his superiors. 'I wish to go by reason, not by feeling,' he said. Yet these very superiors were now bringing up their heavy guns against him.

Newman had not realized, nor had any of the Tractarians, the strength of the feelings roused against them. Tract 90 was not the cause but the occasion of the explosion. People now sometimes express wonder at all that fuss over the interpretation of the Thirty-Nine Articles ; but what really caused so much passion was the revival of Catholicism, and it was the more heated since most people had a distorted picture of it which they had not been able to check against the reality for a long time, owing to the severe penal laws against Catholics in England and Ireland. Aristocratic Catholic families were known to their equals and dependants, but in other classes of society Catholics were simply unknown, and wished to be unknown for safety's sake. Popular feeling against the Catholic Church did not break out in public riots till nearly ten years later, but Tract 90 let loose similar feelings among the educated classes, directed not against Roman Catholics themselves, since, as a body, they had not emerged into sufficient prominence in the national life, but against those clergymen of the Church of England who proclaimed Catholic doctrines and ideals and publicly repudiated the Reformation. To the great majority they appeared as traitors, because the great majority believed the Church of England a Protestant Christian body which had freed itself not only from the jurisdiction of Rome, but from Catholic errors of teaching and practice which were regarded as superstition and idolatry. The seventeenth-century tradition of Laud had never been widely popular, and had been almost lost in the intervening centuries, especially as the chief spiritual revival (Wesley's) had taken on the Lutheran and Calvinistic forms associated with the various kinds of Evangelicals, both within and without the Church of England. People had overlooked the fact that a great deal of Catholic doctrine had been retained in the Prayer Book and they were unfamiliar with the idea of unity as essential to the Christian Church : by the phrase in the Creed they understood merely that all individuals who attained heaven would be there united. When, therefore, Newman proposed to make the Church Universal the standard by which to regulate doctrine in the Church of England, it seemed to them that he was attempting to force on a free Christian society the rule of another, represented by Rome, which they were accustomed to regard as tyrannous, morally corrupt and theologically perverted.

So strong was the revulsion from this that even in people who met Newman every day it affected their opinion of, and their behaviour to him ; those who did not know him were at liberty to imagine him the embodiment of all they righteously detested. Oxford itself was full of caricatures of him, and the Provost, as he once wrote to Tom Mozley this summer, was 'cold as ice'. Bloxam afterwards remembered how Hawkins had perpetually snubbed Newman, on the most trivial pretexts. Oriel was uncomfortably divided into two camps, though of course everyone was too polite to say so. The Provost began to make Tract 90 a test of faith, and refused testimonials to young men seeking ordination if they would not repudiate it. It

cannot have made him feel kinder to Newman that he was forced to
ask Church to be a tutor, for educationally the college was not doing
very well. '*Entre nous*, don't let it get out,' Newman wrote of this
occasion to Tom on Christmas Eve 1841, 'the first glimpse of that
humble pie after which Froude's eyes strained in vain.' Church
refused the tutorship.

In Oriel the situation was strained, but in other colleges warfare
could be open. The chief agitator was still Golightly, who got an
obsessive complex about Newman and the Tractarians; even his
friends admitted it was something abnormal. He declared he was
frightened to go home alone in the dark for fear revengeful Tractarian
young men would set on him; a sign perhaps of a guilty conscience
over his activities against Newman, whose early letters he kept in
some cupboard or drawer all this time. Tract 90 had made him 'a
great man' so that even the Provost, as Church reported, was content
to lose his breakfast 'to hear G. prose'. He went about, as Newman
remarked, 'with the thanks of four bishops in his pockets'. He sent
Newman copies of his pamphlets, with letters imitating the Tractarian style, 'my hostility does not extend to yourself personally, but
to your *opinions*, and I may add, your *mode of advocating* them'. One
of his pamphlets scare-mongered about the visits to Oscott. Tom
Mozley woke up one morning to hear that he was about to go over
to Rome; he lay in bed, he told James, thinking over '30 pages of
jokes at G.'s expense', but, surprising conclusion for Tom, decided
it was best to hold his tongue. Perhaps he thought of Newman's
feelings about his jokes at the expense of Professor Faussett. In
December Newman wrote to Jemima, 'Poor Golightly's friends are
seriously alarmed for his mind'. He quoted the report of a friend
about 'people who are base enough to make him (G.) their tool and
mean enough to shrink from acknowledging their hatred of N.'s views,
chiefly . . . because those views are too strict'. Newman always
felt that a good deal of the opposition in Oxford was aroused not by
his Catholic opinions but by his appeals for a stricter self-discipline
and more penetrating examination of conscience. Of Golightly he
added, 'Thus you see the poor unhappy fellow has left his true and
natural friends to worship asses'.

Not only Oxford was agitated, but the whole country. Pusey
went to preach in St. Mary Redcliffe, Bristol, and the next Sunday
the clergyman there denounced from the pulpit 'the hell-born heresy
of Puseyism which has lately appeared in bodily form among you'.
Sermons were preached everywhere against these crypto-papists;

meetings were held and their proceedings reported in the newspapers ; petitions were sent to the Archbishop of Canterbury — and he received them, though he had refused, in the interests of peace, to hear any from the Tractarians. Dutiful to superiors on principle, they desisted ; not so their enemies.

Hoping all this agitation would die down if they did not fight back, Newman settled down at Littlemore to the translation of St. Athanasius he was doing for the Library of the Fathers. 'I had got but a little way into my work when my trouble returned upon me', he wrote in the *Apologia*. 'The ghost had come a second time.' The Arians turned out worse than the Monophysites as an historical parallel. 'The pure Arians were the Protestants, the semi-Arians were the Anglicans, and Rome now was what it was then. The truth lay, not with the Via Media, but with what was called "the extreme party".' He could not think why, when he had been writing about the Arians before, he had not seen this. But then he had been looking for something else, for the visible and undivided Church in action. Now he was looking at the divisions, and wondering what God willed in the matter, how He intended unity to be preserved. History seemed to show that Rome was the centre of orthodoxy, but if that were so, why was the Church in communion with her in modern times corrupted, in its excessive worship of the Virgin and Saints, and in maintaining its own infallible authority under the supremacy of the Pope ? The identification of the Anglican Via Media with the semi-Arian heretics of the fifth century shook Newman's confidence that Anglo-Catholics were more truly Catholic than Roman Catholics, but it did not explain why modern Rome had changed from ancient Rome. He was left in a miserable state of uncertainty, believing in the Catholic Church but not able to recognize its features in the existing communion which claimed its name.

But it became clearer and clearer that the Church of England did not claim what he believed the Catholic Church must claim. This year its leaders seemed bent on proving that they belonged to the Protestant world. A plan of Count Bunsen's, for combining the Prussians and English in Jerusalem under a Bishop of the Church of England, was promoted in high quarters, chiefly to procure an official footing for Protestants in Palestine, where France and Russia had established themselves as 'protectors' of Catholics and Orthodox. Pusey, typically, was at first enthusiastic ; he thought that the introduction of an Anglican Bishop into German Lutheran Church would soon Catholicize the whole system. Other Tractarians, especially the London group of lawyers and clergy, were horrified at such a compromise with heresy. To Newman it was like the behaviour of semi-Arians, relying on State power and preferring the satisfactions of this world to the maintenance of truth.

Shocking as this scheme appeared, the Protestantism of Church leaders came home to Newman more personally when he found himself under attack from the Bishops. At that time Convocation had been suspended by the State for over a century; it was inconvenient to the government to allow a free assembly of the Clergy during a period when they still enjoyed a wide, if not exactly popular, power and prestige. True, the Bishops still had seats in the house of Lords, and in the nineteenth century took part in debates very frequently; but they acted as individuals and often as members of opposing political parties, divided both on social and ecclesiastical questions. There was thus no way open for public concerted action on religious affairs. The Bishops, however, had a weapon which, as newspapers grew in influence, had become powerful: they issued triennial Charges which were widely reported. It was an individual means of expression, but could become collective if their opinions on any subject coincided. Upon the subject of Tract 90 and its author there was an unprecedented unanimity. Seven Charges against the Tract came out in 1841, more the following year, and by 1844 a hostile pamphleteer could print an appendix of the names of twenty-four Bishops who had anathematized the Tract and all that Newman stood for, and often himself as well. This was the most complete public censure possible in the Church of England at that time; the university statute against Hampden was nothing to it — a slap in the face to a rain of blows. And Tract 90 had already been condemned by the university authorities, though not in full Convocation.

Newman copied out some of the Bishops' Charges. 'At first I intended to protest', he said in the *Apologia*. 'But I gave up the thought in despair.' What was the use? He had all along insisted on the Catholic doctrine of episcopal authority, and when that authority condemned him he was defenceless. In his Lectures on Anglican Difficulties he turned it into a joke, representing the Tractarian as having tied himself to a post by his own principle of obedience, unable to do anything but watch the Bishops at their solemn war-dance round him. The experience certainly had its comic side, but at the time it was more painful than funny. For they attacked not only him and his interpretation of the Articles, but the Catholic doctrines involved. He could no longer say cheerfully that he could bear anything because no doctrine was censured. Late the next year came the most unkindest cut of all, mild though its terms were, the condemnation of Bishop Bagot, who had promised, if Newman gave up the Tracts, not to attack. Newman had certainly tied his own hands more effectively than anyone else could have tied them, in giving up the powerful weapon of the Tracts and promising to say no more about No. 90. He had even given up his other public platform, the *British Critic*, so far as publishing his personal views was concerned. There were was no more he could do, in the way of submission. Yet the Bishops fired again and again, as they had done at no one else, not against the extreme Evangelicals who ignored the Articles concerning Baptism and Justification, not at the Liberals of the school of Arnold and Hampden who applied rationalism to Scripture and thought theology mere private opinion. Nor did some of them scruple to use language more suitable to the denunciation of some revolutionary agitator.

The Bishop of Exeter said the tone of the Tract was offensive and indecent. 'As this is by far the most daring attempt yet made by a minister of the Church of England to neutralize the distinctive doctrines of our Church I shall be excused if . . . I unravel this web of sophistry.' Llandaff (Copleston, the ex-Provost) said the Tract showed want of principle. Ripon said the integrity of subscription was endangered. The Bishop of Durham spoke of error spreading widely and misplaced zeal ; 'the mere love of singularity ; attachment to friends ; the importance arising from leading a party, ay, the very spirit of opposition engendered by our enfeebled nature ; all concur to produce a desire of being noticed for something new and to push that novelty to extremes'. (This to one who appealed to Antiquity !) As well as being an exhibitionist Newman was a cunning manipulator of words and meanings : Hereford talked of 'intricate and subtle explanations'. Winchester, Keble's Bishop, who was refusing to ordain his curate because of his views on the Eucharist, appealed to the Anglican divines so admired by the Tractarians—but in favour of the Reformers. Chester, Pusey's old tutor Sumner, attacked specific Catholic doctrines. The infallibility of Ecumenical Councils was condemned, so, as 'sacraments of the gospel', were confirmation, penance, orders and matrimony, and extreme unction. The elements of the Eucharist remained bread and wine and the Lord's supper was in no sense a propitiatory sacrifice ; Purgatory, Pardons, Adoration of images or relics, Invocation of Saints, were all roundly condemned together. As well, he talked of 'the subtle wiles of that Adversary against whom the Church of Christ is set up' as if Newman were the devil's advocate, and of 'notions which might seem inconsistent with the advancement of reason' as if he himself were Lord Brougham's.

In 1842 came St. David's : 'refined and artificial' ; London : 'the endeavour to give a Tridentine colouring to the Articles'. Salisbury went into three editions, rejoicing at the Bishop of Oxford's interference to end the Tracts ; Ossory was very violent, attacking 'the dishonest casuistry to which the Jesuits have given a name'. He said, 'I should despair of conveying anything like a full impression of the shifting, corrosive, disingenuous sophistry . . .' and spoke of 'one who must have been supposed to have known intimately the minds on which he exercised so baleful an influence', who was 'able to calculate on their readiness to avail themselves of such a mode of escape from the fair force of the most solemn and sacred obligations, by such sophistry and evasion, such shifts and contrivances, as a man could not apply to the very lightest of the engagements of common life, without forfeiting all reputation for integrity and good faith'. The Bishop of Calcutta joined in with a published sermon in which he said : 'Already the mystical piety of the Church of Rome is cast as a cloke over the most unscriptural of doctrines and modes of worship ; and the meek language of penitence and humiliation is used to conceal the worst kind of presumption in explaining away Holy Writ and throwing off the obligation of solemn subscription — one of the most fatal of all symptoms, as it saps the foundations of moral judgment and leads to pure fanaticism, the accounting evil good and good evil. . . . Now let us trace the same affected humility in Mr. Newman in his letter to the Vice-Chancellor of Oxford after the condemnation passed upon the Tract.' Thus even Newman's voluntary submission and readiness to admit his own faults were used in evidence against him.

These are only brief samples of the language of the Charges of the Apostles' successors, repudiating doctrines and practices of the ancient Church and appealing to the Reformers as the founders of the Church of England ; and spurning as sophistry any attempt to take the Articles in a Catholic sense. These were the superiors Newman had obeyed because he believed them to be the divinely appointed guardians and teachers of the truth revealed by God.

No wonder that the Charges, and the affair of the Jerusalem Bishopric, caused bewilderment and despondency among the supporters of the Movement. 'If a number of persons have for years been preaching the existence of the Holy Catholic Church,' wrote

Newman at the end of 1841, 'what is the inevitable and immediate effect of the Church of England by its rulers declaring she is *not* that Holy Catholic Church but to send people to Rome by exhaustion, because there is no other Church ?' There was real danger of this, known not only to Newman, but to Wiseman, who had heard from Mr. Newsham, the priest at Oxford, that as many as forty undergraduates sought him out and questioned him after the Tract 90 row. To James Hope, his lawyer friend, Newman wrote: 'When friends who rely on my word come to me and say, "You *told* us that the English Church was Catholic", what am I to say to this reproach ?'

He had come back to Oriel in September, to correct the proofs of *St. Athanasius*, an even more tiring task than usual because he was writing footnotes when the text was already in type. He was working at them eight, ten and even twelve hours a day, and at the same time coping with the difficulties and despondencies of the Tractarians, in person and by letter. There was this question of Keble's curate, Peter Young, twice refused ordination for holding exactly the same views of the Eucharist as Keble himself held ; at one moment it looked as if *Keble* would have to resign his living. (What would have happened if he had ?) Newman wrote to cheer him up: 'As things have before now been at their worst as regards the clergy, so they are now as regards the Bishops, and they will improve, I think. Recollect the clergy left off their wigs before the Bishops did. All in good time.' He was strongly in favour of Keble's proposed Protest, which he finally made, but he was more doubtful of the propriety of himself making a Protest, as he wished to do, against the Jerusalem Bishopric. '*They* act, why may not I ?' he said of the Bishops to Hope. 'Why may not I be troublesome as well as another ?' But he knew he would only be called 'a bitter fanatic' if he did. In the end, after asking advice from several friends according to his usual custom, he sent a formal protest to his own Bishop and the Archbishop of Canterbury, but did not publish it. Needless to say, it made no difference ; the Jerusalem Bishop, a Lutheran as it turned out, was sent off to Palestine with the blessing of State and Church.

There was another battle going on in Oxford over the Poetry Professorship, in which the bone of contention was the unfortunate Isaac Williams. A furious campaign was got up against him solely because he had been a Tract writer, so that Newman felt bound to support him, though he was not active in the combat. The opposition meanly used the Tractarians' weak point against them : they got the Bishop to ask Williams to retire, so of course he did. 'We are hit because we are dutiful', Newman observed. This battle raged in midwinter and was not settled till January 1842.

Newman had one place still from which he could speak in public : the pulpit of St. Mary's. For the sake of those who reproached him with having told them the English Church was Catholic and were now desperately at a loss, he broke his rule and introduced 'subjects of the day' into his sermons. Not that he referred directly to what was happening, or, like pulpiteers on the other side declaimed against parties and people by name, but he used Scripture, as he had done before, to interpret the situation. But this interpretation was different from earlier ones in being entirely his own, a theory formed for the occasion, and reflecting the uncertainty and bewilderment of the crisis. He drew a parallel between the Church of England and Samaria, the northern kingdom of Israel when it was separated from Judah ; when Elijah the Prophet was raised up in the north he did not command the people of God, corrupted by the influence of paganism though they were, to go up to Jerusalem to worship. This theory appealed strongly to Keble, who could never get himself to believe that God ever meant anyone to move from the place where he had put him at birth. But Keble was puzzled, as were many others, by the Advent series of 1841, because they were so 'methodistical'. Apart from staying put like Samaria, Newman had to have a reason for believing that the Church was still in some real sense Catholic. He fell back on the Sacraments. Whatever the Bishops might say or do Christ was in the Church in His Sacraments, the changeless Lifegiver, and the proof of this was just what he had always refused to count as proof, the experience of God's grace and love which accompanied them. He was afterwards very scornful of himself for this lapse into reliance on subjective feelings. But something had happened which for the moment overwhelmed all other considerations.

What exactly it was we cannot know, because Newman was extremely reticent about his own religious experiences. But at the beginning of Advent he wrote to his friend Samuel Wood, who was his great support in his Littlemore plans, but could take no active part because of his health — he was destined to die in two years' time from tuberculosis. Wood also was 'unsettled' about the Catholicity of the English Church. To him Newman said : 'If it is not presumptuous to say, I trust I have been favoured with a much more definite view of the (promised) inward evidence of the Presence of Christ with us in the Sacraments, now that the outward notes of it are being removed. And I am content to be with Moses in the desert — or with Elijah excommunicated from the Temple.' He mentioned the same thing to Miss Holmes, a young lady whom he had not met, but who had been writing to him for advice and guidance since the year before. To her he spoke of 'something that had happened in connexion with the Most Holy Sacrament (not going so far as to speak of miracles)' by way of encouraging her to persevere in the Church of England.

Hostile eyes were not the only ones watching Newman ; somehow a garbled version of this private experience got out among his admirers and went round as a piece of pious gossip. W. G. Ward told people Newman had 'seen our Lord' in the Sacrament. By the next year the news had got round to the Catholics and Phillipps received a letter from Lord Shrewsbury, who was suspicious of the Oxford men, demanding 'Does not this sufficiently prove Newman's Vision to be an illusion of the Father of Lies, since they take it in evidence of the truth of their system and in Justification of Schism ?' Phillipps did his best to soothe the noble Lord, and begged him not to spread a story he had learned in confidence. That James Mozley, of all people, was writing to Phillipps to deny rumours of supernatural visitations, suggests that Newman may have realized that tales were going about and tried to put an end to them. He had not yet fully realized that whatever he said, even to friends, was bound to come out, sometimes distorted, in public. It was ironic that he should have acquired a reputation for secrecy and mystery-making ; his only contribution to the legend was a natural desire not to have his deepest and most intimate experiences made the gossip of tea tables and the joke of wine parties.

So that we do not know (and why should we know ?) what lay behind the sermon on *The Invisible Presence of Christ*, with its strong but restrained feeling and hints of more than could be said. '. . . If you can recollect times when you visited holy places, and certainly gained there a manifestation such as the world could not give . . . or if your soul has been, as it were, transfigured within you, when you came to the Most Holy Sacrament . . . O ! pause ere you doubt that we have a Divine Presence among us still, and have not to seek it. . . .' But the Life and the Way cannot be separated from the Truth and all experience of God's Love must lead to his Truth, unless the person concerned looks away, back into the world, or is looking out first for himself. However aware Newman was of himself, his mind and heart were fixed first on God. It was the Divine Presence, not his feelings about it, that he put first, even at this moment of deep uncertainty, and perhaps of unexpected wonder.

1842

'Arnold and I bowed'

THE uproar had by no means died down by the next year, and Golightly, Newman remarked to Jemima, was still crying 'stinking fish'. 'If they were to get rid of me, for the moment they would appease the panic,' he said, 'but the evil is in Oxford and removing me would not change Oxford.' His enemies knew his power better than he did ; removing him was to change Oxford so completely that in a few years' time the fashion there was all for liberalism. Now he was planning to go and live altogether at Littlemore, but before he went, an interesting incident occurred : he and Thomas Arnold met face to face.

Arnold had been appointed Regius Professor of Modern History and came to Oxford to deliver a series of lectures ; they were lively and popular, crowded out with eager listeners. The Provost invited him to dinner on the Oriel Gaudy-day, February 2nd, feast of the Purification of the Blessed Virgin Mary. Newman discovered that, as Senior Fellow, he must take the place of Eden, the Dean, who was ill, and assist the Provost in entertaining the distinguished guest. What could be more embarrassing ? Ever since 1833 Arnold had been attacking him, first privately for saying, 'But is Arnold a Christian ?' and then publicly, as the chief of 'the Oxford Malignants'. Nor would the Provost be likely to ease the situation, 'cold as ice' as he was to Newman now. 'My first feeling was to shirk', Newman told his sister Jemima, when, two years later, she asked for the true account of this meeting. 'However, I thought it would be cowardly, so after all I went, knowing that both in Hall and Common-Room the trio at the top of the table would be Provost, Arnold and I, and that in the Common-Room I should sit at the top between them as entertainer.'

He managed to get into his place in Hall before the others came in ; with them as a fourth was Baden-Powell, afterwards a contributor to the famous *Essays and Reviews*, which made such a stir with its

263

liberal views of religion. So that they were three against one.
Newman described his own sensations during the evening to his
sister : 'I was most absolutely cool, or rather calm and unconcerned,
all through the meeting from beginning to end ; but I don't know
whether you have seen me enough in such situations to know (what I
really believe is not any affectation at all on my part ; I am not
conscious of any such thing, though some people would think it) that
I seem, if you will let me say it, to *put on* a very simple, innocent and
modest manner. I sometimes laugh at myself, and at the absurdities
which result from it ; but I really cannot help it, and I really do
believe it to be genuine. On one occasion in the course of our conversation I actually blushed high at some mistake I made, and yet on
the whole I am quite collected. Now, are you not amused at all this ?
or ought not I to blush now ? I never said a word of all this about
myself to anyone in my life before ; though, perhaps, that does not
mend the matter that I should say it now.'

It would have been an inhumanly insensitive person who would
not have felt self-conscious at meeting, in full view of many interested
onlookers, someone who had publicly accused him of malice, cunning
and sham meekness. Newman could have made it an uncomfortable
evening, if he had been stiff and silent, or prickly and argumentative.

'The Provost came up in a brisk, smart way, as if to cut through
an awkward beginning, and said quickly, "Arnold, I don't think you
know Newman ?" on which Arnold and I bowed, and I spoke.' The
introduction was too much for the tease in Newman. 'I was sly
enough to say, very gently and clearly, that I had before then had
the pleasure of meeting Dr. Arnold, for I had disputed with him in
the Divinity School before he took his B.D. degree, when he was
appointed to Rugby. At which Baden-Powell laughed, and Arnold
seemed a little awkward, and said, "Oh, I thought it had been
Pusey".' It might well make him feel awkward, for Newman had
done him a favour in volunteering when he could not find a disputant.
But after that, Newman did his best to make things go easily. 'We
then sat down at table, and I thought of all the matters possible which
it was safe to talk on. I recollected he had travelled with William
Churton, and that made one topic. Others equally felicitous I forget.
But I recollect the productions of North Africa was a fruitful subject ;
and I have some dream of having talked of a great tree, the name of
which I now forget, as big as a hill, and which they bring as an
argument for the indefinite duration of the present earth *a parte ante*.'

The evening was going quite well, but the Provost did not seem

grateful. 'In the Common-Room I had to take a still more prominent part, and the contrast was very marked between Arnold and
the Provost — the Provost so dry and unbending, and seeming to
shrink from whatever I said, and Arnold who was natural and easy,
at least to all appearance.' Others, who were watching with fascination, told Newman afterwards they had been amused, when Baden-
Powell made some irreverent remark, 'to see how Arnold and myself,
in different ways, retired from it'. The meeting ended well. 'At
last the Provost and Arnold rose up to go, and I held out my hand,
which he took, and we parted.' Newman could nearly always get
his professed enemies to shake hands, once they had met him. The
news came round to him later that Arnold had been surprised to find
him not what he fancied. What had he imagined ? A shifty character
with an unctuous manner and a fanatical gleam in his eye ? He told
Stanley, afterwards the famous liberal Dean of Westminster, that it
would not do to meet Newman often. When taken up, he backed
out of saying anything definitely in his favour, merely remarking that
it was not desirable to meet often people one disagreed with. 'For
myself,' said Newman, 'I don't think I was desirous of pleasing him
or not ; but was secretly amused from the idea that he certainly
would be taken aback by coming across me *in propria persona* ; at
least, so I think.'

Next June Arnold, who was only five years older than Newman,
suddenly fell ill and died. Newman immediately made his will,
leaving what he had for the maintenance of Littlemore, in case he
might meet a similarly sudden death. Keble was distressed when
Arnold's works were reissued, but Newman thought there was so
little system in his ideas that they could not have much effect, whereas
his influence as a man and headmaster was good. He always respected
Arnold's good qualities, even though he laughed at his opinions. It
is pleasant that Arnold found out before he died that the Oxford
Malignant was someone he could not help liking, even against his
will.

1842–1843

Strange Doings at Littlemore

'I AM going up to Littlemore and my books are all in motion — part gone, the rest in a day or two', Newman wrote to Jemima a few days later. 'It makes me very downcast ; it is such a nuisance taking *steps*.' Jemima was so alarmed that he had to write again to calm her. Perhaps she was already fearful of Rome, but he was thinking of the difficulty of his position in Oxford and 'the hostility of the Heads, who are now (do not repeat this) taking measures to get men from St. Mary's'. He felt he would rather make the move himself than wait for action to be taken against him. Jemima did not understand his other reason, that he felt out of place in Oxford 'as customs are', with almost everyone his junior. She did understand, however, that he was facing a good deal of suspicion and coldness. 'How I wish you could come here', she said, 'it seems so desolate for you to be all alone.' But to be alone at Littlemore would be a relief.

In February Newman's sixth volume of sermons came out and caused, as Jemima said, 'a hubbub'. It was the first book to come out after Tract 90, and the first in which he put no dedication. He felt he could not associate any friend with himself, now that he was more or less under official censure. Of course the book was eagerly read by those who were on the look-out for secret popery, and they certainly got some Catholic sermons, on fasting, on the Eucharistic Presence, and the life of the Church. What annoyed Protestants so much was that in preaching on both discipline and doctrine Newman did not appeal to medieval custom or to the Fathers, but to Scripture. It was quite shocking the way he could find evidence for popish observances in the actions of Christ and the Apostles. St. Paul, whom they regarded as their private property, Newman seemed to know better than they did. 'St. Paul as *really* i.e. rough, miserable etc not as from king's palaces', he noted at the back of his diary. So these sermons came out like a challenge and showed that Newman was not going to lie down and die because the Tract was condemned.

He had given up polemics but he was not going to give up the Catholic Faith, not even to please the Bishops.   But of course it meant that his influence was undiminished, and even, in some quarters, growing ; consequently the anger aroused by Tract 90 did not die down, but increased.   The Tract, too, was still in print, and still selling.   From the proceeds Newman was able to buy more books for his Library.

The Library, in the barn of his row of stables at Littlemore, was by now sufficiently finished to receive the precious books, which he sorted and arranged himself, 'till my thumbs are quite stiff with the weight of the folios', he said.   He found afterwards he had strained the muscle in his thumb ; it affected his writing, and in after life he was always forgetting and doing the same thing again.   Friends used to inquire anxiously if he were ill when they saw the familiar regular hand turning scratchy and small.   He wrote to Bowden from Littlemore on their joint birthday: 'I have got my books nearly all in their places and talk of insuring them.   Not, one would trust, that there is much danger of fire, but I am somewhat given to fancy mischances, and when they *are* insured I shall dwell on the chance of their being destroyed, as Dr. Priestley's, by a mob shouting "No Popery" as in 1780.'   There was no insurance against mobs, whether protesting against the Unitarian Dr. Priestley or the secret Papist at Littlemore. Newman added: 'The dwelling rooms are still in a damp state, waiting for March winds to blow through them. . . . I hope I shall not get to idolize my Library ; but I assure you, for its size it is a very fine one.   I regret having no observatory here for Charlie.' Charlie Bowden, his godson, was only a little boy still.

The stables were now nearly fit to be lived in.   To get from one room to another you still had to go outside ; there was a covered porch running along the back.   Newman's rooms were at the far end of the long arm of the L, and the farthest was later turned into a small oratory.   (The position has been determined by the plan drawn for Bloxam by Stanton many years later.)   The floors were still uneven bricks, but there were some fireplaces put in.   The furniture was scanty and simple.   Newman had a wooden bed with a straw mattress, a hard chair and a desk at which he could stand, for he often wrote standing.   In the narrow room which afterwards served as a refectory there was a sort of side-board at which the inhabitants stood to take their meagre breakfast; the young men later christened this 'the pig trough'.   But at present there was no one but Newman ; he was alone when he first moved in.

He was not able to do so till April, so Lent was spent in lodgings as usual. By this time his nearest friends were more than suspicious of what he did in Lent. In 1840 Mrs. Bowden had written to Manuel Johnson, a cousin of her husband who was Observer in Oxford, 'So the Great Man is gone to Littlemore, and there I suppose he will practice nobody knows what austerities'. Now Henry Wilberforce wrote to beg him to be careful ; Mr. Babington, the doctor they both consulted, had spoken strongly of the danger that Newman might permanently damage his health. Newman replied cheerfully, 'Carissime, your kind note came to me last night ; — kind but inconsistent, for don't you know you once wished me dead rather than otherwise disposed of'. (Henry had said : 'I do feel it would give me less pain to hear of your death than of your leaving the Church of your Baptism'.) 'And now as to my own matters. I will tell you what I will do. I am going into Oxford in the afternoon. I will call on Dr. Wootten and let him see my throat, and if he forbids me to do as I am doing, I will obey. And I will offer to show myself to him once a week or a fortnight — but I will not tell him *what* I am doing — for Doctors always go *a priori*.' Nor did he tell Henry, though he answered his questions on abstinence generally. He was crafty in going to Dr. Wootten, who was inclined to pooh-pooh any illness that was not mortal, and was unlikely to guess 'what he was doing'. So he could report to Henry : 'As you wished I saw Wootten, who said my throat was a little relaxed but nothing the matter. He said I might have my way and I promised to show myself to him as time went on — the truth is last year I was a good deal in Oxford, where I am obliged to *talk* a great deal, which is to me very wearing when weak. Again, last year I left off milk, which I suspect was my fault and I shall not this year.'

He certainly made it sound as if this year Lent was going to be much easier ; but from his notes it does not seem to have been. True, he decided it was not safe 'to do without all oleaginous substances', and that milk and some butter must be taken, as the equivalent of olives in the east. He was drinking tea, now, milkless, 'the stimulus of which I have much missed in former Lents'. Yet to balance this meagre indulgence he now left off eating dinner altogether and had nothing but breakfast and tea. The notes for the year before had often run : 'I shall do . . . (so I did)'. But this year he twice had to note relaxations, first for milk, then for butter, because he felt so weak and all the eggs and bread had such inconvenient effects. Also sometimes 'they' sent up some fish or pancakes for tea, so, not liking to refuse, he ate them. Poor Mrs. Barnes probably felt he was starving. There was fever in the village, and for a week while he was visiting the sick he drank a glass of wine and ate a piece of bread at midday. And he was arranging his books in his spare time. All the same, he seemed quite surprised to find that he was 'very much exhausted', and that he had failed to be regular with the Breviary offices 'from exhaustion'. Yet this year he tried to sleep on the floor. The experiment did not succeed. 'I cannot get to sleep without being warm and then I am too warm.' Last summer he had tried it, and had to give up ; he took to a straw mattress instead.

He had too much sense to make himself unfit for work by lack of sleep, but he nearly overstepped the bounds of prudence in fasting so severely. In fact the Lent diets of these years probably had a permanent effect on his digestion, for in earlier years there were no references to the miseries caused by indigestible meals, as there were later. The rash generosity of these voluntary privations is reminiscent of similar episodes in the lives of saints in all ages of the world. Such different characters as St. Benedict, St. Ignatius Loyola, and St. Philip Neri, went through a period when they undertook self-discipline which they afterwards considered unsuitable for most people, not allowing their disciples to follow the extremes to which they had been driven by love of Christ and the desire to follow Him. They discovered, too, the psychological dangers lurking in the practice of bodily austerities, and the possibility of controlling physical appetites only at the expense of exalting self-will.

By the time he went to Littlemore Newman already knew much about these dangers, as the sermons show ; he noticed apparently trivial reactions, such as an increase of irritability under fasting. The discipline he advocated in public was not severe, and he always stressed the supreme importance of subduing self-will to the divine will. But when it came to himself he had to do more than he thought it wise to tell others to do. When he was writing to James Hope about the possibility of others joining him at Littlemore he said, 'Men want an outlet for their devotional and penitential feelings'. He certainly wanted it himself, driven by an inward need to express in action the love roused by the contemplation of Christ's sacrifice for an unheeding world. But he did not live in the sort of society where it was possible for someone in love with God to retire to caves and catacombs while he fought out the mysterious conflicts and endured the spiritual and emotional purging that transforms those who are ready to die to live. It needed an extraordinary balance of mind to pursue a course of intense inward adventure while conforming

to the demands of an active life in the civilized intellectual and
critical world of nineteenth-century Oxford.   But somehow that
balance was kept, and no one who knew him, however much they
disapproved both of what he said and what they suspected he did,
ever recorded any eccentricity, or strange behaviour on his part.
Indeed, his cheerfulness and at times gaiety and high spirits, while
he lived at Littlemore, misled some people, including the unimagin-
ative James Mozley, into thinking that he did not feel as deeply as
they thought he should the tragedy of his and their situation.

But now, since the Tract 90 row, he had to contend with more
than just the distractions of the busy world ; he found himself living
in a glare of hostile publicity.   It was only the beginning of the power
of the press, but it began as it was to go on, spreading to thousands
all over the country the unreliable gossip of a few inquisitive people.
Newman was news, and the most fantastic and distorted accounts of
what he did, in or out of church, were eagerly seized and swallowed
whole, and more demanded.   The year before, Bishop Copleston
had written about 'the religious aberrations at Oxford' to Provost
Hawkins, and added, 'strange rumours have reached me about doings
at Littlemoor'.   Now, in April 1842, reports appeared in the papers
that 'a so-called Anglo-Catholic monastery is in process of erection
at Littlemore, and that the cells of dormitories, the chapel, refectory,
the cloisters all may be seen advancing to perfection under the eye of
a parish priest of the diocese of Oxford'.   Poor old Bishop Bagot was
forced into action again, writing to Newman 'to afford him the
opportunity of making an explanation'.

It was a fearful blow, before he had even begun to live in his
retreat ; yet all along he had been afraid he would be stopped.
Rogers, last year, had jeered at the idea of the author of Tract 90
having fears about taking a lease of some cottages, but Newman's
instinct was surer.   In the *Apologia* he related, without giving a date,
an incident which may have occurred now and given rise to these
reports.   'When I entered my house, I found a flight of Undergraduates inside.   Heads of Houses, as mounted patrols, walked their
horses round those poor cottages.   Doctors of Divinity' (Faussett ?
Hampden ?   Symons ?) 'dived into the hidden recesses of that private
tenement uninvited, and drew domestic conclusions from what they
saw there.'   Did these spying colleagues look a little shamefaced when
the owner of the house suddenly appeared among them ?   Or was it
already an accepted thing that no rules of conduct need be observed
when dealing with Newman ?

'What have I done that I am to be called to account by the world for my private actions in a way in which no one else is called ?' he wrote to the Bishop. '. . . I am often accused of being underhand and uncandid . . . but no one likes his own good resolutions noised about, both from mere common delicacy, and from fear lest he should not be able to fulfil them. I feel it very cruel, though the parties in fault do not know what they are doing, that very sacred matters between me and my conscience are made a matter of public talk. May I take a case parallel, though different ? Suppose a person in prospect of marriage : would he like the subject discussed in newspapers, and parties, circumstances etc etc publicly demanded of him, at the penalty of being accused of craft and duplicity ? . . . The resolution I speak of has been taken with reference to myself alone . . . and being a resolution of years, and one to which I feel God has called me, and in which I am violating no rule of the Church any more than if I married, I should have to answer for it if I did not pursue it, as a good Providence made openings for it. In pursuing it I am thinking of myself alone, not aiming at any ecclesiastical or external effects. At the same time of course it would be a great comfort to me to know that God had put it into the hearts of others to pursue their personal edification in the same way, and unnatural not to wish to have the benefit of their presence and encouragement.'

He told the Bishop that he thought his partial retirement from St. Mary's might ease the situation in Oxford, and some young men, he suggested, might be kept in the Church of England who might otherwise look elsewhere. He said he was only providing a parsonage house for Littlemore. 'There is no chapel, no refectory, hardly a dining room or parlour. The "cloisters" are my shed connecting the cottages. . . . I am attempting nothing ecclesiastical, but something personal and private and which can only be made public and not private by newspapers and letter writers.' The Bishop was satisfied, though had he seen the parsonage house he might have been rather surprised. No parson of the time would have dreamed of putting his family into it. After Newman left Littlemore the cottages were tenanted by the poor ; 'a pretty parsonage house' was built for the clergyman. However, Newman was the parson for whom he was providing a parsonage, and the more unlike it was to a gentleman's home the better he loved it. He did not offensively proclaim it to all the gentlemen parsons around him, but one of his chief aims was to escape from that whole condition in which parsons had become gentlemen first and priests afterwards. Hence the poverty and simplicity of the stable-cottages, the plain and meagre fare, the hard chairs and straw mattresses.

Newman moved in alone, but he was not alone for long. The first to come was John Dobrée Dalgairns, a young graduate of twenty-three, extremely clever but immature even for his age ; his writing was like a boy's. He was high-spirited, enthusiastic and rather conceited. His family in Guernsey were alarmed at his Catholic notions, and he was unable to get a Fellowship because of them. He had got his ideas from Newman, but did not know him very well. In July came William Lockhart, a connexion of Sir Walter Scott's, sent by his family to Newman to be kept back from the Church of Rome, for he had already wanted to 'go over'. His ambition was to be 'a Brother of Charity'. Later, he became a priest of the Institute of Charity, and was instrumental in securing St. Ethedreda's, Ely Place, the only pre-reformation Church in London now in Catholic hands. Before he came he promised Newman to stay three years. He was only twenty-two ; three years proved too long an eternity to wait. Frederick Bowles came in December ; an attractive, but rather nervous and unstable young man. A brother of his had been at Oriel, and died young ; one of his sisters, Emily, who first met Newman about now, became a lifelong friend. The Bowles family lived at Abingdon.

Ambrose St. John, Henry's favourite curate, did not arrive till the summer of the next year, 1843, just before Lockhart's defection. He was twenty-eight, though he looked younger, and in character already more mature than the others. He was sensible and straight-forward, and more decided in his Catholic views than Newman, when he came. Newman took to him at once and wrote to Henry : 'St. John goes to-morrow and I ought to thank you for letting me have the great pleasure of making his acquaintance. He wishes to pay me a longer visit — and I assure you *I* do.' St. John's longer visit lasted the rest of his life. He was practical and energetic, brisk, rather blunt and tactless, but generous in trying to make it up to those he offended, and ready to admit it when he had been in the wrong. He had humour and sympathy and was a keen gardener ; he had a pet rose even at Littlemore and wherever he was plants were put in and directions went to and fro about them when he was away. He was not musical, but liked painting ; he was a good linguist, and his favourite studies were Hebrew and Syriac ; he had worked under Pusey and was always grateful to and fond of him. Later, he kept up with German Biblical criticism. But his chief interest was pastoral work and he was good at it ; he liked people, and they liked him, and he was always busy with many little schemes at once.

Others were to come later for a brief stay before their reception as Catholics, and during the whole three years there were many visitors, either for the day or for a longer time. Two who used to come out from Oxford were James Anthony Froude, Hurrell's little brother, the future historian, and Mark Pattison, later the Rector of Lincoln College, and a well-known Victorian character. Both these two lost their faith in Christianity after Newman left Oxford, but half a century later, when he was a Cardinal, he was able to get in touch with them again, and they retained for him a respect and love the more remarkable in that they had turned away from all he stood for.

The fact that the men who joined Newman at Littlemore were all much younger than he, gave the gossip in Oxford a new turn. It became a common jibe against him that he surrounded himself with 'inferior men', and could not do without a circle of junior admirers over whom he exercised an absolute sway. As for the 'inferiority' of the men, when they became Catholics they gave up the opportunity of making a name in academic circles, but they had all done well in the schools and several were considered outstanding. Some of the Littlemore visitors became Jesuits, not considered unintellectual men even by their enemies. But Newman did not choose them for their brains ; in fact, he did not choose them at all. They came. Either they were sent by relations or friends or were drawn to ask Newman's advice. Those who lived there often had nowhere else to go, and Dalgairns, for one, was partly supported by Newman, for his father refused him more than a tiny allowance inadequate to keep him. Newman acted as a kind of buffer between him and his family, calming their anxieties as well as he could, and trying to get the youthful enthusiast to be dutiful and patient. In spite of being so much younger, they were by no means always easy to manage. Lockhart was impetuous, Dalgairns restless and headstrong. Besides this, as Lockhart recorded in his memoir, Newman refused to be treated as a Superior, or even as a don. He wanted them to call him simply 'Newman' but Lockhart said it seemed too familiar, and they usually addressed him direct, without any name !

When Newman's friend Samuel Wood died, in April 1843, he wrote to Jemima : 'But really I ought to be very thankful, or rather, I cannot be thankful as I ought to be, for the wonderful way in which God makes to me new friends, when I lose old ; to be sure they are younger, which is a drawback, as making me feel so very antique ;

but there are compensations even then.' Still he missed the sort of
companionship he would have had if Samuel Wood and Hurrell
Froude had lived, for he was sure that both would have been with him.

Newman did not interfere with the liberty of thought and action
of those who visited, or those who stayed in Littlemore. He warned
Ambrose St. John not to expect discussion ; St. Mary's house at
Littlemore, as he sometimes called it, was not for that, but for study
and prayer. Even the rules of the house were little more than an
order of the day. It began at five with Matins, Lauds and Prime
from the Breviary. At eleven they went to the Church for Morning
Prayer and again at three for Evensong. The main meal of the day, a
simple one, was at six. Silence was kept except between two and
eight. Vespers was at seven and Compline at nine, in English if
visitors were present. A servant came in from the village to do the
fires and cleaning, though Newman hoped they would later do everything themselves. They did their own rooms and other jobs. Between
the hours of prayer there was study and work on the new project :
Lives of the English Saints, when that was started. Until the autumn
of 1843 Newman still had his parish to attend, and although he had
curates, he often walked in and out between Littlemore and St.
Mary's, a good three or four miles, uphill on the way home, several
times a week. Even after he had given up the parish, he went on
visiting the dying Miss Lenthall, as he had done for years. And all
the time he was writing letters every evening, often till midnight.

In spite of their hardworking and ascetic life, and their doubts
about the Church, the atmosphere of the house was homely and full
of laughter. Sometimes Newman got out his violin and played
sonatas with anyone who could or would, in the Library after dinner
— that is, in the old barn lined with books, after their very plain
meal. There were a lot of jokes ; the letters of the young men, when
they went home to their suspicious families, were full of messages to
everyone, reminders, apologies, requests for the door to be left open
at night. When it was Newman who was away, they sent him all the
small domestic news. Well might he say to Jemima, amused, that
there was no chance of his coming north yet, because he was 'a
family man and could not leave home'. The spirit of the Littlemore
house was so like that of St. Philip's Oratory that the Saint must have
had his eye on Newman already.

All this summer of 1842 he was particularly happy and in high
spirits. Anne Mozley was asking for poems for an anthology ; he
allowed her to reprint, 'but as to *new* verses, when my plantations are

grown up into trees and I have built a nest in the top boughs, then you will get me to sing a fresh tune'. He was startled, on looking at a publisher's list, to see advertised 'Louisa the Bride, by the Rev. J. H. Newman'. It was a mistake for Harriett's name! He thought this book of hers the best thing she had done. To Aunt he told the tale of an earnest visitor, who, as he walked out to Littlemore with an enthusiastic Oxford companion 'was so mystified and terrified about the place, which I suppose he thought before to be a sort of rural villa, that when he at length reached us he was as grave and solemn as an old cat, and we could make nothing of him. I thought marriage had spoiled him', added Newman wickedly. The poor visitor was sick all night and fled in the morning to Christ Church, where he 'soon became as lively and chirping as usual, and his face lost all its gibbous effect and swelled into a gleaming glistening full moon — so you see we had our fun without practising any tricks upon him. His *imagination* did it for us.'

Outside in the world excitement still ran high about popery at Oxford. Mr. McGhee, a pugnacious Evangelical, challenged Newman to a public debate 'with stenographists' on St. Paul's epistle to the Romans. '*I* might as well propose a duet on the violin', observed Newman to Keble, 'for I am as little able to contravert on a platform, as, I suspect, he is to execute a concerto.' Legend has addressed this retort to McGhee himself, but to him Newman wrote : 'You need not have told me that you considered me ignorant of the way of Salvation ; I knew it before you said it. . . . You will see, Dear Sir, that your trouble is lost upon me. Alas, there are others up and down the country whom you may be able to terrify, but your cause is a failing one. . . . I am, with sincere respect for your zeal, yours faithfully.' That must have sealed his doom with the Evangelical champion!

Newman was teasing everybody. Miss Giberne was so disgusted with the caricatures that she wanted to draw him herself ; Newman said she might just as well have drawn William Copeland, his curate. 'How do you know that many persons would not think *me* a scarecrow, and my caricature an improvement ?' He reminded her of Westmacott's bust, which he had done on the sly last year, taking Newman's measurements by subterfuge. 'I suspect it is flattered enough to please the most indulgent friend.' But if ever a portrait was done, 'I would not do it by halves, but would prefix the said portrait in every one of my books, sermons and all, and would be represented in an elegant dress and attitude, with my hand between the buttons of my waistcoat, or in a new taglioni'. Miss Giberne took a friendly interest in Littlemore. 'Have you any fellow monks in your quiet retreat?' she inquired. After the September festival that year he told her that there had been a man in church crying '"Popish!" If I had heard him I should have had him turned out for brawling — he was a little man and we had some stout fellows among us. Then he would have said, "What, persecution already! I thought the wily Puseyites would have kept the cloven hoof out of sight a little longer."'

Perhaps it was this year that Emily Bowles, a little vague about dates in her memoir, first saw Newman. She put it in 1840, but mentioned the 'monastery'. When she was old she wrote of that vivid memory, the flowers, the sunshine, the procession of singing children and 'one face, grand, reticent, powerful, both in speaking and at rest, and slightly forbidding, that detached itself from the rest and remained for ever stamped on my mind'. Emily Bowles was a spirited and intelligent girl, who had worked alongside her delicate brother to encourage him, and persuaded him to ride with her for his health; this was the brother who died, not Frederick, who was soon to join Newman at Littlemore. He had given her the *Lyra*, and Newman's poems had come to her like strange oracles, changing all her ideas about religion — for she had been inclined to sceptical doubting. Now she saw the actual man. 'At his voice I trembled all over and at last tears began to flow for no other cause but that of the awful sense of the Invisible Presence which he brought among us.' After the service Newman entertained his guests to luncheon in the 'monastery' and poor Emily, who was quite young, was overcome when he asked her: 'Will you have some cold chicken?' In spite of 'the kind smile as he bent down with his singular chivalrous courtesy, mingled with an indescribable reserve to all women', cold chicken after her pious exaltation was too much for her feelings, and her mother had to answer for her.

No wonder that the lively H. W. continued to tease Newman about the ladies; he had some joke against him which involved cutting out the words 'Mary Mordaunt' from a letter of Newman's and sending them to his friend Acland. Newman said: 'I think all nice persons are called Mary but how could you think I could, with our present unhappy habits, take the liberty of writing (Mary Mordaunt) in the book of a lady I have seen but once? Am I an Archbishop or an Abbot? am I a Monk of the Desert? And yet I wish very much to be civil and kind.'

Kindness certainly led him into situations which might have turned out unfortunately, considering the hostile eyes fixed on his

every action.   He could never say no when anyone begged for help
and advice, however overburdened he was, and however unsuitable
the inquirer.   Mary Holmes first wrote to him in 1840 disguising
herself as ZYX.   She was a clever, headstrong, emotional girl forced
to work as a governess, while she longed for an artistic and musical
life : a real Brontë type.   She was related to Thackeray, met him as
a child, and later became quite a friend of his by letter ; alas, when
he met her he thought her very plain and her nose was red, and he
lost interest in her.   She also corresponded with Trollope.   She
wrote long anxious letters to Newman, asking his advice and rarely
taking it, relentlessly involving him in all her domestic affairs with
her employers, oblivious of the risk of bringing on him the sort of
scandal the newspapers would have seized on with delight.   Oakeley
was soon to be accused of exercising sinister priestly influence on a
young lady.   It could have happened to Newman, though, as he
sometimes mildly complained to her, he found it very difficult to
influence Miss Holmes at all.

In 1842 Miss Holmes had to pass through Oxford on her way to
a new job and begged to be allowed to meet Newman, whose letters
she had now been receiving for two years.   Evidently she imagined
him as the perfect Father, a venerable sage uttering words of unearthly
wisdom, for the real man came as a shock to her.   She was nothing
if not outspoken and must have communicated her disappointment
to the cause of it, for he wrote : 'I fear I made matters worse by
being rude, when I wished to show my sympathy.   As for myself,
you are not the first person who has been disappointed in me.
Romantic people always will be.   I am, in all my ways of going on, a
very ordinary person.   However, ordinary or not, I shall not cease,
if you will suffer me, to speak from time to time when I think a word
may be useful — for though I am not an old man as you expected,
I suppose I am about double your age and have a right to advise.'

Miss Holmes was soon trying to put her idol back in its shrine
again.   Newman said firmly : 'As to myself, be quite sure that if you
saw me again, you would feel as you did when you saw me before.
I am *not* venerable and nothing can make me so.   I am very much
like other people and I do not think it necessary to abstain from
feelings and thoughts, not intrinsically sinful, which other people
have.   I cannot speak words of wisdom ; to some it comes naturally.
Do not suffer any illusive notion about me to spring up in your mind.
No one can treat me with deference and respect who knows me, and
from my heart I trust and pray that no one ever may.   I never have

been in office or station ; people have never bowed to me — and I could not endure it. I tell you frankly my infirmity, I believe, is always to be rude to persons who are deferential in manner to me. I really do fear it is.'

But this personal self-defence did not take up much space in the correspondence, which was chiefly concerned with trying to instil a little patience into Miss Holmes, who expected to become perfect overnight, and was inclined to blame her uncongenial circumstances when she did not. 'Our very work here is to overcome ourselves', he told her after Christmas, 'and to be sensible of our hourly infirmities, to feel them keenly, is but the necessary step towards overcoming them. Never expect to be without such while life lasts — if these were overcome you would discover others, and that both because your eyes would see your real state of imperfection more clearly then than now, and also because they are in great measure the temptations of the Enemy and he has temptations for all states, all occasions.'

There were difficult young men as well as difficult young ladies ; next spring Newman was dealing with one William Davis, just as excitable as Miss Holmes and as ready to turn him into an idol. 'I have been able to recall nearly every word you said to me,' wrote Davis, after he had paid a longed-for visit, 'and the last seemed to glow most in my heart, "when you have a more perfect religion".' Newman had given him the Anglican Bishop Wilson's *Sacra Privata* and poor Davis had no sooner read that sinners should confess their sins than he seized his pen and wrote to Newman in a frenzy, 'I have read no more and can read no more until I do so. I am almost afraid to say Matin Prayer and I dare not approach that Holy Table. Oh take my confession and I will obey whatever you command. Shew me the narrow way for I have never askt for it. I cannot weep, my eyes and forehead are as dry as a piece of parchment.' Newman's answers have not survived, but that they were calming and practical may be inferred from the fact that he got his friend the Radcliffe Observer, Johnson, to take Davis as an assistant. In this capacity the unfortunate young man must have been an unmitigated nuisance, for later that summer (1843) Johnson refused to accept a return of some money he had lent him, said he did not want an assistant and would rather not have another. Two years later, Davis, now finding his feet as a Catholic at Oscott, wrote to Newman wanting to make things up with the good-natured but exasperated Observer — 'Do help me'. Of course Newman did.

It was not only clever young people he assisted, but all and sundry. In 1842 he was trying to persuade Pattison to take on as cook the son of a college servant. 'He is a very presentable looking person and if he does not get too fat would do your college credit — but I know he has a good many competitors. His father is a very respectable worthy man, and his sister is a really good person.' It was like Newman to know the cook's sister well enough to know she was really good. Looking out for a nursery maid for Jemima, he described a family of likely girls : 'The third is a nice interesting child too — but recollect that gentlemen are very bad judges of the female sex and I may be quite out'. He even made use of Miss Holmes to find a place for a lady's maid. During these years, too, Newman taught Latin to a boy in the village whose father was master carpenter on the Queen's yacht ; he got Henry Weltch into St. Mark's College, Chelsea, and went to see him there. Henry later married and visited Newman in Birmingham.

Littlemore was held by Newman in joint tenancy with Wood, Church, Bloxam and William Froude, Hurrell's brother who had become an engineer, and married Miss Holdsworth, daughter of the governor of Dartmouth Castle, whom Newman had known earlier. When he made his will this summer of 1842 Newman must have been full of hope that 'the monastery' would continue even if sudden death removed him from the scene. Everything seemed to be going well there, so that the Bishops' Charges did not intrude themselves unduly. Aunt thought it might be cold in winter, but Newman told her a few sheepskins on the floors would work wonders, and he had invested in a special Arnott stove for the Library, where they worked most of the time. On its vagaries he consulted Bellasis at length, hearing that 'he had taken his degrees in the science of Arnott stoves'. But the stove pursued its own way and the same day in November that Newman wrote to tell Miss Holmes that romantic people would always be disappointed in him, he was saying to Jemima : 'Everything is very quiet in Oxford except the internals of the Heads of Houses and such like, who, I am told, fret and fume the quieter things are. . . . The top (iron) of our Arnott stove has just leapt off without reason and deposited itself on the floor.' He decided to abandon Arnott in favour of the ordinary variety.

Meanwhile the enthusiastic 'R. Catholick' Ambrose Phillipps brought to Oxford Father Gentili of the Institute of Charity. Gentili was born, in Italy, the same year as Newman. A lawyer, and a brilliant, handsome man, he had fallen in love with an English Catholic heiress, whose guardians for some reason refused his suit.

This shock profoundly altered the whole trend of his life, and he joined the Institute, newly founded by the philosopher priest Rosmini, friend of Manzoni and the Italian nationalists. Gentili had come to England to work among the Catholics of the industrial towns, and Phillipps perhaps felt he was the man to convert Newman. They met both Newman and Pusey. Phillipps wrote, 'We were quite enchanted with Newman, whose amiable manners are only equalled by his gigantick learning and talents'. Newman had just brought out a translation of Fleury's Church History, with an introductory essay on Ecclesiastical Miracles. 'It is quite magnificent', Phillipps told the suspicious Lord Shrewsbury. 'Not only Catholick and orthodox, but written with a power of argument perfectly *tremendous*. Newman has the intellect of the cherubim — forcible like the lightning flash, clear as crystal.'

1842–1843

The Idea of Development

IN November 1842 Newman preached four sermons on 'The Christian Empire', tracing the continuity of the Christian with the Jewish Church, the nation chosen by God to receive and guard the Truth as He revealed it. There was no sign of the fumbling of the year before. Arnold had accused the Apostolicals of Judaizing, as if of some atavistic crime ; indeed to him and other liberal thinkers it meant a reversion to a primitive and external type of religion from a Christianity which they believed to be an inward moral ideal. Newman would have none of that. A religion is the bond, both inward and outward, which holds a society together and Christianity is not an ideal but an event : the coming of God to transform the whole human race. 'And consequently', he said, 'Catholic Christians must not be surprised, if, on their submitting to Christianity *as* a religion, and not as a mere philosophy, or an opinion, or a sentiment, they are charged by those who do so treat it, with being Jews or even Pagans.' Christ was not an idea but a Person, both divine and human, and like Him the empire He founded was at once subject to the operation of natural processes and living by a power which transcended them.

In these sermons Newman summed up all he had been thinking for years on the history of God's action in the world and the nature of the Church as a concrete society set up to renew mankind. But now he was looking at this history from another angle, studying the conflicts within the Church in the early centuries, out of which had been born the great definitions of the Creeds. Those who had studied them till now had either recorded the quarrels as historical events, or analysed the ideas of the theological argument as might be done in a philosophical discussion. But Newman was particularly interested in the process of thinking, especially in thinking about the mysteries of faith, and he saw that the ideas themselves had a history : that although the Teaching had always been whole and sufficient, all the implications and consequences of it were not immediately apparent, but had been drawn out by the working of many minds over many centuries. A man may believe what he believed as a child, but his understanding of it has grown and deepened as his own mind was growing. In a similar way the Church had a collective mind, continuous with itself but expanding and deepening through the meditation of many individual minds. The Faith, just because it was concerned with facts, events and persons, admitted of intellectual study, so that the communal understanding of it could not but grow into a complex, though coherent, system of thought, definite but not desiccated.

Christ compared His kingdom to a seed which grew into a tree. This image was generally referred to the expansion of the Church through the ages ; but it can also be taken as a picture of growth from source to complex maturity. Christ called Himself the seed which must fall into the ground and die to bring forth fruit ; the full-grown Church has developed out of Him, though at first sight it looks as different as tree from seed. And as a tree grows not only by the external action of sun and rain and the nourishment of the earth, but according to the internal pattern of the seed, so the Church, in its intrinsic ideas as in its action, must grow to the pattern of the spirit within it, the Spirit of God Himself, the Living and True.

If the idea of development of doctrine does not seem strange to us now, it is because we are familiar with theories of evolutionary process ; not so were those who first heard Newman speak of it. He sketched the theory in the last university sermon he was to deliver, preached on the feast of the Purification of the Blessed Virgin Mary, Candlemas Day, February 2nd, 1843, and completed his *Essay* on it in the autumn of 1845. The sermon was sixteen years before the publication of *The Origin of Species*, when Charles Darwin proposed the theory of biological evolution and startled a society accustomed to believe that each species was created perfect and separate in a world which had never been other than it appeared at present. In the last hundred years such a revolution of thought has taken place that it is almost impossible to imagine what it felt like to live in a world so static ; wonderful and mysterious indeed, but as everlasting and changeless as it appears to a child.

Far more profound, surely, this change in our minds than even that which transformed the imagination of Europeans when they realized that the world moved, rolling like a ball in the heavens. The

world was not the centre of all things, nor stable. But at least everything on it remained as it had always been, and man retained and
increased his supremacy over nature, the supremacy of reason over
unconscious beings and inanimate matter. The great discovery of the
nineteenth century, rapidly invading every field of thought, was that
everything — species, the human race, the earth itself — was involved
in a continuous process of change, only not immediately noticeable
because the periods of it were vastly beyond even the recorded
memories of men. Just as in the sixteenth and seventeenth centuries
people had to get used to losing their cosmological stability in space,
so, during the last hundred years, they have had to lose it in time ;
the heavens do not revolve round the earth, nor is man the centre of
a static world, changeless except for the birth and death of individuals,
and subject to his will under the supreme authority of reason. The
general reaction to this discovery seems to have been double : fear
at being caught up in an inevitable progress uncontrolled by man,
and worship of any form of progress as inevitable. Neither is the
necessary consequence of recognizing the evolutionary process.

Newman grew up in the world which saw itself as static, except
for the improvements brought about by the cleverness of men, whose
cleverness indeed seemed to be exceeding that of all previous generations. It was this which gave birth to the idea of progressive enlightenment, that greater knowledge would bring moral as well as mental
improvement. Newman absolutely rejected this view and consequently, to the march-of-mind men, as Froude had christened them,
he appeared atavistic, determined to cling to outworn forms of the
past. The timelessness of Catholicism makes it look old-fashioned
to the world. Yet though the fault in man's nature made it impossible
for him to change himself for the better by means of his reason, he
could be changed : the whole point of Christianity was that God
could change him. God's entrance into the world of space and time
was the one truly free and dynamic act in its history.

Newman had been familiar since his boyhood with this action,
both in himself as an individual and in his study of the Church in
fact and in theory. He was exceptionally self-aware, and at the same
time acutely perceptive of the world outside himself. The journals,
the sermons, the *Lectures on Justification* show how deeply he meditated the process of setting right and making whole broken and
disfigured human nature ; in this process the mind as well as the
will played its part. His own mind had had to find its way through a
maze of ideas, and he had noticed how what was true in his original

belief remained and grew, while what was distorted or false was gradually recognized as such and dropped. So long as he continued to believe, his search for truth enlarged his understanding of faith — so long too as he acted on his belief, according to his conscience. But those who relied on reason alone lost what elements of truth they had started with. The seed of grace could grow in the soul till it transformed the whole person, his ideas no less than his acts ; its history in the Church, the collective Body of Christ, might be similar. Newman's theory crystallized in his mind while he brooded over the intellectual battles of the fifth century, but his own life must have influenced the way he looked at them.

Thus he made the great jump from a static to a dynamic view of the history of the human race before it was made in scientific fields. His theory dealt with a very special area of thought, the activating ideas of the Christian body, and there was a vital difference between the merely natural evolution of ideas and the development controlled by the Holy Spirit ; he made this distinction especially clear in the *Essay*. But by recognizing the principle of growth in the Church he provided the basis for a constructive approach to the coming secular theories which, indeed, were never a trouble to him as they were to so many Christians, whose mental balance was upset by Darwin very much in the way that it was upset for their ancestors by Galileo. Just as the generation of the Renaissance had imagined that the earth must be stable and central if heaven and hell were real, so that of the mid-nineteenth century imagined that creation could only be instantaneous and that man was totally different from the beasts of the field — still more so from those of the jungle. Still later was to come the further development, confounding the proud Victorian rationalists, of the psychological theories which shook reason in its seat by discovering the jungle not only in remote ancestry but in present unconscious activity in the individual. This would not have worried Newman, to judge from his interest in the passions of beasts and their relation to human sin. But it was his fate to see too deeply into things for his contemporaries to understand him. Liberals thought him anti-rational and authoritarian ; pious conservatives feared him as an innovator, almost a sceptic. His sermon on Development was considered dangerous stuff in Oxford.

He preached on the text : 'And Mary kept all these things and pondered them in her heart'. He did not speak then of Mary, except as the pattern of all Christians who ponder the great mysteries of God's revelation. But he was thinking about her. It was possible that modern Roman teaching about her might be a true and not a false development of the doctrine of the Fathers that she was the Second Eve, Mother of God made man, and Mother of all men living in Him the life of the new creation. About this time Dr. Russell of Maynooth sent Newman some penny leaflets from Rome, and the sermons of St. Alphonso Liguori, extracts from which were used by Protestants to prove that Rome put Mary in Christ's place in worship, just as the Pope was put in Christ's place in the matter of obedience. St. Alphonso was an eighteenth-century lawyer, who, like Gentili later, had given up career and comfort to preach to the poor of the Italian countryside ; the order he founded was known as Redemptorist, sufficiently witnessing to his love for the Redeemer. He might almost be called a Catholic Wesley. Newman was surprised to find what a distorted view the Protestant writers had given. His fears about corruptions were already allayed by habitual reading of the sober Breviary offices, but here was evidence from the popular and contemporary side that Mary and the Pope were not presented as substitutes for Christ but had their own places in the scheme of redemption.

In 1839 Newman had seen the Church simultaneously in two periods of history, at the time when the world was about to become officially Christian, and in his own age, when, as his prophetic insight enabled him to see, it was about to become un-Christian. The two periods paralleled and 'Rome was where she now is' — the centre and standard of unity. What had held him back was his belief that England had the Apostolic Succession, and his conviction that Roman doctrine about Mary and the Pope was corrupt, and not to be found in Antiquity. Since then the Charges of the Bishops against Tract 90 and Catholic doctrine, and their promotion of the union with heretics in Jerusalem, seemed to confirm his suspicion that England was in schism, and the grace of succession suspended. Now he began to wonder if the elaboration of teaching about Mary and Peter's successor might not be examples of development in action, and to trace it back to its beginnings. He had already been struck at the way the early Popes had *behaved* as if they held a divinely appointed special office in the Church, even before the claim was expressed in documents. But he went slowly. The theory of development was intimately connected with his own development.

1843

Hypocrite and Deceiver

FOR one who was supposed to be so crafty, Newman was singularly unable to manage things to his own advantage. Reading Dr. Russell's books had made him realize that he had made unfair and untrue attacks on Rome, relying on the views of Anglican divines. Before Christmas he planned to make a formal Retractation of what he had said ; publication was delayed, and when it came out in January 1843 he was in the thick of his worst newspaper scandal so far. It was this that confirmed the general suspicions of his guile.

Bernard Smith, a young clergyman who had shocked people with the popish goings on in his parish, suddenly seceded to Rome. It was immediately reported that Newman had already advised him to continue in his parish after conforming, in order to subvert his people and take them with him. On being approached by a friendly editor Newman insisted on his printing a direct denial. The editor was dubious of the wisdom of this; and in fact it was not believed. Pusey heard that Smith's Bishop, on being shown the denial, remarked, 'Ah, these Oxford men are disingenuous'. Pusey assisted Newman in tracking the slander to its source : an anxious lady whose words had been misinterpreted. Private apologies followed, but by then (March) it was too late to do anything about it. Bernard Smith had consulted Newman, who had written him a couple of letters, though not advocating deception ; Newman could not therefore deny any contact with the young man. It was in March that the evangelical Dean Close of Cheltenham, speaking at a Tradesmen's Dinner, announced amid applause that he would not trust the author of Tract 90 with his purse.

The Retractation appeared just when everyone was reading about Newman's underhand dealings with the popish Smith, and, as Jemima reported from Derby, it made 'a hubbub in the world'. This was just what Newman had wished to avoid. He knew by now that his name was the signal for thousands who had never read a word of his works to start howling about popery ; therefore he did

not sign the statement he sent to the *Conservative Journal*. Since
he gave the references in his own books, anyone who had read them
would know who was now eating his own words ; anyone who had
not read them did not need to read his recantation. But he reckoned
without Golightly, who never lost any time in letting the world know
the implications of Oxford actions. He wrote to the *Oxford Herald*,
'really boiling over' as Jemima said.

That the statement was unsigned was additional proof of Newman's cowardly underhand ways ; what he said was misunderstood
as well. He said he had published the attacks because it was necessary
to the Anglican case to protest against Rome, and that he had followed
the Anglican divines in doing so — he had 'thrown himself into their
system'. People thought he meant he had not believed the accusations he made, whereas he thought that though he believed them yet
he would not have been justified in publishing them had he not the
example of those he had taken as guides and authorities. With his
usual headlong candour he had also confessed that the violence of the
language in which he had protested was probably due to faults of
character. 'Yet I have reason to fear still, that such language is to
be ascribed, in no small measure, to an impetuous temper, a hope of
approving myself to persons I respect, and a wish to repel the charge
of Romanism.' It was immediately assumed that the charge he
wished to repel had been true all along, and that he knew it, and
merely abused Rome to curry favour with the authorities. Why he
should now let all this out, nobody stopped to inquire.

Newman was simply bewildered to find his admission of mistaken
zeal was taken as a confession of duplicity ; his mind did not easily
comprehend the depths of dishonesty attributed to him. Yet not
only newspapers but people who had known him believed him a
conscious deceiver. Whately wrote to remind Hawkins that even
two years ago he had suggested that 'the Tractites did not preach
and mean the same thing'. He had 'thrown down the cap' then and
now Newman had put it on. 'It is a thing which makes me every
now and then feel as if I were in a dream', he said, 'to find people
going on believing men who *proclaim* themselves liars.' It was now
that he said Newman had nothing to learn from 'the *Slanderer*
himself !' Not content with accusing Newman of intent to deceive,
malice and deliberate lying, he threw in the charge of pride, denoun-
cing 'the tendency in mere men to imitate God or his Prophets and
Apostles in those very points in which imitation of them should be
most carefully guarded against'.

Newman now made everything worse for himself by preaching the sermon on Wisdom and Innocence which so shocked Kingsley because he thought it taught that lying and cunning were the weapons of the Christian against the world. What Newman said, that February Sunday in St. Mary's, was that the world could only recognize two causes for success : force or guile. Since Christians were forbidden to use force, they were credited with guile. It was like him to admit that Christians, when oppressed, had sometimes succumbed to the temptation to use the subterfuges and treacheries of slaves, just as when they were established in power they had often used force against their enemies ; nevertheless he did not, as Kingsley imagined, advocate deception and sanction it with the example of Christ. The Pharisees called Christ a deceiver because they saw and feared His power with the people and yet could not force or surprise from Him any teaching conflicting with the law of God. Newman was comforting himself with the knowledge that others before him, even Christ Himself, had by their very innocence laid themselves open to the charge of guile from a world unable to recognize the invisible power of truth. The world saw the revival of Catholic ideas all over England and could not believe they could spread by conviction ; Newman was credited with raising a Romanizing party by secret diplomacy and masking his cunning with a sham humility and pretence of virtue. What could he do ? The more submissively he behaved the more clever he was thought to be. The Movement kept growing, and all that its members did was referred back to him by its enemies.

But most difficult of all, his mind had just taken, almost against his will, a further step, and he said to Henry, 'I am a Roman in my heart'. He felt more sure that the Church of England was in schism and corrupted with heresy than that Rome was corrupted with superstition ; he thought England was more in the wrong than Rome. He did not yet have a positive conviction that Rome was right in claiming to represent the Church of Antiquity. 'I am much out of heart,' he wrote to Henry, 'merely because I wish to be out of hot water, and something or other is always sousing me again in it. It is so very difficult to steer between being hypocritical and revolutionary.' But now that he was more or less convinced that England was in schism, and that the sense in which he interpreted the Thirty-Nine Articles was not that upheld by the Bishops, the urgent question to be decided was whether he should give up St. Mary's. Not wishing to rely on his own judgment he intended to ask Keble to

consider the question during Lent, and also decided to consult
Rogers, of whose common sense he had a high opinion.

Rogers came down for the Gaudy ; he probably heard Newman's
last university sermon, on Development. This must have been the
occasion of one of the most painful scenes Newman ever had to
endure. What happened can be gathered from letters they exchanged
later, just before Easter. When Newman tried to ask Rogers for his
opinion he recoiled violently, refused to listen, and accused Newman
of deceiving him and others, of leading them in the direction of
Rome while pretending to be satisfied with Anglicanism. The next
day Newman was writing to Henry : 'I am sure I have no wish to
take people in, yet having outgrown former faith by present convictions, I have managed effectually to do so. Yet though there are
those, and intimates too, who take to themselves to accuse me of
"keeping the word of promise to the ear and breaking it to the lips"
like certain not very respectable persons, as if I used language which
said only what I meant, but implied what others meant, I can truly
say that the idea of people's trusting me when I am not trustworthy
has long made me uncomfortable. Yet what can I do ? How is it
possible to give persons a right impression of what I would say when
every word is sure to be misunderstood, every admission to be exaggerated, every avowal to be considered but a hint of what is left
unsaid ? Then there is the certainty of unsettling people, and
then it is far easier to say what I have not confidence in, than what
I have.'

He added : 'I wonder whether I am more apt to be out of heart
than other people — I am very much so just now. The truth is, I
believe, I am pulled down by the blue pill which G. Babington whom
I consulted told me to take, having left it off for something like
eleven years.' This must have been a remedy prescribed after his
breakdown in 1827 and left off before the voyage in the Mediterranean. Babington therefore must have thought he was suffering
from acute nervous strain. It was like Newman to blame the pill
rather than the unkindness of friends for his being out of heart, and
instead of indulging in self pity to wonder if he were melancholic by
nature. Yet he was soon making light of his troubles to Jemima, and
teasing Hope about the *University Sermons* which had just come out.
'You got a headache from *one* — it would be an act of gratitude to
send you *all*. Shall I do so ?'

Rogers was silent during Lent ; he was in London. But the
prospect of meeting Newman again after Easter led him to write a

letter on April 3rd, part of which was printed by Anne Mozley, no
doubt at his wish, as expressing his sense of what he owed to Newman's friendship. But by itself it gives little indication of what was
going on. 'I do not like to meet you again without having said, once
for all, what I hope you will not think hollow or false. I cannot
disguise from myself how very improbable, perhaps impossible — a
recurrence of our former terms is. But I wish, before the time has
passed for such an acknowledgement, to have said how deeply and
painfully I feel — and I may say have more or less felt for *years* —
the greatness of what I am losing, and to thank you for all you have
done and been to me. I know that it is a great measure by my own
act that I am losing this — and I cannot persuade myself that I am
substantially wrong, or that I could have avoided what has happened.'
There was more in the same style, together with an apology for any
irritation he might have shown, and he ended by saying he did not
expect an answer. The whole letter suggests that Newman acquiesced
in, or even initiated, the idea that with such a difference between
them their friendship must be at an end. This was not so.

Newman wrote back at once, scribbling a draft which he kept.
'I have just received your kind letter and I must not let you go on
supposing what I have before now attempted to explain to you. You
have not pained me by differing from me in opinion. I never have
assumed you acted on the notion that you agreed with me. On the
contrary, I have not been slow whenever asked by others to declare
that I did not know what your opinions were, nay, on almost *any*
subject. You never have told me your opinions. What did more
than pain me was first and chiefly your refusing me that advice
which I had a right to ask as a friend, whether he agreed with me or
not, and next your refusing to receive my confidence. I hope you
will not refuse to continue to me the benefit of your prayers.'

This straight reply had the effect of rousing Rogers to justify
himself. His answer shows how he misconceived the whole situation.
He said he thought Newman had been in the habit of consulting
him 'as the conductor of a great movement in the English Church —
I fancy I have been of use to you in habitually showing you in my
own person what ordinary men would think of this or that course
of conduct . . . I cannot feel myself at liberty to occupy this place
in a movement which *I* feel is tending to a secession from England
to Rome. I think it would *in me* be treachery to the English Church
to which I belong, and to which I feel more and more contented to
belong.' But how could it be treachery to receive a friend's

confidence and advise on a practical decision? He was treating Newman
not as a friend but as the leader of a party, and imagining that he was,
and all along had been, acting like a politician, with a view to consequences, and using his best friend to calculate them. Perhaps this
seemed natural to Rogers, now that he was living in the political
world, but it is extraordinary that anyone who had been Newman's
close friend could imagine that he looked at the Movement in such
an external way.

Newman received this letter, which opened such chasms of past
and present incomprehension, in the middle of Holy Week, when he
and his Littlemore companions were making their first retreat, using
a Catholic manual for the purpose. Whether or not he read it then,
Newman did not think of answering it till the retreat ended. On
Easter Eve he scribbled some notes. 'He is wrong in saying that I
used him as a specimen of others. I have gone by his *advice*. I have
not done, or not modified, by his *judgment* what I should have done
by my own. No one has so much restrained me as he. But it is not
worth while to write to him to explain.' But then to leave Rogers
believing such nonsense seemed unbearable. 'Yes, I think I must
write a letter to repudiate such an idea.' Afterwards he noted, 'I did
not write'. He did write, but did not send, some much altered notes.
'My conscience altogether repudiates the idea contained in it and I
am writing in a holy season. But really I hardly know to what
extent you may think me deceiving whether myself or you.' He
thought there was 'a trait of suspiciousness in your character, and
that not as regards myself, which it has not till lately come into my
head to think, but persons and things generally. . . . May you find
others as *reverential* in their feelings towards you as I have been.'
In spite of the fact that Rogers was so much younger Newman had
felt this reverence for him as a person, for his liberty to think and feel
differently, his right to his own life and opinions. Rogers' return for
this was suspicion, just at the moment when Newman most needed
a friend's sympathy. His admiration and gratitude were sincere,
but he was lacking in imagination and understanding.

While Newman was on retreat he made a note : 'Also I prayed
that I might have grace always to look at things, and at my actions
upon them, as I would wish I had looked at them, and shall look at
them, on my death-bed. E.g. the mode in which I ought to behave
to Rogers.' The letter he had tried to write did not pass the death-
bed test ; Newman dropped his self-defence, and his criticism of
Rogers' suspiciousness. It was useless to try to recover an intimacy

which Rogers was determined to relegate to the past. He saw Rogers whenever he was in Oxford ; Rogers paid a public tribute to his general good influence in 1845, in the hope of keeping him in the Church of England ; when he left, he dropped his acquaintance entirely. Yet twenty years later when at last he went to visit Newman in Birmingham he was received without a single reproach, only with delight.

Self-deception was hardly possible to someone so much on the look-out for it as Newman, and he had just been searching his heart even more closely than usual in this first retreat. Six of them made their meditations together three times a day in the chapel, reading out the points from a manual based on the Spiritual Exercises of St. Ignatius, designed to make people realize the continual choice that faces them, between the Standards of Christ and of Satan. The hours of meditation were at 4.30 a.m., 1.30 p.m. and 8.30 in the evening. The chapel, made out of the end room, was tiny, and windowless, for as the only window opened on the village street they had blocked it up and put up in front of it a wide shelf on which stood a cross. The walls were hung with red stuff and behind the *altarino* was an antependium of white material called challis, which Miss Giberne had bought for Newman in Cheltenham. It hung from ceiling to floor, folded over the altar-shelf. When they were all six kneeling in this small shut-in place there cannot have been much room. Newman noted that he found it difficult to realize God's presence when they were all meditating together like this. He kept noticing the time, whether it went fast or slow ; he fidgeted, waiting for the clock to strike and sometimes found himself dozing off or dreaming — 'which is a kind of momentary illusion or scene'. He wondered whether the exercise might not become 'a languid piece of talk' in the mind.

In spite of these difficulties, his self-examination was so drastic that no enemies could have improved on it. The first day was on the End of Man. Newman was most struck by the thought 'that God put it into my heart when I was five or six years old, to ask *what* and *why* I was, yet now I am forty two, and have never answered it in *my conduct* ; that if disobedience is *against nature*, I am in the sight of Angels, like some odious *monster* which people put out of sight ; that I have acted hardly ever for God's glory, that my motive in all my exertions during the last 10 years, has been the pleasure of energizing intellectually, as if my talents were given me to play a game with. . . . Hence that Selflove in one shape or another, e.g.

vanity, desire of the good opinion of friends etc, have been my motive; and that possibly it is *the* sovereign sin in my heart.' Self love is the sovereign sin in all hearts; few go so far as to see it at work in what they have done for God, for intellectual pleasure was certainly not the *only* motive for undertaking the tasks he had done.

'At the end I solemnly gave myself up to God to do what he would with me — to make me what He would — to put what He would upon me.' This was no vague aspiration; later in the day he put down four definite things he might have to endure, and did not want to endure, but was willing to accept from God. 'Various great trials struck me: 1. the having to make a General Confession to some one in our Church, I not having full faith that our Church has the power of Absolution. 2. having to join the Church of Rome. 3. having to give up my Library. 4. bodily pain and hardship. I considered God is used to accept such offers, but I trust he will not exact such.' By the evening he was too tired with the exertions of the day to concentrate and 'could only repeat over, sometimes almost in a doze, such words as "Enable me to follow Thee" etc. I could very little or not at all, realize, that I was in the Lord's Presence; and now I am so sleepy I can hardly write this.'

One of the distractions that beset him was 'that dreadful thought about D.' Dalgairns had the room next to his and during this winter had contracted a bad cough. He also had jaundice. Later he moved to the little two-storey guest-house on the end of the Library building. He was very enthusiastic and headstrong, keen to follow severe ascetic practices, and Newman was tormented with the fear that he would ruin his health. The next year Newman made him consult a doctor when he went home at Easter, who, Dalgairns said 'made light of your terrors on account of blood in the lungs'. He had not contracted the dreaded consumption. 'I think you have a right to know why I treated myself so roughly this Lent', said Dalgairns, in 1844, in his naïve way. 'I believe it arose from restlessness rather than wilfulness; if you had in confession bade me do otherwise I am almost sure I should have obeyed you.' Newman's unwillingness to exercise authority over other people often resulted in their ignoring what they knew well enough to be his opinion and feeling; if they sensed disapproval they sometimes hinted that he should have issued a command. Dalgairns, however, was sure he was right. 'My feeling on this subject is a great dread of being a mere literary man with the accident of holding Catholic opinions, which my intellect shows me to be right. I live among kind friends, read what I please and write books which gain me reputation, besides the accident of my natural disposition makes every body love me.' The unconscious self-satisfaction of the last phrase shows how far he was from knowing himself.

Worry about Dalgairns in 1843 intruded on Newman's meditation on the End of Man. The next day of the retreat was on Sin ; when the subject was his own sins, though it was 'so full of topics, yet I seemed unable to interest or engage my mind. Every thing fell flat and I had to begin again. I went through time past and thought how dreadful it would be to confess to this person or that. But various miserable feelings came over me, and I found I dared not go through some of my sins.' In the evening, thinking over venial sins, 'I put before me, as very frequent ones in my case, distraction in prayer, self complacency, inaccuracy or lying, greediness and want of self control in little things'. He resolved to confess to Lockhart that 'I just now, in excuse for omitting to read out loud something from Stone [the manual] said I thought it came after Compline, whereas in fact I forgot it'. The next morning his clock stopped and he overslept half an hour, starting at 5 a.m. 'Had a feeling of disgust at having confessed to Lockhart last night my fault.' It was humiliating to confess such a common little excuse to someone nearly twenty years his junior whom he was supposed to be guiding, but this only made him wonder if he ought not to force himself to make such avowals regularly, to cure the fault. Did the people who called him a deceiver judge themselves so severely ? That evening 'I considered and prayed against my present great aversion to the very name of penance'. He had no morbid attraction to ascetic practices. On the last evening he remarked with his usual practical insight : 'It has come upon me yesterday and to-day, that I cannot bear contempt, when it comes in palpable instances.'

There had certainly been palpable instances of contempt lately, and were to be more. He had been sounding the Provost on the possibility of giving up St. Mary's and keeping Littlemore ; he even hinted 'as a bribe' that he would give up his Fellowship to obtain this concession. But Hawkins had no desire to perpetuate the 'so-called Anglo-Catholic Monastery'. It seemed more or less settled that if Newman resigned, Eden would be his successor. Eden was six years his junior and had come up to Oriel, the eldest of an orphaned family, as 'Bible Clerk'. Newman had helped him a good deal in his career. He was clever, and had won himself a place in the university by his exertions, but as Tutor and Dean he was unpopular, a disciplinarian full of his own importance. His manners were

aggressive, he was rude to foreigners and slanged servants in public
for trivial offences. He was so pleased with one of his own sermons
that he read its twenty pages again the next Sunday, 'tossing his head
slightly back'. Dean Burgon picked out these stories as the *best* of
the reminiscences of this eccentric character, whom he included in
his book *Twelve Good Men*. Eden married when he was over forty
and retired to a Yorkshire parish. His wife was said to be a sensible
woman, who managed and mellowed him considerably. But this
was the man to whom Newman would have to give up the parish he
had served so long, and Littlemore, which he had built up out of
nothing. Eden said that if he were made Vicar of St. Mary's
he would not allow Newman so much as to read the prayers in
Littlemore Church.

At the beginning of Lent Newman had written to Keble to ask
his advice on resigning St. Mary's; he had sent a further note on
Easter Eve. At last, at the beginning of May Keble answered: he
thought it permissible. But Keble did not know the burden on
Newman's mind, that he feared the Church of England was in schism.
Rogers would not listen; Henry was distressed. But he dared not
rely on his own judgment and must get help from somebody. To
whom could he go but Keble?

'Oh forgive me, my dear Keble, and be merciful to me in a
matter, in which, if I have not your compassion, my faith is so weak
and I have so little sense of my own uprightness, that I shall have no
refuge in the testimony of my own conscience, such as St. Paul felt,
and shall be unable to appeal from you to a higher judgment seat.
But if you do on deliberation accuse me of insincerity still tell me,
for I shall deserve to bear it, and your reproof will be profitable.'
So Newman began his confession, with all the pent-up misery caused
by the suspicions of friends and enemies. He then briefly described
the shock of 1839 and its consequences. 'It broke upon me that we
were in schism . . . at present I fear . . . I consider the Roman Catholic
Communion the Church of the Apostles, and that what grace is
among us . . . is extraordinary and from the overflowings of His
Dispensation.' There is something irrevocable about putting into
definite form any such interior impression, a declaration whether of
belief or love. Newman wrote an introductory letter and sent both
off, tormented by the thought of the pain he would be giving Keble
and the fear that after all the whole thing might be a delusion —
'a hideous dream'.

Keble read Newman's confession, as he recalled next year, 'in a deserted old chalk pit. I cannot tell you with what sort of fancy I look at the place now.' He did not mention that at the time. His reply came, so deliberate was he, *ten days* after Newman's letter was written. 'Believe me, my very dear Newman, that any thought of wilful insincerity in you can find no place in my mind. You have been and are in a most difficult position, and I seem to myself in some degree able to enter into your difficulties : and, although one sees of course how an enemy might misrepresent your continuing in the English Priesthood with such an impression on your mind, I have no thought but of love and esteem and gratitude for you in this as in everything.'

What a relief it must have been to find that Keble did not condemn him! But now, knowing what was on Newman's mind, Keble regarded resignation as 'a perilous step', because it would bring Newman nearer to the 'temptation of going over'; it would also be 'a grievous event', throwing everything back just when there were signs of repentance and renewal in the English Church. Keble had one great argument against moving, which satisfied himself : men were responsible for what was wrong in a position they chose for themselves, not for that where God's providence had placed them. The problem presented itself to him as a moral choice, not as a question of truth ; therefore, for all his kindness he was not able to help Newman. In fact, while he begged his friend not to depend on his advice and hesitated to give it, he could not help exerting a pressure against moving, as an act of self-will, which had all the more influence as Newman was so ready to suspect himself of that particular failing. All the same, Keble's integrity and understanding were the greatest human support that Newman had in the next two years.

Newman replied at once to thank him. 'I feel it to be almost ungenerous to entangle you in my troubles ; at least it would be so, were it not a rule of the Gospel that Christians should not stand alone or depend on themselves. . . . To whom would Hurrell go, or wish me to go, but to you ? . . . I feel no doubt that in consulting you I am doing God's will ; for since I lay claim to no infallible perception of His leadings . . . the alternative lies between self will and consulting you.' People, even Keble, were inclined to think he was influenced by results, and public events ; he asserted that he never had depended on them, and added, with psychological insight: 'Re-actions are, I suppose, sudden ; strong opposite impulses occurring in immediate succession ; but my present feelings have arisen naturally and gradually, and have been resisted. It is true, that I have now laid down my arms rather suddenly.'

To Henry he was writing : 'It was *necessary* to tell him, in honesty and propriety — and I shall in all things go implicitly by his advice. But it is impossible to act in any way without laying oneself open on one side or other to the greatest misrepresentations of enemies — but they are not my Judge.' Then he mentioned something he found bewildering during all this time of inward change. 'Everything external to my own consciousness is most flourishing . . . openings occurring continually — lines of influence offered me etc. Could I trust myself, I have a clear path.' But now he could not trust himself. There was no Via Media any more.

Now it was Pusey's turn for trouble. He preached a sermon on the Eucharist which was condemned by the Hebdomadal Board and he was suspended from preaching in the University for three years. He was treated most unfairly ; after extracting a promise from him not to reveal proceedings they refused to let him know what exactly was condemned, passed sentence without allowing him a defence and then published their own version of the episode. Silencing Pusey was chiefly the work of Provost Hawkins of Oriel and Dr. Symons of Wadham, the college where Evangelicalism had its stronghold in Oxford. This was the way people acted who had disapproved the Tractarians' attack on Hampden, when they had clearly stated the case against him and brought it before Convocation for voting.

Newman wrote to Henry of the verdict, 'or falsi-dict', as he called it : 'Keep your eyes open to what is going on but I have neither time nor will to meddle with these dirty matters'. His sympathy for Pusey made him worry about the strain on his health, but it did not seem possible to take any action. Any interference from him would only make matters worse. Pusey thought he ought to fight ; he believed a principle was at stake, and there was an obstinate bulldog tenacity in him which, once he was forced to fight, would never let go. Protests, pamphlets, legal proceedings followed, to no avail. The unjust sentence stood. But his opponents may well have wished they had let him alone, for injustice made him a martyr in the eyes of many.

Having gained Keble's assent to his resignation Newman put the matter aside, waiting a suitable opportunity. His conscience was clear, and in spite of the burden of decision hanging over him, cheerfulness reasserted itself. 'We have now two families in this place so it is getting quite genteel, and they are both Catholic', he told Henry.

These were the Woodmasons and the Crawleys ; the Woodmasons afterwards became Catholics, the Crawleys stayed at Littlemore. Newman could even tease Henry about his own Romanism now : 'Do you know, though you need not say it, that I have taken a liking to the Jesuits ? You see I am determined to shock you.' And he wrote funny stories to Aunt, who had been thrown out of her carriage but was none the worse. A farmer had called his bull Dr. Pusey. 'You see how Puseyism is spreading. It has reached our very cattle. Here is the first Puseyite bull. . . .' He excused his bad writing, 'My hand is always aching somewhat'.

Dear Aunt suggested embrocation.

1843

Resignation: the Case of Jonah

In August 1843 came the necessary occasion for resigning St. Mary's. Young Lockhart went over to visit Gentili at Loughborough and, unable to bear delay any longer, was received by him into the Catholic Church. Gentili wrote Newman a long letter. 'You know that several months since he wrote to me,' he began, which provoked Newman to note, 'I did *not* know till I received this'. Gentili went on in his friendly, foreign way : 'I say to you all this that no feeling of disaffection or uncharity may ever arise between me and you, whom I love, esteem and highly respect for all reasons. . . . I know that if what is happened to you now had happened to me, it would have been a very great trial indeed to me, and it would have required a great deal of virtue in me to offer it calmly among my other mortifications to the Almighty.' He ended by saying he hoped to have *The Lives of the English Saints*, which Newman was editing, read in the refectory, and urged him to write against State appointments in religion. Newman told Church he had no fault to find with Dr. Gentili's share in the matter.

Lockhart had broken his promise, and Keble for one felt there had been 'some underhand dealing', but Newman found it easy to forgive the young man's impatience. Perhaps he was thinking of him when he drew the portrait of the impetuous young Willis in *Loss and Gain*. Lockhart recalled in his memoir an incident which had influenced him. He had gone to Newman for confession and suddenly asked him : '"Are you sure you can give me absolution ?" He did not speak for a few moments, then said in a tone of deep distress, "Why will you ask me ? Ask Pusey."' He often sent the doubtful to Pusey, who had no doubts. This was the first indication to Lockhart that Newman was uncertain of his position. As he had been living with Newman for a year, this shows how well he hid what was troubling him for fear of increasing the trouble of others. Lockhart joined the Institute of Charity at once. He liked to remember that two years later Newman had gone out of his way to visit him at Ratcliffe College where he was studying, and, when he was a priest, insisted on serving his mass.

Lockhart was easily forgiven, but of course his departure caused a scandal : one of Mr. Newman's young men had run off to be a real Roman monk! The newspapers eagerly fell on it, and letters, signed and unsigned, came pouring in as usual from angry and agitated people. But it gave Newman the pretext for resignation and now he had to break the news to Jemima. He did not yet tell her his doubts about the Church, but naturally the news made her unhappy. 'I am very sorry to put you to so much pain', Newman wrote. 'Your letter (and Anne's to you) would have brought me to many tears unless I had so hard a heart. You must take what I do on faith — at least, if not, I fear I cannot find a better way of consoling you. . . . No time is *the* time. . . . The question is, *ought* it to be done. My dearest Jemima, my circumstances are not of my making. One's duty is to act *under* circumstances. Is it a light thing to give up Littlemore ? Am I not providing dreariness for myself ? If others, whom I am pierced to think about, because I cannot help them, suffer, shall I not suffer in my own way ? Every thing that one does honestly, sincerely, with prayer, with advice, must turn to good. My sweetest Jemima, of whom I am quite unworthy, rather pray that I may be directed aright, rather pray that something may occur to hinder me if I am wrong, than take the matter into your own hands.'

It seemed to be Newman's fate that he could never get through a crisis of his own without having to cope with one in the family as well. This time it was Tom Mozley. Harriett had been overdoing things and suffered from sleeplessness ; so Tom took her and the baby, Grace, to France for a holiday. They had never been abroad before and Catholic Normandy astonished and delighted them. Harriett was excited to find her brother so well known, pleased to find he and not 'Dr. Puzzy' was considered the head of the Movement. There were articles on it in the French and Italian newspapers. But after a while the novelty palled for her, she talked to a French lady who told her less edifying tales of religious life, and she felt England was the best place after all. Not so Tom. He was swept right off his feet. Harriett ignored his hints, so, making the *British Critic* his excuse, he rushed back to England and wrote to tell Newman that he must join the Church of Rome at once.

Surprised and alarmed, Newman left the drafts of the letter he was preparing to send to his Bishop, and made for Cholderton at top

speed. He spent the day walking about the country with the excited
Tom, trying to persuade him to wait. At last he told him about his
own doubts. It was Tom's turn to be surprised, but he allowed
himself to be persuaded and Newman hurried back to Oxford to
complete and post his letter of resignation to the Bishop.

In his Charge Bagot had said that Newman's method could make
the Articles mean 'anything or nothing', and much as he had been
hurt by this Newman now apologized for adding to the Bishop's
anxieties about the Church. 'I am not relaxing my zeal till it has
been disowned by her rulers. I have not retired from her service till
I have lost or forfeited her confidence.' Knowing his man, he politely
begged that he should not be asked to reconsider his decision. Bagot
would certainly have preferred delay, as he said in his answer, dated
September 16th. But since he must accept Newman's resignation
he reminded him that this must be a formal act, done either in his
presence or before a notary. The next day was Sunday, and Newman
was preaching at St. Mary's in the afternoon. He wrote hastily to
say that the delay was due to the absence of the notary from Oxford ;
he was just about to go to London to complete the act there. That
night he could not sleep. It was a sign of the strain put on him by
this surrender, known only to his diary, where he noted it. He went
up to London on Monday 18th and signed away St. Mary's and
Littlemore, and all they had been to him for fifteen years.

He no sooner got back to Oxford when he received 'a sad letter'
from Jemima. Tom could not keep either his own secret or Newman's. 'T. M. forthwith blabbed what I said to him to my sisters,'
Newman noted afterwards, adding charitably, 'But it did not matter
much, for at that time I was telling all my friends'. There was all
the difference, however, between his way of telling, and Tom's
heartless blurting out the bare facts. His home in Derby was thrown
into an uproar, and there was poor Harriett stranded in France, left
to learn by letter that her husband was threatening to throw up his
career and 'go over to Rome' and that her brother was abetting him.
The storm broke over Newman's head just as the news of his resignation became public property and while he was trying to prepare his
farewell sermon for the following week. He sat down and wrote at
once to Tom and to Jemima.

He did not reproach Tom for giving away his secret, but begged
him to try to right things at home. 'I suppose you think you *must*
get it over and that words cannot alter facts and are but so much
palaver ; — but it is not so. . . . Now only think how everything of

this kind will prejudice those nearest and dearest to you against wha
you believe to be the truth, to put it on no other ground. A deep
hopeless, bitter prejudice will sink into the minds of your whole
family as well as into H's. And again, how unseemly to seem to be
acting under excitement! If you ask me, I must plainly tell you tha
you *are* under excitement and in no fit state to act for yourself.' I
would be fatal if Tom's family associated his change of mind with a
change 'from tenderness and affection to cruelty'. Tom ought to
go to Harriett at once, writing first to warn her; if he could not
Newman himself would go. 'Now my dear fellow, enter into wha
I say — and may you be guided to do what God wishes of you. He
does not ask of you anything wanton. Pain enough do changes of
opinion cause in any case, without our going out of our way to
increase it.'

To Jemima he wrote at length to defend graceless Tom, to assure
her that for all his careless way of talking he did feel seriously on the
subject. Probably Newman assumed that Tom's feelings were more
like his own than in fact they proved to be. Meanwhile Harriett
wrote angrily to her brother. He gave up the idea of going to her on
finding she thought what had happened was more or less his fault
But he suggested going to Jemima in Derby, to talk things over
'You will not say, I think, that I am less affectionate to you from the
bottom of my heart and loving than I have ever been.' But by
October 5th the difficulties were weighing on him. 'To you, as to
myself, I think it may be a comfort, but what will it be to Mrs
Mozley or poor Anne or others? I really hardly like to think of it
What am I to say! what consolation, what hope, what guidance can
I give! And then again about my Aunt — this pains me more than
anything. I can make *you* understand me, and others — but it is
absurd to expect that she can but take that view which all her life
she has taken. . . .'

Newman was still trying to explain Tom's behaviour, but it was
he, not Tom, who was worried about his parents, unhappy at his
'want of candour' to his wife, and anxious for Harriett's health. He
need not have worried; Harriett's health was weak but her will was
strong. It was significant that Tom had fled from her when he
wanted to do something he knew she would disapprove; nor was
his instinct wrong. Once she got him back, she never let him slip
out of his groove again. In 1845 Newman expected Tom to come
into the Church; he never did. By the time Harriett died he was
content to stay as he was. As for Harriett, she never forgave her

brother for what she felt to be his fault.   Newman wrote to her,
'Only see what a position we are in — how difficult to please you.
T. you blame for telling you, me for not telling.   T. is cruel and I am
disingenuous.'   Harriett tried to argue John out of his opinions, as
she successfully argued Tom out of his.   She told him that Catholics
in France were not as good as they should be.   But Newman replied,
referring to the early controversies he had studied, 'I saw from them
that Rome was the centre of unity and judge of controversies.   My
views would not be influenced by the surface or the interior of the
present French Church or of any other.'   Harriett was the more
annoyed, the less she could move him.

The total result of Tom's 'indiscretion' as the family referred to
it, was to prevent Newman from making known to them in his own
way that changing his mind had not changed his heart.   It was
unlikely that any of them would have understood his actions any
better, but they might have shown him more sympathy.   As it was,
Jemima was the only one whose feelings remained the same towards
him after this shock, and even she was to take up a different attitude
when the moment for action arrived.

Meanwhile the events of Newman's own life would not wait
while Tom's whirlwind 'conversion' ran its course.   He preached
the last sermon in St. Mary's on Sunday 24th of September, and the
last at Littlemore on Monday 25th, a week after his official resignation in London, and the anniversary feast of the consecration of the
little church.   Many friends came to hear this farewell, including
some from outside Oxford, Henry Wilberforce and the lawyer
Serjeant Bellasis among others.   Pusey took the service.   The church
was full of flowers — dahlias, fuchsias and Passion flowers; the children
were all in new frocks and bonnets, Newman's parting gift.   The
church was crowded, but very still; there were a hundred and forty
communicants and the offertory was for the new seating.   Bellasis
described it all to his wife.   'But the sermon I can never forget, the
faltering voice, the long pauses, the perceptible and hardly successful
efforts at restraining himself, together with the deep interest of the
subject were almost overpowering; Newman's voice was low, but
distinct and clear. . . .'   He did not break down though everyone
else, including Pusey, seemed to be in tears.   When he left the pulpit
he threw his gown and hood over the altar rails ; a gesture of finality.
He received communion, but took no further part in officiating.

For his sermon, which he printed, last of the long series, under
the title *The Parting of Friends*, Newman chose the same text he

had used for the first he had preached : 'Man goeth forth to his work and to his labour until the evening'. He wove together the themes of harvest, earthly and heavenly, the dedication of the church and of the soul in the service of God, the love of friends and the sacrifice of that love for another which is higher, leading up to the famous address to the Church as he had known it : 'O my mother, whence is this unto thee, that thou hast good things poured upon thee and canst not keep them, and bearest children, yet darest not own them ? . . . Who hath put this note upon thee, to have "a miscarrying womb and dry breasts" to be strange to thine own flesh, and thine eye cruel to thy little ones ?' But he broke off from this lament to say in the words of Scripture : 'Bless God, praise Him, and magnify Him, and praise Him for the things which He hath done unto you in the sight of all that live. . . . Leave off from wrath, and let go displeasure ; flee from evil and do the thing that is good. Do that which is good and no evil shall touch you.'

Then at last he made his farewell. 'And O my brethren, O kind and affectionate hearts, O loving friends, should you know any one whose lot it has been, by writing or by word of mouth, in some degree to help you thus to act ; if he has ever told you what you knew about yourselves, or what you did not know ; has read to you your wants or feelings, and has comforted you by the very reading ; has made you feel that there was a higher life than this daily one, and a brighter world than that you see ; or encouraged you, or sobered you, or opened a way to the inquiring, or soothed the perplexed ; if what he has said or done has ever made you take an interest in him, and feel well inclined towards him ; remember such a one in time to come, though you hear him not, and pray for him, that in all things he may know God's will, and at all times he may be ready to fulfil it.'

The farewell was spoken, but life went on. The first anxiety was what would happen at Littlemore ; to their great relief, Eden, whose bark was worse than his bite, allowed Copeland to stay on as curate there. 'Oh my dear Copeland,' Newman wrote to him, half teasing, half serious, 'I am a dangerous untrustworthy fellow, and you had better keep your distance from me.' Eden had behaved well, too, when the Provost tried to refuse him testimonials for St. Mary's unless he would repudiate Tract 90, which was now widely used as a private test of opinions. Eden was not really a Tractarian, but he refused to be tested, and after an exchange of notes, he won the round. But he was something of a trial in himself. His attitude to

Newman was patronizing and tactless. He assumed dignity and importance on becoming the Vicar of the University Church, and wrote Newman tiny notes in tiny writing — surprising for such a heavyweight character — talking about 'my parishioners' and 'our Littlemore'. Newman scribbled on one, when he was an old man, that Eden was 'pompous, though in intention kind', and observed that you could not make a silk purse out of a sow's ear. Eden showed his insensitive nature by referring to Elizabeth Lenthall as 'a poor thing'; Newman could not bear the tone of patronage, for he thought that the woman, who had cancer, was suffering the pains of the martyrs, and in their spirit. Eden asked Newman to go on visiting her, which he did, regularly, till she died two years later.

Newman had resigned his living, but the cottages at Littlemore were his own, and there was no reason why he should not continue to live there as a private person, a clergyman without a benefice. He was still a Fellow of Oriel College, and there was no reason why he should not remain one. He resigned his public office in the Church of England because his views and teaching had been condemned, as officially as it was possible for anything to be condemned while Convocation was suspended. His position was similar in some ways to that of Non-Juring clergymen at the end of the seventeenth century, and he could have lived out his life as William Law had lived his, privately, writing spiritual books and ministering to friends of like opinions, had his doubts about the Catholicity of the Church of England been satisfied. But they were not.

He had told Harriett definitely that he believed Rome was the divinely appointed centre of unity; he had told Keble he thought it the Church of the Apostles. Yet it was two years before he made his submission. People then and later wondered why it took him so long to do it, and various motives were ascribed to him, generally not very creditable ones. It was the common belief among the mass of Protestants who did not know him personally that he was sitting at Littlemore like a spider in his web, luring excitable young men and sending them to the Roman larder, while drawing the pay of both churches. That he was literally in the pay of Rome was reported in the papers. Others, who did not suspect him of such gross treachery, believed him insincere and untrustworthy. Catholics, on the other hand, who had never met him, were inclined to shake their heads over the pride that could not endure to admit being mistaken, and could not bear to give up power as the leader of a growing party in the Established Church — for it still grew in spite of everything. And there were Tractarians who put down his hesitation to personal feelings, thinking that every blast of criticism drove him towards Rome and every breath of praise wafted him back.

To Newman the cause of his waiting was quite simple : he was not yet convinced. He had said to Dr. Russell that he wished to go by reason, not by feeling. Reason had now carried him to the point where he thought Rome was the centre of unity and England in schism, but this had not yet become certitude. In the *Apologia* he said, 'For myself, it was not logic that carried me on — as well might one say that the quicksilver in the barometer changes the weather. It is the concrete being that reasons ; pass a number of years and I find my mind in a new place ; how ? the whole man moves ; paper logic is but the record of it.' This was not merely an explanation after the event ; he was saying the same thing at the time in letters to Mrs. William Froude. His greatest fear was that he might be under a delusion, as he called it. The very clarity of his intellectual vision might be as deceptive as an hallucination. Pusey and Keble did not see the question thus : why should he trust himself to be right against them ? His conviction must be tested in two ways ; intellectually by working out the theory of development of doctrine in detail, for it was that alone which answered for him the question as to whether the changes in the Church of Rome were true or false to the original deposit of faith ; morally, he had to search his heart still more keenly to be sure that he was not acting from wrong motives, whether in wishing to go or in wishing to stay, for of course he felt drawn both ways.

What chiefly drew him to the Catholic Church, apart from the truth of its claims, was his thirst for a life ever more closely lived in union with Christ ; the Sacraments, the Saints drew him, the religious life of poverty, chastity and obedience called him. What pulled the other way, apart from the possible duty of staying, was his personal life, rooted so long in places and among people he loved with passionate tenacity. As well, he could not ignore the fact that by now a very great number of people depended on him, not only those who looked to him as the leader of a party, but countless more, simple and devoted, who had begun to live a spiritual life through his influence. If he had wished to forget them, they did not allow him to do so, for they wrote continually, whether known to him or not, anxious, inquiring. Whatever he did must affect them, and many more ; it was his duty to them to act only when he was certain he was not deluded.

21. THE STABLE COTTAGES AT LITTLEMORE
From a photograph *c*. 1900

22. MARYVALE, OLD OSCOTT

23. NEWMAN AND AMBROSE ST. JOHN IN ROME, 1846
From a painting by M. R. Giberne

24. NEWMAN LECTURING, 1851
From a painting by M. R. Giberne

Time was the only test; it would both dissolve illusions and allow the truth to grow. Again and again he used images of growth in the effort to make his friends understand what he meant, but few of them understood. One of his most tiresome trials was the continual pressure of men like Ward, whose mind seemed to work entirely by that 'solitary, naked, external logical process' that he found, as he said to Mrs. Froude, so unsatisfactory. Ward, with no ill intentions, was always tormenting Newman, pumping him, as he called it, to find out how far he would go, hunting arguments to death and in the process turning living reality into an abstraction. But the whole man must seek the truth, not just his reason. So Newman, beset with spying enemies and inquisitive friends, somehow managed to pursue his own way, fasting and praying and searching his conscience as well as thinking.

Yet no man can try his own heart to the depths. Now was to come a time of suffering. It had begun indeed, but this year he was primarily concerned with the necessity to act, in resigning St. Mary's. Now it was done, and since he was not ready for further action, he could only wait and endure the consequences. In differing ways and degrees this inward trial lasted for over a year, coming to a climax in November 1844 with an anguish so intense that for a short time it physically prostrated him, and left a long wake of weariness and depression of spirits. Yet he rose up from it to fulfil the creative work all the time germinating within, to express the vision of the Christian Church growing like a tree in time, with the informing power and pattern of the directing Spirit. After that the *whole* man at last could move, and by then, having passed through so searching a trial, the man was more whole than before.

Newman did not tell the tale of this suffering. The *Apologia* was the record of his thinking, not of his feelings, except incidentally. There was nothing to show for it, no visible wounds or scars, though wounds indeed there were within the heart which could not but have an effect as lasting as those which can be seen. His letters to Jemima, to Henry and to Keble told something of what he felt, but after all, how can pain be told? And it was a fact that those who lived with him and saw him every day did not realize what he was going through, as their letters witness. This was not due to any grim control over emotion, for Newman was not very good at hiding his feelings, but to the fact that his conscience was at peace, so that he was living all the time in the divine love, and more closely than ever before. In spite of all he had suffered there, he always remembered Littlemore with joy ; when he left he told friends that it was the only place he had lived in which had no association with what he regarded as serious sins of his own. Thus he was happy there, and the happiness was more apparent to visitors than anything else. But since it was based in the spirit it could co-exist with suffering in the heart. An emotionally happy person can suffer as much as a sad person if his body is hurt ; in the same way someone at peace in the spirit can be hurt in his heart. Pain is the inevitable result of injury, whether physical or emotional. Christians have the divine example of Christ's agony in Gethsemane to help them to understand this. They can also realize, from the behaviour of the disciples, how rare it is for human beings to enter into and understand suffering which is not caused by wounds they can see.

Just at the beginning of this time, when he was telling his friends, in warning, of his doubts about the Catholicity of the Church of England, Newman realized that he could not tell them to the one friend now alive with whom it would have been a solace to share his trouble. Bowden, who had been ill some time, was now dying. It took him a year to die, by inches, as Froude had done, of tuberculosis, but this autumn Newman gave up hope that he would ever recover. 'My dear Keble,' he wrote on Michaelmas day, 'I am so cast down by various things, that I have hardly heart to think what I have to say to you. What chiefly presses on me is Bowden's illness. It is hardly right perhaps to say I despair of him. And he is all the while so kind and quiet and happy.' In the *Apologia* he wrote : 'Why should I unsettle that sweet calm tranquility, when I had nothing to offer him instead ? I could not say "Go to Rome" ; else I should have shown him the way. Yet I offered myself for his examination. One day he led the way to my speaking out ; but rightly or wrongly I could not respond.'

The *Apologia* was written to answer the charge of deception and hypocrisy ; such cases as Bowden's made Newman feel like a hypocrite, though his reason for silence was not selfish. The longing for communication, which had to be suppressed for his friend's sake, shows through the letter he wrote to him that same Michaelmas day. 'You are always so kind, that sometimes when I part with you, I am nearly moved to tears, and it would be a relief to be so, at your kindness and at my hardness. I think no one ever had such kind friends as I have.' But it was not hardness that kept him from indulging his feelings at the expense of Bowden's peace of mind. Perhaps Bowden guessed something all the same, for before he died he told his wife to be guided by Newman. Had he lived, he would probably have followed his friend into the Church, as he had followed him so far. Froude, Bowden and Wood all died before the moment of decision came, so that Newman, as far as his old friends were concerned, had to make it alone. With Bowden his own youth seemed to be dying.

The news of Newman's resignation brought in many letters from anxious members of the Movement. Among them was Manning, wanting to know his reasons for the step. Newman instanced the condemnation of the Bishops. 'It seems a dream to call a Communion Catholic when one can neither appeal to any clear statement of Catholic doctrine in its formularies, nor interpret ambiguous formularies by the received and living sense past or present.' Of himself he said, 'It is felt, I am far from denying, justly felt, that I am a foreign material — and cannot assimilate with the Church of England' — a typical image of living bodies, expressing what he felt about the Church. Manning was so alarmed at this confession he sent Newman's letter to Gladstone, his great friend and ally. Manning misunderstood Newman's remarks about the Bishops and thought he was complaining of personal ill-treatment at their hands. His reply was somewhat admonitory. 'Has not God prospered you in the last ten years in a measure which makes it — may I venture to say — impatience something like Jonah's to ask or look for more?' Like so many he thought Newman's aim was to Catholicize the Church of England, in which he was certainly succeeding, as even enemies witnessed. But to Newman, what mattered was to be living in the Church which Christ founded, and if the Church of England was not it, there was no point in men trying to make it so.

'I think the Church of Rome the Catholic Church,' he said straight out, clarifying his position for Manning from Derby, where he had gone after all, at the end of October. Manning was horrified. This letter, too, he sent to Gladstone, who said it made him 'stagger to and fro like a drunken man'. He thought that if it came out Newman would be disgraced and the Movement discredited. Presumably he felt that if it was known that Newman had had doubts for several years all the newspaper tales of hypocrisy would be regarded as confirmed. Manning wrote to Pusey too ; he said he felt betrayed, for he had been using Newman's works to spread the cause and now it turned out that he was secretly a traitor. Yet to Newman himself he wrote an affectionate little note. 'Never think I judged you in my last letter. But ignorant of the one master key of all I was led to shallow thoughts on the matter. May God ever bless and keep you, my dear Newman.' Knowing nothing of the frenzied letters to Gladstone and Pusey, Newman was touched by this kindness, when he came back to Oxford from his painful visit to Derby. He wrote off at once to say that it 'has made my heart ache more and caused more and deeper sighs than any I have had a long while — though I assure you there is much on all sides of me to cause sighing and heart aches — on all sides'.

A few days later Manning went down to Oxford to preach, from the pulpit of St. Mary's, an anti-Roman sermon at the service in commemoration of the Gunpowder Plot, usually boycotted by the Tractarians. Newman had omitted it for years. 'Manning has delivered a No Popery bark,' said Church scornfully. Only Newman could know that it was also, in a sense, a bark against him. But to everyone it looked as if the Archdeacon were taking the opportunity to dissociate himself from those in the Movement who were in disgrace. Yet he walked out to Littlemore the next day. Long afterwards, Anthony Froude said that Newman had refused to see Manning, who had been upset. Froude had walked along the road, bareheaded, with him, trying to comfort him. Nobody else ever referred to this. J. B. Mozley remarked in a letter next day that Manning went out to Littlemore and saw Newman. Newman wrote in his diary 'Manning called', which usually implied a meeting ; nor did Manning refer to any rebuff then or later, to Newman or anyone else. But he certainly felt a little guilty about Newman, as his letters at Christmas show. Whether or not he saw Newman, it was typical of Manning to expect a private welcome after what amounted to a public act of hostility. He never could understand why his friends should mind his attacking their causes and principles in public ; Gladstone was to come up against the same thing, to his bewilderment and indignation. Manning mentally separated everyone into a private and a public personality, and thought he was only attacking the latter. Nevertheless he did not like it at all when he himself was attacked ; private Manning could not help feeling what was directed at public Manning. Unfortunately he did not realize that others were equally vulnerable.

This little incident had an effect on Newman's latest scheme. Tom Mozley had retired from the editorship of the *British Critic* after his abortive conversion, and the magazine died with his retirement. Its last number, however, contained an advertisement for a series of *Lives of the English Saints*, which were to appear in monthly parts, under Newman's editorship. For although Newman had

given up his parish, he was not going to sit still doing nothing.   All
this year, in spite of personal anxieties, he had been busy arranging
with various authors to undertake suitable Saints.   It was his intention to pick up where the Tracts left off, to collect the same public,
but instead of polemics to treat them to history and edification,
following up the success of *The Church of the Fathers*.   The series
was to start with Dalgairns' Life of St. Stephen Harding, the medieval
English Cistercian.   Newman thought it safe because it had 'hardly,
if at all, any miracle in it'.   It was a shock to find that Pusey, on
reading it, thought it pro-Roman and likely to cause another disturbance — so he told Hope, the lawyer.   Soon Newman too was writing
to Hope : 'Now Church history is made up of three elements —
miracles, monkery, Popery.   If any sympathetic feeling is expressed
on behalf of the persons and events of Church history, it is a feeling
in favour of miracles, or monkery, or Popery, one or all.'   But he
suspected that Rivington's, scared by all this, was going to refuse the
undertaking, and it worried him to think of all the work of the authors
going for nothing, without payment.   'I know myself, when I was
younger, how very annoying such a disappointment is ; the more so
because it cannot be, or is not, hinted at.'   Worse still, 'If the plan is
abandoned, the significant question will be, nay, is already asked —
"What then, cannot the Anglican Church bear the Lives of her
Saints !"'

The Anglican Church could not.   Hope asked Gladstone's
opinion, and with Newman's shocking letter to Manning still burnt
into his mind, he was against the whole thing.   Hope's first suggestion
to Newman was that he should tone down certain expressions in
Dalgairns' Life.   Newman was always ready to take advice, but when
he set to work it seemed too ridiculous.   'An alteration of the word
(e.g.) merit was like giving milk and water for a fit of the gout, while it
destroyed its integrity, vigor, in a word, its go.'   He went to bed feeling
discouraged, but got up next morning with a new idea which put him
in high spirits.   It was his name that was the trouble ; it stamped the
series as a party challenge.   Well then, he would give up the editorship, and the books should come out independently, each author
preserving his own freedom and responsibility.   Pleased with himself
at this solution Newman took up his pen and put back 'merit' and
other such expressions into the manuscript.   'Now don't you be
hasty and think this is a great sacrifice,' he wrote cheerfully to Hope,
'and that I am knocking under to people in authority or to such men
as Gladstone ; no such thing. . . . Nor am I abandoning *publication*

because I abandon this particular measure. Rather, I consider I have been silent now for several years on subjects of the day and need not fear now to speak.' In fact, he was once more in fighting form and even talked of starting a new review.

Far from thinking it a sacrifice, Hope felt Newman had scarcely allayed the danger. And in fact people went on thinking he was the Editor ; he was always having to deny it. As long as he was alive and writing he was bound to be what he said he did not want to be, 'a continual blister' to men like Gladstone, whom he respected. The *Lives* did create a commotion, as Pusey had foreseen. Medieval Englishmen were nearer home than Greek and Syrian Fathers, and it was a nasty shock to the public to find them saying mass, confessing their sins to priests and journeying off to Rome with appeals to the Pope. They surely could not be Popish and Saints and Englishmen all at once! Many of the moderate Tractarians wished Newman would keep quiet : 'Why *will* you do anything ?' as he said himself, amused. 'The party is breaking up,' he told Miss Giberne. 'Palmer is going off and so is that most kind and nice-tempered man, Archdeacon Manning.' He might have been nastier about Manning, since it was just after his Fifth of November display.

But by December Manning was feeling guilty. He had been reading Newman's farewell sermon, in his newly published volume *Sermons on Subjects of the Day*, and immediately identified himself with Orpah, the daughter-in-law of Naomi, who, in contrast to the faithful Ruth, kissed her and left her. Manning was an emotional man ; his feelings perhaps all the stronger for being kept in iron control by his still stronger will. 'I felt it bitterly,' he wrote to Newman, 'from the thought that you might think my words the smooth words of one that would leave you for the world. . . . You have a hard life and an empty home before you, and so have I, and I trust we shall walk together long enough to trust the singleness of each other's eye and to love each other as friends. . . . My dear Newman, do not suspect me as an empty pretender if I say that the only thing that has kept me up in the last six years' (since his wife died) 'and more of trial, and the only thing I look for until death is to save the Church in which I was born again. Doubtful thoughts about it are dreadful — and seem to take all things from me.' This was the secret of his violent outburst, both in the pulpit and in his letters to Gladstone. He identified himself with the cause of the Church, and felt Newman's probing mind was undermining his foundations. The same thing was to happen all over again, more seriously, when they were both Catholics. 'I could not help writing to you,' he ended, 'for it has been in my mind day after day, and yet I have shrunk from doing it, until I read your words about Orpah. And after all this may seem to you no better than her kiss.'

It was very funny to think of Manning as Orpah, but he was so serious that Newman answered him, on Christmas Eve, most gently. 'My dear Manning — How can I thank you enough for your most kind letter received last night ? — and what can have led you to entertain the thought that I could ever be crossed by the idea which you consider may have been suggested to me by the name of Orpah ? Really, unless it were so sad a matter, I should smile ; the thought is as far from me as the Antipodes. Rather I am the person who to myself always seem, and reasonably, the criminal ; I cannot afford to have hard thoughts which can more plausibly be exercised against myself. . . . It is no pleasure to me to differ from friends — no comfort to be estranged from them — no satisfaction or boast to have said things which I must unsay. Surely I will remain where I am as long as I can. I think it right to do so. If my misgivings are from above, I shall be carried on in spite of my resistance. . . . It is my constant prayer, that if others are right I may be drawn back — that nothing may part us.'

Manning sent this letter too to Gladstone, who also melted somewhat, and wondered whether the Bishops could not be prevented from Charging and Newman kept in the fold by kindness. 'Cords of silk should one by one be thrown over him to bind him to the Church.' This kind but mistaken policy was to mystify Newman completely. He was always remarking to Henry how queer it was that just at the time when it could be no comfort to him any more, people were beginning to speak well of him in public. Little tributes would appear in pamphlets or the more respectable newspapers, the more successful Tractarians would make graceful references in speeches, and when, in 1845, it was proposed to censure Tract 90 in Convocation, silk cords were flung from every direction, James Mozley and Rogers joining in the exercise. It was all the more incomprehensible to Newman when, on his actual conversion, they all turned round and told him he was selfish and ungrateful, not to say treacherous, to leave them in the lurch. They did not realize that whether the cords were of silk, or used as lashes, they made no difference to his decision, though they could, and did, affect his feelings.

As for his telling Manning that he was the person who always

seemed to himself the criminal, this was no empty phrase. At Littlemore they had been making a retreat again, for Advent. On Wednesday, the day before Manning wrote, Newman was thinking '"I have
been all but damned" — just as when you saw a man fall from a
horse, you might say that he had been all but killed.' His writer's
imagination leapt into action. 'And then this image came on me,
but I could not help beginning to think how it would dress for a
composition of some kind. Suppose their footing giving way, when
persons were on some high ground, and they rolled down with the
swiftness of lightning down, down, a steep descent towards a chasm :
let them fall in it, and let one be caught by a projecting rock. That
was I, but this is not all. I clamber up a little but the sides are
slippery whether with snow or other cause — and the footing scarcely
possible, and the greatest care is necessary to hinder destruction after
all — that is I now.' On Friday he saw the same thing from a
different angle, when they were considering Death and Judgment.
He was struck by 'the horror of a lost soul being stripped of the
graces which were (only) lent it, not made its own — e.g. becoming
cruel, desperate etc etc parallel to the countenance becoming deformed. What seems to throw light on this is my apparently great
inconsistency of character, so that persons who know me well would
be puzzled, saying I was reverent yet profane, considerate yet cruel,
gentle yet violent etc all showing that I have *gifts* contrary to my real
nature.' Would not many have chosen the gentle side as their real
nature, and the violence as the aberration ?

It was very cold weather. Newman was extremely tired. He
kept nearly dropping off to sleep. This same evening, after imagining
himself stripped of all virtue, not yet truly part of himself, he wrote :
'I fear I was asleep some considerable time, but I do not know. The
first point I was alive.' On an earlier evening : 'My limbs have
ached so much from the frost I could hardly kneel and was obliged
to keep more or less in motion . . . what I have been thinking about
I do not know.' On Thursday, having overslept ten minutes, he
commented 'Far too intellectual — all I can say is my head was achy
and almost swimming — and then to urge myself actively to feel
affection etc is to hurt it.' As well as undertaking the exercises he
was thinking about them. 'I have been observing myself narrowly
as I went on ; I cannot tell whether or not improperly so. Such
watching seems to make religious thoughts a sort of art or game.'

It is strange to see Newman as he saw himself, 'all but damned',
and aware on so many different levels of being : aware of cold,

sleepiness, pride within, evil without searching for the weak place in his defences; aware of his own intellect noticing what went on in himself, of his imagination turning thoughts into images and images into composition; and somehow through all this complexity simply aware of God, determined to obey Him whatever the cost, not merely internally but in all the external particulars of the situation in which he found himself. 'I am created here and now, in England in the 19 cent. surely not for myself.' And so he could write : 'I tried to give up to Him, if for His greater glory, my fellowship, my Library, the respect of friends, my health, my talent, my reason — but added, "Lord, be merciful". Texts struck me. 1. who stand in the Presence of God. 2. who I am, and whom I serve. 3. the case of Jonah, who for God's greater glory was cast into the waves, and became a type of Christ.'

1844

'Am I in a Delusion?'

NEWMAN wrote most of his letters late at night. As 1844 was about to begin he wished Jemima a happy new year and told her not to send some watch, perhaps a family one : 'I really am afraid of the charge. I have had so many accidents. Recollect, though this was not in fault as regards the watch, my brick floor. I dashed to pieces on it the other day your poor cayenne pot — which I had carefully kept as a medicine and not begun. It was all lost.' This was doubtless some of the pepper he had asked for before, 'if it is not greedy', from the supply 'which R.H.F. brought from Barbadoes in a vast jar'. Newman had been reading Harriett's latest story, and did not think she understood boys. 'Hers are very unreal. She makes them talk, not like boys, but like Walter Scott's middle age characters. And she makes them think quite wide of the mark.' So much for those who think Harriett's boys an accurate picture of her brothers in their schooldays.

Harriett was still attacking Newman by letter ; he felt it was unfair, for, as he told Jemima, he had not forced his views on her, and did not want to get into an argument. 'And now my dear J, I have written you so cross a letter that you will think my cold has affected my temper — but that is not the case — and I rejoice to say that (whether from being in better health or other cause) I am not so moody as when you, dearest, knew me better. PS. . . . I have been reading Sintram again and it has made me cry.' He had several colds this winter ; they tended to come at times of crisis, and the muscle he had strained in his wrist was aching. 'As to rubbing, I might as well rub my nose as my wrist, or as someone says it is like cutting one's nails for toothache.' His writing got much smaller during these years of stress, but also more definite.

His birthday and Bowden's, the last they shared, fell on Ash Wednesday this year ; Newman had a cold and there was a heavy fall of snow in the morning. 'I am not worthy of friends', he wrote to

Bowden in what he called an Ash Wednesday rather than a birthday letter. 'With my opinions, to the full of which I dare not confess, I feel like a guilty person with others, though I trust I am not so. People kindly think I have much to bear externally — disappointment, slander etc. No, I have nothing to bear but the anxiety which I feel for my friends' anxiety for me, and perplexity.'

Keble had been writing, to deliver, gently, two warnings. The first was against the Evil One, who would certainly seize on any personal weakness in the agents of the Catholic Movement, in order to ruin it. 'Such tendencies one can imagine in your case : among the rest a certain restlessness, a longing after something more, some- thing analogous to a very exquisite ear in music, which would keep you, I should think, in spite of yourself, intellectually and morally dissatisfied wherever you were.' Keble recognized Newman's long- ing for a closer union with God, but he confused it with the desire for certainty in a question of truth. Newman was never satisfied with himself, but his uncertainty about the Church was temporary, though some well-meaning Protestants could never believe it.

Keble's second warning was to impress on Newman the effect of his actions on others. 'I really suppose it would be to *thousands* quite an indescribable shock, a trial almost too hard to be borne, making them sceptical about everything and everybody.' Newman was not allowed to forget for a moment that he must bear the burden of other people's consciences, and the guilt of their loss of faith, if they lost it through the shock of his change of mind. Keble sug- gested that it might be Newman's duty simply to suppress his misgivings, 'nay, what seem your intellectual convictions, as you would any other bad thoughts', on the ground that as the conclusion was 'undutiful' there must be some 'delusion in the premises'.

This was too much for Newman. 'Was it undutifulness to the Mosaic Law to be led on to the Gospel ? was not the Law from God ? How could a Jew, formerly as now, ever become a Christian, if he must at all hazards resist convictions and for ever ?' As for unsettling people : 'There have been events ten thousand times more unsettling than the change of individuals now. St. Paul must have unsettled all the good and conscientious people in the Jewish Church.'

All the same, he was far from insensible to the claims of those who had been guided by his words and views, publicly or in private. Miss Holmes was a vocal representative of the younger generation of those who relied on him. In the autumn, just after his resignation,

she had been writing frantically almost every day, as much about her
affairs as her opinions, her mood changing with every letter. 'Hardly
have I despatched one but another comes', said Newman in mild
despair. He was too kind-hearted to ignore her demands, though
he was always reminding her that she was supposed to be asking for
spiritual advice. She was dreadfully worried by some incident with
her employers, and a clergyman Mr. Villars ; no one would ever
trust her again unless Newman wrote and exonerated her from the
charge of insincerity. 'I feel the incongruity of writing formally to
deny it', he said to Mr. Leigh, her employer, amused at the idea of
such a headlong girl being accused of insincerity, 'just as if I had to
deny she had committed a highway robbery or been found guilty of
treason.' He referred to Mr. Villars, who 'thinks I may be the
insincere, disingenuous and doubleminded person — an opinion he
is quite welcome to entertain, so that he exculpates, as he is bound to
do, Miss Holmes'.

As 1844 went on Miss Holmes became almost hysterical. She
longed to be a Catholic, but could not bear to give up her relationship
with Newman, which, although at a distance, got more and more
emotional in spite of all he could do. She was meeting Catholics,
among them a young nun. 'Oh, I could love her so well, better than
I love you, for she would be affectionate, but you are made of marble.
Those cold words of yours fell on my heart like an iceberg. . . . I
shall think no more of monks. They are too hard and stern — nuns
will suit me better. . . . Cruel, hard-hearted Mr Newman, you would
not even deign to tell me how you are. . . . You keep me in the
Church by a spell I cannot comprehend or break.'

'You are seeking what is not possible in the Catholic Church,'
Newman told her once. 'Such a relation of father and daughter as
you speak of, that is, in the way you conceive of it, natural as is the
idea to a person of your enthusiasm and warmth of feeling, is unrecognized in the Church of Rome, and I think you would not find it there
in fact. . . . Your letter has quite frightened me. I am not conscious
of any elation at the fervency of your expressions.' At these cold
words Miss Holmes decided she had been making an idol of him,
and told him she intended to join the Church of Rome. Newman
wrote to say goodbye. 'I ask you to pardon me in all the various
imperfections of my mode of dealing with you — whatever was harsh
or inconsiderate or unkind. I have much to answer for about it I
know. . . . And I pray that He would bless you every day and guide
you continually and enable you to discern between His voice and

your feelings. In losing you, I lose what I can seldom expect to meet with — an affectionate heart.'

Needless to say, he did not lose her. She was torn in two, feeling her troubles disappear whenever she went into a Catholic Church, but drawn back to Newman again. 'Oh Mr. Newman you do not know what the torture of being a waverer is ! You who are so calm and fixed and immoveable — Oh dear Mr. Newman can it be possible that I can be right and you wrong ? Oh no, it cannot.' She told him a dream in which she had met him in Oxford, looking stout and proud and worldly, when he had snubbed her, turning away 'to intellectual friends. When she got too wild Newman tried again to make her realize that she was not bound to him in any way. He had offered advice, not guidance. 'You have never really been under mine, so do not deceive yourself. I have told you this before as I have told you various things which do not rest upon your mind.' This was just stern monkishness to Miss Holmes, whose cries of despair reached a crescendo in June. 'I hope I may not have said anything to vex you much ; but I love you better than all the world together, a million times better than you love me.' Next week : 'Oh Mr. Newman, how can you be so hard hearted as not to write to me ? I cannot bear to leave you. I am your child and you are my Father.' Two days later : 'Oh Mr. Newman, is it come to this ? Must we part this way, almost in anger ? . . . Oh Mr. Newman, do you wish me to die before your eyes ? . . . I feel as if I were a traitor or like a runaway slave who deserved to die without mercy.' And in a puzzled PS. 'I cannot tell what you may do. I don't think I half know you yet. You look and speak as if you were mildness and gentleness itself; but you can act so sternly.'

Newman said, 'Your distress makes you exaggerate very much what I have said. I would do everything that could be done to remove it.' He did succeed in removing some of it, for at the end of June she was writing, 'Now I see it all. Your letter has explained what seemed so contradictory in your dealings with me. I have been mad for a time. . . . You knew me better than I knew myself when you said my affection was not so strong as I fancied.' She realized now that he had doubts himself. She was received in November into the Catholic Church, and was soon writing in a different vein : 'Oh Mr. Newman, why will you be so long in coming over ? . . . I really feel now I could *almost* be willing to be killed on the railroad if that would make me a martyr and enable me to obtain your conversion from Almighty God.'

Very different from the Brontë-like Miss Holmes was Newman's contemporary Miss Giberne, though she too was a great enthusiast in her way, and depended on him for advice and encouragement. In November 1843 he told her he was surprised and anxious at not having heard from her. 'It looks as if something I had said had perplexed and frightened you. Please, write to me.' She did not resist this invitation, but unlike Miss Holmes she did not pour out everything to him. She felt a great need for confession, and wondered if she could get it in France if she went there. She threw herself enthusiastically into penitential exercises, gathered from books. Living with her evangelical family she could not fast ; everything had to be done in the privacy of her room. She tried sleeping on the floor, wrapped in her cloak. It was not cold which prevented her sleeping, but lack of a pillow. She used to get up at three in the morning to read Matins from a book Newman had given her ; she hit herself with the cords of her trunk as a penance. She did not tell any of this to Newman, but recalled it, as an old nun, in her French memoir, half amused, half nostalgic to remember these midnight efforts at mortification. They came to an end when a visitor was put to sleep in her room ; Selina Bacchus, who became a great friend. She was much younger than Miss Giberne. She was to marry, quite soon, William Copeland's brother George, a Cheltenham doctor. Both became Catholics, and years after Selina's nephew, Francis Bacchus, became a priest of the Oratory when Newman was a Cardinal.

In 1843 Newman had entertained Miss Giberne and some friends of hers at Oriel, and shown them over Littlemore. In 1844 he was visited by Miss Bowles, now a Catholic, and a party of Catholic friends from East Hendred, near her old home, where she was staying with the Eystons, who were descended from Sir Thomas More. Newman showed them the Library and the Church. She had no idea till she read the *Apologia* twenty years later 'what anguish and travail of the soul lay hidden the while beneath that calm face and voice of utter serenity'. She felt melancholy at the time, and as they drove home they all said to each other, 'He will never be a Catholic !'

There were other, very different friends to deal with. William Froude had a hint from Rogers in 1843 and called on Newman. 'It quite put me out when William was here how little I could explain myself to him,' said Newman to Mrs. Froude. 'Everything I said seemed to be shot out like bullets, round and hard and sudden —

arguments ought to grow out of the mind.' After his resignation Mrs. Froude, who had known him before her marriage, when she was one of the young ladies he met at Dartington, picked up the correspondence, wanting to know more. She was clever and sensible, and William was inclined to be a sceptic ; Newman's letters to them contained more of the intellectual progress of his mind than those to any others, and he used them in the *Apologia* for that reason — Mrs. Froude was by then a Catholic too. In Holy Week 1844 she again demanded information, and he wrote, every night, what became a kind of serial letter ; the earlier instalments were punctuated with expressions of disgust at himself for 'thrusting his doubts upon them'. But as they really wanted to know, he went on. 'And now this insufferable prose has exhausted my paper. O my dear Mrs. Froude I am very disgusted at it.' It was because his ideas had grown so much more definite that he felt they were dull. 'I am sure my last letter must have been a regular quietus and by its sedative effect must have tended to undo all the excitement I have caused you (as *Punch* says that a pun of the Duke of W's this day week made the Emperor of Russia go home and sleep sound for 2 hours).' At last he got entangled in the history and theology of the Papacy, which was where the theory of development had landed him at the moment, and having caught himself up he was forced to stop the letters for a while.

When Newman began writing to the Froudes that Easter Pusey was sitting by the bedside of his dying child, Lucy. She was only fifteen. Her first communion had been made on the Trinity Sunday after Tract 90 ; she longed to be a nun and read St. Francis de Sales on her death bed. She was a child of the Movement, too young to be troubled by doubts. 'You may fancy what an heart ache your note of to-day has given me,' Newman wrote to Pusey, when he heard there was no hope of her recovery. 'Dear Lucy has been made His in Baptism, she has been made His in suffering ; now she asks to be made His by love. Well may you find her sweet countenance pleasant to look upon, when here at a distance I feel pleasure in thinking of her. . . . Tell her she is constantly in my thoughts . . . as she who has gone first, is in my mind day by day, morning and evening continually.'

Lucy died on April 22nd, 1844. Pusey wrote : 'The child educated . . . in your sermons has been accepted and is in Paradise.' She had once said she wished she could be a martyr, and her poor father felt the wish was realized in the 'long and severe struggle' she had suffered. 'But all at once her eyes opened wide and I never saw such a gaze as at what was invisible to us; and after this had continued some little while she looked at me full in the face, and there came such an unearthly smile, so full of love also; all expression of pain disappeared and was swallowed up in joy; I never saw anything like that smile: there was no sound, else it was almost a laugh for joy, and I could hardly help laughing for joy in answer. I cannot describe it: it was utterly unlike anything I ever saw: it seemed to me as if she wanted to say "All you have ever longed for me is fulfilled." . . . It turned at once sorrow into joy. . . . A few days ago this seemed the heaviest blow that could fall upon me; she was the one being around whom my thoughts of the future here had wound and now I would not exchange that smile for worlds. . . . I feel certain that it was our Blessed Lord she saw.'

Newman said to Bloxam, 'She was a saint'.

He was, this summer, going back through his life in his mind, searching the past as well as the present for a sin mortal enough to cut him off from the knowledge of truth. Having gone over the intellectual ground with the Froudes, he began to write again to Keble about this moral question. 'I know that I have done enough to provoke Him to give me over and to deserve all that is evil. But still such is not His way, and I cannot get myself to believe that He means evil towards me, yet month by month my convictions grow in one direction.' This was in June. 'When I was a boy of fifteen and living a life of sin, with a very dark conscience and a very profane spirit, He mercifully touched my heart; and, with innumerable sins, yet I have not forsaken Him from that time, nor He me. . . . He then brought me through numberless trials safely and happily on the whole — and why should He now leave me to a blinded mind?' And, as always in times of crisis, he remembered his illness in Sicily, and the devil's attempt to destroy him, body and soul.

From memory he returned to the present; God seemed to grant his prayers for moral and spiritual aid, why should He refuse those for light and guidance in the truth? As for making a move, he had no natural inducements to do so; rather his decision must be made in the teeth of all his feelings and habits. 'The loss of friends, what a great evil it is! the loss of position, of name, of esteem — such a stultification of myself — such a triumph to others. It is no proud thing to unsay what I have said, to pull down what I have attempted to build up. And again, what quite pierces me, the disturbance of mind which a change on my part would cause to so many — the casting adrift, to the loss both of religious stability and comfort —

the temptation to which many would be exposed of scepticism, indifference and even infidelity. . . . I dread it in particular persons. . . .
Indeed, I sometimes feel uncomfortable about myself. A sceptical
unrealizing temper is far from unnatural to me — and I may be
suffered to relapse into it as a judgment. . . . So then I end as I began
— Am I in a delusion and given over to believe a lie ? Am I deceiving
myself and thinking myself convinced when I am not ? Does any
subtle feeling or temptation which I cannot detect, govern me, and
bias my judgment ? But is it possible that Divine Mercy should not
wish me, if so, to discover and escape it ? Has He led me thus far
to destroy me in the wilderness ?'

Keble could not really help him ; to his credit he did not try to
argue with him, still less to judge him. Of one of his letters Newman
wrote : 'Its effect upon me I can compare to nothing but some very
fragrant scent breathing on me — it has been soothing and enlivening
me the whole afternoon.' Keble said affectionately, 'In any case
surely you will be guided, and if others are guided differently, may
not both in some sense be right ?' Characteristically he blamed
himself, and lamented too that he should be cheerful, as he often was,
while such dreadful things were going on, in the Church and in his
friend's heart. He was inclined to put down to his own sins everything that went wrong. Newman answered at once : 'Let me, almost
in self-defence, beg and pray you not to be sorry that you can be
cheerful. What should either you or I do, if things oppressed us as
they might ? I hope it is not wrong to be cheerful, for I cannot help
being so. Surely to keep an equable frame of mind is the only way
to be able to view things healthily and rightly. . . . Do not lament
that you do not lose your sleep. I think sleep is the greatest of our
ordinary blessings. Nothing goes well with the mind without it ;
it heals all trouble.'

Some Fourdrinier cousins had sought him out in Oxford and had
told Jemima that he seemed very cheerful. Jemima did not believe
it. 'You must not suppose I *put on* cheerfulness because people do
not find out I have cares' ; he wrote to her, 'the truth is, (thank
God) I *am* cheerful. And though it so entirely depends on Him that
I might be cast down for good and all any day, and know not of
course what is before me, yet having sound sleep at night and quiet
days and trying to serve Him without aims of this world, however
imperfectly, how can I but be cheerful, as I am. And I trust He
will overrule all painful things which myself or others have to bear,
to our good. Of course the pain of my friends is what cuts me, and

I do not know how I shall bear it ; but He gives us strength according
to our day.'

At midsummer, on St. John the Baptist's day, there suddenly
turned up at Littlemore Father Dominic Barberi, the Italian Passionist, who had been giving a mission in a hayloft near Heythrop. He
had been corresponding, intermittently with Dalgairns ever since that
young man had written a letter about the Movement, in French, to
the *Univers*. As a young countryman in Italy Barberi had received
an interior understanding from God that he would have work to do
in the conversion of England. He always longed to begin it ; yet he
had spent nearly the whole of his life in Rome, teaching theology. It
was only a few years since he had come to England, and he was
fifty-two. He had given up his habit now, and wore a scratch lot of
black clothes, old patched boots and an ancient hat. He was short,
with a round face, and keen eyes. 'His very look had about it something holy', Newman wrote long after. 'When his form came in
sight I was moved to the depths of my being in the strangest way.
The gaiety and affability of his manner in the midst of all his sanctity
was in itself a holy sermon.' Father Dominic was delighted with
Littlemore, with the poverty and simplicity of the house, and with
its inhabitants. He went away, back to his arduous life, preaching in
broken English to all who would listen. In him for the first time
Newman met what he had told Ambrose Phillipps he saw no sign of
in the Roman Catholic Church, holiness in action.

In July Henry Wilberforce persuaded Newman to sit to George
Richmond, because he wanted a portrait of him. 'Richmond will be
delighted to have the honour of drawing you', he said. 'Neither is
there the least danger of his making a fine gentleman of you. I
cautioned him about it to his amusement.' The famous drawing was
taken down to East Farleigh by Miss Giberne. 'I cannot well say
how much I like and value it,' Henry wrote. 'I almost expect to
hear your voice at times. The likeness is no doubt diminished by not
having your glasses which seem to me an almost necessary part of
you.' Years later Henry sketched for the *Dublin Review* Newman as
he had been as a tutor at Oxford, and recalled how, on the rare occasions when he took off his spectacles, he had to grope about on his
desk to find them again. Newman was glad he liked the portrait.
'I feared you would think it sawney and sentimental.' Miss Giberne
evidently agreed with Henry about the glasses, for she made a copy,
putting them in, and giving Newman a more intense expression and
straighter, less tidy hair. To judge from later photographs she was

right about his hair. It was the sort of straight thick soft hair which
flops out of place the minute after it is combed ; it was still dark at
this time. Newman must have been very striking to look at ; no
wonder his friends were annoyed at the caricatures, which made too
much of his nose, at the expense of his equally definite jaw, and gave
him a drooping cadaverous look.

Newman fitted in his sittings to Richmond when he went to
London to visit Bowden. At the end of June he wrote to Keble : 'I
found him very weak, but able to move about on a crutch, and dine
downstairs. He is most wonderfully calm and cheerful — you
cannot understand it unless you saw him. It is difficult to believe
he is so ill. As I sat by him, he could not help half laughing again
and again, and could only say, "It is your face — it reminds me of
old times".' The Bowdens were then at Roehampton ; Newman
went there several times, and gave the sick man Holy Communion —
he only did this now for Bowden. On his way there on the vigil of
St. James' day he suddenly found himself outside the house where
his grandmother and Aunt had lived till 1806. He wrote to tell Aunt
all about it. The day was fearfully hot, 83 in the shade, and it was a
vigil (which meant he was fasting) and he had had to walk carrying
his luggage, first from Littlemore to Oxford station, and then, after
a busy two hours in London, out to Roehampton. Suddenly he came
to the house in Fulham, now turned into a chemist's shop. He went
in and asked for some quinine.

'The good chemist, civil as he was, did not take my hints, so I
saw nothing except the hall through the door. I saw too the staircase
which I had forgotten. . . . I told him where the kitchen was, where
I recollect you going to superintend the making of apple puffs.'
Newman had been no more than five when he was last in that house.
It revived far off memories. 'I recollect coming down in the morning
and seeing the breakfast things bright and still — and I have some
vague reminiscence of dry toast.' And he thought he remembered a
loft 'in which I have a dim vision of apples on the floor and a mangle.
By this time my quinine was compounded and swallowed, and so I
came away.' But to come back like this to the beginning of his
conscious life, just when he was going through it in his mind, following out the course of it, was a strange experience. He could not tell
Aunt all, but he could tell her something of it.

'How strange it is, I wish I could describe it, to stand in a house
which was so much to me, as that house was, and it so different and
I so different ! Whatever good there is in me, I owe, under grace, to

the time I spent in that house and to you and my dear grandmother, its inhabitants. I do not forget her Bible and the prints in it. Alas, my dear Aunt, I am but a sorry bargain, and perhaps if you knew all about me, you would hardly think me now worth claiming ; still I cannot help it — I am what I am — and I have grown into what I am from that time at Fulham. What a strange change 40 years makes ! How little did that little child whom you used to fondle, think of what he thinks now. He had no thoughts.' No ; but it may have been there that he said to himself 'What am I ? Why am I here ?' — the momentous question which started him off on his long quest. But now, thinking of the sorrow he was preparing for his loved and loving old aunt, who could not be expected to understand his present thoughts, he ended : 'May we all meet again in peace, when this troublesome world and its many contentions are over. I really do think I love peace, yet I seem destined to be "a man of strife". I am talking a great deal about myself, but if any one will pardon it, you will.' And he added a PS. : 'Love to Harriett, Jemima, their husbands and the children and kind thoughts to everyone else who will receive them from my worthless self . . .'.

By this time he had come to wish that people in general knew more about his views, not wanting what began to seem inevitable to come as a shock to them. He suggested to Henry that he should tell people about what had happened in 1839, but Henry was too distressed to contemplate it. It seemed to make the move inevitable, and he told Newman of the dreadful effect it would have in a thousand parishes. Newman was amused at this estimate. 'As to the 1000 parishes you so poetically speak of, the sooner my Anglican character is damaged, the safer for those parishes, for the more gradual will be the change in the feelings of others. It is my very dread of surprising or shocking people which makes me wish something known at once. However, I would not for the world put upon you anything so delicate and painful as you feel this to be ; so let us say no more about it — and consider my request quite at an end. . . . It will be little indeed if I save the feelings of strangers by hurting yours.' In an earlier letter he had said : 'I am what I am ; let me be known to be what I am ; for good or for bad, for evil report or for good report. I have never wished to make myself of authority or the head of a party — so if the knowledge of what I am merely makes people give me up οὐ φρόντις Ἱπποκλειδῆ (Hippocleides doesn't care). If they still follow me, let them do it with their eyes open.'

Yet though he had never wanted to be a leader, others had made

him one, and he could not escape the consequences.   He soon had
his wish, to be known — though not for what he was, but for the
traitor he was believed to be — and it came about in the most
shatteringly public and painful way possible.   But before that trial
came another, more personal, more heart-rending.   For now at last
Bowden was dying.

1844–1845

Drinking the Cup out

THE Bowdens spent August in Clifton and Newman went to town
to see them off. Brooding on the imminent loss of this his oldest
friend, who seemed to be taking youth with him, Newman wrote to
Jemima. 'It certainly is strange, Bowden's state just now — and
seems to cut me off from Oxford. I do fancy I am getting changed.
I go into Oxford and find myself out of place. Every thing seems to
say to me, "This is not your home". The college seems strange to
me, and even the college servants seem to look as if I were getting
strange to them. I cannot tell whether it is a fancy or not, but to
myself I seem changing. I am so much more easily touched than I
used to be. Reading St. Wulstan's life just now almost brought tears
into my eyes. What a very mysterious thing the mind is! Yet
nothing that my feelings suggest to me is different from what has
been engraven more or less strongly on my reason long ago. Now I
daresay that if I kept this a day or two it would seem unreal, and I
could not bear to send it; and yet I do think there is truth in it,
making allowance for accidental feeling. . . . Do not be discomposed
by this dismal letter.'

It was no fancy that he was more easily touched. Although he
had grown up in the Romantic period, when the expression of
feeling was not considered unmanly, Newman's friends noticed the
tears in his eyes at the news of Froude's death as something unusual.
Yet now, just at the age when emotions, in the course of nature,
begin to decline in violence and urgency, he became more susceptible;
and this process continued, so that by the time he was an old man he
was afraid to preach at the funerals of friends, knowing he was so
likely to break down, and many people noticed how difficult it was
for him to control his feeling when speaking in public of things which
meant much to him. By that time he had lived into an age when it
was fashionable for men to think themselves above the natural
expression of emotion; tears were only fit for women. Yet coldness

nd stiffness are death beginning, and the hardening of hearts that
ets in with middle age is comparable with stiffening limbs and loss
f physical elasticity.   In this connexion it is remarkable that New-
nan's body remained supple into extreme old age ; it was specifically
noticed in his ninetieth year, the last of his life.   He became weak, but
not stiff.   In the same way his psychological life, instead of the gradual
atrophy and diminishing response of nature left to itself, became ever
more malleable, discriminating, sensitive to experience.   The violence
of youthful passion, which had made him feel he was going to faint
n controlling his anger, had already long since been tempered ; but
t was no rigid suppression, such as too often dries up and hardens
eeling.   The present trial, if he had resisted it, might have shrunk
up his heart with resentment, or over-softened it with self-pity, but
he was able to submit to it so completely that it was no longer a
passive endurance but a creative action.

Newman went to Clifton at the beginning of September to see
Bowden for what turned out to be the last time.   They were planning
to remove to their new house in St. Leonard's for the winter.   Bowden's father had died only a few months before at their house in
own.   Newman described for Keble Bowden's day, how he would
come downstairs as long as he could ; he had to be lifted up them at
night by two servants 'making a sort of low interjection, not of pain
out of relief, "lo, lo, lo", or the like, and says, as he told me, "Well,
another crest has been topped, another billow is over", calling his
days billows, with an allusion to "Who would count the billows
past ?"   He made me come and see what he called his "procession"
— his wife first with the candle, then he in the arms of the two men.
While going up, he turned about his head, to be sure I was looking.'
And Newman said, 'One forgets past feelings, else I would say that
I never had pain like the present'.

Before he had finished writing, news came that Bowden was
already dead.   At first Newman did not know where he was, at
Clifton or St. Leonard's.   But the journey had been too much for
him, they had stopped in London, and there he had died, in his
father's house, at four in the morning on Sunday, September 15th.
As soon as he knew where to go, Newman went up to town at once,
and two days after wrote to Keble : 'He died, and he lies, in a room
I have known these twenty-four years — the principal drawing room.
So many persons have I seen there, so kind to me — they are all
gone.   The furniture is all the same — the ornaments on the mantelpiece — and there lies now my oldest friend, so dear to me — and I

with so little of faith or hope, as dead as a stone and detesting myself.'

Afterwards he wrote a note : 'I sobbed bitterly over his coffin to think that he had left me still dark as to what the way of truth was, and what I ought to do in order to please God and fulfil His will'. As he told Mrs. Bowden in 1846, from the other side of decision : 'I kept praying and looking, if so be, for some sign — through dear John's illness I kept thinking that God's mercy would use him as the means of guiding me, and perhaps my most overpowering thought when we lost him was that now he left me alone in darkness and distress, when he had been kept in tranquillity and taken to his reward without a responsibility which weighed upon me. But so it was, God's ways are not as ours.'

Elizabeth Bowden and the children were almost as familiar and dear to Newman as Bowden himself, and even if her husband had not advised it, it was natural for her to turn to him for help and support in her grief. It was therefore very painful to have to begin by telling her the truth about himself, but it had to be done, if she were not to hear about it first from others. As it turned out, he was only just in time. He had managed to tell all his friends, and even bring it home to Pusey, who for a long time refused to face it, before the storm burst in the newspapers. From Oxford he wrote to Mrs. Bowden, 'You cannot tell what a relief it is to me that you know what I am. Till then I feel to people like a hypocrite.' But of course it was a shock to her. 'I hardly think I ever felt so desolate as that night', she wrote. 'For I had always persuaded myself that it was not so and vehemently contradicted everybody who hinted at it — it seemed to throw me more upon myself, to find you differing from John — yet I had much rather *know* than be in doubt, and your talking with me afterwards made me happier.'

'Your letter,' Newman replied, 'you may suppose, tried me a great deal. I have been and am in very difficult circumstances, and try to act right as I will, I cannot hope to do what is best, nor to be satisfied with myself on looking back. You in your kindness do not make any complaint, and except for the great infirmity which attaches to all I do, I do not think I merit it — and yet I am full of misgivings and am sick of myself, to think how cruel I seem to have been to you. I have had many bitter sighs since I read your note. Yet what could I do ? Dear John has been kind enough to call my friendship for him "true". I do sincerely wish to be true to you and yours and that I may be able, and yet here I begin with what seems to be the most unfriendly of acts, as if I would deny you such service as he

asks of me. Unless my heart is very self-deceived I most profoundly
wish to be a servant to you. O do suffer me to be such, and take me
for what I am, though I cannot be all you might have thought or
could wish. And please, as you think kindly of me, never disguise,
as you have not in this instance, any pain I cause you. Let me bear
it, though I cannot rid you of it — for I assure you I do bear it, and
your letter to-day has pierced me, O so much, yet as I wish to be
pierced. Deny me not this slight make up, if it may be so called, of
the distress I am causing. Your distress is but one out of many, yet
He who I trust is the imposer of this great trial will enable me to
bear it all.'

She at once answered that he was quite right to tell her, and felt
she was 'undeserving of so much thought'. She was a kind person,
noticing little things, like the handwriting of Newman's letter which
she thought unsteady and hoped was due only to tiredness. He said,
'If my hand generally seems better to you than it is, I believe it is
that I have generally shown you my company hand — or sent you
short notes — and that in my last you saw it as it commonly is. I
can't quite make it out though. It is better sometimes without
apparent reason.'

He did not admit he was tired, but in fact he was feeling so
exhausted that he consulted Mr. Babington, at first by letter, to
which he received such a stern reply that he went to see him. Babington, in his note, prophesied 'premature decrepitude'. He said,
'When I last saw you, about the close of Lent I believe, I was much
struck with your appearance which was shrunk and debilitated ; and
it is impossible to avoid the suspicion that, partly from overwork, and
partly by deficient nutriment, you are rendering yourself unfit for
exertion'. He told Newman he might reduce himself to a helpless
invalid. However, the interview proved less alarming. Newman
reported to Jemima, introducing the subject as if he were really only
concerned about his hand ; as its aching affected his writing it was
the only sign of fatigue she could notice in Derby. 'Mr. Babington
has pronounced my difficulty to be a deficiency of nervous power and
to have nothing to do with my hand — and corroborates (tell Aunt)
my assertion that I might as well rub my nose for it as my thumb
or my wrist. I was terribly afraid from his language that he was
going to do something desperate, send me abroad or the like —
but when he saw me he softened, and said I was better than he
expected.'

What would Mr. Babington have said to a recent exchange

between Dalgairns and Father Dominic ? Dalgairns shamelessly only answered the Passionist's long letters when he wanted something. At the beginning of October, with Newman's backing, he was writing: 'Several persons among us are anxious to lead a more mortified life than is common among us ; they have been trying in vain to procure shirts or girdles of haircloth'. He hoped his request would not raise a smile or be considered immodest, 'but forgive me, it is ignorance, not want of modesty'. He hastened to add : 'They will be put into the hands of a person who guides many souls among us, so you need not fear their being indiscreetly used. . . . The person who wishes for them would mind no expense in procuring them. . . . I had almost forgotten to say that he also wants a discipline, such as ordinary persons would use. Of course he wishes his request to be kept a secret.' Father Dominic was in Belgium at the time, but sent them their parcel of haircloth and the discipline. Hairshirts were often worn by men like St. Thomas More, Henry VIII's Chancellor, who had to live in the midst of a rich and worldly society, Christian in name but not very Christian in nature. The discomfort acted as a reminder of Christ's sufferings, and, in a small way, as a voluntary participation in them. Many ascetics have worn more uncomfortable and painful things than these, for the same reason, and sometimes have gone too far with them. A young enthusiast stayed with Newman at Littlemore who was wearing something which he considered so unsuitable he 'pitched it to the other end of the room'.

The use of the discipline shocks some people now quite as much as it shocked the Victorians, perhaps more, since psychological investigations have familiarized them with neurotic perversions in which pain becomes a sexual stimulant, sadistically inflicted on another, or masochistically received. Probably there have been ascetics who have become neurotic over their penances, but there are many more who have not. There is a great difference between satisfying perverted instincts in occasional orgies of painfully pleasurable violence and taking up, for some definite object, a regular exercise which causes physical pain or discomfort. The exercises of some athletes strike ordinary people as tiresome, uncomfortable and even painful. The object of any Christian's exercise of discipline, whether or not it involves his body, is to express in action his penitence for the evil-doing which brought Christ to the cross, and to liberate himself from slavery to his own selfish desire for ease. Of course it would be pointless if it were not part of a life of prayer and charity. But self-denial and voluntary discipline of some kind are necessary if a Christian's life is not to turn into mere emotional self-indulgence, and all the more necessary in a society where material comfort is the practical, if not the recognized, ideal.

Voluntary suffering gains its value from its object ; everyone admires the man who rushes into a burning house to save another, or, like the heroes of prison camps, gives up his food or takes a punishment for the sake of someone else. A Christian doing penance is trying to make this principle part of his daily life. At Littlemore they wanted to follow the ways of monks and saints, who, when the world ceased to persecute Christians, could not bear to live at ease, wanting to follow the Christ who suffered hunger and thirst and was scourged and humiliated and cast out as a criminal. When Newman noted in his retreat his aversion to the very name of penance, he may have been thinking of this particular exercise, which he nevertheless did undertake, probably sometime this autumn.

While Newman was in London an agitation was going on among the Tractarians in Oxford ; James Mozley was organizing a formal protest to be put before convocation objecting to the election of Symons of Wadham as Vice-Chancellor. Newman did not like the idea of protesting against a person, but he supposed he must record his vote in order not to let his friends down. It was to be the last vote he gave. He also felt that it seemed out of place, censured as he was, to take a prominent part, 'and if I act at all, I cannot help seeming prominent', he told Mrs. Bowden. When he was going back to Oxford he found himself on a train crowded with the opposition, all going to vote against the Tractarians. 'It was dark when we entered the carriage at Paddington', he wrote to Mrs. Bowden. '. . . Three persons were in a parallel carriage and they began talking at the pitch of their voices in the dark, forgetting that walls had ears. I cannot give their conversation but "all the world was coming — Lord Faversham, Lord Eldon — a great gathering and triumph, the Church in great danger — they must be put down etc." One man then went on, "I know the soundest divine in the Church — the soundest divine in the Church is Mr. Stanley Faber of Durham, and he said to me, Depend on it, Newman, Newman (very loud) is a Jesuit, a Jesuit". Somehow I could not help interfering, though they had no claim on me. So I put my head through the cross window which separates the carriages and said (in the dark), "Gentlemen, please don't speak so loud, for persons are here whom you would not like to speak before". On which there was a deep silence — but in a while the conversation was resumed at a lower pitch.'

Did anyone recognize the famous voice ? But it was unlikely that any of these had ever met him.

The Protest was defeated by 882 votes to 183. The Tractarians were a losing, an almost routed, side.

Bowden had left Newman £100 and 'a memorandum which he dictated with difficulty and with tears in his eyes', said his widow. 'You know his love for you and it was mutual and it is a pleasure to me to think of it, though it makes me sad.' Newman decided to spend the gift on enlarging his Library. He could not decide whether to get the Bollandists' learned researches into the lives of the Saints, or various classics, and was happily writing about it to a lawyer friend in London, Badeley, when there suddenly appeared in the *Morning Chronicle* at the beginning of November an account of a supposed letter of his to Isaac Williams announcing his secession to Rome. As he had not been writing to Isaac at all lately he dismissed the whole thing as 'a myth', and did not even look at the paper in question.

But the report was so plausible, perhaps because it seems to have originated with Golightly, that it was widely believed, first that he actually had seceded, and then that he was on the point of doing so. The newspapers attacked him so bitterly as to shock and alarm his friends. An avalanche of letters descended on Littlemore, lasting from the beginning of November to the end, abusive, accusing or anguished according to the varying views of the writers. Newman answered all those who signed their names, but he gave no answer to the newspapers : what answer could he give ? He had not gone over to Rome, but he could not say that he believed Rome to be wrong. It was no use talking about paper logic and possible delusion to newspapers.

Public uproars are soon forgotten, even by contemporaries ; a century later it is often difficult to discover the echoes. Newman said very little about this in the *Apologia*, and some have thought him oversensitive to hostility, not knowing the violence and bitterness of the attack. But what is really surprising is that the victim of such abuse and injustice should have let it pass with scarcely any complaint. In answer to Keble's solicitude Newman wrote, on November 21st : 'What I feel as to the attacks made on me, or rather the only thing which I *feel*, is the charge of dishonesty. Really no one but O'Connell is called so distinctly and ordinarily a liar as I am. I think nothing tends to hurt my spirits but this. I am not treated merely as a gentleman, and that by educated people.'

Keble had told him that Sir John Coleridge was thinking of

organizing a Protest in his favour. Although Newman did not know
of the Gladstonian silken cord policy, he was aware that many people
thought his dissatisfaction with the Church of England was caused
by the treatment he received in it ; they were always telling him so.
He did not want to encourage this false impression, as he told Keble.
But he also gave another reason. 'I should value it much — but
then it strikes me I should be removing a cross from me, and that I
might have a heavier one put on me. If there is a cross which is
blessed from those who have borne it from our Lord's own time, it
is this — and it is safest to be content with it.' This was his consolation, that even Christ was called a 'deceiver'. But that he was
allowed to bear this reproach after his master, though it strengthened him in bearing it, did not make it less painful or less humiliating.
For what could be more shameful for the famous preacher of stricter
Christian living than to be held up before everyone as a liar and a
hypocrite, saying one thing and meaning, even doing, another ?

Even if the fury of the attack is realized, it may seem to-day out of
proportion to the event. Religion has ceased to be social and is no
longer a vital part of the national consciousness. The only possible
parallel is to imagine the sensation if it were disclosed in the newspapers that a prominent political leader were not only a secret member
of the Communist party, but actually in the service of a foreign government. The conscious feelings of the English at that time towards
'Rome' were similar. But religion touches deeper regions in human
nature than politics, and below the articulate hatred of Rome as a
foreign tyranny from which England had emancipated itself in the
sixteenth century, there was a dark irrational fear, as of some evil
supernatural power, delusive, irresistible, corrupting, a fascinating
slavery. Newman himself had picked up in boyhood this picture of
Rome as a witch, as Anti-Christ, and it took him long to shake it off,
not from his mind, as he expressly noted, but from his imagination.
When he finally got free of it, he did not dismiss it as nonsense ; it
seemed to him a real, but dark, shadow of the truth. The Catholic
Church was a mystery and had a power over the human imagination
no other thing on earth had ; if it did not look like Christ, it must
look like Satan. That many took it for the embodiment of evil was
often not their fault ; nevertheless, if it was indeed the representative
of Christ, it would arouse, as He did, the forces of evil in the world.
The dark spirit would direct against Christ's Body still the spite, the
jealousy, cruelty, fear and hatred of men, and their pride, which
misused both reason and love.

In English minds in the nineteenth century 'Rome' was still the symbol of religious tyranny, though in England for three hundred years the only tyranny practised was against, not by, its members. The tough little remnant of Roman Catholics had had to keep very quiet to survive at all, and consequently made little impression on the national consciousness. Thus for the ordinary Englishman it was the Oxford Movement which revived the idea of Catholicism, raising it almost from the dead, and it seemed the more dangerous in that it was happening inside their own Church, commonly regarded as freed from the degrading superstition and idolatry practised by Catholics. And Newman was the leader and representative figure of this new revival of an ancient sorcery ; he had already, without any intention of doing so, focused on himself all the fears, rational and irrational, all the hatred and contempt the mass of his countrymen felt at the idea of a priest, the very symbol of what they called, comprehensively, Popery. It was inevitable that when it was noised abroad that he had been all along in the pay of Rome, all the passions aroused by that mysterious body should have been let loose upon him.

The letters which came in day after day reflect something of what was being said. Extracts hardly represent them, because the prejudices are often so ludicrous that they would be laughable but for the violence behind them. Many of the writers lectured Newman at length on his dishonesty, his 'monkish slavish obedience', his 'absurd hobby of his wonderful admiration of the Virgin', his playing with truth ; they demanded how he could without shuddering go near to the Apocalyptic Babylon ; they assured him that Froude would repudiate him now or, alternatively, that this was the result of Froude's silly and wicked attacks on the Reformers ; they advised him to travel. They expected and often demanded answers ; if Newman's answers did not satisfy them they burst into further tirades. Sometimes private answers were not required, as to this anonymous appeal, desiring him to make some statement to 'show that the injury you have done your country and its pure form of worship, has not arisen from your being in the pay of an Italian Bishop called a Pope, as is generally said and believed, but has been caused by an over-heated imagination. . . . May Heaven turn you from your evil doings is the sincere wish of A Briton.'

But far more painful than these crude attacks were the cries of despair from those who had learned Catholic ideas, sometimes faith itself, from Newman, and were utterly bewildered to hear he was going over to a form of religion they had been taught to regard as corrupt, and this from his own earlier works. These were some of the 'thousands' Keble had feared for. Newman had wanted to find some way to warn them, but this was a very painful way, both for them and for him. They implored him not to desert them. They wanted denials and reassurances which he could not give. He did deny he had already seceded, but he was forced to add that he had no cure of souls now, and leave them to draw their own conclusions. 'I am most keenly distressed it is causing such feelings as you express', he wrote to one.

It was indeed almost more than he could bear to know the anguish of all these people and not be able to help them. 'Do not laugh at me,' cried one anonymous woman, 'I know I am ignorant and vile and weak but I sicken at the thought that you have fled from the Church Catholic and called yourself a Romanist leaving a cloud over the blessed words you have written — torturing and puzzling the mind that would be led to *reality* — but oh not that part of the Church of Rome which you have yourself condemned — oh best and holiest you cannot love anything false — you cannot embrace it — Forgive this from a wild and worn spirit — a weak and sinful woman yet who has prayed for you and oh may you — may you also pray for me!'

'Oh my very dear friend,' wrote an old schoolfellow of Ealing, 'can you think of leaving us — I entreat you not to forsake us — we shall be left to scorn and derision ; already pointed at enough for endeavouring to restore church principles in our own little sphere, we shall be made powerless altogether if a master in Israel forsakes our communion. . . . My dear friend Clarke, an Ealing boy, is dying . . . but that separation would be as nothing to my hearing that Newman, who rescued me from low views, and such as now seem scarcely believing views, had ceased to call himself my brother and declared me to be in heresy. Oh! Newman do do stop with us — what shall we do without you!'

'What confusion to our Friends — what triumph to our enemies,' wrote Crawley, one of the two gentlemen who had settled their families at Littlemore the year before, 'and to Rome what an argument to confirm her in all her errors and abuses! What hope, humanly speaking, can remain to our poor humbled Church after such a blow ? . . . To find herself all at once despaired of and deserted by her best champion ; one who under Providence has been the chief instrument of raising her from her degraded state and as it were breathing into her afresh the breath of life!'

Newman had said, only a week or two ago to Mrs. Bowden, that he wished to be pierced by the pain he was causing. Now he was. To her, in answer to her inquiry, he only said : 'I am going through what must be gone through, however painful. It seems wrong to say anything of myself to one who is in such sorrow as you are.' But to Mrs. Froude he wrote on November 18th : 'My spirits have not yet given way. But what with the long continued inward secret trial and the unwearied violence of the attacks on me, most cruel, though they mean it not so, at a time when I most need peace, I am just now in straits. Dying people are commonly left in quiet. If I am, as people think, unsettled, what great thoughtlessness to be watching every look and gesture and reporting it in the market place.'

This was what Golightly, among others, was doing ; it was through private reports from Oxford that all the details and rumours about Newman got into the national press. Golightly congratulated himself on his part in starting the whole outburst. 'I thought they might be entering the communion of saints on All Saints' Day', he joked. He was always writing to the papers ; Pusey too suffered from his attention in this respect. 'It is astonishing what little feeling some people have', Newman wrote to Jemima on November 24th. 'Golightly and the newspapers would think it wrong to put out a statement on doubtful authority to the effect that I had broken my leg, yet they have no remorse in circulating what is adapted to shock friends indefinitely more. But the said G. is a man literally without bowels. I doubt whether he has any inside, or is more than a walking and talking piece of mechanism.' That was the worst he ever said of his ex-pupil, who seemed willing to stick at nothing to dislodge him from Oxford.

Jemima was causing Newman extra pain by leaving out of her letters any comment on what he said about himself ; he felt it an ominous silence and asked the reason for it. Jemima said she did not know what to say ; trying to make up for it, she asked for more news. 'I have gone through a great deal of pain and have been very much cut up', he answered. 'The one predominant distress upon me has been this unsettlement of mind I am causing. This is a thing that has haunted me day by day. And for days I have had a literal pain in and about my heart, which I suppose at any moment I could bring on.' To Edward Coleridge, an Eton master, he said the same thing. 'On Saturday for some time my heart literally ached, and is still uneasy.' Pusey said, 'It even seems to affect his whole frame as one might imagine "a sword piercing", a pain shooting through every part'.

It was too much for him. On November 24th he was adding to his letter to Jemima : 'The other day I was seized with a swelling at my elbow and yesterday there were symptoms of the like at my knee — a collection of water. Dr. Wootten does not think much of it . . . but it shows I am not well. . . . I hit my funny bone violently some months ago.'   But it was as likely to be caused by internal as by external pressure. As usual he tried to blame his weakness on the doctor's treatment, 'He has put me on such low diet and given me so much medicine as to make me weak and almost bring on the face ache again which has troubled me somewhat lately — but I think it will not be necessary to observe it long'.   Nothing kept him down long and on the 30th he was assuring her that he was 'to all appearance quite well again I am thankful to say'.   But he was not at all well, as he admitted to Keble at the beginning of December, when he proposed going up to London to visit Robert Williams (the Breviary translator) who was due for an operation. 'For myself I am just recovering from a severe influenza which wonderfully pulled me down — and I cannot properly stand and walk as it is.'   He went to London all the same, and saw Williams, but it was hardly surprising that in January he collapsed again, with what he called to Henry 'a new attack of something very like influenza'.   It was a strange kind of influenza, for, as he told Mrs. Bowden, who was expecting him for a visit, 'I had no fever, cold or cough, but a wonderful pain in my head and limbs, and prostration of strength so that I could hardly lift myself from my bed — and even at the end of a week could hardly walk'.   To H. W. he made the tell-tale comment, 'I have not been in such poor health (for the time) since 1828 d.g.'

His poor health in 1828 was the result of mental strain, and grief at Mary's sudden death, and this collapse, though he was so determined not to give in to it, was caused by a stress more intense and a grief more exhausting because he felt he was responsible for the pain he was giving others, and yet could not alleviate it, however much he suffered himself.   Yet he would not try to escape from this apparently useless pain. 'I am not unwilling to be in trouble now,' he wrote to Jemima at the end of that dreadful November, 'nor for others to be — for it is what must be — and the more of it, the sooner over.   It is like drinking a cup out.'

Soon after he wrote to his Aunt : 'In a changeable world like this, nothing is certain, after the unchangeable God, but the past. The past is our own. What you have done for me is irrevocable — it is mine — and I can delight in it. I can think of my debt to you, and when you are tempted to be low and despondent, if such feelings ever come on you, as if you were lonely and desolate, do recollect that there is one at a distance who is thinking of you and praying for you ; and into whose eyes tears start at the thought of your having any sorrow or perplexity, especially through him. O what a world is this, and how great are its trials — and none duly knows them but He whose blessed will imposes them, and who can turn them all to blessings.'

All this time, newspapers and letters and influenza notwithstanding, Newman was working on the proofs of St. Athanasius, who always seemed to be in a critical state in times of stress. He could still be amused, too, at certain aspects of the Anglican reaction to the crisis. Of the moderately high party in the Movement he remarked to Mrs. Bowden, 'I should feel very keenly for them if they were not so angry, but they are very angry. Hook is the best of them — and if such is Hook what is Palmer, who seems like a walking folio or a theological nine pounder ? They act as if they had no feeling at all : as different as possible from Manning, Gladstone, Judge Coleridge etc.'

Hook was convinced that Romanism was a temptation of Satan and told Pusey he was glad Newman had been saved for the moment. But he thought he 'was embittered against the Church and so was blinded against the soul-destroying errors of the Romish sect'. It never seemed to occur to people like him that Newman was suffering infinitely more for his 'Romanism' than he had from even the episcopal attacks on Tract 90. 'Newman', Hook insisted later, 'has not had the strength and grace to stand the fiery trial.' Pusey was shocked at such a judgment, yet he too felt, though with sympathy, that the treatment Newman received biased his decision. This could only be a further trial for Newman, though they did not intend it to be ; it was humiliating that his friends thought him too weak to stand up to opposition, and that he was making for Rome as for a bolt-hole. It was hard to bear this imputation not only because he was a fighter by nature and had never shirked the consequences of his actions, but because it made nonsense of those actions. What was the use of acting from conviction against his own inclinations, if everybody thought he was acting from some other motive ?

None of them seemed to visualize, as he did, the actual personal consequences of his secession. He saw no consolations ahead. 'What a forlorn, miserable prospect, humanly speaking, I have before me!' he broke out once to Mrs. Bowden in November. Even if he did not himself give up his Fellowship, he thought it unlikely that the Provost would leave him in peace. He had just invented a new test for candidates for Orders—whether they thought Newman 'an ill-used man'. Rome itself seemed alien. 'No one can have a more unfavourable view than I of the present state of the Roman Catholics', he told Keble. 'So much so, that any who join them would be like the Cistercians of Fountains, living under trees till their house was built. If I must account for it, I should say the want of unity had injured both them and us.'

This was at the end of December. In January 1845 he succeeded in visiting Mrs. Bowden at St. Leonard's, though not as soon as he intended, for on the 8th he was writing, 'I daresay you have expected to hear from me before now, but the influenza got hold of me again. Not that I am ever very bad.' On the way he went to the Wilberforces in Kent and wrote to Jemima, 'Really I think it is hardly a relief going about — for I *see* people pained. It quite made me sick to hear H. Wilberforce's wife sigh. . . . I could not bear to come to you yet — I could not bear the Friary party — you don't know how poor a creature I am now, though I should not, and do not, show it to others.' That he did not show it is witnessed by the letters of his Littlemore companions, who would not have written so gaily if he had left them in a state of feebleness and gloom.

'We have just been unpacking all your books and beautiful editions they are', said Dalgairns. 'St. John opened one but he was so shocked at the immorality that he shut it up again!' St. John himself wrote, 'Do you know I am getting more popish every day so that I am beginning to frighten myself and I want you to row me when you come back'. A few days later, 'Dalgairns thinks his Protestant rags are good enough for his camping here; his popery he puts on with his holiday coat and ring'. Next it was: 'We have heard nothing about Ward's flooring you but are very anxious to hear as it is something new and we consider all our honour is at stake till you have knocked him down and trampled on him'. St. John made do with the minimum of punctuation. He added of some mutual friends: 'Your visit seems to have done good, I don't exactly know how, but I believe because you played with the children'.

The Bowden children could not be played with because when Newman at last got to St. Leonard's they were 'all in the measles'.

He had only been there a day or two when Mrs. Bowden, to her great distress, caught it too, so the visit was after all not much comfort to either of them. Marianne, just better, 'was your representative when I left', Newman wrote afterwards to her mother. 'Dear child — I took her by surprise and wished her goodbye on the staircase — and her manner was so kind, and I wished so much our custom was to give a blessing on leave taking.'

Going to St. Leonard's just then was another mysterious event to Newman, returning him upon his past. 'Here I am where I have not been since 1810', he told Jemima. 'It seems as if I were destined now to be visiting places and persons known to me in youth and childhood. I have made out our house of 1810, and the face of the town is quite familiar to me. I knew where the churches were, was sure certain houses were of recent date as hiding the cliff and recognized the place where my brother Charles and I got up the face of the cliff and could hardly get down. . . . There is something quite mysterious to me which I cannot communicate, in early scenes — not pleasurable, I can't tell why. When the Bowdens in 1836 took me to Ham, my pain was most piercing. I had no pleasure — yet I am drawn to them. I cannot understand it. I have seen the sea but once (in 1835) since 1833.'

1833 . . . and a few weeks later, on the anniversary of Froude's death, he was saying to Keble, thinking of all the changes since then, 'yet how short a time it seems since we had dear R. H. F. with us'.

Thus at the beginning and end of this strange submerging in the tide of other people's feelings, their hatred or their grieving, and in the suffering of their suffering, Newman was taken back, not so much by chance as by the duties of friendship, to childhood and the sea : to the way to that island paradise where the devil met him, and to the house where the little child asked the meaning of his existence. So now this death was completed ; he had gone back to the beginning and brought the whole of himself into that unity which he obscurely felt was necessary before he could act, for it must be an offering, a sacrifice of the whole man. It felt like death, and he called himself, more than once, a dead man ; yet now was the time when he was suddenly possessed with the idea of his book, so strongly that he felt he must begin it at once, in spite of weakness and weariness, must get it out of himself into the objective world : and then the delusion would vanish, if it was a delusion. And if it was the truth, it should be obeyed.

So he went back to Oxford, already dead to the university which had been his life so long, and it was Lent already, Ash Wednesday came early this year, on February 5th, and that was the day he heard, hardly caring whether he heard it or not, that the Hebdomadal Board proposed to introduce into Convocation a formal censure on Tract 90.

1845

'*Scattering the ashes of the dead*'

THE proposed censure of Tract 90, introduced only nine days before the Convocation, took the Tractarians by surprise. They had for months been preparing for battle on behalf of W. G. Ward ; even those who disliked his book, *The Ideal of a Christian Church*, were opposed to his being censured and deprived of his degrees, the measures which were to be put to the vote. Pusey, who certainly did not hold, with Ward, 'the full cycle of Roman doctrine', was shocked that degradation should be applied to the Catholic-minded members of the Church, while the extreme Protestants, who disbelieved in Baptism, and the liberals, who rationalized both doctrine and Scripture, got off scot-free. 'What should you think', he said, 'of a judge who punished adultery with death and appointed a murderer to high station ?'

Newman was also disgusted with the measure, though till then he had been inclined to think 'Ward can take care of himself'. In spite of Ward's tiresome habit of pumping him, Newman liked him, and had once reproached Tom Mozley for something he had said to Ward. 'Did you know him better you would not treat him in such a way that anyone else but a person so singularly sweet tempered as he (for this is his strong point, from being fat I suppose) would have taken offence at it.' This had been in the year after the Tract 90 row, when Ward was already shocking everybody with his Romanist views. The famous book had come out last summer, in 1844 ; Newman did not care for it. The title indicates why : Ward thought of the Church as an ideal to be realized, Newman saw it as a fact to be found.

The attack on Ward followed an unsuccessful attempt at the end of the preceding year to introduce a new Test besides the Articles. It had failed because the liberals, a growing party, though they would have liked to have got rid of the Tractarians, had no desire for a Test even more stringent than the Articles. Of this measure Newman had remarked to Mrs. Bowden : 'The Vice Chancellor would be able and would not scruple to summon a Tutor before him for his lectures on the Articles on the information of his pupils : it would be the reign of Golightlyism. The Statute should have contained another clause, creating a new office for a personage to be called the Oculus Vice Cancellarii and nominating G. to the place.' He could still joke about Golightly even after all his spying and informing.

The Test failed and left the anti-Tractarians dissatisfied, even after they had taken up the case against Ward. To condemn Ward would after all only be a gesture, and Ward represented no one but himself. Nearest to him in views was Frederick Oakeley, whose chapel in Margaret Street was the centre of the London Tractarians. The degradation of Ward would not even affect them and would not condemn the far larger body of Anglo-Catholics who followed Pusey and Newman. Even in September 1844, before the popular outburst against Newman, Hawkins had said to his friends : 'Tract 90 is the real mischief. . . . Admit that interpretation and you have no real remedy against Romanism.' He had used Tract 90 as a private test ; if it could be formally condemned it could be used publicly and with authority. To make the detested Tract a weapon against Catholicizing clergymen would be far more satisfactory than kicking Ward out of Oxford. As well, the university would be backing up the Bishops' censure both of the Tract and its author. And it would force Newman to give up his Fellowship, if the terms on which he held it (by oath) were invalidated. If he did not surrender of his own accord, he too could be degraded and deprived. Evangelicals like Symons, the new Vice Chancellor, who had hunted down Pusey, and liberals like Whately, were at one with the conservatives in approving the introduction of a censure on Tract 90.

The Tractarians did their best in the nine days. Charles Marriott brought out a printed Protest, Gladstone said in public that he felt 'indignation at this prospect to treat Mr. Newman worse than a dog'. Churton was scornful of the 'attempt to overwhelm Newman with Ward, Achilles with Thersites junior'. They felt it chiefly as an attack on Newman, unfair in that the Tract had been four years in print and because he had retired from all public action. Pusey wrote to a friend, 'To me the condemnation of N. when he has retired successively from every means of influence and has won more souls to Christ than any beside, is beyond measure dreadful. I should expect some dreadful chastisement to follow. "They entreated him shamefully and beat him and sent him away empty." He has been, to an amazing extent, God's messenger to us for the good of souls, and now men would cast him out.'

The only person who did not care was Newman ; he half hoped for the condemnation, which he could have taken as a sign that it was time to move. He said to James Mozley, 'I am, as I was saying last week, and as the *English Churchman* has said since, as though a dead man, and Hebdomadal Boards can do me neither good nor harm'. The *English Churchman* had spoken of 'scattering the ashes of the dead'. Two days before the Convocation Newman wrote to Jemima : 'Although I mean to keep silence myself, for really I am not bound to come forward and play the Scaramouch for the amusement of the *Standard* and *Record* papers, yet I am anxious lest things may happen to make it cruel to my friends so to act. However, there is no good in one's bothering oneself beforehand — so goodbye.' He did not go to the Theatre.

The famous meeting took place on February 13th, a cold snowy day, and aroused so much excitement that pictures of Ward and accounts of the proceedings appeared even in such papers as the *Illustrated London News*. Ward spoke for an hour and a half in his own defence, several times declaring 'I hold all Roman doctrine'. There was a large majority in favour of condemning his book, a much smaller one for his degradation, but both measures were passed. Then the proposed censure on Tract 90 was brought forward and pandemonium broke loose, everybody yelling for or against. In the middle of it arose the two Proctors, Guillemard and Church, and Guillemard, the senior, shouted their veto. Tremendous jubilation from all the Tractarians ! And when the company issued forth crowds of undergraduates were waiting to cheer Ward ; their cheers bursting into laughter as the good-natured fat philosopher slipped in the snow and fell down, scattering the papers of his speech broadcast. But they snowballed the Vice Chancellor's retinue. Symons was not popular among the junior members of the University.

So Ward was condemned and Tract 90 was spared. Newman was grateful to Church for his friendly act, but what could it all mean to him now ? It only showed the loyalty of the friends he would soon have to leave. Nor was there much doubt but that without the veto, the University would have rejected him.

1845

Development in Action

NEWMAN made a false start on his *Essay on Development* ; it would not come right, and no wonder, for he was exhausted from the stress of the winter, and tiresome worries seemed to arrive from every direction.   In February a young man called Thomas Meyrick, who had been staying at Littlemore, rushed home in a state of nervous breakdown, making all sorts of wild accusations against Newman, among them that he had extracted a promise from him not to join the Church of Rome.   On this point Newman wrote to set his mind at rest.   'Your letter to me this morning was most kind and this must seem most heartless,' said poor Meyrick.   After he was received he wrote to confess the things he had said against Newman and to ask forgiveness.   'He is a very aimiable and very clever fellow, — but it is impossible to say how he will turn out', said Newman.   Meyrick was to have many ups and downs trying to follow his vocation with the Jesuits.

Then there was Dalgairns, longing to begin a new life, but unable to get his parents to see it as anything but a disaster.   Newman wrote to his father, praising Dalgairns, and trying to reconcile his family by pointing out that he was wasting his life and talents at present.   'He will have a place to fill, a duty to discharge, whereas he, as some others, is at present cast out of society, disowned by all, with a burning heart and an idle hand.'   Dalgairns, however, the first to come, stayed on till the end.

Newman's brother Charles was in trouble and his family had begun to fear he was insane.   According to a plan of Frank's, he had been persuaded to attend Bonn University, where at first he was happy, studying Kant.   But presently he began to quarrel with everybody.   'I was obliged to carry a weapon about', he said, 'to repel the insults aimed at me by several of the students.'   Finally he was sent to gaol for not paying his rent (he had a feud with his landlord) and said he preferred it to his lodgings.   'I found much better people there than I have found anywhere in Bonn.' He added in his lofty way, 'It is necessary that my relations should familiarize themselves with this idea'. It was all part of his Socialism. He had sold his clothes, including the coat that Frank had given him, and John's watch ; then he hurt his foot. But somehow he got back to England, and Frank managed to persuade him to see a doctor. He was pronounced sane, though Frank could not help feeling he had 'a kind of moral insanity'. Charles stayed some time with Harriett and Tom Mozley, and with various doctors. Finally John and Frank decided that they had better make him a regular allowance, to be sent in small instalments, so that he would not squander it at once. This suited Charles quite well. He eventually settled in Tenby, which was a popular health resort in those days, in lodgings with a sympathetic landlady. There he lived simply, wrote pamphlets and rigmarole letters to his brothers, criticizing their characters and enjoying an argument with Frank, who, according to him, was the maddest of a mad family. His mental stability improved as time went on, but during this summer none of his family quite knew what night not happen.

Frank was always more friendly to John when he seemed to be a failure. He urged him to follow his conscience and begged him to count on his person and his house 'as if it were that of a most congenial and *united* brother'. He would take on the burden of Charles entirely if John were to lose his income 'suppose by becoming an R.C. or anything else, for which system I have no sympathy'. He regarded religions as a matter of choice, and urged John to start one of his own ; with his followers and wide influence he could do much more good than by joining the antiquated and unimportant body of English Roman Catholics. John's comment, in a note, was : 'That I could be contemplating questions of Truth and Falsehood never entered into his imagination !' But he thanked Frank for his kindness — this was in August — and briefly explained his position. 'I think the English Church in schism. I think the faith of the Roman Church the only true religion. I do not think there is salvation out of the Church of Rome. This of course does not interfere with my thinking an exception is made for those who are in involuntary ignorance . . . I am no longer in such ignorance.' Frank was pleased to receive his confidence. 'I have no new feeling towards you,' he announced, 'except a lamentation that you are *now* so in the power of others as to lose no small part of your personality.' And he warned John that a convert so important 'will be bound by all the chains which the experience of confessors teaches them how to use towards those whose consciences they see to be devoted to the Church'. He had a Maria Monk view of it all.

In March, at the end of Lent, Newman began telling his family and friends that he intended to give up his Fellowship next autumn. This policy of advance warning meant that he laid himself open to strong emotional and moral pressure which, while it did not alter his conviction, made the prospect of his act more and more painful. Not a single member of his family, not one of his old friends, agreed with him. The friends who would have been with him, Froude, Wood and Bowden, were all dead. It was clear that Pusey and Keble would stay where they were, and could not for all their affection, see why he should do otherwise. When Harriett heard the news she broke silence — for she scarcely ever wrote to him now — to lament the fact, and to say what she thought of the Church of Rome. 'What can become of Anglicans when they have once joined it, I cannot imagine.' Jemima said, 'What can be worse than this ? It is like hearing that some dear friend must die. I cannot shut my eyes to this overpowering event that threatens any longer.'

Newman had always tried to prevent her shutting her eyes to it. He had begged her in the stress of last November to be open, not to be silent, but to tell him what she felt and allow him to tell her his feelings too : 'Indeed there can be no exercise of love between persons without this openness'. She admitted then that she 'could not help feeling a repulsion from that Church which has so many stains upon her', and later she told him she feared his influence. Newman told her that he did not want the responsibility of others as well as his own ; indeed, ever since his first doubts, he had never pressed his views on his family. Now she broke out with her real feelings, that he was making a dreadful mistake, and cutting himself off from them. 'I am much afraid, dear John, you may be taken by surprise by what I say, and expect I shall receive this event more easily.'

Newman was not so much surprised as made extremely miserable by her incomprehension. It induced a crisis in his attitude to the feelings and opinions of those he loved which can be seen in the letter he wrote in reply, for the tone of it changed in the middle. The beginning was a desperate appeal for understanding. 'O dear John can you have thought long enough ?' she had said. He began by reminding her that if he was to give anything worth giving he must not wait too long. 'I see men dying who were boys, almost children, when I was born. Pass a very few years and I am an old man. What means of judging can I have more than I have ? What maturity of mind am I to expect ?' As to his convictions, he could not see why he should be deciding to move except that he believed it to be right, and God's will for him to do so. 'At my time of life men love ease. I love ease myself. I am giving up a maintenance involving no duties and adequate to all my wants. What in the world am I doing this for (I ask *myself* this) except that I think I am called to do so ? I am making a large income by my sermons. I am, to say the very least, risking this ; the chance is that my sermons will have no further sale at all. I have a good name with many ; I am deliberately sacrificing it. I have a bad name with more : I am fulfilling all their worst wishes, and giving them their most coveted triumph. I am distressing all I love, unsettling all I have instructed or aided. I am going to those I do not know, and of whom I expect very little. Oh, what can it be but a stern necessity which causes this ? Pity me, my dear Jemima. What have I done thus to be deserted, thus to be left to take the wrong course, if it is wrong ?'

He told her (what Anne Mozley left out in her transcription) that if he were dying he would call for a priest : could it be right to live as he dared not die ? He felt quite anxious on journeys, lest an accident should cut him off suddenly. 'What is the difference between me and a poor profligate ? We both feel we have a work to do which is un-done.' 'Why should I distress your kind heart with all my miseries ?' he went on. 'Yet you must know them, to avoid the greater misery of looking at me externally and wondering and grieving over what seems incomprehensible.' There was a worse horror still that haunted him. 'Of course the human heart is mysterious. I may have some deep evil in me which I cannot fathom. . . . Continually do I pray that He would discover to me if I am under a delusion ; what can I do more ? What hope have I but in Him ? . . . All is against me — may He not add Himself as an adversary !'

He finished the letter on Palm Sunday, aware of a change in himself, though uncertain how it had come about. The tone is quite different ; this was the resolution, as far as he was concerned, of the problem of balancing the claims of truth with those of human affec-tion. 'I am somehow in better spirits this morning. Have I not a right to ask you not to say, as you have said in your letter, that I shall do wrong ? What right have you to judge me ? . . . Who has the right to judge me but my Judge ? . . . He may have purposes as merciful as they are beyond us. Let us do our best and leave the event to Him ; He will give us strength to bear. Surely I have to bear most ; and if I do not shrink from bearing it, others must not shrink. May I do my best ; am I not trying to do my best ? — may we not trust it will turn to the best ?'

Jemima answered with affection, sure he would do his best, but she could not admit he might be right. It was inevitable that their relationship should lose completeness once this divergence of view was plain, but Newman did not intend it to lose in depth and sympathy. In July he at last got Jemima to come and stay at Littlemore ; Copeland vacated his lodgings at Mrs. Barnes' for her, and St. John arranged for a shoulder of lamb and left a nosegay before he went on his holiday. She brought her eldest boy, Herbert, who had been delighted with a letter from his uncle because the writing was so clear he could read it himself. Newman dined with her, and they walked round the village calling on the villagers whom she had known when she lived at Iffley. He was sorry St. John was away, so that he missed finding out 'what a very sweet gentle person she was'. When Jemima went home she told Anne Mozley she was pleased to hear such praises of Copeland from Mrs. Barnes ; if he stayed the people 'would not go far astray'. Yet Newman had never told the villagers anything about his doubts ; he attended the services in the church till the end and they did not know why he left. If their Mr. Newman chose to live in the old stables, that was just his way. But nothing, said one old woman, seemed quite the same when he had gone.

Newman remained open with Jemima, writing fully and naturally about what he was doing, both before and after his conversion ; he respected her views and did not obtrude his own. But she was not able to respond. She shut out of her mind everything and everyone connected with his new life and at last her silence destroyed his confidence ; she reduced their correspondence, and with it their relationship, to trivialities. This process was not complete till after Newman returned to England in 1848, when Jemima's husband more or less showed him the door, but it was beginning now. On Palm Sunday, however Newman had realized that there was a point beyond which he could not go in subjecting his actions and feelings to others ; he had a right to his own. To submit further would be weakness, not humility.

At the end of April, alone at Littlemore, he wrote to Henry : 'Carissime, since I have no one to talk to, I write to you, a poor compliment perhaps. Tell St. John I have just got his letter — and tell him that his letters are like violets in my forlorn estate. How

thankful I ought to be that if I lose some friends I gain others.'
The reason why he wanted to talk to Henry was because Blanco
White's posthumous autobiography had just appeared — 'the most
dismal and horrible book I ever saw'. Reading through the disintegration of Blanco White's Christianity, the intellectual process
from belief to unbelief, Newman felt that he had long known 'the
lie of the country'. As early as *The Arians* he had said that the
consequence of giving up the idea of Christ's Divinity would be
Pantheism — the belief that there was no divinity beyond the world,
that life was the only divine essence. People did not see the ultimate
consequences of giving up belief in God. 'They really do think it is
no harm whatever being an Atheist, so that you are sincerely so, and
do not cut people's throats and pick their pockets.'

So he was led on to consider the problem of the relation of personal
sincerity to objective truth. He knew Blanco White was sincere, and
had given up country and friends 'all for an idea of truth, or rather
for liberty of thought'. 'I see B. W. going wrong but sincere —
Arnold going wrong yet sincere. They are a puzzle to me. I can
put my finger on this or that point in their character, and say, there
was the fault. But *they* did not know the fault — and so it comes
upon me, How do I know that I too have not my weak points which
occasion me to think as I think ? . . . This is what is so very horrifying,
as you may suppose.' He did not answer his question ; other people,
then and now, have answered it for him, and think they have found
the unconscious fault he was looking for. It is doubtful whether
these critics have tested their own motives as stringently as Newman
tested his. As to the two who puzzled him, the Catholic priest who
had reasoned away his faith, and the Protestant moralist who had
used his reason to scale down Christianity to suit himself, did they
test their own sincerity, or their intellectual arguments ? Can one
imagine Blanco White submitting himself to the scrutiny of another
man, as Newman did to Keble ? Or Arnold keeping silence for fear
he was under a delusion ? Or either of them, upon the onset of
intellectual doubt, taking at once to a rigorous course of fasting,
penance and prayer ? They assumed their own sincerity, as they
assumed that their individual human reasoning powers were sufficient
to discover the meaning of things. Newman made neither of these
assumptions ; he tested his own sincerity by every means he could
think of, as keenly as he tested his intellectual conclusions, and submitted both to the unknown will of God.

Blanco White spoke with affection of Newman in his book, and this touched him. But it also made him realize, quite suddenly, how he had appeared to other people during his youth and prime. At the time he had been so entirely concentrated on the great work, personal and public, of reviving Catholic ideas and practice, that he had only seen his position from the inside. Now, as if in a mirror, he suddenly saw 'Newman'. He found this very bewildering. 'It seems as if people were just now beginning to praise me when I was going. . . . Their praises are valedictions, funeral orations. I do not think it raises feelings of elation as to what I *am* — at least B. W. has not — because he speaks of what is gone and over — it hardly seems I that he speaks of — I this old dry chip who am worthless but of a past I.'

In contrast it showed up, with sudden objective clarity, the conduct of others towards him. 'My friends who have had means of knowing me have spoken against me. Whately and Hawkins have both used opprobrious language about me, till I began to think myself really deceitful and double dealing. Golightly has known me only to lift up his hand against me and to accuse me of many things of which I am guiltless. Eden, who has come near enough to know me, has shown no tenderness, no real respect, no gratitude. Others have kept silent in my greatest troubles. The mass of men in Oxford who knew me a little have shown a coldness and suspicion which I did not deserve . . . I have not thought of all this *indeed* — it comes to me now as a *new* thought, by the contrast of what B. W. says of me, which is like light showing the previous darkness. I say to myself, "Is it possible, was I this ?" And then a second set of feelings succeeds — "It is over". My spring, my summer are over — and what has come of it ? It seems B. W. thought so-and-so of me — others then I suppose thought in a degree the same, but what has come of it ? Heads of Houses whom I have known have been unkind to me and have set the fashion ; and now my prime of life is past and I am nothing.'

It could not but set him wondering to discover that people had thought so highly of his gifts and yet that he had so relentlessly been kept from the position in which he should have exercised them, 'the tuition or the oversight of young men'. It fidgeted him, he said, not morally, but intellectually, to think what his influence might have been in his proper place in the university 'when it has been what it is among people who never saw me'. Thus he had been kept out of the very work for which everyone admitted he had been especially endowed and trained, and which he felt to have been his vocation. It was a mystery which was to haunt him again, still more painfully. 'And now it is all gone and over, and there is no redress, no retrieving — and I say with Job "O that it were with me as in years past when the candle of the Lord shone on me" — and yet, Charissime, I don't think anything of ambition or longing is mixed with these feelings, as far as I can tell. I am so desperately fond of my own ease like an old batchelor, that having duties, being in office, is an idea insupportable to me. Rather I think of it in the way of justice — and with a sort of tenderness towards my former self, now no more.'

The whole period through which that dead self lived, for he was looking at it from the grave, now appeared in perspective, an external history, and he was struck by the injustice of the treatment he had received, the harshness of the judgments of his seniors and the ingratitude of juniors ; what had he done to deserve all this ? For he had not attacked them, had not even retorted on them when they attacked him. Perhaps the most curious thing about this realization is that he was to do exactly the same at the end of another fourteen years, when he saw, for the first time, how his course as a Catholic had gone, on the human level. He never realized it while it was happening because he was absorbed in his object.

For the first time, now, but by no means the last, Newman learned from Albany Christie, a young Tractarian studying medicine in London, that people were 'ascribing (I can hardly get myself to write it) so sad a thing as scepticism to you'. He was surprised, but he knew it was not an impossibility. To Pusey he said : 'I thank God that He has shielded me morally from what intellectually might easily come upon me — general scepticism. Why should I believe the most sacred and fundamental doctrines of our faith, if you cut off from me the ground of development ? But if that ground is given me, I must go further.'

The *Development*! All that he had done so far was now scrapped. His spirits and energy were rising again. When he told Mrs.Froude that he intended to give up his Fellowship in the autumn he said : 'My mind is certainly in a very different state from what it was this time year. It is so made up.' And he added, 'I am getting more callous about consequences, from feeling that there are dangers on all sides, on any course of conduct, so my mind is like the nautical needle in a box cased all round with iron. With love to W(illiam) and all the little children, especially dear R. H. F.' For there was now another little Richard Hurrell Froude.

Summer was here and the book must be done before he could act. By June he was right in the glorious exhausting struggle of it ; and it began to grow, it began to be. Although the longest and perhaps the most complex of his works it was done in four months, though he would never call it finished. As a writer he was careful, full of second thoughts. To Mrs. Froude he wrote : 'Perhaps one gets over-sensitive even about style as one gets on in life — Besides re-writing, every part has to be worked out and defined as in moulding a statue. I get on, as a person walks with a lame ankle, who does get on and gets to his journey's end — but not comfortably. Now after all this you will expect the work to be something out of the way — alack, that is the worst of it — it is much cry and little wool. However, I must do my best and then leave it. I sleep very soundly and am very cheerful externally and now you know pretty well nearly all about me.'

How Newman ever got his books written is a mystery, for he always had half a hundred other things pressing on him at the same time. There were the endless letters to answer, the hours of prayer to observe, the old people to visit in the 'refuge for the destitute' built in 1843, where he had jokingly said he had better retire himself. There was Elizabeth Lenthall bearing the pains of the martyrs in Oxford ; he was still visiting her. She died in July and when Newman went to her funeral it was the last time he was in St. Mary's. There was a continual stream of visitors, worried Tractarians from London or further afield seeking advice, others coming to retreat, some, like Richard Stanton, to stay and join the party living there ; there were also callers from Oxford, who came to dissuade Newman from going over to Rome.

'Barter came up to Littlemore to tell me there was something like madness in my family,' Newman noted on a letter of his, 'or at least great oddity and liability to twists — and this ought to be an intimation to me not to leave the Church of England.' Reports of Newman's madness were circulated after his conversion for some years ; even Robert Wilberforce talked of it. Burgon, the future author of *Twelve Good Men* (including Eden) arrived to deliver a lecture. 'Burgon, well-intentioned fellow, came up and preached to me besides writing this letter,' Newman noted on it. The letter was a thick wad of mournful expostulation. 'Is it fair, is it kind, is it like you — now to turn round and tell us — *what* I know not : perhaps you will not think fit to tell us *anything*. . . . I admit you have had much to bear. . . . We are grown refined and well-bred — it would be shocking and revolting in the extreme to *burn* Mr. Newman ; but we may torture him in a new way and nobody will be shocked at all.'

But Mr. Newman had survived this new form of torture and was not to be turned aside. The letters he got now were more amusing than heart-rending. Westmacott, his old school-fellow, who had done the bust in 1841, wrote to remonstrate, and when Newman carefully gave his reasons, suggested that he had been 'too long cloistered'. Newman replied, 'I am amused at your calling me "cloistered" — it is true, but I am a sharper fellow than you think'. People were inclined to imagine that because he lived a special kind of life he knew nothing of the ways of the world. Some, like an old lady called Mrs. Jones, disapproved of his being cloistered at all ; her stern reprimand on the subject of celibacy ought to approve itself to many to-day who think any perversion more natural than virginity. 'Consider too how often men attempting to live like angels here in their bodies have failed and brought discredit on their sincerity when they did but mistake the powers of their nature. . . . When our clergy live like other good men, how are they blessed, and how do we see their offspring considered and provided for, and the virtues imparted to them diffusing a benefit throughout society.'

There were invited visitors, as well as the unwanted ; Jemima and Herbert, and earlier Mrs. Bowden and her little girls. But Marianne was suddenly and seriously ill ; Newman was anxious about her, relieved at her recovery, worried that it proved so slow. None of Bowden's children were strong. Newman was writing a preface for Bowden's posthumous book, and consulting his widow on it. Then there was Pusey to see off to Ilfracombe. 'How very sad it is to be wounding so many', said Newman to Mrs. Bowden. 'And he is just one of those determined not to look trouble in the face and now that at last he believes it is to be, he is trying to smooth it over — as if it involved no great separation necessarily. God grant it may not! but it is well to expect the worst and then everything is gain, that is a shade better.' Friends kept writing to know what he was going to do ; he could only think of how long the book would take — when it was done he would move, before Christmas probably. 'The nearest and dearest friends are, I think (as they necessarily must) getting annoyed about me,' he told Mrs. Froude, 'and the stupid ungrateful feeling comes upon me in consequence that I am a trouble to everyone I address.'

Of course people did not understand about his book, they

imagined it was a mere manifesto in favour of Rome. Perhaps his companions at Littlemore realized something of what it would be, when they saw him standing at his high desk, writing, re-writing for hours on end, all the hours he could get. The strain told on him and to them he seemed to be getting thinner and paler as the work went on, absorbing his energy. Feeling tired, he began to shrink at the thought of winter coming. It made him remember the misery of the year before. 'I dread this winter', he confessed to William Froude in September, recalling the 'illness' he had made so little of at the time. 'But there is nothing to show for it so to say . . . I am quite sure I am not really unwell, only pulled down.' In the same letter he wrote, 'And so I say of little Hurrell — it would rejoice me indeed to set eyes upon him, but this is not the time of year for a child to travel'.

Perhaps there was another reason for putting off that visit. The younger members of the household at Littlemore could wait no longer and were making their own arrangements for reception into the Catholic Church. Dalgairns, whose parents, still very much against the change, were coming to Oxford on October 1st, decided that it would save them pain in the end if he could meet them as a Catholic. He was nearly twenty-seven. He wrote to Father Dominic, suddenly urgent after all these years, asking how soon it could be done. Very happily did Father Dominic reply, inviting him at once to Stone, where he had founded the first Passionist house in England. 'Dear Littlemore I love thee!' he exclaimed. 'A little more still and we shall see happy results from Littlemore. When the learned and holy Superior of Littlemore will come, then I hope we shall see again the happy days of Augustine, Lanfranc and Thomas. England will be once more the Isle of Saints. . . . I am afraid to tire you with my bad handwriting. *Vale, carissime, et ora pro me.*' That must have sounded familiar to Dalgairns! So he went off to Stone and was received on the feast of St. Michael and All Angels. He came straight back to Littlemore, and Newman, who was just about to send in his resignation to the Provost, wrote to Mrs. Bowden, 'If you could see how happy and altered D. is, you would wonder — I cannot describe it, but it is the manner of a person entrusted with a great gift, though to a stranger he might seem the same'.

Ambrose St. John, three years older than Dalgairns, had also resigned his Studentship at Christ Church and went to Prior Park, near Bath, where he was received on October 2nd, the feast of the holy Guardian Angels, an appropriate feast for him. The next day

Newman sent his resignation to the Provost.   In acknowledging it
Hawkins said : 'And yet I cannot forbear expressing the most earnest
hope (in all sincerity and with feelings of real kindness) that whatever
course you may have resolved upon, you may still be saved from some
of the worst errors of the Church of Rome, praying to human mediators or falling down before Images — because in you, with all the
advantages with which God has blessed and tried you, I must believe
such a course to be most deeply sinful.   But may He protect you!'

Newman wrote to tell his friends that he had resigned his Fellowship and that 'anything may happen to me any day'.   For suddenly,
although the book was not yet complete, he found he had finished
his journey ; the whole man, mind and heart at one, could present
himself to God and be sure that he was doing what he must do with
no other motive than to obey what he believed to be the call of truth.
And now that he *was* certain, the impetuosity he had accused himself
of in retreat, and which was there under all the restraint that had
seemed like delay, suddenly took charge.   St. John must return at
once, Stanton, who had gone off to seek reception elsewhere, must
come back and be received with him ; Father Dominic was to pass
through Oxford on his way abroad and Dalgairns had asked him to
visit Littlemore.   The book was left at the end of a sentence ; the
time had come at last.   It was too good, too providential a chance to
miss ; he could make his general confession to Father Dominic,
whom he knew, and be received here at Littlemore and get the final
step over before anyone could find him out or pry into what he was
doing.   People have talked of Newman's secrecy, as if it were a kind
of mental aberration, but who that had suffered the heartless publicity of the year before would have risked telling anyone his intentions ?   Besides that, he hated to make a fuss, especially about
anything important.

Dalgairns was to meet the coach at three in the afternoon on
October 8th. He later told how 'As I was taking up my stick Newman
said to me in a very low and quiet tone : "When you see your friend,
will you tell him that I wish him to receive me into the Church of
Christ ?" I said "Yes" and no more. I told Father Dominic as he
was dismounting from the top of the coach. He said "God be
praised" and neither of us spoke again till we reached Littlemore.'

It was very late and pouring with rain, the coach had been
delayed by the weather.   Father Dominic had had five hours of it
on top of the coach and was soaked.   They took a chaise out to
Littlemore, arriving about eleven at night. 'I took up my position

by the fire to dry myself', he wrote later to his Superiors. 'The door opened — and what a spectacle it was for me to see at my feet John Henry Newman begging me to hear his confession and admit him into the bosom of the Catholic Church! And there by the fire he began his general confession with extraordinary humility and devotion.'

Earlier that week Newman had stayed indoors all day preparing himself for this confession. It had to be finished next day. Something of what he felt on this occasion, which seems to have been described by everyone except himself, can be gathered from a letter to Mrs. Bowden the next spring, advising her about last-minute trials of spirit. 'Of course I should call them artifices of the enemy. The moment before acting may be, as can easily be imagined, peculiarly dreary — the mind may be confused — no reason for acting may be forthcoming in our mind — and the awful greatness of the step in itself, and without any distinct apprehension of its consequences, may weigh on us. Some persons like to be left to themselves in such a crisis — others find comfort in the presence of others — I could do nothing but shut myself up in my room and lie down on my bed.' Perhaps this withdrawal is the origin of the legend that Newman was half fainting, or in a state of physical and emotional collapse at his reception.

The next morning Father Dominic walked down to St. Clement's to say mass, acquainted the priest, Mr. Newsham, with the situation, and returned in the pouring rain. He heard the rest of Newman's confession and those of Richard Stanton and Frederick Bowles. In the evening at six o'clock, as Father Dominic reported, 'they made their profession of faith in the usual form in their private Oratory, one after another, with such fervour and piety that I was almost out of myself with joy'. He gave them conditional Baptism — baptized them with the proviso 'if you have not been baptized before' — the usual procedure if there was any doubt that the sacrament had not been properly administered. This caused much misunderstanding at the time in Anglican circles; people thought it meant Catholics regarded them as heathens. The next morning Father Dominic said mass in the tiny chapel, using a writing desk of Henry Wilberforce's as an altar, and he gave them all communion. St. John, Dalgairns, Bowles and Stanton were there with Newman. After mass he walked round to see the Woodmasons, one of the two families who had made Littlemore 'quite genteel' and received the husband and wife and two daughters. The rest of the family hesitated. but came in later.

Newman marked his first communion with a little cross in his diary.

Father Dominic had to leave on Saturday after mass. Writing to his Superiors of Newman he said, 'In my judgment he is one of the most humble and lovable men I have met in my life'. Of him, at the same time, Newman was writing to Mrs. Bowden, 'I wish all persons were as charitable as he. I believe he is a very holy man'. Before he went, Father Dominic suggested moderation in their 'practices of penance' which he, a member of an austere Order devoted to Christ's Passion, called extraordinary. He was pleased that they were under Wiseman's jurisdiction; 'they will do what he tells them, for they are docile and teachable beyond words'.

That day Mr. Newsham called; Bloxam said he was the same priest on whom Newman had called years ago, when he was curate of St. Clement's, and, not knowing who he was, had asked him why he did not come to church. If so, it was a curious coincidence. Twenty years had gone by, and Mr. Newman had become one of the most famous, or infamous men in England; and Mr. Newsham was still the Catholic priest in Oxford. Next day, Sunday, the five converts walked down to the Catholic chapel in St. Clement's to attend mass. What a surprise for everybody, Catholic and Protestant alike! Newman had actually achieved the feat of going over to Rome without anybody, even Golightly, knowing anything about it.

1845–1846

'Going out on the open sea'

NEWMAN now reaped some reward for the care he had taken to prepare his friends for his act; at least it could not be a shock to them. While he was waiting for Father Dominic, all that pouring wet day, he wrote about thirty letters to those he felt ought to have the news direct from himself. One was to his old Aunt; Anne Mozley, always inclined to be sentimental, thought his hand was shaking with emotion, not realizing the fatigue of writing the same thing thirty times over. 'I can scarcely bear to think you should have written it', said Rogers in reply to his, but he ended, 'perhaps it is presumptuous but I cannot help saying God bless you for all the great kindness you have shown me.'

Letters came pouring in, from distressed friends, from Catholic priests who had been praying for him, from converts. Ward's wife wrote; she had had a difficult beginning to her married life, for Ward had no sooner been kicked out of Oxford for being practically a Roman priest than he announced his engagement, shocking the earnest and amusing the rest. Typically he explained himself in a letter to *The Times*: 'so complimentary to the lady', as James Mozley remarked. The Wards had been received not long before Newman; Ward was soon to be given a post at St. Edmund's College, Ware, where he taught theology to future priests. This unprecedented step, a convert and a married layman teaching in a seminary, was to have far-reaching effects, though not due to Ward's status, but to his remorselessly theorizing mind. Among Newman's pile of letters were two very different communications: an Apostolic Blessing from the Pope, Gregory XVI, and a note from Norris, the college servant, thanking for his generous parting present.

The immediate practical result of Newman's reception was the loss of even the precarious measure of peace he had secured before. As soon as his act was known everyone expected him to leave Little-more at once. Jemima even told him so in a letter which arrived the

same evening as Father Dominic ; Newman answered it at 5.30 a.m.
the next day, before he was received. 'Why should I go if I think
I am right, as one of a large body which is poured over the earth, and
of which the whole earth is the inheritance according to the prophecies ? Of course I must think any other body to be a usurper, as
having no place, according to the Divine Scheme, in any part of
the earth.' He added, 'All this is quite consistent with believing, as
I firmly do, that individuals in the English Church are invisibly knit
into that True Body of which they are not outwardly members ; and
consistent, too, with thinking it highly injudicious, indiscreet, wanton,
to interfere with them in particular cases'. Aunt was just such a case,
and Newman was most relieved to see her handwriting, when she
sent him a note in Jemima's letter. Jemima replied in grieved tones :
'Dear John, when you spoke in the name of our Church your exhorta-
tions were all powerful, your voice seemed the voice of an angel, you
touched a chord in all our hearts — you seemed to know our very
hearts. Since your new views have gained the ascendancy, how great
the change !' Yet she herself, and many others, were not able, as he
had suggested, to separate the individuals from the body to which they
adhered, and respect their integrity while not recognizing its claims.

As for leaving Littlemore, Newman said : 'So far from its being
a sacrifice to go, as you suppose, it is a great trial to remain — to
remain in the midst of known faces, perplexed, and whose perplexity
I cannot possibly relieve — to remain in a place where I have myself
built up a system against myself : to remain where there are no
outward tokens or means of Catholic Communion. It is said, that
the one support of persons in my case has been the daily Mass —
now mass is only twice a week at St. Clement's, and at a distance of
two or three miles. Nor is it a slight trial, as you may suppose, except
as faith overcomes it, to go to what to outward appearance is a
meeting house.'

St. Clement's chapel stood back from the road, next to an inn.
It was a plain rectangular building of yellow local stone, with a
classical front, and an alcove inside for the altar, flanked by Corinthian
pillars. There were probably no statues ; Catholics had got so used
to hiding everything that differentiated them from their suspicious
neighbours that they even referred to mass, circumspectly, as
'prayers' or 'duties'. Frederick Oakeley came to stay at Littlemore,
and was received by Mr. Newsham in St. Clement's chapel. He
remembered, long after, that now the antiphons of the Blessed Virgin
were heard in the chapel of the house at Littlemore. 'I have always

looked on Littlemore as under the special protection of St. Mary,'
Newman told Jemima, 'and so many providential circumstances have
brought and fixed me where I am, that I fear to move.' There were
practical difficulties too. 'Where am I to go ? — am I to take a house
for my books in the first town I come to ? It is easy to advise, very
difficult to form a plan.'

But soon circumstances made his way plainer. In the first place
his younger companions did not want to separate from him ; they
had all been drawn both to him and to live a kind of regular life, and
hoped to find a common vocation. Newman himself did not expect
to be a priest ; he felt it was not right, after taking so prominent a
part in a schismatic communion, to offer himself. But the others
must go where they could be trained for the priesthood. Dalgairns
had already decided to go to France ; he had left Littlemore by the
end of October, when Father Dominic visited his converts again.
He sent them to Oscott to receive confirmation from Wiseman, who
was now their Bishop, on the Feast of All Saints.

It was Newman's first visit to Oscott, and the first time he had
met Wiseman since he had seen him in Rome in 1833. With St.
John and Walker, he was shown upstairs into a small airy room
looking out over a distant view of Birmingham, the great growing
mass of small factories and smaller red houses that was soon to be
Newman's own field of work, though he had no idea of it now.
Wiseman came in with Mr. Spencer, the convert priest with whom
Newman had refused to dine, on principle, and Bernard Smith,
whose secession had occasioned the first public outburst against
Newman's double dealing — he could hardly have chosen companions more likely to increase the embarrassment of the meeting.
Bernard Smith had visited Littlemore in June to spy out the land ;
Newman had turned up for dinner in grey trousers, which Smith
assured Wiseman was a deliberate hint that he now regarded himself
as a layman. 'I know the man', said Smith. He did not know the
man very well. Newman, in fact, still thought his orders probably
valid ; he even scrupled at re-ordination, though his doubts on this
score were set at rest before Christmas by Bishop Griffiths of the
London District, who explained that even Roman orders were conferred again, if there was any doubt of their validity. The idea that
Newman put on grey trousers as a signal to Bernard Smith is ludicrous, but has been repeated many times. The last thing he wanted,
in June, was a great buzzing at Oscott. Did Smith imagine he had
bought his trousers specially for such an occasion ?

Wiseman himself was embarrassed at this meeting, and could think of nothing to say except to inquire about their journey. Newman was seized with one of his fits of disabling shyness and the others talked hard about nothing to cover the silence. Wiseman literally jumped at the chance of escape when a message came that a boy wanted to go to confession.

This was a bad beginning, but things went better the next day. Newman, St. John and Oakeley were confirmed in Pugin's Gothic chapel; there were ten convert clergymen present. Newman took the name of Mary; in this way he expressed the devotion he always felt for her, the patron of every place with which he was associated. It was All Saints' Day. They were to leave Oscott on the Monday, but before they went much had been accomplished. In a private interview with Wiseman Newman offered him his book, the *Essay on Development*, promising to do with it whatever the Bishop said. Wiseman read it, and had the breadth of mind to decide that it should be printed as it was, without correction. Newman therefore published it on his own responsibility. Other things were discussed besides the book. Wiseman wrote to Dr. Russell of Maynooth, 'He opened his mind completely to me; and I assure you the Church has not received, at any time, a convert who has joined her in more docility and simplicity of faith than Newman'.

There is a note of relief in this, as in many similar remarks by Catholics at the time. Newman was so famous, so brilliant, that he was expected to stand on his dignity and perhaps to be difficult and full of his own importance. Wiseman found him almost too retiring and had to begin by persuading him that he should be a priest. Then there was the question of his young friends, who wanted to stay with him. They could not be expected to make up their minds all at once to offer themselves to an Order, or commit themselves severally to the Bishops of various dioceses. Wiseman wanted to help them to find their feet, and also to keep them near him; he suggested to Newman that they should move to Old Oscott college in the valley, from which they had all, clergy, students and schoolboys, migrated a few years before. There they could live together in community and begin their studies for the priesthood. It would be 'Littlemore continued', said Wiseman, and he himself would be their official Superior, and would lend a priest to say mass for them and be their spiritual director; Newman would keep the same position as he had now. They walked down the hill to look at the house. It was a large rambling building of red brick; the high

outside walls, with their windows barred for fear of intrusion, had an
unpromising look, but through the entrance door was a semicircular
pillared ambulatory, with a vine growing over it, and a big garden.
Inside, the rooms were plain, dark and undistinguished. 'It has
room for 20 or 30 persons — a chapel etc. but is dismally ugly',
Newman told Mrs. Bowden. He thought it looked like Sandford
Mill, near Oxford. Still, 'friends could be educated for orders
without separating from each other or from me'. He accepted
Wiseman's offer. The house he later rechristened Maryvale, a name
it has kept to this day.

They were not to go there till some time in the new year ; meanwhile Newman received many invitations to the various Catholic
Colleges and from some of the Bishops, which it seemed best to
accept. 'We must throw ourselves into the system', he said to St.
John. He was travelling to and fro all through November, in
December, and again in January. He went first to London, and
visited St. Edmund's College at Ware from there. It was a surprise
to find how indomitably English the Catholics were, and practical
in their religion, not at all the politically minded liberals Newman
had feared them to be. He liked the people he met at Ware, and
especially Robert Whitty, 'one of the most striking men I have seen',
he told St. John. 'I hope I see him as he is, for a more winning
person I have not met with, though an Irishman. I really seemed to
form a sudden friendship with him, as the ladies in "the Rovers".'
Whitty came to his rescue when he cut open his eyebrow walking
into a door in the dark. In the same letter Newman said, 'Everything
I saw impressed me with the one idea you got elsewhere, of *simplicity*'.
This was what they felt about him, so the pleasure of the meeting
was mutual.

While he was in London Newman gave Miss Giberne a helping
hand into the Church. She was in a state of great agitation, still
attending Margaret Chapel — though Oakeley had gone — but unable to take communion there. Pusey took the services ; he met
Miss Giberne and told her that though Newman 'had to go' he
should not be taken as an example ; Pusey offered to be her director.
Miss Giberne felt that what was good enough for Newman was
good enough for her, but till he turned up she had not the strength
of mind to take any initiative. 'It's quite easy', he assured her. He
had a cab at the door, she could come and see Father Brownbill, the
Jesuit, now. 'Not yet !' cried Miss Giberne, but she found herself
going all the same. She hung on to Newman's arm, afraid to meet

'the terrible Jesuit'. But he turned out quite gentle, even shy, and shook hands with her, which reassured her. She arranged to come again and when she went out Newman said, 'Now I'm content'. She wrote to him later when she had actually made the plunge. In her old age she recalled what an effort it had been to make her general confession. She stared at Father Brownbill's large red ear and thought, 'Now I have got to tell all my life to that ear!' But once she was a Catholic she was soon pressing all her friends to follow her. A little while later she grumbled to Newman that she was being treated like a child. 'Do you think Mr. Brownbill a clever and deeply learned man?' she asked. 'I do not. I shall never get accustomed to anyone but you.' Newman reminded her that converts had extraordinary gaps in their knowledge, and priests could hardly guess what they did and what they did not know. 'And after all, such unnecessary lectures are a good school for our pride', he said. 'And now I suppose you will say all this is an unnecessary lecture.'

Miss Giberne was by no means the only one who followed Newman's example. He had been so busy explaining himself to friends he felt were unlikely to do as he had done that he had not realized how many there were who were only waiting for his lead. The back pages of his diary rapidly filled up with the names of those to be prayed for, 'and all the converts' as he had to add soon. News of those coming or likely to come was passed to and fro, and he began to wonder whether his long wait at Littlemore, though necessary to him, might not have been dangerous to them. He realized that the psychological moment for turning conviction into action varies for everyone, and that some have to act quickly, or miss their chance. He became acute in discerning when someone needed a helping hand forward, and when it was better to think further.

Although he was surprised at the numbers who followed him, the newspapers were not, though they got more angry the more there were. They took to publishing lists of those who had 'embraced Popery' and headed paragraphs: 'More Perversions!' Exclamation marks sometimes ran into triples. Oakeley, as the London leader of the Tractarians, shared the chief publicity with Newman. Golightly was still busily writing to the papers; he was now exposing Jesuitry in the *Oxford and Cambridge Review* which had wickedly published an article on the Society by a young Catholic law-student. Golius declared: 'Our banner must be: God is my helper, and underneath it, No Peace with Popery'. But Newman was now out of reach of

Golightlyism. It was the Anglican Puseyites, including poor Pusey himself, who suffered from it.

Newman went from London to Oscott at the end of November, inadvertently arriving on the school gala day, St. Cecilia's feast, transferred from Saturday to Monday. The whole place was upside down. Newman and young Charlie Woodmason, whom he had brought with him, 'had to poke in as we might, leaving our luggage at the entrance'. The Oscott people seemed rather taken aback by his arrival, and apologized for all the turmoil. Newman wrote to Bowles at Littlemore, 'we were ushered into the boys' dining-room — the orchestra at the end and the tables plentifully laden for all hearers with cake and (pro pudor) punch — a very sensible way of hearing music. They certainly were scandalized by my detecting the punch — for they said again and again that it was made of lemon and sugar. All I can say is that *ours* at high table was remarkably stiff, and that I was obliged to dilute it to twice or thrice its quantity with water. The concert was capital, the voices remarkably good, and the instruments played with great spirit — but its gem was towards the end. Only fancy the Bishop, me and the whole of the good company, listening to Mynheer Vandunk in honor of St. Cecilia. And the worst is that the tune has been running in my head all this morning.'

By the time he wrote this letter Newman had guessed why there had been so many apologies for the merrymakings. Father Dominic had been writing to the *Tablet* boasting happily of the holiness and austerity of his converts, and the religious poverty at Littlemore. It was embarrassing, but as Newman wrote to St. John, 'One must bear the infliction as one does the stomach ache ; with the feeling that grumbling does no good'. Now he saw the reason for the way they treated him this time at Oscott, overawed and alarmed at the idea of his supposed austerity, and fearing he would disapprove their punch and cake and music. 'They have the most absurd notions about us', he said in his letter to Bowles. 'I think they fancy I never eat, and I have just lost a good dinner in consequence. After returning from Birmingham walking and hungry, I literally have had to pick up a crust from the floor left at breakfast and eat it, from shame at asking again and again for things.'

'This is a most portentously windy place', he told them at Littlemore. 'I am in the Stranger's Room — the chimney almost vibrating — my ankles fanned by a continuous stream of air, and the shrieking and screaming of the casements making me shiver. See what stuff I am putting in my letter for want of matter. But I can't help writing to dear Littlemore, now that I am a pilgrim at a distance from it. I suppose it is a good penance going from home.' He ended his St. Cecilia letter, 'I had more to tell you but Faber has been sitting here for an hour or more, and driven things from my head. This gas makes my head and eyes ache.'

Frederick Faber had been one of those temporarily held back by Newman's advice during the last two years ; he had been living an increasingly Roman, not to say Italian, life in his parish at Elton. On a visit to Rome he had picked up many Catholic devotions, which he practised before leaving the Anglican Church, shocking the fox-hunting gentry with his goings on. He was just over thirty, about the same age as Ambrose St. John. At Oxford he had been known as a poet, and in early portraits he looked the part, with the dark locks of poets of the Romantic period, and large lustrous eyes. An enthusiast, he charmed a great many people, and so fascinated his simple parishioners that there were dramatic scenes when he left, sobs and tears. He took with him a band of country youths, some hardly more than boys, who had been confessing to him, praying, and taking the discipline. At present he was living with them in Birmingham, in a house which, inside, was intended to make them feel they were in Italy, so full of pictures, statues and lights as to astonish some of the sturdy English Catholics who called. Faber was known as Brother Wilfrid, and his young men were known as Wilfridians, though he called them Brothers of the Will of God. Father Dominic, shrewd holy man, called them 'Brothers of the Will of Faber'. It was possibly Faber's excited conversation as well as the gas that made Newman's head ache.

Back at Littlemore in December Newman wrote to Dalgairns, now in France, and told him Father Dominic had written another letter in the *Tablet* 'which no one here can read with a grave face'. Newman's private affairs now came up in the Catholic *Tablet* as well as in the national papers ; both began to argue, taking different sides, as to whether he should have drawn his salary as a Fellow of Oriel while he had doubts about the Anglican Church. 'O my dear sir, cast this affair upon my shoulders and think no more about it', Father Dominic wrote to him. 'That ought rather to be restored to the Catholics which was taken from them by violence, but enough about this.' Newman replied that he himself had never thought he was bound to restitution.

Father Dominic invited them to Stone for Christmas, but Newman-

could not get there till New Year. 'Yes, yes, yes come by all means
with the Revd. St. John', he said. 'Oh! could we pass the Xmas
together! No matter; we shall at least finish one year and begin
another so that we may be two years together.' So Newman and
St. John saw the new year in with midnight Matins and mass at six,
'then a good breakfast' as Newman told Bowles, and several 'gossips
with Father Dominic'. A schoolgirl read her romantic poem on
Newman's conversion, 'poor thing, before Fr. Dominick and me',
Newman noted on his copy; it must have been difficult to keep a
straight face. Father Dominic had the lion's share of the youthful
author's admiration.

> Well may that holy smile now beam
> The scene would almost make
> Him fancy that it was a dream
> But no, he is awake.
>
> And one is kneeling at his feet
> Who though of wealth possest
> With learning and with power replete,
> Solicits to be blest.

Newman must have been amused at the idea of his wealth, and
Littlemore as 'a spacious place'. The moon, and angels looking on,
lent romance to the scene.

At Littlemore itself all was peace, and Newman, finding that
Walker could play the piano, got out his violin and they played
Beethoven and Haydn sonatas after dinner. But to go into Oxford
was no pleasure now. He dined with Observer Johnson and met
Church 'who seems the only person who is not too sore to bear the
meeting'. Even Church dropped contact with Newman when he
left Oxford. Johnson alone remained; meeting Newman by chance
in London on his return from Rome he burst into tears at seeing him
again. He was the only one to call on Newman when he was a
Catholic. Pusey, who had tried to imagine that Newman's change
would make no difference, was now 'thin and pale and upset by all
the conversions'. In October, at the moment of crisis, he had
written generously in the *English Churchman*, 'He seems to me not so
much gone from us as transplanted into another part of the Vine-
yard'. In a Puseyish way he even hoped that Newman would reform
the Church of Rome from within, smoothing the path for eventual
reunion. But the numbers who followed Newman, and the language
of some of them, upset him. Faber wrote a pamphlet which was

widely read by Anglicans and disgusted them. Newman, incidentally, disapproved of it, but he defended Faber to Henry Wilberforce, pointing out how much he had given up, and his zeal in serving God. Pusey said he did not want to hear from Faber again and 'another spirit besides love was at the bottom of the movement of certain persons'.

Human nature being what it is, it was inevitable that the more excitable of the converts should express themselves tactlessly, but it was difficult even for the tactful to please the friends they had left behind. Pusey complained that Newman was 'sharp' with him, and that Rome was already hardening him. 'Alas!' Newman wrote to him in February, 'I have no alternative between silence and saying what would pain.' Pusey would talk about it all, and about his book, and then be hurt if he disagreed. People narrowly watched every word and action of the converts for signs of the moral deterioration they were sure must be setting in ; if they said what they thought they were considered uncharitable ; if they avoided argument it must be because they were already convinced they had made a mistake but were too proud to admit it. Criticism by the converts was bitterly resented, but criticisms of them were freely made.

Everyone was reading the *Essay on Development* ; it came into a second edition in a fortnight, a welcome surprise to Newman, since his income now depended solely on the sale of his books. But so far as Protestant readers were concerned, it was not read for its ideas so much as picked over for evidence of Newman's motives in making the change. Whately thought it more likely to make sceptics than Romanists. He told Hawkins, 'My own suspicion is that N. himself is only seeking to escape Infidelity by a violent plunge into credulity.' Samuel Wilberforce thought the same. 'As for poor Newman, I believe he has been driven to Rome, not by the Bishops . . . but by that spirit of selfwill which has ever driven heretics and schismatics to the accomplishment of their lamentable end! May God give him the grace of repentance before he falls through Rome into infidelity.'

Such comments from clever men show how little they had grasped the theory of Newman's *Essay*; but perhaps it was not surprising, for even Catholics were at first, for the most part, puzzled by his approach. They were like astronomers who had long been plotting the map of the heavens faced with the theory of a mathematical genius which put everything into a different perspective. 'Nor can I believe the R.C.s will like it at all', said Whately. Some of them did, and wrote to Newman, full of interest, but Catholic comment in England was cautious. Protestants tended to fasten on the fact that Newman believed in miracles; they considered this proof of abject credulity. He must either be deluded, perhaps even mad, or else frightened of his own scepticism. For years these two contradictory explanations of his action were put forward, often almost in the same sentence. Because of his reason he was called sceptical, and because of his faith credulous. Once this view was established, people saw evidence for it everywhere, even in his physical appearance.

In January came a rallying of the Anglican Tractarians. The *Christian Remembrancer*, the monthly successor of the *British Critic*, and a new paper, the weekly *Guardian*, started by Rogers, Church and others, both came out with articles and assessments. James Mozley was part owner and co-editor of the *Christian Remembrancer*, and the article 'On the Recent Schism' was by him. It was an obvious moment for the restatement of Anglican views in face of the new situation. Yet Mozley's article on the schism had no theological or practical content whatever; he simply assumed that those who had not moved were right, and went on to analyse Newman's motives for going — since he was wrong, these must be due to some weakness of character. Mozley professed to be unwilling to undertake this self-imposed task; curiously enough neither Keble, to whom he sent it, nor anyone in Derby, felt Newman could be offended. They were all obsessed with his desertion; it did not occur to them that their own position needed defending. Newman was hurt by the article; he felt that James Mozley had exploited in it things which he could only have learned in private conversation, and in confidence. He was also much tried by the common theory among the Anglican members of the Movement that his 'sensitiveness' to hostility had driven him out of the Church of England. Of course by ascribing his change to cowardice they effectively side-stepped the necessity of examining his reasons for thinking the Church of England in schism.

'To us and to the English Church he is now a past and not a present person', said Mozley. 'He was a friend — he is now an antagonist. Nay, the nearer he was to us, the deeper in one sense, is that antagonism: even his continued vicinity to that University which was the scene of his labours, assumes an antagonistic spirit.' It was a hostile act to go on living for a few months in his own house at Littlemore. 'It is melancholy, but it is necessary now, as Mr.

Newman has put himself outside of us, to look at him as a spectator
and observer would . . . regarding him as a phenomenon.' But would
he have thought it necessary for Newman to regard *him* as a phenomenon, and analyse in public the motives of his friends for remaining
in the Church of England ? He might have retorted the charge of
cowardice on them. He never dreamed of doing so. In the *Lectures
on Anglican Difficulties* of 1850 he dealt with the general and intellectual problems, not with the motives of anyone, whether friends or
strangers. He did not defend or explain his own motives till he
wrote the *Apologia* in 1864, to rebut the charge that he was a liar,
and as a Catholic priest believed lying excusable in the cause of the
Church.

Mozley assured Mr. Newman that he would hear nothing petty
from him, and went on to accuse him, in his theological works, of
wanting too much to convince ; criticized him for making size a
criterion of the True Church (which he had never done) ; called him
and his theories bookish and insisted that he 'did not energize as a
parish priest but as an author'. This was good from one whose only
parish experience had been gained lending an occasional hand at St.
Mary's. Mozley led an exclusively academic life till he was forty-
three, when he married and took up a living. He later returned to
the university as Professor of Divinity. Even Church, when he took
a similar course in 1852, marrying at thirty-eight and retiring to
Somerset, confessed that he found it difficult to enter into the minds
of his country parishioners.

James Mozley was essentially a party man ; his letters are full of
the details of every Oxford battle. Although he was thirty-two in
1845 his mind had not yet found its resting place. A few years later
he shocked his Anglo-Catholic friends by agreeing with the Gorham
Judgment, throwing over the doctrine of Baptismal regeneration and
praising the Erastianism of the Establishment as good common sense.
James Mozley thus became a Z at the age when Newman became a
Catholic ; he settled down into the society of the day as a gentleman
parson, going abroad for his holidays and writing books. Newman
said once that James Mozley had never seen the necessity of an
intellectual basis for Anglicanism ; James would probably have
agreed with him.

In January, when this article appeared, Newman was travelling
about England. He was at Oscott for the Epiphany, and then went
to stay with Ambrose Phillipps at Grace Dieu. Probably Phillipps
treated him as 'a lion', for he wrote to St. John, 'I have been seized

with one of my bashful fits and cannot speak two words, if it were to keep me from starving'. From there he went north, calling on various Bishops on the way, to Ushaw College, where he was much impressed with the President, Dr. Newsham, brother of the Oxford priest. Newsham became a real and lasting friend. Then he proceeded to Stonyhurst to visit the Jesuits, an arduous journey ending in a ten-mile walk. Then he went to Preston, back to Birmingham and up to Liverpool. He had hoped to fit in a visit to Aunt in Derby, but the train did not stop long enough. He wrote to her, 'Let me be to you an affectionate friend and faithful helper and minister unseen, since I cannot at present be more than this'. At the end of January he was back in London, but too tired to visit Mrs. Bowden again, as he had at the beginning of his journeying. 'Travelling has a depressing effect on me,' he wrote to her, 'as making me feel a pilgrim and a sojourner. Of course, persons in the highest frame of mind would find themselves raised, not depressed by the thought.'

He came back to Littlemore to pack his things, and clear up letters and papers, an exhausting and melancholy task at the best of times. While he was at it Miss Giberne wrote, complaining that she was losing her dear friend Selina through her conversion, and saying that Newman at least was taking his friends with him. He prefaced and ended his reply with words of encouragement to her, but he told her something of his own trouble too. 'Alas! can you point to anyone who has lost more in the way of friendship, whether by death or alienation than I have ? . . . so many dead, so many separated. My mother gone ; my sisters nothing to me, or rather foreign to me ; of my greatest friends, Froude, Wood, Bowden taken away, all of whom would now be, or be coming to my side. Other dear friends who *are* preserved in life *not* moving with me ; Pusey strongly bent on the opposite course ; Williams protesting against my conduct as rationalist and dying' (Isaac was very ill, but recovered) 'Rogers and J. Mozley viewing it with utter repugnance. Of my friends a dozen years ago, whom have I now ? and what did I know of my present friends a dozen years ago ? Why, they were at school or they were freshmen looking up to me, if they knew my name, as some immense and unapproachable don ; and now they know nothing, can know nothing of my earlier life. . . . And yet I am very happy with them, and I have with them, what I never can have had with others, Catholic hopes and beliefs, Catholic objects. And so in your own case, depend on it, God's mercy will make up to you all you lose, and you will be blessed, not indeed in the same way, but in a higher.'

'In telling me your griefs you soothed my own', said Miss Giberne, thanking him for his 'dear kind letter.' And she added, 'May nothing ever separate us, for though we meet face to face but seldom, I always feel as if you were my strong hold. You have never failed me, and you never will, for I have always loved you in Christ and for him.' She had many difficulties to face with her evangelical family, and in the end had to leave home. A little while later she turned up, in tears, on Newman's doorstep at Maryvale. He gave her tea, and took her up to Oscott in a carriage, as it was pouring with rain, introduced her to Wiseman, and made arrangements for her. At High Mass and Benediction in Pugin's chapel she thought she was in heaven. Some months afterwards she left England for Rome.

But in February Newman was unable to visit her; he was short of time and money. The move was going to cost so much. 'I quite dread the sum total', he told her. For now the time had really come when he must leave Oxford, and the life he had lived for over twenty-five years, ever since he was growing from a boy into a man. No wonder, as he said to St. John, that it felt 'like going out on the open sea'. A frenzy of packing ensued, books once more 'in motion', keys lost, and things to arrange for at the other end. St. John and Stanton went on ahead to Maryvale, and the others followed, so that in the end Newman was left alone in the house, on his birthday, February 21st: he was forty-five. He wrote to H. W., 'I came into this bower by myself — I quit it by myself'. He told Mrs. Froude how happy he had been there: 'The only place I have ever lived in which I can look back on without an evil conscience'. To Mrs. Bowden he said that he had been taking leave of the people; 'and now I must leave off, though unwillingly, for time gets on and I must once more go over to the poor-house before the fly comes'. To Copeland he said, 'I quite tore myself away, and could not help kissing my bed, and mantelpiece and other parts of the house. I have been most happy there, though in a state of suspense. And there it has been that I have both been taught my way and received an answer to my prayers.'

That last day, February 22nd, had begun with walking to mass at St. Clement's; it ended with dinner at the Observatory, where he stayed the night with Johnson. Pattison and Church and some others came to see him there. Last of all, late at night, came Pusey to say good-bye. Newman left Oxford next morning at half-past eight and did not see it again, except from the train, for thirty-two years.

'I am writing next room to the Chapel', he wrote to Henry Wilberforce from Maryvale. 'It is such an incomprehensible blessing to have Christ's bodily presence in one's house, within one's walls, as swallows up all other privileges, and destroys, or should destroy, every pain. To know that He is close by — to be able again and again to go in to Him; and be sure my dearest W., when I am thus in His Presence you are not forgotten. . . . Thus Abraham, our father, pleaded before his hidden Lord and God in the valley.'

ROME AND BIRMINGHAM
(1846–1850)

1846

'Some wild incomprehensible beast'

WHEN Newman left Oxford, his old mathematics tutor, Ogle, said:
'Depend upon it, you will come back to us'. But thinking of the
sacramental presence of Christ, Newman said to Mrs. Bowden, 'With
this great blessing in possession . . . it would indeed be turning
away from heaven itself'. All his letters when he first came to
Maryvale reflected this, the uppermost thought in his mind. Somehow when he had been abroad he had not realized that the tabernacle
lamp was the sign of Christ's presence, in the consecrated Host.
'But now after tasting the awful delight of worshipping God in His
temple, how unspeakably cold is the idea of a temple without that
Divine Presence!'

This special presence of Christ was the continuing source of
comfort in a situation which, on the human side, was full of difficulties and surprises. After the prolonged strain of the last few
years, the hurried travelling of the winter, and uprooting from
Littlemore, what Newman needed most was rest and quiet. But
he did not get it. It had seemed such an advantage to be near
Oscott, but it turned out something of a trial. The reasons for
this were complex, due in part to his own innocence, not to say
ignorance, of the English Catholic situation, partly to that situation
itself. In the supernatural life of the Church, Newman was in his
element, but in his particular human surroundings he was sometimes
at a loss, and, as so often happens to someone thrown among strangers,
more lost than he realized at the time. It was not till much later
that he understood why that first year had been so uncomfortable.
While it was in progress he was carried through the discomforts by
his determination to obey his new Superiors, and fit in as well as
he could to the society he found. In this he was more docile than
some of the Oxford converts, who, disapproving the ways of English
Catholics, as compared with those they had met abroad, were keen
to change them at once.

Oscott was the Catholic show-place of the moment, and the centre of Wiseman's influence, but Wiseman himself was not typical of the Catholics of England. Brought up and educated abroad, living so long in Rome, he knew little of their insular world, and did not much approve what he knew. He thought them stiff, old-fashioned, over-secretive about their faith, and isolated from the trends of modern Catholic thought. Yet though Oscott seemed so suitable a centre for Wiseman, it was not he who had built it, but Dr. Weedall, whose whole life and energy had gone into the College, and who was somewhat unfairly jockeyed aside by distant authorities in Rome to make room for Wiseman. Newman was to preach Weedall's funeral sermon in 1859, when he called him 'the tree beside the waters' and took the opportunity to praise the old English Catholic body from which he sprung. Weedall was typical in his piety, individualism and mild eccentricity, but not in his meekness; most of the 'old' Catholics were sturdy outspoken people, who kept quiet about their religion for safety's sake, but were tenacious of their private opinions.

The whole Catholic body was about to be changed by the influx of Irish, driven out of their country by famine and rack-renting landlords; the immigration indeed had already begun, but it had not been realized, far less assimilated, by the Catholics of England. The Catholics of the two nations shared nothing but their faith and their common human nature; their background was totally dissimilar. In the sixteenth century the Irish people, already ruled from England, lost still more of their liberty and rights, but retained their ancient faith while their rulers went over to the Reform. Thus Catholicism and nationalism became closely inwoven, as happened in Poland, with the difference that in Poland the aristocracy too were Catholic. In Ireland circumstances reduced the upper class Catholics to a handful, and it was natural that to the mass of the people the priests became their guides, acquiring an influence and authority greater than was common in countries whose institutions developed freely. English oppression meant that the people were unable to get education or rise from conditions of direst poverty; the priests had the only learning there was, gained with the greatest difficulty and sacrifice. The Irish immigrants who flocked into the industrial towns of England in the Forties were half-starved illiterates with no love for the country which had so mismanaged their own, and with an inbred conviction that there was no such thing as an English Catholic — they were all persecuting heretics.

But English Catholics there were, with a character all their own, and a history as heroic, in a different way, as that of the Catholics of Ireland. They were not a nation oppressed by foreign rulers of a different religion, but a minority in a nation which regarded them as foreign, though it was their own. Those who survived the violent executions of the State in the sixteenth century were afterwards subjected to the less dramatic but more effective pressure of penal laws, deprivations and fines, forbidden to have Catholic schools, forbidden to send their children abroad to school, fined for not attending the services of the Established Church, their own worship made illegal, and the laws that declared a man a traitor if he was a priest still on the statute book.

English Catholics survived in pockets, the biggest in the north, especially in Lancashire. In the south they congregated round the houses of those Catholic gentlemen who had managed to keep both faith and some of their fortune : many lost either one or the other in the course of the centuries. Priests lived as chaplains and tutors in these great houses and they were not able to organize parishes and live in them till the relaxation that followed the French Revolution, when the government and people of England most generously welcomed priests and nuns of the religion they had done their best to exterminate at home, when they fled as refugees from the Terror. This was a comparatively recent development at the beginning of the nineteenth century, and the Church still depended much on the loyalty and generosity of a few noble families. They built the churches, where their memorials remain to-day, unless the buildings have been pulled down as inadequate and 'Victorian'. They held the purse strings, and they exercised in the world the only power they could — social pressure among their Protestant equals. They intermarried extensively, forming a world of their own, pious and practical, and except for those who travelled abroad and married into continental noble families, they were a race of squires, who knew more about estates, crops, sport and horses than about ideas and art. They provided many priests for the Jesuits and Benedictines, and nuns for the contemplative orders ; the secular priesthood on the whole was recruited from the other ranks of Catholic society. In the rising middle classes there were very few Catholics before the coming of the converts.

All these, whether rich or poor, had deeply ingrained in their minds the long history of legal oppression, popular hatred and outbursts of violence. The pressure of the world was such that they were accustomed to seeing their numbers diminish rather than augment. Conversions were rare, of clergymen rarer, of the learned, practically unknown. Mr. Spencer, the evangelical clergyman of aristocratic family who became a priest, was easily floored in argument by the learned Anglo-Catholic Palmer of Worcester. The Catholics were used to seeing the Protestants all-powerful, the universities in the hands of the Establishment, Bishops of the Church of England sitting in the House of Lords, and its laymen in all the highest posts of the government. It was difficult for many of them to believe all these learned convert clergymen were sincere; even if they were genuine it was feared they were looking down on the meagre intellectual attainments of Catholics. The married converts tended to make friends among the Catholic gentry, but the unmarried, pursuing a priestly vocation, were thrown into surroundings more ecclesiastical and socially less similar to the background they had left. In these circumstances there was bound to be friction.

The effect of the influx of converts on the small Catholic body, though nothing like in numbers to the Irish immigration, was more immediately noticeable. Many, especially the younger ones, had travelled abroad and picked up this and that devotional practice natural to the people where it originated but often not natural at all to English habit and temperament. Faber was the most ardent devotee of these practices, and annoyed the 'old' English Catholics very much by intimating that it was not he who was too exuberant, but they who were not 'Catholic' enough. His Italianism clashed with the Gothicism of the earlier converts, Phillipps and Pugin, and his emotional enthusiasms aroused the suspicions of stolid English theologians. However, his influence at present was hardly felt beyond Birmingham, though he was preparing the first bombshell for the insular English Catholics, translating some Italian lives of (foreign) Saints.

Wiseman had all along encouraged the Oxford men, and Catholics in England and in Rome, though with different feelings, thought of them almost as his converts, the fruits of his policy. In Rome they thought he was doing wonders; in England they were suspicious of him, thinking that he was ignorant of the conditions they knew so well, and that he had too many Roman ideas and too much influence there. It was a great triumph for Wiseman, then, when the converts came pouring in, and they clustered round Oscott, visiting it if they did not stay there, and people curious to meet

them came too. Gossip was endemic. Whatever the converts did
or did not do was the subject of curiosity and suspicion, or of un-
critical enthusiasm. Wiseman, of course, was most anxious they
should show up well. Oscott was the Catholic show place, the
converts were Wiseman's show piece, and the masterpiece of the
collection could only be Newman.

For a shy person, to be on perpetual exhibition was tormenting
enough, but it was doubly so when it became, through the insensi-
tivity of the people concerned, a humiliation. About seventeen
years later, when Newman was over sixty and seemed to himself
to have arrived at a position where his usefulness was as completely
stultified in the Catholic world as it had been by 1845 in the Church
of England, he wrote down what he felt about what had happened
to him since his conversion, in a private journal. 'How dreary my
first year at Maryvale, when I was the gaze of so many eyes at
Oscott, as if some wild incomprehensible beast, caught by the
hunter, and a spectacle for Dr. Wiseman to exhibit to strangers, as
himself being the hunter who captured it! I did not realize this
at the time, except in its discomfort. . . .'

Emily Bowles was the witness of one of these exhibitions of the
incomprehensible beast. She was with some friends in the gallery
of the chapel and saw Newman 'catechized by an Italian priest'.
She said, 'It was almost more than I could bear to see the great
teacher come out to be questioned and taught as a little child'. It
was some comfort to her, she wrote, as an old woman, in her memoir,
that a Catholic friend was reminded of Christ in the temple teaching
the doctors. 'The beauty of his voice and singular lowliness and
unselfconsciousness of his whole bearing so overwhelmed me with
emotion that I have little recollection of what he said except that it
was about the Magi.'

There must have been other such occasions. Newman only
noted two in 1863 : 'I was made an humiliation at my minor orders
and at the examination for them ; and I had to stand at Dr. Wiseman's door waiting for Confession amid the Oscott boys. I did
not realize these as indignities at the time, though, as I have said I
felt their dreariness.'

Someone who demands no special consideration rarely receives
it. Had Newman stalked about looking important, people would
have thought twice before asking him to do this or that. His unassuming manner and readiness to do what he was told led thought-
less people to treat him carelessly ; some of the more obtuse, who

knew little of him but his fame, even thought it would be good for him to realize his new status as neophyte rather than teacher and leader. The contrast between the treatment of Newman, and that of Manning five years later is interesting. By that time, when the second wave of converts came in, after the Gorham case, the first had begun work, but they were by no means fully accepted and trusted. Yet Wiseman ordained Manning within a few weeks, and when he went to Rome, it was to the Accademia, the college for priests of noble birth and the nursery of ecclesiastical diplomats. Old Catholics disapproved of Manning's rapid ordination; but nobody catechized him in public, or expected him to queue up with schoolboys for confession. Manning was a person nobody dreamed of snubbing, yet his position in the Movement was nothing to what Newman's had been, nor had he then an international reputation as a writer and religious leader.

Newman's diffidence and gentleness not only led people to order him about, but to lecture him, as he called it, on what he ought to do, even on his behaviour. One of his trials, he wrote in 1863, was 'the strangeness of ways, habits, religious observances, to which, however, I was urged on to conform without any delicacy towards my feelings'. The Mass, Benediction, the office, praying before the Blessed Sacrament, were all to him wonderful privileges, but there were also a lot of popular devotions and practices suitable to different kinds of people, and at different periods of their lives, of quite secondary importance. Awkwardness and unfamiliarity with these surprised those who had grown up with them; they could not believe anyone who fumbled with them was really a Catholic. Converts were such an unknown tribe; Catholics had come to feel Protestants were almost another race, and could as easily change their religion as the colour of their skins. Newman tried, much too hard, to do what was expected of him; next year, in retreat before ordination, he accused himself as a fault, of failing to enter into all these pieties at once. Yet his whole life was already centred on Christ and on the mass. It was like trying to force the roots of a tree into a tub. In the end he realized that the operation was unnecessary; only humility kept him from discovering it sooner.

Things like this always had to grow slowly and naturally into his life, and it was particularly difficult to make sudden changes in religious practices, which affected the deepest part of himself, at the age of forty-five, when habits are set. It was easier for the younger converts, partly just because they were younger, partly

because they had grown up in the Catholic revival and had not so
far to go.   Perhaps it was the comparative ease with which they
took to the external forms of Catholicism which gave some of them,
without their being aware of it, the notion that they had somehow
arrived on the same spiritual level as Newman.   They were all new
boys together, and some felt they were settling down better than
old Newman, and that something ought to be done to assist the
process of Catholicizing him.   Again, this unconscious attitude of
patronage and criticism towards one who had taught them, directly
or indirectly, most of what they knew of the Catholic faith, and
started them on a spiritual life, could hardly have arisen had Newman
stood on his dignity or even behaved with the self-confidence of one
accustomed to be obeyed.

The first to begin lecturing Newman on his duty was Dalgairns,
who had been a boy of fifteen when Newman, a man of thirty-two,
came back from his illness in Sicily to start the Tracts.   The flatter-
ing reception Dalgairns received in France, and the novelty of
living under the direction of a priest and in a Catholic town, went
to his head, and before the others left Littlemore he was writing to
tell St. John that what they needed was a director.   'I especially
allude to dear Newman. . . . He wants a superior as much as any ;
not, in the least, that he wants to learn obedience, but a delicate
and sensitive mind such as his will not venture to do the great
things the Church requires of him unless he is commanded.'   St.
John took up the idea, and Newman was hurt to think they had been
discussing him behind his back.   'I am not in the habit of criticizing
you,' he told Dalgairns, 'much less on an understanding with other
parties. . . . To tell me I must have a director was unnecessary.'
Dalgairns, among his other criticisms, feared Newman was too
sensitive to the remarks of the 'old' Catholics.   On Easter Eve
Newman wrote : 'As to my "sensitiveness" I suppose you cannot
show where it has ever affected my actions, else I should have left
the English Church long ago.   The English Bishops have said
worse things of me than the "old Catholics".'   But he accepted
Dalgairns' belated apology.   'And now, except that I am very tired
and languid, I would try to say something to make up any pain I
have given you.   But I can only beg you to forgive what I have
done wrong myself in this matter and send you my best Easter love.
If I attempted anything else I should only be stiff and cold as I am
in what I have said above.   God bless you, my dear D.'

There were others besides Dalgairns who could not imagine a

community life without Newman as its centre, and yet who were
unwilling to trust his authority. He found it extremely hard to tell
individuals where they were going wrong, hoping they would take
hints which they were often too careless or too headstrong to notice.
And if he did attempt a remonstrance it was only too easy for a
determined person simply to bear him down by force of will. So
he sometimes took refuge in the written word, both as being more
tactful and as being more likely to make a man admit his mistake.
Thus after Easter he wrote to Jack Morris, who had scared the Vice-
Chancellor out of St. Mary's with his sermon on making animals
fast, and who was now at Maryvale. Morris had been using Maryvale merely as a lodging house, ignoring the rest of the community,
spending his time in his room or up at Oscott. He put up his own
bookshelves without attempting to help anyone else. He did not
bother to do his week's turn of housework ; Newman said nothing,
but did it for him. It was Lent, Morris was not well, and Newman
hoped he would make an effort after Easter. Far from it ; he even
got out of the job of pouring coffee for the others at recreation.
Morris did not realize the selfishness of his ways even after Newman's
letter, although his own to Observer Johnson naïvely relates the same
incidents from his own point of view. He was unashamed in preferring the 'better dinners' and services at Oscott. Now he caught
mumps, retreated up the hill to the new college, and never returned
to community life. He liked Wiseman, who was amused by his
eccentricities, and never let him forget the day he had caught him
at work in an apron and nightcap. Morris discussed Newman with
Wiseman, and then used to descend to Maryvale to lecture his
erstwhile superior on what he ought to do, or not do.

John Walker, 'Dismal Johnny' as the Observer called him, who
played duets with Newman at Littlemore, now took to lecturing
him on theology. Walker talked him over with Dr. Acqueroni, the
Italian priest who lived at Maryvale, though not with the community, and said mass for them — perhaps it was he who so shocked
Miss Bowles by catechizing Newman in public. Walker presently
left them. He came back several times in later years, discontented
with his lot and wondering whether he would not join the Oratory.
But he never could quite bring himself to 'bolt my dogmatics' as
Newman put it.

All this was tiresome, but things went on fairly cheerfully all
the same. Robert Coffin, who had been Vicar of St. Mary Magdalene's church in Oxford during the last years of Newman's

residence, and who was now temporarily acting as tutor to Ambrose Phillipps' boys at Grace Dieu, came over to visit Maryvale towards the end of March. He was about twenty-six, a year younger than Dalgairns. He wrote to Observer Johnson : 'Though they are still in great confusion, the books not being arranged and the house only half furnished, yet I thought they all seemed very happy and well satisfied with their new abode, especially Newman, who was much more so than I had expected to see him after his sore trial in leaving poor old Littlemore : as usual he is the life of the whole party and keeps all cheerful and in good humour. They go on much as they did at Littlemore saving that they are all in *cassocks* which makes them look very ecclesiastical.' Jack Morris, still with them then, wrote to Johnson as well. 'Here I sit with my whiskers shaved off at last in a stiff Roman collar and long Italian cassock which last I hate and on Sundays I mount a biretta, which old Newman is very shy of yet.'

At five o'clock on May morning Newman was ringing the rising bell, and it made him think of the bells on Magdalen Tower ringing to welcome the May, and he wrote to Bloxam, 'Why should they not tune themselves to ours ?' He was anxious about Bloxam, for though he never pushed those who had not made up their minds, he felt that Bloxam had reached the point of conviction, and was delaying putting it into action. On Christmas Eve last he had called on him in his rooms and proposed that he should be received the next day. 'I was not prepared for this and was silent', Bloxam wrote, as an old man. 'Before he left me the choristers were at my door clamourously waiting for me to go into Hall for the Christmas Eve concert.'

Of course Newman was thinking much of the friends he had left. Henry Wilberforce was writing as affectionately as ever, but after feeling he must follow Newman in October, he had sheered off again, persuaded by his brothers, and Manning, his brother-in-law, that it was only love for Newman, not for Rome that prompted him. In March he was saying, 'If you had turned Quaker I would have felt you *must* be right', and he harped so much on Newman's personal influence that in July Newman called it 'nauseous humbug'. 'Have I a grain of influence as *I* to make you *move* ? Not at all.' Afterwards he was afraid he had been 'too severe' in this letter. Henry longed to see him but said, 'So much publicity is thrown about your movements that I fear it would get into the papers'. They met in London in September, just before Newman set off for Rome. Henry was always demanding details of their new life; sometimes he got them from Ambrose St. John, his ex-curate. 'When N. heard of the Pope's sending him the Crucifix he shot out of the Bishop's room like an arrow.' The Crucifix, a silver one, contained a relic of the True Cross, and was venerated in the chapel at Maryvale by all the community. Newman was much struck that this token of friendship from the highest authority arrived on the anniversary of what he called 'the Heads of Houses' Placard with the Pokers against Tract 90'. The Latinity of his reply to Cardinal Fransoni was much admired in Rome, to his amusement when he heard of it.

Mrs. Bowden was on the point of decision, her objections to Rome having melted away during the months after Newman's conversion. But she was under a fierce bombardment from her family, especially from Bowden's brother Henry, a 'military man' who some years later came over himself with all his family; they became some of Newman's dearest friends. Just now, however, he was pressing learned Anglican books on Mrs. Bowden, and she wrote to ask Newman what he advised on his side. 'I will be no party to this baiting of you,' he broke out in June. 'It is a cruel word but the thing is worse. I will not be the man to talk you over this way or that. I protest against it.' It was ridiculous to expect her, a busy mother, to get up a scholars' controversy which she had not the training to judge. God gave every one sufficient grounds for a decision. 'But as to your being driven hither and thither by opposite disputants, I cannot bear to think of it. It is meant kindly, but for me I am not capable of stunning you with arguments or stifling you with folios, or subduing you by an urgent tone and a confident manner.' It was no good trying to calculate the consequences of action, 'Let us leave the consequences to Him who makes them. Excuse me if I have written abruptly, which I am apt to do. I am at your service whenever you send for me.'

She sent for him at once, and he came, travelling on Friday, so that he accidentally missed his dinner. 'The train was first class — eheu — and there was no cheese at Wolverton, but I am set up by some bacon and eggs this morning — how animal!' he wrote cheerfully from London. First class was expensive and he was short of money. He called on Bishop Griffiths, who sent him for confession to Mr. Wilds at the Warwick Street Chapel. Mr. Wilds turned out to be eighty but 'as sharp as the President of Magdalen'. He was one of the old Catholic priests trained at Douay, the first college founded overseas for training priests in the penal times. Newman tried to introduce himself after his confession. 'No, no, I don't want to know your name, goodbye,' said Mr. Wilds uncompromisingly, as Newman told St. John. However, he got the old man to listen at last 'and then his joy was quite great — he wanted to put me in his own armchair — he wanted me to dine with him — he would have a gossip with me, which he had'. A few days later Mr. Wilds received Mrs. Bowden and her younger children. Afterwards she went down to Eton to see her eldest son, John, who was old enough to decide for himself. He was held back for some time by his uncle and friends who represented the change as treachery to his dead father.

Newman stayed a few days longer in London and embarrassed himself by wearing the Catholic clerical dress which he was not yet bound to do. With black knee breeches and old-fashioned skirted coat it made him look like a cross between a Methodist preacher and an Archdeacon ; but the Roman collar, rarely worn in England then, stamped him as a Catholic. 'I am so awkward and gawky that I feel ashamed of myself', he told Dalgairns. 'The only make up is that the poor Catholics recognize it as I go along and touch their hats to me, but fancy me, who has never been in costume, wearing a straight cut collar to my coat and having a long skirt to it. I know I look like a fool from my own intrinsic absurdity.' He felt even worse when he met George Talbot, a convert who had been received by Wiseman, and was farther advanced on the road to the priesthood than Newman, but was wearing no Roman collar. Newman felt self-conscious. 'What a fool I am,' he said helplessly.

He met his brother Frank in London. Frank had just been appointed Latin Professor at University College, a post he was to hold for the rest of his working life. His pupils remembered him as eccentric, wearing three coats, one on top of the other, and pedantic, hating slang and lacking in humour. In London his progress towards free-thinking rationalism was accelerated, and he shocked his Unitarian friends in Manchester by criticizing the character of Jesus ; his biographer cut out all offensive remarks of this nature from the letters she quoted. He was now developing an extreme admiration for Mazzini, the leader of the Italian Liberals. In losing his Christian faith he did not lose his crusading spirit, and his life was a succession of causes and crazes ; one of the most lasting was vegetarianism. He also became a teetotaller, and was later to be shocked when his brother said he did not know whether there were too many public houses in Birmingham or too few. At this time he was about forty, a striking figure with his black, straight hair and intense blue eyes ; he gained a certain fame in intellectual circles. It was typical of Victorian society that the rationalist was so much more easily tolerated than the papist. As for John, Frank was still convinced he was in the toils of fanatics. He wanted to come to Maryvale. 'Why should he come ?' Newman wrote to Stanton. 'I think he has some obscure idea he can decide whether there are thumbscrews or the like at Maryvale.'

After Easter Wiseman had told Newman he had better go to Rome for a time, to the College of Propaganda. At first he thought he was to go alone and at once ; this daunting prospect was later modified. His departure was put off and St. John was to go with him. In June Wiseman himself suddenly went to Belgium ; he left Newman in charge at Maryvale as superior. Newman wrote to David Lewis, who had once been his curate at St. Mary's, but had now opted for a secular life, and had a job on the *Tablet* : 'If you come again you will not have the easy life of it you had — for now we have conferences, and penances, and are altogether on our good behaviour'. Soon afterwards, when he was in London about Mrs. Bowden's reception, he called on a Dr. Fergusson, who drew a harsh picture of the discipline at the College of Propaganda, which was a seminary for students from all the mission fields of the world, Newman retailed the conversation to St. John. Money was to be handed over to the Rector. '"Then there is no good," I asked, "in taking money ?" "No," said Dr. F., "none at all." Next, you may not have *clothes* of your own — the Rector takes away coat, trousers shirts, stockings etc etc and give you some of Propaganda's. "Then it is no use", I asked, "taking a portmanteau." "No," said Dr. F., "it is no use."' St. John replied that they 'could not help laughing at the face you would make when you were putting on a Turkish nightshirt or an American pair of boots'. Newman expected to be treated like the other students, who were mere youths. It did not occur to him to try to get out of the tiresome prospect of going back to school at the age of forty-five.

Before Wiseman left he conferred on them minor orders, following the tonsure. Newman kept some notes of his retreat in preparation for this step. It was very like the retreats at Littlemore, except that the meditations were made privately in their rooms. 'I thought also of the horror, at the judgment, of Christ's saying to me "Here is the end he was made for — look at it — this was the end and this

has been his life — he was made for this end and he has not fulfilled
it.'   Once more he felt he had not yet begun to serve God truly, so
much had been done from liking the work itself. 'But now let me
do some work for Thee before I die — here am I, send me.'

The last hour of meditation was 'interrupted all through with
knockings etc about a letter from the Bishop'.   That evening Newman
was due to receive the tonsure 'which I dread', he noted.   In fact,
he was 'sent for to Oscott to be examined' that night, but the tonsure
and minor orders were given the next morning.   This was the occasion, as Newman noted long after, when he was 'made an humiliation'.

Towards the end of July he spent a few days at Alton Towers, the
seat of Lord Shrewsbury, the most munificent of Catholic noblemen
and the patron of Pugin. 'This is a most superb place', Newman
told Mrs. Bowden. 'I never saw such inside splendour, perhaps
never such outside beauty and grandeur.'   His greatest admiration
was for the chapels, in the house and at the new church in Cheadle
where 'the chapel of the Blessed Sacrament is on entering a blaze of
light, and I could not help saying to myself "Porta Coeli"' — gate
of heaven.

He told Miss Giberne too the current news of Faber and his
Wilfridians ; they had nearly been poisoned by bad meat. 'He has
more adventures than any one.'   Lord Shrewsbury was considering
offering Faber a nearby property, including old Cotton Hall, and
asked Newman to open the subject to him. 'Newman rushed in to
tell me the news,' Faber wrote to his friend Watts Russell.   Newman
thought it would be just the thing for Faber ; in the country he
could form his community in peace, for in Birmingham they were
already being pressed into work although even Faber was not yet a
priest.   By now Faber had three young gentlemen with him as well
as the country boys.   Frederick (Alban) Wells and Henry (Austin)
Mills were only a year or two over twenty, both from Cambridge,
where their careers had been cut short by conversion.   Antony
Hutchison was twenty-four ; he was to be Faber's closest friend and
ally, dying in the same year, although so much younger.   He was
rich, and his first act of friendship was to take Faber off on a tour
abroad.   Faber had little money of his own ; last year he had feared
he must put off his removal from Elton because of the building debts
he had incurred there, but an Anglican friend paid them for him.
On first coming to Birmingham Faber had collapsed ; he was thought
to be dying, but revived after he had received the Last Sacraments.
The tour was taken in order to restore his health.   At the tomb of

St. Thomas of Canterbury in France he was inspired to compose a rule for his community, to whom he wrote long letters of exhortation and enthusiasm. When the travellers returned Hutchison's generosity enabled them to move into a larger house, fitted up according to Faber's taste in the Italian religious style of the day. They now adopted a Habit, a cassock and cloak, with the device (in red) of a cross and the letters V.D. — Voluntas Dei — the Will of God. They all took religious names ; Faber became Brother Wilfrid of the Humanity of Jesus.

Urged on by old Bishop Walsh (to whom Wiseman was Co-adjutor) Faber accepted Lord Shrewsbury's generous offer. He met Newman again at the end of August, at Alton Towers, for the conse-cration of Cheadle Church — 'the house full of people and I looking like a fool', Newman told St. John. He was never comfortable at parties in high society. Faber rather enjoyed country-house visiting , he charmed and converted the upper classes as easily as he did the poor. In a few months he had transformed Cotton Hall into 'St. Wilfrid's' and was building a large Gothic church. Little did Newman know that in a very short time the exuberant Faber, his youthful Wilfridians, and St. Wilfrid's itself, were to become his responsibility.

Meanwhile, in August, Newman had a letter from Pusey, who was ill at Tenby, which sounded as if he were at death's door. Newman waited anxiously for more news ; none came. So he made a hurried dash to Tenby by boat. 'I had a bad passage 12 or 13 hours,' he told St. John, '— thick drizzle half the time — cabins full of people prostrate — myself on deck, never so sick in my life : chairs tumbling about.' When at last he reached Pusey he found him weak but not in serious danger ; he was allowed about two hours talk with him. Pusey was surprised, but pleased to see him. Newman had half hoped his illness might spur him to reconsider his position, but he saw there was no chance of it, and from now on he thought Pusey's conversion would be 'almost a miracle'. When he first left Oxford Newman had written his friend a passionate appeal — which he did not send. The letter he sent was calmer in tone. He felt that Pusey was inventing a religion of his own, neither the High Anglican tradition nor Catholicism, but a mixture of everything for which he had no authority but himself. Perhaps he had a right to maintain this isolated position so long as he believed in it, but he had no right, Newman felt, to forbid his penitents, as he did, even to consider the claims of Rome, but to put aside the whole question as a moral temptation. Newman had often advised people to pause and think — he still did when he thought it necessary — but he had never put them under obedience not to change, or made religious enquiry a sin.

Pusey's isolation comes out in his correspondence with Sam Wilberforce, recently made Bishop of Oxford, and at the start of an active career very different from that of old Bagot, who had moved on to Bath and Wells, where he suitably ended his days. Sam Wilberforce was shocked when Pusey said he now believed in Purgatory because he had just discovered that the early martyrs prayed to and for the dead. It was not in Scripture, said Bishop Wilberforce firmly, and was not mollified when Pusey meekly said he did not teach the doctrine to other people. Sam Wilberforce, moderately high himself, was sure he could unite High and Low in his diocese, but Pusey, a law unto himself, eluded him.

Newman came home from Wales by coach, a complicated journey. 'I go 130 miles to-morrow in 20 hours!' he scribbled to St. John, '. . . price inside being £3 odd — I mount. Have bought a *shawl* to cover my legs on the strength of the difference between inside and out.' In 1875, going through his letters after St. John's death, he noted, 'It rained all day on my return. I got *very* wet. The shawl I still have in use ; but it was too scanty to be of any real use atop of a coach. Two gentlemen on the coach took pity on me. They turned out to be the two Mr. Eystons' — Miss Bowles' Catholic friends from East Hendred, the descendants of St. Thomas More. The 'shawl' which still exists, is a square piece of woven material, what we should call a rug. Folded into a triangle, Newman used it to put round his shoulders when he was an old man. He felt the whole expedition had been a waste of time and money, which he could have spent on books. A paragraph appeared in the papers, bitterly accusing him of causing a serious relapse in Pusey's condition. People imagined him capable of bullying a sick friend to go over to Rome.

He returned to the business of packing for a year abroad, making in the back of his diary lists of clothing, for winter and summer, including that then common item, nightcaps. There were too 'things to get in Birmingham' — soap, sticking plaster, braces, housewife, steel pens, second pair glasses, Greek Testament, Vulgate, English Bible, breviary, private journal, envelopes, string. Last minute agitations occurred about the customs. 'Mr. Moore has frightened me', he wrote to St. John on August 28th — Mr. Moore was chief Catholic missioner for Birmingham — 'he says knit woollen shirts

are the *very things* they seize in France and Italy.' They might pas
if they were washed but there was not much time. From Alto
Towers he wrote : 'As to my woollen things I shall souse them in
pail of water Thursday night when I get to London and get then
all dried on Friday. The shirts I have worn, some of them. Th
socks will soon wet and dry.' Did the new clothes survive sucl
treatment without shrinking? But they may not have all been woollen
for it was not till a few years later that Newman was enlightened b
his friend Lady Olivia Acheson, that what he had always thought wa
'knit wool' was really 'knit cotton'. This, he decided optimistically
must be the reason why he had always felt so cold in winter.

In spite of all the bustle he managed to pay a flying visit to Jemim
in Derby. Perhaps it was on this occasion that, going to see ol
Aunt, he found her reading the psalms verse by verse with his smal
nephew, just as she had done with him long ago. He at once joine
in, taking a verse in his turn. This reassured and 'soothed' the ol
woman, said kind Anne Mozley, relating the incident in a note at th
end of her volumes.

In London Newman saw Henry Wilberforce, who begged to hea
every detail of their lives in Rome ; and was amused by his godso
Charlie Bowden, already an expert on rubrics. St. John told Dal
gairns, 'the very first day he went to mass with Newman he set hin
right'.

Early in September they crossed the channel. Newman ha
not been out of England since 1833.

1846

Snow and Surprises in Rome

THEY slept at Dieppe and went on to Paris next day. Newman was already famous in France, where the Catholic Movement at Oxford had aroused great interest. He had even exchanged some controversial letters with a French Abbé at an earlier date, while he still thought the Church of England Catholic. M. Gondon, the French impresario of the Movement, who was translating the *Essay on Development*, presided over a festive welcome ; public speeches and dinners, introductions and visits to churches followed close on one another. Newman was embraced on both shoulders by the Archbishop, the same who was later assassinated. An enthusiastic account of the visit went into *L'Univers* : Newman charmed everyone with '*sa simplicité et sa modestie*'.

From Paris they went on to Langres to see Dalgairns, and here again they were splendidly welcomed, almost too splendidly for comfort. 'We are all knocked up by their mode of living,' Newman told Bowles, left behind at Maryvale. Meals at 11 a.m. and 7 p.m. all cooked in oil, cold wine to drink instead of hot tea, played havoc with their digestion and the feather beds with their rest. After one sleepless night Newman 'all but fainted at Mass and was obliged to come out of the Church'. The same day at noon there was a state dinner at which he had to talk Latin — as his French was so poor. 'I rejoice to say it went off very well. It was a very elegant dinner.' French manners were elegant too, and Newman was amused to be 'handed as a lady to a sofa. . . . They have never done bowing in the most formal manner . . . and for me, who hardly ever made a formal bow in my life, I can hardly keep my countanance as I put my elbows on my hips and make a segment of a circle, the lower vertebrae being the centre and my head the circumference.'

On they went to Besançon, where they were greeted with more courtesy and Latin and a dish of fricasseed frogs. 'I rather think Newman relished them,' St. John told Dalgairns, 'but I am sure it

was out of obedience that he ate them.' They started for Italy on a
Wednesday, went over the Simplon Pass and arrived in Milan in time
for the last mass in the Duomo on Sunday morning. They had
rooms usually reserved for retreat preachers in the house attached
to the Church of S. Fidelis, 'lofty, cool and quiet in the heart of
Milan'. The quietness was a great blessing after their tiring journey
and Newman fell in love with the church, 'Grecian' as he called it,
in style. He wrote to William Penny, a convert who had recently
joined the Maryvale community, 'It has such a sweet, smiling, open
countenance, and the altar is so gracious and winning — standing
out for all to see and approach'. Indeed he loved Milan at first
sight ; he was ready to do so for the sake of St. Ambrose, who had
held out against an Imperial family which favoured Arian heretics ;
but once there he was almost more overcome by St. Charles Borro-
meo, the holy Cardinal who had done so much, in the sixteenth
century, to put into practice the reforms of the Council of Trent.
'He died at forty-six — scarcely more than the age at which I have
begun to live,' Newman told Mrs. Bowden, and to Penny he wrote,
'He was raised up to resist that dreadful storm under which poor
England fell'. He hoped the saint would help them ; 'and my mind
has been full of him, so that I have even dreamed of him — and we go
most days and kneel at his shrine, not forgetting Maryvale when there'.

They breakfasted every day on rolls and coffee near the Duomo.
'The Duomo is the most beautiful building I ever saw,' Newman
told Penny. 'As you go about the city, its pinnacles are like bright
snow against the blue sky. We have been up to the top twice.' Then
they went home for Italian lessons with a young man who was an
ardent nationalist. 'It did not require him to make us detest the
tyranny of the Austrian government,' Newman wrote to Jemima.
'It is inconceivable.' To their disappointment they just missed
meeting Manzoni, the author of the famous *I promessi sposi* which
Newman had admired so much. 'A Catholic cathedral is a sort of
world', he told H. W., fascinated by the varied life that went on in the
great churches. It had its less pleasant side. 'They spit everywhere,'
he remarked to Penny, 'they spit on the kneeling boards — they
encourage it and as if for amusement go on every ten seconds — I
should not wonder if it encouraged consumption.' His letters were
transcriptions of what was happening, alive with the mood of the
moment. 'I have just asked St. John what else to say and he says
"Tell him you bully me,"' he wrote to Dalgairns. 'This is true,
but he deserves it — I am glad to tell you he is decidedly stronger.

I having been making him take some quinine.' He teased St. John, who came in with his hat over his eyes after his first Italian hair-cut.

They did not go on to Rome till the end of October, reluctant to leave Milan. The journey was so hazardous, owing to floods and to the disturbed state of the country, that reports reached England of their being nearly drowned, or murdered by bandits. They did have to take to boats twice on the way to Genoa; describing it to David Lewis, Newman said 'then we had all our luggage opened under a most threatening sky without any covering — then we were mounted atop of our luggage in two one-horse carts riding backwards sundry miles till nightfall — and then in the dusk and rain to be rowed across the mighty Po'. From Genoa they went to Leghorn by steamer, then to Pisa by railroad, by steamer to Civita Vecchia, and on to Rome by diligence. They went, as he told Jemima, 'to say the Apostles' Creed at St. Peter's tomb, the first thing — and there was the Pope at the tomb saying Mass — so that he was the first person I saw in Rome and I was quite close to him.' This was not the Pope Gregory who had sent him an Apostolic blessing, but the new Pope, Pius IX, destined for a long and stormy pontificate.

The College of Propaganda was still not ready to receive them and they had to stay over a week at an hotel. 'It is a palace of filth', Newman wrote to Stanton at Maryvale. 'We thought it bad enough in France, when in an elegant room they had placed a pie dish and a basin of sugar instead of a wash hand basin and soap — bad enough at Milan where we washed our feet by instalments, but here . . . the carpet is a nest of fleas and they have milk pans for slop pails.' Troubles with clothes began again. 'We are obliged to dress in the queerest fashion, which besides its irksomeness is in this dirty place like dressing up black a moors in muslin.' St. John hated to be different from everyone else and was 'dying for his shorts' — knee breeches — but Newman was more uncomfortable when they arrived. 'It is enough to drive one into an order at once, the extreme torment of this dressing up', he said. 'Buckles at the knees, buckles on the shoes, a dress coat with a sort of undergraduate's gown hanging behind, black stockings which must be without a wrinkle, and a large heavy cocked hat; that I should have lived so long to be so dressed up! A cassock is allowable and as soon as possible I shall shrink into it, but as I may have to go to the Pope directly I have been obliged to provide myself with my miseries first of all.' He found the hat completely useless, for it had no brim to keep off the weather, and blew off at every gust of wind.

When they got to Propaganda at last, on November 9th, they had to buy yet more clothes. Newman groaned over the expense, but he preferred the college cassock to struggling with buckles and stockings. Far from being turned into schoolboys again, they were treated, he felt, with too much deference ; it seemed to be expected that they would use their rooms merely as lodgings. They were papered 'with drawing-room patterns' and new furnished. 'We are treated like princes,' he told Mrs. Bowden, laughing at 'the worked muslin curtains to our beds — it is really quite absurd, considering our habits.' Determined not to be too pampered they 'begged off carpets' and did not light the stove put in for them, because the students did not have such luxuries. For the same reason they gave up the butter put out for them at breakfast. But the Rector insisted on their having tea, for he had installed a wonderful machine to make it, in their rooms. So St. John solemnly made tea every day during Newman's Italian lesson ; when he came in with it Newman was reduced to stammers, too self-conscious to attempt a foreign language with someone listening. St. John, much the better linguist, used to visit the students and talk to them ; he also saved the situation at the recreations with the Jesuit Fathers who ran the college. 'I will say this, that since I cannot even talk English to strangers, it is not wonderful that in a room full I cannot say a word of Italian', said Newman. But he used to call on the Fathers in their rooms and managed to talk a little then, in spite of shyness and English fright at speaking a foreign language.

Latin of course was hardly foreign to him, and the lectures were given in Latin. The students were surprised but respectful at his attending them. (H. W. was fascinated : 'Who examines *Newman* ?' he demanded of St. John.) At first Newman went to all the lectures, but soon, in a joint letter, St. John was accusing him of going to sleep and nodding in morals and dogmatics. He was really wasting his time following a schedule meant for beginners, and the day was already so divided up with devotions, meals, recreations and so on that he could scarcely find leisure to write letters, let alone study. So he gave up lectures and began to turn some of his work on St. Athanasius into Latin dissertations, hoping it would facilitate discussions with Roman theologians.

Meanwhile the weather was terrible, it rained incessantly, and first St. John caught a cold and then Newman. Later it snowed, a fairly rare occurrence in Rome ; Newman was always unlucky with weather. In spite of this they usually went out in the afternoons, visiting churches and making calls. Miss Giberne was in Rome and delighted to see them. 'He used to come often to my lonely lodgings . . . to tell me to take care of myself', she wrote. 'I thank God for him. Everyone makes much of him and all try to be introduced to him.' It did not occur to Newman to go into society. It seemed natural to him to live like a poor student and only go out to pray at shrines, visit religious, or see that Miss Giberne was keeping warm and comfortable ; but no doubt it appeared very odd to the Romans.

It was after a call on Miss Giberne that they were suddenly summoned to the Pope's presence. Newman described it all to Bowles. 'I never saw any city with the tenth part of the quantity of dung in the streets as Rome. When the rain comes this is formed into a thickish fluid. Last Sunday it rained hard, and when we came in our mantellas had a deep fringe of the nastiest stuff I ever saw and all wet. Well, in this state, in came the Rector and said we were to go to the Pope in half an hour. How are we to dress ? You are to go as you are. But our mantellas are dirty. Never mind — we are used to that — we will put them in water. So the tails of our mantellas were dipped in water, not to remove, but to hide the colour of the dirt (this was a simple fact as next morning showed) and in this state we went in Mgr. Brunelli's carriage to be introduced to the Holy Father.' After all that they had to wait an hour and a half before they saw 'the poor Pope, who is overwhelmed with work from morning till night'. Of Pius IX, Newman said, 'He is a vigorous man with a very pleasant countenance, and was most kind'. This was the occasion when, in kissing the Pope's foot, Newman hit his head on his knee. The Holy Father was very friendly, called Newman a recovered sheep, and told them a story about a convert clergyman. 'St. John in his simplicity said, "What is his name ?" on which he with great good humour laid his hand upon his arm and said something like "Do you think I can pronounce your English names ?" . . . He is quick in his movements and ran across the room to open a closet and gave us a beautiful oil painting of the Mater Dolorosa.'

The effect of this good beginning was soon spoilt by an unfortunate incident, which Newman afterwards regarded as 'a presage of his after course'. In 1863 he wrote in his journal, 'O I was a sort of sucking child, just as much knowing what I should say, what I should not say, and saying nothing right, not from want of tact so much as from sheer ignorance'. A niece of Lady Shrewsbury died, and Prince Borghese came in person to ask Newman to preach the funeral oration. All the English in Rome would go, Protestants too ; what a chance to convert them, the Prince thought, imagining that only worldly motives kept them from the Church. Newman tried to get out of it on the score that he was only in minor orders, but Prince Borghese insisted on getting permission. There was no refusing, short of offending all the most devout Catholic aristocrats of Rome and England. So the very next day Newman had to face a large congregation of fashionable strangers ; he did not know them, but of course they all knew about him. He preached from outside the altar rails. The sermon would have been considered a failure in any case, because his delivery was thought even by English people to be odd, so plain and cold. To Italians it seemed even stranger. Miss Giberne loyally defended him. 'His deliberate manner arose from his deep feeling.' Everyone else thought him stern.

But the matter was worse than the manner to the English present. They were all wealthy people who had come to Rome for a winter's amusement. It was a nasty shock to be told that 'Rome was not the place for them, but the very place in the whole world where Michael and the Dragon may almost be seen in battle'. Nothing is more annoying when complacently fulfilling a pious duty than to hear the uncomfortable news that the way of salvation is not easy. Richard Simpson, a lively and intelligent convert clergyman, and his wife were present ; they thought the English Catholics quite as much irritated as the Protestants. 'We all need conversion', Newman said to people who thought they had everything they needed.

But it was the Protestants who felt themselves most aggrieved. St. John said afterwards that Newman expressly excepted those present when he attacked the behaviour of English tourists in Rome, who thought nothing of 'prying like brute animals into the holiest places'. Victorian memoirs are full of the sort of things that he meant ; Protestants were then so ignorant of Catholic worship, and so convinced it was all idolatry, that they felt it a positive duty to ignore the mummery going on round them. Newman perhaps hoped that those present might drop hints to the others. But they all went out feeling insulted, and told everyone that Newman had said they were no better than dogs. On Christmas Day, in the Ara Coeli, Ambrose recorded in his diary, there were lots of Protestants 'looking as if they would eat Newman'. 'The story was made worse, and the anger excited greater, on each successive tradition', Newman told Mrs. Bowden in January, when he had got over the first shock of his

blunder. 'At length the Protestant world got into a regular fury and
Miss Ryder heard a man express the sentiment in a party, that I
ought to be thrown into the Tyber.'   When Newman attacked the
world, it was no vague abstraction, but nineteenth-century society in
all its monumental self-satisfaction, and he pulled no punches.   It
was this telling of home truths that roused such antagonism.   It is
curious how many people used images of physical violence in their
anger against him.

But Newman had not expected to annoy people;   he writhed
inwardly at what he felt was a stupid blunder.   It was all made worse
by George Talbot, who, though he had quite enjoyed the sermon at
the time, changed his mind when he found how unpopular it was,
and repeated the whole story to the Pope.   Pius remarked that on
these occasions honey was more suitable than vinegar and supposed
that Newman must be more of a philosopher than an orator.   'This,
the said person,' Newman told Mrs. Bowden, not naming Talbot,
'who thinks he is my friend, and is in a way, told all over Rome and
gave an edge to the condemnation with which my unhappy sermon
was visited.'   Perhaps it was a presage, for it gave important people
in Rome a distorted impression of Newman as an awkward scholar,
hopeless at managing the human situations of daily life and a tiresome
puritan into the bargain.

This social setback occurred just when Newman was beginning
to hear adverse comments on his Development theory.   The most
famous theologian in Rome, Perrone, was said to be picking out
pieces of the *Essay* to attack in his lectures, and in America a clever
convert from Unitarianism, Orestes Brownson, who ran his own
magazine, was fulminating against the whole conception of development in doctrine.   He thought that to say the doctrine of the Trinity
had been developed was to say that it was not primitive;   since this
was just what the Unitarians asserted, Brownson excitedly denounced
the Development as heretical.   Newman's friends wanted him to
answer Brownson, but he scorned to do so.   Brownson was a layman,
and not a theologian but a journalist;   Newman thought his ungentle-
manly conduct was to be expected of 'a half-converted Yankee'.
But the noise Brownson made thickened the atmosphere of disapproval, for his paper was read and quoted widely.

The attitude of Roman theologians was more serious, and Newman tried to grapple with it, characteristically, by getting to know
the men who were suspicious of him.   In this way, he soon won
round Perrone to a more open-minded, though cautious, approach

to his theory. Newman did not mind its being criticized as a theory, but a piecemeal picking of holes irritated and depressed him. He was well aware that he had not written it in the language of modern Catholic theologians, and that it needed correction, but it was the idea itself he wanted discussed. But he had decided to write no defences, to let the book make its own way, trusting that if it was true it would be accepted in the end. All the same, he thought it worth while to familiarize Catholics with his ideas, and for this reason suggested to Dalgairns that his sermons on Faith and Reason might be translated into French, as a kind of introduction to the *Essay on Development*. In a letter to him he expressed his feelings as an author and thinker.

'And now after reading these sermons I must say I think they are as a whole the best things I have written and I cannot believe they are not Catholic. Indeed there are times (I mean after reading them and the like) that feelings come upon me, which do not often else, but then vividly — I mean the feeling that I have not been done justice to — but I must leave all this to Him who knows what to do with me. People do not know me — and sometimes they half pass me by. It has been the portion of Saints even ; and may well be my portion. He who gives gifts, is the best Judge how to use His own — He has the sole right to do as He will, and He knows what He is doing. Yet sometimes it is marvellous to me how my life is going and I have never been brought out prominently — and now I am less likely than ever — for there seems something of an iron form here, though I may be wrong — but I mean, people are at no trouble to deepen their views. It is natural.'

When he came to Rome, Newman was surprised to find that theology was taught on a system of bits and pieces from second-rate manuals. Not only was St. Augustine unknown, but even the medieval St. Thomas Aquinas was not read. This was partly due to the far-reaching effects of the French Revolution, and the wars, which had closed the great schools of France and attenuated the traditions of other countries. The Austrian Empire was still suffering from the Josephite policy of state control, when religious orders had been out of favour, and seminaries interfered with by government officials. Thus even in 1845 Catholic intellectual studies were at a low ebb, and just at a period when the secular world was in a ferment of scientific discovery, political revolution and criticism of the fundamentals of religion.

Of course, it was not Catholics alone who were intellectually no

match for the new inquirers, but it was Catholics with whom Newman
was now concerned. He said of Perrone to Penny, 'I have as respectful an opinion of him in dogmatics as I think him often most
absurd in polemics. In polemics he does not understand the arguments he has to deal with.' This was Newman's field ; he called
himself a controversialist, not a theologian. It was an inadequate
name for what he was ; controversy for him was not a boxing match,
but a method of seeing more deeply into the truth behind the opposing views. Even the theory of development was an historical and
practical idea, the result of brooding over what had actually happened.
Newman's method was always the same : he started with the Church
as a fact, the faith as an objective system, he then took various
difficulties and objections, putting them in their most acute form,
and answered them, not piecemeal, but integrally, by bringing out
the true perspective in which they should be seen. This was
'deepening views'. It could not be done in abstracts from text-
books, without reference to what people were thinking and feeling
or what was happening in the world. But it is a trouble to think,
a trouble even to feel deeply ; it is easier to repeat a lesson than
to try to understand a difficulty, and easier still to criticize someone
else who is making the attempt.

For Newman there was a further reason why he was not 'brought
out' which he did not realize : there were few minds which could
take in the full import of his views. For he was a creative genius,
and several generations have to pass before smaller minds can
begin to understand the depth of such a one.

Newman wrote to Henry Wilberforce on December 13th, and
his letter reflects his first feeling on these failures of communication,
which came, like the snow to Rome, so soon after he arrived there.
'Both what people here can do for me and what they cannot carries
off the mind to Him who "has fed me all my life long unto this
day", whom I find protecting me most wonderfully under such
new circumstances just as He ever has before, and who can give
me that sympathy which man cannot give.' Perhaps just because
there was this shadow of unhappiness in his public life, he told
Henry how happy he was at Propaganda. This was no passing
mood, for in 1863 he could still refer in his journal to 'the happy
days, thank God, at Propaganda'. 'It is a kind of dream, — and
yet so quiet, so safe, so happy — as if I had always been here — as
if there had been no violent rupture or vicissitude in the course of
my life — nay, more quiet and happy than before.' And he looked

back to his time at Oxford and Littlemore and Maryvale, and felt the same happiness had been his.

So it was, the real happiness of his heart in prayer and work for God. What made for unhappiness was the mysterious way in which he was again and again frustrated in what he felt was his special task, the intellectual battle with the forces of the world at enmity with God. But still, he was not going to give up the fight. He was going to get Perrone and the others to talk things over, and he was going to make up his mind on the difficult question of how best to organize the energies and talents of the community at Maryvale in the service of God.

1847

Philip Neri and the Idea of the Oratory

THE question of Newman's vocation within the Catholic Church was complex, involving not only his unique position and talents, but the lives of so many other converts, for already, as well as his Littlemore companions, others were collecting round him. Much thought and prayer was needed to make the right decision, but no time was wasted. Newman arrived in Rome in November, and by the turn of the year this problem had taken precedence over all else. Before he had left England, Wiseman had suggested the answer might lie in the institute of St. Philip Neri's Oratory. From Milan, where they had attended an 'oratorio' in the evening which had turned out to be simply a concert, Newman had written to Dalgairns, 'It seems rather the age for external secularism with a gentle inward bond of asceticism — and this is just Oratorianism'. But in Rome he did not at once take up the idea, partly because the others were at first more interested in better-known and larger religious orders; Dalgairns in the Dominicans and St. John in the Jesuits.

In Rome Newman talked to an Irish Dominican who disparaged the Movement in England, 'but this may be Irish, not Dominican', he shrewdly observed to Dalgairns, writing him a long letter at the new year. He thought that Order inclined to rigorism. 'I shall be of a (so-called) lax school.' The great Dominican revival had then scarcely begun. The Jesuits Newman admired very much; they were like first-class Oxford men, he told Jemima. Many of the younger Oxford converts did in fact join the Society. After its suppression by the Pope in the eighteenth century the Society had revived with redoubled vigour, and the best education among Catholics in most countries was to be found in its colleges. This had perhaps given the Jesuits more prestige and a certain preponderance over other religious institutions at that time. In 1846, judging from those he met in Rome, their only defect seemed to Newman too much conservatism. He thought them 'suspicious of *change*, with a perfect incapacity to create anything *positive* for the wants of the times'.

But it was not only the Orders themselves that had to be considered, but how to make the best use of the converts in England, and Newman's own influence. He felt doubtful, not only of fitting into an order at his age, but of being any use in it. 'I have the greatest fear of bamboozling myself when I talk of an order,' he said to Dalgairns, 'or that, just as Anglicans talk of being Catholics but feel drawn back when it comes to the point, so I at my time of life shall never be able to give up property and take to new habits. Not that I should not do it had I a clear call, but it is so difficult to know what a clear call is.' It was not material property he was concerned with — he had never had much and there was less than ever now — but his books, his work. 'When it comes upon me how late I am beginning to serve the Church, the obvious answer is, "Even Saints, such as St. Augustine, St. Ignatius, did not begin in earnest till a late age". "Yes, but I am much older than they."' He was some ten to fifteen years older. 'So then I go on to trust that my past life may form . . . a part of future usefulness. Having lived so long in Oxford my name and person are known to a very great many people I do not know, so are my books, and I may have begun a work which I am now to finish. Now the question is whether as a regular I do not at once cut off all this as becoming a sort of instrument of others and so clear beginning life again. . . . As a Jesuit e.g. no one would know that I was speaking my own words or was a continuation as it were of my former self.'

He was to find it hard to convince his countrymen that he was not the mere mouthpiece of others, even without the handicap, as it was in those prejudiced times, of being a Jesuit. Newman's mission had all along been to draw those who were very far from the Church, but sincerely seeking the truth and acting according to conscience, nearer to the fullness of Catholic Faith. As a member of one of these famous Orders he would, in that time and place, be removing himself from any possibility of affecting further those who were disposed still to listen. At this point, only a year or so after his reception, Newman was hopeful that the majority of those who had joined in the Movement would come to see that their true home was in the Catholic Church gathered round the centre of unity at Rome.

Some had suggested that Newman should form his own community, and he had wondered whether at Maryvale they might not be most useful in assisting in the teaching of theology at Oscott, but he disliked the idea of starting something of his own, and now that his theology seemed so unpopular it might be wiser to leave it alone for the present. Faber had started his own community, and written the rule for it, and seemed to be encouraged ; but Newman had not such self-confidence.

'Well then, we said to ourselves, let us see what the Oratorians are like', he wrote to Dalgairns in the middle of January. 'We do not hear much about them — they are said to be good confessors.' Thereupon they visited the Church St. Philip Neri built, the Chiesa Nuova, and the house of the Roman Oratory. Father Theiner, an Oratorian and eminent theologian, said mass for them and gave them communion in 'the small room where St. Philip had his ecstasies'. Of the house Newman said, 'The casa is the most beautiful thing of its kind we have seen in Rome — rather too comfortable, i.e. fine galleries for walking in summer, splendid orange trees etc. etc. If I wished to follow my bent I should join them if I joined any. They have a good library and handsome sets of rooms apparently. It is like a college with barely any rule. They keep their own property and furnish their own rooms.' The Oratory was not, strictly speaking, a religious order ; its members took no vows, and could leave at any time, and each house was completely autonomous. Nevertheless the Fathers lived in obedience to a rule ; they were not a mere collection of individuals living in the same house, but a close-knit body with a carefully balanced constitution. The Father Superior, or Provost, elected every three years, was assisted by a council of four Deputies, elected from among the Decennial Fathers, who had been ten years in the congregation. This council appointed the other officers : in charge of the house, of ceremonies, of the novices and so on. St. Philip was a Florentine, and his institute is a kind of elective republic in which the president, while in office, has limited powers, and the supreme authority is the General Congregation of Decennial Fathers.

These were the bare bones of organization, but the spirit, the personality so to speak, of the Oratory was that of Philip Neri himself, of all founders surely the most original, not to say accidental, for it was a long time before he could be persuaded to leave his little room and live with his disciples. The Pope ordered it, so at last he removed, carrying his frying pan and with a train of friends bringing his other belongings. But the cat was left behind and someone had to go back to feed it twice a day.

Philip Neri, born in 1515 in Florence, left home as a youth ostensibly to seek his fortune under the auspices of an uncle, but he soon abandoned all thought of a career in the world. When he first came to Rome he earned a meagre living by teaching the boys in a house where he was given lodging. But he spent a great deal of his time, often at night, praying in the catacombs, or out in the country. He had no idea of being a priest, but as a dedicated layman he drew many people to him by his attractive personality and some were later organized as a Confraternity, wearing red cloaks and working in the hospitals. Judging by his portraits as an old man, Philip must have been well built and good looking ; there is something solid in his face and the set of his head which does not suggest the physique most people imagine suitable to a visionary. And yet in an age of ecstatic saints he was one of the most extraordinary. Living in a great city amid a crowd of curious observers, his miracles and seizures are more extensively documented than those of many of his more famous contemporaries. We know so little about the natural powers of human beings that it is not possible always to distinguish what is supernatural ; apart from the special gifts of God, Philip may have been a natural seer, and his fits of trembling which he tried in vain to control and hide, occasioned by the particular make up of his own psycho-physical organism. He was always extremely suspicious of supposed supernatural manifestations, and in his direction of others severely practical, setting would-be visionaries to empty hospital slops, and clever people to cook dinners, or do things which made them look silly.

Philip was over thirty when he was persuaded to be a priest by his confessor, over forty when the future members of his congregation began to gather round him and fifty when its rule was approved and it began to stabilize. He was not an organizer ; he liked to let things grow and he was suspicious of formality and abstractions. The Oratory, originally, was just his way of organizing an evening of prayer, meditation, penance and instruction. People, quite often laymen, spoke impromptu, passages from Scripture were read and commented on, and later there was music, often written by Palestrina, Philip's friend, and sung for love by singers in the choirs of great churches. Sometimes the whole thing took place out of doors, or on pilgrimages round the shrines. The freedom and liveliness of the proceedings aroused the suspicions of severe or conservative persons, and several times Philip was called a heretic ; once, under the stern Pope St. Pius V his congregation was on the point of suppression. Somehow he survived, and the Oratory grew in influence.

Philip, whose own life was so simple and austere, rejected nothing of the new world of the Renaissance : not the new learning, the new science, nor the new arts and the new manners. His principle was to plant the seed of real devotion to Christ in the hearts of those who came to him, trusting that as it grew it would cast off all that was doubtful in the pursuits and amusements of his penitents. Worldliness was a disease which he teased and laughed out of countenance. He lived to be eighty, very old for that time, and, right to the last, streams of people visited him, learned and simple, Cardinals and street boys, nobles and students ; among his friends too were women from all ranks of society, mostly living in the world and managing families. As a young man Philip had had some difficulty in keeping the women at a proper distance — he was, after all, a layman, and a young and good-looking, not to say gay, one. His method was to take flight, which caused amusement at the time. When he grew older and after he was a priest, he was able to take a more positive line. He had a special gift for attracting young men and boys, because they found in him a Christianity uncompromising with the world, but human and humorous too. In the Italy of those days sodomy was by no means unknown, and Philip had occasion to speak about it with some of the youths he met when he too was young ; his own kind of friendship, affectionate but detached, attracted more than were drawn by the dangerous variety.

'This great saint', Newman told Jemima, 'reminds me in so many ways of Keble that I can fancy what K. would have been if God's will had been he should have been born in another place and age ; he was formed on the same type of extreme hatred of humbug, playfulness, nay, oddity, tender love for others, and severity, which are lineaments of Keble.' Some of these were the lineaments of someone else too. Newman was born with a very different temperament, physical and psychical, from Philip Neri, but he shared more than might be supposed at first sight with his patron saint.

In January, between the Feasts of St. Peter's Chair and St. Paul's Conversion, Newman and St. John made a *novena* of prayers to St. Peter, at his tomb, for light on their vocation and studied the Oratorian Rule, and the history of the Congregation. St. Philip, who was unwilling to found anything, had never wanted to go further than ensuring the continuance of the Oratory in Rome ; when some of his keenest followers got his reluctant permission to start one at Naples, friction had occurred between the two groups, since Naples developed in a different manner from Rome. After St. Philip died and other Oratories were founded, in Lombardy, Tuscany, Sicily and elsewhere, his principle of independence was maintained, and the only thing that linked the various houses was the Rule. Since the Fathers took no vows, the Rule was also, within each house, its binding force. Thus it had even more importance than the Rule in religious orders organized under vows, where the individual members, and the different houses, were subject to a hierarchy of authority, whether elected or appointed.

But when Newman came to study the Oratorian Rule he found it was more like a list of decrees and customs of the sixteenth-century Oratory, in which essentials were mixed with practices which time had rendered obsolete, or unsuitable to nineteenth-century England. Newman instanced some of these : 'four sermons running every day, disciplining before or with a congregation, going in a troop from Church to Church, sitting down on the grass and singing, getting by heart a finished composition etc. etc.' At first he was told the Rule must not be changed in any particular, and was somewhat daunted. But later he learned that a certain amount of adaptation had gone on in the Italian houses without the Rule being altered, and that for England alteration would probably be sanctioned. In fact, the Italian Oratories were to find it necessary to revise the Rule as time went on, but when Newman studied it, they had not done so. He himself adapted the Rule for England, so carefully that it did not afterwards need revision. He distinguished the binding decrees from the customs, which were to be used according to discretion. The chief change was the insertion of a clause allowing the Fathers, in case of grave necessity, to keep a school. The Oratory was not primarily an educational institute but England was gravely in need of Catholic education and even at the beginning a few boys had lived at the Chiesa Nuova as pupils. Oratorian Fathers were encouraged to pursue intellectual studies ; St. Philip's most faithful disciple, Baronius, was set by him to write the history of the Church. Both it and he became famous, and consequently he came in for a lot of teasing from St. Philip.

The idea of taking the discipline in public, edifying as it no doubt was to Italians of the sixteenth century, was quite impossible in Victorian England. St. John said to Dalgairns, 'Newman has never told you that it is part of the Oratorian Rule to flog, I think in public,

but in the dark during Lent for edification. If this rule is essential
and cannot be abolished, he says he will put you and Irish John in
front as the best floggers, whilst he and Walker retire to the rear and
lay on gently behind a screen.' Irish John was a lay brother at
Maryvale. Luckily publicity was not essential to the exercise. But
as a penance, in private, for the whole community, it was the established custom in St. Philip's time, and Newman, although he put it
among the optional parts of the Rule, intended to follow it. Some
years later he found it had been dropped in most of the north Italian
houses, but he did not know this in 1847 ; nor did he change it when
he did know. This penitential exercise was to take place three times
a week after the spiritual exercises of the Oratory, when half an hour
of meditation was made in common every evening before the formal
communal meal. A Latin narrative of Christ's Passion was recited
and the Psalm Miserere. The room was to be dark except for a dim
light on the crucifix, so that, in fact, publicity was reduced to a
minimum. The Oratory was not intended to be severely ascetic,
and St. Philip had laid the greatest emphasis on inward mortification ;
but the penance of the discipline was one he employed frequently
himself, especially when he was dealing with difficult people or
situations.

The Oratory had grown up as a centre in a large city, drawing to
itself the lost and the curious, the eager and the uncertain, who
needed more help than they could get in the parish churches, or who
perhaps hardly went to churches at all. The Fathers had always
been preachers, instructors and confessors ; confessions were heard
every day, and services and devotions were frequent. They did not
go out and give missions, or travel about as members of large orders
often do, but stayed in their centre, collecting people round them.
It was part of the Rule that Oratories should be in large cities, and
this was just what was needed in England, where, except for the
country gentlemen's estates, Catholics, mostly poor, were congregated
in towns.

Newman saw that, as Wiseman had suggested, there were great
possibilities for the Oratory in England. Its freedom, democratic
constitution and the independence of the houses appealed to Englishmen. Its common life and rule would give strength and support to
priests working in the large towns, while providing a nucleus around
which parishes might grow up. The Fathers would for the most
part support themselves. It was a particularly suitable way of organizing the converts, older than most candidates for the priesthood,

keen but unfamiliar with Catholic life, and for the most part men of
high intellectual training, and with money of their own. In an
Oratory they could work both at books and pastorally, and form
centres where inquirers would naturally come. Although Newman,
like St. Philip, would never look far ahead, or plan for the future, he
saw that it would be possible, and useful, for Oratories to arise in
every big town in England. The institute, although it was small,
and hardly known outside Italy, was remarkably adaptable, and
seemed to be both of 'a so-called lax school' and yet not too conservative to produce 'something positive for the needs of the times'.
Newman made up his mind and wrote a long Latin letter which was
taken to the Pope, who warmly approved. It was settled that
Newman should found the Oratory in England, and settled on his
birthday. He was forty-six.

The same day he wrote to Mrs. Bowden that he did not like to
be starting anything new, and this was not. But for him it was a
new beginning. 'I wish (but perhaps it is not right to wish) I had
more confidence in myself — but I seem to myself to have none. I
cannot realize to myself that my time is not past.' He asked for her
prayers. But though he had doubts of himself, he had none of the
work. He wrote to Wiseman at once, reminding him that the
Oratory had been his suggestion, and that he thought there was a
place for it in Birmingham — where he would still be in Wiseman's
jurisdiction. 'I suppose you would say it ought to be in a populous
part of Birmingham in the midst of the mechanics.' He was anxious
that ground should be bought before the newspapers got on to the
story. As to the house and church he proposed to build: 'I'm
afraid I shall shock Pugin'. He did shock Pugin, whom he met in
Rome. Pugin cried out that he would as soon build a Mechanics'
Institute as an Oratory. Pugin was convinced the classic style was
pagan: the war of the Goths and Pagans was in full swing!

The Pope wanted them to make their novitiate together in Rome
under an Oratorian father; the others were hastily summoned from
England, and Dalgairns from France — he was to bring some six-
penny keepsakes for the boys at Propaganda, medals and so on.
Newman was in high spirits now, joking about the kind of men they
wanted — 'with a good deal of fun in them — for that will especially
be wanted in an Oratory. Fat Marshall, I don't think you saw him,
is the kind of man — to please boys and young men and keep them
together. . . . I should like a good mimic to take off the great Exeter
Hall guns. What stuff I am writing. If we have not spirit it will be

like bottled beer with the cork out.' Exeter Hall was the London
headquarters of the Protestant Evangelical Alliance, a powerful
organization with a strong No-Popery platform. Penny and Stanton
turned up in March, the first from Maryvale ; the others came later,
even Bowles, though Newman had rather wished he would not,
because he was a nervous type and needed so much looking after.
Robert Coffin made a retreat with the Jesuits and decided to throw
in his lot with the Oratory. Even George Talbot suddenly offered
himself. Newman tactfully put him off. It is curious that Talbot,
who played the part of a Catholic Golightly in Newman's life, should,
like Golightly, have come under his spell at first.

Faber had now heard the news in England and wrote some agitated
letters in his decorative handwriting, which, with its archaisms,
scarcely altered all his life and seems so much a part of his personality.
His style was vivid and his view of life highly dramatic. He was
afraid the two communities might suffer from similarity and proxim-
ity. Newman did not think so, and said so. Faber's community
appeared to be much more monastic, ascetic and romantic than the
Oratory, and he would be in the country near Alton Towers, whereas
Newman would be among the mechanics in Birmingham. Back came
a long reply full of reported gossip, which Faber laughed off in a not
very convincing way. 'Some say you craftily got ye Bishop to remove
us from Birmingham that we might not stand in your way.' He had
been at Oscott before Easter for his ordination. 'Of course I heard
a good deal during ye *ennuyante* fortnight spent at distracting gossiping Oscott, and people seemed inclined to doubt and criticize.
What strikes me as oddest is ye way people have mixed you and our
piccola famiglia together, trying to make out we are intersecting each
other and so on.' There were several references to 'Santo Padre, as
we call St. Philip', to show Newman that St. Philip, as well as St.
Wilfrid, was really Faber's property. He had translated an Italian
life of St. Philip. The Saint's ecstasies and miracles greatly appealed
to the romantic Faber, and the anecdotes of the tricks he employed
to hide his fervour and emotion, so that people should not think him
holy because of them.

In the same letter Faber described his triumphal return to St.
Wilfrid's as a priest. He was welcomed with guns and fireworks and
triumphal arches, stayed up till midnight hearing confessions and
next day said mass and preached two sermons in the new church he
had built. The Protestant church was deserted in favour of this
novel exhibition of Popery unashamed. But after this success story

Faber returned to the sore spot, 'I am supposed to be biting my fingers off with rage at your Jesuitical plot for ousting me from Birmingham!' It was not an encouraging prospect, whether it was Faber or others who were watching suspiciously from afar. But there was nothing Newman could do about it.

Meanwhile he was in Rome for Holy Week and Easter. He and St. John went to the Pellegrini on Good Friday to wash the feet of poor pilgrims, feet that evidently needed a wash, for some years later Newman mentioned it as a task unpleasant in itself, but with a certain romantic halo about it, unlike other less spectacular charitable services. From April the 8th till the 17th he made a retreat at St. Eusebio, for ordination, although he was not in fact ordained until Trinity Sunday, June 1st. He kept the Latin notes in which he analysed the state of his heart and soul. 'I have in my mind a wound or cancer, the presence of which prevents me from being a good Oratorian. . . . I creep along the ground, or even run . . . but I cannot fly. I have not in me the elements required for rising and advancing.' He analysed this further : 'It is difficult to explain and strange even to myself, but I have this peculiarity, that in the movement of my affections, whether sacred or human, my physical strength cannot go beyond certain limits. I am always languid in the contemplation of divine things, like a man walking with his feet bound together. I am held as it were by a fetter, by a sort of physical law, so that I cannot be forcible in preaching or speaking, nor fervent in praying and meditating.' It may have been a psycho-physical limitation imposed by his natural temperament ; his feelings were deep and tenacious rather than forceful and warm. But the fact that he felt this as a limitation suggests that in some sense he went beyond it ; to feel his power of loving inadequate to his will was already to love more than those who are quite content with themselves in this respect.

The details of what seemed to him his failure to fly were prosaic and practical as usual. He did not want riches, but he did not like poverty ; the mean was always a temptation. He thought he avoided bodily pain more than he used to. 'I do not like a rule of life, although for eighteen years I have wished to live a more or less regular life. I like tranquility, security, a life among friends, and among books, untroubled by business cares — the life of an Epicurean in fact.' He felt his mind was growing slower as he grew older, he was unready in learning new habits and embarrassed by the unfamiliar in Catholic devotions, blaming himself for this. 'In almost everything I like my own way of acting ; I do not want to change the place or business in which I find myself, to undertake the affairs of others, to walk, to go on a journey to visit others, since I prefer to remain at home. I am querulous, timid, lazy, suspicious ; I crawl along the ground, feeble, downcast and despondent.'

Yet he was about to bind himself as strongly as a man can be bound, to all the things he would rather not do ; not only in his life as a priest but in the laborious task of setting up the Oratory in England, which would inevitably involve him in business cares, housekeeping on a large scale, travelling and publicity. As for the affairs of others, he was about to shoulder the responsibility of trying to form a religious body out of a heterogeneous collection of high spirited individualists, and that in a country where his every movement attracted attention, and even Catholics were on the watch for lapses on the part of the converts. He never had lived the Epicurean life that tempted him, even at Oriel, but now he was going to throw away for ever the chance of it. He would never be on his own again, but bound to work and sacrifice himself for his religious family just as he had done so long for the family he was born in. And now the Catholic practices he had taken up with such enthusiasm years ago were no longer novel : 'now I undergo a reaction as they say, and have not the courage to continue those things which I did willingly in the Anglican Church.' But he was about to bind himself to do them for the rest of his life : fasts, office, retreats, meditations. He was trying to meditate now though it made his head ache. This perseverance he called crawling on the ground, but it required courage to go on, especially as his energy was drained away by the 'wound' not yet healed.

'In a variety of ways I have fallen away from hope. In the Church of England I had many detractors ; a mass of calumny was hurled at me. . . . I became an exile in solitude . . . but not even in that retreat was I safe from those who pursued me with their curiosity. I believe and hope that I did not on that account give way to anger, indignation or the like, for in that respect I am not especially sensitive, but I was oppressed and lost hope. And now the cheerfulness I used to have has almost vanished. And I feel acutely that I am no longer young, but that my best years are spent, and I am sad at the thought of the years that have gone by and I see myself to be fit for nothing, a useless log.'

It was impossible to go through the psychological crisis of the last few years and not suffer for it. There had been no time for rest ; on top of the nervous strain of inward uncertainty and public attack

had come the intense creative work on the Essay, and then the rush
of events in his new life, the loss of old friends becoming ever more
real, the uprooting from all old associations more noticeable under
the pressure of Catholics, new and old, trying to force him at once
into this or that mould. It was a wonder he did not suffer a nervous
collapse. But even in this private analysis he did not complain, but
only feared he was not doing enough. It was less real despondency
than sheer exhaustion. Nor was it visible to others ; the Newman
people saw was full of Oratorian plans, making jokes about flat beer,
and appeared to be ready for anything. But once, in the Vatican
Gallery, Dalgairns stopped 'before a statue of Fate, which was very
striking and stern and melancholy . . . "Who *can* it be like ? I know
the face so well —" presently he added "Why it is you".' This,
which surprised Newman at the time, did not surprise him when he
recorded it in his journal in 1863. He realized then that his face
did look stern ; he was quite afraid of intimidating people. But
photographs of that later time show that the stern look disappeared
when he smiled, and it vanished altogether in old age.   But the
strain of the last few years had set the muscles of his face in heavy
lines.

  After the retreat they made a holiday expedition to Monte Cavo,
where the wild jonquils were 'smelling most piercingly sweet', as
he told Jemima. 'And so at Tivoli the acacia blossoms and other
flowers almost carried me away with their sweetness.' Yet he preferred Monte Cavo to Tivoli : 'I like an extensive view with tracts
bold and barren in it, such as Beethoven's music seems to represent'.
He was reminded of Sicily again, and his earlier return from abroad
'quite a different person' as he told Mrs. Bowden. Writing to
Jemima was beset with difficulties. 'I do not tell you any more news
of myself as it seems not to please you,' he said to her, giving instead
a pleasant picture of the Roman people to balance some earlier
criticisms. On a holy day at St. Peter's 'to look down upon them
from the entrance in their very striking dresses, in the liquid atmosphere, so distinct that it is like a camera obscura, men and women
in white and red — the white delicately clean, is as pretty and
imposing a sight as I have often seen'.

  During this time Newman made a friend of Mgr. Palma, the new
Secretary of Propaganda : all English affairs then came under its
jurisdiction, as one of the missions. Newman liked Palma very much,
in spite of his looks ; he described him later to Miss Giberne : 'He
is a short hideously ugly man — you can't mistake him — with large

cheeks and no nose — and can hardly speak — I doubt whether he
has teeth'. It was just Newman's luck that this real friend was to
be assassinated only a year later, leaving him without any official
contact in Rome. Newman did not expect people to seek him out ;
he did not visit in society, but he took trouble to get to know theologians. St. John said he and Perrone were quite friends now —
'they embraced each other'. The learned Oratorian Theiner was
another, and Passaglia, a Jesuit. He also called on the Passionists, so
as to tell Father Dominic how much he liked them, and their house.
Father Dominic, much in need of novices though he was, left Newman
to make his own decisions, and even asked his advice on relaxations
of his Rule for England : should they leave off sandals ? Newman
advised against it ; he did not believe in altering rules simply to make
things easier for Englishmen. His own alterations were made for
other reasons.

At last, on May 26th, St. Philip's day, Newman and St. John
were ordained subdeacons by Cardinal Fransoni in his private chapel ;
on Saturday they were made deacons at St. John Lateran, and on
Trinity Sunday, June 1st, raised to the priesthood by Cardinal
Fransoni in the church at Propaganda. In a small chapel there
Newman said his first mass on the following Thursday, Corpus
Christi ; St. John said the community mass and the students, according to custom, kissed his hand afterwards. The next day it was
Newman's turn for this. On Saturday he said mass at St. Thomas's
altar at the English College, and on Sunday at the Chiesa Nuova, in
the inner chapel, over St. Philip's body. He said nothing of these
events in his letters, simply recording them in his diary. It was just
his luck that the day before his first mass the weather changed and
he 'caught cold in his throat as if it were winter'. He was very
susceptible to sudden changes of temperature.

At the end of June they all moved out to Santa Croce, to learn
how to be Oratorians, under the supervision of Father Rossi. Santa
Croce, Newman told David Lewis, was 'so called because St.
Helena not only brought the True Cross there, but earth from
Mount Calvary on which the chapel or the Altar there is built —
thus if there be a centre to the Church, we shall be there, when we
are on earth from Jerusalem in the midst of Rome'. Close by was
St. John Lateran, 'the mother Church of Christendom'. Santa
Croce was just outside Rome, ·and they kept talking about walking
into Oxford, as if they had been at Littlemore. The Oratorian
novitiate was not like a monastic one, and they were fairly free. But

they were well out of Rome, which was disturbed with riots. A threatening mob gathered outside Propaganda ; the Father Rector spent the night praying before the Blessed Sacrament. The Jesuits were politically unpopular ; Newman compared them, for Jemima's benefit, with 'the conservatives of 1830 . . . unpopular in the extreme and the butt of journalists — considered the enemies of all improvement and advance'. Unlike the crafty Jesuits of English fiction they had not much worldly wisdom : 'They are continually making false moves by not seeing whom they have to deal with' — a pleasing comment from Newman who was usually in the same predicament. The general situation in Italy was inflammable. Pius IX, who had been, at first, immensely popular as 'the Liberal Pope' was now running into trouble with the revolutionary wing of the Liberals, anti-clerical and violent. Pius was no politician. That shrewd statesman Metternich said he lacked practical sense and prophesied truly that he would be driven out of Rome. 'The Pope has destroyed by his liberalism his own temporal power,' he observed. 'What he is unable to destroy is his spiritual power.'

With this unrest fermenting on the edge of their lives, the Englishmen at Santa Croce settled down to learn Oratorian ways. They were not all there. Francis Knox, who had been to see Newman at Littlemore, was shipwrecked after crossing the Atlantic and had to go home before coming. Knox was twenty-three, the grandson of two earls ; he had taken a first in classics at Trinity College Cambridge in 1845, and was received with Faber later that year. Staying at St. Sulpice he wondered if the discipline there would be good for him ; the students did certain menial tasks — he mentioned among these that they wiped their knives and stuck them in their dinner napkins. Newman said, 'If you were here under Father Rossi of the Chiesa Nuova with us, you would enjoy room sweeping, slop emptying, dinner serving, bed making, shoe blacking, as at St. Sulpice, all but the dirty knives'. Knox evidently thought life was going to be too easy in the Oratory. Newman observed, 'And though Fr Rossi is too prudent to carry out the whole system at once, yet I trust by the time we come to England, we shall have confession and the discipline three times a week and the chapter of faults'. Earlier he had said, 'We would take good care of you, my dear Knox, for it would be one of the greatest of pleasures to see your face again and have hold of your hand after all your wanderings and perils'. Knox came, but not till the autumn.

'How dreary Fr Rossi and Santa Croce', remarked Newman in

his retrospect of 1863, contrasting that time with the 'happy months' at Propaganda ; but he did not say why it was dreary.   Later letters of Birmingham Oratorians who met Fr. Rossi provide some hints. Rossi was a year younger than Newman ; he was very talkative and excitable and extremely opinionated ; he also had his own ideas about reforming the Oratory, and thought he might start pushing them through the new foundation in England.   One of his ideas was that the Oratory needed centralizing ; it would have more power and influence if it were more like the other religious orders in this. He made the suggestion that Newman should retain some sort of hold over all the houses to be founded in England.   When Newman mentioned this later, he said that because he 'shrank' from it a coolness arose between him and Fr. Rossi.   In a letter of explanation to Miss Bowles in 1859 he said 'At Rome Dalgairns and Coffin took part against me'.   These hints indicate that what made Santa Croce dreary were the personal dissensions arising out of Fr. Rossi's way of doing things.   Newman's diffidence in pushing his own opinions made certain determined people fancy they could force him (for his own good) to accept theirs.   When he turned out to be immovable they felt baffled and somehow cheated, as if he had no business to be both gentle and steadfast — soft and yet obstinate as some thought it.

Newman was also harassed by future uncertainties.   Fr. Doyle wrote to offer him St. George's, with a community house, in London. Newman replied that he must consult Wiseman first.   Doyle, annoyed, accused him of wishing to please men rather than God. Newman said he did not think consulting his Bishop came under that head, 'nor do I think that any one is bound to seize upon the most influential post possible without regard to existing engagements and ties'.   Wiseman had first claim on their services, and the papal Brief, which would give Newman authority to set up the Oratory in England, was already in preparation, fixing Newman in Birmingham. Yet changes were in the air.   It was expected that in the next few years England would cease to be reckoned as a mission field, under the direct jurisdiction of Propaganda, and be restored to normal autonomy under a hierarchy and Canon Law.   Two of the senior English bishops were ailing, Walsh in the Midlands and Griffiths in London.   In August this year Griffiths suddenly died.   If and when the hierarchy was restored it was the Roman plan to put Walsh in London, though in England it was doubted if he would survive the translation.   He was appointed, but died soon after and Wiseman succeeded, though the temporary nature of his appointment was indicated by his unusual title, and it was expected that at the restoration he would be recalled to Rome, probably as a Cardinal. The young and energetic Dr. Ullathorne was translated from the Western to the Midland District. Many people thought it only a step on his way to London. For the next two years the position of all these prelates was quite uncertain.

Before he was sent to London as Bishop, Wiseman went back to England on a semi-diplomatic mission ; first he ordained Richard Stanton in Rome on the feast of the Assumption, August 15th. After this, some brief holidays were taken. Newman and St. John, combining business with pleasure, went down to Naples to visit the Oratory there. Newman still thought the hills round Naples lumpish. 'Form is to me even more than colouring,' he said to Jemima, but 'the beauty is in the exuberance of the season and the splendour of the sun and its light. To walk through *woods* of vines and figs, festooned across one's path and intertwined with each other and asking to be eaten, was a new thing to me, and threw one out of the everyday world into some garden of Armida or Alcinous.' The weather was bad at first, but picked up ; they climbed Vesuvius and bathed in the sea and visited Monte Cassino. Newman was disappointed there was no time to visit the Oratories in Sicily and see again that beautiful landscape he never could forget. This active holiday lasted barely ten days ; on their return Newman sent the others off in pairs to Propaganda's villa at Frascati. St. John, who was unwell, was sent too and wrote to Newman from the Prop. Villa as they called it, 'This ink is like paint. I can't write with it.' He used a pencil to say that everyone was disappointed Newman had not come too. But Newman was busy — he was writing a novel. It was all about Oxford and made him laugh out loud while he was writing it.

He wrote it partly to help 'poor Burns' (the convert founder of the firm of Burns and Oates, Catholic publishers), partly to answer, on its own level, a ridiculous novel called *From Oxford to Rome* which was having a great success in England. Its anonymous author turned out to be a young lady ; having pretended to give an inside picture of the repentance of the perverts, she repented herself, and involved poor Oakeley in a shattering newspaper scandal. Miss Harris's brother wrote to the papers about 'mental torture', and it was said, 'Mr. Oakeley *was* an English gentleman before he was a Romish deacon'.

Newman called his novel *Loss and Gain*, a dull title for such an
amusing book.   Although it came out first anonymously, everyone
knew the author, nor did Newman trouble to preserve secrecy.   It
came as a surprise to some, after the *Essay on Development*.   Earnest
Puseyites, as Faber informed Newman later, were soon saying he had
'sunk below Dickens'.   To anyone who received his letters, Newman's novel cannot have been a surprise.   It had the same vivid
immediacy, dry humour, moments of deep feeling, shrewd observation and sudden flights of comic fantasy.   Considering how close it
all was to him, it is remarkably objective and detached.   He put no
real people in, referring to Pusey as 'a great and good man' and
laughing at himself as 'Smith — he never speaks decidedly on difficult
questions'.

At the beginning there is a charming scene where a quartet of
romantic young Tractarians imagine a Catholic Oxford, with Cardinals walking in the Parks.   'Yet I don't quite like, though, the idea
of a Cardinal in Oxford' (said Miss Louisa Bolton).   'Must we be
so very Roman ?   I don't see why we might not be quite Catholic
without the Pope.'   But what would happen to the wives of the
Heads of Houses when they were all converted into Abbots ?   Would
such old ladies be able to stand the life of nuns ?   The conversation
now 'took a more pensive, or even tenderer tone', and Louisa wondered timidly whether 'young persons might not more fitly lead the
way.   "Young persons", said White, "are too delicate for such a
sacrifice."   She was silent ; presently she said, "And what will you
be, Mr. White ?"   "I know not," he answered.   "I have thought
of the Cistercians ; they never speak."   "Oh, the dear Cistercians !"
she said.   "St. Bernard, wasn't it ? — sweet, heavenly man, and so
young !   I have seen his picture : such eyes !"   White was a good-
looking man.   The nun and the monk looked at each other very
respectfully, and bowed ; the other pair went through a similar
ceremony ; then it was performed diagonally.   The two ladies
entered their home ; the two gentlemen retired.'

Near the end of the book Charles Reding — who was not intended
to represent his author but one of the younger generation — was in
a bookshop in Bath when in came 'a young clergyman, with a very
pretty girl on his arm, whom her dress pronounced to be a bride' —
none other than White and Louisa.   'Love was in their eyes, joy
in their voice and affluence in their gait and bearing.   Charles had a
faintish feeling come over him ; somewhat such as might beset a man
on hearing a call for pork-chops when he was seasick.'   Charles was

on the verge of becoming a Catholic. Hastily hiding in a corner he overheard their conversation, as they looked at the books, all about the Bishop's family. '"Oh, what a sweet face!" she said, looking at the frontispiece of a little book she had got hold of; "do look, Henry dear; whom does it put you in mind of?" "Why, it is meant for St. John the Baptist," said Henry. "It's so like little Angelina Primrose," said she, "the hair is just hers. I wonder it doesn't strike you."' Then she wanted a book and could not remember what; White ran through a list of titles : '"Lays of the Apostles" or "The English Church older than the Roman"? or "Anglicanism of the Early Martyrs"? or "Confessions of a Pervert"? or "Modified Celibacy"?' However it turned out to be "Abbeys and Abbots" from which she hoped to get 'some hints for improving the rectory windows, when we get home; and our church wants, you know, a porch for the poor people'.

Newman was anxious to get home by Christmas, but the Brief was not ready till the beginning of December. At the last moment Archdeacon Manning, who had been seriously ill, suddenly turned up. 'As to dear Manning, I must tell you I thought him looking very ill', Newman told Henry Wilberforce. 'He ran up to me as I was getting into a carozza — and I must say fairly that, for the first instant, I did not know him. And when I saw him again and again, his old face did not come out to me, nor did I get over, as one so often does, my first impression.' The next day, December 3rd, Newman went to the Quirinal to present the Brief to the Pope, and a few days later he and St. John started for home. Coffin was just ahead of them; Penny and Stanton had gone via France. Bowles, who had somehow managed to fail his examination for the priesthood, had set his heart on receiving it in Rome, so Newman allowed him to stay at Propaganda, though he was afraid he would feel lonely when they had all gone.

They travelled north in a great hurry, fearing the Brenner Pass would be closed, but Newman wanted to stop at Loreto, the shrine of the Holy House of Nazareth, transported, legend says, by angels from Palestine. 'We went there to get the Blessed Virgin's blessing on us,' Newman wrote to Henry from Maryvale. 'I have ever been under her shadow, if I may say it. My college was St. Mary's, and my church; and when I went to Littlemore, there, by my own previous disposition, our Blessed Lady was waiting for me. Nor did she do nothing for me in that lowly habitation, of which I always think with pleasure.' They arrived at Loreto just at the feast of the Translation of the Holy House ; the angels looked after Newman, for in spite of the crowds he was able to say mass in the house itself at 4 a.m. 'in the midst of as great and strange a crowd as came up to Bethlehem to be taxed', as he wrote back to Bowles, from Frankfurt.

The next day they called on Wiseman's mother ; on the Monday managed to fit in the tombs of St. Dominic and St. Catherine, and then hurried on, travelling through the night over the Brenner, arriving at Innsbruck at two in the morning, where they had an hour's sleep before going on again by courier.   Leaving Italy they had difficulty with the customs over the *corpo santo* — the relics of an early martyr of the name of Valentine, secured in Rome through the determination of St. John.   The customs men threatened to open the casket, St. John got tired trying to explain in German, but at last it was passed, to Newman's amusement, as a mummy !   The story became a favourite locally, for they heard their fame when they came that way again in 1855.   In Munich, after some very uncomfortable stages, they called on Doellinger, the famous German scholar and theologian, and had tea with him.   Sunday Mass was said in the Chapel Royal and then on they went, day and night, arriving in Frankfurt at five in the morning.   St. John collapsed and went to sleep, but Newman sat writing letters, to Jemima for Christmas, to poor lonely Bowles at Propaganda — but Bowles was not at Propaganda, for he had run away, to the Rector's astonishment, the day after he arrived.   He rushed to Genoa, but then lost heart, and returned.   Newman did not know this till he got home.   'I am so cold I can hardly write,' he told Jemima, but he was thinking about the Pope, in the midst of a political crisis.   'Anything may happen to him personally, as to other popes, but when they suffer personally, their cause triumphs.   Yet how it would pierce my heart, if anything happened to him.'

This journey home was typical of Newman, taken at headlong speed, stopping only for the tombs of saints, old ladies and theologians.   It became more modern in Germany, where they went by rail from Cologne to Ostend, crossing to Dover, and arriving in London on Christmas Eve.   'There was snow over everything down to Ostend,' Newman wrote to Jemima from Maryvale, to wish her a happy new year, 'and worse fog going through Belgium than here, or at least as bad.'   His godson Charlie Bowden served his mass on Christmas day.   They had a hunt to 'find an altar' but Dr. Ferguson, who had tried to make Newman's flesh creep with the College discipline at Propaganda, found them one at a chapel in Halsey Street, Chelsea. 'So we began our English life with the Nativity,' Newman wrote to Henry, 'saying mass first in England on that blessed day, as I had said it first in Rome on the feast of Corpus Christi. They are cognate feasts. . . .' His last mass, too, was to be on Christmas Day.

1848

Faber Arrives

NEWMAN and St. John had to eat their Christmas dinner in Hatchett's coffee house, since Mrs. Bowden was dining out. When Newman found that Stanton and Penny had already arrived at Maryvale he was disappointed they had not gone straight down there. However, he was there in time to say mass on New Year's Day, 1848. Before he left London Wiseman had told him that Faber and all his community wished to join the Oratory.

Faber's decision had been taken at the beginning of December, when he and Antony Hutchison, the only two priests in the community, were preparing to take their vows in the presence of Wiseman. 'Decision' is perhaps the wrong word, for to Faber it came as an 'inspiration'. The idea occurred to him during his morning meditation before mass and by the time he had finished his thanksgiving after mass he was convinced that it was God's will. He did not think the matter out, but mentally argued with various saints who all 'seemed to say' it was the will of God. He felt the more inclined to believe this, as he admitted to his friends, because in some ways it went against the grain to give to another all he had built up. He went out from his thanksgiving, he told his friend Michael Watts Russell, in a mood of 'calm brokenheartedness'. 'How everything seemed changed when I went out! everything had ceased to be mine : the rising spire of our magnificent church, the young trees, all seemed buried in one thing, God.'

Without a moment's delay he told the choir brothers, his three young converts, 'whose aversion to the plan was very vehement'. After all, they were all expecting to take vows as monks, and it was Faber they had joined, and his rule they expected to follow. However, 'I took Father Hutchison out, and told him the whole,' said Faber to Watts Russell; 'he immediately said, "It is from God, I will go with you". His repugnance was utterly gone. The same happened with Brother Alban and Brother Austin; this seemed wonderful.' Mills and Wells, dutiful Brothers of the Will of Faber, as Father Dominic called them, how could they doubt his inspiration? Faber thought perhaps they should all make a Jesuit retreat, but the very next day came a letter from Wiseman, fixing the feast of Mary's Immaculate Conception (December 8th) as the day for their vow taking. At once Faber and Hutchison started for London and when they arrived, whom should they find with the Bishop but Stanton, wearing his Oratorian habit, a black full-skirted cassock. It was all very exciting. 'I was up with the Bishop till midnight on Thursday ; he solemnly approved the whole thing as coming from God.' This was only the day after the 'inspiration'.

All this excitement made Faber feel ill. 'I could not get my breath in London, so I asked the Bishop to let me go down by railroad to Tring to sleep, where I could breathe. Father Hutchison, also as white as a corpse and very ill, set off with me on Friday at two p.m. but when we got to Euston Square we were obliged to go to bed. In the evening we got up, and went all the way to Derby, and arrived here on Saturday evening in time for the confessional.' The lay brothers, of course, would follow Faber anywhere, and another young convert who had just joined them, Nicholas Darnell of New College, Oxford, decided to come too. Though it was hardly a question of 'going' anywhere, for Wiseman, Faber told Watts Russell, 'says St. Wilfrid's can, by the Pope's modifications, be kept and become an Oratorian house, and he has pledged himself to me, that our most prosperous mission will be carried on'. All this was decided without the slightest reference to Newman, but Faber's doubts of acceptance were perfunctory. 'I shrink from the prospect before me very, very much ; to fall from founder and superior to novice, and a novice who must naturally be an object of extreme jealousy from his influence over the rest of the brothers ; to meet the ludibrium of all our old-Catholic enemies, to stand the evil opinion of those who think all this from Satan, will require no little grace.'

So here was Newman, arriving back in England to set up the Oratory, with his community not yet formed, faced with the prospect of Faber and his seventeen Wilfridians. Newman had five newly ordained priests, and Bowles and Knox to come ; one or two lay-brothers at Maryvale as well. Faber's community had been living together since their conversion and already had habits and customs formed, and those on a monastic model. Newman wrote to him on the last day of 1847 of his joy at his offer, but hoped he realized what he was doing. 'I will but say that, from the very wish I have that we may come to an understanding, I am anxious you should try if you have fully mastered *what* Oratorianism is. In many important respects it differs from what you are at present. It is not near so ascetic — indeed it is *not* ascetic. It is not poetical — it is not very devotional. Now it is a question what your youths will say to this. Again, as you know, it has but few lay brothers compared to your present society. An Oratorian ought, like a Roman legionary, to stand in his place and fight by himself though in company — instead of being a mere instrument of another, or a member of a phalanx. I am so desirous of our coming together, that I wince while I put down these objections, but no good will come of it, if we don't consider the matter in all its bearings.'

Faber was not good at consideration. He wrote at once to say 'Consider us as giving ourselves over to you in ye spirit of surrender', with their new church, house and all, 'as so much raw material for Oratorianism'. He wanted Newman to come over and visit them at once. This was not possible, since after new year the others had dispersed to their homes and Newman was alone at Maryvale. 'I can't come to you — I am solus here — and am wanted for many things — but I should rejoice if you came here.' Faber did come for a flying visit and the discussion continued by letter. Newman wrote to Dalgairns that St. John and Stanton were for accepting the Wilfridians, 'though it is a very anxious task to have on our hands. We ought to know the *state* of F's people more than we do.' However, to Faber he outlined a plan. He wanted 'our party' to be at Maryvale together 'for a while to get into shape'. After that, an exchange of members might help them to get to know each other, and then Faber himself could come to learn 'the special Oratorian way'.

Faber, in his exalted mood of renunciation, did not want his wishes consulted, but to act in 'blind obedience'. At the same time, while taking Newman's suggestions as commands, he exaggerated their import and imagined all sorts of frustrations in store for himself. He told his fears to everybody, not only in his community, but at Alton Towers and among his village converts, complaining to Watts Russell at the beginning of February, 'My courage fails a little ; I am to remain here a few weeks and then go as a "strict novice" to Maryvale, and I understand I am *never* to return to St. Wilfrid's. So away goes home, church, flock, Eltonian children and all. The people are up in arms about it, memorializing Father Superior, the

Shrewsburys are vexed, the neighbouring priests are writing letters,
the lay brothers are downcast : as to Father Wilfrid himself, he hopes
he is happy.' The petition to Newman, signed in a careful hand with
the villagers' names, still survives. 'Certainly, rickety and ailing as
my health now is, I have occasional fits of low spirits ;' Faber continued 'I cannot move my Library to Maryvale, so I shall be separated
from that as well, neither will Maryvale be my settled home. . . .
Certainly the Oratory has been a bloody husband to me because of
the circumcision ; but I trust that it will also bring with it a fresh
covenant of grace.' All this because Newman had suggested he
should come and learn Oratorian ways, and reminded him that the
Oratory's work was to be in large towns and that he felt Faber's
proper sphere would be in one, probably in London.

'The Oratorians are remarkably kind to us,' Faber admitted, 'and
seem very anxious to make us feel happy and at home ; and I hope
we may have grace not to disappoint them by taking too much upon
us and forgetting our place as novices. But this will be very hard.
. . . I have had a house full of temptations and repugnances to govern
for some weeks past, but by the grace of God and dear Mama's help
I hope to steer my little crew into the port of San Filippo without a
loss.' Dear Mama was Faber's way of referring to the Mother of
God. Newman had wondered what Faber's youths would think of
the change ; he did not realize that they were not consulted, but
merely carried along by Faber on the wings of his inspiration. He
did not know he would have a house full of repugnances to cope with,
under the ardent solicitations for admission, or that Faber, who wrote
to him so keen to give up everything to join the Oratory, was writing
to other friends bewailing the hardness of his lot.

Meanwhile, on the feast of the Purification of the Blessed Virgin,
February 2nd, 1848, Newman had officially set up the Oratory in
England. He admitted five Fathers, one novice (Knox) and three
lay brothers at solemn vespers on the eve of the feast, and next day
blessed and distributed the candles at the mass, which he said.
Candlemas Day, which was Oriel gaudy, now became a special feast
of the Oratory too. It was exactly five years since Newman preached
his last university sermon, the first sketch of the theory of Development, taking Mary as the pattern of the Church meditating the truth
in her heart.

Ten days later he went over to St. Wilfrid's to receive Faber and
his men. Faber recovered his spirits at one bound. He wrote to
Watts Russell, 'Father Superior has now left us, all in our Philippine

habits with turndown collars, like so many good boys brought in after dinner. In the solemn admission on Monday morning, he gave a most wonderful address, full of those marvellous pauses which you know of. He showed how wonderfully we had all been brought together from different parts, and how, in his case and ours, St. Philip seemed to have laid hands on us and taken us for his own, whether we would or not. Since my admission I seem to have lost all attachment to everything but obedience ; I could dance and sing all day, because I am so joyous ; I hardly know what to do with myself for very happiness.' This elation did not last long.

Even before he had received the Wilfridians Newman discovered that he had landed himself with more than the responsibility for eighteen men. As he had told Faber, the Oratory was designed to function in cities, and St. Wilfrid's could be no possible use to it, beautiful as the place was. Therefore he proposed to run the little country mission — Faber's converts, which he estimated as two hundred — by putting in a secular priest. But now it turned out that Lord Shrewsbury had made his gift on condition that a community served the church, and was angry at the prospect of losing Faber. Faber had 'given' himself and the property to Newman without telling him, or perhaps without himself being aware of this condition. Equally worrying was the fact that the Wilfridians' income was all spent ; even Hutchison had temporarily come to the end of his resources, having sunk a large sum in the big church. The eleven lay brothers, village boys from Elton, and the two schoolmasters had no money of their own and had to be supported by the others in any case. Faber's inspiration to join the Oratory was probably not due to the threat of bankruptcy, for he never bothered about money ; friends always turned up providentially to pay off his debts. But Newman found himself with a community twice the size of his own, a large property, no income and an angry earl.

The first thing was to pacify the earl. Newman suggested that the Oratory should supply two priests and three lay brothers to keep things going for a year, till some other community could be found to take over St. Wilfrid's ; meanwhile, owing to their financial difficul-ties, perhaps Lord Shrewsbury would pay £200 towards their keep. The most the noble lord would do was to add £50 to the £150 he already paid to the mission, and when Newman said this was not enough, he blew up, rushed down to see Faber, told him he refused to correspond with Newman any more, that Newman had said Faber was a burden to him, and so on, with much feeling. Faber, aggrieved, repeated all this to Newman. *He* would not have asked Lord Shrews-bury for money, and anyway everything would come right soon, because Antony Hutchison had expectations from an old aunt, and as she was over ninety they could not be long delayed.

By this time March was nearly over, and Newman wrote on 27th to calm Faber and send him a copy of his letter to Shrewsbury. All he had said was 'the house at Maryvale, without its fault, is laden with an expense in consequence of the sums laid out at St. Wilfrid's for the spiritual benefit of the neighbourhood of Alton Towers'. To reassure Faber he said, 'You must realize more than you do how much I admire and love you, and how we all do the same. How can you suppose we think you a burden ? . . . Believe me, if the trouble of St. Wilfrid's were ten times what it is, it would be far more than repaid by your giving us *yourselves* . . . we have got what will do us more good than if we had many patrons.' As to the number of lay brothers, some of whom had already been transferred to Maryvale, it was simply the money question that worried him. 'I know very well I could not find such nice and dear fellows in Birmingham, or, if I had found them in the raw material, could not make them.' As to Lord Shrewsbury 'the simple question was whether, as he in-sinuated, or rather said, I was taking money from you for Maryvale, and *then* coming on him to make up the deficiency which resulted at St. Wilfrid's'. He guessed some of Faber's qualms. 'You must trust us more. . . . It is a great evil we are divided. You are cut off from us, and then again, it is very trying for you to have your plans unsettled and you sit and brood over things — just as I am apt to do. But don't be out of spirits — all will go well, I am sure, with a little care.' If only, too, he added next day, Faber and Shrewsbury would have patience ; they both wanted everything decided at once.

Faber was already out of spirits. He took to his bed with a sick headache, staggering out of it to write to dear Lord Shrewsbury and falling back on it without the energy to write to Newman, as he naïvely told him next day, in a letter which was a long descant on his love and gratitude to the noble earl. And he was much, much too ill to go to Maryvale for his novitiate. 'Ye horrid motion of a railway' nearly always brought on a bilious attack. Newman's reply was brief and soothing ; everything was settled now, and Faber must stop worrying ; he must definitely come to Maryvale after Easter. Faber was relieved, but still begged off his novitiate on the score of health, though he was well enough to take part in a scheme of Oratorian preaching in London in Passion Week, which Newman had undertaken, much against his will, to pacify Wiseman, who wanted to show off his protégés in London.

For Newman had his own affairs to manage as well as Faber's. Everyone, as soon as he set foot in England, seemed to be wanting something or other of him. He was persuaded to undertake sermons in St. Chad's Cathedral, Pugin's Gothic gesture of faith thrown down like a gauntlet in the black middle of Birmingham. He preached eight times, twice in January, twice in February and four times in March, nearly always walking the six miles from Maryvale and sometimes back as well. The way crossed a wild common, and when Knox was coming in January Newman warned him not to come at night, as there were thieves at large. It has an eighteenth-century sound, and shows the disorders that haunted the expansion of the industrial towns. Factories and dwellings proliferated at such speed that slums grew up before anyone realized what was happening. People streamed in from the country and from Ireland and were swallowed up in the rootless mobs, without property, without rights or duties or organization or traditions. No wonder that in this year of Revolutions, England itself was threatened with revolt, and this very Easter was to see the great meeting of the Chartists, which many expected to be the signal for a general rising of the people. It was to the Catholics among this mob of Birmingham operatives that Newman preached some simple but very typical sermons on the dangers of sin and the power of God to transform men.

But Protestants also ventured into Catholic churches in those days, out of curiosity. On Sexagesima Sunday, February 27th, a youth of nineteen slipped into St. Chad's in the evening to see and hear Newman. He was Edward White Benson, a future Archbishop of Canterbury, and he wrote to tell his friend Lightfoot all about it. 'He is a wonderful man truly and spoke with a kind of Angel eloquence . . . sweet, flowing, unlaboured language in short, very short and very pithy and touching sentences.' Newman had given up reading his sermons on finding it was not the custom among Catholics; it must have been difficult to change his habit in middle life. He used to take a little Bible into the pulpit, leafing through to find the texts he wanted. 'His appearance was exceedingly interesting,' said Benson, 'he was very much emaciated, and when he began his voice was very feeble, and he spoke with great difficulty, nay sometimes he gasped for breath ; but his voice was very sweet. . . . But oh, Lightfoot, never you turn Romanist if you are to have a face like that — it was awful — the terrible lines deeply ploughed all over his face, and the craft that sat upon his retreating forehead and sunken eyes. He was a strange spectacle altogether — and to think of that timid-looking, little, weak-voiced man having served old England as he has done.' Benson was perhaps too young to realize that other things beside craft may line a man's face. His attitude shows very clearly how Newman had 'stultified himself' — nullified his message — by turning 'Roman', just as he had known he would. The phantasm of Romanism in the minds of ordinary English people distorted everything he said and did, even his appearance.

Newman spoke, during his exposition of the parable of the Sower, on a favourite theme, illustrating what the lover of Christ feels at hearing of him, and his name, by what a friend feels at the name of a friend. 'Then if you had seen how his eye glistened and his whole face glowed, as he turned round to the Altar, lifting his priest's cap and bowing low, while he pronounced His name, and with such a voice — you could not but have felt your heart yearn towards him.' Benson felt a thrill run through the congregation but for him everything was spoilt by the introduction of the name of Mary. And during Benediction, while the Litany of Loreto was said, 'he went on chanting indeed, but withal somewhat carelessly and looking about', but suddenly at the point where Mary was addressed as Help of Christians, 'he clasped his hands fervently and looked up with an expression of face, I had well-nigh said heavenly, but how far from that!'

The sermons at St. Chad's were broken off to fulfil the promise to Wiseman of Passiontide preaching in London. Unfortunately very few people turned up and Newman felt it was a blunder and a failure, which for years he could not think of 'without raw sensitiveness'. He preached every evening himself, like the rest of the team, in different churches, dashing down to Maryvale for Palm Sunday and back to London for the first days of Holy Week, spending the rest at home 'taking the functions' as the Catholics then called the services — an euphemism dating from penal times. They had their first High Mass at Maryvale on Easter Sunday, and on the Monday, everyone, lay brothers and all went over to St. Wilfrid's for the opening of the new church. For Lord Shrewsbury had apologized and begged Newman to come. He replied from London, then full of rumours about the Chartists' meeting, 'If all is well I will gladly come unless the Chartists and Primitive Methodists have by that time burned the Church down'. It survived, and he was there, and preached; in the evening he gave Benediction and carried the Blessed Sacrament in procession.

After Easter Faber was supposed to come for his novitiate, but
he had one of his attacks, writing a dramatic and detailed account of
his miseries to Newman, all in his neat little handwriting. What with
diarrhoea, vomiting, being rubbed with cod liver oil and taking
anodynes which made him lightheaded, he was in a bad way. 'I
thought I was going; it was ye anodyne, ye sufferings were very
dreadful, besides being half drunk so that I could not pray and had
horrid temptations to blaspheme Almighty God. I have had another
night without sleep and have been screaming for several hours.' All
his friends high and low, rallied round nobly. Brother John waited
on him and tried to tempt his appetite with chicken. 'I see that
Lord S. comes twice a day,' Faber remarked. 'He sent Mr. Tomlin-
son of Cheadle instead of our own medical man — furnished the
hot bath, and has all my slops made at ye Towers.' His next letter
was very gloomy. 'The increasing debility, ye clouded brain, ye
loaded eye, ye continual going off in faints, and ye incessant feeling
of vomiting . . . get more distressing and deject me. The offensive
effluvia of the cod liver oil which has turned rancid on my body and
may not be washed off is rather hard to bear.' The writing suddenly
tails off in a sprawl: 'I cannot write any more, I am so sick'.

Newman was saved from giving up hope by a cheerful letter from
Antony Hutchison, who was used to Faber's collapses. He made a
joke of Faber's 'ancient and fish like smell', thought him better,
remarked that the cat had produced two very promising kittens, and
was shocked at the young Brothers who had let the kitchen fire go
out and run out of doors to play battledore and shuttlecock. Time
went on, and Faber still felt unequal to coming to Maryvale; how
could he transport his library? 'Do come, and bring fine weather
with you', said Newman. 'I suppose you will not stop here so long
that you should dream of bringing your library here.' Faber did
not come; he had to stay with Brother Stanislas, long fatally ill, who
was now dying. 'Father Wilfrid, how long will it be now? Will it
be long?' he kept saying in his death agony. After he had died,
when Faber lifted his head on the pillow 'there came on his face ye
loveliest smile that can be imagined'. This made the young lay
brothers very happy, but Faber felt sad, and next day he felt much
worse. Then he had the bright idea of swallowing three of Brother
Stanislas's hairs in a glass of water. Whether or not this effected a
miraculous cure, Faber was certainly well enough a week later to
indulge in a tremendous row with Pugin and Phillipps, who were
staying at the Towers.

This was one of the great engagements of the War of the Goths and Pagans. Although architecture was the ostensible cause of dissension, there was behind it the suspicion of differences in doctrine. Gothic art was northern, and the Goths were suspected of indulging in Gallican views about the power of the Pope. Gallicanism in its true form had passed away, even in France, since the cataclysm of the French Revolution ; in its heyday it had expressed more of national pride than theology, but the idea animating it was that the Pope's supremacy was more of convenience than divine right and that he was responsible to a General Council. But by the nineteenth century the Church was centralizing more strongly on Rome, and English Catholics, though their theology often came from France, were known for their loyalty to the Holy See. Notwithstanding this, the party in Rome sometimes known as neo-Ultramontanes, who later became the extreme vanguard of the Infallibilists, was inclined to stigmatize as Gallican every more moderate tradition than their own. Faber had picked up this view in Rome, and in his great enthusiasm for everything Roman came back to England convinced that the old English Catholics were Gallicans to a man, half-Protestantized, and in need of conversion to true Catholicism, which he identified with the extreme of Ultramontanism. This view was to dominate the most influential Catholic circles in London, chiefly through Faber, Ward and Manning and the large numbers of converts who took it up. It is the key to Newman's later history that he never accepted it. His central theological and ecclesiastical position eventually brought him closer to the old Catholic tradition and cut him off from the converts and the generation trained in their methods, but now, at the beginning of his Catholic course, the issues were not yet plain, either to him or to anyone else. Consequently he was identified by many, and allowed himself so to be, with the line that Faber took, though privately he tried to restrain Faber's excesses.

Faber's battle with the two eminent Goths took place near 'Mama's statue' outside St. Wilfrid's. Soon rumours were going about that Ambrose Phillipps had lost his temper and cursed the Oratory. Faber wrote a dialogue of the occasion for Newman's benefit. The trouble started because Phillipps asked why there was no screen in St. Wilfrid's, which was built by Pugin. Faber said 'ye Father Superior did not wish it'. He also said that Pugin might as well treat the Blessed Sacrament as Henry VIII's men had, as do what he did at Benediction at Cheadle. 'Pugin : Now hear him ; my dear sir, I never saw such a man as you are : its beastly, positively beastly.' When he asked Faber what he would do with all the sixteenth-century screens, Faber said, 'Burn 'em all'. Naturally such talk bordered on blasphemy to the two Goths, and soon Phillipps cried, 'Father Faber, God for your pride destroyed and brought to naught your first effort (stamp, fist to heaven) He will curse and destroy your order and it will perish if you go on thus'. Pugin was upset, 'Now come, my dear sir, come, hold your tongue, my gracious, what a thing upon my life — really — well, I always thought I was ye only moderate man in ye world.' Phillipps swallowed his wrath and the two Goths ended in dining with Faber.

However, so wild were the rumours, that Newman was soon involved in a correspondence with Phillipps, wondering how he could be so tolerant in discussion of doctrine and so intolerant in matters of ritual. Phillipps thought Newman was accusing him of Gallicanism and retorted 'Gothick is Christian architecture and Italian or Grecian Pagan'. Newman slyly equated Pagan and Pope, like Bunyan, but he assured Phillipps that he did not mean to call him a Gallican. Newman was by no means a strict adherent of classic any more than of Gothic architecture. He said, 'In order that any style of Architecture should exactly suit the living ritual of the nineteenth century, it should be the living architecture of the nineteenth century — it should never have died — else, while the ritual has changed, the architecture has not kept pace with it. . . . Gothic is like an old dress which fitted a man well twenty years back but must be altered to fit him now'. He pointed out that 'for the Oratorians, the birth of the sixteenth century, to assume the architecture simply and unconditionally of the 13th would be as absurd as their putting on them the cowl of the Dominican, or adopting the tonsure of the Carthusian'. Phillipps was pacified, but not converted.

Newman's view was practical; a church was the place where certain forms of worship went on. 'In details Pugin is perfect,' he said to Miss Giberne, 'but his altars are so small you can't have Pontifical High Mass at them, his tabernacles so low that you can scarce have Exposition, his East windows so large that everything else is hidden in the glare, and his skreens so heavy that you might as well have the function in the sacristy for the seeing it by the congregation.' Mrs. Bowden had got Pugin to build a church at Fulham as a memorial to her husband; they quarrelled over the screen, which she did not want. He started putting one up; she had it taken down again. Pugin refused to come to the consecration, at which Newman preached.

In his architectural letter to Miss Giberne Newman also described the first St. Philip's day in England, May 26th, the feast of the Oratory's founder and patron. 'I sang my first High Mass; after which we had a dinner (to which we invited 8 or 10 persons from Oscott) so perfect that it nearly converted one of our guests to be an Oratorian on the spot. We then had a concert, vocal and instrumental, the Red Cross Knight and other favourite glees, some Trios etc of Beethoven and piano duets. Then we had Solemn Vespers — games in the field — a splendid Benediction and at length fireworks when it got dark. . . . I am giving you a dry detail of events, but poetry goes with youth.'

Meanwhile Faber had still not appeared for his novitiate. He had gone up to Scarborough, his home district, to recuperate, but instead of resting he was preaching to crowded churches and holding evening 'Oratories' for ladies in drawing-rooms — even he realized that this was not a custom of St. Philip's. To Newman's mild expostulation he answered airily that he had no idea he was supposed to come at any definite date. Newman then told him to come by Corpus Christi day — and he did. So he actually arrived for his novitiate about half a year after he had lamented that the Oratory was taking from him all he loved. His advent at Maryvale brought to the surface latent disturbances in the doubled group which was struggling to form itself into a coherent body. This first became apparent to Newman in his own feelings; he sensed that he was not in touch with the younger members of the congregation.

He was tired and unwell and suffering from temporary deafness. Ambrose St. John went away at the end of June, visiting his mother at St. Leonard's, and at the beginning of July Newman wrote to him, 'Charissime, my head is so stupid to-day . . . it is a nuisance. It makes me languid and drowsy and then I can't do my duties and people think me reserved etc when I don't mean to be. At times the sense of weight (of responsibility) and of desolateness has come on me so strongly that I could fancy it might grow equal to any pain; and I thought what this Pope must suffer. It is useless to tell you on paper all the little trials which constitute all this — and it is ungrateful in me not to be more cheerful with the improvement of things in some quarters. My great trial is some of the giovani [novices] — not that anything new has occurred, but they have so repelled any thing between us but what is external, shown so little kindness when I have done things for them, treated me with so little confidence, as to throw me back upon myself — And now I

quite dread our fortnightly chapter day, when I have to make them
a little address, as being something so very external, when I have no
means of knowing what is going on in their minds.   In consequence
I feel as if I were not doing my duty by them, yet without any fault.
I don't know what influence I am exerting on them.   It is as if my
time of work were gone by.   Except that one has been led step by step
to where one is, beginning in 1841 with going to Littlemore, one is
tempted to say "How much happier for me to have no liabilities (so
to speak) but to be a single unfettered convert —" but then I should
not have known you, carissime — so good and evil go together.'   He
finished this letter after dinner, remarking that his deafness suddenly
went on his taking some cayenne pepper — 'how odd it is — whether
nervous or what ?'

It was bewildering to Newman to find himself out of touch with
the young men, but the present trouble arose less from his temperament than from theirs.   In their youthful romanticism they formed
expectations of the religious life which had little to do with reality
and their reactions were primarily emotional.   Some were so young
they could have been Newman's sons, and all regarded him as their
Father, both in his capacity as Superior and as the originator of the
Movement which had made them Catholics.   The idea of Fatherhood
appealed to them, perhaps especially as most of them had broken
with their natural fathers, but like Miss Holmes they wanted an
emotional rather than a spiritual father — most of them in any case
confused the emotional and the spiritual spheres.   Consequently
they expected from Newman either domination or indulgent affection,
sometimes both at once.

He neither could nor should have given them what they wanted ;
such an emotional bond would have retarded their personal development and reduced the weaker to permanent dependence on another.
This is a psychological danger in any attempt at community life,
especially at its initiation.   That Newman had the power to exercise
this emotional domination is shown by the excited reactions, affectionate or hostile, he roused in his juniors, but he deeply suspected
such moral pressures and did everything he could to restrain his own
will and encourage the independence of others.   He had done it in
Oxford, giving his curates and co-operators 'full swing', he had
done it at Littlemore, refusing to be treated as a don and a Superior.
But now he was placed in the position of Superior by the Pope ; in
middle life he had to learn how to accept responsibility for the control
of others without exercising the personal force he so much distrusted.

Perhaps it is worth noting that his patron, Philip Neri, had to go through the very same experience. It was to prove far more difficult to Newman than running his Catholic campaign from Oxford.

When things did not turn out as they expected, some of the younger men reacted by criticizing everything to each other. In a Chapter address of June 17th Newman reminded them that if they were dissatisfied with anything, the proper procedure was to bring it to the attention of the person whose concern it was, not just grumble to each other. This indicates something of the atmosphere, difficult to reconstruct in detail, since as they were all together there are few letters about it. Penny later referred to the 'dissensions and disturbances' at Maryvale, and Hutchison admitted that he had 'kicked up his heels'. Francis Knox was to say he must have been mad to have treated Newman as rudely as he had.

Newman's momentary despondency soon passed. He decided that as he did not seem to be managing the young men very well, someone else had better do it. On July 22nd he terminated Faber's novitiate, which had actually lasted only about a month, and made him novice master. Faber, who alone had any experience of directing others, was the obvious choice; but it was a responsible post, and the only one Newman had ever wished to hold. He had told Wiseman this, writing from Rome of his hope that some 'old' Catholic would join them as spiritual director, or even as Superior. 'I am now just where I would be,' Faber wrote to Watts Russell, 'hidden completely, doing a secret work, and one which I love above all other works.' Some six months later he was complaining to Newman that he had given him 'quiet hidden indoors pensive work' which did not suit him, but which he had taken solely out of love for Newman.

About this time Faber made a voluntary surrender of his liberty to Newman: whatever happened, he was to stay with Newman. The offer was welcome to him personally, Newman wrote in a private note, but involved them in further difficulties. 'We are now thrown back into a chaotic state, in number too large for an Oratory and with two different views running through our members. Yet it seems to be the divine will, since F. Wilfrid has done it so religiously.'

Newman thought that twelve was the ideal number for an Oratory; more made it difficult to preserve the intimate family atmosphere he believed essential to it. In Rome, he said in another Chapter address of this year, they had been cautioned that the difficulty of the Oratory as an institute was the living together in community without the bond of vows. A group at once small and permanent

and free was in constant danger of disintegration, either altogether,
or into a mere collection of individuals, unless the common bond
was strong — which it could not be without a certain community of
views and interests. An Oratorian's property was his own, Newman
said, but not his person or his time ; in joining the Oratory he gave up
himself and became the property of others. It was a high ideal, and
Newman had hoped to devote some time to the formation of the
congregation in this spirit before setting to work. 'Oh for a year of
quiet!' he had said on returning to England — so he told Capes,
convert editor of the *Rambler*.

The arrival of Faber and his Wilfridians had not only swelled
the Oratory to three times the ideal size, but had introduced a forceful
personality whose influence tended to make him a centre of the elements which found Newman too slow, cautious and 'cold' for them.
It was by no means a division between Littlemore and St. Wilfrid's,
for Dalgairns and others sympathized with Faber's fervent Italianism
and missionary dash. Faber's surrender may have been inspired by
a wish to prevent what looked like becoming a split, in which the
larger number followed his enthusiasms. But Newman felt that since
there were too many of them for one body, it would be better for
each group to form naturally round its leader ; and he had always
felt that Faber would be better working in a separate sphere from
his own. Faber's submission, therefore, complicated the problem.

Besides this internal difficulty there were many others. The
Oratory was intended to function in large towns, but Newman
found himself landed with two houses in the country. They were in
financial straits, so much so that Newman could not see how they
were going to support themselves among the poor Catholics of
Birmingham. Wiseman, who had drawn them to the Midlands, was
now in London, yet at rumours that they were going to London the new
Bishop, Ullathorne, was offended, not wishing to lose their assistance.
The Brief, too, fixed Newman by name in Birmingham. Although
it was only six months since the Oratory was set up people were
complaining that nothing was being done, even its members were
restless. Yet they were without pastoral experience, untrained in
community life, full of ideas and ideals but with little common sense
and a good deal of conceit.

Newman took his problems to Mount St. Bernard, where he
made a retreat with the Cistercians. When he came back to Maryvale in August he made three decisions. The first was to close with
the offer of a site in Bayswater, in spite of some opposition within

the Congregation. The second was to move the entire community to St. Wilfrid's, as it was impossible to run two country houses, and St. Wilfrid's *could* not be given up. The third decision was to take an offered site in Alcester Street in Birmingham, on which to found the first working Oratory house. It was a gin distillery.

1848

Old Catholics, new Converts, and Saints

THE Bayswater plan fell through, though not because other members of the community disagreed with it. Those who opposed it did so on the ground that it was too far from London, almost in the country, said Dalgairns, with a distant view of two villages. Even St. John said the place was a wilderness and the Oratory would be the last inhabited house. Nobody would walk the three miles from London. 'I find there is a prevailing notion abroad that we are fighting shy of work among the poor,' he said, adding that the speculative builders were trying to keep the poor out of the new area of development. Newman thought this a 'waspish' letter, and it came just when he was struggling with the novices. 'None of your team, Pater carissime,' St. John replied, 'is so obstreperous, so waspish as you know who, and yet I think he will try to obey.' But he stuck to his opinion that Bayswater was not the place for them; he could not see Faber going there. He had said himself, 'I declare I had rather go to Timbuctoo'. But he did not expect to go, since Newman was to stay in Birmingham, 'unless you intend to dismiss your plague or drown your cat'. It was his joke to compare himself to St. Philip's cat. Newman answered, 'Cats are of different kinds, and there are wild cats.'

He thought it would do London young men good to walk three miles to confess their sins; he was sure the neighbourhood would soon grow up and the poor with it, quite enough of them 'for those the Pope has sent to the *rich*'. For the Pope had inserted in the Brief a direction for the Oratory to care especially for the educated and influential people of England. Newman interpreted this widely, to include provincial seats of rising political power and 'Brummagem intellects', but he kept in mind that the Oratory had a special intellectual mission. In spite of this opposition he decided to close with the Bayswater offer; but after a while another difficulty came up. Ground and money were offered, and he wanted to start by building the house. 'A house will build a church but a church will not build a house.' But the Bayswater people wanted the church built first.

In the end Newman gave up the idea, and later the property became Manning's, and his Oblates of St. Charles still live there.

The removal to St. Wilfrid's was accomplished during October. Newman had a bad cold, which hung on him for a whole month, and forced him into bed once though it did not stop him from writing letters, not only to friends and on business but to inquirers ; he had a new one this year, Catherine Ward. Gentili had died, and he wrote to the Fathers of Charity on this tragic loss. Sad to say, Father Dominic, so much better known to Newman, was to die the next year, collapsing at the railway station of Reading, worn out before he was sixty.

Newman was not taking his books to St. Wilfrid's, as they would shortly be required in Birmingham, but a lot of other stuff had to be moved and 'vans' went off every few days. The Fathers and Brothers left in relays. Faber wrote to Newman, 'Now that ye community have come and you are not here, it is very dismal'. Coffin said, 'We only want our dearest Padre and all would look most smiling'. Newman went at the end of October and St. John, left with Frederick Bowles at Maryvale, wrote, 'We both felt horribly mopish after you were gone. F. Frederick still persisted in thinking himself paralytic.' The next day he reported 'F. Fred now informs me he is now able to close his lips'. He also told Newman that there was grumbling at Oscott that they had deserted the mission, though there were few Catholics in the district.

During the move Newman was corresponding with Faber about a new novice, Henry Formby, a convert with a monomania about plain chant. Formby had written a book which Newman and the Deputies thought it not advisable to publish ; it soon became clear that in a choice between the Oratory and his obsession, the Oratory would lose. Newman wrote to Coffin, 'He from literary vanity, thinks that Plain Chant, though predestinated, cannot stand without his viewy recommendation of it. This must be broken, if he is to be a good Oratorian, a good Priest and a man of even second-rate perfection. We must have no literary selfishness and jealousies among us. I own I am hard-hearted towards a mere literary (ethos) for there is nothing I despise and detest more. He is only half a man if he can't put his book into the fire when told by authority. His reluctance only makes me see my way clearer. An't I fierce ?' But he was not fierce to Formby himself, whom he tried to encourage to persevere, as he thought it would be for his good to stay, though perhaps 'for *our* comfort if he goes', he admitted to Faber. He added : 'I wish I felt that keeping F. William [Penny] increased his merit — but that's another matter. He has just left us, having regaled us at recreation last night with a shoeless pair of feet. I thought it was thin gutta percha.'

Penny was turning out an extreme individualist, and Newman had told him already he was not throwing himself into community life. He had grumbled about going to St. Wilfrid's earlier and had bargained for a holiday first. 'I think all this is unreasonable ; who has his way like him ?' Newman had said to St. John. In that same (June) letter he had remarked, 'F. Minister [Coffin] and F. Antony don't get on and F. Minister is turning sulky (*burn* this)'. These difficulties were to grow rather than diminish when they were all at St. Wilfrid's. As for Formby, he decided that he had a vocation to publish his views on plain chant. Wishing to mark his departure from the Oratory with a gift he offered Newman either a model ship (carefully drawn) or an upright music stand. And so he went.

Before he left he tactlessly showed Faber a letter from Newman, who had tried to encourage him to give up his literary aspirations by pointing out that Faber was doing the same 'in a more emphatic way'. Thus Faber learned, in a way Newman did not intend, the probable fate of his cherished project, the *Lives of the Saints*. Faber took it well, but the Saints became the occasion of the first public row the Oratory had to face in the Catholic world, and resulted in a prolonged misunderstanding with Ullathorne, their Bishop.

Faber, who had contributed to Newman's series of English Saints, in 1847 had begun a series of translations from Italian and French hagiographies. When he joined the Oratory it was decided that the volumes in preparation should go on appearing, and meanwhile they would decide in the autumn about taking over the series as an Oratorian work. Faber wrote a memorandum for Newman on his objects ; out of nine reasons, only one referred to those outside the Church, the other eight were directed against the English Catholics, who seemed to Faber 'utterly protestant', lacking in supernaturalism, and in need of a strong dose of 'modernism and foreignism'. Wilfrid Ward printed this memorandum as Newman's in his biography, but nothing could be further from Newman's attitude. 'Charissime,' he said to Faber, 'I cannot see that we have any call, whether as Oratorians or as converts, to begin our course by preaching to the old Catholics — and a good part of your argument is this.' In June he gave the greater part of a Chapter address to relations with others in the English Catholic body. He cautioned them against offending

people by laughing at bad taste ; it was thoughtlessness, but it would
be serious if they got the name of 'uppishness, flippancy, criticalness
etc'.   Referring to the (minor) divisions within the Catholic body he
said '*your* mission is to lessen them . . . do not be fond of finding
fault — take every thing in the best point of view. . . . Do not put
yourselves forward, do not talk much before others — do not argue
much in private.'   They must be on their guard against saying
'strong things or sharp things'.   But some forgot these cautions as
soon as they were in mixed society.

However, Newman was convinced of the supreme value to Christians of the lives of those who had gone furthest towards the goal of
perfection — wholeness in the new life.   'Saints are the popular
evidence of Christianity', he wrote for the preface to this series.
'The life of a saint is a microcosm or whole work of God, a perfect
work from beginning to end, yet one which may be bound between
two boards and mastered by the most unlearned.   The exhibition of
a person, his thoughts, his words, his acts, his trials, his fortunes, his
beginnings, his growth, his end, have a charm to everyone, and when
he is a Saint they have a divine influence and persuasion, a power of
exercising and eliciting the latent elements of divine grace, in individual readers, as no other reading can have.'

To Newman the great value of the lives of Saints was to trace the
development of a living person growing in grace.   In 1859, at the
beginning of a penetrating sketch of St. John Chrysostom, he wrote
'I ask something more than to stumble on the *disiecta membra* of
what ought to be a living whole.   I take but a secondary interest in
books which chop up a saint into chapters of faith, hope and charity
and the cardinal virtues . . . they do not manifest a saint, they mince
him up into spiritual lessons.'   Incredible as it may seem, when he
wrote this, and for years after, a fierce campaign was being kept up,
principally by the converts, for the old style of mincemeat.   A writer
in the *Dublin Review* complained of a new biographical work that he
could not look up the virtues in it and see how the saint displayed
them, as if a man were an encyclopaedia and virtues collected like
a wardrobe.

Unfortunately, the books Faber had chosen to inject supernaturalism into the old Catholics were of this type, which, indeed,
he approved.   But as well as mincing up the saints into spiritual
lessons, so that they ceased to be alive and became static patterns of
every possible virtue, these Italian and French lives loaded their
subjects with miracles, not distinguishing between the authentic and

the legendary, and magnified their heroism into such feats of super-
human endurance as to make them seem as unreal as characters in a
fairy tale.   Faber had chosen St. Rose of Lima, a Spanish American
of the sixteenth century, who lived in a place and time which could
hardly be more remote from Victorian England.   To the imagination
of the English reader the hard and normal side of St. Rose's life was
swamped by her visions and physical austerities, astonishing even in
that fierce age.   Newman admitted that he wished Faber had not
begun with St. Rose, who could not be much help to their contemporaries ;   still, she was a Saint, appearing in a most unpromising
colonial *milieu*, and other saints, less remote, were to follow.   He was
inclined to think the Oratory should sponsor this literary work.

The situation was abruptly changed when *Dolman's Magazine*, a
Catholic publication, came out with a violent attack on the *Lives*
and on Faber, who was actually accused of promoting idolatry.   The
writer was a priest called Price, a convert from Presbyterianism.   It
turned out later that he had been put up to it by Pierce Connelly,
the American Episcopalian convert, who in order to become a priest
had persuaded his wife to enter a convent.   She had now become
the Foundress of a teaching order, of the Holy Child Jesus, and
Connelly was on the point of reverting to Protestantism ;   he was
soon pursuing Mother Cornelia Connelly through the courts of
England demanding restitution of conjugal rights.   The attack on
Faber, so dubiously inspired, was unjust in any case ;   the only
grounds for talking of idolatry were his over-literal translations.   To
take an example from another of the *Lives*, 'Il Crocefisso' in Italian
signifies both Christ, the Crucified, and the object called in English a
Crucifix.   Faber, not only in books but in letters, talked of 'fighting
with my crucifix' which simply sounds ridiculous ;   nobody in their
senses, however, could seriously imagine that he wished English
Catholics to worship brass figures.   It was true that Protestants
misconceived the use of images, so that it was unwise as well as bad
translation to use such phrases ;   but no worse.

After this public attack it was impossible to launch the series as
an Oratorian work without some sort of countenance from authority ;
such a charge, too, against so well-known a convert as Faber ought
to be condemned by his Bishop.   Newman felt he must identify
himself with Faber in this.   'You may be sure, Carissime, that I will
stand by you,' he wrote to him, 'and no reproach shall fall on you
which does not fall on me too.'   With this in mind he went to call
on Ullathorne, before he left Maryvale in October.

William Bernard Ullathorne was a tough little Yorkshireman, five years younger than Newman, who had been present in August at his installation in St. Chad's as Vicar Apostolic of the Midlands District. Ullathorne had been for a short time Vicar Apostolic in the Western District; he was consecrated a Bishop at the age of forty. He had started life as a cabin boy, but when he was seventeen went to Downside Abbey and became a Benedictine novice. In those days English Benedictines were rarely able to live a normal monastic life; Ullathorne was only twenty-six when he was sent out to Australia as Vicar General of the missions there, and official Catholic chaplain to the Government. His great work had been to try to alleviate the lot of the convicts and publicize the shocking conditions imposed by the iniquitous system of transportation; his evidence before a commission did much to assist in abolishing it. His fearless pugnacity stood him in good stead in such work; it was less admirably employed in dealing with missioners older and more experienced than himself. He was attacked in the newspapers throughout his sojourn and defended himself with vigour.

Ullathorne left Australia in 1840, refusing to go back as a Bishop, and spent the next five or six years in charge of the mission at Coventry, where he first met Margaret Hallahan, the wonderful woman who started life as a servant girl and was to become the Mother Prioress of the Dominican nuns of Stone, a community she gathered and formed herself in the active tasks of the Third Order. Mother Margaret and the first of her nuns followed Ullathorne to Clifton from Coventry; when he came to the Midlands he soon got her to Stone. They were great friends and understood each other perfectly. Ullathorne's pugnacity increased rather than diminished with his episcopal consecration; he started off in the West with a tremendous row about the Prior Park finances, and repeated the performance with Oscott when he arrived in Birmingham. He had met Newman once or twice but did not know him except by hearsay. A typical 'old Catholic', Ullathorne thought Wiseman had made too much of the converts, and that they needed taking down a peg, though he had one, Estcourt, closely associated with him in the work of the diocese. 'That goose Estcourt' Newman called him once, for showing other people's letters about, told the other converts what Ullathorne had said about them, and told the Bishop what was said about him — all with the best of intentions, but with doubtful results.

To Newman's great surprise Ullathorne advised him to stop the series altogether. 'He was very kind and easy in manner,' said

Newman, bewildered and silenced by a stream of well-meant criticism, of the *Lives*, of Faber's anti-Gothicism and the general behaviour of the converts. He told Newman he ought to do something to 'soothe the jealousy of the clergy'. 'I did not reply,' said Newman, 'but this strikes me as impertinent — *why* are they jealous ? *what* have we done ? since the day we were Catholics they have all been bursting with "jealousy" — and we are on every occasion to give way to this indefinite terror.' But the important point was that it was 'shameful to recommend us to stop the *Lives*, *before* they have made Price eat his words publicly'. He saw that to suppress the series now would amount to an admission of Faber's idolatry and an acknowledgment that the lives of foreign saints were unsuitable reading for English Catholics. Ullathorne did not see the dangers of suppression, only those of publication. He was convinced that the Italian books would do more harm than good, and that the miracles, visions and austerities would shock Protestants, and put off possible converts. He told Newman he would have liked original works on the lines of the English Saints — and how right he was — but if it was only the style he objected to, the reasonable course would have been to suggest adaptation and revision by a censor, not suspension.

Newman did not know what to say, so he said nothing. But afterwards he wrote, in answer to a letter from Ullathorne, to say that 'Protestants are converted by high views, not low ones ; to hide from them the Lives of the Saints is to escape indeed offending those who would never be converted but at the same time miss those who would ; nay, those who might in the event be Saints themselves'. He observed that 'hostile Protestants know as much and more of the sins and corruptions of foreign Catholics and the mystical devotions of Saints as the Lives in question can tell them'. It was the old story of knowing your enemy ; Ullathorne knew the feelings of old English Catholics, but he could not know the feelings of Protestants as Newman did, who had run the whole course from Evangelicalism to Anglo-Catholicism. 'I thought of trying to set him against Price,' Newman said, 'but I somehow think that our Lady and St. Philip will take our part, if we do not take our own — and even humanly speaking we shall be sure to have defenders if we do not defend ourselves.'

But he was not going to leave Faber to bear the brunt of the attack alone, even though he did not agree with him in matters of style, or in wishing to preach to the old Catholics. He obeyed Ullathorne in stopping the series, but he wrote Faber a letter to be printed in the notification to the subscribers. He did not mention the Bishop, but said it was the Fathers of the Congregation who had decided on suspension. 'It appears there is a strong feeling against it on the part of a portion of the Catholic community in England, on the ground, as we are given to understand, that the lives of foreign saints, however edifying in their respective countries, are unsuited to England and unacceptable to Protestants. To this feeling, we consider it a duty, for the sake of peace, to defer. For myself, you know well, without my saying it, how absolutely I identify myself with you in this matter ; but, as you may have to publish this letter, I make it an opportunity, which has not yet been given me, of declaring that I have no sympathy at all with the feeling to which I have alluded, and, in particular, that no one can assail your name without striking at mine.'

This final hit was directed at Price, in order to show him that he must reckon with Newman in attacking Faber ; in identifying himself with Faber Newman hoped to deflect from him some of the criticism, and perhaps lessen it. But Ullathorne took it as a kind of snort of resentment : don't you realize, he thought Newman was saying, that when you strike Faber you are striking *me*, great man as I am ? He was the more agitated as there was a great outcry from those who wanted more Saints' Lives — not all converts by any means. People were saying that it was Ullathorne who had stopped the series ; annoyed, he demanded his letters back from Newman. As Newman had scribbled drafts of his replies on the backs of them he had to send copies, explaining why, and assuring the Bishop that the circular was directed against Price, who had not been officially censured.

Newman was not much worried by this difference with his Bishop. He wrote to Capes, the editor of *The Rambler*, who often asked his advice and told him the London gossip, 'Don't think we shall not get on with him in Birmingham, I think we shall — but I shall have no delicacy at all with him or fear of offending him. I think he is a kind-hearted man and wishes to get on with us — but that, just as gentlemen make acquaintance with bowing and civil speeches, so the way to be good friends with him is to begin with a boxing bout.' He believed Ullathorne had been misled by Price's article, and that he had heard rumours that Faber had more influence in the Congregation that its Superior. 'I suppose he took it for granted that I wished to have a rap at Faber and should not be unwilling to have the Lives stopped and catch at a good excuse such as his wishing it.' Thus Newman brushed aside the gossip about Faber's position, which was at that very moment receiving fresh confirmation now that the whole community was together at St. Wilfrid's; and supported with quixotic loyalty one who was then making himself unpopular with the old Catholics for no very good reason, and was privately causing his Superior trouble and anxiety.

Newman was anxious that friends like Capes and Lewis who had a platform on which to fight for him, should fight fair. 'Say what you like about the expedience or inexpedience of the Lives', he told Lewis, of *The Tablet*. 'But *don't* (you have not done it yet) accuse Mr. Price of heresy or attack *him* in any way. I wish his article brought to justice, — but a literary warfare (for he will reply) will be nuts to the Puseyites and throw some of them back.' To Capes he wrote, on November 22nd, 'If it will be a come off to persons either to save their dignity or to excuse their changing, you may throw blame on me to them. They may allow themselves perhaps to express regret, if they may say, it is all my fault.'

Ullathorne was one of those who was changing his attitude; he wrote to *The Tablet* to deny that he was the cause of the suspension, but thought that the translations ought to be submitted to a censor. 'Why did he not say so to *me*?' Newman observed to Capes, but he was quite willing to compound on those terms. The Bishop wrote a pastoral letter for Advent, 'beautiful and impressive', as Newman said in thanking him for it, calling on the laity to aim at a more perfect life, and to make friends of the Saints, whose lives were like a garden of Paradise. But in his letter to *The Tablet* Ullathorne had expressed only a mild disapprobation of Price. He said that Catholics would take it as a condemnation, but Wiseman disagreed. 'He has forgotten the difference between disapprobation and condemnation', he said. On the strength of this Newman ventured a slight protest to the Bishop. Justice had not yet been done; a priest of his diocese had been accused of promoting idolatry and the charge had not been rebutted.

This was too much for Ullathorne, who responded with a letter pages long, not about the public question, but about Newman's private character. Although he scarcely knew Newman he delivered a minute and severe lecture, though he wrote in a warm, emotional style. 'I am pained to observe the acute sensitiveness with which several little matters have been viewed of late. Believe me, my dear Mr. Newman, this cannot be without a hidden ingredient of self-love, a most subtle spirit and the object of the fears and combats of the humble saints of God.' In fact, it was sad that the Saints, who were so humble, should be defended by someone who so evidently was not. A warning was issued against 'the more delicate shades of pride, especially of intellectual pride', so difficult to see in ourselves, and 'personal sensitiveness' was discerned in the circular, and in the phrase quoted (erroneously) by Ullathorne as 'the blow struck at *me*'. 'My dear Mr. Newman,' said Ullathorne, 'I can with difficulty refrain from tears whilst I write. I love you so much, and yet I feel so anxious.'

This letter, intended to produce shame and contrition, struck Newman as rather funny, and he rashly sent it to Capes. But Capes' indignation, for he thought the Bishop unfair in treating Newman as an individual instead of as the head of a religious body, made Newman feel guilty. 'I sent you the letter as a piece of fun, but perhaps I had better not,' he said. Capes had shown it to Wiseman, who said Ullathorne had no call to lecture Newman. It was not lecturing that Newman minded, but lecturing off the point instead of taking the necessary action. 'But my dear Lord,' he wrote to Wiseman, 'not only as a bishop, but *any* one may lecture me, and I should be obliged for it. What I had to remark in Dr. Ullathorne was that he spoke about me *without knowing me*. It stands to reason no one can know a person of my age in a moment — and the Bishop has had no experience whatever of persons in my circumstances and he spoke of me on a theory.' It was the old theory that his acts were dictated by his feelings, added to the equally mistaken theory that he was in the habit of disobeying bishops.

Ullathorne had so missed the point that Newman found it difficult to answer him. He could not acknowledge his delicate shades of pride without admitting that his course of action had been wrong, whereas he was convinced it was right. He never would defend his own character, and it was beside the point in this case, which was of justice for Faber. So he sent only a few lines, scarcely more than 'My dear Lord — I feel obliged for your Lordship's letter', and asking if he could send to the press Ullathorne's private gloss on his *Tablet* letter, that in it he had meant to express condemnation of Price. Ullathorne mistook the brevity of the reply for a studied insult, issuing from hurt pride and angry resentment. Estcourt said, 'It was so very short . . . as if you were squaring out for a fight'. When Wiseman heard that Ullathorne thought Newman's letters cold, he remarked, 'Dr. Ullathorne's letters are warmer than his conversation, Newman's the other way'. Newman still refused to be worried ; it was only a Yorkshire boxing bout. To Capes he wrote, 'You seem to think I *was* warm in my published letter. I really believe not : but I will cheerfully bear any such imputation from any one if I have succeeded, as I trust through God's mercy I have, in gaining an important point.'

For Mr. Price had at last come out with a handsome public apology and begged Faber to continue the Lives. Price had once long ago considered calling on Newman at Littlemore. On December 3rd Newman wrote to him, 'Fulfil this long intention now. . . . Meanwhile, pray for us dear Revd Sir, that we may be worthy of your generosity.' Price's answer was enthusiastic, though he at present could not accept the invitation to stay. The *Lives* were to be resumed in January, after passing before a censor. All was now well, except in relation to the Bishop, who was, if possible, more hurt and irritated than before. When Newman wrote to him about his candidates for orders, he got a reply from Estcourt only, and so vague that he was forced to put down what he hoped was correct procedure and ask for corroboration. Next Ullathorne started inquiring into their ecclesiastical position. When Newman said he was sure there would be no differences between them the Bishop insisted on seeing the Brief — he evidently thought Newman, a convert, knew nothing about such things, and was suspicious because he had told him that though the Oratorians received their faculties from the Bishop, he did not have the right of visitation. But it was all correct.

Newman's letters, plain and polite, no doubt still seemed cold and supercilious to Ullathorne, though he did not so intend them. After Christmas he said cheerfully to Capes, 'Dr. Ullathorne has ceased for the present "to torment us with his discipline" as Wisdom in Ecclesiasticus, but he has made up for it to his own satisfaction by going about talking of my intolerable pride. However, we are very good friends ; I have written to him some smooth letters and he has renewed our faculties in a very gracious way.' He was wrong in thinking his smooth letters pacified Ullathorne — they were the very things that convinced him of Newman's intolerable pride. He had started with a prejudice against Newman as a convert, a famous religious leader among the heretics who must be suffering from intellectual pride ; his prejudice seemed confirmed by behaviour he did not understand, and a style of address which was not his own. The curious thing is that later writers have all agreed with Ullathorne that it was Newman who showed sensitiveness in this episode.

1848-49

Community Tensions and Birmingham Back Streets

NEWMAN did not need Capes to tell him the gossip about the Oratory — he told it himself, in the November letter in which he talked of his boxing match with Ullathorne. 'From your letter I am amused to see that it is the feeling of all Catholics, old and new, that the Oratory is hitherto a failure. But my good fellows, you do not know what it is to bring a religious body into form. If a body with vows is difficult to manage, what is one without vows? We have between 30 and 40 as good and dear companions as we could wish in imagination — but the higher, the more gifted, the more spiritual are minds, the more difficult to shape in one course. . . . Then again, we have to learn each other. And we have to learn the genius of the Congregation and to make it work. . . . Meanwhile it is amusing, while we have been hugging ourselves on the *real work* we have done, on the gigantic internal difficulties we have surmounted (I fear to boast, but certainly we have been much blessed) you, gentlemen, at a distance, looking on, and seeing we were not insane enough to waste our strength in flashes in the pan, have said, "It's a failure, the F. Superior is at his old game, sitting still — giving up things — cherishing ideals about Bishops, while souls lie by thousands perishing in our great towns; nibbling at Bayswater and receding, promising to go to the Adelphi, shilly-shallying about Derretend in Birmingham, complaining of the want of funds when he, like some others, should throw himself on a poor population for support and fight (as you say) with brazen weapons.' Capes had said that what Newman lacked was 'brass' and 'tin'.

In spite of all their difficulties, Newman said, they had received a hundred converts during the year and were preaching eight or ten sermons every Sunday. 'But the truth is, these old priests will be satisfied with nothing — they have pursued us with criticisms ever since we were Catholics. Why do you keep together? Why don't you go to Rome? Why *do* you go to Rome? Why do you rush into the Confessional before you are examined in all dogmatics and morals ? Why do you sit idle ? What a short novitiate you have had ! *When* did you read morals ? None of these questions are fictitious, and they are but samples of a hundred. No, we must go our own way ; we must look to the Fount of grace for a blessing, and for guidance — and we must care nothing (and certainly don't care much) for the tongues about us . . . but I must end this long prose.' Capes said he had 'laughed at your picture of the buffetings the Oratory has got. It is so exactly what I have heard people say.'

Some internal difficulties had certainly been surmounted, but others remained to disturb them. The whole community was now under one roof and psychologically if not actually it was Faber's roof. He had built the church and the people were nearly all his converts. 'Father Fable', as they called him, was in constant demand. Thomas Godwin, now Brother Frederick, recalled in later years an occasion when he saw Faber, about to go in to interview an important visitor, pause and ruffle his fine head of hair. Godwin was lost in admiration for what he, and no doubt Faber, considered a gesture of humility. Faber certainly exercised a great fascination on large numbers of people, and his preaching was very popular. He was still asked to preach at Alton Towers to eminent Catholic visitors. Then he and Dalgairns went off on a mission to the Potteries ; their audiences were so crowded that Dalgairns was afraid the floor would collapse. 'F. Wilfrid does not sleep but is very larky', he wrote home. The excitement brought on one of Faber's headaches ; yet he craved excitement and felt frustrated when he was not missionizing.

The mission still came first with him, though when Oratory matters were in question he had very definite opinions. He was inclined to assume that as he had translated a life of St. Philip he knew all about the Oratory — a rash assumption, since the old Lives concentrated on the saint himself and consisted mostly of strings of anecdotes. Time and again Faber was to show his ignorance of the English Rule and its alterations, and Newman's views carried little weight with him. Right at the start he had persuaded Newman against introducing the exercise of the discipline. Faber had a reputation for ascetic ferocity which quite alarmed Francis Knox, who wrote to Newman before he arrived at Maryvale, 'The discipline nights are quite terrible to contemplate with Faber's indurated community, who perhaps are accustomed to chained and spiked discipline besides hair shirts, chain girdles and such like'. But Faber assured Newman that 'ye savagery of Elton' was a thing of the past and was

scarcely admitted before he wrote a memorandum dismissing the
exercise as too ascetic for St. Philip's way — regardless of the fact
that the saint himself had initiated it.   Newman wished to retain it,
and urged as a consideration that it would help to emphasize that
being Oratorians did not mean merely living like gentlemen in a
common house.   He suggested that if Faber disapproved the idea of
its taking place in common, they might take it severally in their
rooms, but at the same time, in order to preserve its communal
character.   Faber dismissed this compromise too.   The convert Dr.
Duke of St. Leonard's then came into the argument with warnings
about health and the question was shelved, but not, by Newman,
abandoned in principle.

But the discipline was a secondary issue.   Newman had started
the regular Oratory exercise, the daily half hour of meditation and
prayers made together in the evening.   Since, like all secular priests,
they said their office privately, this common spiritual exercise was
the distinctive religious bond of the community.   Sunday Vespers,
also, according to the Rule, was said or sung together and in the
Church.   When Newman transferred the base of the Oratory from
Maryvale to St. Wilfrid's, in order to fulfil Faber's commitments
there, he started the exercise again at once.   He had hardly done so
when Faber objected to it as interfering with the mission services
and the routine of the novices.   Antony Hutchison was officially in
charge of the mission, but Faber assisted him, which meant in effect
that he still ran it.   Newman tried one adjustment of time and place
after another, but still Faber complained, so that in the end they were
forced to give up the exercise altogether.

Before he went to Birmingham Newman made a memorandum
for his private record of what had happened ; it was dated January
14th, 1849.   'F. Wilfrid wanted still more power for the Mission in
the Church — we gave him the use of the choir, separated his services
from ours and proposed to have our Sunday Vespers at a different
time.   Not enough still — so we have given up Vespers altogether,
given up Benediction to him and put High Mass at his disposal.'
Newman concluded : 'At this moment the mission is supreme in the
Church and the Oratory is nothing.   This is no home of the Oratory,
but the Oratory is the guest of one of its missions . . . the Missioner
is the sole authority both in the Sacristy and the Church.'   Even the
candlesticks, chalices and vestments belonged to the Mission and not
to the Oratory.

Newman's conclusion was that Birmingham should be primarily

n experiment with the Oratory and only secondarily a mission. If
he could get the Oratory working as such, a London house might be
started from there ; if it failed, he might try to get permission from
Rome for them all to go to London. Evidently he did not consider,
or thought unwise, any direct attempt to make Faber change his ways.
Newman may have been wrong in yielding to Faber in the question
of the Oratory exercise and Sunday Vespers, but Faber was exceedingly difficult to manage. He was so zealous, and so plausible, and
at the least hint of criticism he tended to take to his bed with headache and sickness. Then the row about the Saints' Lives was running
concurrently with the difficulties at St. Wilfrid's. Newman preferred
to try to shape his Oratory in Birmingham first, and see whether time
might not effect what argument perhaps could not. Christmas, anyway, was no time for argument. Newman sang High Mass at midnight, exactly a year after he had landed in England. 'We have had
masses going on literally through the night 36 in all,' he wrote, '— as
if in emulation of the Angels who sang through the night 1800 years
ago "Glory to God, peace on earth". Some of us have not been to
bed at all.'

He began the new year of 1849 with a *novena* of prayers for the
new project in Birmingham. He had bought the lease of the gin
distillery in Alcester Street, and alterations were in progress. There
was a hall a hundred feet long, still full of vats when he first saw it,
which would do for a chapel, and a large room above it which Newman
at once saw as a Library. The house, he said, 'though inconvenient
will make up 7-12 bedrooms.' This elegant property, with a highly
ornate classical front, was situated on a corner site, half way up a rise
in Deritend, then on the outskirts of the growing town. It was a
district full of the small press-work factories for which Birmingham
was famous, and rows of still smaller brick houses. Ramifications
of the canal network ran through it, carrying a large traffic and not
yet eclipsed commercially by the new railways. The area was certainly in the midst of the mechanics, and not very well placed for an
Oratory, which ought to be accessible to all, but Newman thought it
better to take what he could get. The lease was for three years only,
but he hoped to get it extended. He was told his site was swampy
ground and would be intolerable 'from the stenches' but on investigation he decided it was all right. He told Henry Wilberforce that
Birmingham was a healthy town because it was built on gravel and
the houses did not have cellars. Certainly it did not suffer badly in
the great cholera epidemics of the nineteenth century.

'We have been given the hardest town in England to work'
Ambrose St. John cheerfully told Miss Giberne a little later. Birmingham did not endure some of the worst results of the rapid
industrialization of these years, since it was comparatively little
affected by slumps in the market ; it was easy to adapt the presses
and turn out something else. On the other hand its vast and sudden
growth from a mere village to a huge town, where the operatives were
largely unskilled, subjected it to successive waves of often transitory
immigration of the very poorest outcasts of a competitive society,
both in England and Ireland. The men of power were self-made
factory owners and business men ; there were few gentry of the
old-fashioned sort ; not much in the way of skilled workers or such
close knit communities as those of the miners, shipbuilders, potters
and others of the northern towns. The operatives were a shifting
rootless mob : 'Birmingham roughs' were famous in the papers.

As far as religion went, which was not far, it was generally Non-
Conformist ; the most famous and socially responsible community
being that of the Quaker families. There was a small but persistent
group of Catholics centred in the district round Edgbaston ; they
had dared to build themselves a church, in an alley off Broad Street,
keeping the wall of it much like a factory, with small windows high
up. A gallery all round inside helped to accommodate more people.
St. Peter's was lovingly decorated within, but simple. Pugin's cathedral, the size of a moderately big church, near the railway stations in
the middle of the town, was the only other Catholic church, a recent
addition, when Newman opened his gin shop chapel in Alcester
Street.

He was getting ready for Birmingham and Birmingham was
getting ready for him. Protestant militants had suddenly realized
that the arch-traitor was about to start practising idolatry in their
midst. St. John, who was there before Christmas supervising alterations, wrote that Newman would be amused to hear the town was
full of Bible-lovers. Placards were appearing and warning sermons
were being preached — 'quite an uproar'.

Newman had little confidence in himself, though much in his
mission. He wrote to Mrs. Bowden, 'My letters are always dull now,
for somehow I seem to have lost all spring in writing — sometimes I
wonder whether I shall be as wooden in preaching and other work
when I get to Birmingham. — but this is all in His hands who can
make or break His instruments as He pleases. Everything as yet
has turned out well and will continue to do so, I firmly believe, what-

ever be the will of Providence about my personal powers and exertions. We are now on the brink of Birmingham — and you may fancy it is an awful thing ; — an awful thing to begin a new life at my age. But you will pray for me I know, as I do ever.' The less he trusted himself, the more he trusted God.

Newman arrived at Alcester Street on January 26th, 1849, a Friday. On Sunday he described his removal to Coffin, whom he had left in charge at St. Wilfrid's, as Rector. He came in a fly, in which were packed 'a bag of books, a box of rattle traps loose, a large basket of vials and gallipots, a violin and case, a ditto belonging to F. Richard [Stanton], a box of relics, a large black box containing the Spanish crucifix, a large glass case to go over the same, a plaister Madonna, a plaister Crucifix, a saucer of China shells and the plaister decorated cross from the Guest Room. My fly was filled nearly to the top and its a wonder how I got in among them, a greater how I got out, and the greatest how everything was not smashed by the jogging.'

He remarked with satisfaction that in one day he had got his room in order. 'Thus I have perfectly imitated Formby in taking care of number one — and my only excuse is, beyond my having brought from Maryvale sundry valuables which are not my own, that I find, as he doubtless felt, that when one has peace and harmony within and one's room is happy with itself, one works with far greater zeal and spirit for the good of others.' He had begun by saying 'We are working in our several ways like Trojans, all except F. Frederic [Bowles] who yesterday morning when his services were wanted took to reading spiritual books. I know I wish *I* had time for spiritual reading . . . the said Father after all has laboured very hard.'

The chapel was opened as planned on February 2nd, feast of the Purification and first anniversary of the Oratory in England. St. John celebrated and Newman preached ; everything went off quietly. But it was a Friday ; trouble, if any, was expected on Sunday. That day Newman said the mass in the morning, and preached in the evening. Between the two services he was writing to Faber and remarked, 'We expect a row this evening and are sending for two policemen'. Five or six hundred people crammed into the former gin distillery that night, but there was no disturbance. Newman's sermon, probably one of the first in the volume of *Discourses to Mixed Congregations*, was very simple, on the sins of men, God's judgment and the means of salvation : how to escape from slavery to evil and the false worship of the world. There was nothing that could not be understood not only by Protestants, but by the many who were almost entirely ignorant of any religion. As printed, however, they did not fail to shock the worldly, whether Christian or not.

The next week they started talks and evening instructions in the Faith, on week-days, and were astonished to be overwhelmed by a flood of children — forty turned up for the first. 'Boys and girls flow in for instructions as herrings in season', Newman told Capes, adding that he did not expect it to last. But the children went on coming. There was no chance of starting a school for them, as they had intended, for all from the age of seven went out to work from early morning till 7 or 8 in the evening. They worked at the presses which stamped out all the thousand varieties of Birmingham ware. Illiterate, unkempt, overworked, at the mercy of sickness and all the ills of overcrowded and unhealthy lodgings, ignorant and without hope of anything better to come, here they came to the gin-shop-chapel, bright and warm, to the Fathers who were kind, and mostly young, and soon made themselves quite at home — even to the point of invading the house and (sad to say) teasing the lay brothers and throwing ink about. But their new religion did not make their lot easier in the world. 'It is a dreadful trial for the poor girls — they don't get places, they don't get married,' Newman was telling Miss Giberne in April. 'It is a dreadful problem how to provide for them. The poor factory boys seem to have no prejudice against us — many of them literally profess no religion and numbers of them have not been baptized.' Out of these unwanted waifs of the industrial revolution Newman and his colleagues built up a sturdy Catholic community, which took root and flourished, and even after they moved to Edgbaston continued to multiply. To-day there is a Catholic school on the site of the gin shop chapel, so the place is still full of children.

Some of the town boys were less friendly and threw stones ; one of the lay brothers was hit. Some 'bad men and women' made trouble in the evenings and the police had to be fetched again, but on the whole they were let alone. There was a rush of work in the evening, but they had the rest of the day to get the house and the community life into order. One of Newman's first cares was the Library. Books kept arriving in loads from Maryvale, sometimes wet, much to his grief. He arranged most of them himself and strained the muscle in his wrist again. It affected his writing and called forth anxious inquiries from his friends, who thought he must be ill. But when he remembered having done the same thing at

Littlemore he was quite pleased to have hit on the cause, though it did not alleviate the pain. These winter months were very exhausting. Birmingham might be comparatively healthy, but the gin distillery was not the airiest place in it. To Coffin Newman remarked once, 'The room was so excessively hot last night in spite of the windows being open (for they come in an hour before the time) that I all but made a complete break down in my sermon. It was like drinking hydrogen or carbonic gas'. The atmosphere became even thicker when the poor Irish immigrants found them out, as they soon did.

The new work, the unexpected shoals of children, the anxieties of beginning this new venture, were not the heaviest of Newman's responsibilities during these first few months at Alcester Street. All the time he was struggling to solve the complex problem of the future of the whole community, which became more, not less urgent when he had left St. Wilfrid's. For he had scarcely arrived in Birmingham before Faber let loose on him a flood of complaints and sorrows.

1849

'Precious cadavera !'

NEWMAN had hardly gone off in his fly among the violins and crucifixes before Faber wrote him a long letter full of anxieties. On the day of the opening of the chapel Newman replied, 'My dearest F. Wilfrid, I do sincerely feel the great anxieties you have upon you, and the generous loyal way in which you try to support me. God knows how I love you, and how grateful I feel to you.' Faber answered, 'I cannot tell you the consolation your affectionate letter has given me after two days of greater suffering than I ever remember to have had.' Every attack was always the worst.

Excitement and frustration alike brought on these physical collapses, from which he would often recover quite suddenly. Faber was later to suffer from kidney trouble and died of Bright's disease ; our present knowledge of the connexion between psychological and physical symptoms is insufficient to make reliable contemporary diagnoses, let alone retrospectively of the dead. Nevertheless, with so many details of his collapses supplied by Faber himself, it is plain that though the form they took was determined by his physical constitution, the causes were chiefly nervous and emotional. Whenever he got himself into an impossible situation he was seized with violent pains and sickness, which puzzled the doctors and disappeared as suddenly as they came. Of course he made himself worse by his erratic way of living ; sleep, work and food were taken with an irregularity which became more and not less marked as he grew older. Faber dramatized his attacks, as he dramatized everything else, but his suffering was real enough. The discomfort to him, however, did not lessen the inconvenience to others of the pattern of his nervous reactions.

The immediate cause of the present crisis was Francis Knox, one of the novices. Knox, an aristocrat by birth, well-off, clever, obstinate and headstrong, was not one to keep his discontents to himself. Perhaps some compunction for the rudeness he afterwards confessed had visited him in November 1848, when he came to Newman and made a special and voluntary surrender of himself to his Superior. Wishing to improve relations with this difficult young man Newman soon after asked him to join the Birmingham party — and he refused. This wilful repudiation of his recent submission was bad enough, but his reasons for it, as relayed to Newman by Faber, were offensive. He said that Knox so disliked St. John that he would not live in the same house with him; he was also disgusted with the whole plan of starting work in Birmingham. All this must have come up on the eve of Newman's departure, for in his letter Faber confined himself to repeating Knox's complaints of his Superior. It was all Newman's fault, Knox implied, for he had been 'cold' and reserved and had not 'carried out the paternal relation' to him.

With Knox's behaviour in mind, Newman observed that it was difficult to be paternal to someone who would not be filial; he had done his best in trying to get Knox to come with him to Birmingham. But he told Faber that Knox's criticisms arose from youth and inexperience; he had a fund of patience for the vagaries of clever young men. He added: 'P.S. It is true there are persons who can by their manner and bearing *claim* to be loved and obeyed and so would solve the problem at once. I feel deeply I have not that gift, and so far, am unfitted (as also in many other ways) to be a Superior. By the way, it strikes me as amusing that Brother Francis, of all people in the world, who loves his own society so much, should talk of another being reserved.' To Knox himself he wrote soon after, in answer to an apology from him, 'I know your kind affection for me, and I pray God may reward it you a hundred fold by giving you, as you so well deserve, the affection of others. Let us learn by everything short of perfection to go on to perfection, and thus have cause to praise Him more and more who trains us in love and obedience, not only by his holy teaching, but by our own infirmities. God's blessing be ever with you, my dear Brother.'

Faber was not satisfied. It was not only Knox who was discontented; there was a general rebellion among the novices. The Gordon brothers, who had come to Newman the year before at Maryvale, were also grumbling at his coldness. John Gordon was thirty-five; his brother William only twenty. In the Oratory the Fathers keep their own Christian names unless they are already in use, when they take their second or confirmation names. Since Newman was John, Dalgairns had become Bernard, and the elder Gordon took the name of Joseph. As Bowles was Frederick, Faber had stuck to his religious name of Wilfrid, and as Penny was William, the younger Gordon chose to be Philip. Joseph Gordon now wrote lamenting that he had so little contact with Newman and wondering if he had better leave the congregation, where he felt he was not wanted.

Newman told him he did not want to lose him, and to give him personal reassurance he said, 'What can I say in return but that with all my heart I love you ? as you would see if you could look into it, but such is our condition in this world, that persons who love each other, cannot from their respective peculiarities at once enter into the enjoyment of that love.' Gordon answered, 'I had hardly sent off my last letter when I felt ashamed I had written it. I did not deserve so kind an answer.'

Faber had said Philip Gordon too was complaining Newman had shown him no affection. Harassed as he was just now in Birmingham Newman found time to write to the young man : 'Many is the time I have stood over the fire at breakfast time or looked at you at Recreation hunting for something to talk about. The song says that "Love cannot live on flowers" ; not so, yet it requires material, if not for sustenance at least for display. And I have fancied that younger and lighter minds perhaps could not, if they would, care much for one who has had so much to wear him down. All blessing come on you my dear Brother Philip in proportion to my waning.' Philip answered dutifully that it was kind of him to write. 'I never doubted you loved me as one of your children although the most unworthy of all. I have ever had the greatest difficulty in manifesting my affections, and that in proportion to their depth.' Either Philip had not complained, as reported by Faber, or he was one of those who expected Newman to give all the demonstrations of affection.

A long time later, when Philip Gordon was an old man and Superior of the London Oratory, he showed Newman's note to Wilfrid Ward, telling him that Newman had put it into his hands after a period of weeks in which they had met daily without exchanging a word. Ward printed this incident, which never happened, as an instance of Newman's supposed sensitivity ; he placed it with the novitiate troubles mentioned in Newman's letter to St. John the summer before, and thought his anxieties were imaginary. He failed to understand the very real difficulties Newman was facing at this time ; Philip Gordon, being so young, probably did not understand them either. The situation would have been difficult even for an experienced Superior whose subjects never questioned his authority ;

it was explosive with a lot of raw recruits who expected Newman to behave like the Ideal Father and solve every problem instantly, while they retained the right to distrust his judgment and criticize his every action.

Newman was particularly vulnerable to the criticism of reserve, for he knew he was shy. When Antony Hutchison wrote, grumbling about his coldness and asserting that he communicated with him through others, Newman replied — in the midst of the excitements of the first week in Alcester Street, with 'policemen-in-waiting' ready to repel rioters — 'You must make allowances and bear with me, my dear F. Antony ; for I am a shy person, and what that is, only shy persons know. But I will try to move faster in my outward ways than is my nature.' He made the mild retort that far from communicating with Antony through others, he had been surprised to find he knew of things from Faber. It is possible that had Newman admonished his juniors more sharply for their failings, they would have been less vocal about his.

One barrier to understanding was their number ; it was impossible to be on intimate terms with forty people at once. A little later, still thinking over these complaints of his coldness, Newman remarked to Faber that recreation 'which is just the time for showing and eliciting love, is just the stiffest and coldest act of the whole day. For myself, if there is one thing more than another which makes me seem cold, it is our recreations. No one (certainly not I) can talk confidentially and lovingly to a great number.' Newman did not add, as he might have done, that no one could be affectionate with young men who, as he had sadly admitted to St. John in the summer, rebuffed his attempts to get to know them better.

Faber had reinforced his reported complaints of Newman's coldness to the novices with their accusations against Ambrose St. John — that he either snubbed them or condescended to them, and that Newman behaved differently to him. Faber said that when he had delivered a warning against 'particular friendships' to the Gordon brothers — 'ye answer was that you set ye example with F. Ambrose'. The phrase 'particular friendship' (which irritated Newman) was common religious jargon for a preference for the company of the congenial in any community, an exclusiveness that might arouse jealousy or suspicions of favouritism. Although it did not necessarily carry emotional overtones, it was a serious personal charge to bring against a Superior and Newman answered at some length.

'As to your remarks about F. Ambrose, they are very kind of you

— and that they are true, this, I suppose proves, viz., that I have all through the year constantly had the danger of incurring them before my mind, and have exercised continual acts of self denial to avoid them. Still, that my manner betrayed what yours betrays towards F. Antony much against my will, I do not doubt and I will strive to guard against it. . . . As to particular friendships I have much wished a definition of what is meant. St. James and St. John had a sort of particular friendship among the Apostles — so must brothers in a Congregation ever — i.e. there *must* be feelings between them which are not between others. My point, I conceive, is that they should not *show* it — should not act upon it. . . . Again, what is more striking, think of our Lord's love for St. John. For myself, in acts I have been strictly impartial — take one, that I put aside altogether the notion of F. Ambrose coming here and took F. Antony. And I could give other instances of a like effort, though sometimes, as in this case, I have been forced back upon F. Ambrose after all. To me *now* the hopeless thing is this, that when the idea has once got into people's minds, it *cannot* get out ; for if from circumstances I *have* been brought closer to F. Ambrose than to others, let me hide the fact as I will, I can do nothing to undo it, unless I actually did cease to love him as well as I do. All I can do is to try to love others *as well* — which if I omit to try to do is certainly a fault. Take a parallel case and see if it *be possible* for you to persuade the Congregation that you are not more intimate and familiar with F. Antony than with others. The unlucky difference is that F. Antony is more popular than F. Ambrose, and therefore your particular friendship, if it must be so called, can be better borne. Is it not so ? Think over these *facts* and *see* if you can devise *practical* arrangements in consequence. I will listen.'

But Faber was not good at thinking over facts, carefully or otherwise. Instead he dashed off another letter insisting that Newman had missed 'the gravamen of the charge' — that he was *influenced* by F. Ambrose. So the novices believed, he hastened to say, and backed it up with their gossip about Ambrose being so often in Newman's room. He naïvely remarked that in his own case it was *he* who did the influencing, and casually admitted that it had not even occurred to him to 'put any constraint' on his friendship.

If Faber expected Newman to get worked up at this charge he was mistaken ; his reply was calm and amused. If the novices thought he talked about them with Ambrose 'never were they so much out ; it is to you I talk about them' — because Faber was

novice master. 'As to his having been in my room, which how could
they tell except by seeing through the walls, I cannot fancy, I have
been so cautious against it that I will venture to say you were in it
ten times and F. Rector [Coffin] five times to his once. Nay, I have
even rowed him for coming so seldom into mine. I have said, "You
are the only senior father who don't pay me the compliments of the
morning". . . . Tell me if this is enough.' He ended, 'Be of good
heart, my dear F. Wilfrid, and trust and believe that all will be well,
if we are but calm and deliberate in what we do'.

Calmness and deliberateness, unfortunately, were as alien to
Faber as to a child ; in many ways he reacted like a child to people
and to problems. Plainly he had not thought at all about 'particular
friendships'. Newman had made notes on the subject during his
noviciate in Rome. St. Philip had made personal friendship a basic
principle in his Congregation, so that it was part of the Oratorian
vocation ; the whole idea of an Oratory was the free association of a
group of men working together for God as friends in one particular
house. Newman, like St. Philip, was concerned not to crush natural
affections, but to widen their scope and balance them with each other
and with a deepening love of Christ. His approach was always
positive and based on the actual situation — the real feelings, not
the convention of what ought to be felt. But since human feelings
are wild and strong it was not surprising that this method of cultivation rather than suppression led to some collisions and eruptions,
especially at first. To some the internal situation of the Oratory
seemed simply chaotic and they interpreted it as the result of incapacity on Newman's part — inability to impose order. They did
not understand that he had a deep distrust of order imposed from
above ; the only order he desired was that which grew from within.
Because it grew, its development was necessarily slow. Newman
had endless patience for the process of living. Others had not.

Faber could never understand Newman's attitude for his own
was almost its opposite. Absolutism was the only kind of authority
he knew, and he knew it only from above, for during the whole of
his active life he was in a position of command, except for his few
months directly under Newman — and Newman's memorandum on
the fate of the Oratory exercise at St. Wilfrid's demonstrates Faber's
marvellous ability to get his own way in the teeth of his official
superior's wishes. Faber's Rule for his Wilfridians clearly shows his
absolutism in idea, as his behaviour showed it in practice. The Rule,
conceived without relation to the realities of the situation in England,

was a blueprint for a large order, in which the Warden was supreme for life and could command 'manifestations of conscience' from the Brothers once a month, or at any other time if it pleased him. In this spirit Faber had ruled his youthful community; any challenge to his authority was met with stern measures, sometimes with emotional shock tactics which soon reduced the rebels to tearful penitence.

Such methods of emotional dominance might answer, temporarily at any rate, with immature adolescents, but were worse than useless with grown men of trained intelligence. Yet Faber had no other at his command; in the last years before his death he was treating his novices and young priests in just the same way, a sentimental autocrat to the end, alternately punishing and embracing. But Knox and Gordon defeated him, Knox because he was hard-headed and strong-willed and Gordon because he was Faber's equal in years and far more mature in mind. The situation was intolerable to Faber; he only felt happy when he was with young John Bowden, a docile creature who never lost his admiration for this fascinating and unpredictable superior. The novices were unmanageable and Faber soon discovered a reason: they ought to be living a normal Oratorian life under their Father, but Newman — an unsatisfactory Father anyway — had made this impossible by going off to Birmingham and leaving half his subjects behind with nothing to do. It was ruining the chances of the institute and endangering the vocation of its members.

Newman's consciousness of his personal difficulties with some of the young men may have made him too ready to believe what Faber said of their discontent. The reactions of the Gordon brothers suggest that in their case Faber had exaggerated. A few years later Faber wrote from London that *all* the Fathers had turned against him; on investigation Newman discovered it was hardly more than another brush with Knox, then a priest. He said Faber had magnified Knox into all the Fathers, as once he had magnified him into all the novices. This February of 1849 seems to have been the occasion when Knox's intractability was inflated into a rebellion of the whole noviciate.

Newman did not realize this at the time. He found Faber difficult to deal with, but he trusted him. Before Joseph Gordon died, in 1853, he told Newman something which so destroyed his confidence in Faber that he said he could never trust him again. Newman told this, without further detail, to Stanislas Flanagan in 1855, and Flanagan, who had been a novice at St. Wilfrid's, replied that he had

25. FREDERICK W. FABER,
ABOUT 1850

26. JOHN (BERNARD) DALGAIRNS,
AGED ABOUT 30

27. AMBROSE ST. JOHN

28. JOHN (JOSEPH) GORDON,
ABOUT 1850

30. ALCESTER STREET

29. WILLIAM BERNARD ULLATHORNE
IN 1848

31. ST. WILFRID'S

thought Faber unreliable then and had said so to Coffin. It seems likely that there was some discrepancy between what Faber said to Newman and what he said to others. It is noticeable that the tone of his letters to Newman is not that he took with other friends ; sarcastic comments on people and moods of bitter disgust with life are absent. Gordon probably thought Faber played up to Newman for his own ends ; there were to be times when Newman felt this himself, though he usually put in the proviso that it might not have been a conscious intention. Indeed, it was unlikely Faber intended to deceive Newman ; it was himself he deceived, carried away by the force of his own feelings. If a large part of the restlessness at St. Wilfrid's was his own, he did not know it ; if it was he rather than the novices who was jealous of St. John, he did not realize it.

But whether or not the rebellion was as serious as Faber made out, Newman believed him. He was willing to admit his personal failings as a superior, but there remained an element in the impatience at St. Wilfrid's for which he could not honestly take the blame, and which could not be cured by kind letters. He disapproved this impatience, but as it existed he must deal with it. There were too many of them all to live together in Birmingham ; there was no room in the house, not enough work at present for so many, nor money to support them, nor was the place suitable for novices and boy-pupils. Besides, Wiseman was pressing for an Oratory in London — it was the call of London which was really unsettling those who had not been chosen for Birmingham. It seemed to Newman that if they made a provisional decision as to which members should compose the future London House, this would give the discontented something to look forward to and prepare for. He had no thought of immediate separation, but wished for preliminary discussion. He put the suggestion to Faber on February 9th, and more definitely the following day.

Faber reacted with surprising violence. He replied on the 11th in that decorative handwriting of his, so unaffected by the drama of the feelings he expressed : 'My dearest Padre your letter has afflicted me very much. I feel so confident that God will guide you as Superior that I voted with you against ye London House [a suggested site] against all my own convictions ; and so I do not like to seem to contradict you now, especially where I may be so deeply concerned myself.' He repeated that he had no confidence in the novices ; in a letter the day before he had said : 'Suppose I were Superior of a London House, do you imagine that ye eyes which can discern specks

on your brightness would not soon discover a very continent of
blackness on mine ? . . . What they have done to you, they would
a fortiori do to me ; and however great my sins may have been, I feel
that such a penance is above my attainments.' Now he declared,
'Nothing but force would now drive me into an Oratory with them,
apart from you'. He would obey a command from Newman, 'but
it would be not only against my will but against my reason'.
He thought they ought to face the loss of subjects rather than
separate.

Then he launched into a long emotional appeal against being
separated from Newman ; it was based on two themes — his love for
Newman, and Newman's unkindness to him. 'When I was at
Oxford I loved you most intensely when your manner to me showed
openly that you did not think well of me — and rightly. Still, it did
not alter my feeling.' After his conversion 'the *moment* it offered I
came to you. Is it only to go off again ? My dearest Padre, you
don't know how sick I turn at all this. When I joined you I was an
active missioner — preaching etc. in all directions : you threw me
into a different groove. Quiet, hidden, indoor, pensive work has
mine been, ever since I had work at all in ye Congregation ; and it
was hard to bear, and hard to snub ye many risings of my old restless
effusio ad externa. It was ye first time I had worked under obedience ;
it was counter to my whole nature — and I believe it was and is the
will of God and would not have it changed.' He had been supported
by the thought of working with and for Newman. 'Think of all this
before you decide to cut me off from those I love and those who love
[me] to go and govern men who will neither confide in me or bear
with me, when I go a different road from theirs. I have been their
slave these ten days past. . . .'

When this letter arrived Newman had just been writing to him
about Knox : 'Save me from such affection and devotion and give me
a little more tenderness for others and a little less self-will'. After
reading Faber's effusion Newman did not send this ; perhaps he
thought it might be applied to others besides Knox ! Instead he
insisted, 'I am not *advocating* separation — I wish it discussed —
and the notion has arisen *not from me* but from *Br. Francis* and those
others who have said, "Why cannot they do without us ?"' Of Knox
he remarked that he had gone on 'to deduce that *therefore* he must
look sharp lest he go to Birmingham and so get separated from those
he likes best. All this is very offensive 1. because it implies that we
should have no regard to his feelings, but treat him like a bale of

goods 2. because this suspicion and impatience is so utterly inconsistent with his voluntary surrender of himself to me in November.
I am very grieved about him for his own sake — and in [no] small
measure for your sake, since he has caused you such anxiety.'

Having emphasized that the separation was proposed only as a
solution to the impatience at St. Wilfrid's, Newman then underlined
the fact that he himself was going to stay in Birmingham. As to
Faber's worries at the thought of being Superior in London he told
him in confidence that his notion was for Coffin to be Rector, and
Faber to be (spiritual) Director. 'Don't suppose that it would not
be a most dreary and miserable thing for me to be separated from
you — but consider the state of the *giovani* and meditate on the fact
that I don't go to London.'

There were two things that went against the grain for Faber in
these suggestions — that Newman was not proposing to go to London
himself and that if Faber went he would not be in command. His
first reaction, however, was to beg Newman not to be hard on Knox.
'Poor Br. Francis! He has both the Gordons against him as well as
everyone else.' All the same he thought it better Knox should leave
than that the community should divide. He added that Penny was
'getting fidgetty because you take no notice of him'. Needless to
say, a letter arrived from Penny himself. He complained that the
Rule was not stringent enough — regardless of the fact that at St.
Wilfrid's they were not carrying it out. It would have been better
to have formed a new Institute ; they had joined not to be Oratorians
but 'to be with Newman', who, as he truly said, was 'more a father
than ordinarily'. When Newman thanked him for his 'kind and
sensible' letter and tried to make amends for his supposed coldness,
Penny said, '*Silent* I am by nature and always must be so, but that is
from stupidity not reserve — reserved I am *not*, naturally'. Perhaps
Faber had overestimated Penny's fidgetiness. He was devoted to
Newman, but had no idea of communal life. These confusing
letters, full of criticisms and demands for affection, descended on
Newman by every post during February, his first arduous month in
Alcester Street.

By February 15th Faber had gathered his forces together and
fired a broadside on Newman's decision to stay in Birmingham. His
ground of objection was that Birmingham was not a suitable place
for an Oratory and that by fixing himself there Newman was responsible for all their present troubles. 'You yourself cannot find a substitute for your work in London ; you can find dozens for ye work

in Birmingham. This Congregation has been gathered round *you* personally ; you, not others, make separation necessary by taking up a position where you say it is *unreasonable* all should come, and in fact impossible.' He brought the highest authority to bear. 'You sacrifice what ye Pope suggested to you for what you suggested to ye Pope. Is it not so ?' He ended dutifully, 'Decide, my dearest Padre, as you like : God will guide you and I will do what you tell me'.

But it was not only against Newman's practice to decide arbitrarily the course of other people's lives, it was against the spirit of St. Philip, of whom it was said that he never issued a command, but always asked a favour. The Oratory had no vow of obedience, only a promise, and consequently arbitrary decisions by the Superior could have no place in it, especially on so important a matter as this. Newman answered Faber on the 16th, carefully and at length. He did not agree with Faber's interpretation of the Pope's intentions and never had ; he quoted his own letter to Cardinal Franzoni to prove it. 'I rest the matter on this, that Birmingham and the like provincial towns are the main holds of political power at this day among us, and I seriously doubt whether I should ever have felt it my duty to submit to St. Philip, had I considered that the *ordo honestior* etc. was to be our scope — considering that the Oratory did not address itself especially to it' — that is, the Oratory as St. Philip founded it, which was certainly not confined to the upper classes. Newman thought that the Pope only meant to confirm in the Brief what Newman had suggested in the letter ; he had introduced the phrase describing the upper classes simply because he assumed that political power rested with the nobility in the provinces of England, as it did in Italy. 'What can the Pope know of the constitution of English political society ? to him *ordo doctior*, *honestior* etc. was in *great measure* synonymous with the classes I had specified — so that *if there be* a class in Birmingham of sharp intellects who are the recipients of political power, and who can be made Catholics, I think we are fulfilling the Brief, not only in the letter as to Birmingham, but in the spirit as to the *ordo honestior*.'

Newman also made some practical observations. 'When we intended last August to suspend our settlement here, and go first to London, as getting no money here, [Bishop Ullathorne] said distinctly that Propaganda had sent us to him, and Propaganda fully expected us to settle at Birmingham, and I have the gravest doubts whether, if at this minute we tried to get the Brief altered, we could.' Further, when they had voted on the matter in January and taken the house in Alcester Street, they had in effect engaged themselves to work for the Bishop. Faber had said that Newman was needed in London and that anyone would do for Birmingham. Newman replied, 'Now *tell me*, how can there be a House in Birmingham *except* I am here ? *make* a house if you can'. He knew very well that none of them would prefer Birmingham to London, and since they all clamoured to stay with him, some would settle for Birmingham to be with him. He felt strongly that there were too many of them for one Oratory, certainly too many for Alcester Street, physically and financially. Besides that there were many who were eager for London, and London 'earnestly calls for and invites us'. He felt sure the Pope had expected them to make foundations, in time, in all the big towns. With all these things in mind he was convinced that 'so far from being hard to separate, separation of a certain kind is the only thing which will preserve us', and the fact that it would be painful to many was a guarantee that though living in different houses, they would be united in affection.

Newman was looking to the future of the Oratory. Faber had said that Newman was the only bond of union. 'Say I live ten years,' Newman replied '— when I am gone the old feelings will come up again which have been smothered, if you have discordant elements among you. Rather form two houses of concordant elements.' They could not all be together in Birmingham, and on Faber's own showing 'some must be running to seed at St. Wilfrid's and may leave us'. Again he insisted : 'I do not want more than these considerations looked in the face. Meet them and propose something better than separation, or make such a separation as will not be painful in the case of individuals. I proposed a plan, let others be proposed. Moreover I have proposed alleviations, one seems unpopular, the other you have not taken notice of. The first was that here and at London we should for a time be one Oratory with the members moving to and fro — the other — a certain number of our members should be *fixed* in London, with the prospect of being formed into an Oratory at the end of a given time — in both cases my being their Superior till the separate Oratory is established. Make other proposals — but do not confine yourself to mere disapproval. Grapple with things as you find them.'

Faber replied : 'I can make no proposals. . . . We are in such difficulties that nothing but light from above can help us through them.' He insisted that as Superior Newman had special light from above which no one else could have. He endowed Newman with a sort of charism of infallibility for the occasion. 'Ye grand thing is for you to divide us in love and from a sense of duty, and not for a lump to detach itself from ye mass. . . . St. Philip founded Naples, not Tarugi ; so must you found London. I should only cry if I tried to write more.'

Coffin now joined in to say firmly that the division ought to be made soon, to quiet restlessness, that it should be done once for all and entirely by Newman, that the London members should not begin in Birmingham, and that everybody at St. Wilfrid's disagreed about the size of the Congregation and thought a large one better. Newman answered to him and to Faber jointly. He deplored all the haste, and that he was being forced into the position of the advocate of immediate separation. 'I cannot make minds patient and hearts contented and imaginations quiet and wills subdued, which are not so. *I* could live ten years with you all, knowing that then there must be a separation from some — you all cannot — *I* could consent to leave it to the course of events, that is to Providence, gently to work our separation during that time, as fruit ripens on the tree and falls ; you all force me to take a knife and cut it off. I repeat, I cannot fight with facts — but I will not allow anyone to say that I am the direct and immediate author of the projected separation, for I lament it.' This attitude of Newman was in fact much closer than Faber's to St. Philip's, for St. Philip had not wanted Tarugi to set up another Oratory in Naples; not wishing to forbid it, he had hesitated in giving the project his blessing so long as to wear out the temper of some of his brilliant and impatient juniors. Like Newman, he was much older than his disciples. They too called him 'the old man' — much as they loved him — as Newman's juniors were soon calling him.

Faber was upset, writing at once to urge him to 'say no more of early separation if it causes sorrow'. But the day after, February 22nd, he took a new line, on his personal future. He ought not to be sent to London, he said, because a Roman Father ought to be the head ; but if he went in a secondary capacity his weight in the Congregation would lead everyone to think he was virtually Superior. Therefore he must stay in Birmingham, with Newman, and Ambrose and Antony — let Dalgairns and the novices go to London. To this Newman replied : 'I wish you would bring out *how* it is possible for a London Oratory to go on without you. I do not feel the force of the difficulty you put as to your indirect influence in the community. Put down your London House on paper to your exclusion.' Faber's answer was, 'I cannot see my way to putting down names for a

London House; ye division bewilders me'. But Newman inexorably repeated his request. This was the signal for a series of lists, each more fantastic than the last, designed on the simple principle of Faber's being in Newman's house with their personal friends, while the rest were sent to London. Newman patiently pointed out that chaos would result in London from these 'personally heterogeneous elements'. And he said, 'Again it seems to me that there is no principle of *unity* in the Congregation except you and I. Think of this too. Look at things as they are, my dearest F. Wilfrid.'

This was in a private addition to a letter in which Newman explained in detail the history of the various plans and his attitude to them; by now it was the end of February. On March 2nd, Faber answered: 'Your letter makes all plain and everyone seems to understand how matters are. I wish it had been equally plain from ye first: but I do not think it was supposed you had any strong or definite view about ye shifting plan' — where the members should shuffle about till they found their right places. 'My dear Padre,' said Faber, 'I must complain of you about this. You shrink from rough riding people or overlaying by your influence ye sentiments and wishes of your subjects. You hint at your view; you throw it out masked, or as if something of no great importance; anyhow neither as essential or integral to your view. Then you get your *soggetti* to give *their* views; it may happen that what is uppermost in your mind is thwarted by them; perhaps with little consideration or upon insufficient ground; they giving ye matter no more thought than ye way you put it seemed to demand. Then they find themselves *aux prises* with you; you won't act against their view, which you have thus brought out: *you deprive them of ye very benefit of having you for their Superior*. You floor your own plans by it, and you leave them in ye fidgetty and disconsolate temper of mind which naturally follows upon their having unconsciously floored what had your best wishes and mature approval. You don't say — "there is my view — I think well of it: I set much upon it — remember, I have given it mature consideration — now you do the same". . . . You are not a Superior only: you are a Founder as well, and you know how much this implies.'

'I won't allow you the loophole for your criticism of me by which you hope to escape. I won't', said Newman in reply. 'You will observe, in my letters which were to be shown to the rest, I said I could not alter *facts* — again and again. Now observe there is a rebellion of the *giovani* — they won't come to Birmingham — they profess aversion so strong for a particular Father that *you dare not express* how strong it is — then, when you have hushed up matters, you say you fully expect it will break out again. Is not this a fact? is it not the cause of many letters? Then, why are they thus rebellious? because they have no Padre — because they are banished — because the noviciate is broken up — because they are not *in a normal state*. Can all your protestations of being a cadaver in the Superior's hands meet this? — again, you and F. Bernard declare, he most strongly, that it is impossible for a Confessor and Director to be in London *for a time* and *to change*. Is not this a fact? . . . And I must *get at facts* before I form any practical judgment. My first judgment ought not to be so overpowering and decisive as to hinder me knowing facts — it ought to be only so strong as to elicit them.'

These two letters are very important, for they express the ground for so much subsequent misunderstanding, especially of Newman by Faber. In his criticism Faber concentrated on the emotional effect on others of Newman's actions, which he disapproved because he based his view of a Superior's office on an extreme reverence for authority — in theory, if not in practice, he expected a religious Superior to be a dictator. Indeed he acted on this principle when he himself was in a position of authority. This absolutist attitude was already leading him towards the extreme Ultramontanism which became so popular among the converts — perhaps in unconscious reaction against the lack of any decisive religious authority in the Church of England. Newman's attitude, both to his own office and to that of others in authority, was based on a much deeper understanding of human nature, and of the interaction of divine and human power within the structure of the Church. Thus, in a more painful way than he then realized, Newman was right in maintaining that he and Faber formed the two principles of unity in the present congregation — unfortunately, as it turned out, opposing principles. In the event, those who were to feel strongly of the Ultramontane persuasion found themselves gathered round Faber and, though they did not always quite realize why, in opposition to Newman. Faber himself was perhaps the one who least understood the reasons for their difference.

'Persons form *lasting* attachments far more by their *views* of things than their feelings', said Newman with his usual insight, when warning against haste in separation. With time and work 'the glow of affection cools — and they find themselves drawing nearer to others whom they did not like so well, in consequence of *similarity* of view with them . . . also people do not know *themselves*'. Faber

and Knox were to be drawn together by their views, and Dalgairns
to them, after some oscillations of feeling. And in future years
Faber was quite friendly with Coffin, who became a hot Ultramontane, though at present his letters were full of complaints of him.

For although Faber wanted to be an obedient corpse, it was to
Newman, not to Coffin. On March 8th, Faber said to Newman, 'My
being a cadaver in your hands does not of course alter facts ; but it
immolates me on ye altar of those facts'. On March 10th, having
heard of a new prospect in London, he wrote : 'You must think
well about F. Rector . . . every day shows me ye difficulties we shall
have. Bishop Ullathorne is nothing to him ; he does not mean it,
he wishes to be humble ; but it is ye superior each second of ye day.
No one here, not even I, dare offer an opinion, or we should catch
it. . . . No one more considerately wishes to make everyone comfortable
than he does ; no one less understands how to do it. . . . I don't think
he has any notion of government but with a high hand. . . . If you
should appoint him, you know I love him very much, and I will do
my best to support him and keep all smooth ; but I dread it extremely ; it preys upon me daily. Yet who else is there ? for it
ought not to be I. . . . Again he thinks he is out with you ; and it
will never do if ye head of ye London House is not both *communicative*
and sympathetic with you.' Unaware that he was supposed to feel
he was out with Newman, Coffin was writing cheerfully about 'poor
little Rowe', a convert who had just come back from trying his
vocation with the Redemptorists, scared at their austerities. He was
later to join the London Oratory.

Newman, who was so tired, he said, that he could not keep his
pen on the paper, suggested that Whitty might do as Rector in
London, and Coffin as Minister. For Robert Whitty, the Irish priest
whom Newman had liked so much when he met him in 1846 at St.
Edmund's, had at last, after much hesitation about his health, come
to join them. Faber replied that Whitty would make a good Rector
but thought Coffin would not like to be under him. He continued
his campaign against Coffin. 'He is childish ; power is a pleasure
to him, and he cannot conceal it is. He has not men's confidence —
nor a manner of his own to carry things off. He has not abiding
confidence in you. . . . I also think his being superior would be a
spiritual harm to him. Of all ye Fathers he is ye one who ought most to
have had a regular noviciate.' Coffin had shared Newman's noviciate
under Father Rossi in Rome. Soon Faber was saying, 'I scarcely
know anyone whom I should less like to work with in close quarters'.

Newman continued to feel that Coffin's place was in London. His confidence in Coffin's powers of leadership was to be justified later, when, after having left the Oratory, he became Provincial of the Redemptorists in England and then Bishop of Southwark. But since Faber expressed such an aversion to working with him Newman tried to think out other plans. One was for 'the Wilfridians' — Faber and Hutchison chiefly, to make a start in a small way in London. Faber got very excited over this : 'I catch at this plan more than I have done at any other'. His version of it was that Ambrose should come first as Superior — but Newman was to come eventually. Faber was annoyed when Ambrose said he meant to stay in Birmingham till Newman left; here was Ambrose claiming his rights — why should not the rest ?

The situation had now got so complicated that Newman was forced to decide his own position before anything else could be settled. 'I do not deny that if all from the first had been open to choose, I should have chosen London instead of Birmingham , he admitted, but he was not satisfied that it would be best for the Congregation if he went to London, and he was determined to stay his three years as Superior in Birmingham in any case. Then he said that, whatever happened to him, his Library would stay in Birmingham. Study and the evening mission could be combined there, but to attempt it in London would only be to load himself with conflicting duties. 'A man cannot do everything, even that he is fitted for.' He had been saying masses on the subject, and asked for others to seek similar guidance. He still felt he ought to stay in Birmingham ; any variation had risen from 'these two feelings — 1. a great desire (for which you have blamed me) to please you all and to give in to you all. 2. a great fear lest divine Providence should by means of others be offering me light which I was rejecting. Else from first to last my own immoveable view has been that I ought to stay where I am.'

Having forced him to define his own wishes, they did not like the result. Hutchison said Faber had been picturing Newman in London 'in a room with books up to the ceiling where you could be reading and people could come and see you . . . he looked to your converting intellectual infidels, lawyers and heretics rather than hearing the general confessions of dirty paddies'. Faber pressed the question in the form of a choice between Newman's personal and his literary influence, and got an answer he was not expecting. Newman said he thought his influence had been greater 'among

persons who have not known me'. His intimate friends had not
become Catholics. It was at this point that Richard Stanton announced that he was not going to Birmingham if Newman was not
there, and William Penny that he would not give up Birmingham for
London.

'Precious cadavera!' cried Newman, at his wits' end. 'And you
lecture me and say, "My dear F. Superior do take us at our word —
you can make minced meat of us — you can turn us into Bolognas
and Germans — don't be consulting for us — speak, speak out what
you think and all difficulty is at an end".' Even Faber had to 'eat
humble pie', as he said, about being a cadaver. But Newman sent
five lists of the proposed houses for their opinions. In making them
up he had given weight to those who, in answer to his request for
their real wishes, had opted for London, among them Coffin and
Stanton. All had, of course, said first that they wished to stay with
him. The fifth list proved the most popular. Coffin was still on it,
and Whitty was put down as a member. Faber now took a violent
dislike to Whitty, saying he would make difficulties in any house, that
he and Coffin quarrelled, and that Whitty was 'white as a sheet and
trembling with rage'. Faber said he would rejoice if Whitty left :
'he must be under you, for he respects no one else'. But Newman
told Faber he thought he was exaggerating and continued to count
Whitty with the London party — he must go as a novice, and perhaps
later might start a second house in London, where he had the experience of ten years' work. 'Charissimi, thank you all for your opinions',
Newman wrote to them. Nothing would be finally decided till Low
Sunday 'so that meantime you must all pray and not be tossing up
your caps as if all was done'.

Faber took to his bed with spasms.

1849

The Oratory Divides

HUTCHISON told the sad news of Faber's spasms, in one of his cheerful, scribbly, boyish letters. They had some noble guests in retreat with them for Holy Week and Coffin had been putting on special meals for them. The irrepressible Penny had been 'deafening all including Lord Arundel with the bird clapper he constructed for the Holy Week ceremonies'. Lord Arundel, the Duke of Norfolk's heir, was soon to be Faber's greatest friend; already he was pressing him to come to London and offering every assistance. Wiseman too had offered free lodging for any who came up to prospect. Faber began to revive, though he told Newman his letter had agitated him so much it had made him ill. Newman suggested that presently Faber might accept Wiseman's offer and go to London to look round, with Hutchison and perhaps Dalgairns for company. This was more like Faber's favourite plan; but still, he felt very ill. Newman had to give in about Whitty, and asked him to come to Birmingham — none of the London party wanted him. And he asked Coffin to stay on for a while at St. Wilfrid's and join the London group later. Thus it began to look as if Faber would be able to start as he wished, and without the two men he most violently disliked.

Mindful of Faber's cavalier way with the Oratory exercise in the previous autumn, Newman asked him to stay in Birmingham before he went to town, to see how they managed things there. Faber said dismally that he would try, 'but my spirits are so beaten down lately that I doubt my taking an interest in anything. Ever since your plans have been proposed I have done nothing but sit and brood over difficulties. . . . I think I shall be better when I have got fairly away from ye poor people, in whom I have taken such a deep root this time and who *seem* to depend upon me more and more.' He was sick of all his flittings, everyone was angry with Whitty, he was sure revolt would break out again; some were again talking of leaving. And so on. At last he did come, after stipulating for a soft pillow and arrowroot biscuits, as he was not allowed to eat bread.

The division was now settled.   Newman had given three of his best men to the London House : Coffin, Stanton and Dalgairns. Newman told Stanton he and Coffin must be careful about the observance of the Rule, which the others might 'throw overboard'. But he warned him not to act 'the Keeper of the Rule — the less you assume the more will be granted to you'.   Stanton was a meticulous person, with liturgical interests — he was to manage the ceremonies in London.   Dalgairns was sent for his zeal and preaching ability ; Antony Hutchison for his practical common sense and as Faber's friend ;   Coffin had been chosen for his abilities and judgment. Newman kept all those who were not wanted elsewhere : St. John, whose brusque manner was unpopular ;   the eccentric individualist Penny ;   poor unpredictable Bowles ;   Whitty the Irishman, refused by the London party ;   Flanagan, another young Irishman not yet a priest, of whom Faber had said scornfully he would make a good vulgar preacher ;   Joseph Gordon, much cheered by a welcoming letter from St. John, but still rather odd man out ;   Austin Mills, so quiet that nobody ever noticed him ; and Nicholas Darnell, clever but headstrong.   There were to be nine fathers in each house ; novices and lay brothers were divided between each.   In actual fact, Coffin and Mills remained at St. Wilfrid's, Mills to teach the boys ; both were to look after the mission.   The final decision was made on April 15th.

The next day Faber left for London and Newman wrote to Coffin, 'F. Wilfrid to our great sorrow is just gone.   All our hearts are too full to show much ; but it is a great blow and will be of increasing weight.   I trust we have done what God would have us do, and if so, He will support us under any trial. . . . All I can say is, as is plain, that I have not considered my personal likings in the division.   My great objects have been, to put a really good house in London — and a solid House, a House that will stand, in Birmingham.'

Did Faber, who would not have anyone else to rule over him, really want Newman to come to London as Superior ?   It is probable that he did.   The picture he drew for Hutchison of Newman living in splendid isolation in his study revealed the position he designed for him — the ideal Father in the background.   Faber was a much younger son in a large family, isolated from his brothers by the deaths of others and the favourite of his mother, who died when he was fifteen — her loss was instrumental in his conversion while he was at school.   His father died when he was just going to Oxford.   Even now, when he was over thirty, Faber was extraordinarily immature in many

ways, and at Oxford he had already begun to fix on Newman to supply
the image of the missing Father, on which he unconsciously focused
the contradictory feelings aroused by fathers, particularly violent in
a romantic temperament like his, with its alternations of mood and
adolescent emotions. He was only thirteen years younger than
Newman, who naturally expected to have an adult relationship with
him, similar to that which he enjoyed with Faber's contemporaries,
Joseph Gordon and Ambrose St. John. Faber's conduct bewildered
him. Highly self-aware as Newman was, it was difficult for him to
imagine the mental state of someone who rarely, if ever, knew why
he did anything that he did, and lived from moment to moment in
the feelings of the moment.

Unfortunately, Newman's personality reinforced the father-image
in Faber's mind. His balance and deliberation were both an attraction
and an irritant to the excitable Faber, provoking ambivalent desires
to break that apparent invulnerability and to surrender to it. But
Newman's gentleness, and his persistent refusal to dominate, frustrated alike the emotional reactions of rebellion and submission and
roused all Faber's own considerable powers of domination. His
psychological need for Newman's presence appeared to him as a
simple demand of love : he loved him and wanted to be ruled by
him. But in fact he made no real attempt to obey him, and tried
instead to bully and cajole him into doing what he wanted. His love
was the undeveloped selfish love of a spoilt child, a demand for
unlimited affection and indulgence and a resentment of criticism as
unkindness. When Newman opposed him, he took to his bed with
spasms.

It must not be supposed that other people saw the side of Faber's
personality that Newman was forced to see ; none of them coincided
with the image of the father in Faber's mind. What came out as
childishness in dealing with Newman appeared in other circumstances
as a childlike simplicity which often charmed those who did not meet
its primitive elements. With other people, too, it was Faber who
played the dominant role, of spiritual guide and leader, as he was to
do in his friendship with Lord and Lady Arundel ; to his novices in
London he himself became a Father, if a somewhat unpredictable
one. Undoubtedly he helped many to lead more devoted and religious
lives ; it is not necessary to be a balanced and fully developed person
to help others. Most of us expend energy in internal or external
conflicts the significance of which escapes our notice. But the fact
that Faber did not intend, consciously, to hurt or to disobey Newman,

did not make him easier to deal with. In some ways it made it harder, since, whatever happened, Faber felt he could never be wrong. It was Newman who was harsh, unjust and cold to his loving son.

In spite of the anxieties of deciding the division of the community, and the cares of the new house and mission, Newman was in good spirits. The letters dealing with their internal problems were also full of gossip and news. When he called them 'precious cadavera' Newman went on to remark that the newspapers were full of 'shocking murders — but the most cold-blooded announcement I ever read was F. Antony's "Tip was shot". By whom ? for what ? when ? has there been an inquest ? what is the verdict ? Do throw some light on it. Was it by vote of General Congregation ?' 'Tip was basely murdered', said Hutchison darkly. Faber explained that Tip had been bitten by a big dog, madness was feared, and Coffin, nervous about the boys, had him shot. The boys were the two elder sons of George Ryder and the two Bowdens. John Bowden had made up his mind to be a Catholic the previous summer, and now he was a novice, known at present as Brother Edward. He was to have been with Newman, but he was delicate, and his mother was anxious. Newman sent both Bowdens to London, where Mrs. Bowden lived, and both became members of the London Oratory.

Faber's letters too were by no means all composed of sorrows ; he vividly retailed incidents of life at St. Wilfrid's. Penny, he said, thought one of his toe-nails was not growing properly, so he tore it off and came downstairs barefoot and bleeding profusely. Faber met him and felt so sick at the sight he had to gulp some raw gin before he could eat his dinner. He also said that Penny, who had been told there was no confessional for him in Birmingham, was going to knock one up for himself. 'I expect it will be like a bathing machine without wheels,' said Faber exuberantly, 'and will do for a summer house in your little garden.' Penny had to write to explain that Faber's fancy had carried him away ; he had not really embarked on any carpentry.

Newman's little garden was the yard between the house and the chapel, and had a few shrubs in it. Building operations were renewed in the spring. 'We are in the midst of bricks and mortar,' Newman told Capes in April, 'sleeping in the laybrothers' room or rather passage, and almost over the Blessed Sacrament.' April was cold, it was snowing — the snow lay on the ground, Newman noted in his diary. He had a cold, of course. 'Tell me *what* or *whence* those hot lozenges were, you gave me — they suit me,' he said to Faber. Now the permanent members of the Birmingham house were settling in, and he described it to Capes : 'There are our members just forming, some coming, some come, everyone taking his place, as one used in a stage coach, accommodating legs and stowing parcels. You know what a scene there is on deck when a vessel is just under weigh — packages, boxes, mackintoshes, live fowls and qualmish women strewed about in all directions. The school department, the instruction department and the confession department all have to be organized. Then the house is full of masons, carpenters and painters, not to say upholsterers . . . *fervet opus*.'

While Faber had been telling all the tensions at St. Wilfrid's, Newman had been silent about those in Birmingham, but they had not been without them. No record would have remained had not Dalgairns, after he had left for London, felt ill at ease and written to Newman to explain why he had not been to see him alone to say goodbye. 'I could not conceal from myself that you were displeased with my way of going on. You cannot tell how I have felt worn down by the thought that I was, as it were, cast away by you and left singlehanded amidst my work with your coldness chilling me all the while.' He knew Newman well enough to go on, 'You will ask me why I did not change my manner of work when I perceived it'. His defence was that he could not see where he was wrong. The spontaneous affection of the people had touched him ; he could hardly bear to leave them. He asked to be told his fault. It had not occurred to him, evidently, to ask this while he was in the midst of it all.

Newman replied at length, and with great care. 'I should not say a word to your and my pain, did I not know you would wish it, and did I not feel it an office of love towards you.' Dalgairns' great fault 'put harshly' was 'contempt of others'. Newman said : 'No one among us speaks against the old Catholic priests as you do ; no one sŏ laughs at the Bishop as you. You are accustomed to laugh at every way of doing things but your own.' He gave examples of Dalgairns' rudeness to St. John and Stanton and added mildly, 'You never asked my advice from the first in anything'. He then showed Dalgairns how this contempt and conceit came out in the details of his conduct. This was very typical of Newman. He had no use for high aspirations so long as they remained untranslated into the stuff of daily existence, and he knew that even work for others could be done in a selfish way.

Dalgairns had had some success with a group of youths, and he allowed them to be a nuisance to everyone else. 'I found them strumming on the piano, they ate the sugar and the jam and stole the candles ; you laughed when it was complained of.' They made such a noise that St. John could not hear his penitents' confessions. 'They flung about the ink in the guest room, broke the chairs, squandered coal and gas, broke into the closet, took out the Crucifix and put it back head downwards. I told you of the disorder they caused to the laybrothers ; you said the latter ought to sacrifice themselves for these half-converted boys. I forbade them the use of the laybrothers' room ; in spite of me, for I told you my wish, you allowed them to sit in it. You gave them the laybrothers' books and they went away with them. Everything was to give way to them, for they were your penitents, whereas I have observed you making game of the penitents of others. . . .'

Dalgairns' behaviour would have been permissible in his own house, but not in community. The Congregation should be supreme and the people should be encouraged to think of it as a whole, yet Dalgairns, not content with private leave-taking, had preached a farewell sermon, thus, though unintentionally, putting himself above the Congregation and doing all he could 'to embarrass and shake in the minds of the people the idea of solidity and permanence'.

'My dearest F. Bernard, I know all this will pain you, but you are too good not to get good from it, even though you think I over-state it. . . . It is the greatest gain for this to come out boldly and unequivocally *as* an eruption before you enter your permanent home. It will be a vaccination which precludes the disease ever after. You have had it favourably and it is all over. You are too bent on serving God and improving yourself to fall into a like fault again.' He went on, 'Your loss to me, my dearest F. Bernard, is in many ways great indeed. I have the tenderest recollection of you and shall always love you and I hope and know you will always give me your prayers. . . . Alas ! had I been fitted for it, you would willingly have put yourself under my guidance, you would have given me your con-fidence, if I could have claimed it. But I know my own infirmities so far and wish you to pardon them. I have not the self confidence and self possession necessary for exciting confidence in others ; I am old ; and you have fits of reliance on me and fits of mistrust and suspicion.' Dalgairns was to repeat this pattern of behaviour to Newman for the rest of his life, but it was hardly Newman's fault. Not even the most confident Superior can force anyone to correct wrong tendencies ; the most he can do is to point them out. Improve-ment lies with the individual. It is possible, too, that Newman's

humility in this respect still further undermined his authority in the
eyes of his inexperienced and rather conceited juniors : they took
him at his word. 'All grace and peace be with you, my dearest
Brother,' Newman concluded. 'Just write a word to me to say you
do not think me unkind, but believe me, though I may wound you,
yours affectionately. . . .'

Dalgairns answered that the letter gave him great pain, but that
'one element of pain, I suppose, is like some sort of feeling as would
come over a person who had thought herself a beauty on being shown
her face in a looking glass after small pox. I can only now wonder at
your forbearance and indulgence in tolerating me at all. In some
instances I might soften your rough touches or attempt to give another
colour to my motives, but still on the whole I must acknowledge with
pain that your picture is correct.' And now that he had gone away
he remembered acts of kindness from Ambrose and felt he had not
appreciated his character because he had disagreed with his views.
On this occasion, Dalgairns took Newman's warning very well. He
had been with Newman since 1842, and Newman noted sadly that it
was another case of his losing an intimate after seven years of *contubernium*. As with Froude and Rogers, so with Dalgairns. But
Dalgairns had never been in any sense an equal ; he was more like
a much younger brother, or even a son. But Newman was fond of
him. It was painful to part with him.

Ambrose remained in Birmingham. As Dalgairns realized, his
bark was worse than his bite. He did not always agree with Newman,
but at least he considered his opinion worth hearing. He made his
blunders, but he was ready to admit them, and he was always anxious
to be friends even with those he barked at. Some, less given to
barking, went their own way without listening, and were not above
an occasional surreptitious bite.

1849

Gin Palace Chapel in London

THEY were offered another Gin Shop in London, not a distillery like
Newman's, but a place of entertainment in King William Street,
Strand. It was many times the price of the Alcester Street property,
but that was to be expected. There were several hitches in the
negotiations. Objections were raised at the prospect of an organ,
'which is good', observed Faber caustically, 'seeing ye house has
been almost if not quite a brothel and ye long whisky room used to
have orchestra and dancing almost every night'. Newman had once
told Keble that becoming a Catholic in England would mean 'living
under the trees' — in a state of improvisation. In practical terms
this turned out to mean living in Gin Shops, quite a change after
Oriel and St. Mary's. It did not worry Newman, or Faber, who
listed other objections made : 'Item — Catholic priests collect beg-
gars round them, to ye annoyance of ye neighbours. Item — a
Catholic Chapel crowds a street with ye lower classes and deteriorates
ye surrounding property . . . ye devil witnessing to our Lord's
divinity.'

'O my feet are so sore!' Faber remarked in the middle of one of
his graphic accounts of their doings. He had a headache, Hutchison
had a cold and boils, they were keeping themselves going on rum
and water ; but they were doing wonders. Faber, with his usual
whirlwind action, had no sooner secured the lease than he swept in
builders to knock the two buildings into one, and moved in, with
hardly a stick of furniture and a great shortage of cutlery, by April
28th, less than a fortnight after leaving Birmingham. Some of his
companions were already there, others soon came from St. Wilfrid's.
David Lewis and Lord Arundel were in and out all the time. The
Bowdens slept in the attics and their mother was a great help. 'Mrs.
Bowden flits about ye house, visits me in my bedroom, inundates us
with floods of devout Irish charwomen, groans over ye dirt and is a
positive mother and St. Elizabeth of our Chiesa Nuova.' Faber had

chosen a small back room, for the quiet, but although he told Newman
it was as big as his at Maryvale, the others thought it too small and
made him take a front room sixteen feet square, where he was tormented by the traffic : 'ye roar is unbearable'. The smell of paint
made him feel sick too.

Faber had a genius for getting things going, but unfortunately he
also had a genius for offending people, and there were a lot of people
waiting to be offended. At that time there were no religious orders
with houses in London ; the Jesuits' church was opened later that
year, but the Jesuits were practised in not calling attention to themselves. Faber, however, wanted the Oratory to attract notice ; he
not only wanted to convert Protestants, but old Catholics. He was
going to show London just what real Romanism was. He fixed the
opening of the chapel for the end of May, only a month ahead, and
suggested to David Lewis he might write something for *The Tablet*
on the subject ; he also got out advertisements for the ceremony.
Lewis wrote a panegyric which shocked Newman, who had been told
nothing about it, 'advertising them', as he said, 'to the universe as its
destined saviour'. He told Faber : 'We should be a laughing stock
if anything turned us out of the house after such a puff. Everyone
would say "the more fools you".' He was afraid that they might be
turned out of the house because it was held on a Crown lease, and
Lord Carlisle, the Commissioner for Woods and Forests, might make
trouble if they shocked the Protestant public too much.

Newman had wanted them to wear their habits in London, but
not to flaunt themselves ; he was amused, but not altogether pleased
to hear of John Bowden 'spreading out his cloak like a peacock's tail
in the sight of Sir R. Inglis'. Inglis, one of the leaders of the Evangelical Alliance, was the present member for Oxford. Even Faber
wondered whether it would not make them all look ridiculous for
John and Charlie to go and 'feed ye swans in St. James' Park in
habit and mantella'. Wiseman had assured Newman before he left
Rome that the day was past when the English objected to religious
habits, and he instanced two foreigners, who had walked about London
and Brighton unmolested. But he did not know his own countrymen.
It was all very well for poor benighted foreigners to wear the habit of
slavery to the Pope, but to see Englishmen in cassocks and cloaks and
flat round ecclesiastical hats was too much. *Punch* burst into angry
caricatures and for some years the Oratorians were the representatives
of everything Catholic, everything Roman, in all the popular papers.

Newman started by writing what he afterwards called a joking

ote about all this, but he was afraid to send it when he saw, as he
old Faber 'the earnest tone your letters were taking'.   Instead, he
ssued a more serious warning.   He ought to have been consulted on
xternal matters, such as the advertisements and Lewis's article.
Depend on it, Charissime, you all need my control over you in little
hings at this minute, more than you have yet or will again.   You
nay damage everything just now.   It is a very critical time.'

One of his reasons for writing more seriously was that an un-
omfortable situation had arisen with Ullathorne over St. Wilfrid's.
When the community divided, Newman wrote to Ullahtorne to tell
.im they could no longer keep up the mission there ; he suggested
hat either the Bishop should appoint a missioner or they would
ecommend one from Ireland.   Ullathorne, still on his dignity, called
.n May 4th to tell Newman how shocking it was for him to give up
he mission, and to claim the right of patronage to appoint a priest
.imself.   Newman assured him that he had not meant to make any
laim ; he had only wished to save the Bishop trouble.   Ullathorne
vas not pacified.   An Irishman would not do, because the country
;entry did not like it ; to put in an English secular priest would be
o make seculars serve the convenience of religious communities, and
>e very unpopular.   Anyway he wanted the Oratory to keep the
nission.   When Newman pointed out that their Rule did not allow
hem to do so, Ullathorne pooh-poohed the difficulty and said it
vould be easy to get a dispensation from Rome to allow some of
heir members to remain there.   Newman, always ready to compro-
nise, hinted a scheme for a school, but the Bishop did not respond.
n spite of this Newman felt they ought to fall in with his wishes if
>ossible, but he thought Faber and Hutchison ought to be consulted,
.ince they had put so much work and money into St. Wilfrid's.
There was a boundary question which they could settle, too.   Late
.t night he wrote to Faber, 'You can manage the matter better than I'.
Ie was very tired.   'I am so sleepy I can hardly write and cannot spell.'

Unfortunately Faber took this to mean he was to deal with the
question of St. Wilfrid's himself ; he wrote direct to Ullathorne in
>elligerent style, saying that St. Wilfrid's was private property and
1ever had been attached to a district ; the Bishop had no right to
nterfere and Faber, if he so desired, could simply close it.

Unaware of this development Newman was cheerfully writing to
Faber that he hoped St. Wilfrid's could be made useful as a common
>lace of meeting.   'If the Oratories are to keep up one spirit, inter-
:ourse is very desirable in time to come.'   Looking ahead, he saw

that they would need something in the nature of a seminary if they were not to be confined to novices who were already priests, a difficulty he had already come up against in the case of a student at St. Edmund's, McQuoin, who had wished to join them. Perhaps it could be combined with a school — 'the Eton of the Oratory' — and a place for holidays, somewhere for 'treasured memorials, viz a gin bottle or cayenne phial of the Venerabile Servo di Dio Il Padre Wilfredo Faber, an old red biretta of his Eminence Cardinal Robert Coffin, and a double tooth and knuckle bone of St. Aloysius of Birmingham'. Aloysius was a lay brother for whom Newman had a great regard; he once said he was the only saint among them.

This pleasant vision was rudely shattered by a second and even more irate visit from Ullathorne, enraged by Faber's letter. He refused to correspond with him, as he was not the Superior. All ecclesiastical property in England was private, owing to the penal laws against Catholics; if St. Wilfrid's was shut they would incur ecclesiastical censures and he refused to hold confirmation there in consequence of their attitude. Newman had certainly not intended to close St. Wilfrid's and tried to calm him, but Faber was still writing pugnaciously: 'If ye little man won't give way to reason, I think we can do him. . . . O there are lots of ways of roasting that dear little pacific confidential bishop.' Newman disliked his tone and commented in the joking note he did not send that Ullathorne's size 'may be a fact, but it is not a dogmatic fact. . . . I suppose the Church may rule he is a tall man — in the eyes of the Church he *is* a tall man.' But he had to write more seriously now. 'Alas! you need not be afraid of Dr. Wiseman blabbing — I fear it has got out already through Lord S. and Dr. U. that you have threatened to shut up St. Wilfrid's.' Of course Catholics would be very shocked at such behaviour, and it was on the eve of the Oratory's opening in London. He told Faber that he had only wished him to put his view; St. Wilfrid's was Oratorian property now, since Maryvale had been given up to keep it. He explained this to Hutchison too. 'though I would lieve consider it yours'.

Trying to write to Coffin about it all Newman was interrupted : 'there rings the supper bell'. He picked up his pen again at '¼ past 10 p.m. just come from the confessional. . . . I am in a fix for I fear F. Wilfrid will not see his way to withdrawing his letter.' Faber was indeed aggrieved; it made him sick again. 'I thought you wished to be quit of it,' he complained, but he wrote to the Bishop and dutifully sent his letter to Newman first. St. Wilfrid's was already a thing of

the past to him. He was absorbed in his London worries. 'You
have given me a very hard work to do, viz to start ye house, and you
have not laid down my *modus*; you have left it all undefined, which
harasses me extremely.' Wiseman was not worried by anything they
were doing, he said pointedly; he was 'in high spirits now and
exuberantly affectionate'.

'It is a shame I should have put on you the trouble of writing to
the Bishop,' Newman replied, blaming himself as usual. As for the
constitution of the London House, he only wished to be consulted
in external matters; Faber must have control in all domestic affairs.
'Be then at once and hereby Rector of the London community —
Be absolute in all internal matters.' Thus he was forced to leave
Coffin temporarily on one side, still at St. Wilfrid's. Faber had got
his own way and wrote back happily. 'Padre mio, how naughty of
you to make merry with my wondrous *humility* to Dr. U.', he said.
Ullathorne forgave Newman so far as to come and say mass at the
Oratory on St. Philip's day. Lord Shrewsbury too was pacified;
Newman told him the Bishop was applying to Rome for a dispensation for them to continue the mission. In June he went out to St.
Wilfrid's and dined at Alton Towers. Curious eyes were always
watching, and sometimes misinterpreted his demeanour. He laughed
when the rumour came round to him that he and Lord Shrewsbury
had quarrelled.

Meanwhile Faber's happiness was completed by getting into a
back room again, away from the traffic. 'The sun never shines there
and fresh air is at a discount,' he said, 'but a bright yellow and red
paper creates an artificial sunshine, and F. Antony has bought me a
glowing rug and a *gleaming* chintz curtain, and Burns has given me a
brilliantly painted S. Joseph and there is a water closet in my room;
in fact my room was ye lobby to ye refreshment room water closet.
It will make a nice confessional.' By this time there were only a few
days left before the opening, at which Newman was to preach, and
Faber told him of all the people coming.

The more he talked, the more Newman shrank from it. Fashionable audiences, especially after the Roman fiasco, frightened him.
The newspapers had already set the tone: 'Here is Mr. Newman
just clothed in St. Philip's mantle and coming over from the Pope
to convert the English. Only let him rise "several yards high in the
air" in Lincoln's Inn Fields and remain there a proper time "his
countenance shining with a bright light" — and we will promise him
a large harvest of converts.' Faber's Italian *Lives of the Saints* were

a gift to sceptical journalists. Newman was so unwilling to go and make an exhibition of himself in London that he nearly cried off at the last moment. He had a bad cold and lost his voice, as he rather hopefully remarked. 'I would fain have gone to bed last night instead of going into the confessional. Moreover I can never preach with a headache, only break down ; and I dread the railroad which always makes a headache worse. I really think you must load your gun, in case I cannot preach.' He had already reminded Faber that it was an Oratory tradition for the Superior to take a subordinate part in a public function, and stipulated that he should be acolyte at the mass. 'There is no precedent for making me priest assistant, and I murdered it at Fulham.'

But although he felt so low on Sunday, on Wednesday he went up to town as he had promised, to find everything in confusion and builders everywhere. Somehow the place was got ready in time and though the mass was very late in the morning it went off well and Wiseman preached 'a most beautiful sermon from the altar', Newman told Ambrose, writing before the evening service, when his own turn came. The chapel was crowded for the mass, the music was specially composed by Capes and the collection was £30 — which disappointed Faber. 'I am no judge,' observed Newman, whose Alcester Street collections were down to £3 odd. They were so poor that the others had to refuse Faber's invitation and Newman had been doubtful if he could manage it himself unless his expenses were paid. 'O for a private California!' he had remarked recently — it was the year of the Gold Rush.

Continuing his letter to St. John, Newman said : 'It is intolerably hot in London — one cannot go downstairs without breaking into a heat. Dr. Wiseman wetted through to his *alb* which is died blue with his cassock and was put on the fire. He gives Benediction this evening in one of our copes about which F. Richard [Stanton] betrays in consequence great sollicitude.' The dreadful moment approached. 'It is now close upon 5 and the carriages are setting down their burdens. Birmingham is a place of peace. O that I had wings like a dove — for I do dislike this preaching so much. Some Frenchman gave his feelings up [to] the last moment under the influence of charcoal — I am giving mine till F. Richard calls me.' He supposed he ought to have the habit of such occasional sermons by now, but he had not. 'It is sheer misery.' But in a postscript he recorded with relief, 'I was myself in my sermon but with what success *aliorum iudicium est*' — others were to judge.

'Prospects of the Catholic Missioner' was afterwards printed in his volume of *Discourses to Mixed Congregations*. First he drew a picture of the vast and various multitude of London and then of the plight of the Church : 'An antequated cause, noble in its time, but of a past day ; nay, true and divine in its time, as far as anything can be such, but false now, and of the earth now, because it is feeble now, bent with the weight of eighteen hundred years, tottering to its fall ; for with Englishmen, you should know, success is the measure of principle, and power is the exponent of right.' He imagined Englishmen saying, 'What have we to do with the ghosts of an old world ?' But then he traced the pattern of Christian endeavour, always rising by failure, from the time when St. Peter, like an old gipsy, despised and poor, entered the imperial city of Rome and planted the kingdom of Christ in the heart of the kingdom of this world. Catholics could make light of a time of defeat, for the issue was with God. They could quietly go about their work and there was no heroism in their challenge of the overwhelming power of the world, because God overcame the world for them.

Of Peter's boat Newman said, 'We have not chosen it to have fear about it ; we have not entered it to escape out of it ; no, but to go forth in it upon the flood of sin and unbelief, which would sink any other craft'. Knowing that many Tractarians were present he spoke partly to them. The Church was the universal remedy for the universal disease of sin, and all other religions were but partial and local and temporary. He asked them to examine their consciences and their reasons for standing aloof ; but he added that their refusal would hurt only themselves, for though he wished them to come, 'Alas, there is work enough to do, less troublesome, less anxious, than the care of your souls'. Nobody was trying to force them against their will. He knew it was reported that he was already sorry for his change, so he said, 'I have followed His guidance and He has not disappointed me ; I have put myself into His hands and He has given me what I sought'.

The next day Observer Johnson called ; tears came into his eyes at seeing Newman again. He was nearly the only one of Newman's Oxford friends who was not afraid of or averse to meeting him. The following day Newman went back to Birmingham for the ordination of Joseph Gordon and Nicholas Darnell, and on the Thursday he sang his first High Mass in Birmingham on the feast of Corpus Christi, only the second anniversary of his own ordination in Rome.

Things went with a swing in the Gin Shop Oratory in King

William Street. From the first the chapel was crowded out, as Faber reported, with 'poor at ye early masses, nobs at High Mass and afternoon lecture, and shopkeepers at late Benediction'. Even after the Jesuits opened their church in July — Faber preaching for them — the Oratory continued to be the great novelty, with its statues, music, new devotions and its popular hymns, written mostly by Faber. Many Puseyites came to the church, met old Oxford acquaintances, talked things over and made up their minds to be received. Faber was besieged by Tractarian ladies. His chief care was Lady Arundel : it was a moment of triumph when she finally made up her mind. Lord Arundel became even more devoted to Faber in gratitude. Dalgairns turned out a great success with the middle classes and shopkeepers. 'I am not at all surprised to find F. Bernard is popular with one class and you with another,' wrote Newman to Faber, amused. 'This is as it should be — thus you will embrace all the monied people in London. F. Francis [Knox] must preach to the poor and then you will be fully furnished.' Mr. Poncia, one of the pillars of the Oratory parish in Birmingham, had returned from London in raptures, said Newman, 'and thinks small beer of us. He talked to me about you in the Library and did not seem disposed to allow that you had no such good room as it.'

In July Newman was writing to Miss Giberne, whose news from Rome in these days of revolution was eagerly passed round, telling her some of the small beer of Birmingham. Some of their convert factory girls, so unpromising at first that they almost wished them out of the chapel, were now formed into a choir and doing very well ; they sang Compline in English, making the best of such translations as 'the business which walketh in darkness'. Newman had given 'a flash lecture on Poetry', in St. Chad's school hall. 'I said absurd things which I knew they would applaud — and when they did it quite overcame me.' The lecture was reported in a Birmingham paper and Newman's letters were so full of Latin quotations that Faber teased him that it was the result of this success.

Miss Giberne had heard that two ladies had denounced Newman as an idolater in his own church. 'Not two *ladies*,' said Newman, '(for *entre nous* we have not yet found a lady in Birmingham) but two well-meaning Methodists came in among others at the beginning of May, and horror-struck at seeing the real thing, which they thought we only kept in our pockets and dared not produce, viz an image of our Lady, they certainly did ask me, in a fit of enthusiasm, what I could mean by such idolatry or the like.' In answer to her inquiries about the odd penances St. Philip had given people, and his dancing in his old age to the surprise of his pious admirers, Newman said he supposed he did it out of 'his intense dislike of hollow pompous pretence'. He would not care to do a dance himself, he observed, but then he was not in St. Philip's position. But he mischievously added, 'What a thing it would be to extirpate donnishness in England! I think in malice I should like to play the St. Philip among the Heads of Houses at Oxford.' How Froude would have cheered him on! In spite of the heat, the smells, and his penniless state, Newman was in high spirits. Bowles, on holiday at St. Wilfrid's, received a letter addressed 'Al Reverendissimo Padre Il molto Bucolico giovane Il Padre Bŏls'.

1849–50

Bugs, Smells, Cholera, Heavenly Favours

THROUGH all this year and the next the recurrent theme ran through the correspondence between the two houses : What to do with St. Wilfrid's. When Newman returned home after the opening in King William Street he wrote to suggest that it should be served on a rota from both houses, thus providing for the mission as Ullathorne wished and giving the Fathers a chance to meet each other on holiday in the country. At the same time he asked if London, which had the richest members, would consider paying £50 a year towards the expenses of the Birmingham House which had three who could pay nothing towards their living ; this to be regarded as 'the price for letting the rich men be together'. Dalgairns, as Secretary, answered they would give the £50, but they did not like the idea of a rota. It would be no holiday, 'especially with a Drumcondra priest for company', he said rudely, referring to the plan of getting a priest from Ireland to act as curate. Newman tried again, pointing out that there must be some plan for St. Wilfrid's — it could not be left unattended, or Coffin abandoned there for ever. Coffin wanted to join his community in London. But of course they did not want him, or Faber did not want him. Faber said a rota would be 'a great bore for this particular house, but I should think going against you a greater bore'. He added, 'Who can be spared ? Why nobody !' Dalgairns thought any difficulty with secular priests would be preferable to dismembering the communities.

But neither of them let the question go at that. They had Newman's idea of a school or seminary in mind and disapproved of it. The Oratory was not an educational institution and Oratorians were confessors not professors. Newman, they said at great length, was trying to model the English Oratory on the French plan of Cardinal Bérulle, rather than after St. Philip's Italian one. The sting of this lay in the fact that the French Oratory, founded primarily as an educational institute, had been mixed up with Jansenism, a type of Puritanism within the Church, condemned as heretical. Faber's remarks were an echo of Dalgairns, who had gone anti-intellectual. 'I loathe literature,' he said crossly.

Newman thought this storm of protest unwarranted by the occasion. They already had boys living with them who were being educated — Charlie Bowden was doing so in London, and the Ryder boys were still at St. Wilfrid's ; they were also teaching their novices in both houses. A school, and possibly a novitiate later, would subserve the Oratory's interests, without turning them into an educational institute ; he had no wish to rival the Jesuits. All this came out in the course of time. At present he was most concerned with this evidence of a divergent view of the Oratorian vocation. It was not the question of whether or not to keep a school, but the anti-intellectualism of Faber and Dalgairns that worried him. It was true that St. Philip himself was famous as a spiritual director and confessor, not as a scholar, but right from the beginning he had not only encouraged, but commanded, his disciples to pursue intellectual works. This tradition had been carried on from the beginning and Newman reminded Faber of certain Italian Oratorians 'more learned than any Brummagem will ever be'. St. Philip also had always had boys and young men living in the house and studying.

'I do not see that my view of the Oratory is different from yours except that it is larger and more practical,' Newman said to Dalgairns. 'It contains your idea and much else.' He wrote quite lightly, teasing Dalgairns for his narrow opinions. 'You describe a Father of the Oratory as one who is "glued to his confessional" ; but if *every* Father were so glued, you would not get breakfast or dinner, nor indeed a confessional to be glued to. In any *body* there must be different members ; and one must not despise another, for each needs each. Now my view of the Oratory is more "literary" than yours, only in the sense in which it is more *culinary*. *You* have not the office of furnishing clothing and providing, but though it nearly exhausts a Father's day, such duties are very Oratorian, while he and his are in the flesh. It is unsacerdotal to keep accounts, yet it is unchristian to get into debt.' Of Dalgairns' anti-intellectualism he observed, 'It is all very well for you, who have the advantage of Oxford to say "I need none of this ; I despise it —" for you can't undo yourself ; but what is to become of the next generation ?'

Newman told Faber he had written this letter four or five times 'lest I should get into a scrape and quite lose my influence with him ; — yet without satisfying myself'. He said that it was offensive to contrast St. Philip and Berulle and put him with the latter, without sufficient cause. Perhaps when he told Faber this he did not realize that he too was inclined to oppose the sainted founder to Newman. Time was to develop this idea more and more strongly in the London Oratory.

Newman wrote to Faber a satirical forecast of the progress of opinion in the London house, only too like what it turned out to be. 'I fear a course like this : — viz, first an agitation among you to be a separate Oratory, originating in the same *impatience* which first refused to be quiet at Maryvale and St. Wilfrid's and next wishes simply to ignore St. Wilfrid's — then a feeling that the F. Superior of the London House must be wholly London's and under no external influence . . . and then, bolder grown, "our Brummagem cousins take the *French* view of the Oratory — let us have no order or regularity, it is *French* ; no preparation for sermons, it is French ; no care for what friends or enemies think of us, it is French — no guard lest our words or deeds give scandal, it is French — slowness is French, go it, if you would not be French ; disgust the laybrothers as you fear the French, for we all know what came of the French Oratory, *not that* we anticipate the like of the Birmingham".' As to St. Wilfrid's, he said briskly that it should be served from Birmingham. He gave up the idea of the rota, since London would not co-operate, but not his intention of using it for the Oratory in some way.

Faber was pained. 'You let us say our mind, and let our say overrule you', he complained and then, rather inconsistently, 'You do not let our opinion overrule your own against ye secular priest plan ; (nor do I wish you to do so) but you keep your plan and use our expression of intellectual dissent as if it were an act of disobedience or a moral repugnance.' Their intellectual dissent was expressed against the proposal of a school ; it turned out that in spite of having been novice master and now being Rector of the new foundation, Faber had no idea that Newman had altered the Rule to allow of a school being opened in case of necessity. And having admitted now that he did not know it, he at once forgot it, for he, and the others in London, persisted in maintaining that a school was against the Rule. Although Newman's amended Rule was sanctioned by the supreme authority, Faber behaved as if it had none.

'I could not help smiling at your protest, the justice of which I am a thousand leagues off seeing', Newman answered. 'What in the world should I ask your opinion for, but to let it influence me ?

Else, I might have acted without asking.' In a postscript he said,
'I cannot help being amused at you, the more I think. I asked of
you all two things — a testimony and an opinion — an opinion
whether it was *desirable* for the Oratory to serve St. Wilfrid's and a
testimony whether you in London *could*. I have taken your testimony
and rejected your opinion. *I have not given up my view* to yours, but
I have carried it out in that way which, according to your testimony,
was alone possible.' For the moment the problem of St. Wilfrid's
rested there. Nothing could be done in any case till they knew the
result of Ullathorne's application for a dispensation from Rome to
allow any of their members to live there at all.

Meanwhile Faber was consulting Newman on various questions,
usually to do with the other members of his party, whom he found
difficult to manage. He complained that they would all go their own
ways without listening to him. Dalgairns was said to have 'a regular
passion for hearing confessions', even to sitting outside his confessional eagerly looking out for penitents if the flow was reduced. His
success with the shopkeepers, and even more with their wives and
daughters, went to his head as his success with the factory boys had
done. Faber was worried at tales he heard, and said that Dalgairns
had stayed in the church till the small hours talking to a woman, a
possible convert, while a poor lay brother waited to shut the doors.

Newman said, 'One must not mind what words people use but
I do fully think, unless *you* are not on your guard, F. Bernard *will*
be accused of being over intimate with women — what with looking
into their eyes, detaining them through the night "till morning
breaks" and preaching upon our Lord lying on the breasts of His
own, he will hardly escape. You *must* watch over him, and I will
support you. We shall have to send him off to Kamschatcha, if you
do not look sharp.' Dalgairns must have cut down on romantic
appeal, for no further gossip was heard on the subject. But Faber
often found him tiresome. He grumbled to Newman, wondering
why 'men get more selfish the more they pray'. Newman replied
that prayer had two effects, acquired habit and grace, and that habit
was often the stronger ; it was this that might lead to selfishness.
Faber and Dalgairns continued to rub each other up the wrong way,
in spite of their common view that Oratorians ought to be glued to
their confessionals and give up intellectual pursuits.

Faber was having trouble with his young lay brothers, though he
only told Newman that Coffin had spoilt them — Coffin, as Father
Minister at St. Wilfrid's, had had charge of them there. But Coffin

told Penny that Faber was dictatorial with them ; he was always blowing them up, they felt they were treated like servants and they had to sleep three and four together in basement rooms. Penny passed on this information to Newman. When Faber grumbled that the brothers were rebelling about their beer Newman took the opportunity to make some suggestions. 'They were boys at first — they have seen a little more of the world now. I doubt whether the way of severity will succeed with them. Severity soon expends its powder — i.e. you cannot be severe more than once or twice. Think it over carefully whether you must not change your system.' In Birmingham they made special efforts to make the Brothers feel they were part of the community, even relaxing the Rule to allow talking at supper, so that they would know what was going on. Presently Coffin went on a visit to London and reported that the lay brothers were all right now. He said he had 'prosed' till two in the morning with Faber, who wondered how Newman had guessed his methods !

From Faber's own letters it became plain that part of their prosing was about Newman. Coffin's remarks threw Faber into gloom and he accused Newman of being bitter and unkind. 'Your letter is a string of dismals and I don't believe any one thing you say,' said Newman firmly. 'Don't listen to gossip about my talking of your aversion to St. Wilfrid's — what business have you and F. Minister to tittle tattle ? You don't think I am going to defend myself. Shake yourselves and go for a row on the water.'

It was a very hot summer, and both houses were overburdened ; cholera threatened. All this did not improve tempers. When accounts were made up at Midsummer and Newman commented on the size of the London meat bill, Faber got very excited and said he was sure they were starving themselves in Alcester Street. 'Carissime,' said Newman, 'it startles me that you are taking up the matter of beef and mutton so earnestly.' He did not think his community was underfed. 'The Brothers were quite zealous in refuting what they considered a calumny.' Several of the Brothers left about now, and a local man, a servant at St. Wilfrid's who thought of trying his vocation caused Newman to write in July to Faber : 'I could laugh at our misfortunes, were they not worries — have you heard the "last" ? Elkes is gone ! He drank too much beer, laid himself out on the kitchen dresser, packed up and went ! *Omnia tendunt visibiliter ad non esse*, as King Edward says in our Oriel Statutes. Formby, Whitty, McQuoin, Gregory, George, John Baptist and now Elkes ! *Et tu Brute.*'

For Whitty had given up. Although, as he wrote to say, he had got on most happily with 'the converts' he could not bear to stay in Birmingham. His confused reasons for leaving amused Newman. 'His notion is that he is sent to the poor, that is to the Irish poor, that is to those who are in gross sin, that is to those who have in them the materials of saints, that is not to those who are going on to perfection, that is not to the many, for he is not strong enough, that is to London, that is to Lord this or Lady that. Don't tell the Bishop *this*,' he said to Faber. Whitty had second thoughts, and in the end Newman had to decide for him that he had no vocation for the Oratory. Later he joined the Jesuits; he remained Newman's friend all his life. But before he was safely in the Society he alarmed Faber very much by coming back to London and talking about starting another Oratory there in the East End. Newman had certainly encouraged this plan, but for the future; he assured Faber that he had not intended to allow it till Whitty had completed his full three-year novitiate. 'Don't go and take any more Irish, Padre', pleaded Faber, who had been ill at the thought of Whitty rivalling him in the East End. 'Abstain from Irishmen for ye rest of your life.' He even refused, on the score of his being Irish, a cook called Scully, who came to Birmingham and stayed for years. As for Whitty, Faber grumbled so much about his gossiping in London that Newman put them all under obedience not to talk of him to anyone.

Whitty left; Austin Mills was so unwell that Newman sent him to London to see a specialist, who suspiciously asked him if he had been through 'any rigorous course of penances, either self-imposed or put upon you by your superiors?' Mills replied, 'Why *lately*, I must say I *have*', conjuring up visions of sadistic cruelty only to dispel them by adding, 'a severe course of medicine and mustard plasters'. Newman was delighted with this unsuspected gift for poker-faced repartee. Penny, going his own way as usual, suddenly went off to St. Wilfrid's without being told to. Ambrose had to go away too, to St. Leonard's to see his mother, now over eighty and seriously ill. On earlier visits she had never been able to make up her mind whether to allow him to stay in her house or not. Usually he cheered himself up by swimming, but this time he had such a cold that even when he came back Newman had to preach two sermons for him. 'This will account for his dulness, if he was dull', said Newman shortly, in answer to grumbles that Ambrose had been odd and shy when he called at King William Street. He was sent off to St. Wilfrid's, where he was put in Newman's old room, much as he had left it, and 'the most perfect picture of a *nido* I have ever seen', as he wrote back. St. Philip used to call his room his nest, and say that an Oratorian should stay in his nest as much as he could. Ambrose rejoiced in the view and the fresh air, but remarked, 'Coffin and Penny do not hit it off, Penny lives in a room almost without furniture and bolts his food'. He thought Newman was needed there, and wished he could go, the country would do him a world of good.

This was at the end of August, but Newman was too busy to go then. Father Gordon was 'turning out a great gun' as he told Mrs. Bowden, but what with people leaving, away, or ill, he had to do a great deal of the work of the mission himself, and was also preparing his book of sermons for the press. He had a bad cold which would not go, and was bothered with deafness again 'which always, as the mercury in the thermometer, shows my blood is mounting high,' he told Faber. 'I say this to excuse myself, not as if I were not very well.' Faber felt very ill himself. 'I lie on my bed all day', he said once. The doctor, however, told him that apart from some bowel trouble he was 'a fine specimen of ye animal man'. He was somewhat cheered when Mrs. Bowden, 'our mama', gave him a dozen and a half bottles of 'old, old Port' for himself and Lord Arundel a 'sumptuous easy chair and various images. What a purgatory I shall have!' he remarked with delight. Coffin's visit put him in the dumps again, but in August they closed the chapel, so that the decorating, scamped for the hurried May opening, could be finished, and Faber went to Belgium with Hutchison and Wells.

All through these hot months cries of despair were coming from London that the poor were driving out the rich from the church, the collections falling, and conversions too. 'The Irish are swamping us', Faber wrote. '. . . People are made physically ill by the stench and the dirt — old Ward even is made ill in our chapel.' Newman suggested a system of tickets (free) for certain services ; he did not like Faber's plan of dividing the seats, which would make a public distinction between rich and poor. He did not have the same problem in Birmingham because all his congregation were poor, but he had the stench and the dirt. 'Coming up our passage last night at midnight (as I was accidentally taken out) it smelt like one of the "For Gentlemen" on the railroad station', he told Dalgairns. 'Br. Frederick, without my noticing it to him, said it arose from the Irish who had been there at 4 — eight hours before ! F. Ambrose has caught two bugs, one on his face, in the confessional, and now I recognize the smell of bugs in certain penitents strong. Have you learned it ?

I am led to think more and more that cleanliness is next to godliness, though I know you hold the opposite doctrine ever since the article on Mère Angélique.   Prosper you, Charissime, in your hard work ; don't fear the cholera and it won't come to you.'   For the dreaded epidemic had broken out in London and Faber wrote that the poor country Brothers were frightened and crying ; they had seen a corpse carried past.   Newman paid a hurried visit to London at the beginning of September, which cannot have been altogether a happy one, for Faber wrote after it, 'I have had visions of your face with ye expression of pain on it ever since you went away, which interferes with ye pleasant remembrance of ye glimpse of you that we have had'.

Newman had barely got back to Alcester Street when Ullathorne asked him to send someone to help the priest at Bilston, where the cholera was carrying off many victims.   Birmingham remained free of it.   Newman at once decided to go himself, taking St. John with him.   When this was known in the parish a great lament was raised. 'No one can express the sorrow our poor journey to Bilston caused,' Newman told John Bowden afterwards, '— every one crying out as if we were going to be killed.   In this perhaps we excel you in London.   A parish is an onus, but it creates a *local mass* of affection.' Tears went on flowing after they had gone ;   Gordon wrote how miserable they all were, Coffin begged to take Newman's place.   They knew how overtired he was, and how suddenly and violently the disease struck.   He was risking everything by going himself into the dangerous area.   But when they got to Bilston the plague was already abated ;   it dropped as suddenly as it arose.   Newman later told Jemima how terrible was the sight of the sick in the hospitals, and of the devotion of the priest, who had carried the victims there on his back.   This priest, many years later, retired to Edgbaston, and liked to remember Newman's visit in the cholera days.   But as he was not now really needed there, and was so much needed elsewhere, Newman only stayed two days and then went on to St. Wilfrid's, leaving St. John in Bilston.

After eight months in the back streets of Birmingham the country seemed like a dream of beauty.   'This is so delicious a place that I can't conceive how any one can stay here with a safe conscience', he said.   While he was there he heard from a friend, Edward Caswall, whose wife had been struck down with the plague in Torquay and died in fourteen hours.   Caswall brought her body to St. Wilfrid's, where she was buried, and he stayed on with Newman.   Caswall had been at Oxford in the thirties, and became a Catholic after reading

the *Development* four times ; he called on Newman at Propaganda
and was received in Rome by Cardinal Acton. He was now thirty-
five, the same age as Faber, a year older than St. John. In a few
months time he was to join the Birmingham Oratory and remained
one of its chief supports until his death, nearly thirty years later.

The same visitation of the plague had a profound effect on Henry
Wilberforce and his wife in Kent, where it struck the London hop-
pickers in his parish. So many were Catholics he wrote to the
London Oratory for help ; first Knox was sent and then Faber and
Dalgairns came down, and some nuns from the Good Shepherd
Convent in Hammersmith. Newman was half expecting from what
Henry said to be called to go and receive him. 'Charissime, you
must die some day or other,' he wrote. But the time was not yet.
The cholera abated, the London Oratorians left Henry to his thoughts,
Ambrose came home to Birmingham from Bilston and Newman
from St. Wilfrid's. Even during his short absence Newman felt he
was deserting his faithful penitents and asked for a notice to be stuck
on his confessional : 'Father Newman is returning on Tuesday
next'. Now that the plague was over, Darnell said, 'Sarah Giles,
your devoted slave, is beginning to look pert again'. Glad to get
him safely back, more people than ever crowded into the Gin distillery chapel. 'The congregation forcibly pushes back the church
doors,' Newman wrote to Mrs. Bowden at the beginning of October,
'the porch is crowded and we give Benediction right into the street,
people kneeling on the opposite pavement.'

Bishop Ullathorne, in the public letter he wrote to Newman on
the occasion of the *Apologia* referred with admiration to the Bilston
episode, but at the time, owing to the sudden slacking of the disease,
it passed unnoticed. In October the Bishop was so full of complaints
that St. John and Gordon were sent to him to straighten things out.
Newman wrote, with amusement, to Faber that there was 'a report
that we were so familiar with our female penitents that they said they
could marry us next morning — and that I was so reserved and had
such notions about the line of delicacy, that he did not know how to
come here and judge for himself of the reports circulated against us.
Thus we all got it.' He thought it might help to invite the Bishop
to preach ; he accepted, but called it off at the last moment on Saturday evening, having been seen during the day showing a lady visitor
round the town. Newman, who 'had to rummage up a sermon on
purgatory' in consequence, remarked 'Some of our Fathers take deep
views of this — but I attribute it simply to the rudeness and incon-

siderateness of the old Catholic school'. He added, 'To this day
the Bishop will not call me Father. I suppose he speaks of Mr.
Dominic and Mr. Spencer.' Newman was perpetually restraining
Faber and the younger converts from rudeness to the old Catholics,
but they tended to judge all the converts together by the most
vociferous, and Newman as their representative. Ullathorne, so
downright and Yorkshire, and dropping his aitches, long suspected
Newman's courtesy as diplomacy. He learned better in time.

In November Ullathorne got a shock, when a Rescript arrived
from Rome, flatly refusing permission for some of the Fathers to
live at St. Wilfrid's and telling the Oratorians to keep their Rule.
Doubt was even cast on the propriety of their running a mission in
Birmingham. The Chiesa Nuova had been consulted. Ullathorne
had all along pooh-poohed the difficulty of the Rule ; his not calling
Newman, the head of a religious institute, Father, was a sign of his
attitude — he treated the Oratory as if it were simply a collection
of Newman's friends who could be organized as he pleased. It was
not a pleasant surprise for Newman either, for Dr. Grant, who had
presented the request to Propaganda, had made out it was Newman's,
not the Bishop's. The Fathers of the Chiesa Nuova immediately
suspected Newman of wanting to alter the institute, and centralize it
in England under his own control. This absurd misunderstanding
could never have come about had Newman's friend Palma been the
Secretary of Propaganda still. But poor Palma had been shot in the
troubles last year ; Newman had sung a requiem for him at Maryvale,
grieved at his loss. He had now no 'friend at Rome' and this mattered
more as time went on.

Meanwhile St. Wilfrid's, which had now earned him what was
almost a reprimand from Rome, was a problem more than ever in-
soluble. 'There is the famous story,' he wrote to London, 'of the
man who bought an Elephant, and was too poor to keep and too
merciful to kill it, and was unable to persuade any one to accept of
it.' He made a list of propositions.

'1. We cannot live at St. Wilfrid's because it is against our Rule.

2. We cannot shut it up because we are bound to keep up the
   mission.

3. We cannot return it to the Earl because it is ecclesiastical
   property.

4. We cannot give it away, for no one, neither District nor Religious
   Body, will accept so expensive a gift.

5. We cannot, much less, sell it, for no one will buy.

6. We cannot let it to a family for the Earl will not hear of it.

7. We cannot let it for a school for the Bishop protests against it.

8. Yet we cannot keep it because of the expense.

Problem, like the quadrature of the circle, what is to be done with St. Wilfrid's ?'

Faber's reaction was to feel ill. Newman was corresponding with his Anglican brother, Frank Faber, at the time, and said, 'Your brother certainly has grown very large the last year or two and is subject to very unequal health — and yet he gets through a great deal of work.' All his letters were full of praise for the amount they were doing in London. Some of them were seven hours a day in the confessional. 'Their success is prodigious,' Newman told Miss Giberne. They had a constant stream of presents 'of monstrances, chalices, hardware, Bass pale ale, painted walls etc. etc'. On October 30th they had a 'great function' with Wiseman preaching and praising them, and another on December 8th, the feast of the Immaculate Conception, when Darnell, who was staying there, dropped his shoe in the soup. Poor Coffin was still mouldering at St. Wilfrid's, missing all the excitements, feeling aggrieved and suffering from indigestion.

In November Newman's book of sermons came out, dedicated to Wiseman. They were considered stern by many, including Dalgairns, who picked, to Newman's amusement, the one he said he had taken from St. Alphonso Liguori: 'Neglect of Divine Calls and Warnings'. 'I have but made easy going Catholics in danger of hell,' he said. He once said Catholics were like Evangelicals, expecting all Christian doctrine in one sermon. 'How is it', he wondered, 'that if I am on the *whole* so stern, that my Parochial Sermons, which I suppose are not less so, are so liked by a lot of women ?' Of one reviewer he remarked that he had 'skipped the discourses which were *not* especially stern and intellectual'. In truth his sternness was the result of his spiritual insight ; he could not bear to see people lost in the fog of their own ignorance and wilfulness, slipping from one sin and illusion to another, deeper into darkness and decay, while they might appear to the world respectable and successful people. The picture he painted of the self-satisfied person discovering himself in hell was an attempt to rouse the sleepers to action, made out of compassion for them, not from any desire to condemn. The Birmingham people did not think him stern ; they cried when he went to Bilston and it seemed he might never come back.

In Birmingham they were as busy as their brothers in London, but there were no rich friends to give them presents, and their

Bishop, far from praising them, was continually complaining. London received the splendid gift of £400 a year from W. G. Ward, who had just come into the property of a rich uncle — wondering if it was a sin to rejoice at his death! In Birmingham the Sunday offertories were never much over £3, and their running expenses were not decreased by 'various boys loitering about the house who eat freely'. When they found themselves in debt, Newman said, 'It has taken all the shine and go out of us and we talk of giving up candles at the altar, shutting up every day and turning schoolmasters'. It was partly poverty that made him so often turn over the plan of a school; though it seemed also that there was no Catholic school in England quite suitable for the children of the converts. However, they did not turn schoolmasters yet. Newman was personally poor ; his income had dropped to under £50 a year and he was £60 in debt. 'I could not make out whether you said my sermons were "selling" or "telling" he wrote to Capes, 'I wish them to "tell" but I am very much interested, I must own, in their sale.' The book went into a second edition but Newman's agreement was such that he did not receive payment till the end of the following year. At the end of this year he confessed to Stanton, 'I have not been able to buy shoes and stockings for the year past, and am ashamed to think how little I have given in Charity'.

In spite of poverty he did not really lose much shine and go. Capes, who continued to consult him about *The Rambler* — Newman told him to get out of his unreadable double columns as soon as possible — wanted contributions. Newman said they had no time to write, and he was afraid to offend Wiseman by sending things to *The Rambler* rather than *The Dublin Review*. But Capes could print their verses if he liked. Faber, that prolific versifier, teased Newman for saying he was so busy and yet having time for poetry ; Newman said he made his verses while he was shaving and wrote them down afterwards.

> The Angel-lights of Christmas morn,
> Which shot across the sky,
> Away they pass at Candlemas,
> They sparkle and they die.

Thus began one of the hymn-verses of this time, and another :

> There sat a Lady
> all on the ground,
> Rays of the morning
> circled her round . . .

Somehow he found time to read the novels of friends, though he told Lady Georgiana Fullerton of one of hers, 'I am too old to take as much pleasure as I ought in tragedy — and especially in the very good suffering in mind very dreadfully, not simply for the truth, but for their venial faults'. But his criticisms, though sometimes trenchant, were always full of friendly interest, and the recipients came back for more.

Dismal Johnny Walker came to see them and Newman retailed their interview to Faber in great delight. 'We then went off about theology and he took the same demure way which an old maid would with a Magdalene or a puritan with a papist . . . he shivered while I spoke of Malebranche's objects and ideas (this reminding him of the Development) just as if they were *double entendres*. . . . Old Formby has cookooed (I can't spell it) him out of the convent and he is on the wide world . . . he is going into retreat to determine whether he can bolt my dogmatics.' Walker was considering joining the London Oratory ; Faber was not at all pleased at the prospect. He did not ; Newman's dogmatics stuck in his throat.

Several times this autumn Newman mentioned in his letters '*grazie*' from St. Philip, graces, favours from heaven — cures effected by means of his patron's relics. Blessed with the relic, a bedridden convert of Ambrose's heard a voice within saying, 'Dust and ashes, get up and walk', which she did. A child of eight was cured, and a young woman with dropsy. Thus St. Philip gave them his blessing.

This was the first Christmas in Birmingham. Not having a crib or 'cave' they used a little picture copied by Miss Giberne, 'beflowered and belighted' as Newman told her, which delighted everyone. He was playing the organ for the services himself. 'Just now I am obliged to be trying to learn the organ,' he told Stanton in his letter at the end of December, 'and have from a forlorn hope of anything being better than nothing, played Vespers and Benediction all through last week, for we cannot afford an organist.' He did not think much of his powers as an organist and decorated his new duty with exclamation marks in brackets. The violin lay unused ; there was no time for Beethoven. On St. John Evangelist's day, his own feast, he said mass for all the Johns in the congregation. He had another bad cold and the weather was terrible. Writing a new-year letter to Jemima he inquired kindly after 'my dear Anne Mozley — I am always thinking of her and wish my thoughts could do her good. . . . I hope this weather has not given her rheumatic feelings.'

Newman began the year 1850 with a *novena* of prayer to decide

the fate of St. Wilfrid's.   At the same time a crisis arose in the affairs
of the London House.   A frenzied letter came from Faber : Hutchison had rounded on him and retailed to him a string of complaints
made against him in the house, that he was a hypochondriac, that
he spent the Congregation's money on himself, and other wounding
criticisms.   Faber was in despair ; he could not go on.   'My dearest
Padre, I wish you would release me from my office here,' he wrote
on December 29th.   'It is four years since I have had no rest and I
am ill and cowed.   I am sure if it were not for my intense love of you
I don't know what I should do.'   Newman replied kindly, 'You have
a great deal to bear and I should feel as you do — but I think you
exaggerate as to the Fathers.'   Since they had been grumbling at
being ordered about by Faber, he made the practical suggestion that
they should have four Deputies, Coffin, Faber himself, Dalgairns and
Stanton.   Thus orders would come from four, not one, and they
would be a step nearer self-government.   Since the Rescript from
Rome in November Newman was more anxious to establish the
London House on its own, to refute the idea that he wished for any
sort of permanent 'generalate'.   But knowing how chaotic things
still were there he hoped to keep an eye on them for some time to
come.   His future position in regard to them was already being discussed ;   Faber always suggested the most sweeping powers, which
Newman repudiated.   At present, of course, they were still members
of his Oratory and in his charge, until the second house was formally
constituted.

Newman was still trying to get them to accept Coffin, who had
no idea how averse they were to him.   To Stanton he wrote : 'It is
impossible that things should go on in the random way that now
obtains. . . . I am rendered gravely anxious by what you say that
"some of you would not obey [Coffin] merely because he was
Superior".   I believe it to be true, but still could hardly believe I
read aright.   Let us be true to ourselves and S. Philip will carry us
through everything — but round St. Philip we must rally and recollect his words even in the case of Baronius ;   *aut pareat aut abeat* ' —
let him obey or let him go away.   'But while this deeply governs
your heart, do not *say* it ; it would but irritate.'   He insisted : 'You
must rally round F. Wilfrid as in St. Philip's place and have no fear'.
The rebellion subsided and Faber cheered up, reminding Newman
of the time he had made rabbits on the wall, shocking the pompous
Berkeley long ago in Oxford.

But Coffin, unaware that he was not wanted in London, and of all Newman was trying to effect on his behalf, was demanding replies to his complaining letters. In February Newman asked Stanton to be ready to replace him if necessary. 'He is the greatest plague to me I have — I mean literally, for nothing I say or do will satisfy him. I have several times before now strongly pressed on him going to London. "No," he says, "I can't" and then he adds aside, "because, though I wish it, I know you don't. I am obeying you in staying." . . . If ever he grumbles again I will have nothing to do with keeping him.' To Coffin he said at last in desperation, 'I don't *make* events — and as time *stops* for no one, so it hastens for no one'. His letters were bound to be unsatisfactory to Coffin until matters were settled. His wrist, as he told Faber, 'had got worn again', and he said to Coffin, 'You little think how it *hurts* my hand writing *this* letter'. His underlining did not have much effect; Coffin's unwilling isolation gave him indigestion, and he thought Newman unfeeling.

At the end of the *novena* in January Newman made several decisions. He organized the London House, giving the senior Fathers 'decennial' status, so that they could make elections. They elected Faber as Rector and novice master, and Hutchison as Minister. Money matters were still to be supervised by Newman. In Birmingham they decided to begin strict observance of the Rule at once. As for St. Wilfrid's, Newman determined to turn it into a college. The London Fathers agreed unanimously to this plan, not, it turned out later, because they approved of it, but to please Newman, to shelve a problem they could not be bothered to solve and perhaps to keep Coffin away a little longer. Newman had just told them that they had shown 'the utmost apathy on the subject'. He had proposed one plan after another : 'I have had the responsibility without thanks, as if I were proposing and planning for myself'. In another letter he remarked, 'We don't forget and shall not forget what you so pointedly wished us to consider, that St. Wilfrid's is useless for *your* purposes'. He had tried again and again to get them to propose a plan if they did not like his; they never did anything but criticize. Now, at this plain intimation of disapproval, they did what they thought he wanted, like lazy boys placating a schoolmaster. Thus a train was laid for explosions of trouble in the future. But Newman, full of energy at the prospect of something definite, got out a circular on the proposed college and wrote round to existing Catholic colleges for their opinions.

It was now, just before their first year in Birmingham was out, that Edward Caswall gave Newman £1000, as an endowment to ensure yearly masses for his dead wife. Soon after he settled £4000 on the Oratory, so that Newman, who had been looking out for a better place for a permanent home, was able to secure a site in Edgbaston and plan to build. Caswall made up his mind to join them, and on Good Friday that year he received the habit from Newman. This was the best possible answer to all their prayers. On the eve of the anniversary of their foundation Newman wrote to Faber of a prospective novice in London, 'Let Rowe don the habit to-morrow and I suppose you may be my commissary to admit him to fight with the ancient serpent'. He was quoting from the form for admission of novices ; the Pope had referred to this text from the Apocalypse of St. John. It was a phrase which well expressed Newman's view of their vocation. He preached a double sermon on St. Philip about this time, later enlarged and included in the *Sermons on Various Occasions* (1857) in which, setting St. Philip in his Renaissance background, he drew out the essence of the spirit he had bequeathed to his sons. St. Philip's favourite maxim had already become his own, 'To despise the whole world, to despise no member of it, to despise oneself, *to despise being despised*'. It was Newman who underlined the last clause. His prayer for his own Oratory was that 'by the world you should be overlooked . . . that you should work for God alone'. This prayer was to be answered, like so many of Newman's, in a way he could not foresee, most painful to himself.

His Alcester Street people were not the only Catholics who thought well of Newman and loved him. An old Catholic, Miss Moore, sister of the principal mission priest of Birmingham, told Miss Munro, a pious but headstrong lady, that Father Newman was a saint ; Miss Munro tactlessly passed on this information to the object of devotion. Newman did not do a dance, like St. Philip, but his reply was rather like one. 'You must undeceive her about me, though I suppose she uses words in a general sense,' he said. 'I have nothing of a Saint about me as every one knows, and it is a severe (and salutary) mortification to be thought next door to one. I may have a high view of many things, but it is the consequence of education and of a peculiar cast of intellect — but this is very different from *being* what I admire. I have no tendency to be a saint — it is a sad thing to say so. Saints are not literary men, they do not love the classics, they do not write Tales. I may be well enough in my way, but it is not the "high line". People ought to feel this, most people do. But those who are at a distance have fee-fa-fum notions about me. It is enough for me to black the saints' shoes — if St. Philip uses blacking, in heaven.'

Ambrose Phillipps wrote in an ecstasy over Newman's two sermons on the Glories of Mary and he replied : 'I do not know in what terms to answer your glowing letter, which has only this drawback on the beauty with which it is written, that it is expended on me. . . . However it is not less pleasant to have such affectionate words from you, though I have gained them by false pretences and strut about in stolen feathers ; and I value them exceedingly. They are a memorial I trust, that we are both of us children of Mary, you because you have liked what I said of her ; I because I have said it. And may she bless us both, you in your wide field of influence, amid your primaeval rocks, under your bright sun and with your holy monks — me and mine in Birmingham amid our labyrinth of lanes and beneath our firmament of smoke.'

TRIAL BY FURY
(1850–1853)

1850

Difficulties of Anglicans — and Converts

UNTIL this year Newman had been out of the public eye since his conversion, indeed, since 1843. But in November 1849, Wiseman, impressed with his Sermons, persuaded him to undertake some lectures in London. Anglicans were in a renewed ferment over the Gorham case, which had raised again the issue of state interference with doctrine. The Bishop of Exeter refused to institute an evangelical clergyman who did not believe Baptism effected regeneration ; the various courts cancelled each other's verdicts until the final decision, which went against the orthodox Bishop. This was the crisis which was to make Catholics of many of Newman's friends among the lawyers, and of Manning.

Newman was unwilling to undertake the lectures ; even after he had agreed he felt, he said, 'troubled by a bad dream, seeking I know not what'. It was so hard to find the right approach, especially as he himself had been the centre of the Movement. To touch the question at all was to risk alienating more than he might win over, and he had no desire to offend Anglican friends like Pusey, who continued to believe the Church of England was, or might be made, Catholic.

Not that Anglicans were so careful of offending him ; even friends had said hard things. Mrs. Wootten, the widow of Newman's Oxford doctor, had finally decided to disobey Pusey and become a Catholic ; she told Newman that even Copeland was accusing him of cutting himself off from his old friends. Newman replied to her : 'I have taken every opportunity or made every excuse for writing to him and sometimes he has not answered my letters — from pain, I believe, but certainly not from want of encouragement from me. No friend has come near me I have not been glad to see — the other day I rejoiced to see Mr. Marriott, though he said he felt it a duty not to be easy with me. . . . No, it is only dear Copeland's extreme sensitiveness. I recollect his coming to our Breviary services after we had become Catholics at Littlemore and we were glad of his coming. But he soon ceased, not from our repelling him, but because (as he said) he could not bear our Italian pronunciation of Latin, nor, I suspect, the Holy Water.'

This notion that Newman was avoiding Anglicans as heretics sprang from the old Apostolical rule ; he explained to Mrs. Wootten that in the Catholic Church this ancient discipline had been modified. 'There are two reasons why I should not dream of avoiding a member of the Church of England ; first because he may not be formally and really a heretic, secondly because, though he were, he is to be loved and reclaimed by love, not by repulsion.' This suited his own nature much better than the stern rule of avoidance. As to their avoidance of him, he could not discover that it was done on any principle. Henry Wilberforce repudiated such a suggestion ; it was not principle but publicity which kept him away. Newman was sometimes annoyed, sometimes amused at Henry ; he was so reverential even in keeping his distance. 'Charissime,' Newman wrote to him in the autumn of 1848, 'what mean you by talking of my "honoring you with my intimacy" ? Come near me and I will revenge myself by kissing your feet. What have I done to be so treated ?'

The silence of friends hurt him, but public misrepresentation roused his indignation, since the lies which circulated destroyed not only his character but his witness to the claims of conscience. When he was in the throes of starting the mission in Birmingham Henry had retailed one of these rumours ; Newman replied with a list of the rest. A Liverpool print had reported that it was perfectly well known to Mr. Newman's friends that his mind was gone : mental aberration, of course, rendered his testimony to Catholicism worthless. 'It was a grave, sleek, imposing lie, which made one smile. People sucked it in greedily and smacked their lips.' He gave a string of further lies. 'Wonderful, it is a psychological fact, this greediness to believe rumours against a Catholic, or against me — and if I don't tell you to show this letter to any one you meet . . . it is because I suspect [your friend] will find something in it "painfully unlike my former tone" — something of "levity" "harshness" or the like, which would make him wish he had never seen it, which would interfere with his former happy recollection of what I was ; it would form to him the best argument that though I was *not* mad, *not* at enmity with Dr. Wiseman, *not* sent out of the country, *not* suspended, *not* refused orders, *not* seceding from the Romish communion, yet there was quite enough in what I said to show that it would argue a much better state of mind if I were. . . . What a donkey in top boots your friend must be !'

Last summer Newman had broken out to Mrs. Froude, not addressing her personally but as if to those he had known : 'Do you take me for a hot-headed dreamer ? have you the face to say so ? yes — you have. When you can't get out of the difficulty otherwise, you hint I am mad. . . . O shame — how will that plea stand at the last day ? — nothing is sacred, private feelings are not sacred, when a way to Rome is laid open. Close that way, though with the bodies of your friends — yes, to the letter, for others said to me "I had rather see you die than join the Church of Rome".' Such an impassioned outburst, even in private, was rare ; in public he had said nothing, except that he had got Stanley Faber, Faber's uncle, to retract the charge he had made in a newspaper, asserting that Newman had been secretly a Romanist when he was Vicar of St. Mary's.

Although so many unworthy motives were imputed to him, Newman was determined not to retaliate in kind. Two years ago he had taken Lucas to task for attacking Lord Shrewsbury in this way in the *Tablet*. 'It seems to me an unfair mode of fighting, like punching a man in the stomach. Perhaps feeling it so much myself, makes me quite angry when I see it used to another. The question is not whether the imputative is true or not, but whether it is fair. . . . And whether it is your business to judge a man . . . instead of confining yourself to judging his writings or his actions. . . . I like others may be tempted to them and transgress — but still I hate them, as I may hate sin. You can't tell how I hate them.' Therefore, though so many bad reasons for becoming a Catholic had been assigned to him by Anglicans, in his lectures he assigned none to them for remaining in the Church of England. He treated the Movement historically and generally.

In the first seven lectures Newman traced the origin and development of the Movement and showed how far removed were its Catholic principles from those which animated the national Church as a living institution. In the last five he defended the Sanctity, Unity, Catholicity and Apostolicity of the Catholic Church against various arguments, or dissuasives, urged against it on each of these essential notes. Throughout he was careful to address the Anglo-Catholics, not the generality of Church of England members who were proud of their Protestantism. Thus he did not even attack the Establishment, though he laughed at it, as he and Froude had done from the earliest days. The whole Movement had been built on the idea of the sacred independence of the Church from any national state, and he had not changed his mind about that. But for all his care, some took his laughter as a sneer at the religion of the individuals in the national Church—the last thing he intended. Whenever he could he squeezed in a tribute, to some Caroline divine or to his old Bishop Bagot ; even the Establishment had, at that time, some use as a 'breakwater' against the tide of sin and unbelief, though he doubted if it could withstand the full force of the storm he saw coming. It was not his intention to destroy anything, but to help those who already accepted Catholic principles to draw out the full consequences of them.

It must be remembered that the Establishment which Newman teased in 1850 was an exceedingly powerful institution, and that as a Catholic he spoke from a tiny minority, despised and civically helpless. The Church of England had recovered from its lethargy and was full of charitable and missionary activity. Christian belief was vague but general ; unbelief was confined to certain intellectual circles or to the town mobs, where it was due to ignorance, not doubt. The national Church, moreover, had the prestige of the nation, and England was rapidly extending her power and influence in the world. England led the field in industrial and commercial expansion, and Englishmen, intoxicated by success, assumed that they were natural leaders in every other respect also. They could not but be shocked when Newman told them that all this vigorous life would pass away, as other empires and their religions had done, and only that would remain which had a vital connexion with the revelation of Christ in the universal Church. 'All is vanity but what is done to the glory of God,' he said in the last of the lectures. 'It glitters and it fades away ; it makes a noise and is gone.'

Sure as he was of his position, Newman found the task of composing these lectures, in the midst of his multifarious activities, exceedingly wearisome. Faber, excited at the prospect of new successes, wrote to Newman for his birthday, 'Masses were said and *dolce* eaten in your honour'. Newman replied, 'Thank you for your congratulations, masses and *dolce*, though you have kept the last as your reward for the former'. A few months ago, in a similar vein, he had hopefully demanded 'some of David Lewis' bride cake'. He went on : 'I congratulate you in your turn on your sermons being ready, and marvel how you do things. Every year I get more languid and cumbersome. To move my mind is like putting a machine in motion, not an act of volition ; yet Aristotle puts down 49 as the acme of mental vigour. But the body affects it. This time ten years was my severest fast, now the most trifling deprivation makes me unable to hold up my limbs.' He enclosed a review of his sermons. 'The poor fellow whose criticism I enclose talks of iron wills ; I would I had some portion of such galvanic power within me.'

The truth was that his strength was heavily overtaxed ; he had now had two years' continuous work and responsibility without rest or holiday. The severe colds which beset him one after another show how his physical energy was reduced by the strain ; yet he never had the sort of illness which necessitated a complete relaxation. And he was living all the time in the industrial slums, working as an ordinary priest alongside the others ; the time tables of the early years in Alcester Street survive, with Newman's turns of preaching and instructing and confessing through week after week and month after month. After Christmas this year, too, he had been doubling and trebling his own hours in the confessional to give the other Fathers a brief respite.

People in the world he had left did not realize the sort of life he was leading now, in bug-ridden confessionals, teaching illiterates the Faith ; his letters only mentioned such things casually and when he emerged occasionally at the call of friendship, there was nothing to show it. Sam Wilberforce saw him at the funeral of George Ryder's wife, who died this March. Sophia was the third of the beautiful Sargent brides to die young. Manning lost his Caroline in 1837, Sam Wilberforce his Emily in 1841 ; now Henry's Mary was the only survivor. Mrs. Sargent, after caring first for the childless widower, Manning, had gone to live at Cuddesdon with Sam to supervise the upbringing of his children. Sam wrote to his brother Robert that Newman was at the funeral, 'But I thought it best not to see him ; I heard that unmistakeable voice, like a volcano's roar tamed to the softness of a flute-stop, and got a glimpse (may I say it to you ?) of a serpentine form through an open door — "the Father Superior".'

George Ryder wrote often for comfort and advice ; and now Henry Wilberforce and his wife were on the brink of becoming Catholics. In the midst of writing his lectures and visiting the dentist, Newman offered to rush down to Kent '*in plain clothes*' and receive Henry's wife, who had made up her mind. Newman, in whatever clothes, was hard to disguise, and the Wilberforces hastily put him off ; Henry had not yet resigned his living. Mary was received in June by Mr. Brownbill, Henry not till the autumn and in Brussels. Daring publicity, he came to at least one lecture, for his presence was noted by a reporter. All the Wilberforces were well

known in society, Sam a Bishop, Robert an Archdeacon, and even
Henry had preached at Court.

The lectures had been put off from Lent to May ; Newman wrote
them, as he nearly always wrote everything, at the last minute and at
high pressure. 'How am I to write two a week ! two a week ! two a
week ! I can't imagine,' he cried, when Faber told him this was
expected. 'You are a bad fellow for not *telling* me Monsignore's
observations as to my Lectures. I am writing them intellectually
against the grain more than I ever recollect doing anything — and
now you bother me by putting an additional fetter on. So please
tell me at once.' It turned out that Wiseman merely hoped Newman
would say he had never advised waiting *after* conviction. 'Voilà
tout!' said Faber. At the end of April Newman was writing all day
and half the night. 'If I were younger I should knock myself up
from sheer excitement,' he told Stanton. 'I cannot convey the misery
it is to me.' He worked on some right up to the moment of delivery.
Mentioning this to George Ryder he added, 'having had a face ache
all night and a headache now and its being a fast day, you shall put
up with only a line or two'.

A few days before Newman began his lectures in London his
brother Frank started a course of a very different kind, which he
made into a book, *Phases of Faith*. He told of his progressive emancipation from the doctrines of Christianity, criticized Christ's character
as a man and declared 'I now with deliberate approval "love the
world and the things of the world".' He still retained a vague belief
in God, but as he held that 'Religion is created by the inward instincts
of the soul : it has afterwards to be pruned and chastened by the
sceptical understanding', there was nothing to stop him jettisoning
Deism too. 'People seem to be talking a good deal about him,' Faber
told Newman, 'and he has been writing on Oxford in a new infidel
paper, *The Leader*.' Frank found many to sympathize with him
among the liberal intellectuals of the day, though to the mass of
Englishmen his ideas were as unpopular as his brother's.

Of Frank's book Newman said to Miss Giberne, 'I can't be
surprised — he must with his independent mind, work out his principles and they tend to atheism. God grant he may be arrested in
his course !' Yet many people were saying that it was John Henry
Newman's ideas that made atheists : too much credulity reacts in
scepticism. Anthony Froude's novel, *The Nemesis of Faith*, published in 1849, was taken as proof of this thesis. His hero plunged
from Tractarianism into a general scepticism ; his admiration of

Newman (who appeared in person) only convinced his shocked readers of his pernicious influence. That terrible leader with his fascinating mixture of severity and tenderness seemed capable of drawing the young only to the devil of Rome or the deep sea of scepticism. The novel reminded people of Newman just when he was coming back into the public eye.

It was certain that a great many would come to Newman's lectures out of curiosity, and this did not make their composition easier. 'I am perplexed,' he said to Faber at the end of April, 'either some of them will be most impressively dull — or they will be too much on the other tack ; and I am frightened at the chance of being satirical etc before the Blessed Sacrament.' In the event the Sacrament was not in the room where he gave the lectures. At King William Street there were an upper and a lower chapel, the latter being divided and used for other purposes besides services. In these, the old assembly and whiskey rooms, Newman executed his cutting-out expedition, to detach the stragglers of the Movement from the solid army of the Establishment and carry them off to the fortress built on the Rock. Nobody was bored. Among the visitors was Doyle, the *Punch* artist, Thackeray, and a friend of his, a literary clergyman called Robert Montgomery.

'The aspect of the outer man', pronounced Montgomery in an account for the newspapers, 'seems very like an embodied illustration of a Romanizing article in the *British Critic* ten years ago.' It was luck for the critics that Newman was thin ; fat Ward, the jolly opera-goer, the author of so many Romanizing articles, would not have represented so satisfactorily the unnatural monkishness of the perverts. 'His face is thoughtful, cold, acute, somewhat rigid and almost repulsive in its nasal expression ; but touched now and then with shades of religious bearing which redeem it from what would otherwise be by no means an attractive countenance. Mr. Newman reads his lectures : his delivery is simple, earnest, untheatrical and devoid of impassioned gesture or exciting declamation. His voice too is not only agreeable but at times artistically intoned with a touching pathos and spiritual melancholy such as emotional ladies delight to hear. Doubtless a great deal of this was artificially *put on* by Mr. Newman but the assumption is beginning to be incorporated with the real man and will soon become a vital part of his oratorical representations.'

Quite another impression was made on a liberal-minded young man, R. H. Hutton, afterwards editor of the *Spectator*, who was to come to know Newman personally after Kingsley's attack in 1864. This was the first time he saw him. 'Never did a voice seem better adapted to persuade without irritating,' he said of this occasion. 'Singularly sweet, perfectly free from any dictatorial note, and yet rich in all the cadences proper to the expression of pathos, of wonder and of ridicule, there was still nothing in it that anyone could properly describe as insinuating.' Thus do eye-witnesses agree, each seeing what he is disposed to see.

Montgomery was shocked at the 'unseemly mirth' which Newman excited in his audience. 'The Fathers of the Oratory were heard to titter, the Romish ladies to giggle, while a scarcely suppressed laughter arose from the *heretical* Protestants.' Wiseman laughed outright, rocking in his chair at Newman's description of the Apostolicals baited by the Anglican bishops — Newman was laughing at his own predicament after Tract 90. 'It was a solemn war-dance, which they executed round victims, who by their very principles were bound hand and foot, and could only eye with disgust and perplexity this most unaccountable movement, on the part of their "Holy Fathers, the representatives of the Apostles and the Angels of the Churches".' Newman was quoting himself of course, and he apologized for doing it so often, saying that at least he was sure of not misrepresenting this author or hurting his feelings. For the same reason his other quotations were drawn from the works of his dead friends, Froude and Bowden. So as not to refer constantly to himself by name he often quoted from his anonymous Tracts and articles.

But he was most himself in the last lectures, defending the Church against all comers. Montgomery was shocked when Newman said that a lazy, filthy, beggar woman 'not over scrupulous of truth' who believed in God and tried to fulfil her duties to Him, had a better chance of Heaven than 'the state's pattern man' who relied on himself. Montgomery noticed disapprovingly, 'Mr. Newman seemed amazingly to enjoy this part of his lecture'. Hutton saw him laugh at this point, trying to hide behind his manuscript, and making the sign of the cross before he went on. He knew perfectly well that he would shock the virtuous with this declaration that Christianity was not just a morality, and he did shock them. This passage was brought up again and again to prove that Newman and Rome winked at lying. Later, Newman observed that Christ himself had told the virtuous Pharisees that sinners went into the kingdom of heaven before them. Yet everybody was equally shocked when he said that it was better for the sun to fall out of the sky than for a single sin to be committed.

Newman's paradoxes on moral evil startled because those of the gospel had become too familiar to impress the imagination.

The lectures contributed to the conversion of many hesitating Tractarians, among them T. W. Allies, a clever clergyman, well known in his day, who had long been a thorn in the flesh of Sam Wilberforce, Bishop of Oxford. Friends of his, including the artist John Hungerford Pollen, were to come in later. Newman himself received Mrs. Allies. Allies became secretary of the Catholic Poor School commission.

Public reactions to the lectures among the Anglo-Catholics disappointed Newman, for they followed the familiar line of attacking the motives of the converts instead of answering their theological and historical arguments. The *Guardian* began a series of articles which Newman learned were by Rogers. He told William Froude he was astonished 'how so clever a man can argue so weakly!' It was so negative an approach. 'And this is what I think so unfair in their argument — that they dare not, won't say *what* they believe and *why* — they fence off.' A favourite excuse was that logic was not everything. 'People love to reason till they are beaten,' observed Newman, 'then they talk of inexorable logic — as others talk of sophistry, jesuitry etc. Give a dog an ill name and hang him — our Anglo-Catholic friends enjoyed my logic while it attacked the evangelicals, Hampden etc, but when it went *too far* then it was inexorable and I deteriorated.'

Rogers' personal position puzzled Newman. He said he dreamed of him one night 'through sheer amazement'. 'The inexorable logic *topos* may parry my attack, but how can it satisfy himself? his "remaining where he is" does not *ipso facto* give him a creed. . . . He has to answer God, not me — it is not a question of polemics but of personal duty.' Brooding over the problem he said, 'I think it is a deep scepticism — i.e. a shrinking from receiving absolutely what another tells him — an utter suspicion of what does not approve itself to his moral feeling — i.e. in substance the very principle which rules my brother, though not so boldly expressed. Of course I don't say all this to anyone but you. . . .'

William Froude, and others, often wondered if Newman was as sure as he seemed that the Catholic Church was the home of the one true faith. Newman said : 'After coming from before the tabernacle, after hearing Mass or attending Benediction what a mere dream and absurdity and talk do these objections seem! *Here* is the reality — Why don't you force me to argue in proof of my having two legs, you declaring I have only a cork one!'

In February of the next year, 1851, Newman protested privately to
John Duke Coleridge, son of Keble's friend the Judge, against the
persistent attacks on the converts in the *Guardian*. As Anglo-
Catholics refused to meet them in person, print was the only medium
of intercourse left, and here it was being used to separate friends still
further. '*I* am the *only* person to whom they have *not* assigned
unworthy motives for the change of religion,' Newman said. 'This
is a proceeding so unspeakably mean, that I do not know how to
allude to it without saying more than I like to say.' They had not
even the excuse of not knowing their victims personally, as had often
been the case when Evangelicals attacked the motives of the Tractarians. 'And why all this ungenerousness and unreasonableness ?
To find some *plea* for their own remaining apart from the Catholic
Church. This surely is want of sincerity, or hypocrisy — I use the
word, not from personal feeling as you imply, but from a feeling I
do not know how to suppress ; of disdain and disapprobation of such
an exhibition.'

But he only expressed this disapprobation privately. Some
Anglicans, too, remained on courteous terms : ancient Martin Routh
of Magdalen sent Newman a book, and Newman in return gave him
his Latin dissertations on St. Athanasius. But when Newman expressed his sympathy at Copleston's death to Provost Hawkins, the
Provost did not reply. 'Poor Copleston's course, what a vanity !'
Newman commented to Jemima, thinking of that brilliant scholar's
ecclesiastical opportunism. Yet still he felt 'This dying out of people
is most affecting, and almost more than I can bear'.

In July he revised the Lectures for publication, telling Miss
Holmes, 'Let no one suppose that my books do not cost me labour —
they are as severe a trial as hedging and ditching, though it is not
one's back that aches, or one's muscles that are worked'. Hedging
and ditching was an apt description for what he was doing in these
lectures, in contrast to the ploughing and sowing of other works. He
was all the more surprised to receive from Rome in August an
honorary Doctorate of Divinity. 'I have no claims on so great an
honour, except what would be sufficient to make every sincere
Catholic a doctor, an earnest desire to serve my Mother the Church,
of which I am the latest and most unformed son.' He told Mrs.
Bowden not to direct to him as Doctor 'but Father, which is my
proper title — I don't know myself in so strange a dress'.

All the same, it was tiresome when Ward expressed surprise that
Rome should confer a doctorate on one whose opinions were 'some-

what novel'. Newman said, 'And then my notions of faith — I don't at all twig them. But really you make me anxious. Old Brownson will be coming down upon me — and finding a thousand and one heresies in my Discourses and Lectures.' In the last number of his magazine Brownson had included 'three several attacks' on the Development. 'He seems to think he has a mission in opposing me ; why, I know not.'

The renewal of publicity about Newman upset his sister Jemima. It was reported to him that she was always telling people she knew John better than anyone and that he was sure to come back. To him she lamented that she was 'only half resigned to an ever new misfortune'. This gave Newman an opportunity to tell her some of his real feelings. He ended, 'O my dear Jemima, bear with me in thus writing to you ; you have led me to do so ; you will not be troubled with such words often'. He told Mrs. Bowden that he sometimes wondered if Jemima had made her husband promise not to speak to him for a fixed period, sure he would return by then. But Jemima and her husband were united in not wanting Newman to come into contact with their children. Herbert had just won a scholarship to Eton ; it would not do for growing boys to be exposed to the influence of their famous uncle, with his insidious charm for the young.

From their own point of view the Mozleys may have been wise. What boy could have resisted Newman's gentle nonsensical humour ? The *Family Herald*, after criticizing a sermon of St. John's, had offered to insert his reply. Newman sketched a reply for him — that he regretted he could not oblige 'as he is engaged to exhibit of the tight rope at Vauxhall for every evening of the ensuing week'.

1850

Showdown over St. Wilfrid's

In July it became plain to Newman that he was going to get no
further co-operation from the London House in solving the problem
of St. Wilfrid's. In January they had all agreed to his plan of using
it as a college and a place of meeting, but the moment anyone was
asked to go there reasons were found why it was impossible. 'Now
the time has come for fulfilling your engagement — and to my disgust
you break it, and that on no grounds but what you must have been
able to urge at the time you made it.' He was especially annoyed
because he had purposely shown no eagerness in presenting his
proposals, in order that they should say freely what they thought.
It was this habit of promising and then finding excuses for not acting
that made decisions for the community so difficult. And now he
discovered, by accident, that the London House had calmly been
making plans of its own for a holiday residence without any reference
to St. Wilfrid's at all. 'Ward would have given you your travelling
expenses but you let him give you money for a house at Lancing —
for the convenience of running up and down for a day — as if you
were to suffer no inconvenience of any kind as the price of keeping
St. Wilfrid's. For myself, I had not a dream that you were not likely
to keep your engagement till the day I came to town . . . and found
that next week you were going to Lancing not for a night or a day
but for three weeks consecutive. And now my dear F. Wilfrid I
have unburdened myself. The whole plan of St. Wilfrid's is overset.
I do not see how I can ask any of our Fathers to go there next year.'

Apart from the responsibility to the Bishop and Lord Shrewsbury
in which Faber had involved him, what chiefly worried Newman was
the loss of a common place of meeting. He had always felt strongly
the necessity for some kind of moral unity between the houses of the
Oratory in England, and the difficulty of preserving it with the independence guaranteed to each community by the Rule. In Italy the
situation was quite different. Italy was divided into regions, politi-

cally and geographically, so that the sphere of each Oratory did not
impinge on that of any other ; in a Catholic population, too, with
other religious houses fully established, Oratories fitted into their
place without all the talk and publicity they were bound to occasion
in England. 'Here such strangeness is impossible ; Birmingham is
a 3-hour train journey from London and Oxford would be just half
way between. Difference of spirit and opinion would be as clearly
seen and felt as between members of the same house, yet without
any arbitrating power. Jealousy, rivalry and distance would be sure
to follow. All this would be a great scandal — there would be continual gossipping, talebearing etc. etc.' He knew human nature all
too well. He knew too how divergent already were the opinions and
feelings of the London House from his own, how impatient they
were of his criticisms, how little they consulted him, though he was
still officially their Superior — witness the business of the Lancing
house.

Faber had suggested that if he remained Superior of both
houses they could not be disunited. 'It is idle, and worse than idle,'
said Newman, in this long letter of July 18th, 'to talk of the expedient,
for it is nothing else, of having me for a Superior a while, when the
root of the matter is left untouched. A common Superior no more
makes united houses, than England and Ireland would be one, with
one queen, after the repeal of the Union.' At the end of the letter
he said : 'I *can't* make you all wish to keep up intimacy with us all,
if you won't, so I must give this up. In saying this, I know quite
well that you love *me*. I know quite well that some of you love some
of us ; but I know too that the continuance of that love depends on
intercourse, which you are now breaking off.'

Before he had this letter, Faber, writing about an 'unpleasant
note from ye Padre' on the arrangements for St. Wilfrid's, said to
Stanton, 'I fear it looks as if he wished to drive matters to a separation'. After he had it, on July 24th, he wrote again to Stanton about
his 'peck of troubles', saying 'Ye Padre scouts all notion of a common
Superior if ye Oratories are not united. . . . You see now, *caro mio*,
where we are : — enter a *generalizio* or a forfeiture of ye Padre's
blessing and countenance. If we adopt the first what of ye institute ?
If the second, dare we do what ye *Padre* solemnly declares will make
ye Oratory *a great scandal* ?' He was at Lancing when he wrote this.
From this it is plain that Faber viewed Newman's plan for St.
Wilfrid's as an attempt to introduce a kind of generalate ; he never
told *Newman* this. Yet it was he who wanted to keep Newman as

Superior (in name at any rate) of London as well as Birmingham, a
position unwarranted by the Rule, and much more likely to lead to
a generalate than a common house of meeting.

Newman now set about the problem of disentangling the Oratory
from St. Wilfrid's, and very tiresome it was, involving an arbitration
with Lord Shrewsbury, who for a long time refused every arbitrator
that Newman suggested. At the end of July he went out there ;
the country he found so beautiful put on a veil of rain. 'The only
thing I know of out of doors is to have got very wet attempting to
accompany a stranger on his way to the rail,' he told Jemima, at the
same time assuring her that he was not ill, as she had heard he was.
In September he went again, and to Alton Towers to have a long talk
with Lord Shrewsbury : 'No — *he* talked for an hour and a half,'
Newman told Antony Hutchison. 'At length I charged in column,
broke his line, and threw him into confusion.' He succeeded in
making Lord Shrewsbury understand that it was impossible for the
Oratory to keep a community there. 'All this was unpleasant, though
I am glad it came out.' He was writing to Hutchison because so
much of his money had been sunk in the building there. By the end
of September everything seemed to be settled, and that the Redemptorists would buy the house.

Faber was not grateful for the settlement. He told Newman how
sad the loss of St. Wilfrid's made him ; he thought the Birmingham
Fathers were much more set against it than those in London. They
had been more affectionate and communicative than the Birmingham
Fathers. He complained that Joseph Gordon had said, 'St. Wilfrid's
is a millstone round our necks and Father Wilfrid tied it there'. If
Gordon had said that, it was only the truth. This statement was to
undergo several transformations in Faber's mind during the next
few years so that in the end he turned it into a declaration by Newman
that the *Wilfridians* — Faber himself, in fact — were the millstone
round his neck. At the present moment he accused Newman merely
of being harsh and bitter in his letters to them. Newman refused
to rake over the past. 'I love you and all of you too tenderly to be
able to enter into a discussion with you,' he answered. 'And I know
you love me. Why will you bring up what is done and over ? I may
be wrong on this or that matter of detail — but on the whole lie of
the matter, I don't think I can be persuaded that I am wrong.'

Meanwhile he had been proceeding with the steps which would
give the London House formal self-government. It was hurried on
because they wanted to get Wiseman to sign the formal act, as patron

of the Oratory in England, and almost the only person in authority
not suspicious of it. He had just been summoned to Rome to be
made a Cardinal, and everyone, including himself, thought he would
not return to England. He was sad and talked of golden bonds. The
introduction of the hierarchy was now imminent, and promotion
would take him away just when, as he felt, his policy was bearing
fruit. Before he went, on August 15th, feast of the Assumption, he
ratified the act. Next day Stanton wrote to Newman: 'We are all
much pleased that you drew it up in such a form as not to make it a
final act, and thank you for this consideration'.

They all said they wanted Newman's continued control. Faber
made extravagant suggestions : that he should censor all books and
articles they wrote, control all public developments, transactions with
Bishops, customs, and petitions to Rome. What was this but to
introduce the very *generalizio* he had suspected Newman of wishing
to impose through St. Wilfrid's ? Newman refused it, as he had
refused similar suggestions earlier, as unconstitutional. He proposed
instead three resolutions to be put before their members for voting :
that he should have the right to give advice, that he should be able
to propose, through the Father Superior, matters to be voted on by
the four Deputies, and that in this council of Deputies a minority of
two might appeal to him. This position for himself he proposed for
three years only. The resolutions were passed unanimously by the
London House. 'Very Revd. and dear Father,' Newman teased
Faber a few days later, 'I congratulate your Very Reverence on your
establishment as a House of St. Philip and on your own elevation in
particular . . . love to all of you.'

Now that the London House was constituted, what of Coffin ?
Since the visit of the Redemptorist Father Lans, his complaints had
taken a new form. There was no tradition of spiritual direction in
the Oratory, he told Newman ; it was obvious that he was wondering
whether he would not leave altogether. Newman was in a difficult
position. He could not send Coffin to London, when they did not
want him ; he knew he would not come to Birmingham because he
did not get on with St. John. He therefore made the attractive suggestion that Coffin should go and study theology at the Florence Oratory,
with a view to founding a house in Bristol later — he was a west-
countryman. Coffin accepted this solution and Newman wrote to
Florence at once ; a welcoming reply arrived in November just after
Coffin had announced his intention of joining the Redemptorists.

'Coffin's resolve surprised me,' said Newman mildly to Faber on

November 22nd. At first, looking at it simply as an intention to live a stricter life, he wrote to Coffin, 'How could you suppose it would be a distress to me? I never can be distressed at any one being called to what he considers a more religious life than he is leading at present. . . . St. Philip would never wish to keep any one who did not wish to be kept.' To Faber he said, 'But he will have so much to go through and no one to *sfogue* to, that it is kill or cure'. (*Sfogue* was Faber's word for letting off steam.) Both Coffin's and Faber's replies made Newman realize that he had been misunderstood, and his approval of giving up lukewarmness taken as an admission that a true religious life could not be lived in the Oratory. He hastened to explain the distinction to Coffin, and told him 'in reality I have no sympathy with what you are doing'.

Faber, with little regard for Newman's feelings, or Coffin's, who had confided in him, reported a long rigmarole of accusations. Coffin had said Newman had never been open, or a Father, or a religious superior to him — 'You manœuvre and are diplomatic'. Diplomacy was the word used by a certain Baron Schroeter, who was living at St. Wilfrid's, painting murals for the church, a job Newman had rashly given him out of kindness. The Baron repaid it by gossiping and encouraging the discontented to think their troubles were due to Newman's failings as a Superior. It was very easy to undermine the converts' confidence in Newman; because he had been a Catholic no longer than they, his opinions had little authority with them. Coffin, said Faber, asserted that for the five months they had been at Santa Croce they were all leading 'wicked' lives, kept from grave sin only by frequent confession. Their only chance of sanctifying themselves was to separate and put themselves under experienced directors. Thus, having chosen to stay with Newman, they excused themselves from obeying him (for Coffin was not the only one), and on the score that sanctity could only be achieved under strict obedience! It was Catholic to obey a Superior, but not if that Superior happened to be Newman.

Newman understood Coffin's state of mind very well. 'The solitude was the mother of unreal slights, neglects and injuries, and most real irritation and alienation', he told Faber. 'The Baron has given an imaginary intellectual basis to this moral disease — and his present illusion is the consequence.' No one knew better than Newman, who so rigorously tested his own motives, how easy it is to find reasons to justify acts which are not free, but determined by selfish desires. Instead of subduing his self-will, Coffin blamed the

Rule and his Superior ; the Redemptorists offered a way out of his difficulties. He fell on his feet in that order, which had few English members at the time, rapidly rising in importance to become the Provincial in England. Newman had been right in thinking he had the materials of leadership in him. He and a rich friend, Douglas, did much for the order; he made friends in Rome and exercised a good deal of influence there ; he was instrumental in helping to secure the appointment of Manning as Archbishop and became a keen supporter of the extreme infallibilists. He was to be one of Newman's most implacable opponents in London.

The Baron's part in this defection was despicable and Newman wrote to ask him to leave. He crossed out of his draft a passage in which he accused the Baron of 'breathing out a sort of moral infection', true though it was, but he told him what he thought of his returning their hospitality by trying to 'ruin the Institute of St. Philip and make its subjects despise it. Not that I fear you,' he added, 'St. Philip has guarded this body and will still ; but from charity to the souls you may have tempted, I am bound to make this request.' He ended, 'And now all good angels go with you and God bring you to a truer knowledge of yourself'. The Baron decamped, leaving a number of oddments, including his passport, behind him.

Coffin's charge of diplomacy puzzled Newman. 'I suppose the word means either having some secret end, or using some underhand means,' he said to Faber, repudiating any such design. 'But I am quite conscious *always* of not liking to tell people how keenly I feel things, both from tenderness to them, and again from a consciousness that, when once I begin, I am apt to let out and blow them out of the water.' Thus casually he revealed the cause of much misunderstanding, of his letters and his behaviour, both while he lived and after his death. People are apt to think there are only two possible reasons for emotional self-control : one is that there are no emotions to control and the other that they are controlled in order to manipulate others for a desired end. So some people thought Newman cold, a man without natural passions, and others thought him calculating, hiding a lust for power under a gentle manner. Any sign of disappointment was taken as soured ambition. The proof that this interpretation was not the true one lies in the domestic Oratory letters. Any desire for domination could have found easy satisfaction in a body in which he was officially supreme, especially as its members so often asked, explicitly, to be absolutely commanded. He would not do so ; nor would he use their personal affection to bully them into doing what he wanted. They must learn to fight on their own feet and obey freely ; it was to allow them freedom that he restrained his own strong feelings. But while he was trying not to blow people out of the water, and forcing himself into action when he would have preferred, by nature, to lapse into an Epicurean content, others thought he was scheming to use them and rule them for his own ends. He was too simple for some people to understand.

From the unhappy affair of Coffin he drew this conclusion for Faber : 'Any how what has happened is certainly a call on all of us to greater personal exactness and devotedness to God. St. Philip means it for this. He means, by means of it, to make us more serious, collected and sober, though not less cheerful and childlike. These are indeed times which impress upon us the necessity of being men, of pruning luxuriances, lest we get thin and shabby about the roots.'

For the times had suddenly become dangerous ; all the Catholics of England had been caught up in the storm let loose by the restoration of the hierarchy which the newspapers called the Papal Aggression.

1850

'No Popery! Down with the Oratorians!'

WISEMAN was not kept in Rome but sent back to England as Cardinal Archbishop of Westminster at the head of the restored hierarchy. He was so delighted that he wrote an exuberant pastoral letter dated 'From out the Flaminian Gate' and posted it on ahead. 'Catholic England', he joyfully announced, 'has been restored to its orbit in the ecclesiastical firmament.' Some cautious clergy doubted the wisdom of reading this effusion from the pulpits, but read it was, at the end of October. Since Emancipation the restoration was only a matter of time ; government circles had been familiar with the scheme for years and some approved it, as making English Catholics less directly dependent on Rome. No difficulty was expected. But *The Times* took umbrage at Wiseman's phrases and regarded the measure as a Papal insult aimed at Queen Victoria, the Church of England and a Protestant nation. Who did the Pope think he was, appointing ecclesiastical rulers — the Government's job — with territorial dioceses, and a Cardinal Archbishop to Westminster itself ? With *The Times* in the lead all the other papers took up the cry of Papal Aggression. The crisis might have been resolved had the government issued a calming statement, but instead the Prime Minister, Lord John Russell, wrote a public letter to the Bishop of Durham, just in time for Guy Fawkes Day, in which he threw all his weight on the side of popular indignation against 'the pretension of supremacy over the realm of England'.

Instantly Bedlam was let loose, the tone of the papers changed from shocked incredulity to violent rage, meetings were held up and down the country, not only in large towns but in remote country districts, the Pope was burned, Wiseman (in red hat) was burned, crucifixes were mutilated and burned, clowns dressed up as Romish clergymen were lucky not to get burned, real Romish clergymen — if recognized — were pelted with mud and stones, windows were broken in chapels and houses belonging to Catholics, and the crowd, unable to distinguish theological differences, menaced Puseyite clergymen whose discreet brass crosses might have been idolatrous crucifixes for all they cared.

Two years before, England had trembled on the brink of revolution, at the time of the Chartists' agitation ; now all classes united in an orgy of righteous violence.   For although it was the mob who threw the stones, it was the gentry and the magistrates who called the meetings that excited them.   Members of Parliament, squires, mayors, judges, parsons, bishops, and all the respectable joined in the outcry, convened and addressed the meetings, petitioned the Queen and preached to the people not to yield to the tyranny of the Pope.   Education had not eradicated the irrational association of the images of the Devil and the Pope, but merely provided reasons for indulging in the pleasures of horror and hatred with a clear conscience.   It was a kind of madness while it lasted, and after a little while people began to try and shuffle out of the consequences of actions taken while under its potent influence.   Fanatics were disgusted at such feebleness, which did not make itself apparent till Christmas.

Punch, which took a leading part in the outcry, went on for months trying to keep the fires of indignation burning, and in the country as a whole they did not simmer down for a long while. *Punch's* circulation went up enormously, as it generously supplied the fare that was wanted.   It was ironical that all this fear and anger at the Pope's supposed aggression came at a time when Pio Nono could not get even Catholics to help him in his temporal difficulties ; he had already been driven out of his own capital once, and his position was extremely precarious.   But to England the Pope was not a man, but the symbol of tyranny, natural and supernatural.   *Punch* and the other papers all assumed that he was about to order all heretics to be burned alive, that Wiseman, if he had the power, would torture Protestants in his cellars, and that all Romish priests were traitors and sadists, actual or potential.

Unaware of the pandemonium he had let loose Wiseman was sailing home on a wave of euphoria ; Catholics were afraid he would be lynched on arrival.   Newman feared that this violent opposition would break his heart.   He reached England the very day of one of the biggest meetings in London, at which Lord Ashley (Shaftesbury) took the chair.   But Wiseman rose to the occasion ; he wrote at high speed an 'Appeal to the English People' which was printed in all the leading newspapers, including a reluctant *Times*.   He asked for fair play in true English style. He had been accused of claiming power in setting up his See in Westminster ; he said he left the seats of government to those who used them, all he wanted was the miserable warren of slums behind them and the poor who lived there. Ulla- thorne also wrote to the papers in the same spirit ; nobody in their senses could think either of them foreigners or slippery customers. This was the point at which the more thoughtful began to wonder if the Pope were not simply reorganizing the spiritual affairs of Catholics, and not attempting to unseat Queen Victoria from her throne and the supreme governorship of the national church. But these Papist appeals were ascribed to unscrupulous cunning by Lord Ashley and his Evangelical friends at Exeter Hall ; and by *Punch*, which only a few months ago had been sneering at Ashley's Puritanism. No- Popery wonderfully united discordant elements in the country. So far as the populace was concerned, the storm raged on unabated.

Newman's first reaction on hearing of the restoration was a doubt of its practicability : 'they can't fill up the sees, positively can't', he remarked. He doubted the wisdom of sending a Cardinal to England, since a Cardinal's was 'an office of this world' and 'who is there who knows anything of the world to put about the Cardinal ?' He wrote to Talbot in Rome, 'Don't interpret me to be the advocate of fears. Fear is the worst of counsellors. We must not retreat a foot — but we must be very cautious.' But it was soon apparent that caution was useless, and once the battle was on his spirits rose to meet it. Ullathorne asked him to preach at his installation as first Bishop of Birmingham ; Newman wrote up the sermon immediately afterwards and had it printed under the title *Christ upon the Waters*. 'I hope you will not think me very *violent*,' he wrote to Ullathorne, asking his permission to bring it out as a pamphlet, 'but my experience tells me, that the more you show a bold front to the world, so cowardly is it, the more you gain. Also, following your Lordship's hint, I think it not a bad move to draw the world's indignation on myself who, not being in a place of authority, cannot suffer for it.' The Catholic Bishops were threatened with old laws, with new laws, penalties, prison, and even, in moments of excitement, deportation or death. Newman was prompted by the same desire to draw the fire of the enemy which Ullathorne had misunderstood in the affair of the Saints' Lives.

He succeeded in his object, for all the papers fell on it at once. *The Times* misreported Newman as comparing Ullathorne's installa- tion with the resurrection of Christ. Tait, the Dean of Carlisle, who had denounced Newman nine years ago for Tract 90, now denounced him for blasphemy. 'Poor Doctor Newman,' said *Punch* pityingly, '. . . gets up on a chair and states that the grave is opened and its awful tenant has arisen.' Newman had said that the Church, like Christ, was always dying and rising again. In a public correspondence with Tait Newman succeeded in getting him to admit he had read the false report in *The Times*, not the sermon, but Tait refused to retract the charge of blasphemy. Tait was to go on to London and Canterbury — to Sam Wilberforce's sorrow, for he was growing ever more liberal in his religious opinions.

Punch found Newman the most suitable representative of Popery; he was second only to Wiseman in the cartoons and more quoted in the letterpress — much easier to caricature than the genial Wiseman. As a 'pervert' he could also be used as a stick to beat the Puseyites, who were pursued with implacable scorn and disgust in its pages. Newman was identified with what *Punch* called Oratorianism — really Faber's Italianate Catholicism. *Punch*, though it was violent, could be funny too. '"Every road", says the ancient proverb, "leads to Rome"; but of all roads none will take you there so quickly as the small Tracts that run through Oxford.' A programme of 'Puseyite histrionics' announced at the end that a certain clergyman 'the Oxford Wizard, will shortly deliver a lecture . . . in which he will perform the ASTOUNDING MARVEL OF SWALLOWING (in a non-natural sense) ANY GIVEN NUMBER OF NO LESS THAN THIRTY-NINE ARTICLES ! ! !' Yet it published a revolting cartoon of a monkey got up as the Pope roasting the paws of a Puseyite cat entitled 'The Cat's paw, or Poor Pus(s)ey'.

In his sermon, as published, Newman had put some observations on the English character. 'Private judgment commonly means passive impression. Most men in this country like opinions to be brought to them, rather than to be at pains to go out and seek for them. . . . As great men have their slaves or their body servants for every need of the day, so, in an age like this, when every one reads and has a voice in public matters, it is indispensable that they should have persons to provide them with their ideas, the clothing of the mind, and that of the best fashion. Hence the extreme influence of periodical publications at this day . . . they teach the multitude what to think and what to say. . . . Is it to be supposed that a man will take the trouble of finding out the truth, when he can pay for it ? So his only object is to have cheap knowledge ; that he may have his views of revelation, and dogma, and policy and conduct — in short of right and wrong — ready to hand, as he has his cloth laid for his breakfast.' The Englishman, said Newman, 'is bent on action, but as to opinion, he takes what comes, only he bargains not to be teased and troubled about it. He gets his opinions any how, some from the nursery, some at school, some from the world, and has a zeal for them, because they are his own . . . he makes light of their incongruity and thinks it a proof of common sense, good sense, strong shrewd sense, to do so.'

Such remarks were incidental to the sermon, which was a call to faith in face of the hostility of the world. The only real danger came from within : 'the open scandal, the secret sin known only to God, these form the Devil's real host'. This was Newman's list of real foes : 'Corruption, hollowness, neglect of mercies, deadness of heart, worldliness'. But as for the present agitation he said : 'We love you, O men of this generation, but we fear you not. Understand well and lay it to heart, that we will do the work of God and fulfil our mission, with your consent, if we can get it, but, in spite of you, if we cannot. . . . We know our place and our fortunes : to give a witness and to be reviled ; to be cast out as evil and to succeed.'

'The people of this great country are such (moral) *cowards* that nothing is likely so to prevail with them as firmness', he told Talbot. 'They will rush forward, if you retreat, but they will be cowed and fall back, if you calmly keep your ground. We must not budge an inch, nor will anyone I am sure.' He praised the Cardinal and Bishop Ullathorne for the stand they had made. Badeley, one of Newman's lawyer friends in London, not yet a Catholic, asked his opinion and he answered, 'My line is not that of external manifestation, still I do believe that St. Peter has come out of the Flaminian Gate and not simply Nicholas Wiseman. . . . And to tell the truth, though I hate rows, I hate (I hope) humbug quite as much — and so much had got about at home and abroad to the effect that the British Lion had become a lamb and that John Bull had become instinct with a diviner spirit, that liberals were Catholics and the race of squires and parsons was extinct, that I do think it is a good thing to have matters put on their true basis.' He said he hated rows, but in fact he enjoyed a straight fight.

Newman had no illusions as to the difficulty of making Englishmen Catholics, just as he had none about the even greater difficulty of making Catholics holy ; but Faber was writing sadly to a Catholic friend : 'We have all been too *cocky*. . . . We have gone on as if the game was in our hands.' The public attack, though he met its emergencies bravely, was a shock and discouragement to him. He had a series of violent sick headaches, from one of which he was instantaneously cured by a relic of St. Mary Magdalene Pazzi, at whose tomb the children of some friends were praying for him. The London Oratorians were one of the principal targets of abuse. They were cursed as they went about in their habits, 'even *gentlemen* shout from their carriage windows at us', Faber told a friend. The streets were full of placards exhorting London to 'Beware of the Oratorians!' Faber's favourite, which he felt revealed the real feelings of the mob, announced in Leicester Square : 'No Popery! Down with the Oratorians! No religion at all!' At the very beginning of the row there were threats that the Oratory would be burned down on Guy Fawkes Day, and police were called in. Afterwards Faber reported that all were safe and sound 'having only been carried (*in effigie*) as Guys and been duly burned — crackers were thrown on ye roof of ye chapel, and ye like. We gave our policemen supper.'

Soon after, he was feeling anxious and Newman wrote in his most mettlesome style, 'You must not be cast down, for the battle is just beginning'. Faber must expect to have spies at his sermons. 'Don't be saddened. . . . Could you sell my sermon at your door ? or is it against the rule ?' He was saying mass for them, had started a *novena* for the hierarchy and was all ready to use St. Wilfrid's as a refuge if a proposed Bill became law, which was to prohibit priests living together. For the Redemptorists had after all refused St. Wilfrid's and it was on their hands again. (It was eventually taken by the Passionists.) Newman was ready for anything and thought the behaviour of English mobs more funny than dangerous. Caswall's brother 'was followed by the rabble the other day in London, having on a long cloke, which they took for an Oratorian. He faced round, pulled aside the cloke and showed his trousers — when they saw him all sound below, they gave a cheer and left him.'

Birmingham was not without its excitements. 'Some furious Protestants threatened to tear our gowns off us in the street', Newman told Badeley. There were some Poles who claimed to have been priests (though it turned out they were impostors) who were 'going about describing horrors and saying they doubt not our hands are red with blood'. This was no joke, for cheap books of the *Maria Monk* variety had convinced people that priests were always perpetrating secret murders — their own illegitimate babies were the favourite victims, but monks were also credited with torturing each other to death, and Oratorians were all monks in the popular view. At the height of the public fury, on November 12th, Father John

Cooke suddenly died. He was an 'old' Catholic, a young priest who
had put on the habit last year ; he had been ill with consumption a
long time, but his death was unexpected. His body lay in the chapel
before the altar ; hostile townspeople suspected foul play and a mob
surrounded the Oratory. The police had to be sent for again. 'The
people are making a great row under my window, while Father
Joseph is preaching', Newman wrote calmly to Faber.

They had the Blessed Sacrament exposed in the chapel and special
prayers ; Newman was singing the High Mass of Exposition when
the grand Protestant meeting was held in the Town Hall. It was a
flop for the fanatics, owing to the firm stand taken by the Quaker
Joseph Sturge and the Baptist and Radical leaders, who checked the
violence of the mob. They turned the tide so effectively that the
Oratorians, to their surprise, found themselves saluted in the streets
with 'Hurrah for the Catholics !' After that there was no more
violence, though Newman remained the target for many a rumour.
One amused him very much, no doubt the result of the publicity that
attended Pierce Connelly's campaign for the restitution of conjugal
rights. He told Faber, 'The report grows stronger and stronger here,
that I am married, and have shut up my wife in a convent'.

The publication of his sermon drew on Newman a number of
private and personal attacks, as well as the scorn of *The Times*. There
was one John Allen, who felt it a duty to write Newman private
protests at his behaviour, all through his life. He sent one now about
idolatry ; Newman replied politely, 'I cannot conceive you wish me
to argue with you'. Allen immediately protested again. Newman
said, 'Do you not think, forgive me for saying it, you have sent me
enough protests ?'

Some of the attacks came from people Newman had known. A
big meeting was held at Reading, at which the younger John Walter,
who, after the *Catholicus* letters, had given Newman a picture of the
Virgin, made an angry speech, referring to Newman by name, and
saying that the converts ought to be kicked out of the country.
Newman wrote to him : 'Once upon a time a young man made his
Senior a present in token of his esteem for him. It was a Madonna,
and that Senior put her over his bed head and whenever any one
spoke of it, he used to say "John Walter gave me that picture" and
he never said so without thinking kindly of him. And so the years
passed and changes came with them, and at length there was a day
when the young man made a speech before a whole county ; and
after speaking by name of that elderly man, of whom he had once

felt esteem, he said that he wished that all who were such as that elderly man was, were kicked out of the kingdom. What then could that elderly man do, before he was kicked out, but send back to that young man, who once had an innocent conscience and a gentle heart, that same sweet Madonna, to plead with the dear Child whom she holds in her arms for him, and with her gentle look and calm eyes to soften him towards that elderly man to whom he once gave it, and who had kept it so safely.' Walter was touched, and perhaps ashamed of his outburst, for he wrote back with respect and affection.

During all this time of excitement Newman had been dealing with Coffin's case. In December, when he had gone, he wrote to Faber, sadly, 'He has done a bad thing under bad feelings, in a bad manner, and it is this which frightens me about his future'. To Dalgairns he said : 'If Coffin declares we are not Saints, there's no denying it ; we can but try to be. Meanwhile, neither God, nor our Lady, nor St. Philip despises his own little ones — and others may as well not despise them either.'

Recent events, internal and external, drew them closer together and to the Rule. Faber wrote saying they had decided to introduce the exercise of the community discipline. Newman thought it 'a fit offering on your part for Coffin's defection'. He added, '*We* have been thinking of it lately — one difficulty is a room — but I trust we shall overcome it, nearly as soon as you'. He said he was glad Faber had changed his mind about the exercise. Faber had totally forgotten his opposition ; all he could remember was some odd scheme of Newman's for all to take the discipline at the same time in their rooms. Newman sent him his own memorandum and reminded him that this plan had merely been his last (unsuccessful) attempt to overcome Faber's objections. This incident shows the way Faber's memory worked and how unreliable it was ; also how his views changed without his being aware of it.

Faber wrote his usual graphic account of the first evening's discipline in London, making it sound like a comic turn. 'The sound was horrid, like hailstones on flesh', he said, and described how they laughed afterwards when they discovered that the dim light on the crucifix had been achieved by putting a bull's-eye lantern on top of a hatbox, on top of a chair, on the altar. 'The length made it very severe, more severe than some of us reckoned for', he commented on the exercise, which lasted for the time it took to recite the Latin Passion, the Miserere and some Psalms. Faber was now so enthusiastic for this form of penance that he wanted to imitate St.

Philip in introducing it to the Brothers of the Little Oratory, lay associates. He was amused when their wives got wind of it and began to imagine all sorts of fatalities. Newman wrote, 'Are you not afraid of this getting into *Punch*, with a picture of Father Faber in the act?' However, next April, Faber was able to write triumphantly, 'You prophesied *we Londoners* should be there *cum disciplina*, instead of which it is *you*'. *Punch* no doubt merely thought it a suitable joke against the monkish Newman, but in fact the Birmingham House had also started the exercise, and from then onwards it was kept up, three times a week after the evening Oratory, according to the tradition of St. Philip. About this time Newman was writing to George Ryder about mortifications : 'I will tell you what is the greatest — viz to do well the duties of the day. Determine to rise at a certain hour — to go through certain devotions. . . . Don't oppress yourself with them but *keep* to your rules and you will find it a sufficient trial.' There is room in a Christian's life for both mental and physical discipline ; the second is often despised because the first is more important, but who gives up walking because thinking is a higher activity?

Faber was upset because in the House of Commons a member called Drummond had said, 'That fellow Faber goes about the country seducing young women'. As this slander was not in the papers and had been left out of Hansard, Newman advised him to take no notice. He noticed it himself in his 1851 lectures, defending a nameless friend 'for whose purity and honour I would die' from the charge. They were watched eagerly for scandals, but those that got into the papers turned out to be fakes ; the Catholic community emerged very creditably from the ordeal. But such watching naturally made some people over-anxious about scandals. Knox wrote to Newman for advice about a convert lady, who had tried her vocation in a convent and came to him with complaints of the behaviour of the chaplains there. Newman read her accusations and made some shrewd comments. He guessed that she was on the verge of mental derangement and so it proved. She saw sinister intentions in what were merely unfamiliar manners and imagined that every priest she met was making advances to her. They managed to elude her and her like ; even *Punch* could find nothing to do but mock at their cassocks and hats.

Coffin was hardly gone when Penny followed. He had met a Capuchin, thought he would like to be one himself, and came out with the usual objections on the laxity of the Oratory. Newman told him he had always had doubts of his Oratorian vocation, even in Rome, 'and ever since that time you have deepened that confusion by (I am obliged to say it) systematically and habitually ignoring, or ridiculing, or violating our Rule, as I have before now intimated to you'. After a general Congregation he declared their considered view, 'We know perfectly how bent you are on serving God, but there are many ways of serving him and yours is not the Oratorian way'. It proved not to be the Capuchin way either ; Penny never tried his vocation with them but became a secular priest in the Birmingham diocese. He remained on good terms with his old companions, and the month after he left, February 1851, Newman was remarking that he was to dine with them 'and we have some good plum cake for him'. It was undoubtedly better that he should go, but his going removes a certain not unpleasing dottiness from the annals of the Oratory.

In December, Newman suddenly realized that the continual grousing about his 'coldness' was not always his own fault. Alban Wells visited Birmingham. He had heard that a new convert wanted a spiritual director to go abroad with him, to Madeira where he was ordered for his health ; he would pay all expenses. Wells was also supposed to go abroad, but he was only twenty-five and not suitable for the job ; moreover, he was quite well off. Newman wrote to Faber : 'I find Alban thought me "wretchedly cold". *I knew he would.*' (Twice underlined.) 'It is the way with some of you. *So I went out of my way* to be kind to him. I ran about the house for him and talked to him till I had a chance of having no time to read Pius VI's life for my lecture — and, as it was, I lost the Oratory for him. Next time I shall take it easy and he will say how delightful I am. The truth is, he was *disappointed* I would not consent to B's paying his expenses.'

About this time, the turn of the year, Newman kept hearing reports that he was going to be made a Bishop — the difficulty of finding suitable men for the new hierarchy was pressing. He was alarmed at the prospect, and when the possibility was mentioned in *The Tablet* he wrote to Talbot to get him to see that it did not happen. Talbot was now a Papal Chamberlain and had great influence in Rome. 'My *line* is different, it is to oppose the infidels of the day', Newman wrote anxiously. 'They are *just* beginning to attend to me. A fearful battle is coming on and my place seems to be in it. Make me a bishop and I am involved in canon law, rubrics and the working of a diocese, about which I know nothing.' The scare passed off and he breathed again.

'Birmingham has resisted the No Popery agitation', he told Mrs. Bowden in March — she was abroad with her delicate family. The government had just been defeated. 'Lord John has struck his foot against a rock and has fallen. A sunken rock, for they did not believe so insignificant a thing as British Catholicism would harm them — but it has shivered them — and as *The Times* truly but blindly says, they have gone down in a smooth sea and under a smiling heaven.' In the same letter he said, 'Our house is rising at Edgbaston. We have been able to build all through the winter. It is quite frightful, the space of ground it covers.'

1851

The Eye of the Beholder

NEWMAN'S personal fame was such that a certain Reverend Mr. Coxe of Grace Church, Baltimore, knew that readers in America would eagerly fall on several columns of print about him. On his travels in darkest England Mr. Coxe bravely ventured into the unknown territory of Deritend in search of his prey. He found what he called a low and dirty-looking chapel with a leather curtain in the doorway like a foreign church. Boldly pushing his way in he was brought up short by the sight of 'an immense doll of ludicrous aspect' — a statue of the Virgin. This was the idol the two Methodists had reproached Newman for worshipping. Mr. Coxe would have been surprised had he known Newman had a 'perfect hatred' of this statue, and contrived to leave it behind when he moved to Edgbaston. 'Before this image several youths with broad tonsures and in long cassocks were kneeling in a manner truly histrionic', said Mr. Coxe, relating his adventures among the aborigines in detail. One of the young Oratorians showed him the Library, in which he saw more baize than books ; the staircase was dark and narrow. But they told him when Newman was next preaching and, nothing daunted, he went back on the first Sunday after Easter, in the evening.

'The room was well lighted and filled with the sort of people usually frequenting Romish chapels in this country', he observed with conscious superiority. 'A few well-dressed persons seemed to be strangers, and like myself were treated with great civility.' Now the altar excited his disgust, 'looking more like the shelves of a conservatory than the table of the Lord. Above this horticultural display towered a thing of wax and spangles and glass, or what seemed to be such, as the apparent divinity of the shrine. It was a shameful burlesque of the Virgin . . . surrounded with tawdry finery, and looked like the idol of a pagoda.' Mr. Coxe had no more idea of the thoughts and feelings of the people round him than if he had indeed been in a Chinese temple. And now, to his embarrassment, everyone began to sing a hymn, just like Methodists. But at last he saw what he had come to see.

'While the singing was going on a lank and spectral figure appeared at the door of the chancel — stalked in and prostrated himself before the altar. This was followed by a succession of elevations and prostrations awkward in the extreme and both violent and excessive, but whether required by the rubric or dictated by personal fervour only, they added nothing to the solemnity of the scene. Meanwhile the hymn was continued by the disciples as fanatically as the pantomime was performed by the Master.' Mr. Coxe was one of those who first call ritual play-acting and then complain that priests are not good actors. 'Could this be the man ? Could this be he who once stood in the first pulpit of Christendom and from his watch tower in St. Mary's told us what of the night ? Was this the burning and shining light who for a season allowed us to rejoice in his light ? What an eclipse ! I felt a chill creep over me as he mounted his rostrum, and turned towards us his almost maniacal visage. There could be no mistake. It was indeed poor fallen Newman.'

Newman's lined face had suggested craft to young Benson three years ago, and now mad fanaticism to this transatlantic visitor. Mr. Coxe went on to describe the sermon, apparently unaware that he was contradicting his own picture of the religious maniac. 'He crossed himself, unfolded a bit of broad ribbon' (stole) 'kissed it, put it over his shoulders, opened his little Bible and gave his text from the Vulgate — Surrexit enim, sicut dixit — "He is risen, *as He said*". The preaching was extemporaneous ; the manner not fluent ; the matter not well arranged ; gesticulations not violent nor immoderate ; the tone affectedly earnest' — why affectedly, unless Mr. Coxe could not imagine anyone believing what did not approve itself to him ? — 'and the whole thing from first to last painfully suggestive of a sham ; of something not heartily believed ; of something felt to be unreal by the speaker himself. And yet', he concluded, with happy inconsistency, '"the hand of Joab was in it". There was no denying the craft of no common artist.' Like Kingsley afterwards, he wanted Newman to be both a fool and a knave, deluded and yet a wily deceiver, a sceptic putting on a show to catch the credulous. It did not occur to Mr. Coxe to wonder why, in that case, he should ever have left the splendid stage of Oxford for a gin-shop chapel in Deritend.

Not all the well-dressed persons were strangers. Last year, when Miss Giberne was casting about for an occupation, Newman told her that they thought of taking a house where some feminine helpers might live, 'not nuns, but nunnish ladies', who would assist with the girls and women of the parish. Mrs. Wootten would be there, and Lady Olivia Acheson, another convert, and others. Miss Giberne was so keen to be a nunnish lady that Newman's next letter was full of warnings and doubts; St. John scribbled on it, 'Come and do not mind the Padre's caution. Birmingham is a very Protestant place. We have the hardest town in England to work.' She did come. Six nunnish ladies were living in the house by May 1851, who would have been surprised and shocked had they known Newman's visage appeared maniacal to anyone. On May 27th they wrote him a little note: 'We the undersigned in all humility entreat our kind and indulgent father not to deprive our thirsty souls of the conclusion of his most attractive sermon, the comparison of the saints of different nations, but to continue it for our instruction, from where the bell interrupted it viz The Seraphic St. Francis'. Newman made his reply in the form of comments written alongside their signatures.

'*Olivia Acheson* — if she will contrive to hear me sitting at home in her easy chair.

'*Elinor French* — as soon as she can go through the saints of the names of Colman, Finian, Kieran, Kentigern and Kebby.

'*C. A. Bathurst* — when her school can show a saint younger than St. Rose and wiser than St. Theresa.

'*M. Georgina St. John* — must learn first to chirp, and must have a little down on her wings.

'*Elizabeth Moore* — when she has made and illuminated vestments of the Spanish, Italian, cockney and every other cut.

'*M. R. Giberne* — if she will be good enough to canonize half a dozen on occasion and give me their measure.   JHN'

Lady Olivia should have been sitting at home in her easy chair because she was not well; before this time next year she was dead, after a long illness. She left a bequest to Newman for the Oratory. It was she who enlightened Newman that what he had always thought was knit wool, was only knit cotton. He always spoke of her with respect and affection, even admiration.

This summer another visitor recorded an impression of Newman, Cecil, Marchioness of Lothian, a widow who came into the Church with Manning and others after the Gorham judgment. She had great difficulty with the guardians of her children. Her eldest son, already at Oxford, did not go with her, but the girls were allowed to become Catholics. The two younger boys outwitted the tutor set to watch them and ran off in the small hours of the night with their mother, to be received. The youngest, Lord John Kerr, wanted to be a priest and was sent to Ushaw, but it was difficult to know what to do with Lord Ralph, who was sixteen, and no intellectual, but a good straightforward boy. He was later to go into the army. Lady Lothian called at the Oratory to consult Newman, and as a result Lord Ralph joined Lisle Ryder, boarding with the Fathers as a pupil. Lady Lothian had never met Newman before. 'I was nervous,' she wrote at the time, 'but without cause, for he is so full of sympathy and Christian love that he is the last person one need be afraid of. That which struck me most was his childlike sympathy and humility, and next to that, the vivid clearness with which he gives an opinion. He is a very striking looking person. His saying of Mass is most striking. I do not know what makes the difference, but one is conscious of a difference. It appeared to me very unearthly.'

1851

Braving the Devil: Attacking Achilli

IT was inexplicable to the majority of Englishmen that conversions still continued. At the beginning of April 1851 Newman was summoned to Leeds to receive nearly all the clergy of Pusey's memorial church of St. Saviour's. Hook, the fiery Vicar of Leeds, who had thought Newman's moral stamina failed under the attacks on Tract 90, was enraged, and poor Pusey's reputation took a further plunge. The St. Saviour's clergy were Oxford men, living together and working in the slums, on Pusey's principle of priestly 'colleges'. Other Oxford men had frequently stayed with them and shared their work and routine. Newman hoped that this body of converts might form another Oratory, perhaps in Leeds itself, but in the end they all separated. Only one joined Newman, an anxious, vague young man called William Paine Neville. He was to spend the rest of his life in the Birmingham Oratory, acting as Newman's secretary and infirmarian in his old age.

At this time, although those outside the Church saw Newman as a representative figure of Catholicism, those within, especially in England, were still somewhat suspicious of him. When he came back from Leeds, he wrote to comfort Allies, who was suffering the usual trials of the married clerical converts. Newman reminded him 'but those who are unmarried have their own. They are solitary and thrown among strangers more intimately and intensely than married people can be. You have a home. We have not had one. The very object aimed at has been first, to separate us from each other, secondly to bring us individually under discipline, thirdly to mortify us. I believe all this *in substance* is right, but it may be trying when it is right and it may be done untenderly and rudely when the substance is good. We have been (necessarily) treated as children, being grown men. This is not a trial to one's pride in the common sense of the word, but it is to one's desire of sympathy and to those habits of refinement and good breeding and mutual consideration which

University life more or less creates.' This had been the atmosphere during his first years among Catholics, but now something was to happen which made them identify themselves with him in a way they had not done before and were not to do again so entirely till he was a Cardinal. The event which effected this transformation of feeling was his trial for libel on the renegade priest Achilli.

The Achilli trial has seemed to some such an incongruous event in Newman's life that they have passed it over as a tiresome interruption of more important things. It was certainly that, but to him it had a deeper significance. He believed from the beginning that in attacking Achilli he was 'braving the Devil' and what followed, though he could not foresee its details, did not surprise him. In another way the affair was important in marking the climax of the first half of his public life, as the focus of the feelings aroused by the Catholic revival. As, in the Church of England, he had been the centre of attack for those who hated what they felt he stood for, so now, and much more since his open identification with the Popery of the international and supernational Catholic Church, he became the symbol of all that the great mass of his countrymen feared and hated and despised, and wished to crush and cast out. As an Anglican he had roused the opposition of the educated and powerful, but as a Catholic at this critical moment of popular fury it was a more general and primitive reaction he had to face. Not that the trial did not affect his reputation with the upper classes ; it did, and in a very typical way. It was considered a dreadful social disgrace. The whole episode was thought so shockingly vulgar that it was scarcely ever mentioned later on, and any allusions in Victorian biographies so veiled as to be almost unintelligible. After this, when he reached the lowest depth of ignominy in the opinion of the world, a quite different attitude began to form, which was to be, to Newman himself, a more subtle and searching trial.

The Achilli drama began with Newman's lectures in the Birmingham Corn Exchange on *The Present Position of Catholics in England*, and these were given with the object of making people see the absurdity of their gross suspicions of Catholics, and the injustice of their consequent treatment of them. Newman always believed in the personal and immediate approach ; people can get very fierce when they do not know personally those whom they are attacking. In trying to open their eyes he used his favourite weapon of laughter, and took his examples from local incidents. Typical of the more silly and less dangerous of these was the fuss caused by the house he

was building in Edgbaston. It was designed by a cousin of John
(Stanislas) Flanagan, the only Irish member of the Oratory. 'Mr.
Flanagan is a most capital architect,' Newman was writing in May
'— everyone is admiring the strength of our building, which they
say will last for ever (we are using 1,700,000 bricks) but I don't
suppose he has much taste.'   Some people have unkindly seen
interior resemblances to the railway station in Ireland which Flanagan
also designed, perhaps because the rooms are very high, in mid-
Victorian style, and everything very plain.   Outside, the house (the
same that now stands fronting the roar of the Hagley Road traffic)
presented a pleasant face in the classic domestic style with tall sash
windows and a large Georgian front door.   There was nothing in the
least Gothic or monastic about it, but it aroused fearful suspicions
in Birmingham, which suddenly spread to the national press when
Mr. Spooner, M.P., denounced in the House the 'underground cells'
incorporated in the foundations.   Dungeons for recalcitrant monks
were actually being constructed in Birmingham!

Newman found it difficult to take this view of his cellars seriously,
but as others did, he was forced to notice it.   In those days a public
attack was often answered by publishing a supposedly private correspondence between the principals in a newspaper.   Sometimes it was
conducted through an intermediary, no doubt a relic of the not so
distant days when gentlemen crossed swords rather than words.
Newman's 'second' this time was Henry Wilberforce (though he only
appeared as Mr. —— —— in print) because Mr. Spooner happened
to be his maternal uncle.   Newman informed Mr. Spooner, through
Henry, that the 'cells' were intended for larders, coal-holes and
possibly for brewing beer.   Perhaps the last intention had better
have been left out, for to some the thought of 'monks' brewing beer
was almost as shocking as the fantasy of their walling up each other
(or some unfortunate female) in underground dungeons ; indeed,
one depravity might lead to the other.   One newspaper headed the
correspondence, 'The Apostate Newman's defence of Underground
Cells in Convents'.   Mr. Spooner was not put off by subtleties about
beer and coal ; he produced an even more ludicrous charge — that
the Fathers were disguising themselves as workmen, the better to
achieve their nefarious purposes.   Newman denied this too ; but
some still preferred the evidence of their own imaginations.

It was this sort of prejudice, whose manifestations were often
dangerous, that Newman hoped to drive out with laughter in his
lectures.   He did not set out to defend Catholicism or attack Pro-

testantism, but to destroy an evil fantasy which had only an accidental connexion with either and did harm both to the victims and to the aggressors. As usual he was writing up to the last moment at high pressure, though this time with more ease, and he was afraid his satire might miss fire with his provincial audience. 'I am fidgetted', he wrote to Dalgairns. 'I fear these Brummagems will take my first lecture as serious — and then to make up for it, all my others, which (alas) are getting prosy, for irony.'

On the day of the first lecture, June 30th, he developed a 'hoarseness' — this often happened at moments of crisis. But all was well : the Brummagems laughed. Indeed, they laughed so loud that Miss Giberne heard them in the street outside, where she prowled frustrated, for ladies were not admitted. Like most public lectures of the time, they were delivered to an audience of men. They were to continue every Monday till September. Among the listeners was Manning, who had submitted to Rome at Easter, leaving behind his friend Gladstone. Wiseman had already raised Manning to the priesthood ; he was to do his studies in Rome as a priest. Conservative Catholics were shocked by this rapid transformation, partly due to Wiseman's enthusiasm, partly to Manning's forceful personality. As an Anglican, Henry Wilberforce had complained that, though he was exactly the same age as his brother-in-law, people were always hushing him to give way to the Archdeacon. Henry's bubbling humour made him seem youthful beside Manning's serious intensity. Manning did not demand attention, he simply claimed it by his authoritative manner.

Newman concluded the first lecture with a set-piece in which he ridiculed the No-Popery campaign by reading a supposed newspaper report of a great meeting in Russia against 'John Bullism' —Russia being sufficiently unknown to serve as a suitable Cloud-cuckoo-land. The chief speaker was a Count who knew nothing of England, having spent the last thirty years in the wars of the Caucasus, where he 'had acquired the title of Bloodsucker'. The Count attacked the wickedness and blasphemy of the British constitution with all the fire and unction of a No-Popery orator from Exeter Hall, using Blackstone as his source-book. 'I open the book, gentlemen, and what are the first words that meet my eyes ? *The King can do no wrong*. . . . This British Bible, as I may call it, distinctly ascribes an absolute sinlessness to the King of Great Britain and Ireland.' When he spoke of the effrontery of imputing ABSOLUTE PERFECTION to 'their crowned and sceptred idol, to their doll, this puppet they have dressed up with a lion and a unicorn' there was an interruption from a Scottish resident : 'You cowardly liar, our dear good little Queen!' He was thrown out and the Count went on from strength to strength, piling up his nonsensical evidences. 'Alexander Pope too, calls Queen Anne, a goddess ; and Addison, with a servility only equalled by its profaneness, cries out "thee goddess, thee Britannia's isle adores". Nay, even at this very time, when public attention has been drawn to the subject, Queen Victoria causes herself to be represented on her coins as the goddess of the seas, with a pagan trident in her hand.' Triumphantly he proved Queen Victoria to be marked with the number of the Beast. 'Now she came to the throne in the year thirty-seven at which date she was eighteen years old. Multiply thirty-seven by eighteen and you have the very number 666 which is the mystical emblem of the lawless King ! ! !' Did Queen Victoria ever hear of this naughty tease by Dr. Newman ?

The Count worked himself into a frenzy of peroration. 'If, as I believe, you are resolved to resist unflinchingly the flood of satanical nonsense and foul ambition . . . if, not from hatred of the English — far from it — from *love* to them (for a distinction must ever be drawn between the nation and its dominant John Bullism) ; if, I say, from love of them as brothers, from a generous determination to fight their battles, from an intimate consciousness that they are in their hearts *Russians*, that they are champing the bit of their iron lot, and are longing for you as their deliverers . . . you will form a high resolve to annihilate this dishonesty of humanity ; if you loathe its sophisms. . . . "Possession is nine parts of the law" and "the greater the truth the greater the libel" — principles which sap the very foundations of morals ; if you wage war to the knife with its blighting superstitions of primogeniture, gavelkind, mortmain and contingent remainders ; if you detest, abhor and abjure the tortuous maxims and perfidious provisions of its *habeas corpus*, *quare impedit* and *qui tam* (hear, hear) ; if you scorn the mummeries of its wigs and bands and coifs and ermine (vehement cheering) ; if you trample and spit upon its accursed fee simple and fee tail, villanage and free soccage, fiefs, heriots, seizins, feuds (a burst of cheers, the whole meeting in commotion) ; its shares, its premiums, its post obits, its percentages, its tariffs, its broad and narrow gauge — here the cheers became frantic and drowned the speaker's voice and a most extraordinary scene of enthusiasm followed, one half of the meeting embracing the other half ; till, as if by the force of a sudden resolution they all poured out into the square, and proceeded to break the windows of the

British residents. They then formed into a procession and directing their course to the great square before the Kremlin, they dragged through the mud and then solemnly burnt, the effigy of John Bull, which had been provided beforehand by the managing committee, a lion and unicorn and a Queen Victoria. These being fully consumed they dispersed quietly ; and by ten o'clock at night the streets were profoundly still ; and the silver moon looked down in untroubled lustre on the city of the Czars.'

The rest of the lectures were not, as Newman had feared, prosy ; but for all the fun he contrived to expose not only the popular fables of the time but the whole psychological map of the tradition which gave rise to them. Newman had one great advantage in the battle : people listened to him. Even the fanatically hostile noticed what he said. He used his fame. He hired the Corn Exchange, he printed each lecture and had it sold at the door, and collected them in a volume which was brought out without delay so as to reach the wider audience of the whole country. Individual Catholics sometimes protested in the county and town meetings, but no one had the power to command attention which Newman had, or the freedom to make it felt, for bishops and noble lords naturally had to express themselves and their loyalty more solemnly and gravely. Though indeed it is hard to imagine anyone but Newman in that year of crisis choosing to attack, rather than defend, and to attack with such vigour and irony just what fed the fires of self-righteous anger.

One of his objects was to try to shame people out of the fantastic beliefs about Catholicism which made them ill treat actual Catholics, to stop the stone throwing, the spying at convents, the jeers and the threats, by showing up the ignorance, the hearsay and the lying tradition on which they were based. This was why he chose contemporary and local examples, and he did not take them at random but as representing several recurring lines of Protestant attack. In each case he touched a vital spot, for furious controversies instantly broke out both in the Birmingham and the national newspapers.

One of the things generally believed was that nearly all Catholic priests were sceptics at heart ; Newman drew the portrait of the real one he had known, Blanco White, and used his evidence against the legend. A clergyman had affirmed that one in twelve Catholic priests in Birmingham was an infidel ; Newman had not met any. People were shocked by his retort : 'What if a Catholic who knew nothing of the establishment said in print he believed that one in twelve of Protestant clergymen was an adulterer ?' He never could make them

realize that sins of the mind were as bad as sins of the flesh, and tha
to call a priest an infidel was worse than to call him a seducer. H
complained that priests were not treated as men but as griffins an
wiverns, fabulous monsters without feelings, so that people wer
actually surprised that they resented being called liars and hypocrites

Of course this was a favourite charge against Newman himsel
Faber's uncle Stanley, who had been brought to retract his statemen
that Newman was a conscious Romanist while he was Vicar of St
Mary's, now chose to retract his retractation. Frank Faber, throug
whom their subsequent correspondence was conducted, complaine
at Newman for using hard words. 'I have called him "generous" —
he has called me a *liar*', Newman retorted. 'God will to a certainty
judge between us.' The public would take Stanley Faber's side
because, as Newman scornfully said, 'A Romish priest always lie
for the good of the Church — I am a Romish priest — therefore thi
need not be true'. This popular syllogism defeated his every attemp
to defend his own honesty and that of Catholic priests in England
He had let such calumnies pass when he was a private person i
Oxford, but he could not do so in Birmingham, where he was no
personally known, but was identified with the Oratory and th
Catholic priests of the diocese. All the same, when a clergyman calle
Minton asserted in *Aris's Gazette*, a Birmingham paper, that 'th
whole of Newman's life was one unmitigated lie' he simply wrote t
say he was burning all communications from Minton unread.

That priests in general and Newman in particular were sceptic
and liars was regarded as an established fact ; nevertheless they wer
also weak, credulous creatures who believed in miracles. In thes
lectures Newman once more affirmed that miracles were possibl
and that some had occurred. 'Melancholy Case of Mental Aberration', announced the newspapers, and another controversy ensued
When the lectures appeared as a book the reviewer in the *Record* fel
on the defence of miracles, not answering Newman, but discrediting
him. The late Bishop Copleston was quoted as saying he was not
even a good classical scholar ; it was not thought necessary to notic
that Copleston had been attacking examinations, instancing Newma
as an example of a man of intellectual worth who might have been
passed over in the Oriel election had they been so narrow-minded a
to go by mere tests. Having disposed of Newman's past intellectua
attainments, the *Record* went on to demolish the present. 'If he
writes with even more than his usual vigour and felicity, it is because
he has got rid of the restraints that fetter a merely fallible writer and

has become intellectually reckless. He has thrown off the burden of
his responsibility at the feet of infallibility and goes on, gay, careless
and indifferent, so long as his writings are sanctioned by his self-
chosen superiors.'

This was the attitude of the educated, but what did the mob care
if Catholics were credulous and their priests liars ? They were
credulous themselves and 'not over scrupulous of truth'. What
moved them to stone priests and break into convents and burn
effigies of the Pope was a more simple and horrible wickedness of
which they believed them guilty : secret tortures and murders and
profligacy among the professedly celibate. The chief source of this
legend was the book of Maria Monk, which had just gone into a huge
second edition, a cheap and exciting form of spiritual reading. Newman, early in the lectures, told what he had been able to find out of
her true history. She was an illiterate and mentally deficient Canadian
girl, who had been a servant in a convent and later had been put in a
reformatory ; she had confused her experiences into a lurid fantasy
of criminal nuns who murdered their illegitimate babies, and occasionally each other — Newman noticed the story of a pretty novice
who refused the sinful commands of the priests and was squashed
to death under a table at a bishop's orders, the callous nuns laughing
as they bounced up and down on it. This was the sort of atrocity
story that led to No Popery riots, and no wonder.

Maria Monk's book had been written for her by others, and the
cleverness of it lay, as Newman pointed out, in the accuracy of the
descriptions of ordinary Catholic rites and practices. Any reader
who dropped in at the chapel at Alcester Street and saw the mass
going on would recognize it from the book, and would conclude that
Maria was equally reliable in describing the private habits of the
celebrating priests. Later in the lectures, illustrating the fact that
people see what they expect to see, Newman read an account by a
Scripture Reader who had gone to Benediction at the London Oratory
and written a pamphlet about it. He had no idea what was going on,
but was quite sure he knew all there was to know. He was not
suspecting murder and fornication, but idolatry, and of course he
saw it. He saw a horde of priests, boys and men ('he thinks we are
born priests' Newman observed) lighting candles and lifting up a
metal Star to be worshipped by the people. Not observing the boy
with the bell, who rang it at the elevation of the monstrance with the
Host, the Scripture reader thought the priest was secretly waggling
a bell concealed in the foot of the Star, to delude the people that it

rang of itself. Apart from the bell his description was accurate enough, and anyone who had read his pamphlet and then went along to a Catholic chapel, would have seen the astonishing vision of nine-teenth-century English people bowing down before a metal star, and ex-Oxford dons acting the conjurer before them.

Newman made fun of such nonsense, but he knew it could be dangerous. It was Maria Monk who convinced people that murders and tortures went on in monasteries; she was behind the interest taken in Newman's cellars, she created the atmosphere in which individual accusers were so readily believed. The extent of the book's influence is shown by the fact that its defence was immedi-ately and furiously taken up by clergymen and others in the news-papers. Father Joseph Gordon took over this tedious controversy for Newman, but his facts about Maria made no impression on his opponents, who could not bear to give her up. Her fantasy had taken so strong a hold of the popular imagination that facts could not loosen it. Newman instanced the recent unmasking of an impostor who had accused the Cistercian monks of imprisoning and ill-treating him; but such evidence was always forgotten whenever a new exponent of the legend appeared with his tales of torture and vice. Such a one was the ex-priest Achilli, who was travelling about the country, sponsored by the Evangelical Alliance, making speeches in all the big towns which invariably inflamed feeling against the Catholics, and led to some very unpleasant incidents. It was to prevent these consequences to his fellow Catholics, helpless as they were, that Newman decided to attack Achilli, not for the mere pleasure of abusing a rascal in public.

A century later Achilli seems as unreal as Maria Monk, but at the time his power to incite the mob was real enough, and he was the more dangerous as his antecedents gave him the confidence of the respectable. After the publicity of the trial they dropped him, but before it he was basking in general approval. He came to England to escape the Pope's tyranny, he said; because he had given up his native idolatry for the light of evangelical Protestantism he had been imprisoned and tortured by the Roman Inquisition and forced to fly from Italy. 'Hail Roman prisoner, Hail!' he was greeted in a hymn of welcome, specially written, at Exeter Hall, the stronghold of the puritans. The powerful Protestant Alliance took him up, gave him a chapel in London on Wiseman's doorstep and a commis-sion to convert poor Italians of the district, and sponsored his appearance on platforms all over the country. His book *Dealings with the Inquisition* was sold everywhere. Achilli was not yet fifty, a vigorous and clever man. He had been a Dominican, and entrusted with offices of practical and intellectual importance in his Order, and after leaving it, had held other positions as a secular priest. It was natural that Protestants should believe what he said about his ex-colleagues. They thought Catholic priests and bishops cruel tyrants : Achilli's tale proved it. They believed celibacy unnatural and that it led to vicious behaviour : this was one of Achilli's chief charges against the Italian priesthood. He showed his good sense, Protestants thought, in marrying a smart and pretty young woman now that he was in a free country.

Achilli was dangerous just because he seemed respectable, a persecuted hero, an unctuous preacher, a married man. But Newman had read an article in the *Dublin Review* which gave the real facts of his career. He had indeed come up before the Inquisition in Rome, not for heresy but for persistent misconduct. This was why he had had to leave the Dominican order. He had been brought to the courts for offences, chiefly the seduction of virgins. His sentence from the Holy Office, of detention in a monastery, was the reason for his flight from Italy. His Protestant ideas were picked up on his travels, and enabled him to live by opening chapels and preaching to gullible Protestants resident in the Mediterranean islands. Eventually he was appointed to the staff of a newly founded Protestant college in Malta, of which Lord Ashley, soon to become Earl of Shaftesbury, was the chairman. Achilli left and the college closed rather suddenly, but nothing was heard about it in England, where Achilli repaired, ready for new conquests.

It was clear from all this that Achilli was the last man to be trusted to give true evidence about the lives of his ex-colleagues. Newman planned his attack to demonstrate this untrustworthiness, not to blacken his character. Unfortunately, where sexual offences are concerned, the attention of the public is fixed entirely on them. Thus most people thought Newman was trying to prove Achilli a seducer of virgins, when his real intention was to show him a liar whose word, whose solemn oath, was of no value. Newman's unworldliness put him at a disadvantage. He was continually surprised at the barefaced lying that went on against him, and at the way respectable and educated people were shocked and disgusted, not by Achilli's false witness, but by Newman's vulgarity and coarseness in accusing him publicly of improper, not to say unmentionable behaviour.

For he did not mince matters, but delivered a catalogue of Achilli's offences, with dates, to the audience in the Corn Exchange ; printed it and sold it at the door and included it in the first edition of the lectures, with his own name on the title-page. He introduced Achilli after a passage in which he recounted the many recent instances of 'persecution' of Catholics by the very Protestants who accused them of being 'persecutors', ending with what aroused all his chivalrous instincts, the newspaper attacks on nuns which had resulted in stones being thrown at women and schoolgirls. This was the consequence of such platform oratory as Achilli's. 'And it is in the midst of outrages such as these,' Newman said of the crowd with indignation, 'wiping its mouth and clasping its hands and turning up its eyes, it trudges to the Town Hall to hear Dr. Achilli expose the Inquisition. . . . The Protestant world flocks to hear him, because he has something to tell of the Catholic Church. He *has* something to tell, it is true ; he *has* a scandal to reveal, he *has* an argument to exhibit. . . . That one argument is himself ; it is his presence which is the triumph of Protestants ; it is the sight of him which is a Catholic's confusion. . . . "Mothers of families," he seems to say, "gentle maidens, innocent children, look at me, for I am worth looking at. . . . Can any Church live over the imputation of such a birth as I am ? I have been a Catholic and an infidel ; I have been a Roman priest and a hypocrite ; I have been a profligate under a cowl. I am that Father Achilli, who, as early as 1826, was deprived of my faculty to lecture, for an offence which my superiors did their best to conceal. . . . I am that Achilli, who in the diocese of Viterbo in February 1831, robbed of her honour a young woman of eighteen. . . . I am that son of St. Dominic who is known to have repeated the offence . . . at Naples again, in 1840, in the case of a child of fifteen. I am he who chose the sacristy of the church for one of these crimes and Good Friday for another. . . . And now attend to me, such as I am, and you shall see what you shall see about the barbarity and profligacy of the Inquisitors of Rome.' There were some ten offences mentioned, besides Achilli's general reputation for others which had never reached the courts of law.

When the case eventually began Lord Shrewsbury remarked to Ambrose Phillipps ; 'What a mess poor Newman is in ! How could he be so *extremely imprudent* ?' But he was not imprudent. He did what he did with full knowledge and deliberation, and prayer. He was aware that he might be summoned for libel and wrote to several lawyer friends to find out the position before he spoke. He asked Hope : 'Could I be had up for a libel in criminal court for saying

against Dr. Achilli the contents of the article in the *Dublin* since
published as a pamphlet ? I can't make out that he has answered it.'
Hope's opinion that an action was possible, but not probable, did
not satisfy Newman. He wrote to David Lewis of *The Tablet* : 'I
am in a great stew lest what I say of Dr. Achilli be indictable, on
Monday next. (1) Is it a libel to say what has been *proved* in a court
of justice ? (2) is to accuse a man of seduction a libel, he being at the
time not what he is now ? It would be such nuts to have me in court,
but Achilli has not had Dr. Wiseman up. How solemn the *Times*
would be!' David Lewis did not take the risk very seriously ; he
thought Newman safe because he could plead justification, according
to a recent amendment of the libel laws. He remarked, 'It will be a
marvellous evidence of your great deterioration, if you should go
down to posterity as a convicted libeller!' Newman had made his
moral decline a joke among the converts, but it was the simple truth
to English society, as the event showed.

In giving advice Hope, Lewis and others did not reckon on two
things, Newman's power of making everything he said tell, and the
blind hatred his name aroused in those who knew him only as the
most effective exponent of Popery in England, their enemy for twenty
years. For in attacking Achilli Newman was attacking his sponsors,
the Protestant Alliance ; they knew it and he knew it. Alone,
Achilli was a mere rascal, unlikely to challenge the facts of his past.
He had left Wiseman severely alone. But he could not afford to let
down his backers. Nobody except Catholics and a few Puseyites
read the *Dublin Review*, and he had safely ignored it for over a year,
but everyone read Newman, or rather read the newspaper reports
and controversies he provoked. The leaders of the Alliance thought
it a heaven-sent opportunity to bring Newman to the public disgrace
he so richly deserved ; Achilli could hardly do other than deny the
truth of the charges, to them. After all, he was already an accomplished liar and perjurer, and he knew the British public would
swallow anything from a Catholic turned Protestant, and refuse any
evidence from a Protestant turned Catholic, just as Newman was
complaining in his lectures. It was one of the curious facts of the
case that both, in the eyes of the people, were converts; Achilli was not
the nonentity to them which he seems to us and Newman appeared
in the distorted image of the press, the cunning traitor and deceiver.

From the beginning Newman had one of his intuitions of trouble,
and before deciding his course he prayed before the Blessed Sacrament, asking that he might be stopped if it were the wrong thing to

do. But the advice of his London friends suggested that his position was legally secure ; what he was planning to say was the truth, and if Achilli were shown up it would put a stop to the petty persecution of nuns and religious. Also he thought he had his proofs to hand : Wiseman's documents. But he was well aware that in attacking Achilli he was challenging the whole underworld of militant Protestantism — not the intellectual, moral or spiritual side of their religion, but its negative emotional undercurrent of ignorant hatred of everything Catholic, something so dark that he ascribed its inspiration to Satan, the father of lies, the deceiver of men and the Adversary of Christ and his people. It was because he believed the Prince of this world was using Achilli and the prejudices of his backers that he expected the worst, in spite of his friends' reassurances.

Within a few weeks he heard rumours of a prosecution ; but his Anglo-Catholic friend, the lawyer Badeley, did not believe Achilli would act, since in bringing a criminal information he would have to swear on oath to the falsity of each charge. On August 31st Newman wrote : 'I have just heard they are trying to find someone who will swear to my words. This shows they are in earnest.' But Badeley and his London friends continued to think he was fussing unduly. The fuss, such as it was, did not arise from panic but from the desire to have his evidence ready. Far from shrinking from the battle Newman alarmed Badeley by the fighting preface he drafted for the published edition of the lectures. Among other things, he said that in England 'To reject the Saviour of man is a far less political offence than to acknowledge His earthly Vicar'. In deference to Badeley he modified some expressions, but he was amused at his taking fright. 'I see you consider me one of the maddest headstrongest fellows that ever a man of 50 was.'

Newman's silences always made people forget what a fighter he was ; they did not realize he was only silent when he felt he was under censure from an authority he accepted — they thought he had gone into a melancholic dream out of disappointment. It had happened at Littlemore and was to happen again, in a different way. But in a straight fight he leapt up at the first sniff of gunpowder and startled his supporters ; he was still doing it when he was eighty-five. And just now his bishop, Ullathorne, made a public gesture of confidence. He presided over a meeting of Catholics in the Corn Exchange at the conclusion of the lectures when Newman was thanked and received 'an immense acclamation'. He was taken by surprise and quite overcome. He was reported as saying, 'It was a curious thing, though he was now of mature age, and had been very busy in many ways, yet this was the first time in his life he had ever received any praise'.

Thus, identified by both friend and foe with the Catholic cause and attacking the temporary mouthpiece of the Protestant underworld, he let himself in for something more than a trial for libel. It was like the fight of two champions in a ring, with thousands watching, and cheering or hissing the combatants.

1851

'He has let me be bound as in a net'

As usual when there was a public crisis in his affairs, a number of other things contributed to harass Newman. Before the lectures began Archbishop Cullen came over from Ireland to sound him on the project of a Catholic University, and soon after invited him to take a personal part in the work. Newman, anxious that any new duties should not conflict with his primary responsibility for the Oratory, at first suggested that he should merely be Prefect of Studies, but both Cullen and his English friends insisted that he must be Rector. Cullen wanted the prestige of his name to launch his enterprise ; Newman's friends wanted to be sure that he would be in control of the policy of the new institution. Plans and questions were going to and fro while the Protestant Alliance were debating their next move. 'Say a Hail Mary for me now and then, for this miserable Achilli has the power of annoying me', Newman wrote to Ornsby, a convert who was already in Ireland. He was married to Dalgairns' sister, but on his conversion his wife had refused to live with him, and was still alienated from him. He kept Newman informed of the position in Ireland.

At the end of September Newman went there for the first time. He took with him Stuart Bathurst, a new convert and recruit to the Oratory ; his health was very delicate and Newman hoped the change of air would do him good. On October 1st he wrote to Lady Olivia Acheson, 'Tell them at the Oratory that we got here quite safe at eleven this morning. We had a bad passage . . . tell F. Ambrose I have spilt I can't say how much of my precious medicine over the amice and other contents of my portmanteau owing to the stiffness of the leather cover ; making everything very sticky and going the way to take the skin off my hands.' To St. John himself he wrote a few days later, 'I generally am careful about strange houses — but alas slept with my windows open the first night here — which has given me such a cold in my tongue that I can hardly speak a word and seem half drunk when I attempt to make a speech'.

It was not an easy beginning, but things seemed to be going well, and he came back to England full of enthusiasm. From Birmingham he wrote to Mrs. Froude : 'It is a most daring attempt but first it is a religious one and next it has the Pope's blessing on it. Curious it will be if Oxford is imported into Ireland, not in members only but in its principles, methods, ways and arguments. The battle there will be what it was in Oxford twenty years ago. Curious too that there I shall be opposed, the Whigs having Lord Clarendon instead of Lord Melborne — that Whately will be there *in propria persona* — and that while I found my tools breaking under me at Oxford, for Protestantism is not susceptible of so high a temper, I am renewing the struggle in Dublin with the Catholic Church to support me. It is very wonderful.' It was to be still more wonderful how the tools broke again, not this time the tools of faith, but of ecclesiastical and secular policy. At the moment, however, his mind was again possessed with the idea of a University, dedicated to the study of truth, divine and human.

He came back from Ireland to a house of sick and weary members. Bathurst was no better for his trip and was sent off to Scarborough. In the end he was not strong enough to follow his vocation in the Oratory, and had to leave. Joseph Gordon, who had turned out such a 'great gun' was so unwell that he was sent abroad for the winter ; he was to collect the evidence against Achilli in Italy. Nicholas Darnell, who was also in a low state of health was sent with him. Edward Caswall, not yet a priest, was seriously ill at Malvern, and Stanislas Flanagan had to be sent to nurse him. Brother Aloysius, whom Newman thought a saint, was slowly dying of consumption.

The London House was not much better off. Faber had written, full of groans, that the doctor attributed his pains to gout. 'I should be glad your ailments took a tangible shape like gout', Newman observed. Ambrose, though not ill, had gone away — 'run off to Belgium with Mrs. Phillips (whose children were pursued by a wicked giant called Chancery and their cruel uncles) and just now writes me word that he likes Belgium better than six hours a day in the confessional. He is larking away to Paris.' This Mrs. Phillips was the sister of a headmaster of Harrow. On his way back Ambrose stopped at the London House and Dalgairns wrote, 'It is great fun to have him with us, he is so fat and jolly and enlivens this house very much'. Faber was still suffering and in a highly nervous state ; the doctor insisted he must have six months complete rest. Newman wrote to Stanton, who had described his excitable state, 'It is a great evil he cannot control his mental activity — else he will wear himself out'. To Faber himself he said, 'All is well — and St. Philip knows what he is at — but it is very mysterious that both your house and we should have so many invalids'. The consequence of all this was that Newman was overworked himself ; so much so that he wrote to Philip Gordon to find out the hours of Dr. Brodie, a well-known specialist, so that he could see him when he came to town at the end of October. 'Don't tell this, or I shall have a paragraph in the papers to the effect that I am dying.' Brodie did not think much of him. Thus he *began* the long trial, which was to last for over a year, in a state of strain and fatigue.

Meanwhile he had failed to get any of the evidence out of Wiseman. On September 6th he had written to the London Oratory, 'My dear F. Philip or anyone, is there anyone who is bold enough to tell the Cardinal I come up to Town on Tuesday and will call at Golden Square, as I come from the railroad, for the documents about Achilli. If he has them not, will he tell me where to find them at once.' Philip Gordon did call on Wiseman, but he was just leaving for St. Leonard's, where he combined a holiday by the sea with visiting Mother Connelly at her convent of the Holy Child ; her husband, having persuaded her to go into religion so that he could be a priest, was now indefatigably litigating to get her out again. Wiseman supported her throughout, and he was so concerned with Mother Connelly that he paid little attention to Newman's predicament. He did not think Achilli would press the case. Yes, he would look for the documents. He did not look for them. Until the legal proceedings actually began Newman had the utmost difficulty in persuading anyone to do anything ; even his friends in the Oratory thought he had no need to worry.

He had barely arrived in London at the end of October when Faber rushed off abroad for his six months' rest, leaving Dalgairns as Rector in London. The suddenness of his moves always disconcerted Newman, but he had no time to be concerned over this one, for on October 27th Achilli urged a criminal information of libel. It was first laid against the publishers, and Newman's name was only substituted on November 5th — a suitable date. This technical delay was represented in the papers as cowardice on Newman's part — he was trying to hide behind his publishers. It annoyed him, but his lawyers would not allow him to answer at once. 'Charissime,' he wrote to St. John in these first bewildering days, 'my hand is so cold and I have so little time for writing that I don't know how I can

32. 'MR. NEWBOY HOLDING UP MR. WISEBOY'S TAIL'
From a Punch cartoon of 1850

33. MR. PUNCH AND DR. NEWMAN
From a Punch cartoon of April 1851

34. G. G. ACHILLI
From a Protestant Alliance pamphlet

35. JOHN HENRY NEWMAN IN THE SIXTIES

write or you will read.' He was amazed that Achilli could swear in
court that the charges were false, knowing that if they were proved
he would incur transportation. 'I fear he knows just what evidence
is producible against him and knows it cannot be produced.   On
Thursday I may come down to you, if Brodie lets me.   I am better
and worse, as if someone were praying for me from time to time.
It seems to me that *suspense* is a trial to which our Blessed Lord could
not be subjected.'   The consultation with the lawyers was put off
till the next day. 'Alas! another day of suspense.'

On November 6th he told St. John, 'I now know the worst and
it is very bad. But I am not so troubled as I was, and hope the calm
will continue.' The consultation was trying.   Sir Alexander Cockburn, the Attorney-General, who had been engaged by Newman's
laywers in his defence, was 'evidently hostile'. He called it 'a bitter
libel' because it imputed 'a pretence of religion as a cloke for bad
practices'. Newman told Ambrose that he 'asked whether I thought
of knocking under, and if so, the quicker the better'.   Every charge
would have to be proved with evidence, the judges would send the
matter to trial if they could, there would be no chance at all with a
jury, they would come down more heavily on Newman than on the
publisher and Lord Campbell, who was likely to try the case, had
already shown his bias by proclaiming it 'ribaldry'. The only hope
was to try to postpone it till the Easter term. If Achilli's confession
in the Court of Inquisition could be proved 'it would go a very great
way indeed'. Newman had already written to Talbot in Rome for
these documents and was expecting them daily.

When Newman was alone he wrote a long memorandum, weighing up the question of whether to continue. He thought it would not
be right 'to suffer for the sake of suffering', but he said, 'I will gladly
risk all, if the Catholic pastors and people make my cause theirs'.
This they were to do, far beyond his expectation. He finished his
letter to Ambrose : 'I said this morning I never would be sad again ;
I will try not to be. May He who was on the cross, enable me to bear
whatever He gives me, in love, of His sufferings.' He had known
the risk when he attacked Achilli, but knowing is not the same as
feeling, any more than volunteering for a dangerous task is the same
as performing it.

St. John was worried as to the effect all this would have on him,
but when he came back to Birmingham he reported to one of the
others, 'The Father is now in excellent spirits, having made up his
mind to be floored ; it was a great effort to him'. To fight the case

knowing he was likely to lose it was not an exhilarating prospect, but he had made up his mind to it when he found that the Cardinal, and the various influential Catholics whose opinion was asked, thought it would be a great scandal to the Church if he gave in. He had no wish to 'knock under' but he knew the expenses were beyond him ; this problem was solved by the opening of a defence fund. St. John remarked, 'The Cardinal is most strange, he has lost all the papers and hopes we shall have a great triumph ! He has, however, subscribed £100.' In Birmingham there was the same loyal support, both from the Bishop, and from Mr. Hardman, head of the Church furnishing firm, a leading layman who was in charge of the fund there. Even the simplest Catholics wanted to help a good priest in unmasking a bad one, and Newman was touched by the contributions of the poor — indeed, he could hardly bear to receive those from Ireland.

Once the decision was made Newman was so ready to fight that his lawyers had to restrain him from reprinting his 'libel' with his signature. 'Already I have been charged with shirking', he complained to Badeley. But he was not allowed to say anything till after he had been called into court. Even now that proceedings had begun he found it difficult to get people to move. He told Ward that in September people simply laughed at him, and he told Gordon that the week before the criminal information was laid he had said to Ambrose and Stanislas : '"Now you must pray, for this is the critical time". They both laughed as if I was fond.' But he had this uncanny way of knowing what was going to happen to him ; it was not a clear vision but like touching something in the dark.

As for the Cardinal, in spite of contributing to the fund he was so sure Achilli would not brazen it out that he still did nothing. He told Badeley he would write to the Pope ; Badeley, who was not yet a Catholic, was impressed. Newman was cynical. 'I was bitterly amused at the way the Cardinal in his usual sanguine way was taking you in,' he observed. But to his surprise Badeley did succeed in alarming Wiseman. 'What a wonderful thing it is to be a lawyer,' Newman said. 'Put your scorn on once more and he really will wake up.' To Dalgairns he wrote, 'The poor Cardinal is now at length frightened and making amends — the hitch at Naples is for want of his stirring himself'. For when Gordon arrived in Naples he found Wiseman's introduction not strong enough to persuade the police to open their records to him. Nor was Wiseman the only one. Weeks had gone by, and there was still no answer from Talbot in

Rome, no Inquisition documents. The time for the hearing approached and Newman had absolutely no evidence to present in justification of his charges.

He was in court on November 21st, 'called up to town by Electric Telegraph' as St. John reported to Joseph Gordon. Asking for masses at special altars in Rome, he went on, 'our Father D.G. was in good spirits when he started yesterday. . . . Do not think from my last that the Father is in any way breaking under the trial, he is coming out more and more and one sees a special providence in it for his sanctification and he half feels it will eventually raise him up. He said : "Don't suppose I shall be damaged by it. It is my fate to fail and rise out of failure".' The very same day Newman was writing back to tell him the result of the hearing. 'The Judges are clean against — will grant nothing — determined to bring on a trial and have the witnesses in the box instead of affidavits — the people present humming assent. . . . Badeley last night thought I should have a year in prison.' This was no idle scare, but the general opinion of the lawyers on both sides, and Achilli's were pressing to the end for such a penalty. Newman put in his scrapbook a newspaper cutting of a case in which a member of the aristocracy was sent to prison for libel ; he was disgusted at having to put on prison clothes like any other convict. If that could happen to a Lord, it could still more easily happen to a Catholic priest. It was only recently that their very calling had ceased to be illegal and in most people's opinion prison was the proper place for them. This threat of prison hung over Newman's head for the whole of the year that followed.

The question of submission came up again ; there was still time before the Rule was made absolute. Newman could say that he had not spoken from personal knowledge, but from the article in the *Dublin Review*. It was true, but it amounted to abandoning the charge. As usual, Newman asked advice, from Archbishop Cullen, from the Cardinal and from his friend Hope. He asked St. John to consult Ullathorne. Besides the general issue, there was the personal one. 'How will it look *in me* ?' he asked Hope. 'I could not withdraw the charges in such sense as to imply I did not believe them or was sorry for saying them.' He wanted to know what would be the effect on the Catholic body of thus apparently giving them up as liars and slanderers. Hope replied, 'You cannot avoid fighting except by retractations,' adding, 'complete legal victory is not essential to the cause of the Church or your own justification.'

This advice fell in with Newman's own feeling — submission might be a duty, but it did not appeal to him. As soon as it was decided that he must go on he was eagerly asking to be called as a witness. 'I could bear (I trust) turning inside out.' He thought a jury would be prejudiced against a person they never saw. He was quite right, but the law did not allow a man accused of criminal libel to be witness in his own case. He was forced to be passive, another trial to his energetic temperament. The lawyers also would not allow him to suggest that Cockburn might 'like to get out of it'. Newman did not want to be defended by someone whose heart was not in it. Later, he was to feel this even more strongly, but each time was forced to submit. Cockburn increased his reputation by his brilliant speeches, but he was said to live a profligate life himself, and Newman would have preferred a clean conscience to any amount of brilliance.

Newman went home to Birmingham to find the pugnacious Ullathorne surprisingly in favour of compromise; but it was too late now. At Alcester Street the Blessed Sacrament was exposed on the altar and a *novena* kept to the Holy Ghost 'to have strength to bear God's most blessed will' as Newman told Sister Imelda Poole. Sister Imelda was a convert who had joined Mother Margaret Hallahan; her community were still at Clifton, but were on the point of removing to Stone. Sister Imelda carried on most of the correspondence, but Mother Margaret and all the nuns followed every move of the trial with sympathy and prayers. Mother Margaret, the ex-servant girl, with her energy, humour, good sense and holiness, had immediately made friends with Newman, notwithstanding the gulf between them of social and intellectual difference. It was she who eventually persuaded her friend Ullathorne to trust Newman. Just now she and her nuns were all praying for absolute victory.

Newman wrote to Sister Imelda, 'Your good Mother may if she will and I will thank her, *add* the intention of my deliverance from the snare of the hunter, but let the main intention be that we — that I, may have fortitude, patience, peace, to bear his sweet will withal. Since the middle of August I have been saying with St. Andrew *O bona crux, diu desiderata.*' (O good cross, so long desired.) 'You will see I expect the matter will go on. I hope, I pray it will *not*. I may be fanciful, but I cannot divest myself of the notion that it *will* . . . any how it is no harm to offer myself in expectation and in will, a sacrifice to Him who bore the judgment seat and the prison

of the unbeliever. . . . Everything has gone on so wonderfully hitherto
— as if our dear Lord were taking the matter into his own hands, and
utterly destroying all human means.   He has let me be bound as in
a net . . . nothing but prayer can break the bond. . . . When it flashed
on my mind at the beginning of September that I might go to prison,
I said "May I come out a Saint!"   I don't say that now when things
are more real, but "May it be accepted for my sins".   I have all my
life been speaking about suffering for the Truth — now it has come
upon me.'

It certainly was strange the way everything went against him.
He had taken every means to get evidence : none arrived.   On
Bowles' letter to Gordon he wrote, 'The cruel suspense, day after
day, the post coming in and no letters from abroad.   You cannot
conceive it . . . we cannot make affidavits even that anything is coming.
. . . We are thrown upon God simply — for man has deserted us.   I
wrote to Talbot on 27th October for all his documents — not one
has come yet, November 26th !'   They did not arrive till after the
Rule was made absolute, so that because of Talbot's twelve days'
delay a trial became inevitable.   Talbot afterwards grumbled that
Newman had not realized that he could not do everything in a minute,
but even if that were so he might have written to tell him about it.
Wiseman's documents were also missing still.   Newman told Ward
that one of the sources of his trouble was 'the Cardinal, who *did not
look* for his documents till the hour when the Rule was made absolute and it was too late.   In that hour he looked and he found.
Father Hutchison brought them to me.   I took up my hat and
went to Lewin.   He had just returned from Westminster.   It was
all over.'

Newman vividly expressed his feelings about all this to Capes :
'The series of strange occurrences connected with this matter, it is
impossible to convey to any one who is not with me.   If the devil
raised a physical whirlwind, rolled me up in sand, whirled me round
and then transported me some thousands of miles, it would not be
more strange, though it would be more imposing a visitation.   I have
been kept in ignorance and suspense, incomprehensibly, every now
and then a burst of malignant light showing some new and unexpected
prospect.'   It was even a relief to know that the Rule was made
absolute.   'There is no settlement but a fight', he wrote to Hope on
St. Andrew's day, November 30th.   'It is a great comfort to be out
of suspense, and out of responsibility on the point.'   Money too was
'amply forthcoming'.

But no sooner was one suspense ended than others began. The trial was fixed for February, the soonest possible date ; it was evident that Newman's enemies hoped that in such a short time he would not be able to collect witnesses. 'It is one awful crisis but the *only thing* we want is prayer', Newman wrote to Gordon. 'If we duly pray we must succeed one way or other. In that case defeat will have to be victory. . . . Suspense is what tires one ; but the great suspense is over now that the documents have come. Till then *no one* knew what we had to say for ourselves — it was a land of clouds. The lawyers looked blank.' He went on : 'Some people say it will dish my influence for ever if I go to prison for a day. I don't think so, but of course it will be a severe trial to us. I am parting with all my property and arranging my papers as if I were to die, that I may be quite expeditious.' Authors are more prone than most to feel they have left bits of themselves lying about in writing. Apart from making him arrange his private affairs the threat of prison seemed likely to reflect on the Oratory, so that he was rather glad he was due to go to Ireland again, hoping to draw attention away from it. 'I am afraid of a mob bullying us', he said. But Birmingham had already begun to respect him. It was only the little boys who ran after him shouting 'Six months in quod !'

Newman's lawyers now allowed him to send a letter to the *Morning Chronicle* to refute the charge of evasion that irked him so much. He gave his reasons for his attack on Achilli. 'And what I said against him I said simply in self-defence. It was an answer to the imputation which in this town he had cast upon persons whom I revere and on a religion I hold to be divine, to the prejudice of every Catholic here. These charges rested on his personal testimony, that testimony on his former position in the Catholic Church. I was desirous of pointing out, as I expect to be able to prove, what his testimony, founded on his history, was worth.' After this the newspapers gave up their talk of Newman's shuffling and instead were disgusted at his coarse vulgarity.

Achilli's lawyers wrote to demand if Newman were the author of this letter. They did not file the criminal information at once, in order, it was suspected, to get their agents off to Italy before Newman's. He wrote to Hutchison, 'We are told on good authority (1) that Achilli's party is well organized (2) that it has been preparing for a year and is now quite prepared for anything we can do (3) that it intends to *expose* the state of the Catholic Church'. This made him fear the co-operation of anti-clerical secret societies abroad, 'vanishing witnesses and counter witnesses swearing to the depravity of priests etc.'.   They faced more ordinary difficulties trying to subpoena witnesses who were in England.   'This very day dear F. Stanislas (Flanagan) is running over England *chasing* F. Vincent who is running away from our lawyers, to great expense and the murder of the vespers of the Immaculate Conception !'   F. Vincent was an Italian now a Passionist, a native of Viterbo ; unfortunately he had been only thirteen at the time of Achilli's offences there. Flanagan caught him at Taunton.   Another witness, Mr. Hadfield, once head of the Malta College, Newman pursued himself, by letter ; his extraordinary memory recalled for him the fact that he had once examined Hadfield, some twenty-four years ago.   Bloxam was pressed into service ;   Newman succeeded in hooking his man.   He wrote cheerfully to Henry Wilberforce that in the event of failure, 'we shall at least be like Samson — seize the two pillars, Lord Shaftesbury and Sir Cullen Eardley, and pull at once the Malta College and the Evangelical Alliance, about our ears to grace the catastrophe'.

His friends now began to realize what was happening, though they spoke more euphemistically than he would allow.   'My suit is no suit but I am tried as a criminal', he told Ryder.   When he said that God had let him be bound as in a net, he did not mean he had accidentally got himself into a mess, as Lord Shrewsbury and others thought. 'I did what I did most deliberately', he told Stanton, who was abroad with the Bowdens again, for his health.   'I went before the Blessed Sacrament and begged to be kept from doing it, if wrong. I have no misgiving.   I cannot wish otherwise.   It is God's hand ; it is His purpose.   We shall see in time why.'   This complete confidence in God's providence and the justice of his cause did not mean that he did nothing to save himself from the consequences.   He was fighting as hard as he could for success, even though it seemed unlikely to be his.

The same day as he wrote to Stanton he asked Hutchison in London : 'What is the best way for an unprotected female to go to Rome by ?   Will she be made a barricade of in Paris just now ?' (Louis Napoleon's *coup d'état* had taken place on December 2nd) 'or can she get through the snows of Germany the papers speak of ? . . . Miss Giberne is on the point of setting out for Italy — she is to pounce on one woman at Naples, another at Viterbo, and forthwith return with one in each hand.'   He told H. W. the reason he had asked her to do this.   'A woman can persuade women and men will be *watched* by the opposite party', whom he thought 'most

exceedingly sharp and I daresay not very scrupulous. Her movements had better be as quiet as possible.'

This request came as a complete surprise to Miss Giberne, but
she rose to the occasion. A year later she wrote a private account of
her adventures in a little book. She had been to confession one
evening, the confessional being in a guest room, and afterwards 'the
Father, leaning against a mantelpiece, said to me "I think you can be
very useful to us in this affair". Without thinking how or when, or
in what capacity I could be useful to him, I arose and said, "I am
ready at your service".' She found she was to leave the day after
next. Her account was written when the issue was still in the balance,
and she was in a state of high emotion about Newman's trials and
sufferings ; her language matched her feelings. On the day she left
Birmingham 'the dear Father gave me communion somewhere about
6 a.m. then I heard a mass, after which breakfast was provided for
me in the reception room to save time. He sat with me giving me
directions about my journey. Then came the parting. He lifted up
his hand and blessed me, which gave me courage and strength to face
my solitary journey.' Off she went in the middle of the winter, a
single lady of fifty with only one bag, so that she was several times
taken for a servant on her momentous voyage — for in the end she
went by boat.

At Marseilles she had a fearful experience, which Newman did
not hear of till her letter came in January. The boiler of the ship
burst, while they were in port. 'I heard awful shrieks and hollowing
and water rushing into my cabin from above.' Through the thick
steam she struggled up on deck, half suffocated, to see some terrible
sights — a lady's maid, 'all the skin rolled off her right hand hanging
down like a white glove and her hand the colour of crimson'. Twelve
died from the accident, including the culpable engineer ; if Newman
had not made her promise to travel first-class she would probably
have been fatally scalded herself. She was taken by some friendly
'Paddies' back to her hotel, and set off again almost at once on another
boat. Time was vital. The new captain thought she must be a
relative of Napoleon's, she looked so like him !

Meanwhile Newman was writing out and saying litanies to the
saints of Malta, Corfu, Viterbo and London, and to all the saints
John — 'St. John the Evangelist, cast without harm into a caldron
of boiling oil : St. John Pope thrown into a loathsome dungeon :
St. John Chrysostom, victim of an unjust sentence : St. John of God,
seized and confined for mad : St. John of Egypt, for forty years shut

up in thy cell: St. John of the Cross, imprisoned by the envious'. Achilli's name was John too: Giovanni Giacinto. Newman also composed this prayer: 'God the lover and keeper of peace, grant peace and true love to all our enemies and give them remission of all their sins, and rescue us powerfully from their snares'.

1852

Eruption in the London House

AT the turn of the year, just when there was so much external anxiety, a storm broke in the London community which had been brewing some time. The excitements of starting were over, the work continued very heavy, and the young and strong-willed team began to feel the strain of personal tensions. Although they were now self-governing, Newman still held the position of adviser which they had voted him for three years. Among other things he still looked over their accounts. Last year, when they consulted him on their debt he had said bluntly, 'I think your expenses of board have been *immoral*, and you will all suffer in purgatory if you don't diminish it. To increase means of getting money which you are to squander, is but to increase your purgatory and not to relieve your need.' Some economy was effected, in spite of grumbles, and in May he was able to say 'unless the accounts are infamously cooked, they present a most satisfactory reduction'. But he was against Faber's new idea of moving from King William Street. They had scorned Bayswater only to fall for the charm of Brompton, then another expanding village at the end of an exceptionally miry road. Living in central London had not turned out as they had expected. Newman thought that with their Lancing house they ought to be able to manage; although he did not say so, in Birmingham they had at present nowhere to escape for a rest from the noise and smells of Alcester Street.

Newman's hardheaded carefulness and the austere patience with which he would endure prolonged discomfort rather than run up debts, did not appeal to Faber's happy-go-lucky temperament. He could not bear delays and he knew his rich friends would subsidize him — and they always did. He could work like a team of six in a fit of enthusiasm, but he would then collapse with nervous prostration and have to take a holiday, coming back to begin the cycle again. It was not surprising that members of his community began to find this instability almost unbearable. The moment they were relieved of his presence, when he dashed off abroad in October, they felt his rule unendurable — even Antony Hutchison was grumbling. They discussed it among themselves but said nothing about it to Newman till they suddenly heard Faber was already on his way home, before even half the term ordered by the doctors was up. The prospect of having him back was too much for them ; they wanted to know from Newman if they could ask him to resign, on grounds of health. It was Dalgairns, as Rector, who made the request, in a depressed and despairing letter.

'You must not dream of deposing F. Wilfrid', Newman wrote earnestly, after praying before the Blessed Sacrament and asking the help of our Lady and St. Philip. 'You have chosen him for three years. St. Philip will not bless you for undoing his arrangement. Three years is no intolerable period ; if it be a trial you must get him to teach you to bear it. Everything will go wrong, even as a matter of human calculation, if you depose F. Wilfrid. It will be like a private judgment and like waters running out. It will be imitating the restlessness you complain of. The community will crumble into units. If F. Wilfrid is not good enough for you, no one will be.' But he understood their personal difficulties and he knew Dalgairns himself very well. 'You must not droop. I feel this strongly. You tend to make matters worse than they are.' Dalgairns had not long since told St. John that they had at least six men 'who perfectly understood each other'. Newman said, 'I will not believe this is not a basis for Carità . . .' (Christian love) . . . 'your business is to strengthen the bonds and deepen the feelings which unite these Fathers to each other'. But they must have 'prudence and caution to avoid the appearance of a clique'.

This was too bracing for Dalgairns in his present state of despondency. Two days after Christmas he poured out all his woes at length. Faber's trying ways came out pell-mell. His was a despotic rule, but not exercised in a distant overawing manner. 'He consults too *much* and then chafes and is irritated' — when there was disagreement. 'He brooks no opposition. If there be any he goes from room to room, painting the opponent's conduct in the most extravagant colours. . . . He governs the house by sarcasms.' Dalgairns was in the mood to exaggerate, but Faber had certainly behaved like this at St. Wilfrid's. His sarcasm does not appear in his letters to Newman, but is plain in those to Antony Hutchison. Dalgairns went on to pour out all his misery and dissatisfaction. 'You say I take gloomy views and you talk of a basis of carità. I acknowledge my gloom and disbelieve in the carità. Of the six you mention, James [Rowe] and Edward [Bagshawe] are non entities, Philip [Gordon] has not the slightest strength of character, F. Richard [Stanton] is not. [i.e. not there] As for F. Antony [Hutchison] I love him much but I disagree utterly in his views about Philippine government. . . . We have kept together by necessity, by F. Wilfrid's strong character, by a certain feeling of sticking to St. Philip. As for myself, I am broken in spirit. I write to you now as I would to a director. All this has filled me with temptations to leave the Congregation. I feel at home with no one. I cannot be certain that anyone will not turn round upon me at any moment and be rude. I utterly disapprove of our blurting out to each other what we think. Merciless criticism and unsparing ridicule is what we meet with from each other's hand under pretence of English bluntness. But above all there is no peace in the house. . . . Now under such circumstances how can I "strengthen bonds and deepen feelings" ? . . . Dearest Padre, it is a shame to send you this when you have troubles enough of your own. But I have no one to tell it to, but to you. Advise me what to do.'

It was ten years since Dalgairns had gone to live with Newman at Littlemore ; he was now over thirty and had come to the point where people realize the world is not what they would like it to be. Horizons close in, many vague hopes disappear, self and other selves show how intractable they are, how difficult to change. Dalgairns' enthusiasm had its shadow of impatience, nor could enthusiasm alone carry him through this interior crisis. When he had left Birmingham Newman had analysed his chief failing for him, to wake him up to it. Now he did not need shock, but encouragement. 'Charissime,' Newman replied, 'I know how difficult it is to rouse and raise up the mind when it is floored and prostrate, and I see perfectly how much you must have had to beat all spirit out of you, yet I still think you exaggerate, and let despondency bear too hard upon reason and good sense, as I think I can show you in your own words. It is not necessary for carità, even humanly considered, that the objects of it should be strong minded, or should agree with us in opinion, but that they should be *amiable*. Now you say of Antony "I love him much but etc". Surely here is sure material of a basis ; where hearts are one, things find their place, and where there is a will there is a way. Then again you say of Philip he "has not the slightest strength of character" — still I think he is a person whom you could easily *love*. And why are James and Edward nonentities ? because they are still

novices ? but what hindrance is that to your loving them and they
you ? . . . F. Richard again is away, but I trust not for ever. I think
any one could love him who tried. . . .' His advice shows very clearly
the attitude of openness towards people he himself took up, not
dwelling on what was tiresome to him in them, but expecting to be
able to love them. This was the fruit of long practice, so long as to
be almost a second nature ; but Dalgairns had started off on the
wrong foot, criticizing others more than himself. All the same
Newman shrewdly surmised that the difficulty now did not lie in
these grumbles but in 'troubles unnamed'.

'Your complaint about the want of tenderness, gentleness, courtesy and sympathy in your congregation is, alas, most true, and I
think most unphilippine. Had you not said it, I should not have
ventured to have a clear opinion that it was so.' This too was typical
of Newman ; he did not criticize them till they criticized themselves,
and then not destructively, but in hopes of a change being effected.
He, who could so skilfully use ridicule against prejudice, humbug or
ideas he thought false, never used it against persons. Even in dealing
with Achilli his tone was changed to indignation ; he did not diminish
an opponent by mocking him. Sarcasm is like a whip, forcing inferiority on the victim, rousing resentment, destroying equality and
the chance of love. So, even though he agreed to some of the causes
of discontent given by Dalgairns, he pulled none of the persons to
pieces, nor criticized the community as a whole, but tried to make
him realize that the difficulties he complained of were not singular to
the situation in which he found himself, but the common lot of
human beings in their present condition. They could not be evaded
anywhere, they must be understood and overcome.

'In conclusion I will remind you that all acclimation is painful,'
he said, 'and acclimation in a religious body as much as any. No one
but a Jesuit or a Trappist knows what a Jesuit or a Trappist goes
through in becoming a Jesuit or a Trappist ; but the vow bends
them, and they must go through it. What do women go through in
accommodating their lives to the will of a husband ! when they have
done it, it is their happiness. *We* have no vows, and there is an
urgent temptation to break away from that from which we can break
away — we are able to speculate on want of peace or rest, for we
have no vow to hinder us. But will our impatience benefit us ?
What religious order would suit us better than St. Philip's light yoke ?
As to the secular clergy see how all our own friends and those who
seem most like them rush away into the ranks of the regulars. . . .

You indeed *could* go to France, but somehow I do not think you could feel you had a call to desert poor benighted England — However, I will say no more to-day.'

So he encouraged Dalgairns to persevere ; but there was Faber to deal with. Dalgairns complained that before he went abroad 'he remained in his room creating rows in the house and living apart from the community. . . . I cannot conceive what he will do when he comes home, in the first joy of getting back, and finds out the present feeling of the house. He will go wild unless you come and help us.' Months ago, when he was Director, Dalgairns had said he dared not tell Fabor his faults, and that he would listen to Newman as he would to no one else. Newman was their only hope.

Nothing could stop Faber arriving, and arrive he did, with the new year, on a wave of high spirits. Newman felt that for his own good and for that of the house he ought to finish out the six months' rest he had been ordered. 'I am going to write you a very ungracious letter, that is, to express my *sorrow* at your return', he said, taking as light a tone as possible. 'The truth is, I have been fuming ever since you went, at the way you have been going on.' Indeed, instead of resting, Faber had been gallivanting round the Mediterranean, sight-seeing, preaching and taking part in public functions. 'I wrote to Malta to protest against your preaching,' Newman sternly said, '— the letter missed you, and next I heard of you as lecturing . . . in Italian. The tone of your letter from Palermo pleased me not at all — I had no confidence in your sudden restoration, and I thought your letter excited. Then suddenly you were making for Rome, which was *forbidden* you' (by the doctors) 'and before a letter could hit you, you are, against all medical orders, in England. St. Philip used to obey his physicians. Have you taken one of the few opportunities a father Superior has for obedience ? I saw his letter — he prescribed six months for you. You are *not* recovered. The very impatience with which you have come back shows it. . . . Your life is precious. This I know is very ungracious, but I am bound to say it.' He reminded Faber, in a postscript, that he himself was likely to have to submit to 'Ἀναγκὴ — fate, necessity. Faber had shown little interest in Newman's trial ; Newman once remarked he did not believe Faber had said one Hail Mary for him since the trouble began. But he did not reproach him now ; he wanted him to realize that he was not alone in submitting to the decree of others.

Faber replied with a long wail of despair. It would be a penance to go abroad again. He excused his restlessness. 'I am not well

when I halt abroad, for I fidget or mope, and I can't controul it, try
as I will.   My dearest Padre, I am afraid to speak exaggeratedly ;
but I am sure you don't know how I suffer.   I can hardly ever say
mass ;   people are near or they see my face, and I get flurried and
break ye rubrics. . . . New altars distract me and I am never very well
when I haven't said mass. . . . I can't get well while I am unhappy —
I am unhappy abroad.'   Yet he had written in high spirits to friends
from various places.   Whether the dislike of his face being seen at
mass was self-consciousness, or whether he felt he was like St. Philip,
who did not like to be seen when he was in ecstasy and not in control
of himself, Faber's own description of his behaviour merely underlined Newman's contention that his nerves were not yet calm. 'Don't
think from all this that I don't see how kind your letter is,' Faber
ended, 'but it has mortified me so much.'

  This arrived on the first day of 1852. 'Your letter was a pleasant
New Year present as regards its affectionateness and its good account
of yourself,' Newman replied on the same day, 'but it does not make
me alter my former view.   You are going to act like the spendthrift
who having gained in his low estate a £50 note from a friend sets off
at once to have one or two jolly blow outs and to secure his being
just where he was or worse some three weeks hence.'   Faber had
suggested that the Fathers of his house should decide.   Newman
retorted 'the decision of medical men cannot be set right by a resolution of the Cong. Deputata. . . . You say you are restless abroad
— I have no proof that you are not as restless and more so at
home.'

  Antony Hutchison now took up the correspondence.   He had
grumbled about Faber's overbearing ways in his absence, but the
moment he returned he fell under the old spell again and wrote to
suggest that a country house should be taken for him. 'How can
you afford a separate establishment ?' Newman asked doubtfully.
But London was certainly out of the question. 'Of all places London
is a place to bring on again the excitement of the brain — It is killing
him to be there. . . . If he is not well his subjects will annoy him and
then it stands to reason he will annoy his subjects.'   The next day,
January 3rd, Hutchison reported that Faber had collapsed with a
headache the day before 'thanks to the cold veal and ham of which
he had too much the first day he came'.   It was more likely due to the
mortification of Newman's letter telling him he ought to obey his
doctors. 'To-day he is well again,' said F. Antony airily, 'and leaves
on Tuesday.'

Newman received this startling information just as he was answering an urgent request from Dalgairns that he should come up to London himself. 'Here you are,' he broke out, 'scheming, arguing, *deciding* — off F. Wilfrid is to go like a shot or a comet, as he has gone, and as he has been travelling, and as he has come back, without sufficient deliberation. Surely the first thing is to call on the doctors. Again — you ask me to town and then, without giving me time to answer by post, whether I will or no, off he is to go on Tuesday morning, the Epiphany ! Now the truth is, I had made arrangements to go up to you to-morrow (Monday morning) and shall do so. Is the whole house possessed of the genius of restlessness ? If so perhaps when my cab stops I may find the whole concern gone like Aladin's palace. . . . How can you do anything well if you do it so fast ?' He insisted that he wanted to see Faber after the doctor had seen him, and went up on a day ticket.

A compromise was effected ; Faber was allowed to stay in England, but he must find a country lodging and observe a strict 'cordon sanitaire' as Newman called it — he was not to visit London, nor were the Fathers to visit him, though apparently they did not realize this. Faber was installed in a house at Hither Green, with a fat housekeeper to look after him and a maid to wait at meals. 'I am quite, quite well but they won't believe me', he told Lady Arundel. When Alban Wells visited him, Faber almost walked him off his legs, he was so full of energy. He wrote long cheerful letters to everyone, in January, mostly about his travels. Telling Stanton, who was still abroad, about his medical examination, he said, 'Ye old Padre affectionately came up to assist'. On January 14th he remarked in passing : 'The Padre has lost a front tooth and is looking old. He has clearly suffered greatly about ye trial and he is like a regular quaint old saint about it now.'

But he was most interested to tell Stanton about the conversations he had had at the Chiesa Nuova with various Oratorian Fathers. There were some differences of opinion there and, according to Faber, the Roman House was see-sawing between absolutism and an over-dependence on the Deputies, according to who was Superior. 'Even ye revolutionary F. Rossi speaks of ye Superior's power in a manner very different from what any of us do, and so strongly as would shock F. Francis [Knox]', he remarked. '. . . By the way, I should also add that so strongly is F. Rossi set against our Padre that he declares he has corrupted ye Birmingham Oratory to Jesuitism, and that he has acted in a manner unworthy of a Filippine *in re*

Achilli, as charity is our calling, and not *calpistare* people.   It is a
bore speaking against F. Rossi ; but I am clear he cannot be followed. . . .'

In these letters there were scornful remarks about the Dean,
Dalgairns.   Hutchison, writing to tell Newman that a succession of
brothers and novices were cheering Faber's exile at Hither Green,
was so entirely won back to him that he could say, 'he completely
outweighs the rest of us ; he is like a first rate line of battle ship
sailing among a lot of frigates'.   But one of the frigates could not take
it.   Dalgairns broke down, and *he* had to go and rest, not at Hither
Green, needless to say, but in Norwood.   London Oratorians were
dotted widely around, recovering from each other.   But Dalgairns,
even when he returned, was seriously unhappy and unsettled, and
clinging to Newman more than he had for years.

1852

The Devil plays Cat and Mouse

MISS GIBERNE arrived in Italy in the middle of January, met Father Gordon and went to see the witnesses he had found. The girls Achilli had seduced fifteen or twenty years ago were now mostly respectable married women ; it was difficult to persuade them to go to far-off England and give evidence of their past misfortunes. Rosa, who had a large family and was pregnant, could not do so. Miss Giberne finally started back with one, Elena, and her husband Vincenzo. Elena at first thought the English lady another of Achilli's victims ; Miss Giberne was not flattered at this reflection on her taste and judgment. Elena was dreadfully sick on the boat and declared she was dying. Talbot had given them the address of a Mrs. Foljambe, in Paris. There they were presently joined by a Neapolitan family, including grandmother and baby — this was the girl who had been seduced in the sacristy at the age of fifteen and whose parents had brought a case against Achilli. Miss Giberne liked the Neapolitans for their simplicity, but they were dirty and verminous and Elena and her husband turned up their noses at them. Lodging-house troubles rapidly developed. Miss Giberne kept them all in order somehow. Unable to stand the state of the baby, she bathed her and cut her hair, and was pleased at the improvement. Elena was pacified with some smart stays that opened in front and a box of magnetic fishes and ducks. All this and more Miss Giberne detailed to Newman, filling thin sheets of foreign writing paper.

Achilli's supporters were alarmed to hear that witnesses had been procured, though they did not know where they were, and towards the end of January they changed their tactics from hurry to delay. They well knew it would be hard to keep poor Italians away from home for a long period without bribery, which would cancel their witness. Therefore when the defendant's Pleas were lodged they put in a Demurrer. Since the charges had to be put in legal language for the Pleas, sharp lawyers could find technical loopholes. Newman gave Miss Giberne a sample. The Plea charged 'criminal intercourse with a female child', and it was objected 'that it did not show she was chaste or had any honour to lose'. Although the Judge allowed the Pleas to be amended, the trial, which was just due to come on, was postponed. Newman told Miss Giberne the news, underlining the words, '*I think Achilli has put it off because you are come*'. To Stanton he wrote a few days later, 'Cowardly curs as they are — who fly at one's heels, and then scour away when one looks round. . . . What *are* we to do with the witnesses in the interval ?' He was anxious about Miss Giberne and assured her, 'Don't suppose that we mean to let you remain in your present uncomfortable circumstances'.

'I assure you I am not uncomfortable, only now and again like everybody else', said Miss Giberne bravely. 'But prayer does everything.' She had met the famous Père de Ravignan, a Jesuit, who turned out most sympathetic, and allowed her to go to communion very frequently, which was unusual then. She was careful not to complain in her letters to England. She wrote gaily to St. John : 'I do not even mind the creatures of which I left six or eight the other day in the warm bath ; when I vacated my place they remained kicking about on the surface. . . . Give my affectionate love to the light of our eyes as well as to all the dear Fathers and Brothers.' All the same the postponement made everything much more trying. Before she had heard of it she was writing to Newman about London lodgings, warning him that the baby would spoil the bed — 'Excuse my troubling you with such matters but I do not know who else to tell about it'. No more than the prospective English landlady, did the French one like her bed being spoiled. Tensions increased and the French maid grew so quarrelsome that Miss Giberne took to sweeping out the Neapolitans' room herself, to keep her out of it.

Vincenzo was her worst trial ; he was gross, grumpy and quarrelled with his wife, who told everybody he might go off his head at any moment. Luckily he showed no signs of doing this, but his table manners disgusted Miss Giberne and she had no idea how to keep him amused. She allowed him two cigars a day. Perhaps prompted by St. John, who enjoyed a cigar himself, Newman suggested she should increase the ration. But Elena put her foot down. 'Signorina,' she said firmly, 'there are three Persons in the Blessed Trinity, but two cigars are enough for Vinci.' How on earth was Vincenzo to be entertained ? Newman said : 'Is there no equestrial exhibition ? no harmless play ? no giant or dwarf ? no panorama, cormorama, diorama, dissolving views, steam incubation of chickens, or *menagerie* (the jardin des plantes !) which he would like to see ? Surely beasts are just the thing for him.' Miss Giberne replied, 'Unfortunately all the animals are shut up'. However, with drives and little presents, and by drawing all their portraits, she managed to keep them on the whole content. Poor Miss Giberne ! She had gone off in such a hurry and never expected to spend months abroad. She had so few clothes with her. On the end of one of her letters to Newman she scribbled directions for Mrs. Wootten to find and send some shifts and a grey dress. Sometimes she felt she could bear it no longer, sometimes she cried, but she never told Newman this. She would do what was most use to him. 'I like what you like — I have no will but God's will which is also yours, so mine is yours.' Unlike some people, she showed she meant what she said, by faithfully fulfilling instructions and making fun of her trials.

All the same, it was a delight to see St. John, when Newman sent him over in February for a brief visit. 'I miss that dear angel face', she said sentimentally, when he had gone. The others might have laughed at Ambrose's angel face, for he was getting fat, and more brusque than ever. It was his kindness and reliability that comforted Miss Giberne. While St. John was in France things moved again at home and Newman wrote cheerfully to him, 'Charissime, or my child since you so call yourself and a very fine babby you are — we have carried the Pleas — the Judges have given it for us and the cause stands for trial, but I expect a new dodge. . . . Love to Miss Giberne.' At the bottom he scribbled another letter in formal terms : 'My dear Mr. St. John,' informing him of an order on the bank for £20 and ending, 'Believe me with much esteem, your faithful servant.' This was on February 19th. A few days before, he had written to Capes, 'Achilli is waving his white feather most ostentatiously — but also very artistically, and I am tired of his exhibition. We have, I don't know how many witnesses, eating their heads off.'

By now there was evidence of Achilli's continued activities in London ; adulteries with servant girls which were to support the general charge against his character in the original attack. That he was afraid of this evidence is proved by the fact that he tried to cajole, bribe and intimidate these girls to withhold their evidence. Newman's lawyers had been considering indicting Achilli for perjury, but they gave up the idea as impracticable. This news arrived on Newman's birthday. 'Never have I had such a Xmas, never such a birthday', he told St. John. 'I think I could make up my mind to

anything but the suspense and the spending money and the keeping
witnesses in good humour and such great trials. I only hope my pain
may go to some good purpose, it is so like physical, that I seem to
understand how the soul can suffer physically in purgatory. . . . I am
so tired out I am scarcely able to pray.'

For nothing stopped while the legal scares and delays took their
course. This Lent they effected the transfer of the community from
Alcester Street to Edgbaston. The chapel at Alcester Street and the
people there they served for some time, until it became a regular
parish, but moved themselves, in relays. In March Newman said,
' As we creep in head foremost I have gone up first, these three weeks,
and am battling with the workmen, who, like aboriginal inhabitants,
do not brook being dispossessed'. He was reminding Dalgairns how
they had 'fought out' drunken Jim Blasy and the painters at Littlemore. The first mass at Edgbaston was a *missa cantata* 'the two
Fredericks and the choir astonishing the corridors, the workmen, and
the public of Edgbaston with their voices'.

Nor was this all, for his private correspondence was heavy all
through these months. Two earnest gentlemen, Lord Charles
Thynne and Mr. Wegg Prosser, wavering on the brink of conversion,
were writing frequently, the latter every few days, requiring answers
to intricate historical and theological problems. Both were eventually
received. Dodsworth, a recent convert, a London clergyman, made
necessary further excursions into theology. Then there was Allies,
anxious for a possible job on the staff of the Irish University; Ryder,
with his motherless family; Mrs. Bowden's daughter, Marianne, needing advice about her vocation; and poor Miss Holmes, restless and
unhappy, unable to find the job she wanted. All these received
letters as if Newman had nothing but their welfare in mind ; he was
able to concentrate entirely on each person he addressed. And in the
midst of all this, not knowing when he might not be tried and sent to
prison, He was trying to compose the lectures on the Idea of a University, to be delivered in Dublin as soon as a firm date could be fixed.

Sorrows as well as anxieties beset him. There was no hope left
for the saintly Brother Aloysius, nor for Lady Olivia Acheson, so
kind and helpful. Newman anointed Aloysius in February, but he
lingered on till March. The two died within a few days of each other.
Lady Olivia was in acute pain, suffering a slow suffocation, but 'to the
last thinking of others'. It was Newman who gave her Viaticum and
watched by her death-bed. No wonder that he said, 'I am so tired
out, I am scarcely able to pray'.

All the same he was praying, and anxiously asking the prayers of others. To the nuns at Clifton he spoke of the case from its supernatural angle. He was severely (but affectionately) ticked off by Mother Margaret in her own sprawling hand, for obstinately sticking to his feeling that he was going to suffer for challenging all that Achilli represented. 'I was afraid our Blessed Lady would have put you in prison herself when I read it', she said. 'It would not be putting much confidence in her were we only to ask her for possible things ; I wish you could have heard twenty Nuns scolding you for wanting confidence in my own Beloved Mother.' She was inclined to blame St. Philip for this lapse. Thanking her for her prayers, Newman wrote, 'Thank you also for the reproof you have administered to me. I know well I am an unbelieving old beast ; and so perhaps in this instance. Recollect, however, dear Reverend Mother, that our house in Birmingham is erected under the invocation of the Immaculate Mother of God as beseems an Oratory of St. Philip — and is dedicated to her for ever, and that you will not please *her* by abusing *him*.'

Sister Imelda reported that Mother Margaret was horrified at the names he called himself. They all went on praying. 'As I told Sister Mary Agnes months ago,' Newman observed, 'if I failed I should say "It's all those idle nuns", so, if I succeed, through God's mercy ; I shall say, "It's all those good zealous persevering nuns".' Sister Imelda told him they were also praying for Achilli — 'who is our brother, though an apostate'. Newman said that 'the great Independent preacher here, Mr. Abyell Jones, assures the young men of Achilli's innocence. He would not assure them unless they *needed* assurance.' Nevertheless, the ordinary Protestant was more likely to believe the word of a Protestant than that of a Catholic. And of such would the jury be made.

'They have the front to ask me to try before a common, not a special jury,' Newman said, '— i.e. not by my peers who have characters to lose, but by a set of pot-house fellows.' Common London juries had already shown, in a case concerning the Hammersmith convent, that so firm was their faith in Maria Monk that no facts could shake it. Newman was to be tried by those already convinced that all priests were liars and conspirators. 'I will not repeat Is it not wonderful ? for nothing is wonderful — be sure of that. I thought I knew it. I have said for years "nothing is wonderful against the Truth" — so much I have had in the way of personal experience of this for twenty years, that I have always said "Anything may happen ;

men are up to anything" — but still there seems a lower depth. It is
intellectually wonderful — this is what I mean ; it is *no* wonder there
are bad men in the world. I muse over the analysis of such ways of
acting, as over a problem. To explain and account for such face,
front, or whatever you call it, is as difficult as squaring the circle.'
He had said to Miss Giberne in January, 'Depend upon it, the nearer
we are to success the more the devil will try to defeat us'. The devil's
campaign was clear enough ; it was the twists of the human wills
through which he carried out his operation that puzzled Newman.
It was the reverse side of the picture he had drawn in the sermon on
Wisdom and Innocence, where he had traced the hand of God working out his purpose through the obedient wills of the humble and
gentle, and with their weakness confounding the empires of the world
of power and glory.

Meanwhile the devil's cat-and-mouse tactics proceeded madden-
ingly. At the end of April, Newman was telling Sister Imelda the
trial would come on at the beginning of May. 'Now your Madonna'
(a specially venerated picture) 'must play her part — for still I am
haunted with the idea that the Church will gain and I suffer. Still
I have prayed for absolute success and triumph.' Yet this date too
receded. Ten days later he was writing to Hope, 'The opposite party
will not agree to bring the trial on. . . . I don't think they will *ever*
bring it on while I keep the women who have come over.' The
objection raised was that Achilli was expecting an important witness
from Corfu who would not arrive till May 20th. Lewin suggested
that Newman should write to the papers to bring pressure to bear
for a speedy trial, but he refused : it was a question for the law, not
for private influence. All the same this new delay was a sore vexation.
To Dalgairns he said, 'It is strange that a matter which, had I the
little finger of a saint in me, I should think nothing of, should so try
me — hamper is the word'. But a cross is no cross that does not
weigh on the one who carries it : to each the instrument of suffering
crosses his own nature, not another's. Many times Newman said
that suspense was harder to him than conviction would be, or prison.
This prolonged anxiety and uncertainty was the sentence he served
as the penalty for attacking Achilli ; and it lasted longer than the
year's imprisonment forecast by Badeley.

Meanwhile domestic troubles continued. William Neville had
smallpox, and several nights they had to sit up with him. St. John
and Darnell were ill too, and young Lisle Ryder. 'St. Philip is
determined we shall not enter the house in too high spirits', Newman

wrote to Faber, who had now returned to King William Street. He celebrated his return by telling Newman a long tale of woe, mostly of the faults of other members of his house, for he felt quite as dissatisfied with them as they did with him. Moving into a new house Newman always found rather a comic operation, tiresome as it was. This was to be his last removal, except for one in Ireland. 'The first result of coming into a new house', he told Faber, 'is to find out all the defects — no door here, and a dreadful draught there, pannels put in awry and locks which will not catch. We are all immersed in these great cares, as many as are not tending the sick.'

On May 2nd he heard that the trial was put off till June. He wrote at once to Cullen, 'Therefore I will wait no longer, and shall make my appearance in Dublin, unless pulled back by the leg here, very shortly'. In a few days he crossed over to Ireland, to deliver the famous lectures on *The Idea of a University*.

1852

The Idea of a University

Just before he went to Dublin, Newman had asked Ornsby to find him rooms in a central position. 'And if I *could* have a low iron bed with a single hard mattress (and no curtains) it would be the greatest boon you could do me. If such things are to be had in Dublin I would buy one. To a large fourpost bed which I cannot *make* myself I will have nothing to say.' Huge feather beds were to him one of the chief trials of travel. He had no sooner arrived than he was invited by a Protestant clergyman to meet a convert *from* Rome in public dispute in the Rotunda. 'Dr. Newman does not see any reason for his taking so extraordinary a step, which he should feel to be a great humiliation', Newman replied, 'respectfully' declining. It was quite enough to have to grapple with Irish Catholics, let alone Protestants. He had meant to stay with Henry Wilberforce, who was living in Ireland as Secretary of the Catholic Defence League, but he denied himself the pleasure when he heard it would offend Irish patriots if he was too much with other Englishmen.

Newman had thrown himself into the project of the Catholic University under the impression that it was to be a centre for higher studies for all English speaking Catholics, from England as well as Ireland, from the colonies, and even perhaps from the other side of the Atlantic, where Catholics in the United States were then a poor minority, struggling with many problems. He had in mind both the newly founded University of Louvain, and the times in the 'Dark' ages when Celtic scholars and preachers from Ireland carried faith and learning all over northern Europe. There was no reason why such an institution should not have grown up in nineteenth-century Dublin — no reason but the narrowness of vision, the jealousies and prejudices of human beings on both sides of the Irish sea. English prejudice against Ireland had as much to do with it as Irish prejudice against England, for few were the English Catholics of means who dreamt of sending their sons to a university in Dublin, even if Newman was to be the head of it. And in Ireland itself the situation was complicated by episcopal differences which Newman did not realize at first.

Cullen was not popular with many of the other bishops ; like Wiseman in England he was regarded as too Roman in outlook and ignorant of conditions in his native land. The university, which was his project, was for that very reason suspect, and became an occasion of further differences. There was a party in favour of utilizing the new Queen's Colleges, which were intended to be non-religious. The policy of the Holy See, that Catholics should be educated entirely in Catholic institutions, was based on conditions in Europe, where secular education was introduced and run by militant anti-clericals who were either freethinkers, freemasons or atheists. English Protestantism was a half-way house not at all understood in Rome. And in Ireland, English Catholicism was hardly recognized. Cullen's chief opponent in the hierarchy was John MacHale, Archbishop of Tuam, nicknamed the Lion of the West ; he was an intransigent patriot, and set his face against the university from the first. Others were less determined, but equally without enthusiasm. Newman was warmly welcomed as a person ; as an Englishman, and from Oxford, he was suspect from the beginning.

He knew this was so, and that, considering the history of the two nations, it was natural. Although he was so English himself and indulged in occasional gibes at Irish 'fickleness' he had great sympathy for the people of Ireland, both individually and as a nation. He knew how much they had suffered from famine and cholera and bad government ; he knew the immigrants in Birmingham, filthy but faithful. A little later, in the university paper he started, he wrote of 'the Catholic Saxon' in Ireland : 'He has but one imagination before his mind, that he is in the midst of those who will not despise him for his faith's sake. . . . He penetrates into the heart of the country ; he recognizes an innocence in the young face and a piety and patience in the aged voice, which strikingly and sadly contrast with the habits of his own rural population. . . . How shall he not . . . exult in his new friends and feel words deficient to express both his deep reverence for their virtues, and his strong sympathy in their heavy trials ? But alas, feelings which are so just and natural in themselves, which are so congruous in the breast of a Frenchman or Italian, are impertinent in him. He does not at first recollect, as he ought to recollect, that he comes among the Irish people as the representative of persons and actions, and catastrophes, which it is not pleasant to think about ; that he is responsible for the deeds of his forefathers, and of his contemporary Parliament and Executive ; that he is one of a strong unscrupulous tyrannous race, standing upon the soil of the injured.' Shrewdly, he saw that with Englishmen, as had recently been the case in India, 'it was that passionate indignation at insurgent feebleness, which has made them in past times so cruel and unjust to the Irish'. Newman was convinced that the great flaw in the English character was the habit of measuring everything by the standard of success.

Thus, in composing the lectures which were to express his ideal, he had to contend not only with the complexity of the subject but the difficulty of so presenting it, and himself, as not to prejudice the whole scheme from the start. He chose to disarm criticism by acknowledging his debt to Oxford and to the distinguished Protestants from whom he had first derived his educational theories, while showing that the principle of intellectual liberty need not develop into anti-Christian secularism, as it seemed to be doing in England, but could, and should, flourish in the context of the Catholic Faith. 'My lectures have taken me more trouble than any one could by a stretch of fancy conceive', he had told Ornsby in April. 'I have written almost reams of paper ; — finished, set aside — then taken them up and plucked them — and so on. The truth is, I have the utmost difficulty of writing to people I do not know, and commonly have failed when I have addressed strangers, as in the St. Isidore's oration at Rome.' No one could tell this from the clarity and precision of thought, perfectly expressed, in these lectures, perhaps the most generally admired of all Newman's works. The first was given in the Exhibition Room of the Rotunda, on Monday, May 10th, 1852.

'You are all expecting news and I have no one to be my trumpeter', Newman wrote to Ambrose the next day. 'The lecture, I suppose, thanks to our dear Lady, has been a hit, and now I am beginning to be anxious lest the others should not duly follow up the blow. The word "hit" is Dr. Cooper's word. The room is very good for my purpose, being small. It is just the room I like, having want of light ; I cannot make myself heard to many and few care to hear me : *paucorum hominum sum*.' He guessed there were about 400 present. On the train to Kingstown afterwards, as he was going to dine with Henry Wilberforce, he met Mr. Duffy the publisher, who was to issue the lectures as they were given, and he 'said he had never seen so literary an assemblage — all the intellect, almost, of Dublin was there. There were 13 Trinity Fellows etc, 8 Jesuits, a great many clergy and most intent attention. . . . I was heard distinctly, or rather my voice filled the room and I had such perfect command of it, that people would not believe I could not be heard in a great church — but I know myself better. It was just the room I have ever coveted and never had. . . . There were a number of ladies and I *fancied* a slight sensation when I said not Ladies and Gentlemen, but Gentlemen.' Ladies were not supposed to go to public lectures. Newman did not disapprove of women thinking, but he did not judge the publicity proper for them.

Ambrose wrote of their delight that things were going so well ; they were all hilarious at a mistake in the printing of the first lecture : 'Peter went out with holy water and venison' instead of benison. '*Punch* won't forget this,' said Ambrose. 'It is indeed most jolly.' Feeling that the book should have an Irish publisher, Newman had almost made it a gift to Duffy. His English friends were somewhat annoyed at this, especially when the bound edition appeared. Duffy had wanted it dressed up in morocco with gold lettering. Newman, who liked things plain, managed at least to evade the morocco.

Many and various were the hazards of life in Dublin. Newman told Gordon he had bought some 'villainous tea' at great expense 'which spoilt my night's rest and left me quite weak. I don't think there was one tea leaf in the whole — though the man who sold it to me was very great about it.' On Sunday he wrote to Nicholas Darnell : 'I am amused at the great cleverness of the Irish, which far surpasses anything I ever saw elsewhere. The very ticket taker in the room followed my arguments and gave an analysis of the discourse afterwards. The printer makes the most judicious remarks and alterations in the proofs, always clever and well meant, though generally wrong. As to the poor servant girl here, she is supernaturally sharp and subnaturally dirty ; but her eyes are everywhere and she anticipates every want, and how she discovers some things I really find a deep mystery. She closed up both windows in my bedroom with the shutters the first night — when I went to bed I opened the right, after putting out my candle ; first thing in the morning I opened the left also. How she found it out I cannot conceive — but the next night and ever since the left was closed up and the right open. She has taken to sort my papers and put away books and fill my drawers — but here she is beyond her province and I have been obliged to snub her just now. As I generally seem very cross and very stupid, sometimes both, she puts me down doubtless as a specimen of English priest.'

During the week he was offered, in a double house in Harcourt Street used as a school, 'a beautiful room with a chandelier and (perhaps) pagan paintings of alto relievos on the walls, *unfurnished*'. There was a staircase separate from that used by the boys, and 'a chapel and meals (unless the mutton is too tough) in the house . . . so I shall transport my iron bed there, and buy a table, chairs and drawers, and I am complete'. He was pleased to think he could leave his things there undisturbed while he was away from Ireland — a vain hope, as it turned out. Ambrose had just been wishing he could be with Newman because, as he said, 'You have no anvil,' and now teased him, 'what can you mean by removing your iron bed ? Mind, *I* am your iron bed.' But he was still unwell, and far from allowing him to come to Ireland, Newman told Darnell to see that he stayed indoors till he was better.

The second lecture was almost more agitating than the first. 'Charissime, 2 o'clock — the lecture at 4 — the anniversary of my mother's death — your letter just come', he began breathlessly to Ambrose on May 17th. 'I never have been in such a state of confusion as to-day, since the day when I was in Leonforte in Sicily ill of the fever . . . or again that day in Oriel Hall, when I was standing for the fellowship. . . . But, thank God, my nerves are not so acute as then — or where should I be ? Yet I am dreadfully afraid of want of strength. I have just discovered *how* I ought to have written my lectures, what would have been the true rhetoric and how I have plunged into a maze of metaphysics, from which I may be unable to heave myself. When this broke on me I half thought of lecturing extempore quite a different lecture — but I am not equal to it . . . and now I shall eat my dinner — and try to banish every thought.' One source of anxiety was that he was not to have the nice room again, but one much larger and higher. However, on the end of the letter he scribbled : 'Lecture just over — brass band playing a good part of the time. H. W. liked it.' The band was outside the window, part of another entertainment.

Newman dashed back to England for St. Philip's day (May 26th). It was the first to be held in the Edgbaston House, Ullathorne was the guest of honour and among others invited was their ex-colleague Penny. Newman had sent advice about the preparations from afar. Although he was feeling unwell, everything went off as planned and he was back in Dublin on 29th. From Birmingham he had written to Miss Giberne, 'I trust I am doing good in Ireland, but really it is like drawing blood — so much am I pulled down'. Pulled down was

Newman's phrase for nervous exhaustion, brought on by the combination of anxiety and intellectual concentration. A week or two later, writing to tell Faber the date of his trial, he compared his state with the time when he was finishing *The Arians* 'in a state of fainting for days'. He had now got sufficiently toughened not to faint; indeed other people did not realize how near he was to breaking down.

Just before his fourth lecture, on his return from England, he transferred himself to Harcourt Street, not without some initial mishaps, as he related to Austin Mills — he wrote to each of the Fathers in turn. 'When I got here I found that the housekeeper, who would not let any of the other servants do it, had arranged not only my clothes but all my papers for me. I had put my letters in various compartments according to my relation towards them and my Discourse papers according as I had done with them or not. She had mixed everything, laying them out neatly according to their *sizes*. To this moment I have not had the courage to attempt to set them right — and one bit which was to have come in, I have from despair not even looked for. And so of my linen; I had put the linen in wear separate from the linen in reserve. All was revolutionized. I could find nothing of any kind. Pencils, pens, pen knife, toothbrush, boots, 'twas a new world — the only thing left, I suppose from a certain awe was (woe's me) my discipline. Mind, everything was closed up, as far as they could be without lock and key, which I had not. She then came in to make an apology, but was so much amused at her own mischief, as to show she had no deep sense of its enormity.' Not surprising, perhaps, so long as Dr. Newman did not rage at her. 'I have found all sorts of useful books in the bookcase', he went on cheerfully, enumerating a list of English poets, Swift, the Waverley novels, Ovid and Gibbon. In spite of all this confusion and his increasing fatigue 'the lecture went off well yesterday', he told Bowles on June 1st, asking him to post two pairs of 'philippine iron shoe buttons' from a writing-case stuffed among his Shakespeares — 'take it out carefully'. He added, 'the room full — people seem pleased'.

The only people not pleased were the militant Protestants, represented by *The Dublin Warder*, which tried to make out the lectures were an utter failure. 'Mammy Newman', the *Warder* said, 'was employed by "Peter the Perpetual", husband of Pharaoh's daughter, to nurse and cherish with papal milk his own bantling, whose gestation-place was Oxford, and its birthplace Rome.' The next issue saw him off from Ireland with the assurance that his audience had shrunk up to nothing, that thirteen people had left the Church after hearing the lectures which, when published, would only be 'the drone of a disordered barrel organ after the waltz was over'.

Newman left Dublin without finishing the course as he originally planned it ; the last lectures in the printed version were never spoken. It was not entirely due to his fatigue but to Achilli, for he now heard that the trial was fixed for June 21st. With it came a piece of good news : Badeley had at last made up his mind to be a Catholic. 'I take it as an omen of success,' Newman said, in his letter of congratulation.

At this critical moment he received an enthusiastic and affectionate letter from Dr. Newsham at Ushaw. 'Go on, my dear Dr. Newman. Providence is making use of you for great ends — ends much beyond the reach of your own view, and extending much beyond the short period of your own life. Your valuable writings will speak to thousands long after your tongue is silent and your humble soul is in a better place — in God's eternal rest.' Newman was touched by his kindness. 'It's extreme friendliness,' he said of the letter, 'just at this moment too, when I am a good deal tried, quite affected me.' To so sympathetic a listener he could tell something of what the lectures had cost him, and why, even apart from the trial, he would have had to interrupt them. 'For three days I sat at my desk nearly from morning to night, and put aside as worthless at night what I had been doing all day. Then I gave it up and came here — hoping I shall be strengthened to begin again. I am ashamed so to speak, as if I were achieving any great thing, but at my age I do not work things out as easily as I once did.' Then he asked Newsham's prayers, 'to gain for me the light of Divine Grace, that I may say what is profitable and true, and nothing else'. This letter was written from Birmingham. He got back there in time for Corpus Christi.

1852

The Trial

THE first thing Newman did on hearing the date of his trial was to print a little circular which he sent round to convents and monasteries, asking for prayers 'that God in His mercy may grant that His own honor and that of His Church, if not the Rev. Dr. Newman's personal safety, may come unimpaired out of the ordeal'. There were many friendly replies, little notes carefully written, promising prayers and offering sympathy.

When the trial was expected for May, Miss Giberne had brought her party to Dover. During the second period of waiting they had to lie so low that her sister Charlotte, as she told Newman, thought she was 'conducting a secret embassy between you and the Pope ! ! !' Miss Giberne was not in the best of health ; she had a boil, but some sea-bathing set her up. The Neapolitans were frightened of England, expecting everyone to be heathen, but they fell in love with the fair-haired children, calling them angels, just as St. Gregory had done long ago. Vincenzo was the biggest nuisance, as usual, although he had been allowed 'to rig himself out according to his fancy' in Paris, as Newman had advised. Miss Giberne read Newman's Irish lectures as they came out. 'I hope it is not wrong, but I do feel so very proud of you, just as if you were my son', she said incongruously, since they were the same age. He was still worrying about her discomforts but she begged him : 'Do not trouble your kindest of all kind hearts — if you will do me a kindness it is to take great care of your own self.' This was a vain hope ; Newman went on working till the last moment in Birmingham and only came up to London the day the trial began. Miss Giberne and her charges were already there, the women terrified of meeting Achilli, who had been trying to bribe the London girl Jane Legge not to give evidence. But Vincenzo wanted to walk about and see the sights. To Miss Giberne's amusement he asked her who was the saint on top of the column in Trafalgar Square.

While Newman was still in Birmingham, Faber had sent a telegram:

there was talk of prohibiting the wearing of a religious habit, and what were they to do ? Newman thought it was better to leave it off than to be forced to take it off. He wrote to the Secretary of State, hoping to find out the position, but he refused to pronounce an opinion. Faber wrote to say that the London House was against 'unfrocking' though its members had been hooted at and insulted in the street. It was as a result of this agitation that Catholic religious do not to this day wear their habits out of their houses in England. Newman said that Ambrose, who was going to town ahead of him, could be his plenipotentiary in their discussions. He arrived in ordinary clothes and was greeted with laughter. 'He looks ye *loudest* snob I ever saw', said Faber. Newman wore the clothes then customary for secular priests when he went to London. In January Faber had told Stanton : 'Ye Padre looks quite awful in his seculars ; he is so lean and his clothes fit so badly and he is so black and shirtless about ye neck, that almost any jury would convict him of horse stealing on a mere view, without evidence ; whereas, you know, he looks positively grand in his habit.' On one occasion Newman was lent a flamboyant French coat belonging to Faber to go home to Birmingham ; someone in the London house drew a caricature of him going off in this vast and incongruous garment.

He was unlikely to be called into court, but he had to be at hand in case of need. He spent most of his time in the tribune at the King William Street chapel, praying before the Blessed Sacrament, but out of sight of the people coming in and out. Friends came round to tell him how things were going. On the first day the prosecution showed their game ; instead of putting Achilli in the witness box at once, as was usual in libel cases, they reserved him till after they should have heard all the evidence brought on Newman's side. Some play was even made when he was sent out of court with the other witnesses ; Sir Frederic Thesiger implying that it was unfair that the innocent Achilli should not hear the slanders alleged against him. The jury fell for this and one rose to protest. Campbell, the Judge, said 'if the other side insist', as if he could have done otherwise than overrule this objection. His bias was plain from the beginning. The jury too were just the 'pothouse fellows' Newman had expected, well-read in Maria Monk, and not shocked at Achilli's misdemeanours, to judge by their laughter.

Cockburn's first speech in Newman's defence was mainly devoted to an attempt to remove the case from the sphere of religious prejudice. He laid stress on the violence of Achilli's attacks on the

Catholic Church and the clergy, and appealed for fair play. 'It would be a mockery to talk of "toleration" — it would be a farce to say that religious opinions were free — if you would only listen to accusations against the Catholic Church, and not allow its members to raise their voices in its vindication.' This, he emphasized, was Newman's motive, not personal malice. He also made the point that Achilli had taken no steps against the *Dublin Review*.

Elena was the first witness, examined through an interpreter ; she was almost two hours in the box, and came through well enough, in spite of an attempt to make it appear that she had been sent to testify by a conspiracy of priests. Father Vincent, the Passionist, and Maria, the girl who had been seduced in the sacristy, also gave evidence that day ; Maria and her mother were cross-examined the next day, Miss Giberne holding the baby in their lodgings. There were two Italian witnesses from Corfu and Mr. Reynolds, a government customs clerk, now retired. In Zante his house overlooked Achilli's and he had had the blinds of his windows drawn down to save the modesty of his family from the scenes he observed. A Swiss girl who had worked for him, supported her former employer ; both were Protestants. Thesiger tried to make out that Achilli had incurred Reynolds' displeasure by rebuking him for drunkenness. 'Certainly not!' cried the retired customs officer indignantly. 'If I had been intemperate I should not have served the Ionian government for twenty-five years.' Somehow the prosecution had got hold of a letter to a friend whom Reynolds had tried to persuade to give evidence in which he said that Newman's lawyers were 'disposed to be liberal'. He said he was referring only to expenses, but the words gave an unfortunate impression.

Next came Hadfield, ex-Principal of the Malta College, and Watts, the secretary. The *pièce de résistance* was the great Earl of Shaftesbury himself. Shaftesbury was willing to give the reasons for Achilli's dismissal, which had been kept quiet at the time, but the prosecution objected and the judge upheld it. Shaftesbury had been ordered abroad by his doctor ; his Parliamentary and social work, his new inheritance and the excitements of all the Papal Aggression meetings had worn him down. His Victorian biographer did not allude to this unpleasant episode.

Then there were the London girls ; one, a Catholic, had by the advice of her confessor, left Achilli's service, thus avoiding his advances ; Jane Legge, less wary, had succumbed and afterwards had a baby. Her sister, with whom she lived, was called and related how

Achilli had come to see them, how he had said that Dr. Newman was a very bad man and he hoped to have him sent to prison, and how, when she said they had been summoned, he had told her to shut the door in the faces of those who came to serve subpoenas on them. Then there was Sarah Wood, who, after having an illegitimate baby at the age of sixteen, had been sent to a House of Mercy run by Tractarian ladies. They sent her to be servant to Mr. and Mrs. Achilli ; she related how he was always trying to put his arm round her waist while she was dusting the bedrooms. He also gave her a book called 'Come to Jesus'. A fortnight later, she said, when she was cleaning his dressing-room, he locked the door and seduced her by force. The prosecution tried to make out that she was a Catholic (and therefore a perjurer) on the strength of the Anglo-Catholic practices at the House of Mercy.

The last witnesses were called on the decisions of the Inquisition court in Rome ; Harting, Wiseman's lawyer, who had been there to collect the evidence and Dr. Grant, who had blotted Newman's copybook at Rome over the dispensation for St. Wilfrid's. He was now Bishop of Southwark and Achilli's lawyers started by demanding of what see he was the Bishop, hoping to involve *him* in legal proceedings, since the new law had just made territorial titles illegal for Catholics. Grant was silent, and the point was passed ; but they went on to question, interminably, the authority of the court of Inquisition and Bishop Grant's knowledge of its procedure. For nearly two hours they fought against the admission of the Inquisition documents — with reason, since they contained a copy of Achilli's signed confession. Lord Campbell eventually allowed the documents, but in a way that prejudiced the simple jurymen. 'I am not considering whether it is evidence under which Dr. Achilli could be led out to be burnt alive, or to be imprisoned for life in the dungeons of the Inquisition,' he said, as if this were common routine in nineteenth-century Italy ; 'but merely whether it sustains the allegations of the plea. We must not be frightened of the word "Inquisition!" Thank God the thing has no place in this country!' This sally was greeted with stamping of feet and applause from the back of the court, and expressions of disgust from the more dignified present, including lawyers and clergy. Lord Campbell did not check the applause, as he later checked some on the other side ; indeed he invited it again a moment later, thanking God once more, this time that the Inquisition's jurisdiction did not extend to England. He got another round of applause from people who identified the Roman court with the Spanish Inquisition of the sixteenth century. Ecclesiastical courts in England, which had just been overruled (as usual) by the State's, in the Gorham decision, went by a less unpopular name.

Finally Cockburn put in Achilli's book as evidence and the court adjourned at quarter-past eight. Badeley sent a message to Newman to say that all was safe : things seemed to be going well. The Inquisition documents alone justified a great deal of what he had said.

The next day Achilli was called. He was in the witness box altogether for seven hours. *The Times* thus described him : 'He is a plain featured middle-sized man and his face is strongly Italian. His forehead is low and receding, his nose prominent, the mouth and muscles around full of resolution and courage. He wears a black wig, the hair of which is perfectly straight and as he close shaves this wig gives to his appearance a certain air of the conventicle. His eyes are dark and deepset ; and with his black wig, sallow complexion and sombre aspect, leave an impression on the mind of the observer by no means agreeable and not readily to be forgotten. . . . The questions put to him by his own counsel he answered with great clearness, and in a calm unwavering manner without any trace of strong excitement, or feeling deeply roused. Some times a slight contemptuous smile accompanied his denials, and once or twice he seemed to treat points angrily. His general bearing was cautious and careful — replying with great reflection and precision.' As well it might be. Although he understood and spoke English quite well, he chose to have an interpreter ; this dodge several times gave him vital moments for consideration. It was noticed that sometimes he began to answer in English and stopped himself.

Achilli simply denied the charges. Confronted with Elena he said, 'I never saw her !' The same with Maria and her mother, though the latter had brought him to court in Naples. Mr. Reynolds drank and he could have seen nothing, since his windows were lower than those of the house in which Achilli stayed. He denied the Malta charges, the seductions in London, and that the Inquisition had suspended him for moral rather than dogmatic deviations. When Cockburn asked him if chastity were not part of the vocation of a priest he said 'Yes', with a sardonic smile, and when pressed about his intercourse with women other than those named he refused to answer, but went on smiling 'the same unpleasant smile, half convulsive' as the lawyer Finlason noted. Finlason printed a report of the trial and he thought Achilli was afraid to make a straight denial for fear of being indicted for perjury. It was the only time there was a sensation in court which was not in Achilli's favour.

Achilli had not many witnesses, the chief were another renegade priest from Malta and the wife of the jealous tailor in Corfu. It was obvious why he had secured her, for she was very ugly, her nose being broken. 'Why should I carry on with her?' was the implication. The plain looks of poor Jane and Sarah were later sneered at, and as a contrast they brought in Mrs. Achilli, smart and attractive, who appeared, it seems, for no other reason.

All this day Miss Giberne was looking after the baby, while 'news came from time to time that the trial was going wrong'. The next day began with a four-hour speech by Sir Alexander Cockburn, considered by *The Times* a masterpiece of pleading, and rousing applause even in that prejudiced assembly — instantly checked, of course, by the Judge. But the Attorney-General, Thesiger, was just as clever as Cockburn and he knew his jury. Although he had chosen to speak last he made out that it was a disadvantage. 'All that the bitterest hate, the most unwearied industry, the most unbounded resources, and unlimited means could combine for the destruction of one man' had been done, he said, as if the prosecuting Achilli were the accused. Had Newman no personal motive? 'We must judge men by their acts, and if we find, in coarse language, serious attacks upon the character of Dr. Achilli, we must presume there is some motive which actuated him; and we can attribute it to nothing else but that feeling of hatred which does not require personal knowledge of the individual to be engendered. Dr. Newman has exhibited all the energy and zeal of a proselyte . . . and his hatred may be as strong as if they had come into personal collision.'

After dwelling on the number of charges for which Newman had been unable to bring evidence Thesiger picked up the accusation that Achilli was 'a hypocrite under a cowl' acting as a priest while not believing (according to his book) in what he did. Thesiger drew a moving comparison with Luther, still a great hero in England in spite of Hurrell Froude, and then turned sharply upon Newman: 'Was he suddenly converted? . . . Did he lie down at night a satisfied and contented Protestant, disbelieving in transubstantiation, confession and absolution — and rise up in the morning a full blown Romanist? Strange that such an argument should proceed from such a course!' He ignored the whole history of the High Church party in this sneer, and Newman's scrupulous retirement from positions of authority as his doubts grew. Thus was Newman's conversion compared unfavourably with Achilli's. The depth of Achilli's belief in evangelical doctrine may be measured from the fact that when he later went to America he first called himself a Unitarian, and then set up for himself in a religion of his own — still leaving a trail of seduced women in his wake.

Having thus discredited Newman, Thesiger went on to discredit the witnesses as far as possible. He could hardly discredit Shaftesbury, but when that noble lord was recalled he was again prevented from giving evidence on Achilli's misdemeanours in Malta, because they had been left unspecified in the charges. Newman afterwards told William Froude : 'Lord Shaftesbury behaved *very well*. Thesiger would not let him speak.' As for the London girls Thesiger represented Newman's party as saying, 'Get the servants of every house he has been in ! If Catholics all the better !' It was then that he compared their looks unfavourably to Mrs. Achilli's. He ended full of confidence that the jury would condemn Newman for his 'foul slanders'.

All might not have been lost had Lord Campbell made a fair summing up. But even *The Times*, no lover of Papists, was shocked at his bias. There was no religious prejudice involved, he said, for even if Achilli had committed the offences, he was a Roman Catholic priest at the time ! The only credit he allowed Newman was for openly avowing his Romanism ; this gave him a chance to sneer at the Puseyites. He shook his head over Elena's remark that the priest at home had advised her to give evidence because it was for the glory of God and the honour of Mother Church. 'Gentlemen, these are extraordinary circumstances, but you must decide !' he said, implying that some sinister conspiracy was on foot. He dismissed much of the evidence and suggested that Mr. Reynolds had hoped to make something out of his. As to the documents from the Inquisition, they proved there had been a judgment, but was it for immorality or heresy ? 'We should rather suppose it was heresy ! Dr. Achilli says it was.' As for the vow of celibacy : 'We must remember that Luther married, and married a nun !' One up to Luther ; Achilli's wife had broken no vows to marry him. Lord Campbell even took Achilli's refusal to answer about intercourse with women unnamed as evidence in favour of his honesty. If even the Judge spoke as if it were Achilli's sexual morality in question, and not his untrustworthiness as a breaker of oaths, what chance was there of a jury of pot-house fellows seeing it otherwise ?

It was half-past eight when Campbell finished. The jury did not come back, according to the report of the trial, till nearly eleven. They found one of Newman's charges proved — that Achilli had been deprived of his lectureship! All the rest, not proved. The foreman got rather mixed up with his 'Guilty' and 'Not guilty' — for people could not help feeling as if it were Achilli who had stood his trial ; but with the Judge's assistance he soon made it clear that in the jury's opinion it was Newman who was the guilty one. Vigorous cheers resounded through the thronged court. Everyone thoroughly agreed with the twelve good pot-house fellows.

The verdict was more of a shock to Newman's friends than to himself, for he had more or less expected it all along. Miss Giberne, released at last from her charges, went round to the Oratory chapel in the evening, while the decision was still in the balance. 'Close behind me sat the dear object of all our cares, pale and still, calm and heavenly', she wrote in her account, a few months later. 'He retired soon after and at the beginning of one of the hymns Father Ambrose came and said "All is lost, and the Father thinks you had better take the people to Boulogne lest they should be imprisoned for perjury". I remained as if dead till the sermon began.' Then she went out and asked what had become of Newman. He was just about to go off to catch the express back to Birmingham. 'Soon after he entered and spoke to me in a calm and soothing manner. I could not help crying a little when he was gone, but roused up . . .' and embarked, poor Miss Giberne, on the tiresome task of getting the Italians over to France again. Father Gordon was detailed to help her, so it was not as bad as she feared.

'I almost stole away like a thief last night,' Newman wrote to Faber from Birmingham, 'but since I must go to Ireland, I wished to be here some little time first. I intend to go to-morrow. It strikes me to say *you must none of you be doleful*. We are floored if we think ourselves floored. Of course we *are* floored, whether we think ourselves so or not, in a worldly standard, but we must steadily recollect that we are above the world, above the feelings of society — and therefore we must cultivate a lightness of heart and elasticity of feeling which, while deeply based on faith, looks at first sight to others as mere good spirits. These good spirits are not enough — but bad spirits will be a *positive* hallucination. We are done if we feel beaten. We must have no indignation against judge or jury or anything else — they act according to their nature, and accomplish according to God's will. Poor shadows, what are they to us ? You must make your Brothers meditate on the nothingness of the world, unless the subject be too intellectual.'

These encouragements may have been prompted by the reception he got in Birmingham from the faithful parishioners, to whom it was dreadful and bewildering news that, after all their prayers, the Father was *not* delivered, but condemned. St. John in Alcester Street sent a hurried note up to Newman in Edgbaston, telling him he could not go off to Ireland and leave them in this state. 'Well, I will stop if it is necessary,' Newman scribbled on it, returning it to him, 'though you must explain to me how.' He thought there was no other train that would make the connexions in time. Again the piece of paper made a journey: Bowles had found out another train. Newman stayed a little longer. To Badeley, who had written to say how the verdict had grieved him, he replied 'I am in the midst of my University Discourses, with one foot in the train for Ireland, and trying to put my thoughts in order to console our people here with a sermon, for they think I am going at least to be transported outright — so you must excuse a hasty line'. He asked Badeley to thank everybody; he had already written himself to thank Cockburn.

Letters were already arriving and some he answered before he left. 'You see how Almighty wisdom has determined things', he said to Sister Imelda, and to Mother Margaret: 'In gaining so many prayers I gain an inestimable benefit. Whoever loses; I gain. I went on saying till the last moment "I will not believe it till I see it that our Lady and St. Philip will suffer it" and now I am quite sure that it is only for some greater good. . . . When I came down here I feared we should have placards in the street against us and that there might be a mob about the chapel. Nothing of the kind — the ultra Protestant publisher Ragg, has not even put up in his windows any notice about Achilli and me.' His only fear was that the poor witnesses would be prosecuted for perjury; there had been talk of it in London. 'I was advised to go off to France! I did send the poor Italians off to France directly. They can only account for my many witnesses by calling it a conspiracy of priests, and that I have bribed them all; but everyone sees through it.' To Mrs. Bowden he wrote, 'Achilli's party will call it a triumph, no one else but will call it not a triumph *for him* but simply a triumph over *me*. . . . Achilli's single word undid a *proof* — so that his single oath put me on trial and his single oath condemns me in the face of a number of witnesses.' Mrs. Bowden felt he must be hurt by the verdict but he wrote again to assure her he had no pain at all. 'Anxiety, cares, suspense, all this

is pain — certainty is no pain. My friends have pain now, not I —
and this is pain to me, but my only pain. You see the feeling is so
strong that even *The Times* is taking my part.'

For *The Times* had said that such a trial would give substance to
Catholics' complaints that they could not get justice in their own
country. To shock *The Times* was a triumph in itself : Bellasis
called it 'a real success'. Indeed part of Newman's aim in attacking
Achilli was already achieved, if the leading newspaper recognized
that prejudice acted even in an English court of law. Newman was
touched when Mrs. William Froude wrote from Devon that the old
Archdeacon was disgusted ; Hurrell's father did not condemn him.
William Froude, although none of his family were yet Catholics,
insisting on subscribing to the defence fund.

Catholic friends were shocked and horrified by the verdict. Allies
was 'in a stupor. An enormous violation of justice gives one a shock,'
he said. Wiseman had had a sleepless night 'from pain and amazement' and sent affectionate sympathy and a request that Newman
should preach at the first Synod of the new hierarchy. Manning said,
'I was behind you yesterday in the tribune' — of the Oratory chapel
in London. He had said mass for Newman every day of the trial.
Warm-hearted Dr. Newsham felt it worst of all. 'What can I say,
in the present state of things, but "Holy Martyr of Christ, pray for
us,"' he lamented. 'For your religion you are suffering' — since
he would not have been condemned had he not been a Catholic.
'I know you are not, my Dear Friend, cast down. I know you are
prepared to suffer this, and infinitely more than this, for Christ.
But *we here* are not so perfect as you. I cannot convey to you the
feelings that at the moment pervade the whole college — grief, indignation, shame for their country.'

Having tried to comfort his people against this defeat on Sunday,
Newman hurried off for Ireland in the evening. It was for the meeting
of the University Committee that he went and he said of it to Hope,
'it was not pleasant'. He was beginning to realize what he was up
against there. Two days later he was warning Bowles of his imminent
return 'and we shall bring with us a wild elephant in the person of
the Rt. Rev. Dr. Olyffi Bishop of Agra. So let a room be ready for
him.' He was back by July 4th, answering letters again.

'God be praised you are not in a dungeon yet', said Sister Imelda.
Newman replied: 'I hope none of you are moping. . . . Our great
and awful difficulty is the expense, say £6000 ! Sympathy is doing
for me here what success would not have done. I am not certain I

shall not be obliged even yet to confess that your Madonna has got me off. If I am not called up to judgment I shall consider that she has, and shall feel bound to present myself at Clifton.' For he had promised to carry the holy picture in procession if the nuns' prayers were answered. Now he composed a circular to thank all the convents and monasteries where prayers had been offered ; he would say mass for his benefactors every Tuesday and Friday for a year. It was headed : *Noli aemulari in malignantibus.* (Be not envious of evil-doers.)

1852

Waiting for Judgment

THE first Synod of the reconstituted hierarchy was held at Oscott in July and it was there, in the high pulpit of Pugin's chapel, that Newman preached his famous sermon on the Second Spring, best known of all his sermons to Catholics in England. 'Shall the grave open ? Shall the Saxons live again to God ? . . . Yes ; for grace can, where nature cannot. The world grows old, but the Church is ever young.' It was what Newman was saying all his life long, in one context or another : the apparent omnipotence of the world, the real omnipotence of God ; and that strange mystery of evil — the suffering of the innocent — which Christ made fruitful. 'Something, for what we know, remains to be undergone, to complete the necessary sacrifice', he said, after recalling the English martyrs. 'May God forbid it for this poor nation's sake ! But still, could we be surprised, my Fathers and my Brothers, if the winter even now should be not quite over ? Have we any right to take it strange, if, in this English land, the spring time of the Church should turn out to be an English spring, an uncertain, anxious time of hope and fear, of joy and suffering — of bright promises and budding hopes, yet withal, of keen blasts, and cold showers and sudden storms.'

Manning also delivered a sermon at this Synod : 'Help nearest when need greatest'. It was just over a year since his reception ; he was at the Accademia Ecclesiastica in Rome, 'the nursery of Cardinals', and already personally known to Pope Pius IX ; every summer he spent in England, lodging with the Jesuits. He preached both in Rome and in London with success, drew large crowds and received many converts, including an elder brother and his family. Manning was the youngest of seven ; his favourite sister, though not converted, remained as affectionate as ever and he stayed in her house, and with other relations in London and in the country. His brother-in-law John Anderdon, who had been very kind and helpful to him in his youth, became a Catholic, and an Anderdon nephew was to be a priest. Manning had temporarily lost touch with Gladstone, but remained on close terms of intimacy with his friend and brother-in-law, Robert Wilberforce, who was slowly coming nearer to the Church. Even so early, there was this great contrast between Manning's fate and Newman's.

The Synod, Newman told Henry Wilberforce, 'ended in great triumph, joy and charity'. He went home to receive the news of his sister Harriett's sudden death. 'It is to me *most* unexpected,' he wrote to Mrs. Bowden '— and indeed the whole matter is a most painful mystery. I can hardly make out poor T. M.'s letter.' The next day he was still complaining '*nothing* is told me'. At last he heard that Harriet had died in her sleep. He had not seen her for nine years, since Tom's abortive conversion in 1843; after her brother left the Church of England she had scarcely written to him once. She had always suffered a great deal from 'nerves', and Newman said to Mrs. Bowden, 'I suppose she died worn out with years of mental *fidget*'. To H. W. he wrote : 'I daresay I have spoken severely of her to my sister Jemima before now — but I am not aware that I have ever felt unkindly. Poor Harriett, what a change from what it was when you first knew us ! What a world this is.'

A few weeks later poor old Aunt died. The shock of Harriett's death, and the pain of hearing her loved nephew John was likely to be sent to prison like any common criminal, perhaps hastened her end. It was one of the most painful consequences of Newman's conversion that he was forced against his will to become a source of shame and grief and bewilderment to the family he loved and had so spent himself to assist in the years of his youth.

The surprise of his sister's sudden death and the emotions and memories it aroused, brought home to Newman how exhausted he was. On July 22nd he wrote to Dalgairns : 'I want a holiday so badly, and have not had one for two years ; not a week of uninterrupted rest, and I have to go to Ireland next week and these lectures lie like a tremendous load on me. . . . I am out on the ocean with them, out of sight of land, with nothing but the stars, and I so dread controversy. How I should like a quiet week with some of you at Sydenham, but even if you were in your house it would be impossible.' The London Oratory had given up Lancing and were building a large villa at Sydenham, then a fashionable place of residence on the outskirts of London. Faber enjoyed laying out the gardens, as he had done at St. Wilfrid's ; he and all the London Fathers were to be buried there — but now development has overtaken the place and the bodies have had to be removed and buried elsewhere.

Already tired out, when he reached Ireland Newman was swept up in a whirl of activities — some expected, like the University committee meeting and the sermon he had rashly promised in Limerick, others the result of his sudden popularity : for what surer road to Irish hearts than to be unjustly condemned by an English court for defending the Church against a lying renegade ? His reception overwhelmed him. 'I am being killed with kindness', he told Observer Johnson, when he had come near to breaking down completely. '*Words cannot express* the exuberant hearty affection which all men, the priests and the multitude in the streets embrace me — but my life all along has to be in quiet and in solitude and no one but I can *understand* how things tire me which would not tire another. I am speaking of *physical* strength — for I think my mind and soul, through God's grace, are up to any thing, and I never had my intellect more vigorous.' He had got over the feeling of a few years back, that it was like moving a machine to set his mind in motion. As to the strain of meeting crowds of people every day, temperaments differ ; those who find it exhausting can never convince those who enjoy it that they are not simply misanthropists. 'But thought wears one down', Newman said, attributing his weariness mostly to the effort of composing the lectures.

Soon he was writing home telling a funny story of a big dinner at which Henry Wilberforce had his health drunk, and afterwards made a speech, 'with one floor' reported Newman, amused by the running commentary of the Irish priest sitting next to him. '"I have loved Ireland long, though this is the first time I have visited it,"' said Henry, and the priest commented, '"Good fellow ! very good." "I knew the Irish poor long before I was a Catholic." "Very well said, nice fellow, very nice." "I did them all the good in my power." "Does he mean he tried to make them *heretics* ?" I interposed,' said Newman, 'to say that he meant he had relieved them in temporals but I cannot be sure I wiped out the impression.'

But although as Achilli's adversary he was so popular, Newman was discovering that the work which brought him to Ireland was beset with problems. 'Very little was done at the university meeting', he told Ambrose, '— nothing is given me to do. I am as yet unrecognized. It would be a comfort to think that this would go on to such an extent as to justify my backing out of the whole matter — but I don't think there is a chance of this. I have only then to be quiet and bide my time, for certainly I will have to keep to my own terms, though I am silent just now.' One of the handicaps was that he,

Rector of the University to be, had no seat on the committee. They could, and did, decide things without reference to him.

Somehow or other Newman survived his hearty welcome till at the beginning of August he reached Limerick. Here at Tervoe, his friend Monsell, afterwards Lord Emly and a convert of highly individual stamp, had a house, at present empty ; he had offered it to Newman as a resting place. He arrived there almost in a state of collapse. To Johnson he wrote : 'With over exertion I am so done up and feel so shivering, I could fancy I had some fever, but I believe it is want of sleep. I cannot sleep in strange places, or on feather beds . . . and yesterday I had a fatiguing journey in an Irish car, which jolts, in a most grievous rain, all in the air — and I am too old for that sort of thing . . . I have been driven over here, and I dare say, if I put my feet in water and go to bed, I shall (please God) be well to-morrow.' The same day he began a letter to Ambrose, saying he was 'quite knocked up' — his usual phrase for being on the point of breakdown. 'Only think of feather beds this weather ! I have been tempted to sleep on the floor. I took it off the first night at the Bishop's, but I suspect they were cruel enough to substitute some sort of soft bed for the hard mattress on which I slept tolerably, and on Sunday night I had very little good sleep.' Sunday was altogether a day of torment. After describing his jolting ride to Tervoe, he remarked on 'all this coming upon my sermon on Sunday and a dinner of *five hours* after it, I am weakened beyond description. I was barely strong enough to preach but these accompaniments are simply beyond me and will knock me up if they go on.' But he added, 'here I am in peace and in great quiet, and I doubt not I shall get well'.

The next day, feeling better, he continued : 'Tell Stanislas with my love that even for his sake I cannot take pleasure in large legs of coarse veal, boiled mutton as red as in the shambles and bloodshot kidneys. However, the bacon is capital — only unluckily people think it too common to give me.' For it was all done out of kindness, and Newman would suffer anything rather than hurt the feelings of his hosts. He dared not sleep on the floor or refuse the tough underdone meat, not only from courtesy but because if he did he was admired for his asceticism, when he only wanted to escape indigestion and insomnia.

He had only a week in that 'silent empty place in a large park' — he called it 'a whole week'. The rare relief of being left entirely alone revived him even in that short time. Writing to Johnson again, to congratulate him on the birth of a child, he said, 'The quiet set me up. It is the only thing for me ever. I never have been tired of being by myself since I was a boy.' A few weeks later he was wishing Dalgairns could have a similar rest and said of his week of solitude 'it was like going to sleep for that time ; everything was so still'.

As soon as he got back to England one thing after another came to harass him. A lay brother, James Pitts, one of the two boys who had run away from their father in Elton to join Faber, showed signs of mental derangement ; he was sent temporarily to his brother in London to see how he got on. Faber welcomed him with open arms, but Pitts was soon crawling under the beds with lighted matches and doing other less dangerous but more unpleasant things. Newman decided that James must be sent home to his father. In order that Faber should be spared the ordeal of meeting Mr. Pitts, he arranged that the youth should be fetched from Sydenham.

Then there was the shock of the expenses of the trial. Lewin's bill, merely one out of several, came to £2300. 'This has made me quite aghast', Newman wrote to Badeley. 'The whole congregational subscription in England and Ireland will hardly cover it.' To Hope he wrote : 'I cannot spend other men's money. I have nothing of my own but £1000 which was my patrimony for the priesthood. It, if given, would be a drop in such an ocean. His simple bill for seven months is more than twice all I have — how preposterous! Surely this must be *stopped*. Better I should not defend myself in October, and let things take their course, than suffer such wanton extravagance.' But the committee for his defence would not hear of his giving up the fight. In vain Newman totted up his accounts and was horrified ; they got up an indemnity fund and the cause spread from England to Europe and America. Such was Newman's fame that everywhere it was enthusiastically taken up by Catholic people. In the end he had over two thousand pounds more than he needed, which eventually went to the building of his University Church in Dublin.

Suddenly trouble blew up from another quarter. *The Tablet* took up 'old Brownson' and repeated his strictures on the *Essay*, so that Newman remarked to Dalgairns, 'I should not wonder if I had a Development controversy in addition to everything else'. It was trying at such a moment to have spread among English Catholics Brownson's assertions that Newman's theory was a novelty and the result of vanity, that he did not believe in the infallibility of the Church, when it was the kingpin of his thought, and that he was not to be trusted, as if he were a theological confidence trickster. Why *The Tablet* chose this moment to relay Brownson to England is a mystery. Newman wrote to the editor : 'This I trust I may say, that if there be a man in the whole Church, who from faith, obedience and love towards her, would rejoice and exult in sacrificing any opinion of his own at the bidding of his ecclesiastical superiors (if I dare speak of myself) I am the man. I have ever detested the spirit of shuffling and concealment of opinion, so recklessly imputed to me when I was a Protestant. . . . Perhaps the able and (I am sure) excellent writer of the strictures which you have republished will live to be sorry, whatever becomes of *me*, for judgments which he had no right to form, and no call to put into circulation.' He did, but not yet.

Two days before this letter to *The Tablet*, on September 12th, Newman was writing to Dalgairns and said, 'I don't seem a bit the better for all this trouble, nay seem not to have strength given me to bear it'. He was surprised at what seemed to him a weakness. Dalgairns was another problem, for he was still unhappy in the London House. After a visit to Edgbaston he wrote nostalgically, 'It seemed somehow as if old times had come back again'. Faber was just now in Dublin, preaching, and such a success that he said he was quite tired of dining out. Newman sent him some rosaries to give away, one for 'my sacristan, viz the housemaid', and the other for the boy who served his mass there — it was typical of him not to forget them in the midst of his troubles. 'Do come — and come soon', he wrote to Stanton in August, '— and have some long chats — and write one of my Discourses for me, or at least lighten the writing.' For although they were never to be delivered he was finishing the rest of the series for publication. And he asked Stanton to find out if John Waite, a Trinity College servant in Oxford, had left anything in his will to his sister Mary Anne. She and her husband had turned up on the doorstep at Alcester Street some years before, remembering Newman's kindness long ago when they were his parishioners in St. Clement's. They had settled in Birmingham and become Catholics.

The same day as he wrote to Dalgairns, Newman also wrote to Mother Margaret to thank her for money, which he hardly liked to take, and for sympathy : 'Indeed I need that sympathy, for things seem to be getting worse daily. Yet I have no right to complain, as I have felt from the first, I have for some time been braving the devil. I knew I was doing so, and that one was commonly in such

cases taken at one's word — but still when the trial comes it is bad
to bear. There are times in one's life when, after the similitude of
holy Job, one experiences a multitude of trials at once. . . . You will
smile at this accumulation of complaints . . . so you see I really do
need your prayers very much.'

Because he went on working and seemed cheerful, people did not
realize how worn out he was ; one week at Tervoe was not nearly
enough to restore him. At the end of September he broke down in
what he called 'a common lecture' — one of the week-day talks at the
Oratory. And now the legal processes were nagging again like a bad
tooth. Telling Sister Imelda how marvellously their prayers had
been answered with regard to money, he said : 'It is impossible to
tell how my matter will turn out. Every day brings a different view,
and it is the suspense and change of prospect which is the trial. It
is like having the pupil of the eye exposed to a shifting light, now
strong, now dim, now darkness — and then the blaze again.' How
curious that Newman should have suffered, in Victorian England,
the same sort of mental torture of threats and anxiety and uncertainty
with which so many to-day are sadly familiar and that he used this
image, of light made the instrument of the torturers. But in his case
the torment was all within and unseen.

Other people saw the effect of the prolonged strain when he
reached the point of physical breakdown — though it was not a
complete collapse even then. Babington, whom he consulted in
October, and who had known him now for some twenty-five years,
prophesied an early death if he did not stop living at such high
pressure. His lawyers wanted medical affidavits, to lessen the chance
of actual imprisonment, so he saw two other doctors as well. Lord
Feilding, an ardent convert, invited him to stay, but he felt it best to
stay at home. 'My people are very kind to me, take all the work and
let me eat, drink, sleep and be idle', he told him. He was also invited
to Abbotsford, Sir Walter Scott's old home, by his friend James
Hope, who, having married Scott's granddaughter and heir, Charlotte
Lockhart, had added Scott to his name. Newman found it difficult
at first to call him 'Hope-Scott'. At present he refused the invitation.
Hope-Scott had come into the Church with Manning ; he too was
a friend of Gladstone.

About this time Newman wrote to Mrs. Bowden : 'I am fit for
nothing but to lie on the sofa. I say this to account for my silence
. . . it will be very long before I write another book.' He still blamed
his exhaustion mainly on the Lectures. The phrase 'lying on the

sofa', which he often used, meant in fact that he lay, or sat propped up, on his bed, fully dressed, and usually writing letters. It was only exceptionally heavy colds which induced him to give up the duties or exercises of community life, when he noted in his diary 'kept my room' or occasionally 'kept my bed'. A sign of being really 'knocked up' was the note 'did not say mass'. Even when he was a very old man and ill, someone noticed he was lying on his bed in his cassock. He liked to feel ready for anything ; to be undressed in a crisis was to be caught at a disadvantage, like Achilles without his armour. At various times bad news did catch him while dressing or undressing ; the fact always came into any account of the events, emphasizing for him the excitement and suddenness of the catastrophe. So now he lay on his sofa, but ready to get up at a moment's notice. In spite of the doctors' warning, he said to Wiseman, who anxiously inquired how he was, 'Physicians may be out in their calculations as well as lawyers'.

In this state of exhaustion, at the beginning of November, he was called up, at a week's notice, for the judgment.

Among all the stern necessities of the occasion was one simply tiresome, which had not occurred to Newman till this moment. He wrote off to Henry Wilberforce in Ireland, in a great hurry, 'I am sorry to give you so much trouble but (*entre nous*) I have no clothes here to appear before Lord Campbell in, and leave for London Friday. I am to be had up next Monday — we have just heard it.' The clothes were those he wore in Ireland, which he called semi-archidiaconal, because of the breeches and gaiters. But with them went a Roman collar, then only worn by Catholic priests. Ambrose had found that his Roman collar excited almost as much undesirable attention in the streets of London as a habit or cassock. These garments, carefully described, were to be packed by Henry in an 'old yellow brown leather small portmanteau' and despatched at once. Alas, on November 11th Newman was writing anxiously : 'It is six p.m. and the portmanteau has not come. As you pass down to Kingstown to-morrow put your head into the booking office and see if it is still there.' It must have come in the end. Anyway, in whatever clothes, he went to London, fully expecting to receive a prison sentence.

On arrival he was met with a new change, another shift of the invisible beam that so confused his inward vision. This time it was his own lawyers who altered the perspective by offering a fresh solution : they wanted to ask for a new trial. Bewildered, Newman wrote

the same day to Joseph Gordon in Birmingham, 'So I am to be in a
sea of trouble again, having just got to shore. At least, this I suppose
will be the result of to-day's consultation, which I am to attend.
What is the good of my attending, if I am told beforehand I *must* do
what counsel advise ? For myself, the more I think of it, the more
I am against this moving for a new trial. My misery for a year was
suspense and not seeing my way. I have a clear short way before
me, and I am to be hurried back into the thick darkness.' He could
see no use in it anyway. 'I don't wish to give the judges a clear
conscience — I wish to be an injured man.' And still more expense !
'Well it is in higher Hands than mine, but if anything is likely to
break me down it is this going on. Sir B. Brodie told me yesterday
that unless I got out of anxiety and let my nerves rest, I should die
Swift's death.' Babington prophesied physical, and Brodie mental,
breakdown, not an encouraging prospect in any event.

Next day, after the consultation, it was Bowles' turn to get the
news. 'The lawyers were very kind and delicate yesterday — they
said I alone could decide. Sir A. Cockburn, who shook hands in a
very friendly way . . . was strongly against moving with a notion of
frightening off Achilli. He said I ought not to move unless I had a
bona fide intention of getting the witnesses again and raising funds.'
Newman replied that in that case he could not do it ; but the decision
was again postponed. He did not realize till later that the lawyers,
as he told Mrs. Bowden after all was over, 'were thrown on their
backs' by his refusal. 'Since they deferred to me I thought I had it
all my own way.' So now he imagined that all idea of a new trial
was at an end, and went to pack his portmanteau for prison. St. John
got leave from the Cardinal for him to say mass in gaol if he was sent
there, and in King William Street they packed up a portable altar
and vestments. Newman was not staying at the Oratory, but with
Lord Arundel, who had persuaded him that it would have a good
effect on public opinion. Convict or no, the Catholic nobility would
show their respect to Dr. Newman, and English people in general
had a great reverence for noble lords, whatever their religion.

Arundel was not the only Catholic gentleman of note who accompanied Newman next day to Westminster Hall where, amid the
splendid memorials of the past history of England, the judgment was
to be given. It was November 22nd, St. Cecilia's day, one of the
special patrons of the Oratory, as well as of music. There were
crowds, both inside and outside the court, come to see the famous
Dr. Newman sentenced ; not all were hostile, for in the street were

many Catholics. Newman wrote an account of the proceedings the same day for Joseph Gordon, and later another for Mrs. Bowden to be handed round to other friends. In the latter he said, 'Sir A. Cockburn leant over the back of my bench, for I was under him, and said, "Well, new trial or not ?" I thought he asked for form's sake, so I answered briefly "not". Then I heard him grumbling behind me and began to suspect that he and the rest had got up their speeches with a view to moving for a new trial.' He found Serjeant Wilkins had been up half the night getting up evidence. 'When the judge came in Sir A. C. leant over once again. "You have now", he said, "a last chance, yes or no." I answered No and he went out of court.'

To Father Joseph, on the day itself, he said : 'Cockburn walked out in disgust. I said to Bellasis, who was beside me, "It is all over, is it not ?" He said yes. Other lawyers then came to Bellasis *who was on my side of opinion strongly*. At last he said, "Well you must not stand out longer — all your lawyers are against you." I said, "It is too late". "No," he answered, "it is not." "Very well then," I said, "let them have their way." It was done.' He yielded when the lawyers were unanimous, because Wiseman and Grant had told him to obey them as he would a physician — and he knew St. Philip's submission to that necessity. Afterwards he heard that Cockburn had said to Badeley, 'We can make nothing of Dr. Newman — you must persuade him'. It was Badeley who got Bellasis on his side, thus presenting Newman with a united front. Later Newman acknowledged that they had been right, but now it seemed to mean nothing but more delay, anxiety and waste of money.

Newman continued his account to Father Joseph : 'After a most tedious reading of the Judge's notes, from ten to half past one, Cockburn rose and began speaking. Campbell in a condescending, considerate way said, "Sir Alexander, Dr. Newman doubtless has an affidavit ?" as if setting him right in my power. Cockburn then said, "My Lord, I wish to suggest the court that there are grounds for a *new trial*". The effect was wonderful, no one had known what was to be. Campbell at once showed great agitation. Thesiger threw himself back. Tonna and another of Achilli's friends who were opposite to me *vanished*.' In the other account he said of Campbell : 'I did not look at the poor old man, but had I any resentment against him, alas ! at that moment and in the rest of the proceedings it would have been gratified to the very full. He changed colour, shook and his voice trembled. A military friend who was at my elbow said his head quivered as if he had been shot in the ear. Serjeant Bellasis

said to me "Do you see how Campbell is agitated?"' The military
friend was none other than Henry Bowden, who had so opposed his
brother's widow in her wish to become a Catholic, but was now one
himself. Newman's letter to Father Joseph concluded: 'Then he
(Cockburn) began a most masterly exposure of judge and jury, till
there was a loud cheering from the audience, which of course was
instantly put down. The judges have allowed the matter to be argued
(which comes on perhaps next month). As I went out of Westminster
Hall a vast number of persons took off their hats etc. etc.' The etc.
was probably cheering, as on a later occasion.

Everyone was now in high spirits and prophesying victory; only
Newman was still doubtful. In December he was writing to Stanton,
again abroad for his health: 'I told you that all the lawyers think I
have gained a great victory on St. Cecilia's day and are in high satisfaction. In an ordinary case I should have, but I have to do with
enemies who hate me so much that one cannot judge by ordinary
rules.' He meant not only Achilli, but his backers of the Protestant
Alliance. He asked Stanton to get him in Rome 'one of the small
recumbent St. Cecilia's' — the famous statue modelled after the body
found in this early martyr's tomb. Perhaps Newman was thinking
of its calm and simple beauty when he wrote of Callista after her
martyrdom.

Newman returned to Birmingham and immediately went down
with influenza, just as he had after the November crisis of 1844. He
noticed himself the curious fact that nearly all the crises of his life
took place in November. February, his birthday month, was also
frequently a time for troubles to descend. Of the influenza, Newman
said to Hope, 'at present it has taken the shape of lumbago'. After
the excitements at Westminster everyone had combined to urge
Newman to take a holiday and rest. He would have preferred to stay
quietly at home, but when Wiseman, Grant and Ullathorne all
insisted — a Cardinal and two Bishops, one his own — he felt he
ought to obey. So he accepted Hope's pressing invitation to Abbotsford. Influenza altered his plans to the extent of leaving London
out of his itinerary; he went straight up north instead, for his first
holiday in years, in the middle of December.

1852–1853

Newman in Scotland: Crisis in Birmingham

'YOU have all heard from Robert that the train was half an hour late,' Newman wrote from Abbotsford to Joseph Gordon — Robert Tillotson was a young American novice — 'and by the time I got to Derby that half hour had become an hour. Accordingly I gave up all hope of the Express, but there it was at the Derby station waiting for me. In I got in a hurry with a more promiscuous freightage than I have ever seen, hardly a seat to be had, what with boys from school squandering shillings on Uncle Tom's relations and imitations, cattle fanciers and black looking quakeresses. I had no time to eat, but abandoned myself to my good luck in gaining the Express, and centred my energies upon the attempt to improve it the first opportunity by seizing on a seat with the back to the motion and the wind. As we drew near York however, and stopped to present our tickets, though I was ticketed to "Newcastle, Express", the policeman told us that the Express had gone some time, and a passenger confirmed the evidence, on his view of the antecedent probability suggested by his local experience. In spite of this we *did* go on as an express, and at once, without a moment to eat. It was now past four, and as the train stopped but once (at Darlington) before Durham, I abandoned myself to sleep, and woke near the end of the run so exhausted that I did not know what was coming. When the train stopped, the man wanted to take my ticket, and on my resisting on the ground that my ticket was for Newcastle, not Durham I found we had run past Durham and were at Newcastle, and the Express gone — but we were to be sent on again by express. I flung myself on the mercy of a Samaritan of a policeman who literally ran with me to the ticket office and then to the refreshment room, where, with great fear lest it would get into my head (which it didn't) I swallowed down a glass of sherry, and carried off to the carriage some sandwiches. On went the Express for Berwick, an hour and a half past its time and with not above four passengers in it, as I was told. I tried to get out of my

616

travelling companion, whether I ought to stop at Tweedmouth or
Berwick, but he was too Scotch to give me a plain answer, and I
could not learn more than that he knew of two good hotels in Berwick,
the Cross Keys and the King's Arms, that railway hotels did not
answer, and that for that matter he did not like railways and the
rest of it at all, but preferred the old coaching proceedings. When we
got to Tweedmouth I prepared to solve my difficulty when I heard
the railwayman's voice running along from carriage to carriage, "Is
a gentleman of the name of Newman here?" and soon I found that
Lord Arundel had sent his servant for me and that I was in fact his
or Hope's guest. My bed was ready, a fire in the parlour, dinner
served up in a trice, a piece of excellent mutton, a fowl, and a pudding! *Quanta patimur!* Then tea. This morning, a fish breakfast.
I sent for my bill — *all* of course settled. I got here without further
adventures. . . . Lord A's servant had expected me by the first
Express, then gone on to Berwick in search of me and returned to
Tweedmouth giving me up — when in came my express. In future
I must say that I travel by an Express of my own. . . . I am longing to
hear something about you. Love to all. . . . P.S. I have nothing the
matter with me, except being a little stiff.'

They were all delighted with this vivid account 'and mentally
chew the roast mutton and chicken provided for you', said Ambrose.
Joseph Gordon, a great fan of Walter Scott, was longing to hear about
Abbotsford, and it was to him Newman began a description of it —
but as usual soon slipped into the human scene. 'The House itself
is dark and the rooms low. The first floor passage is not so broad
(not above half) as the "Newman Alley" leading to my room from
our corridor.' This was at Edgbaston; the Newman Alley was a
short passage which could just be used to pace in on wet days. 'Very
dark withal and winding — I could shake hands with the nursery
maids in the room opposite me without leaving my own room — and
sometimes of a morning or evening in going downstairs, seeing
nothing, I hear a step approaching and am obliged to stand
still where I am for fear of the consequences, and then a little light
figure shoots past me on the right or left, she having better eyes
than I. Once there was an awful moral stoppage, neither daring to
move.'

The Hopes had a private chapel, and the Blessed Sacrament
reserved so long as a priest was with them. When Newman arrived,
a Conceptionist left, for there was a great shortage of priests in the
north. The Bishop at once gave Newman faculties, which in effect

meant that he would be responsible for the local Catholics over Christmas. He wrote to St. John, that indefatigable missioner, 'You will feel it a drawback on this goodness that I have begged off the sick calls. . . . Hope asked me to preach this evening — which however he recalled directly he found I was coward enough to scruple at it. All this will give you true satisfaction.' Far from it : Ambrose wrote protesting at 'your sacrificing your leisure time to missionizing in Scotland. I shall write to Hope myself if you go on as you do.' Newman's cheerfulness made people forget the doctors' verdicts on him. He was still suffering from the after effects of the influenza, and remarked, 'I cannot get rid of my lumbago, so to call it, which annoys me, because, till it is gone, it may get worse'. It certainly did not get better, for he mentioned it in other letters.

The weather, as so often when he got the chance of going into the country, was terrible. Scotch mists, rain and a 'nasty whistling wind' made walking out of doors impossible, and did not increase the comfort of Gothic Abbotsford. Just after Christmas, Newman was writing to Ambrose : 'What weather! We have only got out for two days walking since I have been here. The wind violently blowing the flame into the room. I have put up an old *Tablet* as a blower . . . one day I was obliged to sit without fire. Everything too covered with soot! one's fingers (in which you will sympathize) beastly.' Not very conducive to rest and recuperation after prolonged strain and overwork, but Newman wrote triumphantly to Henry Wilberforce, 'It is to me a proof how much is in me, true as it is of course what Mr. Babington says, that I rally so quickly — I never had so bad, or at least a worse attack, yet I was able to travel in ten days and have no sort of cold on me now, or any weakness more than ordinary.' And to Joseph Gordon, himself dangerously ill, who had been anxiously inquiring how he felt, he boasted : 'I have been struck at my latent vivaciousness. How few people could pick up so quickly as I did, after so severe a touch of influenza! To my own feeling, this is a great point.' But he told him too his feeling of being held in a 'moral tether' so that in everything he could do just so much and no more. 'I cannot feel more pain than a certain quantity without *fainting* and it is my way all over. I cannot feel more devotion, unless something happened to my heart like St. Philip's. I am like an instrument which cannot be played on except in a certain way . . . the difficulty will be to persuade others *that I am doing as much as I can.*' Actually the difficulty was to prevent them from forcing him to do more than he could ; his habitual courtesy and

gaiety, mentioned by so many, made them think that nothing cost
him any effort.

But although the party at Abbotsford was congenial, this was not
to him a happy time. It was nothing to do with the Hopes and the
Arundels who, he said, were 'quite saints — I do not know which of
them is in the chapel most'. Nor with their aristocratic way of life,
though it amused him. A drive was a formal occasion, taken in a
procession of carriages, 'Hope and his wife and Lord and Lady
Arundel first, with outriders in the form of Lady Victoria or little
Henry, and I and Badeley to bring up the rear'. Newman told
Gordon in January, 'Never was a party which got on so well together,
yet even here there is considerable cause for anxiety and I am not at
my ease. It is from no over fidget that I am led to recollect the
proverb "Familiarity breeds contempt". The very absoluteness
with which I feel at home is certainly dangerous and I have to be ever
on my guard lest I go too far. I am in danger of arguing too much,
or laughing too much, and though I ought not *personally* to care that
persons should go away with a lower and truer notion of me, the
thought of giving scandal comes before me and annoys me.'

It was not that he thought it wrong to argue and laugh, or that he
wanted to appear dignified, for there was nothing he hated more than
pious pretensions ; but he was too acute an observer not to notice
that sometimes people were shocked at what they considered levity
or frivolity, and knew that to many he was not just a private person
but a Catholic priest and the representative of the Oratory. It was
just because it was natural to him to behave casually that he had
qualms about it. In later years he gave up bothering and visitors to
the Oratory often remarked afterwards with surprise that he was
'not at all like a Roman priest' — like what they had imagined he
ought to be, whether on the suave, crafty or saintly model. Badeley,
the new convert, was certainly not shocked on this occasion, for
shortly afterwards Ambrose met him in London and reported :
'Badeley says you are so cheerful and so jolly and tell such good
stories. They seemed to have enjoyed you much.'

Yet it was when Badeley left, after Epiphany 1853, that Newman
nearly let out his unhappiness in public. He told Joseph Gordon,
'It came upon me with such a thrill of horror that I might have cried
out before everyone when I heard it "O that I were going with you !"'
The reason for this inward cry of anguish, suppressed so that his
hosts remained unaware of what he felt, was a sudden crisis in his
community in Birmingham which painfully revealed its weaknesses

and the instability of its enthusiastic but youthful and headstrong members. Newman had been thinking of his community from the moment he left them ; as well as writing almost every day he had planned a surprise for them at Christmas, the first he had spent away from them. 'A large supply of eatables' was ordered through Philip Gordon in London, 'e.g. tongues hams beef Yorkshire pies etc. . . . I think we are falling ill from want of generous living' — some consolation for the Londoners with their high meat bills ! The Christmas 'suck' as Ambrose called it, was much appreciated, but Newman had another surprise in preparation, 'not suck, tell F. Ambrose, but a real spiritual present'. Sitting in his Gothic room with the fire blowing out into it, he was arranging St. Philip's life in portions to suit the ecclesiastical year, to be read in the Refectory. In doing this he was thinking of their common vocation and family life, as he was when he wrote special letters to be read at the chapter meetings, and the ordinary daily letters which were passed round at recreation. It was therefore a shock to his feelings as well as to his confidence in them when, on a scandal and a quarrel breaking out at home, they acted precipitately, giving him no time to advise.

No wonder they were alarmed, living in the full glare of Newman's publicity, with Protestant militants and newspaper reporters watching like hawks for scandals among monks — Oratorians were all monks to them ; nor were they able to distinguish between priests vowed to chastity and lay brothers who were not bound by vows and could, if they wished, return to the world and marry. The scandal in Birmingham was caused by Brother Bernard Henin, who had more education than some of the others, and was a frequent visitor at the house of the 'nunnish ladies'. Ambrose's first letter, which arrived soon after Christmas, was so incoherent that Newman could hardly make out what had happened and feared it was worse than it turned out to be ; it seemed that Brother Bernard had been making advances to Mrs. Wootten, under the pretext of cherishing a 'spiritual love' for her ; that she had told Darnell in the confessional, giving him leave to speak to Bernard ; that Bernard had been rude to Darnell ; and that Gordon, who as Father Minister was in charge of the lay brothers, had become very excited and made himself more ill than ever.

Darnell's first statement Newman burnt, probably for fear the servants might see it ; he afterwards regretted he had done this. He wrote home at once, giving his immediate reactions. 'Bernard's delusion', as he called it, about 'spiritual love' he found distasteful.

'I suppose Miss Giberne has encouraged him. Doubtless she has talked to him in the most idiotic way of her spiritual love for me — and doubtless B. has thought that my impatience *at* seeing her rose from my fear that I felt too much spiritual love for her.' But he said to Darnell : 'As to the thing itself I do not indulge the disgust and indignation I feel, thinking I may, for what I know, feel more its bad taste and absurdity than its sinfulness. But I cannot get over his deceit. . . . Had he committed an act of fornication, and then come and said "Listen to what I have done" it would have been a most bitter piercing trial to me, but I should have felt, I think, no anger with him — for strong temptation may come upon anyone — but to go on deliberately month after month keeping secrets from us, making a confidant of a woman, and asking no counsel of his fathers and brothers . . . shows that there has been some great mistake in his original casting and he needs melting up again.' It was this deceit and disloyalty that prompted Newman's first severe judgment : 'I can stand anything but unfaithfulness — he has committed the unpardonable sin. Confidence is simply at an end with him. I shall not live long enough for him to regain my confidence.' But he added : 'He may lose his soul if he goes — yet to keep him is to keep a traitor. I am very much perplexed what to do.' And to Ambrose, in the heat of the moment he had said, 'He must go — St. Philip has no need of men'.

But he did not mean that Bernard must go at once ; indeed he had asked him to write a statement of his own case. Such was the excitement in Birmingham, however, that Brother Bernard was virtually dismissed from the Congregation at once ; to hide the scandal of his sudden departure he was sent to the Redemptorists for a retreat. From there he wrote a letter full of contrition. Meanwhile, instead of a statement from the culprit, Newman received two letters from Ambrose so incoherent that he began to fear he had not realized the full extent of Bernard's delinquency. He quoted Ambrose's words back to him, saying of the first letter : 'It ran "Mrs. W. positively denies that B. kissed her hand at all. This is a dead block." (a dead block to *what* ?) ". . . B goes to Liverpool to-morrow. I am relieved from the most intense anxiety."' Newman said he had hardly deciphered this before the second came, announcing : 'I think we all feel the trials of the last week have been worse than *death* in the house. *Horrible* as the reality was when it broke upon me. . . .' Newman said, 'Is it wonderful that from letters such as these, the most wild thoughts rushed upon me, — that he had forced someone, that he had lived for months in a state of sin with half a dozen people, that someone else had turned out a reprobate, nothing seemed too great for such expressions — and nothing but my utter helplessness here and that I *must* submit, whether I would or no, kept me quiet'. At last came a more explicit letter : 'and I discover poor B's offence is not any open scandal or extraordinary depravity, but what I thought it at first, a gross, a very gross case of self-deception. Such a case is afflicting but not horrible — for who does not, in his measure, deceive himself ?'

Unfortunately for Brother Bernard, Newman with his common sense and wide understanding of human frailties, was not there to check the less balanced reactions of the younger Fathers. For silly and dangerous as the young man's behaviour was, that of others concerned, in a different way, was almost worse. Bernard's deceit and gossiping about the affairs of the house to outsiders, were worse than his delusions about spiritual love ; but there was Darnell's extraordinary independence, in not referring to his Superior a moral problem of such gravity, and one that he had apparently known about for months. As if this were not disturbing enough the supposedly responsible members of the community had acted precipitately, without consulting their Superior, in sending the Brother away, and thoughtlessly in sending him to Father Lans, of all people, who had unsettled Penny and carried off Coffin, and generally treated the Oratory as he would never have dreamed of treating an established religious house. It seemed to Newman that if they acted like this the moment he went away they could not have much respect for his authority, or love for him. 'Does it not come to this, that I am unnecessary to you ?' he said sadly to Ambrose. He felt such behaviour must arise from a lack of confidence in himself, and he was the more hurt because he had been trying so hard to keep the bonds close during his absence. 'I bought 5/- worth of stamps,' he said, 'all are gone but eight.' The chapter addresses, the little book of St. Philip, had never even been acknowledged.

In spite of this feeling that they simply did not care what he thought, and could not be bothered to consult him, he wrote a careful letter to the headstrong Darnell, telling him where he thought he had acted as wrongly, in a different way, as Bernard. Darnell had learned Bernard's secret and kept it to himself, so that to the lay brother he must seem to have a private hold over him. Putting himself in the place of the culprit, Newman said, 'If I had been an Italian and a man of unsubdued mind, I should be sorely tempted to use a stiletto against that confessor'. Brother Bernard, being English and mild, had simply taken it out in rudeness. Darnell took this correction hard; he had been so sure it was the lay brother who was the only delinquent in the affair. Newman said: 'If I wound you and him [Ambrose] I am wounded myself — and have had the words "Heal our wounds, heal our wounds" — in my mouth for some days. Alas, alas, they are bleeding wounds — as if we had not enough to bear without these in addition.'

In Birmingham there was sorrow and alarm, and letters of apology and explanation went rushing north. Ambrose swore he had thought Newman meant him to send Bernard away at once. Realizing that his first reply might have given that impression, Newman said, 'I retract what I said on that point'. What he complained of was not their excitement but that they had acted while under its influence. 'All is at an end — as far as it is my fault, I am very sorry. . . . And now let us close the painful subject, and make much of each other, and love each other better because we are one the fewer.' Ambrose was so very upset by his censure that Newman again begged his pardon for calling him careless, 'I am very sorry if I have hurt you'. He posted this on Wednesday, January 12th; on Sunday he was writing again: 'I trust it comforted you, as I meant it to do. I have been anxiously looking out for a letter since to have this hope confirmed — when I had none yesterday (Saturday) evening, I got quite sad, kept thinking about it when I was in bed, and now am quite unsettled. For me, I did not delay an hour in sending you a kind word when I found I could, and this makes me uneasy at not hearing from you, as if there were some hitch some where.'

There was no hitch beyond the fact that Ambrose was travelling to and from London on the trial business. He felt sad, he said, to think they had all forgotten to thank Newman for the St. Philip. 'Only the other day I was boasting to F. Bernard [Dalgairns] in London that you had been working for us all the time you had been away. Well, it is no good saying this now it is too late.' And in another letter: 'I hope we all acted according to our lights but oh, how we want a head and backbone!' It was on this trip he met Badeley, who had said how much he had enjoyed Newman's company and stories. Newman said himself, 'I do not allow myself to think of anything — but go on at a jog trot through the day, seeming very merry and cheerful, but with an aching heart'. He would not let his hosts know an unhappiness they could do nothing to assuage; nor did he mention it when writing to Gordon, for Caswall had told him how much worse he seemed, emaciated, his legs mere spindles. Gordon said of Newman's letters to him that they were 'as good as a chapter in Scott's novels'. Newman decided that when he came home it would be better to say no more about it. 'It will only give rise to warm and keen feelings. Mine own are such that I do not know how I could restrain them, if I once began — and if I so feel others will too on their side. The thing is done.' But he was determined that no expulsion should be made so precipitately again, and suggested a decree should be passed to prevent it.

As to Brother Bernard, at first he did not want to leave the Oratory altogether and went to ask Faber to take him in. Faber wrote to ask for information, and Newman's reply was a plain report, unlike those he had received himself. 'B attempted to kiss Mrs. W's face four times. This is his own confession sent to me at Abbotsford. He tried but was not able to kiss her hand. . . .' It was not possible to have him in Birmingham, since they had a parish, which at that time the London Oratorians had not. 'We could not cut him off from Mrs. this and Miss that . . . if you break him you will have a most valuable brother — he has, I need not tell you, a hundred good qualities — but he is hopeless till he ceases to be selfish.' He added in a postscript that his impression was that 'all B cared for was to get Mrs. W's approval. If he had, he would not have cared for any of us, he would not have mentioned anything in confession, but would have gone to almost any extent of sin with her. Lucky or rather providential is it, that he did not address some other person. Mrs. W has behaved as well as could be from the first, whatever B may seem to imply.' Bernard Henin was not cut out to be a Brother. He left, got married, and later brought his wife to see Newman.

Thus ended Newman's holiday, and needless to say he did not feel much the better for it. The Hopes took him to visit the ruins of Melrose Abbey and insisted on paying the expenses of his journey; he was grateful for their kindness but glad to be going home. Darnell was to come for a holiday and be their temporary chaplain, but they need not pay his expenses, Newman told Hope, for he was rich. He asked Gordon anxiously about tips, 'Speak O man of the world'. He went back to Birmingham on January 25th, arriving unexpectedly, and found Gordon sitting up, looking dreadfully ill. 'I was greatly shocked at the change', Newman wrote in his diary. He went to London at once, where the arguments for the new trial had already begun.

1853

Newman passes into his Autumn

THE day Newman was looking at the ruins of Melrose Abbey, January 20th, the arguments for a new trial were heard in London. Ambrose was there as observer. 'Thesiger got very bitter', he reported. 'He said your words charged Achilli with an *unnatural* offence at Malta.' Lord Campbell had to pull him up. On the third day, 'Ellis began exceeding in bitterness everything that had gone before, declaring that the case had been hatched "where the black adder gathers her poison"'. Newman's lawyers, however, more than held their own. On 23rd, Ambrose gave an enthusiastic account of the opening of their case by Serjeant Wilkins.

'I think you would yourself willingly have endured all Thesiger's muck to have heard this good old honest fellow's hearty approbation both of yourself and of the Church.' Wilkins said of Newman's becoming a Catholic from conviction, 'for my part I *honour* him for it', and, reported Ambrose, 'he continued a long time in the same way, in the most hearty way, censuring most strongly the conduct of counsel, jury, and England in general for their scandalous belief of any lies that might be said against Catholics, turning round and speaking into Thesiger's face in the most delightful way. Afterwards he for 3 hours and a half took to pieces Achilli's own evidence and in a masterly way showed how he had corroborated our witnesses in the whole or the greater part of their statements, one felt and Badeley admitted that Achilli *must* have broken down under his cross examination, he far far surpassed Cockburn's best analysis of the evidence, and the great attention of the Judges, though they had heard the whole twice gone through before, showed that they felt him quite irresistible. I really felt quite carried away by the old boy's energy and set to work saying Hail Mary's for him then and there.'

For all that, they could not get over the technical point that not all the original charges were proved. It was on this ground that the Judges refused a new trial. On January 25th Newman was back in

Birmingham ; two days later the adverse decision was given and he went up to London to be sentenced. His movements were determined by cryptic messages on the Electric Telegraph, the code worked out beforehand. This time he refused the invitations of influential lay friends and stayed at the Oratory. But he could not refuse their invitation to dinner.

It was W. G. Ward who drove him to court on Monday 31st for the judgment. The court itself and 'all the avenues leading to it were crowded to excess', the newspapers reported. As well as Lord Campbell, that strong Evangelical, there was Mr. Justice Coleridge, a High Churchman, Keble's friend and future biographer. Both his sons had been admirers of Newman at Oxford ; the younger, Henry James Coleridge, had only recently submitted to Rome, and was to become a well-known member of the Society of Jesus. The Judge felt this as a great blow, and it may have embittered his feelings. The situation was curious in many ways. By now respectable opinion agreed with *The Times* that the first trial had been unfair ; yet a second would be an insult to Campbell, who was after all the Lord Chief Justice. Nobody knew what to expect. 'Prison is still on the cards', Newman had told Bowles earlier that month. In relating to Miss Giberne what happened he said : 'My counsel rose one after another and said I retracted not a word of the so-called libel. Thesiger was very angry and called on the Judges to inflict on me, for such audacity, a severe punishment. But the Judges said nothing.'

Newman only wanted one thing, to be allowed to say a few words himself. 'It is my day,' he said to Badeley, 'I seem to have a right to it.' He had drafted, last November, what he wished to say ; it was quite short, written out on a sheet of paper. 'The paper that I held in my hands' could have been written by no one else. Newman was aiming less at the people in court than at the vast invisible audience of newspaper readers, who had seen so many aspersions cast on his motives and had so little understanding of the real issue. 'So clear was I of all personal feeling against the individual to whom it (the libel) referred, that ever since the verdict, I have in dreams fancied I was falling on his neck and embracing him. . . . My Lords I cheerfully submit myself to the law that condemns me. That law put me on trial on the oath of one man. . . . That man is the very man against whom I made my charge ; and my very charge against that man, was that his word could not safely be taken. I accused him of breaking oaths ; he convicts me by taking his oath that he has not broken them. . . . A prison can but shorten my life ; a fine can but drive me to beg ; the world's reproach and scorn can but inflict on me, what they have already inflicted on me for a long twenty years.'

This speech was never heard. When Newman was called out on to the floor of the court to be sentenced, he asked permission to say a few words. He was questioned as to whether his lawyers knew of it ; in general, he answered, but not in particulars. The judges seem to have taken fright at this, for though he began, he was not allowed to continue. All the newspapers got out of the incident was that he tried to read something but was stopped. 'He accordingly stood with arms folded on the floor of the court and was addressed as follows by Mr. Justice Coleridge.' Coleridge proceeded to lecture Newman for half an hour ; during that time Newman had no idea what sort of sentence was coming to him at the end of it. He wrote afterwards, 'There was apparently an expectation all over the court that I should suffer some considerable imprisonment — in which I certainly had participated up to the time of the sentence and when I left the London Oratory in the morning, my dear brothers parted from me as if for prison'.

He had even prepared, in case of necessity, a Chapter address for the Birmingham Oratory to be read if he were sent to gaol. Among other things in it he characteristically remarked that one result of the trial which might be expected had not come to pass : his own advancement in the spiritual life. 'When it broke upon me last August year, that I might have to go to prison, I involuntarily said, "Well, if so, I ought to come out a saint". Yet all that interval has passed, and judging from it, never, never was there less appearance of religious good accruing to a soul from an external trial than in this case. This is my real discouragement and trouble. At most I shall be doing some slight penance for sin past ; to speak of more than this, is a romance or a dream. My children, what you are, depends much on what I am. You must pray for me and you will be praying for yourselves.'

Judge Coleridge was not aware of what went on in Newman's mind and heart. He could only see the traitor who had left Keble and Pusey in the lurch. It seemed a fit punishment for such an action that his character should have been corrupted and his taste coarsened by Rome. There was no necessity for Coleridge to lecture Newman for his personal conduct in public ; the temptation, however, proved irresistible. Newman listened to what he called cheerfully 'a horrible jobation from Coleridge — the theme of which was deterioration. I *had* been one of the brightest lights of Protestantism — he had delighted in my books — he had loved my meek spirit etc. etc.' But now Coleridge, as reported in the papers, had read the attack on Achilli 'with infinite shame and disgust', thinking it conceived 'partly in what may be called ferocious merriment, partly in triumph, partly in exultation over the unhappy man whose foul offences you were producing before your hearers'. Achilli's backers cannot have cared for what amounted to an admission of his guilt. To the high-minded Judge, however, Achilli's guilt (and he had been a Roman Catholic at the time) was less shocking than Newman's. But *he* was not going to exult over a fallen Newman, he declared virtuously ; he merely suggested that he should try in future not to be so personal and so bitter. The Judge entreated Newman to show a spirit of charity and humility.

This lecture was intended to make Newman feel ashamed of himself. Indeed, in the eyes of the world, what greater social disgrace could there be for so famous a Christian than to be condemned for criminal libel and severely reprimanded by an esteemed authority for extremely unchristian behaviour, for indulging in malice, scorn, slander and coarse invective merely for the fun of it ? And it was typical of polite society that it did indeed take the Judge's view ; the injustice of the trial which led to Newman's condemnation was forgotten, the damage Achilli had done to Catholics was forgotten — all that was remembered was the shocking fact that the supposedly saintly Newman had called someone a liar and a seducer in a public lecture. Even in later years, when Newman became respectable again, this episode was never referred to by the well bred.

Catholic friends were extremely annoyed at Coleridge, and Newman had to write pacifying letters to them. 'I could not help being amused at poor Coleridge's prose', he said to Capes. 'I have no doubt it gave him pain — and I think he wished to impress me. I trust I behaved respectfully, but he must have seen that I was as perfectly unconcerned as if I had been in my own room. But so it was — putting aside supernatural views and motives (of which alas I have not overmuch) mere habit as in the case of skinned eels would keep me from being annoyed. I have not been the butt of slander and scorn for twenty years for nothing.' To Henry Wilberforce he said : 'I had not the least awkwardness or confusion before Coleridge. Poor fellow, I think he seemed hurt I was not moved — but it was impossible. Catholics view these things so differently from Protestants.' Perhaps because it was so obvious that he was not ashamed, as he stood there with his arms folded, Coleridge, whose exhortation seemed to be going on for ever, brought it suddenly to a close and pronounced sentence : A hundred-pound fine and imprisonment till it was paid.

The light sentence surprised everybody ; Achilli's counsel were plainly disappointed. In a moment Newman's friends jumped up and crowded round to congratulate him, and, said the reporters, he seemed quite pleased about it himself. 'Of course the said fine was paid there and then', Ambrose scribbled off to Birmingham, hoping they had made out the telegram dispatched earlier, 'and we walked off in triumph amid the hurrahs of 200 Paddies. The whole outside of the court rung with these acclamations.' Newman wrote on the same page that the opinions they had heard so far were 'to the effect that I had gained a victory'. The letter was addressed to Bowles, the absent-minded, and he said : 'Don't put this in your pocket but let everyone see it. Love to all.' At the bottom he wrote, 'They would not let me speak'.

When the newspapers came out, with Coleridge's 'jobation', Newman's indignant friends wanted him to make some public answer ; Bellasis was especially pressing. To Northcote, a convert clergyman, Newman wrote : 'I suspect all my friends are down in the mouth as if I had got a fatal snub — *which I doubt not the judges meant*. All depends on what *I* feel about it. If I *am* dead, I am — if I am not, I am not. I don't feel dead at all.' All very well, his friends argued, but did it not matter that people in general might assume the snub had extinguished him ? After some deliberation Newman dealt with the question in the public letters of thanks he wrote to the contributors to his defence fund, which were printed in both the local and national papers.

In Birmingham he addressed Mr. Hardman, and after warmly thanking him went on to say, 'I said that Catholics had no fair play in the Protestant world ; is my statement confirmed or refuted by the trial which followed upon it ? I have been running the gauntlet of Protestantism in its many varieties from the Evangelical Alliance to the High Anglicanism of a Judge. It is a strange history, but I am not going to complain of it. . . . I have been too surprised at what I have undergone to be indignant, and too well satisfied with what I have done to be resentful. I have struck at the Protestant world and the Protestant world has struck at me, and I trust I have given as good as I received, or rather better. I trust my own blows have been fair. I cannot say so much of those which have been levelled against

me ; but any how I have gained by falsehood ; and I am content
with my bargain. . . .' And he quoted his 1850 sermon : 'We love
you, O men of this generation, but we fear you not !' The London
letter was addressed to Whitty, and contained a generous tribute to
Wiseman, considering what a nuisance his carelessness had been.
But now it was all over Newman said, 'What is good endures ; what
is evil comes to naught'. For years he prayed for his benefactors in
this trial.

Coleridge's eldest son, who was to be the Judge in the Tichborne
case and later Lord Chief Justice and a great admirer of Newman,
saw one of these letters at Hursley, where he was visiting Keble. 'I
never saw a letter of his so bad in taste, and seldom one so unfair . . .'
he said to his father, to whom he was devoted. 'I should not myself
have said exactly what you said (I mean as to substance) and I could
quite understand his not agreeing or feeling pleased — he stands at
a different point of sight — but I cannot think he was right to sneer
and laugh. . . .' (The dots of omission are those of Lord Coleridge's
biographer.) Yet Newman had not sneered at Coleridge senior, nor
defended himself against his charges of moral deterioration ; if he
laughed at the Protestant world in its No-Popery aspect, that world
was powerful enough to bear it. Throughout he had said no word
against the belief or morals of Protestants ; his protest was directed
at their negative and aggressive acts against Catholics. Nor was he
ever one to defend such persecuting acts on the part of Catholics, in
countries where they had the majority, against Protestants.

On February 1st, the day after the judgment, Newman went back
to Birmingham ; the next day he was distributing the blessed candles
and singing High Mass for the feast of the Purification, four years
since the opening in Alcester Street, five from the setting up of the
Oratory in England. But after all it was a sad homecoming, for
Father Joseph was so ill he was sent home to Bath. Yet none of them
realized how near the end was. Only next Sunday, during Vespers,
a telegraph came to say he was sinking. Newman took it as an
immediate summons and set off at once, arriving at Bath at midnight,
only to find he was not expected by Gordon's family. The doctor
was so determined not to alarm his patient that he refused either to
let Newman see him or to allow the local priest to be called. In the
end Newman got his way, and when he went into Father Joseph's
room it was plain that it was just what he had been longing for.
'When he saw me he broke into a cry of joy', Newman wrote to
Ambrose. 'I said "Hush", he said "No I can talk to you as to my

mother". I then brought in the Priest — He was anointed and then said "I am so happy". I said "Go to sleep" and he is now trying to do so. I ought to be most thankful. Remember me, O God, for the bitter things Thou bringest on me. The doctor says he is sinking — a true loyal son of St. Philip — he has a relic of him round his neck.' He asked Ambrose to send him in Latin directions for washing and vesting the body, but at 8 o'clock he was writing again : 'The anointing had almost a miraculous effect on him. All nervousness and anxiety is gone — he is cheerful, smiling and happy and the doctor says he will probably so continue till the last.' The next day the change for the better seemed so pronounced that the doctor became more hopeful still, and Newman went back to Birmingham for Ash Wednesday, distributing the ashes and singing the High Mass. But the next Sunday, at ten o'clock at night, came the news that Joseph Gordon had died at five that evening. The funeral was the following Thursday, and Newman went over to Bath for it. Gordon had left all his property to the Oratory.

To Joseph's brother, Philip, Newman wrote : 'We are brought into the Church to go to heaven. We cannot choose our own time, there may be but one time, as there is but one gate.' To Nicholas Darnell he said, 'He is an inexpressible loss to us — to me a special loss, never could any one be more loyal to me personally than he has been from first to last'. Darnell was feeling unhappy, because of his quarrel with Gordon over Brother Bernard, and because they had not always got on well. To comfort him, Newman said : 'When I gained him the Last Sacraments he said "Now I am in unity — before I was here and there". . . . He was two persons.' Newman admitted that Gordon had sometimes been hard to please. A mature man when he joined the Oratory, his novitiate had coincided with all the tensions caused by the incorporation of Faber's community. He had survived it all, turned out a 'great gun' at Alcester Street, hunted up the Achilli witnesses, and now he was taken away. Newman felt his loss more rather than less as time went on. When he bought land at Rednal for their holiday retreat and burial ground, he would not sleep in the house till Father Joseph's body had been brought to its final resting place there. In 1865, twelve years after Gordon's death, Newman dedicated to his memory *The Dream of Gerontius*.

For himself, this blow made him feel, with his strange groping foresight, that he had come to the end of a season in his life, that a change was coming. 'What a year and a half I have had ! When will the strokes end ?' he wrote to Henry Wilberforce, to whom he always turned for sympathy in moments of personal crisis. 'I recollect in 1826 when I was serving Rickards' church at Ulcombe during the Long Vacation, after a most glorious summer, there was a week of pouring rain, and then it was fine again, and the sky as radiant for weeks as before. But the season was changed — the ground had been thoroughly chilled — and never recovered itself. Autumn had unequivocally set in, and the week of wet divided the two seasons as by a river. And so I think I have now passed into my Autumn, though I trust grace will more than make up for me what nature takes away.'

He may have been thinking chiefly of the physical effect of the intense and prolonged strain of the last eighteen months; but although it was not immediately apparent a change was setting in which would entirely alter his position, and make an autumn in his inner, as well as in his outward, world. Now, for the last time until he was an old man nearing eighty, he had the full support and confidence of his contemporaries in the Catholic Church, high and low, clerical and lay, at home and abroad — for letters were still going out to all parts of the world to thank the thousands who had contributed so generously to 'The Newman Indemnity Fund'. Catholics accepted him as their champion when he attacked a renegade and the power and prejudice of a hostile world. They admired the fearless fighter who laughed at the disgrace to which he was consigned by society. But there was another battle going on which was not so easy to understand, nor the issue so simple, the battle for the minds of men, and this was the field where Newman had long ago chosen, or been chosen, to fight. He might be braving the devil in trying to blow away the smoke of lies that in England obscured the real issues, but he was daring the empire of darkness much more in his campaign to reintegrate reason and faith and to show his contemporaries that Christianity was not just an abstract idea immobilized in static forms, but a living and developing body.

In the *Essay on Development* he had stressed that growth takes place by means of assimilation; he sketched some of the lines of growth, in government and ideas, in the early Christian Church. Christianity had successfully assimilated a great many useful discoveries of pagan Greeks and Romans: philosophic, scientific and practical, discarding only what proved incompatible with revealed teaching. So, after some initial and instructive blunders, the Copernican revolution in scientific cosmology had been accepted and with it the whole concept of experimental investigation. Newman was convinced that another great mental effort was necessary to understand and assimilate what was true and positive in the discoveries of the new age, and it distressed him when he found Christians too often reacting, as in the first renaissance, with a rigid, narrow and suspicious conservatism not only unnecessary but dangerous.

The speed of change during the middle of the nineteenth century, from about 1830 to 1860, was extraordinary ; the pace then slackened till the final decades presented a false appearance of security, which can now be seen as the dead centre of a cyclone, in the second wild phase of which we are now living. All our problems and most of our general ideas have developed out of what was thought and done in that fierce uprush of creative energy — the breakthrough from a static to a dynamic conception of the world, taking so many and such various forms, from railways and revolutions to the idea of natural evolution and the awakening of the self-consciousness of the masses. This second renaissance, with all its opportunities and dangers, centred on the ideas of time and progress, as the first on those of space and enlightenment, was recognized by Newman for what it was : a great period of challenge to Christians, comparable to the sixteenth century, but also to the fourth and fifth, which he knew so well, the Church of the Fathers, who plumbed the abysses of the mysteries of the Faith with their Greek philosophic minds.

Why was Newman drawn so early to the Fathers ? Why did he so much love St. Paul, who presented the Gospel to pagans without the long moral and spiritual training of the Jewish nation ? Why did he choose St. Philip Neri for his patron, who had been accused of Protestantizing in his day, because he wished to bring Christian holiness within the reach and understanding of the man in the street — that new renaissance man, experimenting with everything, questioning everything, an individualist as the medieval man had not been ? St. Philip was not afraid of that new development ; he assisted in the process of transmuting a mere individualism into personal responsibility. Why did Newman bring St. Philip's institute to England in the revolutionary year of 1848, except that he wanted to present to Englishmen Christianity as wisdom in harmony with love, both obedient and adventurous ? He did not expect the Oratory to do original work, in theology for instance ; that was more likely to come from the religious orders — Jesuits, Benedictines and Dominicans — once they were free to expand. What he wanted to do was to provide centres where ordinary people could realize the best of the new knowledge in a Christian context, and find answers they could understand to the problems created by it. This was why he was concerned both with the cultured and educated and with the 'snobbish intellects' of the provincial middle and lower classes. In an age when statesmen were still all aristocrats he recognized that the rising political power was in the industrial towns. Thus he hoped to found Oratories as centres of Catholic activities, social and intellectual, in all the leading towns : Leeds, Bristol and Liverpool were all seriously considered. Oxford was always only one of his desired goals.

For Newman the proposed university in Ireland was a more specific application of these ideals to higher education ; he intended that 'Modern' subjects and sciences should run alongside the old classical curriculum and the medical school from the first played a large part in his plans. It was extremely necessary that those Catholics capable of receiving intellectual and cultural training should get it, but as far as Newman's own vocation was concerned, he felt the university to be secondary to the Oratory ; he was willing to help start it off, but never meant to transfer himself entirely to its affairs, as he told Archbishop Cullen from the beginning. For him, the Oratory expressed something wider and more general ; like his books, it could address everyone and anyone.

In 1853, tired as he was with the extraordinary stresses of the last ten years, fifty-two, and feeling at times considerably more, Newman was all ready for the double battle, to train the next generation of Christians to face not wild beasts but wild ideas, and to win back to Christ those who were being led into a sterile scepticism. Besides his own unique reputation and long experience at Oxford, he had then the whole-hearted support of the Catholic people in England and their spiritual leaders, the Pope's blessing for both Oratory and University, and two teams of intelligent and keen Englishmen, full of zeal and enthusiasm. It was only five years since he had started the Oratory, but the two houses had already settled into their respective spheres and both were in full work and still expanding. The stream of educated converts had not yet stopped flowing and it was reasonable to suppose that many would join St. Philip's Congregation and help in setting up other Oratories.

Yet these prospects were to be destroyed, and all the supports broken or weakened until at the end of the next ten years Newman was to be left almost helpless and to all appearance useless. There were many reasons for this series of defeats, but the ultimate cause was the acute internal crisis of the Catholic Church on the question of the right relation of Reason and Authority in intellectual, political and ecclesiastical affairs.   Catholics became deeply divided, some over-emphasizing the rights of reason and freedom for the individual, others going to the opposite extreme of authoritarianism, with its dangers of tyranny and suppression of truth.   Catholics believe that the Church will never fail because of Christ's promise ; nevertheless it is often in a state of moral crisis or collapse, according to the human beings which at any time compose it.

We are familiar with the state of moral laxity and corruption at the end of the Middle Ages, which was the chief cause that so many reforming movements ended in separatism and became confused with nascent and competitive nationalism.   Christendom lost its physical cohesion and spiritual unity because Christians had allowed the growing forces of individualism to swamp the sense of community ; the Church did not lose it, but inevitably in the chaos that ensued, the form it took in the minds of Catholics tended to be both aggressive and defensive.   By the nineteenth century it was clear that Protestants in the northern countries, and secularists and atheists in the south, had the ascendancy in Europe and were the leaders of material progress ; this of itself gave educated Catholics an inferiority complex, which led to romanticism about the past, an exaggerated scorn for modern achievements, or an excited determination to keep up with the rich relations at all costs, according to temperament.   The Church was fully reformed as to morals and discipline, full of charitable works and missionary zeal : just what it ought to have been three centuries before.   Christians, like the English nation, are always ready for the war before the one they actually have to face.

The great crisis of the nineteenth century was not moral but intellectual, and as Newman discovered so sadly when he went to Rome in 1846, the Church, in the persons of its rulers and teachers, could hardly have been worse equipped for the battle.   They were like generals trained in ground tactics suddenly attacked from the air. In him they had, if they had realized it, one who had already anticipated lines of attack which even the enemy had not yet thought of. But as the Lord himself observed, the children of light are not so quick in the uptake as the children of this world, and are blind to their own advantages.   Newman was to be misunderstood and denounced as a Liberal by the leaders of the extreme authoritarian party, who associated him with a critical individualism which he had given up before 1830, perhaps, one might even say, at the age of fifteen when he put aside Paine and Hume, humanism and scepticism, and turned to God made Man.

These inter-related problems of Reason and Faith, Freedom and Authority, agitated the Catholic body for some twenty years with a violence which is now forgotten, though its effects continued long after, perhaps still continue. Such a fierce internal dissension, resolved at last without very much loss by open schism, though probably with a large lapse of those unable to stand the strain, was a sign of latent vitality, but was mistaken by outsiders for death throes. Outsiders, too, thought then, and perhaps think now, that authoritarianism won the day because the Vatican Council defined the Pope's Infallibility. But in fact the moderation of the definition limited the power the extremists claimed for the Vicar of Christ; and also, a greater relief at the time, put a brake on their heresy-hunting inclinations. Religion is not the only field where doctrinaires rampage and real or supposed deviationists go through the mill, as we know only too well to-day. Since human nature is fallen from its original virtue, these weeds crop up in any society, small or large. They are failings we have to allow for and contend with in building up any communal enterprise, and give to Newman's story a personal and psychological interest even apart from the fascination of the ideas involved.

The first half of this campaign, of successive failures for Newman, was dominated for him by the divergence of the London Oratory, which allied itself with the extremists of the authoritarian party, and his consequent isolation and alienation from the leaders of policy in London and Rome. The second ten years more or less coincided with the sudden revival of his world-wide influence on the writing of the *Apologia*, which at once made him appear more dangerous, and so called down a determined campaign of attrition from Ward and Manning, the brain and the ruling hand of the English authoritarians. All doctrinaires think they are right, but religious doctrinaires think they are divinely right. Ward thought if he said what the Pope said he must be infallible — and then said more than the Pope said. Because the Church was inspired by the Holy Ghost Manning often felt the Archbishop of Westminster was too, and that anyone who disagreed was in danger of committing the unforgivable sin. It was perhaps the greatest shock of his life when Newman, whose books in his opinion were riddled with heresy, was made a Cardinal by the successor of Pius IX, the great Leo XIII.

Undreamed of, that final apotheosis, in the stress and anxieties of the fifties — undreamed of then the long second lifetime of defeat, desertion, rejection, suspicion, and the consequent feeling of uselessness, watching the opportunities wasted and the enemy advance. Newman did not know all that was to come, and yet he felt that a change had begun, when he said to Henry, 'And so I think I have now passed into my Autumn'.

NOTE ON SOURCES

Birmingham Oratory Archives

(1) *Letters by Newman.* There are estimated to be about 20,000 extant. A complete edition, which will run to about 30 volumes, is in preparation by the Very Rev. Charles Stephen Dessain, the present Superior of the Birmingham Oratory, to be published by Nelson. Two card indexes have been compiled of the letters, one chronological and the other under the names of correspondents. In order to avoid unnecessarily overloading the text with references I have tried to give the name of the correspondent and some indication of the date for all quotations, which can thus be verified fairly easily. In every case where these letters have been published before, I have quoted from the originals.

Autograph Letters. Correspondence with individuals fill 150 Personal Files; 80 are devoted to the various public crises of Newman's life; 60 to the domestic Oratory Letters. The latter are invaluable for the study of Newman's character and everyday life and show how his Oratorian vocation worked out in practice.

Missing Letters. The most unfortunate gap occurs in Newman's letters to Rogers, Lord Blachford, during the Oxford years. Rogers lent some to Anne Mozley, but nothing has been heard of them since. Francis Newman must have destroyed his brother's letters to him, except for one or two early ones.

(2) *Memoranda by Newman.* These are usually in the files dealing with the particular events concerned. Some are notes made at the time, others written afterwards but based on letters and diaries of the period concerned. The most important of those on the Irish University is printed at the end of *Autobiographical Writings.*

(3) *Autobiographical Journals, etc.* These have been published in *Autobiographical Writings* (Sheed and Ward), edited by the late Fr. Henry Tristram, with some additional notes by Fr. Charles Stephen Dessain. Unpublished: a few pages of prayers, etc. from 1817. Some other notes have been used in recent books on Newman, and printed in part.

(4) *Private Diaries,* 1824–79. Very few gaps in these, which provide a useful skeleton of Newman's life.

(5) *Historical, Philosophical and Theological Papers.* Much used by students of Newman's thought; some have been published in periodicals.

(6) *Irish University Papers* arranged by Newman himself and used by students of his educational theory and practice; also 30 bundles of miscellaneous papers concerned with affairs of the university.

(7) *Unpublished Sermons, Sermon notes, etc.* Some of the latter published 1913 with preface, by Fathers of the Birmingham Oratory. The only

unpublished sermon I have quoted is that written for Marianne Bowden's clothing in 1854.

(8) *Chapter Addresses* and Papers on the Oratorian life, of various periods : extremely interesting records of Newman's spiritual and practical teaching in the context of his religious life ; I have quoted especially those dealing with particular situations.

(9) *Letters to Newman* from friends, enemies, popes, children, bishops, governesses, statesmen, editors, nuns, evangelicals, atheists, aunts, Jesuits, lords, servants, cardinals and anonymous angry people. Some are in the personal files, some in the 65 boxes of Miscellaneous letters. They provide an interesting cross-section of current opinions.

(10) *Pamphlets, Scrapbooks of newspaper cuttings*, copies of the *Dublin Review, Weekly Register, Tablet*, etc., reviews of Newman's works and controversial correspondence.

(11) *Copied Letters* : 5000. Neville appealed for letters after Newman's death and was nearly buried under the response.

(12) *Letters by and to Neville* and other members of the Oratory relating to Newman, after his death, and to various articles, books, etc. about him, and about Purcell's life of Manning, etc. Also notes on these compiled by Fr. Henry Tristram.

(13) *Notes made by Neville* on conversations with Newman in old age, and for his introduction to *Meditations and Devotions*. From the former I have taken some stories of Newman's schooldays not (I think) used before.

(14) A detailed account of Ambrose St. John's last illness and death written by Newman, originally for Miss Bowles. Neville also wrote some incomplete accounts.

(15) Memoirs written by Miss Giberne, in French and in English, and her account of the Achilli trial ; memoir written by Miss Bowles.

(16) *Photostats of Newman's Letters* from the collections owned by Oriel College, Magdalen, Trinity, Pembroke, Keble and Pusey House ; by the Bodleian Library ; and of those to Henry Wilberforce owned by the Catholic College at Ushaw, and by Georgetown University, Washington, U.S.A.

(17) *Photostats from the Archives of Propaganda, Rome*, relating to Newman's delation for heresy in 1859, by Bishop Brown ; these were secured by Fr. Vincent Blehl, S.J., whose article on the Delation was published in the *Dublin Review* for Winter 1960–61. Fr. Blehl has also published an article in *Thought*, the Fordham University Quarterly, for Spring 1960, on Newman's Bishopric that never materialized, using letters of Archbishop Cullen from the Propaganda Archives. The same Irish material was used by J. H. Whyte in the *Dublin Review*, Spring 1960. Documents from the Archives are made available for general use exactly one hundred years from the date of writing.

MATERIAL FROM THE BIRMINGHAM ARCHIVES IN PRINT

Many letters from Newman's Anglican period are included in the *Letters and Correspondence of J. H. Newman*, edited by Anne Mozley in 1890, but few are printed entire, and Miss Mozley made many small alterations and omissions as was customary then in editing the letters of contemporaries. From *My Illness in Sicily* she cut out all Newman's references to the devil and to his bowels.

Entire letters of the period 1839–45 are printed in the *Correspondence of John Henry Newman with John Keble and Others*, edited by Fathers of the Birmingham Oratory in 1917.

A number of letters of the period 1845–90 are printed in *The Life of John Henry Cardinal Newman*, by Wilfrid Ward, 1912. They are necessarily a selection and are rarely printed entire ; some passages have been altered and edited.

Autobiographical Writings, edited by Fr. Tristram with additional notes by Fr. Dessain (1956), contains complete and unaltered Newman's early journals, his account of his illness in Sicily, his memorandum on the Irish university, his private journals 1859–79, various retreat notes, etc., and the memoir of his early Oxford period written in 1874.

Odd letters have been published in various articles and books.

It would be invidious to comment on the many modern Lives and studies of Newman, but mention must be made of Fr. Fergal McGrath's book, *Newman's University Idea and Reality* (Longmans, 1951), if only because, knowing this excellent and detailed study by an Irishman existed, I have treated the Catholic University in Ireland very summarily, concentrating on Newman's personal activities.

Material from the Archives for the early period has been used by Maisie Ward in *Young Mr. Newman* (Sheed and Ward, 1952) and by Sean O'Faolain in *Newman's Way* (Longmans, 1952). Mr. O'Faolain's research uncovered much relating to the vicissitudes of the Newman family, before and after the Bank failure, for which all subsequent writers are indebted to him. Both authors have also used much Mozley family material and have covered the ground so thoroughly that there seems little new to reveal, though everyone has his own way of looking at things. However, I have put in some things from the Archives not printed before, relating to Newman's pastoral visiting in St. Clement's, his work as a college tutor and details of events from letters received by him.

Fr. Louis Bouyer, in his penetrating study *Newman, his Life and Spirituality*, used the material which has appeared in *Autobiographical Writings* ; though he relied much on Ward, his interpretation is new and discriminating.

RECENT ADDITION TO THE BIRMINGHAM ARCHIVES

A collection of letters from Richard Hurrell Froude to his father, and from friends to him, and to his father after his death, has recently (1960) been given to the Oratory by the grandchildren of William Froude, Mary Froude (also descended from Ryder) and Beatrice and William Froude (Wilberforce descendants). I have quoted from these in introducing Hurrell Froude to the reader.

LONDON ORATORY ARCHIVES

Quotations from Faber's letters to other members of his Oratory, and theirs to him, are taken from the files of correspondence at the London Oratory ; also from Faber's letters to the Duke of Norfolk's family. Quotations from his letters to Michael Watts Russell and others are taken from the *Life* by J. E. Bowden, 1865. Also consulted : the collection of documents relating to the quarrel between the two Oratories (1855–56) copied by Stanton as Secretary of the Congregation ; and some notes in French made by Fr. Dalgairns on retreat in Paris in 1855, which refer to Newman, his methods, etc. as seen by Dalgairns ; other letters to and from Dalgairns. Much of this material has been used for the first time by Ronald Chapman in his book *Father Faber* (Burns and Oates, 1961), and he has also printed some of Newman's memoranda on the Quarrel, from the Birmingham Oratory Archives. My account was written when his appeared ; I take a different view of the same events.

The Manning Papers at St. Mary of the Angels, Bayswater

Unfortunately these have been through many vicissitudes since Purcell used them for his biography of Manning in 1896. Due to enemy action the Talbot correspondence seems to have been one of the major casualties. Purcell's judgments are not always reliable, and he was careless, but presumably his transcripts of actual letters were correct ; I have had to rely on him for quotations from the letters between Talbot and Manning. The originals of many letters to and from Herbert Vaughan, who succeeded Manning as Cardinal Archbishop of Westminster, remain, and these have been used for the period of the sixties, and later. There is also a digest of reports on the question of university education drawn up for Manning by Dalgairns, undated, but probably done in 1872.

College Correspondence at Oriel

My quotations from letters of Whately, Hawkins, Arnold and Hampden to each other are taken from these files, two on the Hampden affair addressed to the protagonist, and others from volumes 1, 2, 3, 5, 8, 10 and 11 ; President Routh's letter on Newman's election for the Moral Professorship from Vol. 12.

Material Supplied by Mr. Basil Johnson

Notes on Newman's ancestry, from old wills and parish records, on the site of his birthplace, on the Bowden family, on the previous ownership of the Littlemore stables, on the cricketing record of Fr. Nicholas Darnell and many other matters. I have quoted from some of the letters by Coffin and others to Observer Johnson, in Mr. Johnson's possession, concerning Newman in the early days at Maryvale in 1846, and from Mrs. Bowden's letters to her husband concerning Newman's fasting at Littlemore in 1840.

Material Supplied by Miss Dorothea Mozley

Miss Mozley kindly showed me letters, pictures, photographs, etc. I have quoted from Maria Mozley's letter about Jemima Newman's wedding in 1836, and used, though not quoted, Harriett's letters on her visit to France in 1843. I regret that considerations of space prevented me from making more use of this material.

SOME PUBLISHED WORKS CONSULTED

CONTEMPORARY MEMOIRS, BIOGRAPHIES, ETC.

(Alphabetically under subject)

Thomas William Allies — Mary H. Allies, 1907.
Life of Thomas Arnold, D.D. — Arthur Penrhyn Stanley, 1844. Pop. edn. 1904.
Passages in a Wandering Life — Thomas Arnold (junior), 1900.
Memorials of Mr. Serjeant Bellasis — Edward Bellasis, 1895.
Coram Cardinali — Edward Bellasis, 1916.
Life of Edward White Benson Abp. of Canterbury — A. C. Benson, 1899.
Lives of Twelve Good Men — J. W. Burgon, 1888.
The Oxford Movement — R. W. Church, 1891.
Occasional Papers (Vol. 2) — R. W. Church, 1866.
Life and Letters of Dean Church — Mary Church (daughter), 1894.
Life and Correspondence of Lord Coleridge — Ernest Hartley Coleridge, 1904.
Life and Letters of Frederick W. Faber — J. E. Bowden, 1869.
The Nemesis of Faith (novel) — James Anthony Froude, 1849.
The Oxford Counter-Reformation (in Short Studies) — J. A. Froude, 1885.
Remains — Richard Hurrell Froude — ed. J. H. Newman and J. Keble, 1838.
Memoirs of James Robert Hope-Scott — Robert Ornsby, 1884.
A Memoir of the Rev. John Keble — Rt. Hon. Sir John T. Coleridge, 1869.
Cecil, Marchioness of Lothian — Cecil Kerr (granddaughter), n.d.
Charles Kingsley, Letters and Memories of his Life — ed. his wife, 1876.
Memorials of William C. Lake Dean of Durham — ed. his widow (K. Lake), 1901.
Life of Cardinal Manning Abp. of Westminster — Edmund Sheridan Purcell, 1896.
Letters of the Rev. J. B. Mozley — ed. his sister (Anne Mozley), 1885.
Reminiscences of Oriel and Oxford — T. Mozley, 1882.
Report of the Trial, etc. G. Achilli v. *Dr. Newman* — W. Finlason, 1852.
Cardinal Newman — R. H. Hutton, 1891.
Cardinal Newman: Reminiscences of 50 Years — William Lockhart, 1891.
Historical Notes of the Oxford Movement — Frederick Oakeley.
Phases of Faith (religious autobiography) — Francis W. Newman, 1850.
Contributions to the Early History of Cardinal Newman — Francis W. Newman, 1891.
Memoirs — Mark Pattison, 1885.
Narrative of 5 Years at St. Saviour's Leeds — John H. Pollen, 1851.
John Hungerford Pollen — Anne Pollen (daughter), 1912.
Life of Edward Bouverie Pusey — Henry Parry Liddon, 1893.
Letters of Frederic Rogers Lord Blachford — G. E. Marindin, 1896.

Life and Work of the 7th Earl of Shaftesbury — Edwin Hodder, 1886. Pop.
  edn. 1887.
Life of Arthur Penrhyn Stanley — Rowland Prothero, 1893. Pop. edn. 1909.
Reminiscences of Oxford — W. Tuckwell, 1901.
Life of Cardinal Vaughan — J. G. Snead-Cox, 1910.
Recollections — Aubrey de Vere, 1897.
W. G. Ward and the Oxford Movement — Wilfrid Ward, 1889.
W. G. Ward and the Catholic Revival — Wilfrid Ward, 1893.
Life and Correspondence of Richard Whately Abp. of Dublin—Jane Whately, 1866.
Life of Blanco White — ed. J. H. Thom, 1845.
Life of the Rt. Rev. Samuel Wilberforce — A. R. Ashwell, R. Wilberforce,
  1880–82.
Autobiography — Isaac Williams.
Recollections of the Last Four Popes — Nicholas Cardinal Wiseman, 1858.
Fabiola (novel) — Nicholas Cardinal Wiseman, 1855.
Life and Times of Cardinal Wiseman — Wilfrid Ward, 1897.

LATER WORKS

(Besides those mentioned in note on unpublished sources :
alphabetically under authors.)

Aubert, R. *Le Pontificat de Pie IX.* Paris, 1952.
Bamford, T. W. *Thomas Arnold.* 1960.
Butler, Dom Cuthbert. *The Life and Times of Bishop Ullathorne.* 1926.
Butler, Dom Cuthbert. *The Vatican Council.* 1930.
Cockshut, A. O. J. *Anglican Attitudes* (Victorian Religious controversy).
  1959.
Culler, A. Dwight. *The Imperial Intellect.* New Haven, 1955.
Dawson, Christopher. *The Spirit of the Oxford Movement.* 1933.
Gasquet, Abbot. *Lord Acton and his Circle.* 1906.
Green, V. H. H. *Oxford Common Room* (Pattison, etc.). 1957.
Gwynn, Denis. *Lord Shrewsbury, Pugin and the Catholic Revival.* 1946.
Gwynn, Denis. *Father Dominic Barberi.* 1947.
Hales, E. E. Y. *Pio Nono.* 1954.
Leslie, Sir Shane. *Henry Edward Manning, his Life and Labours.* 1921.
Lock, W. *John Keble.* 1905.
Magnus, Philip. *Gladstone.* 1954.
Martin, R. B. *The Dust of Combat* (Charles Kingsley). 1960.
Mathew, Abp. David. *Acton, the Formative Years.* 1946.
Middleton, R. D. *Newman and Bloxam.* 1947.
Middleton, R. D. *Newman at Oxford.* 1950.
Pope-Hennessy, Una. *Canon Charles Kingsley.* 1948.
Reynolds, E. E. *Three Cardinals.* 1958.
Sieveking, I. Giberne. *Memoir and Letters of Francis W. Newman.* 1909.
Smith, B. A. *Dean Church, the Anglican Response to Newman.* 1958.
Tristram, Henry. *Newman and his Friends.* 1933.
Walgrave, J. H. *Newman the Theologian* (trans. Littledale). 1960.
Ward, Wilfrid. *Last Lectures.* 1918.
Young, Urban. C. P. *Dominic Barberi in England.* 1935.

INDEX OF PERSONS

THE END